The Architecture of Experience

Flowers in the basket,
Basket on the bed,
Bed in the chamber,
Chamber in the house,
House in the weedy yard,
Yard in the winding lane,
Lane in the broad street,
Street in the high town,
Town in the city,
City in the kingdom:
  This is the key of
  the kingdom.
      (Traditional)

*For Lewis and Aidan
and all others learning to
'construct' the world*

GRAHAM DUNSTAN MARTIN

THE ARCHITECTURE
OF EXPERIENCE

*A Discussion
of the Role of Language
and Literature
in the Construction
of the World*

*

AT THE UNIVERSITY PRESS

EDINBURGH

© G. D. Martin 1981
Edinburgh University Press
22 George Square
Edinburgh
ISBN 0 85224 409 6
The Publishers acknowledge the
financial assistance of the
Scottish Arts Council.

Set in Monotype Bell
by Speedspools, Edinburgh
and printed in Great Britain by
Clark Constable Ltd
Edinburgh

Contents

Preface

One of my basic themes is that categories and classifications limit thought. The initial publishing history of this book is a case in point. Some readers of it were disturbed because it does not fall into a category. It is not exactly philosophy, so *what is it*? I am reminded of the game that children often play – as I used to myself – on the way to school. They run along the pavement taking care not to step on the lines between the big square paving-stones. For if you do the Devil will get you.

ACKNOWLEDGEMENTS. Some of the material in Chapter 4 has appeared in article form in *Comparison* and in the *British Journal of Aesthetics*. I am grateful for these reviews' permission to republish.

G. D. M.

Introduction

Literary critics often make great claims for literature; and to many of these claims I should assent. Relatively little has been done, however, to vindicate them except from within the horizons of literature itself; for to justify them properly would force the critic onto dangerously unfamiliar ground. But we cannot be content with a prohibition which makes it in principle impossible even to attempt to defend one's values. If literature is important because of its blending of perception and reality, we must look at the relation between perception and reality; if literature is important for social and political reasons, we must look at those reasons; if literature is important because of its celebration of consciousness, we must look at the value of consciousness. Trespass is obligatory.

This book is therefore an effort towards a dialogue across the boundaries of subjects as they are usually narrowly defined. I admit the dangers of this procedure. No doubt some of what I say here is said in error. But, since 'the art of being correct lies in making the weakest possible statements' (Anon., in Good 1961, p. 213), anyone who wishes to say something meaningful must accept the risk of error. We should not fear to err; as Karl Popper shows, the road towards truth is strewn with well-intentioned errors, and only by their progressive correction do we learn to accommodate our beliefs to reality.

There is, in any case, a strong justification for interdisciplinary thinking. We judge the validity of a theory by (among other things) its self-consistency. We judge it also by its consistency with other theories. Thus, if Mendelian heredity had turned out to clash with the theory of genes and, ultimately, with that of molecular structure, some rethinking would have had to be done. Telepathy, despite some strong experimental evidence for it, is not yet accepted by the scientific community as proven, and this is because it cannot at present be reconciled with the scientific world-view (cf. Martin 1975a). I think scientists are right to take this view of telepathy. For the sum of our theories about the world should, ideally, be self-consistent. And this makes interdisciplinary thinking a necessity for anyone who wishes his world-view to be better than an untidy heap of disconnected fragments.

The starting-point of this book is consciousness. Upon consciousness depends perception. And out of perception we construct reality, a medley of concrete and abstract, of certain, less certain and downright dubious. This book attempts to explore, not only something of these processes, but also how literature stands in opposition to a false under-

1

standing of reality, since it promotes perception as against habits and stereotypes.

In Chapter 1 I posit consciousness as the ground of all understanding, scientific or other. I explore the way in which we may be presumed to construct reality out of our initial perceptions, and how these constructions are increasingly abstract as they lie further from concrete and verifiable perception. The secret of science's success is in 'reversibility', or its readiness to check its more abstract constructions against perceptual data. Society is 'less real' than the physical world in that it is dependent on human belief and practice. As for the social constructs of common sense, they are still less real, still less reliable.

In Chapter 3 linguistic and conceptual categories are seen as necessary to thought, but at times misleading about the nature of reality. Reference is discussed, and a model for abstract reference proposed. A number of linguistic 'optical illusions' are analysed, to demonstrate the misleading nature of some abstractions. But possibly an awareness of language and literature, and preferably of more than one language, of more than one literature, may help us to treat such abstract stereotypes with caution. Thus, it is not the ordered harmonies of literature that are its principal glory, but its aptness to disrupt our categories; not so much its presentation of apparent truth as its questioning of unnoticed falsity.

In the fourth chapter language is shown to be misleading too in the incompleteness of its reference to reality. Polanyi's notions of 'tacit knowing' are drawn upon to support the argument of there being ineffable elements in experience. How may we express such inexpressibles? An answer may be found through what the 'information processing' school of modern psychology has to tell us of mental imagery. The inexpressible may be imprinted on the memory, and it may be possible, by way of poetic imagery, to evoke it. Hence *ut pictura poesis* may be explained. This chapter deepens the discussion of metaphor which I presented in my earlier *Language, Truth and Poetry*, and deals, therefore, with one of the mechanisms by which literature refreshes perception.

Finally, Chapter 5 proposes that henceforth we should speak, not of 'culture' but of 'socio-culture' and 'value-culture'. The arts having been established as a perceptual tool, and as a reminder and expression of consciousness, the definition of value-culture in purely sociological terms can be dismissed. Though implicated in society, it is, more interestingly, useful in its own right, and justifiable on non-sociological grounds. The attempt of certain sociologists of knowledge to refute this view, by claiming that all human values are relative to particular human societies, is in its turn refuted. Value-culture should take its proper place in education. It reminds us of the value of ordinary people; and there are two tests of human progress, one of which is the personal progress of the individual human being.

It will be seen that this book therefore constitutes a defence of art, and an endeavour to restore it to the every-day world where it belongs, alongside the rest of human experience. Art is not a thing apart.

The concept of 'aesthetic consciousness', in distinction and isolation from 'nonaesthetic' realms of experience, is relatively modern. . . . According to this conception the subject contemplating the aesthetic object is an empty consciousness receiving perceptions and somehow enjoying the immediacy of pure sensuous form. The 'aesthetic experience' is thus isolated and discontinuous from other, more pragmatic realms; it is not measurable in terms of 'content', since it is a response to form. It does not relate itself to the self-understanding of the subject, or to time; it is seen as an atemporal moment without reference to anything but itself.

The consequences of such a conception are many. In the first place, no adequate way is left to account for art except perceptual enjoyment. There can be no contentual measures for art, since art is not knowledge. . . . Art no longer has any clear place in the world, since neither it nor the artist himself belongs to the world in any specific way. Art is left without function and the artist without place in society. The evident 'holiness' of art, which we sense in our outrage at any senseless destruction of a great work of art, is left without legitimation. And certainly the artist can hardly claim to be a prophet if all he is creating is a formal expression of feeling or aesthetic pleasure.

But such a conception of the aesthetic phenomenon is contradicted by our own experience of any great work of art. The experience of encountering a work of art opens up a world; it is not mere gaping in sensuous pleasure at the outsides of forms. . . . Art is not sense perception but knowledge. When we meet art, the horizons of our own world and self-understanding are broadened so that we see the world 'in a new light' – as if for the first time. Even common and ordinary objects of life appear in a new light when illuminated by art. . . . In an encounter with a work of art we do not go into a foreign universe, stepping outside of time and history; we do not separate ourselves from ourselves or from the non-aesthetic. Rather we become more fully present, . . . we bring what we have experienced and who we are into play. Our whole self-understanding is placed in the balance, it is *risked*. It is not we who are interrogating an object; the work of art is putting a question to us, the question that called it into being. The experience of a work of art . . . takes place in the unity and continuity of our own self-understanding. (Palmer 1969, pp. 167–8)

Such (in summary) are some of Gadamer's complaints against those who seek to amputate aesthetic experience from reality. Though there is nothing Gadamerian about my approach, he and I share an enemy if not a method; and this quotation would make an apt conclusion to the present book. Nothing illuminates reality more vividly than the imagination; nothing is more relevant to truth than fiction.

1. Outwards from Perception

[The self] is not capable of proof, nor does it need any, for it is self-proven. Though itself inconceivable, it is the ground of every possibility of conceiving, of every act of knowledge. Even he who denies it presupposes it in so far as he thinks.

(Radhakrishnan, *Eastern Religions and Western Thought*)

Intellect to Senses

νόμῳ χροιή, νόμῳ γλυκύ, νόμῳ πικρόν, ἐτεῇ δ' ἄτομα καὶ κενόν.
Ostensibly there is colour, sweetness, bitterness; actually only atoms and void.

Senses to Intellect

τάλαινα φρήν, παρ' ἡμέων λαβοῦσα τὰς πίστεις ἡμέας καταβάλλεις; πτῶμα τοι τὸ κατάβλημα.
Poor intellect! You get your evidence from us, and you hope to overthrow us? Your victory is your defeat.   (Democritus)[1]

Thus nature gets credit which should in truth be reserved for ourselves : the rose for its scent : the nightingale for his song : and the sun for his radiance. The poets are entirely mistaken. They should address their lyrics to themselves, and should turn them into odes of self-congratulation on the excellency of the human mind. Nature is a dull affair, soundless, scentless, colourless; merely the hurrying of material, endlessly, meaninglessly.

(Whitehead, *Science and the Modern World*)

It is well known that carbon is required to make physicists.

(Dicke, *Nature* vol. 192)

Où est le monde? En dehors de moi ou en moi? Ni l'un ni l'autre, et les deux à la fois.
[Where is the world? Outside me or inside me? Neither one nor the other, and both at once.]

(Lefebve, *L'Image fascinante et le surréel*)

1. Consciousness

CONSCIOUSNESS is so familiar a condition of our existence that we overlook its importance. Just as a man watching an absorbing play forgets the eyes through which he looks, just as a man driving a car pays no heed to the muscles with which he turns the wheel, so we remain most of the time engrossed in our surroundings, and fail to notice the conditions which alone permit us to perceive them.

But consciousness is the primary condition of our lives. Without it, the world and ourselves are blotted out. With it, the world and ourselves

5

are perceptible, imaginable and even sometimes manageable. Without it, the tree in the garden might as well not be there. Even with it, of course, the tree in the garden may still not be there, for it may be an external mirage or an inner hallucination. But there are only three ways of deciding whether it is there or not, and all involve consciousness. The first is to go up to it and look at it, touch it, smell it, measure it, strike its trunk and listen to the sound; all these actions are perceptual, and in performing them we are checking the evidence of one sense against another; and it is by way of our consciousness that we make this comparison. The second is an extension of the same principle of checking: we ask other people; and they in turn have to mediate their perception of the tree through their consciousness, and then communicate their knowledge through ours. The third is to reason with ourselves: if the tree was not there yesterday, how could it have got there today, considering what we know of the world? And our perception of the tree's presence, of its absence, and what we know of the world, all came to us through consciousness.

I have hardly started, and I am already deep into a thicket of the most hoary and intractable of problems. For instance, (1) how can I 'prove' that consciousness exists? (2) What is consciousness? Is it not incapable of definition, and what can usefully be said about the indefinable? (3) Can pure consciousness without sensory perception exist? Or if not sensory perception, at least awareness of something other than consciousness itself? Is awareness not always awareness *of*?

The first objection is easy to answer. No-one has seriously denied the reality of consciousness, since to do so would be to deny that he knew what he was doing (let alone what he was denying). If anyone were to declare : 'I am not conscious, and neither are you,' one might well reply : 'Perhaps you'd better go home in a taxi.' This is not so facetious as it sounds. All assertions in argument depend on terms like 'knowing', 'thinking', 'believing' and 'acting', which imply consciousness. To deny the very basis of the assertions one is making is itself irresponsible or facetious. Philosophers who have appeared to deny consciousness, such as William James, have normally intended merely to reject some view of consciousness that they found objectionable. And others who have denied consciousness, such as the behaviourist psychologists, have in fact simply been refusing to talk about it.[2] As Ornstein says, consciousness was for a long time regarded as an unsuitable subject for psychological research because it could not be investigated scientifically. 'The *reductio ad absurdum* of this position was that of the "logical positivists", who maintained that any question not amenable to a perfectly logical answer should not even be asked' (Ornstein 1975, p. 5). But I have already, in a previous book, talked sufficiently about the absurdities of refusing to ask such questions. For how can one know what answers there may be until one has asked the questions? It is one thing to object to the answers which have so far been given; but to complain that no answer could possibly make sense is to take the way of the ostrich, and bury one's head in the sand of defeatism.

Let us turn then to our second question: 'What is consciousness?' If this requires us to give a definition of the thing itself, we shall be hard put to give one. I shall simply reply that 'we all know what consciousness is like, from our own experience of it'. This is not a mere evasion . . . or if it is one, it is an evasion that one also has to perform with certain other basic experiences, such as Time. We might say: 'Time can be defined in terms of "before" and "after".' But 'before' and 'after' then need a definition, which will inevitably involve the concept of time. There is no escape that way. Or we might say: 'Time is movement in the temporal dimension.' It will be clear that this definition is circular too. Or we might compare movement in time to movement in space. But for our analogy to be understood, we should already have to have a concept of time to apply it to. Or we might treat time as a fourth dimension, along with the other three spatial ones, as Einsteinian mathematicians do. In so far as their equations apply to real time and space, however, we should have to have some notion of both these indefinables. Or we might describe time in terms of the processes we see going on around us (such as entropy) or those we feel within our own bodies. Perhaps indeed such processes do give us our sense of time. But we have still not defined 'time' itself, for the notion of time is inseparably involved with the notion of 'process'. All such treatments of time have an element of circularity, and like Jurgen we end up where we started, facing our own front doors.[3] But it will be admitted that we cannot do without the notion of time.

In short, there are at least a few basic experiences so fundamental to our natures as human beings that we cannot step backwards out of them to examine them. It would be surprising if this were not so, for if we could, would we not have an infinite regress? In the case of consciousness, an infinite regress has sometimes been stated to be an absurdity. Yet we do sometimes feel we should like to claim that 'I am conscious of being conscious' and that 'I am conscious of being conscious of being conscious' and so on; and if we set foot on this unholy merry-go-round, it is difficult to see how we can stop. Perhaps the solution is to be found in this way: consciousness can be seen as an infinite regress, precisely *because* we cannot step backwards out of it and are locked, as if spinning, in its infinite circularity.[4]

In any case, even if we cannot define certain experiences, we can at least say *something* about them. For what do we do with our basic experiences in practice, when we talk about them? Describing the smell of roses is impossible, for instance, except by analogy with other similar smells : I cannot describe *the smell itself*. But I can certainly talk about the sense of smell as opposed to the other senses, about the parts of the anatomy that seem to mediate them to us, about their apparent relative strength, sweetness and so on. Similarly, without being able to define time *as such*, we can still say quite a lot about it.

And in doing so, we have to appeal to other people for validation of our statements. There is nothing in the least shocking about this procedure, for upon it depend each and every one of the statements of science itself. Even the most behaviourist of scientific proofs depends for its validation on the assent of other behaviourist scientists. Skinner's, Watson's or Bloomfield's assertions are not proven by God, Truth, Objective Evidence, or any other deity with a capital letter—and in such beings behaviourists do not in any case believe. Scientists' assertions are in practice either accepted or rejected by other people, namely by their scientific peers, whose training and grasp of the evidence is sufficient to allow them to judge. Is this assent a matter of conditioned reflex? Or is it a matter of an individual mind assessing and judging? Are these two statements the same statement? No matter : in either case, the final judge and jury is the same; it is a number of individuals, all separate from each other by virtue of their separate consciousnesses —or, as the behaviourists might put it, by virtue of their separately functioning sense organs and brains. In short, individuals themselves are the final arbiters, whatever definition we put upon 'individual'. A 'community of scholars' has no existence except as a number of individuals; a 'community of men' has no existence except as a number of individuals; Man's senses divide him and his opinions from his fellow men; we do not only die, but live, alone, in an isolation that can be assuaged but never healed.

This inaccessibility of individual experience to other individuals need not perturb us too much. So long as most individuals report roughly the same things of their own personal experience, we can accept that 'it is probably so' (which is the most that any branch of science can usually assert). And it is this that justifies those scientific investigators who proceed by asking people what they feel (as doctors do) or what they see (as psychologists like Richard Gregory do). I shall here proceed on a rather similar basis. I shall, admittedly, state what I think to be the case, but I shall always do so with an implicit appeal to the reader's experience. My statements are not assertions but questions : Do you find it to be so? Would you agree?

And so it is with consciousness. Do you think you possess something of the sort? (We shall all think you are cheating if you do not!) And if you do, is the analysis that follows in accord with your own experience?

One final point : what are we to answer to my third question, namely 'Can pure consciousness be said to exist without consciousness *of* anything?' This problem has preoccupied philosophers since time immemorial, and I shall not have the temerity to discuss it here, for it is irrelevant to my argument. Whether one thinks that pure consciousness is the prime datum of experience, or whether one gives that status to consciousness *of* memories, sense experience, thoughts, desires, dreams, etc. is not important; I am merely interested that the reader should admit *one* of these alternatives to be correct. Consciousness-*of* is as fundamental an experience as my argument requires, for I am not concerned here to proceed inwards into the mysterious regions of inner awareness, but outwards into the daylight of sensation, perception and the phenomenal world.[5]

2. Constructing the World

Let me start, then, with the way in which we construct our world upon consciousness. For I am not of course insinuating that 'there is nothing out there'. It is clear that there is a great deal 'out there', but it is consciousness that allows us to be aware of it; and it is even to some extent consciousness that allows us to distinguish between real and imaginary worlds. 'Knowableness to mind', says Eddington, is

a property which differentiates the actual world of our experience from imaginary worlds in which the same general laws of Nature are supposed to hold true. Consider a world – Utopia, let us say – governed by all the laws of Nature known and unknown which govern our own world, but containing better stars, planets, cities, animals, etc. – a world which might exist, but it just happens that it doesn't. How can the physicist test that Utopia is not the actual world? We refer to a piece of matter in it; it is not real matter but it attracts any other piece of (unreal) matter in Utopia according to the law of gravitation. . . . As soon as any element in it has been shown to be unreal, Utopia collapses; but so long as we keep to the cycles of physics we can never find the vulnerable point, for each element is correctly linked to the rest of the cycle, all our laws of Nature expressed by the cycle being obeyed in Utopia by hypothesis. The unreal stars emit unreal light which falls on unreal retinas and ultimately reaches unreal brains. The next step takes it outside the cycle and gives the opportunity of exposing the whole deception. Is the brain disturbance translated into consciousness? That will test whether the brain is real or unreal. There is no question about consciousness being real or not; consciousness is self-knowing and the epithet real adds nothing to that. Of the infinite number of worlds which are examples of what might be possible under the laws of Nature, there is one which does something more than fulfil those laws of Nature. [This is the *actual* world, whose actuality we recognize] because it is that world alone with which consciousness interacts. . . . Each of us is armed with this touchstone of actuality; by applying it we decide that this sorry world of ours is actual and Utopia is a dream. As our individual consciousnesses are different, so our touchstones are different; but fortunately they all agree in their indication of actuality – or at any rate those which agree are in sufficient majority to shut the others up in lunatic asylums.   (Eddington 1928, pp. 265–6)

Nor is any element of reality lost to us by taking the view that consciousness is the ground on which we build all the rest; as Natanson says, when he embarks on a similar examination of reality from the centre (consciousness) instead of some hypothetically objective position, some distance out into the world, 'no item of experience is lost to consciousness in the process; rather, everything thought of and entertained in perception is taken *as* thought of and *as* entertained' (Natanson 1970, p. 10). None of our usual apprehensions about the world is lost, but everything is seen in a new perspective.

Consciousness, then, is the touchstone of reality : the world is distinguished from utopia by the fact that consciousness knows it, and that different consciousnesses agree about this knowledge.

Edmond Wright (1977*a*, *b*), however, has pointed out that it is not agreement pure and simple, unhaunted by any ghost of disagreement, that constitutes our yardstick for reality. For if everyone else always and in every respect agreed with *me* about reality, how could I be confident in the independence of reality – and of other people – from myself? I should have no persuasive argument against solipsism, against the view that the world was a figment of my own (no doubt fevered) imagination. For everyone I met would merely reflect my own perceptions, and the world and its inhabitants would be reduced to a mere hall of mirrors. (And the rigid-minded individual, who will accept no-one else's insight or perception, is indeed a kind of solipsist.) As Wright points out, outer reality can be shown to be independent of me *only* if it does *not* correspond, always and invariably, to my own prejudices; only when my observations are *corrected* by someone else; only when someone says to me : 'Look here : you're not seeing that properly : it's not a dried leaf you're looking at, it's an insect!' or 'Now do you hear the clarinet notes in that passage ?' and I reply : 'Goodness yes, I hadn't noticed that!' At the same time this process gives me unmistakeable proof of the reality of other people. This is a two-way process, however : 'sometimes I correct [the other], and all my ancestors and mentors' (Wright 1977*b*, p. 285). The touchstone of reality is thus (1) consciousness and (2) the mutual correction of consciousnesses by other consciousnesses. One of the necessary bases of truth is *variousness of perception*.

Consciousness is indeed so primary that, though Newtonian science believed it had got rid of it altogether, many modern scientists have admitted it back into the centre of their world. 'Classical physics', writes Max Jammer,

> described physical reality as composed of entities devoid of sensuous qualities . . . ; but the theory achieved its validity only by virtue of its verifiability (or falsifiability), that is, by virtue of the fact that its predictions could be tested, an operation which, in the last analysis, had to involve human consciousness (1975, p. 471).

For the perceptions of scientists were always involved in the verification or falsification of a theory. In classical physics, however, the effect of these observers on the observed evidence was regarded as so negligible that it could be disregarded; and the 'psycho-physical problem' could accordingly be banished outside the bounds of physics.

But the situation in quantum mechanics is quite different: here the effect of observer on observed may be of the same order of magnitude as the effect of observed on observer. For instance, the experimenter may measure a subatomic particle's *position* exactly, or its *momentum*; but he may not measure *both*. In short, his act of measurement determines what he measures. A number of quantum physicists have contended that human consciousness has to be inserted into the physicist's mathematical equations, as it were. For instance, von Neumann says that 'it is impossible to formulate a complete and consistent theory of quantum mechanical measurement without reference to human consciousness'. F. W. London and E. Bauer claim more validity for the state of the mind perceived by introspection than they do for 'objective' perceptions (Jammer 1975, pp. 480, 484). And Wigner asserts that consciousness or mind influences the physico-chemical conditions of living systems, just as it is influenced *by* them (Jammer 1975, pp. 499–500). At the very least we may conclude that consciousness, in modern physics, is now a factor to be reckoned with.

Wigner, indeed, goes quite far along this line. He asserts that there are, as it were, two realities: the primary one is consciousness; the secondary one is the world that we 'construct' on the basis of our consciousness and of what it seems to 'show' us of external reality. He writes:

> Does a magnetic field exist in a vacuum? Most of us physicists would say that it does. But, if we analyse the meaning of this statement that a magnetic field exists in a vacuum, we find that it means that it is *convenient* for us to think of such a field, that it enters our calculations, and that we can explain these calculations more easily if we are allowed to refer to the magnetic field as being everywhere, even in interstellar space. The reality of the magnetic field in a vacuum thus consists in the usefulness of the concept of a magnetic field existing everywhere; and reality is in this case

synonymous with the usefulness of the concept, both in our own thinking, and in communicating with others.

One has to go but one step further to realize that the existence of the book I am holding in my hand is of the same nature. Its existence manifests itself in the fact that I cannot bring my fingers together, in my knowledge that if I stopped pressing them together I should hear a loud bang, and in the possibility that I might open it and read it. The book is a convenient expression for describing some of the sensations which I have, some of the sensations which I know I might have, and some of the sensations I could cause in someone else . . . if I, for instance, threw the book at him!

The only difference between the existence of the book and the existence of the magnetic field in interstellar space is that the concept of the book is much more directly useful, both for guiding my own actions and for communicating with other people. There is only one concept whose reality is not merely a convenience but also an absolute: the content of my consciousness, including my sensations.[6]

It might well be thought that Wigner goes too far here in disparaging the reality of books in the same way as he has just disparaged that of magnetic fields in empty space. We should most of us suppose that the reality of books is hard to deny, since we all see them, feel them, and can agree about their existence. But this, of course, is precisely why consciousness must be said to be primary: for we can only assert the reality of books by relying on our sensations, namely by seeing books and feeling them, and on the sensations of others, namely by appealing to others to confirm that they have the same sensations. And if the intellect denies the reality of sensation, on the ground that there are only interactions between atoms, it can do so only on the basis of the information that innumerable scientific minds have built up over the generations; and this information was obtained through the mediation of the senses, through the use of rulers, microscopes and thermometers, and through the use of the senses to perceive the readings on them. One cannot deny the validity of the senses without denying the validity of the information obtained through them. We obtain no information at all, except through the senses.[7]

Wigner's argument is a difficult one to counter, for it perfectly fits the way in which we must be presumed to construct reality, as it were, out of our own sensations. We are not, of course, as adults, aware of this process. As Huxley writes, 'it is possible, by inhibiting the activity of the interpreting mind, to catch a hint of the raw *sensum*, as it presents itself to the eyes of the new-born child. But such hints are very imperfect at the best, and of brief duration' (1943, p. 17). Nor can we actually *recall* what it was like to be a new-born child before we had begun to assemble our sensations into a set of orderly, classified patterns. But it may be that in certain abnormal conditions, when the upper levels of the mind have been temporarily put out of action by drugs or anaesthetics, returning to consciousness may give us some inkling of what the child's slow and immeasurably longer construction of the world might have been like. It is at least interesting to speculate that an experience such as the one Huxley himself describes, 'coming round' after an anaesthetic administered in the dentist's chair, may give us some clue as to how our initial process of 'constructing' the world operated.

'Returning awareness', writes Huxley,

> began with pure visual sensations completely devoid of signi-ficance. These, as I can remember them, were not of objects existing 'out there' in the familiar, three-dimensional world of everyday experience. They were just coloured patches, existing in and for themselves, unrelated not only to the external world, but also to myself – for the knowledge of self was still wholly lacking, and these meaningless and unattached sense impressions were not *mine*; they simply *were*. This kind of awareness lasted for a minute or two; then as the effect of the anaesthetic wore off a little further, a notable change took place. The coloured patches were no longer sensed merely as coloured patches, but became associated with certain objects 'out there' in the external three-dimensional world – specifically, the façades of houses seen through the window facing the chair in which I was reclining. Attention travelled across the visual field selecting successive parts of it and perceiving these selected parts as physical objects. From being vague and meaning-less, the *sensa* had developed into manifestations of definite things belonging to a familiar category and situated in a familiar world of solid objects. Thus recognized and classified, these perceptions (I do not call them 'my' perceptions, for 'I' had not yet made any appearance on the scene) became immediately clearer, while all sorts of details, unnoticed so long as the *sensa* lacked significance, were now perceived and evaluated. That which was now being apprehended was no longer a set of mere coloured patches, but a set of aspects of the known, because remembered, world. Known and remembered by whom? For a time there was no indication of an answer. But after a little while, imperceptibly, there emerged myself, the subject of the experience. And with this emergence there came, as I remember, a further clarification of vision. What had been at first raw *sensa* and had then become, by interpretation, the appearances of known varieties of objects, underwent a further transformation and became objects consciously related to a self, an organized pattern of memories, habits and desires. By becoming related to the self, the perceived objects became more visible,

13

inasmuch as the self, to which they had now entered into relation, was interested in more aspects of external reality than had been the merely physiological being which had sensed the coloured patches, and the more developed, but still un-self-conscious being which had perceived these *sensa* as appearances of familiar objects 'out there' in a familiar kind of world. 'I' had now returned; and since 'I' happened to take an interest in architectural details and their history, the things seen through the window were immediately thought of as a member of a new category – not merely as houses, but as houses of particular style and date, and as such possessed of distinguishing characteristics [which] were now perceived . . . because my mind was once more in a condition to look for them and register their significance.[8]

(Huxley 1943, pp. 17 – 19)

We should not take such an experience too literally, as a repetition of the child's own slow construction of reality from its initial sense perceptions. It will serve us, however, as an analogy for that process. It must also be remembered that what follows is largely speculative, for we can none of us remember our earliest experiences. None the less, it is a commonly held view of child psychologists that the newborn infant has no clear sense of separation from the persons and objects that surround it.[9] It is not even aware of the true boundaries of its own body. It experiences its mother and itself as practically a single entity. As it grows, it begins to recognize and to establish a separation, or have that separation imposed upon it. In the beginning was sensation : sights, sounds, feelings and tastes. From the regularity of these sensations, the existence of solid objects in the world around us is deduced. And their separateness from us is progressively revealed by the fact that we cannot manipulate all of them, and can manipulate some of them only up to a point. As Piaget writes, the object is 'constructed by intelligence itself' (1950, p. 110). As Richard Gregory puts it, 'the perceived object is a hypothesis, suggested and tested by sensory data' (1972, pp. 11 – 12).[10] And, of course, once we have learned to do so, we see it as an object, not as a mere assemblage of shapes and colours. Thus, in Gregory's experiments with perception, we interpret what are *in fact* mere assemblages of shapes and colours as objects. Piaget writes :

Quand je perçois une maison, je ne vois pas d'abord la couleur d'une tuile, la grandeur d'une cheminée, etc., et finalement la maison! Je perçois d'emblée la maison comme 'Gestalt' et ne passe qu'ensuite à l'analyse du détail. (Piaget 1970, p. 83)

[When I see a house, I do not see first of all the colour of a tile, the size of a chimney, etc., and finally the house! I perceive the house as a 'Gestalt' from the start, and only secondly do I proceed to the analysis of detail.]

14

At the same time we deduce the existence of persons (seen first, according to Piaget, as notable 'centres of activity') to whom we similarly attribute stability and permanence, and whose existence interacts with our own to give us a sense of their individuality and our own.[11] We learn, in fact, to perceive persons, and not mere patches of colour and movement, just as we learn to perceive objects and not mere regularities of shape and behaviour.

This is, so to speak, the first stage. The next stage is to place the various individual objects and persons we see around us in categories, or classes. The tree is seen as an instance of a tree, the individual horse as an instance of a horse. As Bruner says, we 'go beyond sense data to the class identity of the object being perceived. . . . William James wrote picturesquely of this process, remarking that cognitive life begins when one is able to exclaim, "Hullo! Thingumbob again".' (1974, p. 219) We further see relationships between the objects around us, and in Piaget's system, these two processes, namely (1) classifying phenomena, and (2) positing relationships, seem to lie at the basis of what he sees as the fundamental operations of thought (Piaget 1950, p. 43). But on the basis of the relationships we deduce from the happenings we see around us, we would then go on, it seems, to deduce *causes* for those happenings : we infer physical causes which make objects behave as they do, and psychic causes which make persons behave as they do. 'Heaviness', we shall say, 'causes' objects like stones, bricks and blocks of wood to fall to the ground, 'lightness' causes balloons and feathers to float upwards; 'jealousy' causes John, who loves Mary, to hate Peter, whom she loves; and so on. Scientists, in seeking causes for the behaviour of physical objects, were led eventually to posit the existence of atoms and molecules, and still more recently, of the fundamental particles. And these particles are then fitted into a framework of theory : quantum theory and relativity describe the relations between the fundamental objects of the world, as deduced by scientists, and give an account of the presumed structure of the universe. Thus we proceed, in our dealings with the world, from basic sensory data to the positing of objects, from objects to the positing of relations from them again to the positing of further hidden objects and hidden relations, in an effort, it would seem, to reduce all the physical phenomena we see about us to a comprehensible and unitary system. We perceive diversity, and in our struggle to comprehend it we reduce it progressively to identity – or at least seek to do so.

> We are not content to accept diversity as so given. We have a hunger and thirst for explanation and, for the human mind, explanation consists in the discovery of identity behind diversity. Any theory which postulates the existence of identities behind diversities strikes us as being intrinsically plausible.[12]

By processes such as these we construct our world progressively out of the raw sense-data that are initially presented to us. A very simplified picture of a scientific world-structure would look something like this:

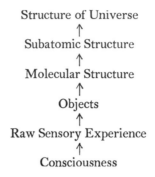

Structure of Universe

↑

Subatomic Structure

↑

Molecular Structure

↑

Objects

↑

Raw Sensory Experience

↑

Consciousness

Now it will be noted that the constructs at a 'higher' level (such as 'structure of the universe' or 'subatomic structure') are invariably inferred from things at a lower level. They *depend* upon these 'lower' level constructs as rigorously as a logical proof depends upon its premises. For if *A* makes a 'higher-level' statement, and is asked 'How do you know?', he may reply by referring to the consistency of the structure as a whole, and may even refer his questioner to a yet 'higher' level. But ultimately, when asked in turn how he knows that, and how he knows that again, he will invariably be obliged to refer to 'lower-level' constructs, to the data of sense experience, to justify the correspondence of the whole structure to reality. We have thus, as we proceed upwards through this hierarchy, a diminishing perspective of certainty. We are 'directly' aware of objects, for instance; but a little thought will show that, when we say this, we see objects 'as' objects because of the data they provide for our senses, and because of the way that we have learnt to interpret these data, integrating them into a unitary 'perception' of the object. Any theory about the behaviour of molecules, or fundamental particles, or gravitational forces, is dependent not only on theory but on data drawn from levels below the theory, that is from the observed behaviour of solid bodies in space, from observations through microscopes, from droplets in cloud-chambers, and so on.

Does this diagram represent the true sequence of events? Do we build up our picture of the world in a strictly progressive way, building from the lower to the higher levels, and never leaping a storey and filling in the one below it later? This would be too much to claim. It has been pointed out, for instance, that even in the first stages of learning about the world, children do not always acquire more particular terms first, and more general terms later. They do not, for instance, usually learn to use such terms as 'elm' or 'oak' before they learn the more general term 'tree'.[13] None the less the broad passage from objects to notions of relations between objects, would seem to be correct. And in any case, the diagram represents in an approximate way the nature of the structure that is built up: it demonstrates the dependency of the 'higher' levels upon the 'lower'.

As for our construction of the human world, the world, that is, of personal and social relationships, the picture is similar. We may schematize it as follows:

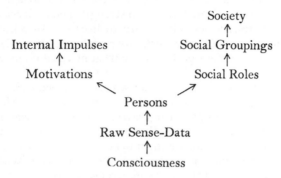

Again this is very rough and over-simplified. However, it must be admitted that we never meet a 'person' as such, but only go through a series of experiences which we interpret as the effect of the actions of a 'person'. But doubtless this interpretation is unavoidable. So it must at least be admitted that we never meet a 'social role' as such, but only persons acting 'in their social role'; that we never meet a 'motivation' as such, but only deduce such motivations from the consistencies and inconsistencies of people's behaviour; and that we never confront 'society' as such, but only people acting 'in society's name'. Thus, none of the levels depends on anything but the levels below it. It might be argued that we can to some extent perceive our own motivations, our own inner impulses, and even the effect upon us of having to take on roles ourselves. But as this is again an appeal to our own conscious experience, the validation of such concepts is again dependent on consciousness. Again, therefore, we have a diminishing perspective of certainty as we look upwards to these 'higher' levels. We build, but as with solid towers of stone, it is the upper storeys that are shakiest. Besides, as we gaze upwards at our stone tower, we see its upper levels in increasingly vaguer focus: the patches of moss, the flaking stone, so evident at eye-level, become indistinguishable from the tower's uniform greyness four storeys up; similarly, generalizations about 'roles', 'classes' and 'society' inevitably submerge the particularity and variety of individual behaviour into a set of vaguer impressions and more general assumptions. Completeness and certainty are both reduced.

3. Constructing Science

None may arrive at the Truth until he is able to think that the Path itself may be wrong.   (Idries Shah, *Thinkers of the East*, p. 38)

How, then, are we to obtain certainty about the outside world? How can we achieve a complete picture of it? Of all human activities, the scientific is that which lays greatest claim to certainty; and the amazing success of many areas of scientific endeavour lends credence to this claim. Our grasp over Nature has been strengthened remarkably in the past hundred years, and our vulnerability to disease and death singularly reduced. But to what degree of certainty can science attain? How complete is its picture of the world? And by what means does it achieve its results?

The first point to be noticed is that science is indeed *incomplete*. One reason for this is that it (*a*) *abstracts from reality*. Henry Margenau's picture of the way we progress from raw sensory data to scientific hypothesis is as follows. We start with complexes of sensory data, which we contemplate, and pronounce them to be 'a desk' or 'a tree'. In doing so we fit raw experience into categories. We then, on the basis of these categories of objects, develop more general categories, which relate to all solid physical objects, such as 'mass', 'weight', 'solidity'. The scientist then abstracts further from these categories, to reduce them to 'pointer-readings', which can be dealt with in a consistent and rational way within the procedures of science: thus the notion of 'mass' or 'solid state' in science is a further abstraction from the commonsense notions of 'mass' and 'solidity'. At each stage of this process we are further from the raw sense experience.[14]

Polanyi's view of things resembles this. He lists in order of distance from sensory reality,

(1) the descriptive sciences, (2) the exact sciences, (3) the deductive sciences. [This] is a sequence of increasing formalization and symbolic manipulation, combined with decreasing contact with experience. Higher degrees of formalization make the statements of science more precise, its inferences more impersonal and correspondingly more 'reversible';[15] but every step towards this ideal is achieved by a progressive sacrifice of content. The immense wealth of living shapes governed by the descriptive sciences is narrowed down to bare pointer-readings for the purpose of the exact sciences, and experience vanishes altogether from our direct sight as we pass on to pure mathematics.' (Polanyi 1958, p. 86)

Secondly, science is *incomplete* because it (*b*) arrives at an understanding of Nature *progressively*. It is clear that we do not start out knowing everything. We have to gradually and painfully plumb the depths of nature. Margenau writes :

> one cannot follow the development of optics, the changes in our conceptions of heat, sound, electricity, chemical affinity, combustion, the firmament, or our notions about the human soul without being impressed by the multitude of ways in which Man has endeavoured to link Nature with reason. Nor can one maintain, in view of such evidence, that the method now in vogue has any likelihood of being ultimate.[16]

Thus for instance Newtonian physics, on which nineteenth-century science had based its alleged certainties, was supplanted (or rather supplemented) by Einstein's theories of relativity around the turn of the century. It is now regarded as a special case of the more complete Einsteinian system. But Einstein's system itself is not necessarily watertight; and from time to time proposals are made to amend it. Thus again, the accepted notions about the internal processes of stars and of our own star, the sun, are currently being reappraised; and the present state of the physics of fundamental particles is one of rapidly proceeding discovery, great controversy, and many conflicting theories.

Of course, the fact that Nature can be discovered only progressively is in fact an advantage. For if it could be discovered only *in toto*, we should never have been able to make a start. As Geoffrey Chew says,

> A key discovery of Western culture has been [this]: that different aspects of nature can be individually 'understood' in an approximate sense without everything's being understood at once. All phenomena ultimately are interconnected, so an attempt to understand only a part necessarily leads to some error, but the error often is sufficiently small for the partial approach to be meaningful. Save for this remarkable and far from obvious property of nature, scientific progress would be impossible. Current examples of the partial approach in science are a cosmology that ignores quantum effects; a biology that ignores almost all hadrons;[17] a particle physics that ignores gravitation; a natural science that ignores the mechanism underlying consciousness.   (1968, p. 763)

Thus science is, although progressive, (*c*) *approximate and partial*. It can also (*d*) *rarely be 100% certain*. Consider the business of weather forecasts : observation stations are set up in (or flown over) particular areas. The happenings within range of these stations are observed; and from these observations a prediction can be made. However, there are always areas between these stations where happenings might be occurring out of range of the stations; and these may well affect the actual outcome of the weather. Science is a system of measurements; but what slips out *between* the measurements can in the nature of things never be taken into account.[18]

19

These limitations on the 'perfection' of science – limitations which are imposed by the nature of the physical universe – *impose certain conditions on the nature of scientific inquiry*. In the first place, it has to be (*a*) *a gradual and progressive approach* to an understanding of reality. It follows therefore that reaching new understanding must always depend on the activities of individuals and groups of scientists who have a new contribution to make, new ideas which are in conflict to some extent with the conventional scientific wisdom. Total anarchy would of course be unproductive; but some fairly large degree of (*b*) *free inquiry* is an absolute essential if science is not to grind to a halt altogether. It follows therefore that a totalitarian or absolutist mentality is damaging to science. And since this observation logically follows from the nature of scientific inquiry and from the nature of the universe itself, we may say that (*c*) *an absolutist attitude is not in accord with the nature of reality*.[19]

Do scientific ideas, then, correspond to reality? The answer is that they do so approximately; and that we may speak, not of an exact match between science and reality, but only of a progressive approach of science to reality. As Victor Hugo wrote (remarkably, for his period) : 'La science est l'asymptote de la vérité. Elle approche sans cesse et ne touche jamais.' (Science is truth's asymptote.[20] It moves ever closer, but never coincides.) And the whole history of science bears witness to this. Indeed, even if one day we had advanced so far that our notions of the universe were exact in every respect, *how should we ever know this*? We might have observed an exact fit between our theories and reality on every verifiable occasion; but we should still be unable to assert the impossibility of some new evidence occurring which might one day disprove our theories. Even if we knew everything, we could never know that we knew.[21]

Furthermore, (*d*) *the observer*, in modern science, *is an essential part of scientific discovery*. Pure 'objectivity' totally divorced from the individual observing consciousness, is no longer possible. This is particularly the case in quantum physics, where (as I have already mentioned) the experimenter may decide to measure *either* the momentum of a subatomic particle, *or* its position; but he may not do both at once. Thus, what we discover is dependent on his decision. And in Einstein's relativity theory, the manifold different points of view that hypothetical observers may inspect the data from, have to be taken into account before a true picture of the whole can be obtained. Mendel Sachs remarks :

> The real revolution that came with Einstein's theory was the abandonment of the idea that the space–time coordinate system has objective significance as a separate physical entity. Instead of this idea, relativity theory implies that the space and time co-

ordinates are only the elements of a language that is used by an observer to describe his environment.[22]   (Sachs 1969, p. 53)

However, as a matter of fact scientific 'objectivity' always did depend ultimately on individual subjectivity. The report of an isolated individual subjectivity. The report of an isolated individual as to his scientific findings is, it is true, not necessarily disbelieved; nor is the experiment always repeated. However, experiments should always be in principle repeatable, since a scientific finding should be true at all times for all (competent) observers. For there will certainly be times when the experiment has been wrongly set up, wrongly interpreted, etc. The only check on this is to bring in other observers who can repeat the experiment to their own satisfaction. And this is what affirms the 'objectivity' of the findings. (e) 'Objectivity' in science, then, as elsewhere, is simply this and nothing more: the *agreement between subjectivities*. For the presence of observers is essential: nothing can be known if there is no-one to know it.[23]

It must be added, however, that equally nothing can be known if the people who know something conceal that knowledge. Objectivity in science depends on scientists' reporting their observations accurately. Not that accurate report is any guarantee in itself that they are not mistaken; but in a social system where they are obliged, on pain of ostracism, dismissal, jail or the firing-squad, to falsify their observations, we cannot even know *what* their observations were, let alone whether they were mistaken or not! The warrant of accurate perception is thus not merely the assent of other individuals: to be valid such assent must be freely given. But who, it will be asked, is free? To this I shall reply that everyone knows what I mean: nobody is entirely free, of prejudice, error, parti-pris or the pressures of social approval; but there are degrees of coercion and independence, and these bear on the reliability of the evidence people offer. It would seem, then, that one of the conditions of objectivity is the existence of (relatively) free individuals.

We must also remember that what we can discover about reality may well be limited by the nature of our senses and our minds. Many of the concepts of modern science are, as it happens, quite strictly unimaginable. It is hard to imagine a thing like an electron, for instance, which is both wave and particle at once, and which is *twice a perfect sphere* (sic). And can the space–time continuum, consisting of three spatial dimensions and one of time, be imagined? So far we have managed to extend our concepts of reality beyond the imaginable, by utilizing the strange structures of modern mathematics, for instance. But it may be that we shall one day come up against the brick wall of the incomprehensible, even the unmathematizable, and no further progress will be possible.

Finally, it is worth at least canvassing the possibility that consciousness may ultimately be found to be an essential fundamental component

21

of the universe 'so that even elementary particles would be endowed with it in some degree' (Firsoff 1967, p. 102). Charles S. Peirce suggested, long ago, that mind is matter seen from the inside; and that matter is mind seen from the outside.[24] A number of eminent modern scientists have toyed with possibilities of this kind. Eddington observed that the basic entities of which the modern scientist believes the world to be made (electrons, neutrons, and so forth) resemble 'mind-stuff' rather than matter. D. F. Lawden has proposed that there might be an elementary mental particle called a 'mindon'.[25] The quantum mathematician Schrödinger seems to hold that consciousness is the basic world-stuff.[26] Geoffrey Chew speculates that perhaps 'the existence of consciousness, along with all other aspects of nature, is necessary for self-consistency of the whole' (Chew 1968, p. 317). A similar conjecture is made by Misner, Thorne & Wheeler (1973, pp. 1216–7).[27]

What, then, is our conclusion about the relationship of science to the world? Science is a construction. The foundation of this construction is, as with all other human constructions, consciousness.

However, there is certainly something more reliable about the constructions of science than about most of our human notions. Polanyi's concept of 'reversibility' will show us just why this higher degree of certainty can be achieved. 'Reversibility' is the possibility of tracing an inference back to its premises (Polanyi 1958, p. 75). It is, in other words, the possibility of examining the plausibility of a theory in the light of the concrete evidence, of the experimental data, and of retracing the logical steps which link the theory to its premises, and the premises to the physical evidence. Admittedly, the scientist reduces diversity to identity; he looks for a single guiding system beyond the diversity of phenomena. He will therefore always tend to assume that if one theory is more all-embracing, more elegant, more powerful in an explanatory way than other competing theories, then it is more likely to be correct. But he has other criteria too. As well as having explanatory power, a theory must ultimately be capable of giving concrete results, it must predict experimental findings and agree with the observed evidence. A scientist's final test is always to return to direct experience, and see if his theory works in practice. Science, in other words, exists in the tension between beautiful theories and stubborn facts. Numerous are the elegant scientific theories which have obtained the total adherence of the experts for a time, but which, under the dual pressure of brute facts and still more elegant theories, have had to be abandoned. In the last resort, no matter how beautiful a theory is, it is the test of its agreement with raw sensory experience that is applied. Science is more certain than other fields of human endeavour simply because of this: the higher storeys of the scientific tower are always regarded as hypotheses, to be dismantled or rebuilt if, on investigation, they do not accord with the particular observable facts on which they are poised. The ultimate test of abstract constructs is concrete sense-data. We have to verify our hypotheses in science by returning to the levels nearer to consciousness.

But this, of course, merely repeats the conclusion already suggested : human consciousness is, in one way or another, always the final arbiter.

4. Constructing Social Science

The attempt to discover a genuine deeper reality is also the ambition of the social sciences. But even the physical sciences find it extremely difficult to deal with complex phenomena. The more variables that are involved, the more difficult it becomes. Every human being is a complex of a very large number of variables; and every social system is of course a complex of such complexes. It is indeed impossible to enumerate the variables contained within a social system (Margenau 1964, pp. 62– 74). Analyses of society are thus always simplifications. I once saw a photograph of a girl's face which had been obtained by exposing briefly upon the same negative the faces of more than a hundred different girls. The result was a generalized face, a little misty, touchingly beautiful, but corresponding to none of the originals. One could not predict the features of a single girl from seeing the features of the generalized face. Nor could one predict the behaviour of any individual from reading an analysis of society.

But could one predict the behaviour of society as a whole? That perhaps has some greater likelihood, and Margenau suggests that, just as we may predict the behaviour of masses of elementary particles by the use of statistical laws, so we might be able to predict the behaviour of masses of people (Ibid.). However, it must be remembered that electrons are identical to each other, whereas people are all different. It must also be remembered that

> Physical objects are indifferent to the knowledge man acquires of them; they display a kind of stability or inertness which makes predictions possible. Stars continue to move in a manner expressible by laws whether or not those laws are known, whether or not predictions are applied to their motion . . . In psychology the state of affairs is different. If a subject knows what a psychologist knows about it, he may spontaneously act to make the latter's knowledge false. There is, furthermore, the possibility of simulation or of making erroneous answers to an inquiry, deliberately or otherwise. (Ibid., p. 73)

Thus William H. Whyte, in his *Organization of Man*, actually includes a long (and morally responsible) appendix on 'How to cheat on personality tests'. And one recalls the

> legendary story in psychology of a well-known researcher into the

behaviour of apes who devised a complex experiment for one of his animals. He set up the materials in the ape's cell, a room purposely cut off from view by a wooden door. As soon as everything was ready, he placed the chimpanzee in the cell, closed the door, and immediately kneeled at the keyhole to observe. As he peered in, his glance was met by a large brown eye peering out.[28]

Thus the social scientist's 'society' will tend always to *automatize the deliberate, mechanize the conscious, freeze the flowing, and simplify the complex*. In short, it is an abstraction from reality (cf. Dahrendorf 1973). But there is a still more fundamental problem.

For what is the *mode of being* of society and of social forces? An electron has, supposedly, real external existence, as has a gene, a neuron, the force of gravity, or the earth's magnetic field. That is, such things exist in some sense independently of what we think of them, though the mode of being that we ascribe to them is dependent on our human consciousnesses. But what is the ontological status of a social law? What is the ontological status of, say, a taboo (such as is common in some societies) on having one's mother-in-law's shadow fall upon one, or on seducing one's own sister? Such social imperatives exist only in the minds of those who have been taught them. They have no objective external existence, since there is no scientific law that condemns sons-in-law or incestuous brothers to death. And only to the extent that they are believed in and adhered to by a large number of the individual members of a given society, have they any subjective existence either. The structures of science depend on the consciousness of individuals, not for the reality that lies behind them, but for the fact of their discovery and the way in which they are understood. But the structures of social science are dependent on the consciousness of individuals for their very operation and *their very being*.

Thus we know that 'we cannot walk through brick walls or move a seven-foot wardrobe upright through a six-foot door' (Kelvin 1970, pp. 22–3). In science we are working with a reality that can be to some extent manipulated, but not changed or recreated. By contrast, there are few such constraints upon our social behaviour. (There are of course some, such as the facts of procreation, the limitations of language and, perhaps, the aggressive instinct.) But 'apart from the constraints due to certain physical limitations, . . . the social environment as such has no inherent constraints, no 'facts' other than those which man himself creates' (Ibid., p. 35). Kelvin therefore contrasts the 'laws' of physical science with the 'values' of the social order : we find the former, we create the latter. As he observes, we probably create our social orders because we need order and regularity; but this need places few restraints on the kind of order and regularity that we establish. There are some such restraints, of course; remarkable though it is for its immense flexibility, human society none the less does not exist in the same degree of variety that animal and insect societies do; but within the limits of human possibilities, the *form* that our societies take is always conventional. The nature of 'fact' in science and in social science is thus quite different. In both science and social science our knowledge of the 'facts' is relative; but the facts of science are approximations to a natural order whose laws are outside our control; whereas the 'facts' of social science, however generally accepted, however unexpected or unconscious, are created by ourselves.

> Ultimately any consistent patterns of social behaviour and relationship rest on consensus, on the consensus that this shall be done and that shall not. But the consensus, however arrived at . . . , can always be ignored or revoked, and the 'laws' which govern such behaviour may be changed or even reversed.   (Ibid., p. 24)

In short, unless a 'social force' or a 'social law' or a particular 'conception of society' is (consciously or unconsciously) assented to by the individuals belonging to that society, it ceases to operate and therefore to exist. Now this is not at all the case with physical laws. Whether an atomic bomb explodes and kills thousands of the inhabitants of Nagasaki is not dependent on the beliefs of the Japanese. But whether or not it is a sin to be rude to the old, or to be married to more than one wife, depends entirely on belief.

At this point an objection must be considered. It is often (and rightly) said that we would not be fully human without our social environment. An 'asocial' man would be an abstraction, or (like wolf-children) not completely human. Society 'creates' us: it creates our language, our customs, our behaviour and our attitudes to each other. Nor could we have evolved as we have, even genetically, were it not for the human and prehuman societies through which our ancestors were 'selected'. Without language, a man would be less than human; and language is 'a social fact'.

Language, however, is just as dependent on individual consciousness as (for a Britisher) a bride wearing white at weddings, or (for a traditional Sicilian) avenging adultery by murder. Now it is true that Saussure, in his discussion of *langue* and *parole* (or 'language', the socially accepted common denominator of language, and 'speech', the individual speech acts accomplished by individual speakers), does not seem at first sight to agree with me here. He writes that

> in separating language from speaking we are at the same time separating (1) what is social from what is individual and (2) what is essential from what is accessory and more or less accidental. Language is not a function of the speaker; it is a product that is passively assimilated by the individual . . . Language is a well-defined object in the heterogeneous mass of speech facts. It can be

localized in the limited segment of the speaking-circuit where an auditory image becomes associated with a concept. It is the social side of speech, outside the individual who can never create nor modify it by himself; it exists only by virtue of a sort of contract signed by the members of a community.   (Saussure 1966, p. 14)

This reads as if Saussure thinks there is automatic imprinting of meanings on individual brains – a process which allows no variation in individual meanings, or even shadings between such meanings, and which would be, in effect, behaviourist *avant la lettre*. However, considerable caution is needed. Saussure's great *Course in General Linguistics* was the result of compiling the notes of students; he did not write it himself. One may wonder whether these words truly represent Saussure's thought. For immediately before this passage he gives a very different picture. Language, he says,

is a storehouse filled by the members of a given community through their active use of speaking, a grammatical system that has a potential existence in each brain, or, more specifically, in the brains of a group of individuals. For language is not complete in any speaker; it exists perfectly only within a collectivety.

(Ibid., pp. 13–14)

In other words, *langue* (language) is an abstraction. The 'French language', for instance, is the common denominator of a number of individual speech acts. What are real are the speech acts and the individual language systems within the brain of each individual speaker. Every man has his *own* language system; in so far as it is very similar to those of most of the other speakers he meets, he and they will understand each other. Understanding depends on the similarity of these individual language systems, not on some abstraction inhabiting the cave of Plato or the grove of Academe. Moreover, the act of learning meanings, the long process of assimilating a language, is not a passively undergone process like the stamping of an image on a coin; it is, as Saussure says, an active process, requiring the participatory understanding of each individual. It is thus just as dependent on individuals as is any other social phenomenon, be it a taboo, a handshake or the comprehension of a gesture.

The point of view that I am putting forward here has some eminent supporters. Let me quote, for example, Karl Popper:

all social phenomena, and especially the functioning of all social institutions, should always be understood as resulting from the decisions, actions, attitudes, etc of human individuals, and . . . we should never be satisfied by an explanation in terms of so-called 'collectives'.   (Popper 1966, vol. 2, p. 98)

Steven Lukes, in a lucid essay, undertakes to 'render harmless' the views of Popper (or 'methodological individualism' as these views are termed). He protests (1) that it would be inordinately clumsy to refrain from talking about social institutions. He is right. It would, he says, be 'futile linguistic purism' to forbid us to use the words 'bank', 'voting', 'saluting' or 'tribe' (Lukes 1973, p. 127). Indeed, I am not proposing that people should cease to utter them. I am merely proposing that when they talk about such things they should remember that they are using constructs. He also says (2) that 'some social phenomena can simply be observed (as both trees and forests can)'. Again, it is true in a sense that we can observe social phenomena, but only in the way that we can observe forests, namely as a large number of individuals which interact in certain ways. Lukes goes on to say that the procedures of a court can be observed more easily than the intentions of an individual. True again, but 'observed' is the wrong term. In fact not even the procedures of a court can be observed as such. Both they and our guesses about people's intentions are deductions from the actual behaviour of human beings. He also complains (3) that social phenomena are easier to understand than individual phenomena, so that to explain the former by the latter does not promote ease of explanation. Again, I should agree. Indeed, it is a part of my case in this book that we need general constructs so as to make large complexes of individual phenomena intelligible and manageable; but that this requirement may lead us to overlook the concrete reality of our experience. Certainly if we seek ease of explanation, we will use convenient shorthand terms like 'society' and 'tribe'; but we must not forget that these terms conceal the complexities of individual behaviour; and that they are shorthand for the similarities in people's dispositions, learning patterns and activities. It is not ease of explanation I am seeking here, but the basic realities of the matter; not simplifications, however approximate, but truths, however complex. Lukes remarks (4) that 'individuals do not exist independently of groups and institutions' (Ibid., pp. 123–4). This is also true. However, what is the manner of being of these groups and institutions? They consist of individuals.

Thus, all those of Lukes's objections which I have noted, are in one sense justified. But the reason why they are correct (up to a point) and justified (up to a point) is that they are concerned with what it is convenient or customary or easy to say; not with what is fundamentally the case. In a sense, therefore, there is no real disagreement between Lukes and myself at all! For he writes at the start of his essay:

> Let us begin with a set of truisms. Society consists of people. Groups consist of people. Institutions consist of people plus rules and roles. Rules are followed (or alternatively not followed) by people and roles are filled by people. Also there are traditions, customs, ideologies, kinship systems, languages: these are ways people act, think, talk. At the risk of pomposity, these truisms may

be said to constitute a theory (let us call it 'Truistic Social Atom-
ism') made up of banal propositions about the world that are
analytically true, i.e. in virtue of the meaning of words.

(Ibid., p. 121)

Lukes thus defines 'society', 'group', 'institution', 'rule', 'custom',
'language', etc., as 'ways people act, think and talk'. This, he says, is
the *meaning* of these words. I agree. Lukes is not, as far as I can see,
asserting that such constructs have any reality apart from the existence
of the men who operate them in virtue of their beliefs and dispositions.
He wants, of course, to be allowed to *employ* the terms in question. But
there is no objection to his doing so, provided that he does not overlook
the concrete realities which justify their use. (I should merely remind
him that there are some political thinkers who would benefit from his
advice.)

On the other hand, society has *subjective* existence, that is, it is
regarded by individuals as existing : it is a mental construct, to which
we attribute some degree of reality, and this fact profoundly affects our
dealings with other people. Provided these rather limited definitions
are given to the word 'exist', therefore, I should agree '(1) that nations,
schools, groups, etc., *exist*, and (2) that social trends *operate*. What [I
deny] is that (1) group entities are self-existent and (2) social institutions or societies self-propelling' (Chattopadhyaya 1975, p. 46).[29] I
should assert in fact that

> The social world . . . does not constitute a reality *sui generis*
> divorced from the human beings who constitute its membership.
> Rather, the social world is the external product of human activity
> and is sustained and changed by such activity. Insofar as the social
> world is intersubjectively produced by its members, it becomes
> externalized *vis-à-vis* them – that is, it comes to possess a degree of
> objective [reality . . . but this] resides in the manner by which its
> members apprehend it. [Thus] the social world [is not] an
> object world in the same sense as the natural world. [For] the
> natural world does not depend upon human recognition for its
> existence . . . In contrast, a given social world *would necessarily
> cease to exist if human recognition were withdrawn from it*, since it
> has no existence apart from such recognition.

(Walsh 1972, pp. 18–19, my italics)

We have thus to attribute different orders of reality to the hypotheses of
science and to the structures of society : to the former, we must attribute
the status of approximate facts; to the latter, that of inventions, conventions, or even fictions. We may deny that an objective *physical* reality
can be *known* independently of a knowing human subject; but we must
deny that an objective *social* reality can *exist* independently of a knowing
human subject.

If the 'reality' of the constructs of physical science is somewhat hazier and flimsier than the reality of our own consciousness – which is the founder and guarantor of such constructs – how much more hazy and flimsy is the 'reality' of the constructs of social life : we have good reason for saying that society and its 'laws' are less real than the individuals which create them. For it is not merely our *knowledge* of society which depends on our consciousness : it is society's very *existence*.

And this, to tell the truth, is just as well. For if each particular social order were primary, then it would be impossible to find a vantage point outside it, from which to judge between it and any other. This would be an intolerable situation; and it is not in any case one that is ever in practice accepted by the critics of human society, of whatever political persuasion. We should be trapped in relativism : each society would be assumed to *create* human beings in its own terms; and since this would be in its own terms, it would be by definition their *perfect* creator. Fortunately, however, consciousness is prior to society, as also are certain other basic features of mankind such as the human perceptual and nervous system, the fact of difference between different individuals, the common logic embedded in all languages (see pp. 21–2), and so on. For the human infant is not a *tabula rasa* : consciousness and perceptual faculties are necessary for the process of socialization itself.

The primacy of consciousness and perception offers us an escape from the spectre of moral relativism. And it must be noted that it is not the *individualist* but the *individual* that I am identifying here as the basis of a common humanity. That is, I am not speaking of the selfish Western 'individual', but of an entity much more fundamental, namely that amalgam of consciousness and perception, judgment and reason, which is the bedrock of the human individual in *all* societies. This entity I term the 'essential individual'. If it is, as I have suggested, *by*, *of* and *through* him that society exists, then it should, by Lincolnian logic, also be *for* him.

5. The Social Constructs of 'Common Sense'

In the generality of human affairs, we do not deal even in the partly verified and shakily verifiable concepts of sociology, but with abstractions of a much more doubtful nature that we have learnt from growing up in our own particular society. As we grow, we imbibe 'commonsense' notions of human character, of human motives, of social class, and of 'the State'. We talk as if 'the people's will' had 'spoken' when an election is held; we talk as if the working class 'wants' the welfare state, as if Britain 'decided' to declare war in the autumn of 1939. When we discuss our own or others' countries, we constantly use abstractions which are intensely familiar to us and to the people we talk to, but which are rarely, if ever, examined for their real content. As Huxley writes, we have a duty to analyse the words currently used in newspapers, on platforms, by preachers and broadcasters. What, for example, does the word 'nation' mean? To what extent are speakers and writers justified in talking of a nation as a person? Who precisely is the 'she', of whom people speak when discussing a nation's foreign politics? ('Britain is an imperial power. She must defend her Empire.') In what sense can a nation be described as having a will or national interests? Are these interests and will the interests and will of the entire population? or of a majority? or of a ruling caste and a few professional politicians? In what way, if any, does 'the state' differ from Messrs Smith, Brown, Jones and the other gentlemen who happen for the moment to have secured political power? Given the character of Brown, Jones, etc., why should 'the state' be regarded as an institution worthy of almost religious respect? Where does national honour reside? Why would the loss of Hong-Kong, for example, be a mortal blow to Britain's honour, while its seizure after a war in which Britain attempted to force the Chinese to buy opium is in no way a stain upon the same honour? And so on. 'Nation' is only one of several dozens of rich and resonant words which are ordinarily accepted without a thought, but which it is essential, if we would think clearly, that we should subject to the most searching analysis.

(1937, pp. 214–15)

The language of politics is still exactly the same. I read for instance in *The Sunday Times* the reproaches of a journalist to President Carter for having publicly protested to Latin American countries who practise torture on their own citizens. His 'biggest mistake is to have made a public show of [this] pressure . . .', he writes. 'In doing this, [he has] offended national pride' (6 May 1977). Echoing Huxley, we may ask: Why is it not a stain on national pride to practise torture, whereas it is such a stain to be told that you do?

Besides, exactly who *feels* this pride? Five or six military dictators, possibly . . . and how many other individuals? 'National pride' is a content-less excuse for depriving a nation of its liberties, as 'the States' rights' was in the sixties a content-less excuse for depriving Southern negroes of the vote.

We might add: how can the U.S.A. and the U.S.S.R. both be 'democracies'? Who are 'the masses'? What are 'culture', 'equality' and 'socialism'? When General Videla, described as 'the *de facto* Argentine president', sends a 'remarkably warm message to the Pinochet regime and the Chilean people' (Ibid.), who precisely are 'the Chilean people'? He can't mean *all* of them, surely? And when President Carter protests about human rights in the U.S.S.R., thereby reminding that government of one of the clauses agreed under the treaty of 'détente', why is this commonly regarded as an action liable to 'destroy *détente* and bring back the cold war'?[30] *Détente* must be a strange sort of thing if it is destroyed by one of the criteria for its own existence, as if a four-legged table ceased to be a four-legged table the moment it had more than three legs.

Roger Caillois, in *Babel*, wonders at one point what the term 'a young nation' can possibly mean. That its constitution is recent? Or that it has a high proportion of young people? Or that its leaders are younger than usual? Or more impetuous than most? Or is it an expanding and rapidly developing country? And are these virtues or advantages? Perhaps not, and if so,

> 'Jeune' n'exprime pas . . . une réalité, mais un prestige qui se dissipe, si on insiste, c'est-à-dire si on demande des explications afin de savoir ce qu'il recouvre. Il ne recouvrait rien. C'était une sorte de chèque sans provision.
>
> Le malheur est que, par paresse, il s'en trouve peu qui pensent à la présenter au guichet de la banque. La plupart l'endossent les yeux fermés et le passent à une autre dupe.'
>
> (Caillois 1948, pp. 186–7)
>
> ['Young' does not express a reality but an aura, which fades the moment you probe, the moment you press for an explanation of what lies behind it. Nothing lies behind it. If it were a cheque, it would bounce.
>
> Unfortunately, apathy is such that few think of presenting it at the counter of a bank. Most endorse it with their eyes closed and pass it on to another dupe.]

If we want to know what reality such constructs have, we should apply the scientist's rule of 'reversibility': we should see if they connect with the stubborn facts of experience, and trace their meaning back to the individual events without which they are a mere concatenation of specious syllables.

6. Coda

I conclude then that knowledge is as much a construction by individuals as paintings are constructions by artists. When a representational artist attempts to reproduce the world around him, its shapes and colours have to be registered on his mind before his hand can register them on canvas. Similarly, the statements of science presuppose the existence of human consciousnesses which have interpreted the world and appealed to others for approval or dissent. Science is not the model herself; it is consciousness's painting of the model.

Our knowledge of society is still more dependent on consciousness. Sociology is the study of how people interact; and they interact according to rules of interaction they have learned from other people. Sociology is not therefore a painting of something which has reality in its own right; that something has partial or qualified reality, because it exists only in the form of people's conscious or unconscious notions of it, and of the behaviour that is a consequence of those notions. In sociology, there is no model save consciousness's paintings of other consciousnesses' paintings.

This is at once a source of confidence and a motive for diffidence. If knowledge is a product of individuals, then these individuals are of primary importance. On the other hand, since knowledge is not identical with its objects, and since it is mediated through individual consciousnesses, it can be seen to be an image, an interpretation, a simulacrum of reality. Consciousness is a window: without it we should be sunk in darkness. Yet it none the less separates us from reality as a window separates us from the air outside. Nor is there any help to be found in appealing to the authority of some political, religious or philosophical creed; for all these things are equally the product of consciousness. And in any case, the *differences* between individual consciousnesses' assessments of reality is (as we saw above) a vital factor in evaluating and enlarging our own knowledge. To swallow without question the fixed menu which is all that society, the state or the dominant creed offers us, would be (to mix my metaphor) merely to offer ourselves the blinkers of a fixed and single view on the world rather than the possibility of altered and expanding perspectives.

> The logically 'convergent' world of concepts which each man fabricates for himself during the first two decades of his life with the aid of language is, of course, essential for everyday activity. It provides him with the mental and behavioural map of the world he needs to act rationally . . . Society must have its maps of 'real events' if it is to function properly. But however truthful it may be, however accurately it may meet utilitarian needs and guide courses of action over the terrain, a map *is* not an actual landscape. As the key to a conglomeration of concepts, it is not the reality it indicates; which latter is always infinitely richer in possible forms than any conceptual reduction of it that can be made. And when one's customary map comes to impose its own conceptual limitations on the landscape, preventing one from even experiencing any aspects or forms of the reality which are beyond its scope, then it becomes an insidiously comfortable prison. The ordinary, non-artistic usages of language help every day in forging that prison's bars by reinforcing the conventional patterns of perception and experience. (Rawson 1978, p. 37)

In short, we 'construct' reality for ourselves. But that construction cannot be treated with total credence (any more than it can be treated with total disbelief).

It is therefore with a moderated scepticism that we should accept the constructs, structures and systems that our thought has built for us. A certain openness, a certain tentative willingness to experiment and to listen : these are invaluable qualities. We have to lay ourselves open to the experiences of others; and this, as we shall see (and as we have just seen Rawson implying) includes an openness to the *non*-ordinary, artistic usages of language, in which such experiences are mediated.

2. The Key of the Kingdom

Lack of interest in literature is often a sign of indifference to concrete reality.   (Milan Kundera)

1. Knowledge and the Individual

AFTER the long semi-philosophical discursus of Chapter 1, I shall now try to see what we have established, and show how, in the light of the importance of the individual consciousness, we may be led to revalue the function of literature.

Knowledge, as we saw above depends on (*a*) consciousness (pp. 9–10), (*b*) agreement between different consciousnesses (pp. 10, 20–1), and (*c*) the possibility of their disagreeing; for this is the guarantee of their difference and hence of the value of their agreement (p. 10). It has also been shown to depend on the individuals in question being (*d*) free to report their perceptions (pp. 20, 21). Variety of perception among different individuals is thus a most important feature of experience. We should, for instance, notice something new much less often if it were not for others who tell us of things we should never have observed for ourselves. An imposed authoritarian unity of viewpoint thus hides, and does not reveal, truth.

Hence it is important to be able to recognize the reality of others, the possibility that there might be a sincere difference in their view of things, and that their perceptions might be, on occasion more, on occasion less accurate than our own. A forced conformity of viewpoint is to be regretted because it falsifies the conditions of knowledge and makes it impossible to progress towards greater understanding.

Moreover, although it is partly through reason and the principle of consistency that we arrive at new understanding, *reversibility* is the final test of such understanding : it must be possible to return from theory to observed and observable data. And it is only through individual consciousness that data are observed (pp. 22–3).

Individual consciousness must therefore be given a sort of primacy : it is more 'real' in a sense than exterior reality, because only *through it* can reality be judged, reassessed, or even initially apprehended. It is a striking fact that science has usually scored its greatest successes in countries where the protestant world-view has been dominant, that is, a world-view in which individual interpretation of reality is given precedence over the diktat of some supreme authority.

How does this relate to literature? The answer is: very well. The techniques of novels are consciousness-centred. However large the canvas (as in Tolstoy's *War and Peace*), however political the intention (as in Jules Vallès, or Koestler's *Darkness at Noon*), the action tends to be seen through the eyes of an individual human being or human beings: we are closely associated with a character's experience, and he appears to us as an individual identity. Forster mentions two essential techniques for the novelist: that of establishing a point of view, and that of drawing character. The latter needs no comment here; the former concerns the question of whether the action of the novel is seen through the eyes of one individual, either speaking in the first person or described in the third; whether it is seen through the eyes of several; or whether it is impersonally narrated from outside them all (but of course such 'impersonal' narration always associates us with the handful of characters that the book contains); or whether and to what extent the novelist himself may intervene. These matters are all concerned with individual identity; the novel cannot do without *someone's* consciousness; and some of its characters at least are usually complex enough to be recognizably human. We may conclude that the vantage-point of human consciousness and the analysis of human personality seem in practice to be two of the essential prerequisites for fiction. Where even characters are absent, as in Philippe Sollers's *Nombres*, we are still left with the author's personality. The issue of consciousness is thus always at the forefront of the novel.

So is the issue of variousness of perception. Within each novel, characters are differentiated; as between each novelist, perceptions and attitudes are differentiated. For Proust, it is only through art that the inner quality of a person's consciousness can be communicated:

Le style pour l'écrivain . . . est une question non de technique mais de vision. Il est la révélation, qui serait impossible par des moyens directs et conscients, de la différence qualitative qu'il y a dans la façon dont nous apparaît le monde, différence qui, s'il n'y avait pas l'art, resterait le secret éternel de chacun. Par l'art seulement nous pouvons sortir de nous, savoir ce que voit un autre de cet univers qui n'est pas le même que le nôtre, et dont les paysages nous seraient restés aussi inconnus que ceux qu'il peut y avoir dans la lune. Grâce à l'art, au lieu de voir un seul monde, le nôtre, nous le voyons se multiplier, et, autant qu'il y a d'artistes originaux, autant nous avons de mondes à notre disposition, plus différents les uns des autres que ceux qui roulent dans l'infini et, bien des siècles après qu'est éteint le foyer dont il émanait, qui'il s'appelât Rembrandt ou Ver Meer, nous envoient encore leur rayon spécial.

(Proust 1965–7)

[For the writer, . . . style is a matter not of technique but of vision. It is the revelation (impossible by direct and conscious means) of the qualitative difference in the way the world appears to us, a difference which, if it were not for art, would eternally remain each person's secret. Through art alone can we step outside ourselves, and know what another human being perceives of this universe that is not the same as ours, and whose landscapes would have remained as unknown to us as the landscapes of the moon. Thanks to art, instead of perceiving only a single world, our own, we can see it divide and multiply; and the more original artists there are, the more worlds we have at our disposal, more different from each other than those which spin in infinite space and, many centuries after the source from which it came has been snuffed out, be it named Rembrandt or Vermeer, still transmit to us their own particular light.]

In Proust's account of things, therefore, 'la vraie vie . . . c'est la littérature.' (The only real life is literature.)

We do not have to go as far as this, of course. Proust's pessimism was unusually complete : for him, all normal communication between human beings was frustrating and misleading. None the less, we may regard works of art as invaluable supplements to what we know of human beings in our face-to-face contacts with them; works of art may serve as the lenses and mirrors through which we may become more conscious of the nature of our fellow beings; and they are, besides, the only record that any of us can leave of the individual quality of ourselves. As such, their value is beyond price.

As a general rule literature tends to display great interest in personal differences of viewpoint; and we value writers themselves because of the originality of their styles and hence their perceptions. Literature constitutes therefore a kind of 'science' of the individual, or rather an exploration of a vast range of different perceptions and attitudes. It is thus an indispensable reminder of the bases of understanding and knowledge itself.

Turning now to my remarks about the social world in Chapter 1, we see that there is a clash between the apparent certainty and solidity of many social constructs (and particularly those of common sense) and their true nature as the constructions of a social group (pp. 23ff). Any element of our experience which might disturb the certainty we too often attribute to such constructs would be most salutary. Social science itself, of course, has the immense value of disturbing our commonsense beliefs about the social world. It points for instance to unconscious elements in the workings of society (such as the different taboos on touching other people that different societies institute); it analyzes society in different and mutually inconsistent ways; it disturbs our sense of 'knowing how society functions'. It thereby sets up a set of clashing schemata, which it progressively criticizes and corrects as time goes on. This is an entirely healthy situation: the reader of social science cannot rest content with either the stable constructs of convention or the progressively elaborated theories of social science itself: he has to develop flexibility of mind.

Social anthropology too has its vital contribution to make. It clashes one society against another; it shows the vast variety of ways in which human beings may function together socially; it demonstrates that the commonsense constructs of one society are not those of another, and that they may even be mutually incompatible (as in the case of the impossibility of even thinking of the notion 'fatherhood' in Trobriand society; so that our own notions of social roles are inconceivable to the Trobrianders).

Literature too however may provide social criticism of the unconscious workings of society. One thinks of Dickens's *Great Expectations*, where the economic underpinnings of society are (by instance and example) shown to be crime (in the person of Magwitch) and parasitism (in the person of Estella). It too, like social anthropology, may offer alternative visions of social possibilities, such as the utopia or the anti-utopia. It too breaks down our naive assumptions.

There is, however, a persistent current of relativism in social science, a belief that all societies are equally valid on their own terms. This is healthy in so far as it is an additional weapon with which to destroy our belief in the self-evident rightness of our own society, certainly. But relativism is not a tenable position (see Chapter 5). And the relativist thinks by definition that all societies are utopias, which is a bizarrely improbable proposition.[1] The utopian or anti-utopian novelist on the other hand demonstrates beyond the possibility of doubt that certain societies (such as Zamyatin's *We*, or that of Kafka's *Trial* or Orwell's *1984*) are at odds with the nature of man. And the realistic novelist too may show that, for example, the society of late-nineteenth-century France (I am thinking partly of Zola) is at odds with the nature of man.

Moreover, what of the pain of the individual facing an uncomprehending and apparently 'concrete' social reality? This is most trenchantly expressed in novels such as Camus's *L'Etranger* or Kafka's *Castle*. For social science is not competent to discuss the individual. Yet, as I showed in Chapter 1, the individual is the foundation of society. He is more 'real' than it, for it is he (in combination with other individuals) who creates it. Literature is the product of society (in a rather vague and general way) but no more so than social science itself is. Both are the product of individuals who may equally criticize the society in which they find themselves. And in some ways perhaps, the literary artist may be as competent as the social scientist to do so. For he must, by the nature of his trade, be always *concrete*.

Take for example moral judgments. The insight of many novelists is that morality is based, not on the conflict between one set of social values and another, nor on some arbitrary authority, but on something more fundamental: consciousness and perception themselves. George Orwell's famous account of 'A hanging' witnessed by him in Burma, offers us this insight:

> It was about forty yards to the gallows. I watched the bare brown back of the prisoner marching in front of me. He walked clumsily with his bound arms, but quite steadily, with that bobbing gait of the Indian who never straightens his knees. At each step his muscles slid neatly into place, the lock of hair on his scalp danced up and down, his feet printed themselves on the wet gravel. And once, in spite of the men who gripped him by each shoulder, he stepped slightly aside to avoid a puddle on the path.
>
> It is curious, but till that moment I had never realized what it means to destroy a healthy, conscious man. When I saw the prisoner step aside to avoid the puddle, I saw the mystery, the unspeakable wrongness, of cutting a life short when it is in full tide. This man was not dying, he was alive just as we were alive. All the organs of his body were working – bowels digesting food, skin renewing itself, nails growing, tissues forming – all toiling away in solemn foolery. His nails would still be growing when he stood on the drop, when he was falling through the air with a tenth of a second to live. His eyes saw the yellow gravel and the grey walls, and his brain still remembered, foresaw, reasoned – reasoned even about puddles. He and we were a party of men walking together, seeing, hearing, feeling, understanding the same world; and in two minutes, with a sudden snap, one of us would be gone – one mind less, one world less.

Let me briefly analyze this description. To begin with, the prisoner is a mere member of a category: he is an Indian with the characteristic gait of an Indian: the description is detached and objective; the mechanisms of his walk are repetitive and automatic. Half category and half machine, he is not yet completely a human being. But suddenly a transformation takes place: resisting the pressure of the hands upon his shoulders, he steps aside to avoid a puddle. The condemned man asserts his will and his identity, and the scales fall from Orwell's eyes: the man is alive and conscious. Moreover, he is like the other men there, alive and conscious in precisely the same way as they are. Should one consciousness take it upon itself to destroy another? The man *sees* the yellow gravel and the grey walls; 'his brain still remembered, foresaw, reasoned' – all fundamental characteristics of the 'essential individual'. Orwell appeals to human solidarity ('he and we were a party of men walking together . . .'), to the consciousness and to the world they all share. There is consciousness and likeness of consciousness; yet each consciousness is a world unto itself, an irreplaceable individual experience. But Orwell's condemned Indian remains anonymous and universal: in his solitude and his uniqueness he resembles us all.

The mere fact of individual consciousness, then, is sufficient to question law and morality. Since it is itself the source of all values, in the name of what values may we eliminate it? Why do we punish an individual? Because he has committed a crime. What is a crime? It is an action regarded by people as damaging to society. What is damage to society? It is damage to individuals within society, for, ultimately, society consists of nothing else. At every turn, therefore, we are brought back to the basic datum of consciousness. It is right, then, that Orwell should clash the demands of the conscious individual against those of society, and should draw our attention to the mystery of consciousness itself.

But the issues can be posed at a still more fundamental level. The final message of *Cancer Ward* is communicated through Kostoglotov's visit to the zoo where he sees the rhesus monkey's cage empty, and a notice of simple explanation pinned upon it: 'A wicked man threw pepper in the rhesus monkey's eyes.' Carried at last to freedom on his train, he weeps for the meaningless suffering of his world, his friends, himself and the tortured monkey ... and for the recognition of simple wickedness contained in that notice hanging in the zoo. For what is wickedness? It is unmotivated cruelty, casual and pointless indifference to the suffering of others. Morality is based upon the horror of suffering; and without an awareness of that suffering, without sympathy for the pure sensation of pain in others, morality and justice have no sense. Morality, in short, has not so much to do with the social system, with the official code, with the legal conventions; it has not so much to do with a man's social identity; it has to do with the 'essential individual', with the pain and suffering that are the most acute, the most instinctively abhorred, experiences of consciousness. Consciousness is prior to society; and hurting people is therefore wrong even if there is no society at all. On consciousness's priority we can base a morality that is also prior to society, and which can judge it, weigh it in the balance and (on occasion) find it wanting. The demands of society cannot overrule the demands of individual consciousness unless they are based on those demands themselves.

And this is made very clear by Solzhenitsyn's use of an *animal's* suffering. For it is not merely that the animal has done nothing wrong; that it is innocent. There is a further message: an animal's suffering is, like a man's, a more fundamental factor than any social or political theory. For the animal belongs to no society, it is isolated from its kind, is alone, exists outside conventions, social systems and politics. In such a case we can see with full clarity what is the fundamental reason for the principle 'Do unto others as you would be done by': it is the fact of consciousness and the fact of suffering. Similarly, in Ivan Karamazov's terrifying disquisition on evil in the fifth book of *The Brothers Karamazov*, we are shown first the picture of a peasant beating his horse over the eyes; then a catalogue of brutalities inflicted on innocent children; then the grief of a mother who becomes insane as her child is chased and torn apart by a noble's wolf-hounds. Cruelty and injustice are not wrong because they are cruelty to 'individuals' seen as sophisticated, isolated individuals 'peculiar to Western culture', but because they assail *essential individuals*, torment the senses of conscious beings. We move from the simple animal (pure uncomprehending pain) to the innocent child (pure uncomprehending pain and mental suffering) to the innocent mother (pure comprehending mental suffering); and with her (as with Alyosha Karamazov's horrified sympathy) we come to the second ground of morality: we step beyond pain to the understanding of pain, to the recognition of it in others, and to the empathy which (as I shall later argue) is also one of the bases of human consciousness. Again this is prior to social systems and political dogmas: it is therefore only *upon* such recognitions that social systems and political dogmas can be justified, only *upon* such recognitions that they can be judged and condemned.

Thus, in Graham Greene's *Quiet American*, the apparently indifferent and sceptical Fowler, who believes that you can't reasonably expect 'to do good, not to any individual person but to a country, to a continent, to a world,' (Ch. 1), is driven to dislike of the politically active Pyle because 'when he saw a dead body, he didn't even see the wounds' (Ch. 2), and finally forced into performing a political act himself (betraying Pyle to his communist enemies) when he witnesses the consequences of Pyle's activities, namely a terrorist bomb-attack on a crowded square: 'A woman sat on the ground with what was left of her baby in her lap; with a kind of modesty she had covered it with her straw peasant hat. She was still and silent, and what struck me most in the square was the silence. It was like a church I had once visited during Mass . . .' (Part 3, Ch. 2). Human suffering is a fundamental experience: it is more profound than categories and abstractions; it demands a religious respect; it is a consequence of political action, but its prevention is the only proper motive *for* political action. 'How many dead colonels justify a child's or a rickshaw driver's death when you are building a national democratic front?' (Ibid.). Those who would discount such questions merely demonstrate that they do not themselves understand what politics is for.

Whatever the sins of the popular novel – and ironically these sins are caused by their authors' taste for cliché, by the habitual forcing of plot, emotion and character into predetermined categories – they at least illustrate that the ordinary reader has a healthy mistrust of abstract motives for action. For if, in a popular novel like Geoffrey Household's *Rogue Male* (1939), the hero fights injustice, it is usually because his girl-friend has been oppressed or killed by it, and not because he objects to it 'only on principle'. Now of course from one point of view this demeans and belittles his decision, because it gives it the note of a merely personal grudge. It is also a failure of imagination if one cannot picture injustice with sufficient immediacy to be forced to action, and this failure of imagination no doubt afflicts the average reader as it seems to afflict the hero. Yet the fact that this personalization of a political motive occurs so often in popular literature casts an interesting light on the popular mind: perhaps we instinctively realize that the reason for attacking injustice is that it is inflicted upon *people*; that it is not abstract, general and irrelevant, but is injustice to real individuals; and that a genuine act of justice cannot be done coldly and for abstract reasons, but must be given the stamp of authentic human feeling.

The 'villain' of many books is the 'abstract man', the Antipov of whom Lara thinks: 'It was as if something abstract had crept into his face and made it colourless. As if a living human face had become the embodiment of a principle, the image of an idea.' Thus, as Trilling writes of Henry James's Princess Casamassima:

> the great irony of her fate is that the more passionately she seeks reality and the happier she becomes in her belief that she is close to it, the further removed she is. Inevitably she must turn away from Hyacinth because she reads his moral seriousness as frivolousness; and inevitably she is led to Paul who, as she thinks, affirms her in a morality which is as real and serious as anything can be, an absolute morality which gives her permission to devaluate and even destroy all that she has known of human good because it has been connected with her own frivolous, self-betraying past. She cannot but mistake the nature of reality, for she believes it is a thing, a position, a finality, a bedrock. She is, in short, the very embodiment of that modern will which masks itself in virtue, making itself appear harmless, the will that hates itself and finds its manifestations guilty and is able to exist only if it operates in the name of virtue, that despises the variety and modulations of the human story and longs for an absolute humanity, which is but another way of saying a nothingness...' (Trilling 1961, pp. 91–2)

The Princess Casamassima's great error is to attribute more reality to abstractions than to experience, to constructs than to human beings, to the absolute than to the relative. Abstractions are deadly things unless they are checked, verified and given credibility by the realities of conscious experience.

So too are social mechanisms. In *War and Peace*, when Pierre

Bezukhov is taken to witness the execution of supposed fire-raisers as 'an example to others', and thinks he is himself destined for the firing-squad, Tolstoy clashes this scene against the shamefaced behaviour of the French soldiers who are carrying out the executions : they themselves feel sickenly guilty. He contrasts it too with Pierre's interview with the French general, and with the moment when he and Pierre look each other in the eye and recognize that they are both 'brothers', 'children of humanity'. And again this is set against Pierre's feeling that he is 'an insignificant chip that had fallen into the wheels of an unseen but smoothly running machine' and that it is 'system, the accidental pattern of circumstance' which threatens him with death. Implicitly the message of human suffering, human consciousness, human fellowship is clashed against the impersonal blindness of the machinery of politics or destiny.

To take another and final instance, where does Huck Finn's morality come from ? It has been said, correctly, that he has natural goodness ; and this is illustratsd already in *Tom Sawyer* when he says : 'That's a mighty good nigger, Tom. He likes me, becuz I don't ever act as if I was above him. Sometimes I've set right down and eat with him . . .' And Twain himself later wrote in a notebook that *Huckleberry Finn* was 'a book of mine where a sound heart and a deformed conscience come into collision and conscience suffers defeat'. When, in Chapter 16, Huck has resolved to go and give Jim up (he is running away from slavery), Huck says, 'I felt easy and light as a feather, straight off.' He paddles off 'to tell on Jim'; but feels a sudden terrible reluctance when Jim says, 'Jim won't ever forgit you, Huck; you's de bes' fren' Jim's ever had; en you's de *only* fren' ole Jim's got now.'

> Right then, along comes a skiff with two men in it, with guns, and they stopped and I stopped . . . 'Well, there's five niggers run off tonight, up yonder above the head of the bend. Is your man white or black ?' I didn't answer up prompt. I tried to, but the words wouldn't come. I tried, for a second or two, to brace up and out with it, but I warn't man enough – hadn't the spunk of a rabbit. I see I was weakening; so I just give up trying, and up and says : 'He's white.'

Happily, Huck wins the fight with his conscience. For it had indeed been deformed. The morality of his society declares that slavery is right and good; and that helping a slave to escape is wicked. Is it merely, then, Huck's natural goodness (which he himself mistakes for wickedness) which leads him to protect Jim, and lie to save him being captured ?

Certainly. But what *is* 'natural goodness' ? Why does Huck's paralysis of the will, what he takes for 'cowardice', have more force, more reality for him than the principles of his society and his religion ? Consider this later passage (Ch. 31) when again Huck struggles with his perverted conscience :

At last I had an idea; and I says, I'll go and write the letter – and *then* see if I can pray. Why, it was astonishing, the way I felt as light as a feather, right straight off, and my troubles all gone. So I got a piece of paper and a pencil, all glad and excited and set down and wrote : 'Miss Watson your runaway nigger Jim is down here two miles below Pikesville and Mr Phelps has got him and he will give him up for the reward if you send. – Huck Finn.' I felt good and all washed clean of sin for the first time I had ever felt so in my life, and I knowed I could pray now. But I . . . went on thinking. And got to thinking over our trip down the river; and I see Jim before me, all the time, in the day, and in the night-time, sometimes moonlight, sometimes storms, and we a-floating along, talking, and singing, and laughing. But somehow I couldn't seem to strike no places to harden me against him, but only the other kind. I'd see him standing my watch on top of his'n, stead of calling me, so I could go on sleeping; and see him how glad he was when I come back out of the fog; and when I come to him again in the swamp, up there where the feud was; . . . ; and would always call me honey, and pet me, and do everything he could think of for me, and how good he always was; . . . ; and then I happened to look around, and see that paper.

It was a close place. I took it up, and held it in my hand. I was a-trembling, because I'd got to decide, for ever, betwixt two things, and I knowed it. I studied a minute, sort of holding my breath, and then says to myself : 'All right, then, I'll go to hell' – and tore it up. It was awful thoughts, and awful words, but they was said. And I let them stay said; and never thought no more about reforming . . . and said I would take up wickedness again, which was in my line, being brung up to it, and the other warn't. And for a starter, I would go to work and steal Jim out of slavery again . . .

The source both of Huck's moral feelings and of their ability to overcome his 'conscience' is the recognition of the reality, the humanity, the warmth, the trust of another human being. The human individual, Jim, is more real and more important to Huck than abstract laws of social 'morality'. It is this that is the true source and driving-force of moral feelings.

By contrast, Tom Sawyer has been successfully socialized, and lost his sense of reality. He prefers to play an absurdly bookish and romantic game of 'rescuing the prisoner', rather than getting on, as Huck would like, with the job of setting Jim free. As Huck observes in Chapter 42, Tom couldn't have set a 'nigger' free . . . and didn't! For he knew all along that Jim had been freed anyway by Miss Watson's will. Tom's plan to free Jim was doubly a sham : it was designed to imitate bad fiction, not to have practical results; and Jim was in any case free already.

This makes Tom's grasp of reality look particularly slim : by playing his literary game out in real life, he endangers Huck, Jim and himself; and it is only an ironic twist of authorial justice when he gets himself shot in the leg for his pains. The contrast between Huck and Tom could not be stronger : Huck's is a genuine morality, arising from a sense of the reality of other people and from mutual affection; Tom, however, prefers fiction to real life, books to people; his plan delights him just as much after he has been shot – for it was 'fun', it was 'elegant', it was 'adventure'. As his imagination cannot rise above the clichés of romantic fiction, so his morality cannot rise above the clichés of social custom.

And here the message may be that to put one's trust in fictions which conceal the truth from us, hanging like a gaily embroidered curtain across the windows of reality, is not merely error, but potentially dangerous error.

We must recall one of the conclusions of the first chapter : the concrete cannot be proved by the abstract; the abstract can only be proved (if at all) by the concrete (pp. 22–3). Fiction can be seen as a testing-ground for the applicability of moral laws and social conventions.

2. Consciousness and Love

The longing for an awareness which transcends the conventions of social understanding – an awareness which would be totally concrete, totally lacking in abstraction, and which would regard the other person as a moral purpose in his own right, not a conventional role to be played to or a social demand to be conformed with – this is the meaning, perhaps, of the Western myth of love.

Not the only reason, no doubt, for the obsession with love that is found in the majority of Western novels. One of these is social, as is shown by the relative absence of love-interest in the literature of some other times and other continents. Another is more *generally* human. We are unusual among animals in making love, not seasonally, but through-out the year. But we may also see the love-interest of the traditional novel as a part of the novel's narrow and delicate focus upon the reality of individuals : the obsessive fascination of the sexual relationship is a microcosm of relationship in general. It explores the fundamental urge of two consciousnesses to contact each other, and to contact reality.

Thus, in *Howard's End* Forster writes : 'But in public who shall express the unseen adequately? It is private life that holds out the mirror to infinity; personal intercourse, and that alone, that ever hints at a personality beyond our daily vision.' In *A Room with a View*, reality frightens people : when the Emersons offer Lucy and Charlotte their rooms at the beginning of the book – or when the elder Mr Emerson hurries off to apologize to the vicar he has unwittingly offended – his kindness holds for them all the terrors of an unpredictable jungle. 'He is kind to people because he loves them', says his son George; 'and they find him out, and are offended, or frightened' (Ch. 2). Meanwhile the vicar's voice soars up from the next chapel : 'full of innate sympathy . . . quickness to perceive good in others . . . vision of the brotherhood of man.' How deep is the gulf between *saying* 'full of innate sympathy', when you are gazing at the work of some artist safely dead for centuries, and between *feeling* it, acting or knowing it. Reality is locked away behind the superficialities of Miss Lavish's romantic novel : she is unconventional in only a conventional way. It is locked away behind chivalry, the 'respect' that a man owes a woman : George, who has a strong sense of reality, 'lacked chivalry : his thoughts, like his behaviour, would not be modified by awe' (Ch. 4). Reality is locked away behind convention, withering politeness, or academic learning. Yet Forster hopes that 'the traveller who has gone to Italy to study the tactile values of Giotto, or the corruption of the Papacy, may return remembering nothing but the blue sky and the men and women who live under it.' Not that the Emersons are mere 'noble savages' : their culture is in fact more profound than that of the other characters.

The conventional opposition is strong : Charlotte gazes at the mysterious question-mark pinned on her wall : 'Meaningless at first, it gradually became menacing, obnoxious, portentous with evil.' (Ch. 1) And the vicar comments on Lucy's piano-playing : 'I do not consider her choice of a piece happy. Beethoven is usually so simple and direct in his appeal that it is sheer perversity to choose a thing like that, which, if anything, disturbs.' (Ch. 3) There is a glimpse here of the disturbing function of art : it questions our categories and must at all costs, if one fears reality, be prevented from smashing them. There is a glimpse too of the categorizing function of language : Lucy, having been kissed by George, 'thought not so much of what had happened as of how she should describe it' (Ch. 7). And she feels 'almost happy' thus turning her half-comprehended feelings into the mere clarity of statement.

Yet even the individual who fears reality and stays therefore on the surface of art, and of human relationships, may feel lurking within himself the force of reality : it is this that occasions Charlotte's terror of the question-mark, this that fuels the neurotic self-pity that she uses as a weapon to manipulate others. It is this too that by a peculiar (but suddenly credible) act of grace at the end of the book, leads her not to interfere in Lucy's final interview with the elder Mr Emerson.

But most importantly, it is through honest sexual love that reality is conveyed. 'To be driven by lovers' (Ch. 6) is to be sure of travelling in the right direction. Lucy's unawakened senses are a token of her uncertain grasp of reality, and when she realizes them only so as to suppress them, she suppresses reality too. Reality is rejected also by those who will not let others be themselves, a constriction from which women, in the society Forster describes, particularly suffer. Cecil is attacked by the author for not letting Lucy be herself, for not daring to let a woman decide (Part II, Ch. 16). And earlier Forster writes of him, 'Nor did he realize a more important point – that if [Lucy] was too great for this society, she was too great for all society, and had reached a stage where personal intercourse would alone satisfy her. A rebel she was, but not of the kind he understood – a rebel who desired, not a wider dwelling-room, but equality beside the man she loved. For Italy was offering her the most priceless of all possessions – her own soul' (Part II, Ch. 10). *A Room with a View* is not primarily a love-story (girl meets, girl loses, girl finds again true love) but rather a quest for reality; and love is both the symbol and the means of its achievement. 'The contest', writes Forster,

> lay not between love and duty. Perhaps there never is such a contest. It lay between the real and the pretended . . . The armour of falsehood is subtly wrought out of darkness, and hides a man not only from others, but from his own soul. (Part II, Ch. 16)

George's father tells Lucy quite early in the book :

> 'Pull out from the depths those thoughts that you do not understand, and spread them out in the sunlight and know the meaning of them. By understanding George you may learn to understand yourself. It will be good for both of you.' (Ch. 2)

And when George and Lucy walk back to their *pension* together,

> she stopped and leant her elbows against the parapet of the embankment. He did likewise. There is at times a magic in identity of position; it is one of the things that have suggested to us eternal comradeship. (Ch. 4)

By 'putting ourselves in someone else's place' we may learn to understand ourselves as well as them. The barriers between self and other may fall; and with them the barriers between self and deeper self. The image of love in Forster is the image of reality, the reality of oneself and others; and the quest for love is the symbol of knowledge, communication and profound awareness. Men and women, divided, are the forked lightning of Urizen's internecine creation. Unite them and you rediscover the unity, within, of the divided mind; the unity, without, of self with universe. The last words of *A Room with a View* are : 'The song died away; they heard the river, bearing down the snows of winter into the Mediterranean.'

In *Women in Love*, the purpose of love seems to be to remain separate, but to know oneself better; and to know oneself better at some deeper and more unconscious level. We are not, says Lawrence, 'broken fragments of one whole' :

> Passion is the further separating of this mixture, that which is manly being taken into the being of the man, that which is womanly

passing to the woman, till the two are clear and whole as angels, the admixture of sex in the highest sense surpassed, leaving two beings constellated together like two stars . . . In each, the individual is primal, sex is subordinate, but perfectly polarized. Each has a single, separate being, with its own laws. The man has his pure freedom, the woman hers. Each acknowledges the perfection of the polarized sex-circuit. Each admits the different nature of the other.

(Ch. 16)

Thus self and other remain self and other, but achieve communication. It is by this means too that a sense of something further is given : the two are not merely related to each other, but to something outside themselves. In Ursula and Birkin's love-making in Sherwood Forest, sex gives 'the mystic body of reality' :

She had her desire of him, she touched, she received the maximum of unspeakable communication in touch, dark, subtle, positively silent, a magnificent gift and give again, a perfect acceptance and yielding, a mystery, the reality of that which can never be known, vital, sensuous reality that can never be transmuted into mind content, but remains outside, living body of darkness and silence and subtlety, the mystic body of reality. She had her desire fulfilled. He had his desire fulfilled. For she was to him what he was to her, the immemorial magnificence of mystic, palpable, real otherness.

(Ch. 23)

Here we touch again upon the mystery of self and other, to be different and know that difference most vividly, to be oneself and know that self most clearly, to feel the presence of the mystery lying *behind* consciousness, Sex and love are in Lawrence the path to this knowledge. 'I do think', says Birkin, 'that the world is only held together by the mystic conjunction, the ultimate unison between people – a bond. And the immediate bond is between man and woman.' (Ch. 13) This in itself explains Birkin's unsatisfied longing to love a man, to have communication with him too. The experience would be another, different mode of communion with reality.

My final example is John Fowles's collection of variations on a theme, *The Ebony Tower*. In the opening title story, we are presented, in the narrator's first meeting with his possible 'Muse', 'The Mouse', with a series of shifting perspectives on the girl, half-glimpses, hints at what might be knowledge, alternations of conflicting guesswork, information that might not be information. He fits different, fleetingly successive theories to his meeting with her. She offers him brief phrases that contain half-meanings – like all our initial words, which contain mere schemata of what might be.

She opened the second door they came to and went a step in, holding the handle, watching him, uncannily like the *patronne* at the hotel

47

where he had stayed the previous night. He almost expected to hear a price . . .

She closed the door. There was something preternaturally grave about her, almost Victorian, despite the *galabiya* . . .

'Henry calls me the Mouse.'

At last a tiny dryness in her face; or a challenge, he wasn't sure . . .

She was trying to tell him something, very plainly; perhaps just that if he *had* seen her in the garden,[2] this was the real distance she kept from visitors. She was apparently some kind of equivalent of his hostess; and yet she behaved as if the house had nothing much to do with her . . .

She hesitated a moment, as if she knew she was being too cool and sibylline. There was even a faint hint of diffidence, a final poor shadow of a welcoming smile. Then she looked down and turned away and padded silently back towards the garden; as she went out through the door the *galabiya* momentarily lost its opacity against the sunlight beyond; a fleeting naked shadow . . .

(Fowles 1974, pp. 14–15)

This sexual touch is important: the impulse to know is given its extremest, most urgent and most nagging intensity by sexual interest – or better, by sexual and personal interest combined. Hence the importance in Fowles's *Ebony Tower* of the sexual element. And of the revolution wrought (in Fowles's view) in European literature by the *matière de Bretagne*.

For why is the theme of love, of pursuit and marriage, so universal a theme in European literature? Why, since its emergence in the literature of the troubadours and of Marie de France, has it been the constant central theme of our writers? Fowles's personal, explanatory myth is, I think, something like this. With the *matière de Bretagne*, the Grail became the woman. The inner secret of the self was no longer seen in terms of a religious symbol, but in terms of the secret of the self of another. We (or Fowles) might even contrast the conceptions of self and other given by the tradition of love with that other early medieval tradition, the religion of the Albigensians: for them the soul was divine, the world was darkness, and these two opposing principles for ever in conflict. And in Fowles's final story in this volume, sun and darkness are clashed together in a tragedy of despair and death. Against this we may put the optimistic image of self and other presented by the troubadours and by the Arthurian romances: the self was the poet or the knight, the other was the woman, his spiritual or physical mistress. The problem of self and other is solved, not this time by hatred, but by love: for self and other seen as God and Devil is substituted self and other seen as man and woman.

For Fowles, then, woman in European literature is not merely the sexual object (though of course she is that too). She is a psychological reality whose knowledge is intimately involved with the knowledge of oneself. And the narrator of the title story fails as an artist and as a person because he rejects the knowledge for which the Mouse stands.

In 'The Enigma', another story in this collection, Fielding, a Tory M.P., disappears. The police investigate; but there is nothing to be found. There is no body, no demand for ransom, no evidence of a threat to the M.P.'s life, no financial difficulties, no family problems. The man seemed happy and contented. There are no sexual affaires. Eventually the sergeant in charge of the case interviews the M.P.'s son's girl-friend. Her comment is :

> 'Nothing is real. All is fiction . . . Let's pretend everything to do
> with the Fieldings, even you and me sitting here now, is a novel.
> A detective story. Yes? Somewhere there's someone writing us,
> we're not real. He or she decides who we are, what we do, all about
> us . . . A story has to have an ending. You can't have a mystery
> without a solution. If you're the writer you have to think of some-
> thing.'   (Ibid., p. 229)

At this point our 'willing suspension of disbelief' is jolted abruptly away : the author's presence suddenly shrivels his story's reality in our hands, like a flame set to paper. It becomes clear that Fowles has deliberately designed his story in such a way that no solution is conceivable : the mystery has no key, because no keyhole has been provided into which one might fit. All exits from the maze are blocked, by Daedalus himself.

We must therefore read the story another way to appreciate its psychology and movement. Fielding has emerged as a conformist without creative powers, but with a suppressed inner feeling of frustration, of being trapped. 'He feels more and more like this minor character in a bad book' (Ibid., p. 234). But the story ends with the problem unsolved, and with the detective and the girl making love. He is an inquirer into people's actions, motives; she, one who understands them intuitively. In other words, out of the enigma emerges a personal reality; out of what Fielding the vanished M.P. stands for, namely a killing conventionality, a blockage of feeling, of alternatives, of exits and of all possible solutions, out of cold detection and the inability of reason to provide an answer, emerges a warm, human, telepathic understanding, and its validation in the sexual act. The girl (who provides also the psychological explanation, namely that Fielding has felt trapped in an exit-less maze like the plot of the story, and commits suicide : his only escape) is herself the key : intuition, the probing of consciousness, real human contact. There are no clues, there is no evidence, logic cannot provide a solution; because reality is in the self, hidden, inaccessible to external understanding, invisible to the world of social exchanges. As the sergeant thinks to himself:

> The act was done; taking it to bits, discovering how it had been done in detail, was not the point. The point was a living face with brown eyes, half challenging and half teasing; not committing a crime against that. (Ibid., p. 237)

In the West we have substituted for the religious myth of unity with the absolute, two other myths: that of the omnipotence of analytic reason; and the sexual metaphor of consciousness speaking to consciousness, of human understanding. Fowles's message is that this last myth is invaluably ours: we abandon it at the peril of an inner death. Thus, Catherine in the last story in the collection sacrifices herself on the black stone of a male sun; and the story ends with storm, darkness, desertion and the threat of death. Thus the 'Mouse' in the title story is so named because she is Vagina (o) and Muse: in rejecting her, the protagonist rejects, or rather confirms his previous rejection of, reality, both within and outwith himself.

> He remembered the old man's crude and outlandish pun on the word Mouse; if one wanted signs as to the real nature of the rejection. Bungling the adventure of the body was trivial, part of the sexual comedy. But he had never really had, or even attempted to give himself, the greater existential chance. (Ibid., p. 109)

The search for reality, both inner and outer, is expressed in terms of the right relationship with the right person: consciousness must find its complement, its own deeper heart; and this is the fundamental meaning of the age-old Western myth of the artist's physical and human Muse. It will be clear why the epigraph to this present book is appropriate: the flowers in the basket can be seen as both consciousness and sexual love, the centre of a Room with a View, around which the wide world may be constructed.

3. Coda

Literature has an important function to perform, namely to remind us of the facts of experience, of the relative uncertainty of abstractions, of the central role of the individual as the creator of a world-view, of the importance of other people as ultimate moral purposes; and to disturb and make us question the apparent certainties and delusory solidities of the social world. Literature is in a sense less fictional than they, for it deals in the concrete.

But this is not a lesson that we can draw from the uncertainties merely of social fictions. We have seen in Chapter 1 (pp. 18–21) that there is a clash between the apparent 'certainty' of the constructs of science as seen by the uninitiated, and what science in fact tells us of itself. Science is a structure of hypotheses, progressive but not final discoveries, and reasonable approximations; it is incomplete and is likely for ever to remain so. Yet science is the most certain of our certainties. We need to draw this overriding moral : that we should cultivate a flexible and provisional attitude towards constructs in general, whether they be scientific, social or commonsensical. Their seeming solidity and certainty is often an illusion; and we need to develop habits of mind which will regard such abstractions with a healthy scepticism. No more, perhaps, than the proverbial grain of salt; yet that grain, as every cook knows, makes all the difference.

But exactly what techniques are used by literature (among other activities) to question and disrupt the accepted, we shall see in the next chapter.

3. Concrete and Abstract

> So then of course they could see that she really was a Princess, because she had felt the pea right through the twenty mattresses and the twenty feather-beds. Nobody but a real Princess could have such a tender skin as all that.
>
> (Hans Christian Andersen, *Fairy Tales*)

> A *picture* held us captive. And we could not get outside it, for it lay in our language and language seemed to repeat it to us inexorably. (Wittgenstein, *Philosophical Investigations*)

1. Imprisoned in Categories

ACCORDING to Jerome Bruner, the very act of perception entails categorization.

> As we mature, we attempt to make more and more consistent 'sense' out of the mass of information arriving at our receptors. We develop stereotyped systems, or *categories*, for sorting the input. The set of categories we develop is limited, much more limited than the input. . . . We expect cars to make a certain noise, traffic lights to be a certain colour, food to smell a certain way, and certain people to say certain things. But what we actually experience, according to Bruner and others, is the *category* which is evoked by a particular stimulus, *not* the occurrence in the external world.[1]

Thus we may be said to experience objects and persons *directly*. As I said earlier, I do not experience a patch of colour of a certain shape : I at once experience it as a book. And some of the ambiguous objects that Richard Gregory presents to his subjects, though they are mere stereoscopic patterns, are experienced as 'real' cubes (Gregory 1971, 1972). Similarly, I interpret persons *as* persons, not the mere 'centres of activity' that (according to Piaget) the baby at first perceives.

Now the usefulness of this categorizing tendency of ours is not in doubt. Bruner comments on categorization that it reduces the complexity of the environment (which otherwise would overburden us with irrelevant information), gives us a means of identifying objects and persons, reduces the need to be constantly learning new things, provides a direction for our acting upon the world, manipulating it and using it, and (finally) orders and relates classes of events together in a useful way (Bruner *et al.* 1956, pp. 12 – 13).[2] All this is highly valuable to us : it enables us to put our world in order, to be able to recognize it and manipulate it, to progress from rudimentary guesses to a deeper understanding.[3]

No doubt all this is fair enough. None the less, even breaking down our more reasonable categories may sometimes have its uses. For the moment, however, let us consider some of our less reasonable ones. Here, the trouble may come when we start to attribute genuine reality to constructs which are 'higher' on my scale of certainty, which are further from direct experience, and when we have not properly checked the validity of these 'higher realities' against more direct experience. Among the criteria we use for validating our categories, according to Bruner, there are some which may betray us into error and prejudice. For not merely do we check some of our concepts empirically (an admirable thing) against more direct experience; not merely do we demand consistency in them, in the sense that they must fit each other and our world-view (again this test may have its validity); but we prefer one concept to another on more doubtful grounds, namely that it fits our prejudices, or the consensus of people in our social group, or that it has what Bruner calls 'affective congruence', that is, that it appeals to our emotions, comfortably arousing them or lulling them to rest as the case may be (Bruner *et al.* 1956, pp. 17–21). Our social concepts are affected by prejudice, desire and need, by political standpoint and social pressure.

Moreover, in the very tendency of human beings to set up firm and solid categories and concepts through which to view the world, a tendency that doubtless is inborn, there is the risk of dreadful error. Some psychologists have suggested that people tend to reify their concepts, to think of them as *objects*. And indeed the fact that Western languages treat abstract nouns like 'virtue', 'truth', 'kindness' and 'society' *as* nouns, itself may suggest the delusion that they are akin to the solid objects we see around us in the ordinary world, like stones, books and motorcars, Bruner and his associates suggest that people need to give their concepts 'definite reality', that they are dissatisfied with less.[4] Bartlett claimed that when we 'rationalize' we seek 'to render material acceptable, understandable, comfortable, straightforward, to rob it of all puzzling elements' (Bartlett 1932, p. 89). There may be a natural tendency to flee ambiguity and seek firm, well-determined concepts. Some writers claim that the dislike of ambiguity is particularly strong in people who are prejudiced or hold extremely rigid views. Else Frenkel-Brunswik, in one experiment, faced a number of subjects with a series of ambiguous pictures, in which a dog changed progressively into a cat; and she reports that people with a rigid frame of reference tend to hold on longer to the initial object and to respond more slowly to the changes in the picture (1949, p. 28).[5] Now, if the world is to some extent ambiguous and uncertain, if the realities for which abstractions stand are shifting and multifarious, and if they are not of the same kind as the solid objects we see and touch every day, then it is evidently dangerous to think in such misleadingly 'materialistic' terms.

The same nature cannot be attributed to concepts on different levels of reality. We might attribute solidity to electrons, as if they were like the solid tables, rocks and metals which are built of them, but we should be wrong to do so, for subatomic particles such as electrons are 'packets of probability'; or we might attribute consciousness to social classes, as if they were of the same nature as the individuals that make them up. Another problem is that we build up whole batches of vocabulary which apply to each level of 'reality', and that the elements of this vocabulary work harmoniously together, giving us the illusion of a consistent world-picture. Normally we have no difficulty in refuting objections to our view of the world, because within it, everything fits. Thus the anthropologist Evans-Pritchard reported of the African Zande people that they were quite unimpressed by his European objections to their beliefs. Their oracle might answer 'Yes' to a question put to it; and might immediately afterwards reply 'No' to the same question. This, to Evans-Pritchard (1937), seemed decisive proof of the unreliability of the oracle. But to the Zande it was nothing of the kind, for they had at least eight ways of explaining such a failure in the oracle's powers. For instance, the wrong variety of poisonous creeper might have been gathered, or a taboo might have been broken, or the owners of the forest where the creeper grew might have been angered and spoiled the poison; and so forth.

The poisonous creeper in question, which is called *benge*, is supposed only to become efficacious if it has been addressed according to the proper ritual forms. When Evans-Pritchard inquired what would happen if the Zande were to administer the oracle-poison without delivering an address, they responded with indifference.

> The Zande does not know what would happen, and is not interested in what would happen; no one has been fool enough to waste good oracle-poison in making such pointless experiments which only a European would imagine . . . Were a European to make a test which in his view proved Zande opinion wrong they would stand amazed at the credulity of the European. If the fowl dies they would simply say that it was not good *benge*. The very fact of the fowl dying proves to them its badness.
>
> (Evans-Pritchard 1937, pp. 314–15)[6]

Our own beliefs are of course just as firmly held, just as studiously defended with reasons, as are those of the Zande. Polanyi quotes Arthur Koestler to this effect:

> My party education had equipped my mind with such elaborate

shock-absorbing buffers and elastic defences that everything seen
and heard became automatically transformed to fit a preconceived
pattern.   (Crossman 1950, p. 68)

And Karen Horney to this:

The system of theories which Freud has gradually developed is so
consistent that when one is once entrenched in them it is difficult
to make observations unbiased by his way of thinking.

(Horney 1939, p. 7)

One might well comment that man is not so much an adept at reasoning
as at finding reasons: he is not so much a reasoning as a rationalizing
animal.

But of course the determination with which we stick to our own world-
view is not surprising. As Bruner remarks, if a belief has often seemed
justified in the past, is held at the moment, is widely supported by one's
in-group, and is necessary for one's proper adjustment to that in-group,
then 'the least pip of confirming information' will seem to bear it out.
And if we are dealing with the kind of perception for which information
is inherently poor – such as the perception of other people's characteristics – our resistance to seeing things that do not fit into our world-view
is all the greater. 'We might have here a good description of the bigot,
the anti-Semite, the xenophobe, or, for that matter, the starry-eyed
idealist who can see only good in all men' (Bruner 1974*a*, p. 95).[7] The
very act of perceiving, according to Bruner, begins with an expectation.
In a particular situation we expect certain things to happen. When we
perceive something, we check it against our hypothesis. Where the
perception is ambiguous, we are less likely to abandon our hypothesis
(Ibid., pp. 91–2, 101). And, as we have just seen Bruner asserting, our
perception of other people's behaviour and motives is often highly
ambiguous.

With people and with social events, in fact, we tend to stick by our
preconceived ideas, and to resolve possible ambiguities and uncertainties
in harmony with those preconceived ideas. Our perceptions of physical
objects are much more ingenious and flexible than our perceptions of
people's behaviour; and so we can entertain a series of different hypotheses as to what it is that we are really seeing. We are much cleverer at
seeing through an optical, than an emotional or political, illusion. Which
is doubtless why science could not progress until it began to dip its
hands into the rough sensory earth of direct experiential evidence, and
to mistrust the high flights of metaphysics. Richard Gregory writes:

Why should the perceptual system be so active in seeking alternative solutions, as we see it to be in ambiguous situations?
Indeed, it seems more active, and more intellectually honest in
refusing to stick with one of many possible solutions, than is the
cerebral cortex as a whole – if we may judge by the tenacity of

irrational belief in politics or religion. The perceptual system has been of biological significance for far longer than the calculating intellect. The regions of the cerebral cortex concerned with thought are comparatively juvenile. They are self-opinionated by comparison with the [area of the brain that is] responsible for seeing. (Gregory 1972, pp. 223–4)

What cure can we offer for this malady? Our tendency to generalize out diversity, and to seek for neat and unitary explanations, is a basic condition of our thought and of our language. For the whole of human speech (with the exception of proper names) is based on this principle of classifying differences away. Nor could we act in the real world without a world-view of some kind. If we always and invariably, at every turn, had to think out our attitudes from scratch, we should end up doing and understanding very little. However, the choice is not between either having a world-view or having none; it is between having a better or a worse world-view; and between a willingness and an unwillingness to amend or alter our world-view once it has been shown to be inadequate or doubtful. Like the Zande, we are rarely willing to change our minds at so profound a level. And I am disturbed by Jacques Monod's suggestion that our tendency to desire clear and certain, comforting and unitary mythologies, is genetically inbuilt.

> Pendant des centaines de milliers d'années la destinée d'un homme se confondait avec celle de son groupe, de sa tribu, hors laquelle il ne pouvait survivre. La tribu, quant à elle, ne pouvait survivre et se défendre que par sa cohésion. D'où l'extrême puissance subjective des lois qui organisaient et garantissaient cette cohésion ... Etant donnée l'immense importance sélective qu'ont nécessairement assumée de telles structures soliales, et pendant de si longues durées, il est difficile de ne pas penser qu'elles ont dû influencer l'évolution génétique des catégories innées du cerveau humain. Cette évolution devait non seulement faciliter l'acceptation de la loi tribale, mais créer le *besoin* de l'explication mythique qui la fonde en lui conférant la souveraineté. Nous sommes les descendants de ces hommes. C'est d'eux sans doute que nous avons hérité l'exigence d'une explication, l'angoisse qui nous contraint à chercher le sens de l'existence ... Angoisse créatrice de tous les mythes, de toutes les religions, de toutes les philosophies et de la science elle-même ... S'il n'en était pas ainsi, comment expliquer l'universalité, dans notre espèce, du phénomène religieux à la base de la structure sociale? Comment expliquer en outre que dans l'immense diversité des mythes, des religions ou des idéologies, la même 'forme' essentielle se retrouve?

(Monod 1970, pp. 182–3)

[For hundreds of thousands of years the destiny of each man

was linked with that of his group, his tribe, outside which his survival was impossible. As for the tribe, it could only survive and defend itself by its cohesion. Whence the enormous subjective power of the laws which organized and guaranteed that cohesion . . . Given the immense selective importance which such social structures must necessarily have assumed, and for such lengthy periods, it is difficult not to think that they must have influenced the genetic evolution of the inborn categories of the human brain. This evolution must not only have facilitated the acceptance of the tribal law, but have created the *need* for the mythical explanation which gives it sovereignty and so justifies it. We are the descendants of those men. It is from them that we have no doubt inherited the need for explanations, the anguish that drives us to seek for the meaning of existence. An anguish which has created all myths, all religions, all philosophies and even science itself . . . If it were not so, how could one explain the universality, in our species, of the phenomenon of religion as the basis of the social structure? How could we explain that despite the enormous diversity of myths, religions and ideologies, the same essential 'form' is always present?]

Perhaps there is no alternative to this pessimistic prospect. The best we can do is to hold tight (as science does) to the sense-data, and to the ambiguities which, we also know from science's attestation, are a condition of the universe. But let us hold tight to language also, for despite its capacity to generalize out diversity, it too has a considerable measure of ambiguity; morcover, it reflects not only the world-view of the peoples who speak it, but also of each individual among them. It is flexible, infinitely adaptable to individual statement and individual perception; and this very fact may offer us a partial defence against the demon of absolutism. Let us turn therefore to an investigation of abstraction in language, in the light of the 'levels of reference' suggested above, and of my remarks on abstract reference in *Language, Truth and Poetry*.

2. Reference

What is abstract reference? To answer this question, we shall first have to deal with the question of what reference itself is. When we are engaged in the normal business of living, we constantly refer to objects and events in the world around us. Reference is simply the act of so referring; and our *referents* are simply the objects, events, situations or relationships *to* which we then refer. Thus, 'He tossed a pebble over the wall' is a sentence which is (1) composed of words which (2) suggest a set of concepts to the listener, and these in turn (3) refer to certain events and objects in the outside world, namely (*a*) a particular male individual already known or indicated to the listener, (*b*) a past action of throwing, (*c*) a rough indication of the pebble's trajectory relative to (*d*) the object 'wall'. By this the reader will see that my definition of 'referent' is wider than usual : I use it to stand for all those objects, events and relationships in the world that are being referred to by a piece of language.[8]

The reader may perhaps interject at this point : 'Wait a minute! Didn't you say only a short while ago that all objects, events, persons, social roles, scientific theories and so on, are merely "constructs" which we use to comprehend the world, and which suffer from varying degrees of uncertainty? Just what "reality" do the objects and events we refer to in the outside world have? How do we distinguish between the outside world and what we think of it? Surely a referent is always no more than a hypothesis, a figment of the human mind, a mere concept?' This point of view is well expressed by Jabès, who writes : 'L'univers se désigne par sa ressemblance avec l'univers intime dans lequel nous évoluons; par sa projection au tréfonds de nous-mêmes, où l'on ne distingue plus ce qui est de ce qui n'est que sa ressemblance avouée, épousée' (Jabès 1976, p. 30). (The world is determined by its resemblance to the inner world in which we develop; by its projection into the depths of ourselves, where one can no longer distinguish what is from what is merely its avowed, adopted likeness.) And Lefebve says : 'le référent n'est pas vraiment la réalité : cela résulterait d'une vue substantialiste des choses; il est l'*image* que nous nous faisons de la réalité. Car . . . le référent ne peut pas être l'objet lui même : cet objet, en effet, n'est qu'une hypothèse, un postulat . . . Je ne l'atteins jamais que par une certaine expérience, et ce qui résulte de notre expérience est mental' (Lefebve 1970, p. 273). (The referent is not truly reality : that would be a substantialist view of the matter; it is the *image* that we form of reality. For . . . the referent cannot be the object itself : that object, in fact, is merely a hypothesis, a postulate . . . I can only arrive at it by experience, and what results from our experience is always mental.)

All this is perfectly true. There none the less subsists a difference between 'concept' and 'referent'. Lefebve goes on to say that 'le référent est un signifié déterminé par une intention portée vers les choses' (Ibid.) (the referent is a 'signified' defined by our intention to refer to objects) : that is, we mean the referent when we refer, not to the notions of objects that we carry about in our heads, but to the presumed objects themselves in the outside world. And indeed, we can distinguish perfectly well between (1) what we conceive an object to be, (2) what we experience of objects through our senses, and (3) what more they might be than we know of them. It is precisely the failure to distinguish between concept and referent, between our image of the world, our experience of the world, and what the world might be, that is the source of the errors described later in this chapter. There are (1) the picture of reality that we have constructed through our perceptions; (2) those perceptions themselves; and (3) the objects of perception.

Word and world do not correspond. The 'real nature' of the referent in its totality, is for ever unknown. So our concept of it cannot fit it. It follows that our words are all, in a sense, metaphoric. Just as 'fire' is not love, in that love is different in some respects from fire; so 'fire' is not any given instance of fire, for the latter is always different in some respects from what we schematically and approximately think of it. The whole of human thinking is metaphoric – though some parts of it are, of course, more so than others.

Caution and clarity are therefore the order of the day. We must always be prepared to ask : to what does a construct refer? What sort of 'thing' is its referent? Is it an object (like 'stone'), a relationship (like 'love'), a causal structure (like 'relativity'), a person, or a relationship between persons (like 'society')? Is it merely a grouping of objects or persons together (like 'nation-state')? What lower-level facts does it imply? Is its relationship to them explanatory (like 'relativity') or does it merely assemble them in a convenient fashion so that they can all be examined together (like 'class')? Does it exist at all except as the lower-level facts it in turn refers to ('Greek thought' for instance means 'what various Greeks have variously thought')? How accurately does it represent what it refers to? How rough or ambiguous is the description? 'John is a socialist' is for instance both rough and ambiguous : precisely what sort of socialism is meant here? We must ask : 'What in practice does John strive for?' In short, what justifies one's use of the word? What facts does it refer to? And do its connotations fit those facts? In military contexts, for instance, 'initiative' is quite commonly used to suggest that the soldier is acting responsibly, voluntarily and 'off his own bat'; but he will only be praised for 'initiative' if he anticipates with sufficient accuracy what authority requires of him. Or take Wilfred Owen's famous poem 'Dulce et Decorum est', which horrifyingly clashes the facts of death in battle against the pompous and sentimental false-hoods of convention.

It will be clear enough from these remarks what definition I give to 'abstraction'. However, I should carry out my promise to define it more exactly. The words 'abstract' and 'concrete' are used in various over-lapping but different ways. (1) 'Abstraction' may be defined as 'degree of generality'. Thus 'plant' is more abstract than 'tree', 'tree' more abstract than 'oak', 'oak' more abstract than 'the Headingley Shire Oak'. (2) The generality of 'tree' and 'oak' is achieved by the selection and isolation of common elements in all oaks and all trees. Thus a 'tree' is so called because it has branches, leaves, a trunk, roots, and is of a certain size. An 'oak' is defined additionally by its having leaves, seeds, etc., of a certain shape. Here 'abstraction' is a process, and means the selection of features which are used to classify phenomena. (3) There is an additional group of 'abstractions' which are not directly related to sensory perception. We may divide this group into three subgroups : (*a*) objects such as atoms, electrons, pi-mesons, etc, which are presumed to be real and concrete, but which are not directly perceived or sensed; (*b*) relationships between sensory objects, relationships which are not themselves capable, even in principle, of being sensed directly, but which have some explanatory power, such as 'relativity', 'gravity', 'weight', 'distance' and so on; (*c*) abstractions which are *relatively* artificial classifications of phenomena, such as 'the state', 'class' and 'culture', of which different and often contradictory definitions are possible because they are not relationships or groupings in their own right, but rather relationships or groupings which we, as human beings, assume for convenience, and which correspond in only a vague and shifting way to reality.

All these different sorts of 'abstraction' have, however, something in common, namely a certain distance from direct sensory experience, for we sense only *particular* phenomena and only *directly* sensed phenomena. Basically, then, I use 'abstraction' to signify 'relative distance from direct sensory experience'.

As for the question of 'abstract reference', we may refer to an abstraction as readily as we like; but *valid reference* to an abstraction depends on the abstraction's being supported by concrete instances. Thus, we may schematize abstract reference as follows :

$$\text{SPEAKER} \xrightarrow{\text{(abstract reference)}} \text{'The State'}$$

Here, we refer to an abstraction as such. But our reference to it is only *valid* provided that the reference can be taken further, in that 'the State' itself refers to concrete data which are capable of being perceived, thus :

There are thus degrees of validation : abstractions tend to be true *in part*. Some of their uses are valid, others only partly so. A phrase such as 'The community has resolved to do F' is true just in so far as x people within that community have resolved it, approximate in that the decision of y others has been delegated by them to x, untrue in so far as

z others disagree or have not been consulted.

And if there is no concrete reference and no sensory validation, we may say that the abstraction in question is a fiction, or an 'optical illusion'.

It should be added that scientific constructs such as 'relativity', 'gravity', 'mass', etc., are as incapable of being directly sensed as is 'the State' or 'democracy'. When we refer to such scientific constructs, the process is identical to the one that I have just outlined. Thus :

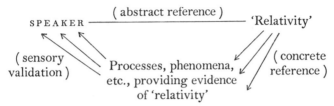

This linguistic-imaginative process of abstraction thus makes the great victories of science possible. Were it not for our capacity to conceive of hidden causes, processes and relations, we should never have been able to delve beneath the surfaces of sensory experience. But the weapon is a double-edged one. Some constructs are factitious. Our capacity for abstraction makes possible not only the great conquests of science and philosophy, but also the terrible errors of superstition, self-deception and political ideology.

3. Constructs as Optical Illusions

> Man's overweening mind uttered the Word, and the Word was
> God.   (Lawrence, *Phoenix*, p. 704)

Let us look at a number of such optical illusions. Here is our first. We tend to assume that, if a word exists, it must stand for a *coherent reality*. It is true that words like 'elm' and 'duck' exist, and that they do stand for relatively coherent organized wholes (though their definition is not as devoid of problems as one might think). But a term like 'poetry' or 'religion' is not in the same case. I recently had a discussion with someone who maintained, though with some puzzlement, that free verse was not poetry. She recognized that there was a problem since, if it was not poetry, how was such verse to be defined? What sort of 'thing' was it? I suggested that she was holding firm to the traditional definition of poetry, which is that it (a) contains a large number of figures of speech, (b) uses musical devices such as alliteration, and (c) employs a regular verse-rhythm. This conjunction of features she saw as 'a thing', 'a phenomenal object'; she did not perceive that it was a mere combination of features. Her difficulty was that she did not know how to categorize poetry that contained, say, features (a) and (b), but not feature (c). To resolve this conundrum one has to see that what we call 'poetry' is a large and varied group of texts,[9] which may have certain purposes and effects in common, but which differ in the linguistic methods by which they produce these effects . . . and perhaps that there is no *intrinsic* difference between poetry and other types of discourse.

Similarly, I once met an enthusiast whose ambition was to discover the 'true definition' of the word 'religion', in the hope that, once this had been established, Christianity would be found to be the most religious of all religions, and hence the truest, Islam would be found to be less true, and Buddhism would be found not to be a religion at all. This proposition seems to rest not only upon a belief in the definite reality of constructs (i.e. that since there must be a 'thing' called 'religion', there must be a proper way to define it), but also on a confusion over the word 'true' (i.e. that if we can find 'religion's true definition' then 'religion' so defined must be 'true'). But the truth of a creed does not depend on its conforming to a certain (arbitrarily defined) category : that is to put the wrong cart before the wrong horse. It is true (i.e. veridical) only if it corresponds to the facts in the outside world.

Let us not suppose that it is always easy to avoid this fallacy. Even Sartre, in his *Defence of Intellectuals*, spends some paragraphs attempting to prove that 'any true intellectual' must be opposed to all ideologies that are not of the left (Sartre 1972, pp. 53–9).

Constructs may not only be seen as coherent realities of a thing-like kind. They may almost be seen as having the attributes of *persons*. We saw in Chapter 1 how the nation-state may often be given such attributes. It is more worrying, however, when a philosopher reproduces the same attitude :

> Yes, the state is not put together, but lives; it is not a heap nor a machine; it is no mere extravagance when a poet talks of a nation's soul. It is the objective mind which is subjective and self-conscious in its citizens : it feels and knows itself in the heart of each. It speaks the word of command and gives the field of accomplishment, and in the activity of obedience it has and bestows individual life and satisfaction and happiness. (Bradley 1876, p. 167)

Similarly, the notion that personal consciousness is secondary to the 'spirit of the race' is a commonplace of Nazi thought; that it is secondary to the 'consciousness of the masses' is a commonplace of communist thought. Bukharin spoke of 'a conscious collective subject [developing] : it is the proletarian State along with the organs which depend on it' (Glucksmann 1975, p. 88). And Paul Nizan is said to have visited Russia in the hope that he might find that men there were no longer afraid of death, because their identities had been submerged in the collectivity![10] The twentieth century, it would seem, is tempted by a strange delusion : the myth of the conscious State.

Both the social functions of individuals and social institutions them-selves may be seen as more 'active', more 'real', than the individuals themselves. As Berger and Pullberg say, one may falsify the actions of people by 'reifying' them, turning them into realities more 'genuine' than the people who perform them.

> For instance, one reifies action by saying that it is performed *because* (or, one may say – *because of course*) the actor is an X-type person . . . Actions are perceived as standing separately from their performer. In other words, actions are conceived of as roles and the actor as an embodiment of roles. When one now reflects about these perceptions, the world is seen as inhabited by people who not only perform but are the embodiments of roles. To put this a little facetiously, role-playing precedes existence – or, even better, replaces it. If one now goes on to theorize on the basis of this con-sciousness, one may develop a sociology that regards roles rather than people as the prime reality. Such a sociology effectively mystifies concrete situations, but goes on to operate as a self-fulfilling prophecy by producing more social situations in which this whole process of reification can take place. It may even happen that the world concocted by this kind of theorizing becomes the taken-for-granted world of everyday life and even finds its ex-pression in everyday language . . . [People] may then act in the false consciousness that they 'have no choice' – *because* they are the bearers of this or that role . . . The executioner who kills his victim mimes the prototypical action of the gods, of abstract justice or of the state in upholding right and punishing wrong – 'ultimately' it is not he but these abstractions that engage in killing. The businessman . . . mimes the prototypical actions that . . . dwell in some Platonic heaven of economic abstractions – 'ultimately' it is not he who is doing business but the economic system is conceived of as acting *through* him . . . The deviant from these institutionally defined courses of action may thus be perceived, and theoretically annihilated, as one who offends against the very 'nature of things', against the 'natural order' of the world or of his own being . . . [Among such reifications of institutions] are 'the economy', 'the state', 'the nation', or 'the revolutionary movement' . . .
>
> (Berger & Pullberg 1964, pp. 205–7)

The reality of persons has been taken from them, and transferred to insentient entities, constructs and abstractions. We should note how the victims of this kind of thinking, 'deviants' and nonconformists, are dehumanized in the minds of the rulers, and how there is nothing 'theoretical' about the annihilation they suffer in certain states which are constructed on these principles. And I would rather speak here, not of reification, but of personification : institutions and roles are turned into quasi-persons, and have attributed to them the reality which properly belongs to individual human beings.

While on the subject of the personalization of abstractions, and the depersonalization of human beings which goes with it, one should note that in many recent cases where innocent people have been held hostage by criminals or terrorists, it has been the practice for the authorities to hold out for several days, *talking* to the criminals, in the hope that some sort of human rapport might grow up between them and the hostages. This, the theory goes, makes it more difficult for them to carry out their murderous threats. For they then may cease to see their innocent victims as merely objects, and begin to perceive that they are persons.

Do those left-wing revolutionaries of our time who advocate the destruction of whole classes, whole groups of people, deliberately regard their victims as mere objects? (For that matter, did Stalin's minions do likewise when they liquidated millions, and created the great Russian famine?) The answer, I think, must be Yes. Here, for instance, is Dotson Rader, a 1968 Columbia University revolutionist, admitting in so many words that, for such revolutionary 'idealists', the abstraction 'justice' had been turned into a reality; and that the realities, people, had to be deliberately regarded as things.' *Had* to be. For otherwise the revolutionary would not have the heart to murder them.

> *Beichman:* I don't quite understand the politics of the word 'revolution'. What would be the power structure? Would it be a politburo? Would it be a dictatorship?
>
> *Rader:* What you're asking is what comes after the revolution. I don't know . . . We're fundamentally interested in justice, which means we have a greater tolerance for ideas of liquidating a class and so on . . .
>
> *B:* You're talking about murder. This is the way people get categorized – a class, Jews, gypsies, Catholics, you don't see people.
>
> *R:* The whole . . . ability to function as a revolutionary, which I'm not, depends upon the ability to depersonalize your enemy . . . If you personalize your enemy, you can't act . . .
>
> (Beichman 1975, p. 20)

No clearer instance could be given of the way 'justice' loses its meaning if it is not seen as justice *to people*.

Another danger is that, instead of exploring the content of a construct, its connotations, its multiple reference to experience, we may remain on the surface of it, regarding it as an object having existence in its own right, as a *reality independent of its content*. In some cases, the word may then be separated totally from any reality that it might have had: it floats, like an imaginary bubble, far above the gross world of significance. Thus, a shipyard worker is reported to have said: 'All right, I'll be on the dole, but I'll have parity.' [11] Or take two verbal dishonesties for which bureaucracies are responsible. First, there is the case of a worker who was refused compensation for an industrial accident on the grounds that to give him compensation 'would have spoiled the factory's accident-free record'. Secondly, in correspondence with an education committee, a citizen complained that there was no supervision in local primary school playgrounds. The Authority replied that, on the contrary, there was 'supervision at all times'. But this, by the Authority's own admission, did not mean that there was anyone in the playground actually supervising. [12]

The absurdity of such cases is self-evident : we are hardly likely to be deceived by the bureaucratic pretence that if you call it supervision it is supervision, and that if you don't call it an accident it isn't an accident. But there are more confusing instances. Take the term 'tolerance'. It is often objected to those who favour the principle of tolerance in human affairs, that it leads to contradictory results. For, if we tolerate all modes of opinion, all political complexions, we will, among them, be tolerating the views of people who have themselves no respect for tolerance, and who would, if they achieved political power, eliminate the tolerant. How then can tolerance be a valid principle ? If we are not willing, in the name of tolerance, to permit its destruction, are we not deceiving ourselves in calling ourselves tolerant ? And if we are willing for tolerance to be destroyed, does this not demonstrate the sentimental impracticality of liberal thinking ?

The paradox is neatly stated, but false. We need to ask (1) for a definition of tolerance; and (2) for its reference to reality. The definition can be sought quite simply in terms of tolerance's referents. When does tolerance occur ? And what is its purpose ? Tolerance occurs, for instance, when we have a group of individuals, A, B, C, D and E, among whom it is agreed that they shall all be allowed to speak their mind. Tolerance's purpose, in this instance, is to allow free speech. If now E wishes to silence the others, and is unable to do so, the principle of free speech has not been infringed. If, however, he goes further and threatens to silence them by superior force, free speech is then at risk. Since tolerance has no meaning unless it is given an actual content, namely the actual free speech of actual individuals, the others will be acting consistently with that meaning if they prevent E from silencing them. And, indeed, if they did not do so, they would actually be infringing the reality of tolerance itself.

The political consequences of this analysis are quite clear. They imply that a democratic government is acting consistently with its principles – or rather with the practice that alone gives meaning to principles – if it tolerates anti-democratic groups such as fascists and communists *only so long as* these groups do not constitute a danger to tolerance itself. The point at which that might come about is a matter of practical politics; but the principle is clear; and it is, if I may say so, quite unsentimental and pragmatic.[13]

The sort of dangers that result from regarding abstractions as more real than facts can be glaringly illustrated in Robin Blackburn. He tells us that it is a 'bourgeois' error to identify Hitlerian Germany with Stalinist Russia and call both 'totalitarian'. For one system was of the right, the other of the left. The 'bourgeois' should therefore not see the 'essence' of both as the same. Now I do not suppose for a moment that democratic theorists think there is such a thing as 'essence': 'totalitarian' is simply a useful adjective which points to the centralist and coercive features which both societies had in common. There is nothing objectionable about such a term provided it refers to actual identifiable data, and not to invisible entities like 'essences'. However, even if we were to concede Blackburn's point (and one must in any case concede that Nazism and Communism are different in some respects), he himself goes straight on to commit the same error which he has just stigmatized in others. The differences between the Chinese, Cuban, Romanian, Yugoslav and Russian experiences, he says, 'have conclusively demonstrated that Stalin's Russia was an extreme, rather than a typical, instance of a Communist attempt to build a socialist society . . . The error of the bourgeois theorists was again empiricism: that is, identifying the essence of a form of society (socialism) with its immediately given forms (Stalinism)' (Blackburn & Cockburn 1969, p. 193). According to him, therefore, Stalinism is still socialism despite its 'immediately given forms'! Now if it is wrong to call two systems 'totalitarian' because they are in some respects different, it is equally wrong to call two systems 'socialist' despite their being in some respects different.

Blackburn cannot have it both ways. His argument is being conducted at quite the wrong level. It is the actual features of a society that should determine what we call it, not its 'essence' or the customary labels for it. For otherwise we should never consider what a man is or does, but only his name for what he is or does; and I could commit any crime I liked provided that I asserted I was 'really good' or that I was acting in the name of some 'really high ideal'. Which is precisely the objection to the two systems in question, Nazism and Stalinism. They do have something in common, and it is at the level of practice, rather than of metaphysics, that this can be seen.

When, in December 1976, Luis Corvalán and Vladimir Bukovski, who had been imprisoned for their beliefs by the Chilean and Russian regimes respectively, were exchanged for each other by international agreement, the Italian communist newspaper *L'Unità* wrote that Corvalán's case 'highlights the necessity to eliminate the fascist regime' in Chile, but that 'Bukovski is an entirely different episode which signals the difficulties of a great country, which has lived through a great revolution, to extend its own conquests into the field of individual rights and liberties' (*The Sunday Times*, 19 December 1976). There could be no clearer case of the double-think whereby tyrannies contrive to apologize for themselves.

Marcuse, in Chapter 4 of *One-Dimensional Man*, launches an attack on the principle of reducing generalizations and abstractions to concrete instances. He discusses a study of labour relations in an American firm, in which the workers' generalized complaints ('The wages are too low', 'The toilets are dirty') were followed up to see what concrete content they might yield. The authors found that they could always reduce the general complaint to the specific instance ('The wages are too low' to 'Now B's wife is ill, he's not earning enough to make ends meet'). The complaint could then be dealt with at that level, and the workers' generalized dissatisfaction evaporated.

Marcuse protests that this method of dealing with workers' grievances is a manipulation, since it reduces complaints against the social order to the level of mere personal discontents. But this begs the question. Because 'The wages are too low' is a general statement does not necessarily mean that it has a general reference. The question is, What did the workers *mean* by it? One could only discover this by asking them. And indeed, had the complaint been that most workers felt underpaid, and had there been no way of altering their distress save by altering the social system, Marcuse's interpretation would be correct. But he would be right, not because 'The wages are too low' must and always be a politico-social grievance, but because of its particular reference in *this* case.

It is entirely possible that there was an element of manipulation in the researchers' treatment of these grievances. However, if the grievances really were personal and isolated, there might have been an element of manipulation in advising them to engage in political action. I wish to make no judgment on this particular case, only to point out that, even if the workers' statement was general, it had to relate to specific particulars or it would have had no valid reference. The question is, what are those specific particulars, and do they in fact need to be cured by altering the social system, or by some other action? The sentence at issue may or may not mean what Marcuse would like it to mean; but we shall not know what to think of it until its content has been examined.

All these difficulties are at their most acute in politics; for it is here that practical consequences are often hardest to judge, and emotion most powerfully builds a person's world-view into an impregnable fortress. A letter in *The Times*, 8 April 1976, reads:

In the course of reading the verbatim report of Alexander Solzhenitsyn's radio talk published in *The Times*, I was appalled by the venom with which he attacked socialism. For sixty years I have considered myself a socialist because I had embraced the Utopian idea that the world would be a better place for all to live in if it was organized on the basis of '*From* each according to his ability and *to* each according to his need.'

I am well aware that the name – socialism – has been usurped by tyrants and authoritarian regimes, and so brought into disrepute, but I see no reason to discard the name on that account. We should rather seek to counter the oppressors by winning over the hearts and minds of men to the ideals we aspire to.

(Mrs Winifred Griffiths)

Here the confusion wrought by using one word, 'socialism', to describe a totally disparate set of regimes and policies, is quite clear. For Solzhenitsyn, 'socialism' naturally has its usual Russian denotation, namely the current political system in the U.S.S.R.; for Mrs Griffiths it presumably means some form of Western European social democracy. There are numerous difficulties here : the first is that 'socialism' (like 'poetry' or 'religion') is not a coherent reality, which has a true and easily discernible referent. Her final remark, however, seems on the right lines : the label is nothing : it is more practical matters, such as are suggested by 'the ideals we aspire to', which are important.

The label, however, has considerable emotive power, as do the other labels of politics. We may reasonably complain that conventional political language is a set of completely *inadequate constructs*, inadequate (that is) to represent the realities that underlie them. Why, for instance, do we reduce all political meanings to the simple one-dimensional scale of *left* and *right*? If there were only two ways of doing things, well and good. But there are many ways of doing things, and many fields of human activity to apply these methods to. The polemical advantage of tarring all opponents with the term 'rightist' or the term 'leftist' according to taste, is probably the reason why the habit is so widespread. But it hardly leads to clarity of mind. It leads in fact to Solzhenitsyn's damning all 'socialisms' out of hand, regardless of their actual content; or to the communist attitude of damning all non-communist systems as 'bourgeois reactionary'. Such a one-dimensional way of looking at politics is dangerously misleading; for it leaves some of the most important areas of political life quite out of account. The crude simplicity of the 'right–left' model implies nothing about political and judicial freedoms, nothing about the actual methods used by governments, whether these be of force, of persuasion, or of some form of popular influence and control.

Yet this is the most important aspect of politics. We need at the very least a two-dimensional model, including (1) left versus right, and (2) coercive versus humane, dimensions.[14] However, this is not the place for such proposals; and all I am concerned to show is that the single 'left–right' dimension is a total over-simplification of the vast variety of human political systems. All constructs are misleading, but this one is worse than most.

'Left' and 'right' are two of those terms which politicians deliberately use to confuse their opponents. And we can see the Marxist thinker Althusser explicitly recommending this procedure :

> In scientific and philosophical reasoning, words . . . are 'instruments' of knowledge. But in political, ideological and philosophical struggle, words are also weapons, explosives, or tranquillizers and poisons. Occasionally, the whole class struggle may be summed up in the struggle for one word against another.

(Althusser, *New Left Review* no. 64, p. 10)

There is something peculiarly suspicious in a political attitude which seeks to confuse people : we may reasonably suspect that its own grasp of the facts is tenuous if its method of presenting them is to conceal and distort them. An example of the suppression of facts by the employment of misleading terms is the Nazi use of 'materialism' and the Zhdanovite use of 'idealism' as hostile labels for modern science. Both of these terms refer to precisely the same features of science, and conceal a precisely similar attitude to it. These terms, ostensibly so opposed to each other, turn out to have the same semantic content. They are like two different proprietorial labels on two different bottles, concealing identical quantities of the same drug.

'Indoctrination' is another favourite word used as a weapon. In normal parlance it signifies 'the instilling (possibly by force) of (false) doctrines', and suggests that no alternative ways of thinking are offered for the victims to decide between. As used by some of the sociologists of knowledge or by neo-Marxists of the Blackburn school, it seems to be used interchangeably with 'teaching' or 'learning'. Raymond Williams is unfortunately prone to a similar insinuation when he writes 'a distinction is now clearly made between our *teaching*, your *indoctrination* . . .' (Williams 1976, under 'Doctrinaire'). It is thus an assertion that the knowledge imparted by teachers or simply assimilated through one's living in a particular society, is invariably false and relative. It carries also with it the suggestion that it was forced upon the learner, and that there is a social conspiracy to permit only slanted views to be presented. Again a conjuring trick has been performed, so rapidly that we may have difficulty in discerning precisely what has happened. From the neutral sense of 'indoctrination' (namely 'the instilling of an opinion') the leap has been made to the implication that all opinions are false, and that all methods of propagating them are equally detestable. It behoves us again to be on our guard. We must ask : what *are* the opinions in question? Are some of them facts? (It would be difficult to assert the 'indoctrination' of facts.) What *methods* are used in instilling them?

The conjurer's trick will then be unmasked. There are two sorts of 'doctrine' or philosophy : the rigid, which admits of no alternative views; and the flexible, which admits that there are other reasonable opinions. There are also facts, and some of them are more certain than others. There is more than one way of teaching : views may be forced upon the learner; or they may be offered as the only possible views; or they may be offered as an alternative among others. The learner may be allowed no choice; or he may be allowed a free one. 'Indoctrination' will remain a useful word only if it assists us in making these vitally important distinctions : if we use it, that is, to mean the instilling of rigid worldviews without any possibility of dissent. The presentation of a flexible world-view, allowing dissent and offering alternative views, is thus not a form of indoctrination at all : *it is its opposite.*

Again we see, then, that we must not treat all the interpretations of a word as being inseparable from its meaning; lest, in accepting some connotations, we should be committed in advance to others which are not a part of *our* meaning. Abstract words do not stand for coherent realities; they are not like persons, whose faults we have to put up with for the sake of their virtues. Their meanings have to be subdivided and analyzed, and we are free to assent to just as much of them as we wish.

The consequences of regarding constructs as coherent realities are particularly virulent in racism.

> In Rhodesia a white truck driver passed a group of idle natives and muttered, 'They're lazy brutes.' A few hours later he saw natives heaving two-hundred pound sacks of grain onto a truck, singing in rhythm to their work. 'Savages', he grumbled. 'What do you expect?' (Allport 1954, p. 3)

What indeed? The racist always sees what he expects : he is incapable of seeing anything else. As for the victim of prejudice, he cannot win. Whatever he does, it will be regarded unfavourably; because it is not what he does that determines how people think of him, but how people think of him that determines how what he does will be seen.

On the basis of one attribute (namely blackness) the man is assigned to a category. The category carries with it a large number of connotations, including laziness and savagery. Whichever of these can be made to fit (and irrespective of whichever others may not) is then assigned to the man. We may be reminded of Luria's patients suffering from damage to the frontal lobe, who, when asked to look at a realistic picture and say what it showed, would fasten on some one feature of the picture, ignoring all the rest. A death-bed scene might be described as a wedding, for instance, because of a white dress, or as someone suffering from a cold, because of a handkerchief (Luria 1973, pp. 213–7).

The Rhodesian story illustrates the linguistic disease of abstracto-latry: people and things are seen solely through the categories which a predetermined world-view has imposed upon them: communists are seen solely as communists, blacks purely as 'niggers', people with upper-class accents purely as 'upper class', miners from Barnsley purely as 'working men'. The process is strictly one of abstraction: people are assigned to categories on the basis of some characteristic that they have in common. The similarity may be as trivial as you like, but the effect is still the same: most of the reality of the people in question is thereby lost.

Take this little exchange:

X: The trouble with Jews is that they only take care of their own group.

Y: But the record of the Community Chest campaign shows that they give more generously, in proportion to their numbers, to the general charities of the community, than do non-Jews.

X: That shows that they are always trying to buy favour and intrude into Christian affairs. They think of nothing but money; that is why there are so many Jewish bankers.

Y: But a recent study shows that the percentage of Jews in the banking business is negligible, far smaller than the percentage of non-Jews.

X: That's just it: they don't go in for respectable business; they are only in the movie business or run night-clubs.

(Allport 1954, pp. 13–14)

Here prejudice slips from point to point; as it concedes one point, it usurps another. And prejudice finds this easy to do, for whatever objection is raised, some aspect of it is fitted into some part of the scheme of thinking. The prejudiced person observes only those connotations of words which fit into his pre-established scheme; he ignores the others. Facts are looked at for how they fit the ideology, the ideology is not looked at for how it fits the facts. The abstract system takes precedence over the realities it is supposed to 'explain'.

Abstract language may thus have practical consequences of the most unfortunate kind. Not that these consequences are inevitable; nor are they entirely the fault of language, and certainly not of language *alone*. But since language allows man to stabilize his categories, to give them permanence and a sort of imagined reality, language and categories interact. Language was given to man to enable him to grasp and manipulate reality, and to imagine alternative possibilities to it. But the gift of imagination is also the gift of error. Perhaps it does not at first sight look as if turning the simple statement 'He was far from certain what was going to happen' into some more abstract version such as 'He

71

little knew the fate that lay in store for him' could be in any way 'dangerous'. But a typical polemical sentence from a modern French writer – 'They are the negation of our specificity' – is a different matter. This abstract phrase means merely : 'They don't agree with what we think.' But it is couched in such a way that an absolute black and white opposition is established : it is no longer a matter of disagreement over points of view, but of incompatibility between the natures or essences of two opposing groups; it sounds as if the very existence of the one threatens the other; as if they should not properly belong in the same world; and it is hence a call to conflict, not a statement of difference of opinion.

Orwell in his 'Politics and the English language' writes :

> Consider for instance some comfortable English professor defending Russian totalitarianism. He cannot say outright, 'I believe in the killing of your opponents when you can get good results by doing so.' Probably, therefore, he will say something like this : 'While freely conceding that the Soviet regime exhibits certain features which the humanitarian may be inclined to deplore, we must, I think, agree that a certain curtailment of the right to political opposition is an unavoidable concomitant of transitional periods, and that the rigours which the Russian people have been called upon to undergo have been amply justified in the sphere of concrete achievement.'

This sentence is hilarious. It is also alarmingly true to type. The reality of death and suffering has been hidden behind a mask of abstractions; the audience are at liberty to forget the facts if they are so inclined; and forget them they therefore will. And did.

One sometimes wonders if some languages are not more prone to abstractolatry than others. Joseph Berger makes the following disturbing remarks about his experiences in Sovet Russia :

> Here I must make a short digression : The discussion about *pravda* ('truth') and *istina* (also 'truth') went on endlessly in the camps and prisons. Russian was not my mother-tongue and I could not at first fathom the distinction, but a philologist explained it to me. The equivalent of 'truth', *'vérité'* or *'Wahrheit'*, is *istina*, which denotes the correspondence between the notion and the objective reality. *Pravda* is a unique and specifically Russian concept : it means the higher concept of truth, a truth elevated to the rank of an idea . . .
>
> In the rooms of the N.K.V.D. and at Party meetings, *istina* was nothing – it was relative and it could easily be changed : only *pravda* was absolute. It seemed to me, as it must do to millions of others who have not been through this school, hard to understand how a philological distinction could have such an effect on the lives

of so many. But in fact this small difference – this tyranny of *pravda* over *istina* – was the level by which white was turned into black; no such dialectic had existed since the Inquisition. The notion of *pravda* was the basis of power.

In 1936 I eventually succeeded in persuading one of my most intelligent interrogators to answer my question: 'Are you not in the least interested in what actually happened? Do you really only want the pre-selected truth that is the "Party" truth?' He gave this trenchant reply. '*Pravda* is what appeared in today's leading article in *Pravda* [the newspaper]. Anything that doesn't fit into this framework is, for us, *objectively, not* true. What have we to do with your petty *istinas*?'   (J. Berger 1971, pp. 52–3)

Pravda is thought amputated from reality: it is the never-never land of wishful thinking, the deification of falsity.

But we do not have to travel to Russia or the Southern States to observe prejudice being given its automatic assent. That a good deal of thought is merely the rehearsal of habitual stereotypes is a matter of everyday experience. I recently overheard the following exchange, when the queue at a bus-stop had been waiting for some time and had had their hopes raised and then dashed by the appearance of a bus driven by a learner driver. Here is an attempt to reproduce the conversation:

A: Ye canna get drivers for the buses. They dinna want to work these days.

B: Aye, it's all they people on the burroo.[15] But Mrs Thatcher'll sort the scroungers oot.

A: Mind you, they're no to blame entirely, wi' all they foreigners comin' in gettin' oor jobs.

B: Aye, things are gettin' real bad.

A: Aye, they should bring back hangin' and birchin'.

B: Aye, but the M.P.'s voted against it. Mind you, Mrs Thatcher has some sense: she voted for it.

A: Och, but will she be able to stand up to the unions? It's no a woman's job, that!

And so on.

Abstractolatry is comforting: this is indeed its *raison d'être*. We fear disorder; and if we fear it enough, we shall seek at all costs to impose order on experience, to recoil in disbelief and horror from all indications of things not being exactly as we so desperately wish them to be. Abstractolatry is also a powerful weapon: it is a method of blinding oneself to facts one does not wish to see, of withdrawing sympathy from people one wishes to oppress, of distancing oneself from human suffering. But it is also dangerous: if things are not in fact as we wish them to be, then one of these days we are likely to receive a nasty surprise or two. Classification is like a medieval cannon: it can knock down the walls of an enemy castle; it may also blow up in our faces. What is to be done? We need *some* sort of world-view, or the behaviour of others and of ourselves would be for ever incomprehensible to us. We have to classify and categorize, to tuck reality away in neat pigeonholes, or we should never have time to act upon it, but would spend our days contemplating its ineffable essence. We have already seen Bruner asserting the utility of classification; and besides, it is a fundamental psychological process.

> Dr Horn at Cambridge has recently found single nerve cells in the mid-brain of a rabbit which respond promptly to a tone sounded at a frequency of 1000 cycles per second, but cease to respond after several repetitions of the stimulus. Habituation to the 1000-tone cycle does not, however, prevent a strong response of the same cell when an only slightly different, 900-cycle tone is sounded. Dr Horn presented examples of similar phenomena in animals as different as locusts, squids and cats.   (Koestler 1974, p. 127)

As for human beings, we may instance the curious 'Bowery El' effect. When the famous overhead railway known as the Bowery El was removed from New York, the inhabitants of neighbouring houses began to report strange creakings and 'bumps in the night': there were burglars on the prowl, they reported to the police. The police investigated, but there was never any evidence of intruders, let alone of 'ghoulies, ghosties and long-leggedy beasties'. And then it dawned on someone that the times when these mysterious incidents were reported coincided exactly with the times that the old Bowery El train used to pass. The *absence* of a customary noise (which they had become used to over the years, and never noticed) had alerted the inhabitants to the silence – or rather to the small insignificant noises with which silence is usually filled (Ornstein 1975, p. 29; see Pribram 1969).

The process of habituation is fundamental to our perceptions, it would seem. Everyone knows that a smell of gas, for instance, is quite distinct when first it is noticed; but a few minutes' acclimatization to it, and it totally disappears.

> Charles Furst has studied the effect of repeated viewing of the same picture on the way we look at it. He found that eye movements tend to become more and more stereotyped as the same visual stimulus is presented. When we see a new image, our eyes tend to move in a new pattern around it, but as we see it again and again, as we see the rooms in our house, we tend to look in a fixed way at fixed portions of it, and ignore or tune out the rest. The 'Bowery El' effect, the 'Furst' effect, and other studies on habituation suggest that we tune out the recurrences of the world by making a 'model' of the external world within our nervous system, and testing input against it. We somehow can program, and continu-

ally revise or reprogram, our models of the external world. If the input and the model agree, as they do most often for the constancies of the world, then the input stays out of consciousness. If there is any disagreement, if the new input is recognizably different, slower, softer, louder, different in form or colour, or even absent, we become aware of the input once again. [And it should be noted that this is inbuilt physically into our perception:] the cells in the visual cortex and retina, for example, are specialized to detect *changes* in input and to ignore constancies.

(Ornstein 1975, pp. 31, 27; see Furst 1971)

And this of course is the answer to the problem posed above. Categorization is basic; and it is valuable as we are aware of its limitations. But difference may produce a new alertness: surprise may make us freshly aware of the facts, or lead us to reappraise them.

We may not be properly aware of our own beliefs, our own frame of reference, our own 'horizon of expectations', as Popper puts it, until one of those expectations is disappointed.

We become aware of many expectations only when they are disappointed – for example, when we come upon an unexpected step. (Only the unexpectedness of the step shows us that we expected an even surface.) Expectation disappointments force us to correct our expectations. (Popper 1949)

It is by departures from normality that we see (1) what we took normality to be, and (2) what more it is than we had thought.

Further support is given to this view by communication theory, which is, as Colin Cherry writes, 'a rigid scientific theory ... [begotten] by Mathematics [upon] Telegraphy' (Cherry 1955, p. 48; see Shannon & Weaver 1949). 'Information' in communication theory is a technical term, but is none the less applied in a way that seems thoroughly in harmony with intuition and common sense. For 'in everyday speech we say that we have received Information when we know something that we did not know before: when 'what we know' has changed' (Mackay 1969, p. 156). For if someone tells us something that we know already in every detail, we do not say that we have received information. And the more surprising the news that we receive, the more information we say that we have obtained. Thus, according to communication theorists, the more probable a message is the less information it conveys (cf. Hintikka 1970, p. 8). To take an extremely simple example: in English the letter *q* is almost always followed by the letter *u*; and indeed, in most contexts of the use of *q*, we can predict with total certainty that the letter *u* will follow. Thus the letter *u* in such contexts provides no information.

This observation can be extrapolated to communication situations in general. We take no interest in some acquaintance's lengthy description of how they put the kettle on for tea at 4 p.m. yesterday, and people who persist in telling us things of this kind are commonly stigmatized as self-centred bores. For such a description contains little 'information': it would only do so if something untoward were to happen, such as the tea being spilt over the acquaintance's best carpet, or the unaccountable explosion of the kettle! Similarly, news bulletins concern themselves with 'information': they do not report the birth of Mrs Smith's latest baby unless there is something unusual about the baby, its parents or the circumstances of its birth. If it is the first to be conceived by artificial insemination, or the first to be born on the way to the moon, then it might figure in a news bulletin.

Thus, the 'information' content of a statement is, to the communication theorist, in inverse relation to its probability. It follows therefore that 'information can be received only where there is doubt; and doubt implies the existence of alternatives' (Cherry 1961, p. 168). For if one has no doubt beforehand what X is going to say, his going on to say it can provide no 'information'. A further consequence of this is that a 'receiver' which is programmed to 'comprehend' only what it already 'knows' is incapable of receiving 'information'. We may extrapolate from this observation to the ordinary business of human communication, and say that a human being of unusually rigid attitudes and beliefs would be unable to grasp new information that was being signalled to him. And here we have precisely the case of those sufferers from blind prejudice whose failings were noted earlier in this chapter. An attitude of flexibility, a capacity for doubt, a tolerance of uncertainty is a prior condition for our learning things about the world. And the same goes for human societies themselves:

> All social systems are open systems, interacting with the external environment and therefore receiving and producing activities and energies across the boundary. Such exchange is bound to present the social system with situations it has not experienced before. If the social system does not allow any disorganization, such encounter[s] will either decrease the efficiency of the system or damage the system severely enough to threaten its survival.
>
> (Lin 1973, p. 189)

Rigidity spells damage and, ultimately, death. And the perfectly organized state would, by that very fact, be incapable of assimilating the new.

What are the consequences of all this for artistic communication? John Lyons sums up the case I am making here as follows:

> (i) All communication rests upon the possibility of *choice*, or selection from a set of alternatives.
>
>   . . . We shall see that this principle provides us with an interpretation of the term 'meaningful' (in one of its senses): a linguistic unit, of whatever level, has no meaning in a given context

if it is completely predictable in that context.

(ii) Information-content varies inversely with probability. The more predictable a unit is, the less meaning it has. This principle is in accord with the commonly-expressed view of writers on style, that clichés (or 'hackneyed expressions' and 'dead metaphors') are less effective than more 'original' turns of phrase.

(Lyons 1968, p. 89)

4. Disrupting the Categories I

The moral of all this is that the unexpected is particularly valuable. It provides 'information', it directs our attention to the new, it directs it also to our hitherto unrecognized assumptions. Art utilizes this fundamental psychological principle to a remarkable degree.

> Thus, Maurice-Jean Lefebve asks us to consider what happens when two sensations which come from a single object and which normally coincide, suddenly seem *out of phase* with one another. This simple disturbance of our perceptions leads us to question reality. Such is the case with a scene watched from a distance, when the sounds which come from it arrive fractionally later than our visual perception of it . . .

(as with watching a cricket-match *before* we become familiar with this experience)

> The same phenomenon explains the way events like a horse-race, or children playing ball on the beach, can seem slowed down when we look at them through binoculars. Or think again of the feeling of unfamiliarity we get if we're walking about a town that we know perfectly well, but suddenly come out in front of a building we had never seen before from quite that angle. (Lefebve 1971, p. 94)

Our vision is refreshed. Certain surrealist techniques had precisely this purpose. Think for example of the sugar-lumps sitting in a sugar-bowl at one famous surrealist exhibition: when you picked them up, they were extraordinarily heavy, so that you sometimes dropped them – for they weren't sugar-lumps at all, but made of marble! Or think of Max Ernst's pictures of men with the heads of birds of prey, or of the canvases of Delvaux, showing naked women walking unconcernedly down a station platform.

But the technique is not exclusively surrealist. A similar effect was produced by Manet's *Le Déjeuner sur l'herbe*, where men in town clothes sat around a naked woman on the grass. The picture shocked the nineteenth-century public (despite the theme's being common in traditional art) because of the modernity of the men's clothes: reality had broken in upon the conventions of academic art, and the protesting howls of public and critics could be heard several frontiers away. Nor is the technique confined to painting. It is in fact closely akin to the poetic use of metaphor, where a word is inserted in a surprising context, as when Yeats has an ominous vision of a 'rough beast . . . slouching towards Bethlemen to be born', or Dylan Thomas 'refuses' to mourn the death, by fire, of a child in London. Though it has been much criticized for this very reason, the special effectiveness of the *trompe-l'oeil* type of surrealism is largely due to its pedestrian realism : Magritte for instance paints things in as ordinary a way as possible, precisely so that the shock to the mind is greater. A *trompe-l'oeil* man in a bowler hat gazing into a mirror – which then reflects, not his face, but the back of his head : such pictures *have* to resemble our cheapest and most commonplace images of reality so as to produce the maximum shock. There is a sort of purity of effect in Magritte's paintings : everything is flatly commonplace except the essential thing, and that is totally impossible!

The philistine, puzzled by such pictures, asserts perhaps that they do not show us anything real, but something absurd, irrelevant, unreal. But of course this is not so. The reversal of the reflection is like Popper's unexpected step that interrupts a flat surface and so shows us what our expectations had been. We suddenly become freshly aware of what, in the constancies of normal life, we take for granted, namely the orientation of reflections, the laws of light. Our two principles of psychological functioning, that is to say habituation and the refreshment of perception through surprise, lie also behind Magritte's picture of a castle standing on the summit of an immense rocky crag . . . only the crag itself is shown suspended above ground in the midst of a bright blue sky. An intense sense of discomfort is generated : we are at once aware that the laws of gravity are being infringed. And so we (as it were) sense the massiveness of the rock much more consciously than we do on viewing a 'realistic' picture of a cliff surmounted by a castle. Our perception of weight has been refreshed, and we realize how important a role the unconscious acceptance of gravity plays in our reactions.

To quote the Russian formalist critic Shklovski :

> People living by the seaside grow so accustomed to the murmur of the waves that they never hear it. By the same token, we scarcely ever hear the words we utter . . . We look at each other, but we do not see each other any more. Our perception of the world has withered away, what remains is mere recognition.
>
> (Quoted in Erlich 1954, p. 150)

Similarly, Zamyatin, no doubt under formalist influence, writes : 'most people suffer from hereditary sleeping sickness, and those who are sick with this ailment must not be allowed to sleep, or they will go to their last sleep, the sleep of death' (Quoted in Howe 1971). Consequently the formalists proposed the notion of *ostranniye* or strange-making, as a criterial characteristic of literature. And of course some sort of deviation from the expected norms of language has been seen as the clue to literary discourse by a large number of authorities. I am following the example of these critics : I am proposing 'oddness' as one of the criterial features of literature, and as a feature which may help to heal us of the ills of categorization. What is *new* in my presentation of this theory? (1) That 'oddness' can be shown to have a firm basis in human psychology; for it has a discernible *modus operandi*. And (2) that there are powerful philosophical justifications for thus 'showing the concrete'.

I am not, of course, making the over-ambitious claim that art is the sole method of disturbing or forcing us to become conscious of our categories. I have already mentioned, in the previous chapter, social science as performing a part of this function as far as social categories are concerned; I have spent some pages of the present chapter using analysis to dispel illusion; and I shall end it with some examples of how the study of two different languages may have a similar salutary effect. However, to spend some time 'within' a work of art, such as a novel or a play, is to spend some time with a particularly concretely realized experience. We may therefore assert it to be one of the principal methods of perceptual refreshment that mankind has so far invented for itself. As a Greek philosopher might have put it,

> Well then, by Heaven, we have to ask ourselves if there is any faculty which sets vivid images of reality before a man's senses or imagination, so that he is compelled to view them in a new light; one that complexifies the commonplace simplicities of perception, reveals our habit of seeing trees merely as instances of the category 'tree', refreshes the stalenesses of our thought, disrupts our uniformities, and leads us to question our commonsense understanding of the world, of human motive and behaviour.

The 'faculty' of art fits these requirements to perfection.

I shall not assert, by the way, that the only feature of art itself which shows us the concrete is its capacity to disrupt expectation. There are in fact two main methods whereby literature embeds itself in concrete experience : (1) by imaginative identification, that is, by associating the reader closely with the individual consciousness of a character, and (2) by 'oddness'. The *isonic process*, which is a special and particularly concrete mode of this second technique, will be discussed in Chapter 4. Here I shall briefly comment upon the first of these techniques, and give a number of examples of the second.

(1) *Imaginative identification.* It is clear enough in the case of the modern technique of the interior monologue or stream of consciousness, that the reader is asked to follow closely and in 'all' its detail, the rhythms, meanderings, switches of attention, perceptions, associations, etc., of a particular consciousness. But the traditional novel, though less detailed and vivid in this respect, habitually performs something of a similar function. Let me cite for instance :

Emma's eyes were instantly withdrawn; and she sat silently meditating, in a fixed attitude, for a few minutes. A few minutes were sufficient for making her acquainted with her own heart. A mind like hers, once opening to suspicion, made rapid progress. She touched – she admitted – she acknowledged the whole truth. Why was it so much worse that Harriet should be in love with Mr Knightley, than with Frank Churchill? Why was the evil so dreadfully increased by Harriet's having some hope of a return? It darted through her, with the speed of an arrow, that Mr Knightley must marry no one but herself!

Her own conduct, as well as her own heart, was before her in the same few minutes. She saw it all with a clearness which had never blessed her before. How improperly had she been acting by Harriet! How inconsiderate, how indelicate, how irrational, how unfeeling had been her conduct! What blindness, what madness, had led her on! It struck her with dreadful force, and she was ready to give it every bad name in the world. Some portion of respect for herself, however, in spite of all these demerits – some concern for her own appearance, and a strong sense of justice by Harriet – (there would be no need of *compassion* to the girl who believed herself loved by Mr Knightley – but justice required that she should not be made unhappy by any coldness now), gave Emma the resolution to sit and endure farther with calmness, with even apparent kindness.

This is far from the techniques of the stream of consciousness. The author can be heard, dimly, looking over the character's shoulder (as in 'Some portion of respect for herself . . .'). The words which describe her feelings in the second paragraph mostly convey a moral judgment, and constitute a sort of abstraction from the texture of her feelings. None the less their broken rhythms, the exclamatory phrases, the parenthesis that breaks into the final long sentence, the force of disapproval present in the choice of words, re-enact the mental emphases and rhythms of Emma's self-disgust. When she reaches more calmness (or rather more resolution) in the final lines of the paragraph (but these I have not quoted), so does the rhythm of the sentences. The character's tendency to impulsiveness, linked with an underlying balance and a capacity for moral self-observation, find themselves not only pointed to, but to some extent syntactically and rhythmically depicted. And indeed any further degree of depiction would perhaps have been too much for the moral perceptiveness which Jane Austen requires of her heroine. This is a *controlled* turmoil of emotion, and as such it suits Emma perfectly. Not as concrete as Joyce or Woolf, no doubt; but none the less we are being shown something of the inner processes of a self-critical mind.

And now a twentieth-century example :

Je peux dire qu'au fond l'été a très vite remplacé l'été. Je savais qu'avec la montée des premières chaleurs surviendrait quelque chose de nouveau pour moi. Mon affaire était inscrite à la dernière session de la cour d'assises et cette session se terminerait avec le mois de juin. Les débats se sont ouverts avec, au-dehors, tout le plein du soleil. Mon avocat m'avait assuré qu'ils ne dureraient pas plus de deux ou trois jours. 'D'ailleurs, avait-il ajouté, la cour sera pressée parce que votre affaire n'est pas la plus importante de la session. Il y a un parricide qui passera tout de suite après.'

A sept heures et demie du matin, on est venu me chercher et la voiture cellulaire m'a conduit au Palais de justice. Les deux gendarmes m'ont fait entrer dans une petite pièce qui sentait l'ombre. Nous avons attendu, assis près d'une porte derrière laquelle on entendait des voix, des appels, des bruits de chaises et tout un remue-ménage qui m'a fait penser à ces fêtes de quartier où, après le concert, on range la salle pour pouvoir danser. Les gendarmes m'ont dit qu'il fallait attendre la cour et l'un d'eux m'a offert une cigarette que j'ai refusée. Il m'a demandé peu après 'si j'avais le trac'. J'ai répondu que non. Et même, dans un sens, cela m'intéressait de voir un procès. Je n'en avais jamais eu l'occasion dans ma vie : 'Oui, a dit le second gendarme, mais cela finit par fatiguer.'   (Camus, *L'Etranger*, Part 2, Ch. 3)

[I may say that, after all, summer very quickly succeeded summer. I knew that with the coming of the first heat-waves there would be something new for me. My case was fixed for the last sitting of the court of assizes and that sitting would end in the month of June. The public hearings opened with the sun, out of doors, at its full strength. My barrister had assured me that they wouldn't last more than two or three days. 'Besides', he had added, 'the court will be in a hurry because your case isn't the most important one. There's a parricide to deal with immediately after.'

At half past seven in the morning, they came to fetch me and the prison van drove me to the Law Courts. The two policemen took me into a little room which smelled of shade. We waited, sitting by a door behind which you could hear voices, requests, the sound of chairs and a great stir which made me think of those local fêtes where, after the concert, the room is got ready for dancing. The policemen told me that I would have to wait for the trial and one of them offered me a cigarette which I refused. Soon after he asked me if I'd 'got the wind up'. I answered no. And even, in a way, I found it interesting to be going to see a trial. I'd never had the opportunity in my life : 'Yes', said the second policeman, 'but you get tired of it in the end'.]

Meursault's world : the simplest of vocabulary, the shortest of sentences; only one image ('a little room which smelled of shade'). The past historic, the customary tense for literary works, has been replaced by the conversational perfect. It has been claimed that this brings us closer to the passing moments of Meursault's narrative. For he lives in the present: largely unreflecting, somewhat passive, open to what life has to offer moment by moment. His passivity is evident here: he does not recount his feelings, save for the curiously detached: 'I found it interesting to be going to see a trial.' But the trial is his own, and he is accused of murder! Otherwise emotion is remarkable only by its absence. The world in which Meursault lives is one that offers with one hand and takes away with the other: he regards this passing scene with stoical fatalism.

Barthes described this style as 'le degré zéro de l'écriture'. But it is not really so. The absence of the usual stylistic conventions is like the absence of the step in Popper's example: it directs our attention to what is absent. Hence we grasp the particular quality of the narrator's world: a succession of events, a bareness and emptiness, a persistent quality of understatement. For instance 'Je peux dire qu'au fond . . .' (I may say that, after all . . .) is a colloquial phrase that understates the effect of the passage of time, and fails to mention any emotional force it may have for Meursault. Much the same could be said of 'quelque chose de nouveau pour moi' (something new for me). The narrator is not a man for the great emotional gesture: in his world things just *are*, and have to be accepted as such. Moreover, the causality of things is as it were reduced by this phrase: the trial just happens with the inevitability of an accidental event. Meursault considers that not much sense can be seen in the passing spectacle of things: hence his detachment and his openness to experience – and experience, to be sure, of the simplest kind. Experience is a good (even the experience of his own trial), but his attitude towards it is that of an ascetic.

Thus it is that the quality of someone else's world (to echo Proust) may be brought home to us.

(2) *Disturbance of expectation.* In *Language, Truth and Poetry* (Martin 1975a) I catalogued a number of literary effects under the heading 'Some varieties of oddness'. All of these effects depended on difference, deviation, unfamiliarity, surprise, the disruption of some established rhythm or expected pattern, the violation of some conventional use of language. The catalogue that follows will act to supplement that list, and to make my case here through a few suggestive examples.

(*a*) The *content* of a work is often unexpected. A reader used to the optimistic conventions of such utopias as Morris's *News from Nowhere* would be disturbed in his expectations by an anti-utopia like *Brave New World*. Indeed, this is a particularly subtle example of the genre, since it has attractive as well as unattractive features and poses in a worrying way the problem of death and suffering. There is no simple solution to the dilemmas present in the book. Such deviation from conventional patterns is extremely common in the novel. Indeed, John Sturrock has reminded us that the term 'anti-novel' goes back in France to 1633 (Charles Sorel's *Anti-roman*), that such classics as *Don Quixote, Joseph Andrews, Northanger Abbey* and *Madame Bovary* are blasts against the conventions of the novel of their time; and he argues that

> all considerable novelists of the past have been anti-novelists, since they must all have found something unsatisfactory about the conventions which they inherited . . . and have been determined to give new life to the novel as a tradition by restoring its vital ties with reality.   (Sturrock 1969, pp. 5–6)

(*b*) Many of these deviations from the novel's expected content are acts of *moral disturbance*. Shoddy sentimentality or simplistic black and white moralities are shown up, and their moral effects lampooned. Conventional notions of 'glory' are questioned by Fabrice's experiences at Waterloo in *La Chartreuse de Parme*, or by the work of the English poets of the First World War. People's habitual categories are directly questioned, as by such lines as Owen's

'I am the enemy you killed, my friend.'   ('Strange Meeting') Another example of explicit moral questioning is Molière's satire on religious hypocrisy in *Le Tartuffe* and in *Dom Juan*, plays which aroused the censors of his time to fury. For, that piety might not be identical with its appearances or with outward declarations of piety was a most dangerous proposition : it might lead people to question the abstraction 'piety' and to demand its concrete content. This is a particularly clear case of the questioning of abstract constructs by the literary presentation of reality.

Coming closer to our own times, the plays of Genet and the poetry of Plath have been attacked for presenting a demoralizing picture of reality. Yet Genet's and Plath's pictures of the world are (by virtue of their being authentic reflections of the writers' own minds) really existent therefore real ones, and require an answer. Such an answer will not be provided by simple condemnation of their work, but rather by using it to clarify and reassess our moral positions. And if their work is so used, even the moralist will come to see that it has considerable value.

Thus, both of these writers demonstrate the presence of dark and destructive forces in the human psyche, forces whose influence should not be underestimated. Closing one's eyes to such things is not satisfactory, for they are a part of the practical problems which have to be taken into account when dealing with moral issues. Solutions can never be found to problems unless all the facts, however pleasant or unpleasant, have been faced.

(*c*) The writer may pretend to disturb the conditions of *reality* itself.

Thus, our certainties about the world are momentarily upset by such incidents as the narrator of *A la recherche du temps perdu* pursuing the sound of a watch around the room : the sound moves until he at last discovers the location of the watch, at which moment its ticking becomes stabilized in that place. Or the episode of Albertines's beauty-spot, which moves around her face during the narrator's first encounters with her. Such episodes as these have an important effect : they make us aware of the uncertainties of perception, of our lapses of memory, but above all they remind us that experience is not a simple objective entity, but a combination of outside reality and inner perception. What we perceive is often affected by the fact that it is we who perceive it.

Realism is thus not the only way of arousing awareness of the real (as indeed we have already seen through the example of Magritte's surrealist pictures). The zigzag and repetitive structure of Heller's *Catch 22*, where event does not succeed event in temporal sequence, but we move from place to place and from time to time in an apparently arbitrary way, and episodes repeat themselves as in a bad dream – this, it might be said is 'unrealistic'. However, no better method could be found for communicating the desperate situation of the characters in the book, caught in the repetitive exitless labyrinth of death and fear that was the Second World War. Their situation is precisely that of people living through a nightmare.

Similarly, Kafka's dark fantasies *The Trial* and *The Castle* practise reality-enhancement by distorting the normal situations of life. The author has been dignified (as few are) by having caused the adjective 'Kafka-esque' to be added to our language – a word that in situations where the world or society seems particularly threatening, indifferent or absurd, indicates well the connexion between Kafka's nightmares and normal human experience.

We may conclude that there is no good novel which is not realistic, and that realism is not always the appropriate technique for achieving realism.

(*d*) Fourthly, there is the question of the *characters* of fiction. Here it may be said that it is precisely when a character is *purely* conventional that he is least satisfactory. For example, it has often been objected that the working-class characters in *Hard Times*, such as Stephen Blackpool and Slackbridge the union leader, are mere assemblages of clichés and that, moreover, these clichés are the comfortable middle-class ones of the period. As representatives of the working-class these characters are simply (respectively) a cardboard martyr and a cardboard villain, and it is for largely maudlin purposes that Stephen's death is exploited in the chapter entitled 'The Starlight'. Thus, though Dickens's broader canvasses of working-class life in Coketown have much to commend them, he fails to bring any refreshment to his readers' understanding of working-class life once he turns to specific individuals.

Oddness is even more spectacularly lacking in popular novels such as those of Edgar Rice Burroughs. The following passage strikes upon the ear with a din of clichés:

> That she had been carried off her feet by the strength of the young giant when his great arms were about her in the distant African forest, and again today, in the Wisconsin woods, seemed to her only attributable to a temporary mental reversion to type on her part – to the psychological appeal of the primeval man to the primeval woman in her nature . . .
>
> Again she glanced at Clayton. He was very handsome and every inch a gentleman. She should be very proud of such a husband.
>
> And then he spoke – a minute sooner or a minute later might have made all the difference in the world to three lives – but chance stepped in and pointed out to Clayton the psychological moment.
>
> (Quoted from Leavis 1979, p. 191)

Tarzan's Jane has the mind of her author: she is an assemblage of platitudes. There is an attempt in the words 'Then he spoke . . .' to inject surprise into the passage; but these words are exactly the expected words for such moments. One is not going to learn anything more about the workings of the human mind from this sort of writing than is already contained in the commonplaces of popular 'psychology'.

No, the true writer surprises us. Either his view of human personality is more profound than normal, or he may inject actual elements of surprise into his characters. Proust's characters are never predictable: M. and Mme Verdurin, who have tormented Saniette continually, turn in the end and settle money upon him – an act of extraordinary kindness in which one none the less manages to believe. For it is Proust's skill to persuade us of the verisimilitude of this incident. Perhaps it is the right and duty of novelists to remind us that in fact human beings are *not* very predictable.

Novelists also ring the changes on the sorts of character that have become conventional. One of the best examples of this is the anti-hero, such as Don Quixote, who surprised the readers of his time by not being a 'parfit gentil knight' but rather a victim of sentimental delusions – and who surprised them further by turning out, despite all his delusions, to be after all a 'parfit gentil knight'!

The anti-hero is a persistent feature of the novel throughout its history, yet for some reason readers have never become used to this. The common reader is still likely to protest that Meursault, or the narrator of *Notes from Underground*, is a disappointing and unsatisfactory character; but this of course is the whole point of such books. No doubt the anti-hero continues to be effective because there is a persistent tendency in human beings to prefer black and white contrasts between good and evil – another basic category which it is the writer's task to assail.

So whereas it is conventional to think of babies crying and nursery nurses being sweet and kind, Lowell writes:

> Gone now the baby's nurse,
> a lioness who ruled the roost
> and made the Mother cry.

('Home after Three Months Away')

And whereas love is conventionally tender, Char makes us feel its rapacious and predatory qualities:

> Mon éloge tournoie sur les boucles de ton front, comme un
> épervier à bec droit. ('Lettera amorosa')

For reality is never as simple as the categories of habit.

(*e*) Fifthly, there is the matter of *genre*. The moderns in particular have a great love of producing texts that do not fit into any previously known category, so as to force the reader to consider the text *in itself*, without any preconceptions as to its type. I shall use the example of Francis Ponge, whose description of an orange begins thus:

> Comme dans l'éponge il y a dans l'orange une aspiration à reprendre contenance aprés avoir subi l'épreuve de l'expression. Mais où l'éponge réussit toujours, l'orange jamais : car ses cellules ont éclaté, ses tissus se sont déchirés. Tandis que l'écorce seule se rétablit mollement dans sa forme grâce à son élasticité, un liquide d'ambre s'est répandu, accompagné de rafraîchissement, de parfum suaves, certes, – mais souvent aussi de la conscience amère d'une expulsion prématurée de pépins. (From *Le Parti pris des choses*)
> [As with the sponge, there is in the orange an aspiration to recover countenance after undergoing the ordeal of expression. But whereas the sponge always succeeds, the orange never does : for its cells have burst, its tissues have been torn. While the rind alone softly re-establishes its shape thanks to its elasticity, an amber liquid has been shed, accompanied by sweet refreshment and perfume, certainly – but often also by the bitter awareness of premature expulsion of pips.]

The tone of this paragraph is detached; it contains a large number of abstractions, some of them scientific ones; its syntax and progression are those of an argument, or a quasi-logical sequence of ideas. It resembles in short a scientist's taxonomic description, and does so even in its comparison of one thing with another, for scientists often take care to tell one how to distinguish one phenomenon from others that are treacherously similar, or compare it with an object from some disparate area of experience. However, this particular comparison is unlike any a scientist would use, for there is no very obvious first-sight resemblance between an orange and a sponge. Moreover, there is probably more insistence on the pleasurable sensations experienced by a human being contemplating an orange, than there would be in a scientific text. Furthermore, the writer is consciously using onomatopoeic effects when he speaks of 'une expulsion prématurée de pépins', which vividly imitates the spluttering and spitting of a man with his mouth full of pips.

Is the passage a poem, then? Perhaps in some respects it is more like a joke. It is full of punning phrases which anthropomorphize the orange, perhaps in a faintly absurd way. 'Reprendre contenance' for example means both 'to swell up into a container again' and 'to start putting a good face on things once more'. And 'conscience amère' suggests a bitter taste in the mouth as well as a regretful sentiment. There is also the facetious 'après avoir subi l'épreuve de l'expression', as if the orange were like Ponge himself struggling to express itself – at the same time as 'expression' means 'being squeezed on a lemon-squeezer'. And at this point one may well suspect there is a further concealed joke. Ponge is punning on his own name and on the word 'éponge'. He himself is like the poor squeezed orange, struggling to 'express' himself.

The language and the semantic content are both, therefore, in some ways like a taxonomic description, in some ways like a poem; but unlike either of these, there is also a note of self-parody. Moreover, in limiting itself to *nothing but* description, the text does not resemble a poem . . . though it does in the way it forces the powers of language. What sort of text is it, then? It does not quite fit into any known genre : it is a mode of discourse invented by Ponge himself. Now what is the function of fitting (as we usually do, when we are confronted by some fragment of language) a text into a certain category? It helps us to 'read the text correctly'. Thus, a taxonomic description seen in some manual on the oyster, will be immediately interpreted as 'guidance on how to recognize an oyster'. But when we categorize a text, we are in danger of overlooking aspects of it which do not harmonize with the category : when reading a taxonomic description of an oyster, we automatically overlook any felicities of expression that the scientist may have employed. Ponge's purpose here may be to prevent us from reading his text as a poem : for if we have a conventional view of what poems are, we may oveflook his principal intention, which is to evoke the concrete impression of the orange. Ponge is trying to be precise *both* as a poet *and* as a scientist.

As for the note of self-parody which erupts into the text from time to time – well, the purpose of this is to make us realize that (as Ponge knows perfectly well) his project is impossible : a poem cannot replace an orange, and the gulf between language and the world is thereby persuasively demonstrated. Language, the realm of abstract categories, is not a substitute for the real world.

(*f*) And finally there are all those *textual oddnesses* which writers employ for the purpose of arousing our attention. Some of these entail the *isonic process* proper, which I shall be describing in the next chapter; some of them have been noted already in 'Some varieties of oddness' (Martin 1975*a*). I shall give here merely a random selection of such features from two short prose texts. As will be seen, there are a number of rhythmic, syntactic and semantic disturbances in the text's smooth current, and each of these disturbances is particularly productive of awareness of the real.

> An engagement is so potent a thing that sooner or later it reduces all who speak of it to this state of cheerful awe. Away from it, in the solitude of their rooms, Mr Beebe, and even Freddy, might again be critical. But in its presence and in the presence of each other they were sincerely hilarious. It has a strange power, for it compels not only the lips, but the very heart. The chief parallel – to compare one great thing with another – is the power over us of a temple of some alien creed. Standing outside, we deride or oppose it, or at the most feel sentimental. Inside, though the saints and gods are not ours, we become true believers, in case any true believer should be present. (Forster, *A Room with a View*, Ch. 8)

Here the interruption of the rhythm after the words 'The chief parallel', underlines the absurdity of comparing an engagement with an alien temple, and the irony of calling them both 'great things'. Key phrases are couched in strange terms. 'Cheerful awe', for instance, what is that? And what is 'sincerely hilarious'? And the comparison of temple with engagement is a most curiously chosen one. Each of these details, however, is precisely right. Each avoids the conventional categorization of engagements, and substitutes for it a mixture of feelings that is much more complex. 'Cheerful awe', for instance, is both too hilarious and too awesome for a conventional reaction: indeed, the engagement is 'awesome' precisely because it is inappropriate to feel such solemnity in the face of such an unexpected match. None the less, some wonder remains among the mirth. As for the temple, it precisely delineates that mingled respect, incomprehension, disbelief yet awareness of the importance to someone else of things quite alien to oneself, that is the spectators' feeling. Such oddnesses in fact carry revelatory force.

My second example is still more colourful. It is taken from Chapter 5 of Nabokov's *King, Queen, Knave*:

> Presently the bed stirred into motion. It glided off on its journey creaking discreetly as does a sleeping car when the express pulls out of a dreamy station. 'You, you, you', uttered Martha, softly squeezing him between her knees at every gasp, and following with moist eyes the shadows of angels waving their handkerchiefs on the ceiling, which was moving away faster and faster.

Now the room was empty. Objects lay, stood, sat, hung in the carefree postures man-made things adopt in man's absence. The mock crocodile lay on the floor. A blue tinted cork, which had been recently removed from a small ink bottle when a fountain pen had to be refilled hesitated for an instant, then rolled in a semi-circle to the edge of the oilcloth-covered table, hesitated again, and jumped off. With the help of the lashing rain the wind tried to open the window but failed. In the rickety wardrobe a blue black-spotted tie slithered off its twig like a snake. A paperback novelette on the chest-of-drawers left open at Chapter Five skipped several pages.

Suddenly the looking-glass made a signal – a warning gleam. It reflected a bluish armpit and a lovely bare arm. The arm stretched – and fell back lifeless. Slowly, the bed returned to Berlin from Eden. The rhythms help to enact the movement. The first sentence is brief, as the motion of love-making begins. It is succeeded by a longer sentence describing its continuation. The suddenness of 'a warning gleam' is expressed by the dash, and by the brevity of the phrase. The reluctant gradualness of the return of the lovers to awareness of their surroundings is conveyed in the last sentence by the withholding of the word 'Eden'.

Most striking, however, are the metaphors. The bed, the angels, the ceiling, the 'objects', the cork, the wind, the tie, the novelette, the looking-glass, and finally the bed again, are all given independent life by verbs which denote human actions. The intense life thereby given to the objects about the room, makes the whole scene extraordinarily vivid. Fragments of reality intrude with great insistence upon our vision. And this fits also with the pattern of the book : Fritz, the anti-hero of this novel, is at the mercy of events : things happen to him, he does not make them happen. And this is true right down to the eventual blackly happy ending.

Along with the attribution of life to objects goes a total withdrawal (after the first paragraph) of description from the human characters. 'Now the room was empty.' For they are absent in 'Eden'; they are in the trance-like otherwhere of the moments after love-making. The author too (he hints) cannot follow them into ecstasy; for the novelette, surely, is the book we are reading, open precisely at this fifth chapter, and wittily censoring itself by skipping several pages. As for Martha's bare arm, which reappears suddenly like a ghost in the mirror, it is separated from her, it has a moment of independent life. She thinks she is in control of her own life, but is she ? Perhaps, indeed, there is something faintly sinister about the activities of these objects in paragraph two. Objects may start to creep up on you when you aren't looking. Martha had better beware, for some day the unexpected is going to happen.

There are many other points that could be made. The scatterment of the objects that 'lay, stood, sat, hung' is enacted by the catalogue of verbs. More interestingly, perhaps, the sentence ' "You, you, you", uttered Martha,' presents an odd use of the verb 'uttered'. We speak of 'uttering a word' or 'uttering a sound' : we do not use it when the actual words are being quoted. But these are half-automatic noises, reflexes rather than meaningful words. Hence 'uttered' is exactly right.

But this will suffice to make the point. The passage is bursting with life, with density, with the realities and the implications of experience. Our vision of the world is indeed truly refreshed. And it is refreshed above all by means of the oddnesses of language.

Many modern authors are particularly conscious of literature's vocation to disrupt the conventions of language, and even of literary language itself. Thus, in some interviews dating from 1967, Philippe Sollers addressed Francis Ponge as follows (thereby reflecting the concerns of both writers) :

> Si je me référe à mon expérience personnelle, j'ai lu pour la première fois un texte de vous, par hasard, dans une anthologie.
>
> J'étais très jeune, mais l'impression ressentie a été immédiatement celle d'un antilyrisme, d'une volonté de communication neuve, d'une 'sortie du manège', comme vous diriez, d'une sortie du 'ronron poétique', et d'une reconsidération élémentaire, lexicale, organique, à la mesure d'une crise radicale.
>
> (Ponge & Sollers 1970, p. 11)
>
> [If I may refer to my personal experience, I read one of your texts for the first time, by chance, in an anthology.
>
> I was very young, but my immediate impression was that of antilyricism, of a determination to communicate freshly, of someone who had 'stepped off the merry-go-round' (as you would put it), who had turned his back on the routine poetic singsong, and of a radical, lexical, organic reassessment on a scale measuring up to a fundamental crisis.]

Ponge replied :

> Une société, c'est un ensemble de langages dont le principal est la langue elle-même, j'entends la langue commune, celle qui se parle et qui s'écrit. Il s'agit de savoir si l'on accepte ce langage, si ce langage est de votre *goût*, au sens le plus absolu du terme, si votre goût ne le refuse pas, si vous *pouvez* employer ce langage.
>
> Eh bien! je dois dire, quant à moi, que c'est par *dégoût* de ce langage que j'en suis venu à écrire. Il s'agira donc pour moi, pour pouvoir vivre, de modifier ce langage.
>
> [A society is an ensemble of languages, the main one being language itself, I mean ordinary language, the one that people speak and write. It all depends if you accept this language, if it is to

your *taste*, in the most absolute sense of the word, if your taste does not reject it, if you can *use* this language.

Well, I must say for my part that it is out of *distaste* for this language that I came to write. If I'm to keep going, I have to modify this language.]

And he goes on to complain that this attempt to disrupt the categories of language meets immediate resistance from society. It retaliates by categorizing *him*, by terming him 'a poet' :

... la société, et son ou ses langages, ont mille moyens de se défendre, de se *conserver*. Par exemple, c'est ce qui m'est arrivé, on va aussitôt vous traiter de 'poète'. On va essayer de noyer le poisson.

[. . . . society and its language or languages have a thousand ways of defending themselves, of *preserving* themselves. For example – and this is what happened to me – they'll immediately start treating you as a 'poet'. They'll try to wear you down.]

For once a new mode of perception is safely classified as 'poetry', it can be pigeonholed, imprisoned behind the bars of the already familiar, the already understood.

And perhaps this process is particularly damaging with art, which is regarded by so many as a thing apart, a 'privileged experience', and consequently one that has nothing to do with experience itself. 'Art is wonderful', a young philosopher said to me the other day. 'It is wonderful *because* it has nothing to do with real life.' It is thus that the otherwise intelligent defend themselves against the explorers of life's frontiers.

Whereas in fact the whole purpose of art is to reposition the floodlights of reality, to refocus the lenses of experience, to jolt people out of their complacent lassitude.

May it not be, indeed, that reality is itself irreducibly ambiguous and elusive? At all events, human language is inadequate, by the nature of things, to pin it down, to 'say the last word', to confine it within the simplicities of human reason. How salutary (for nothing could be more disturbing to the certainties of our wishful thinking) is the poetry of that supreme master of ambiguity, Stéphane Mallarmé! And I would refer the reader to Malcolm Bowie's (1978) excellent book on his work, in which he shows that Mallarmé's poetry will not allow us even to work *towards* a final stable interpretation of his meanings, but continues to shift under the gaze as long as one contemplates it. There is no ultimate satisfying sense here, even of a complex kind, and Mallarmé thus achieves perhaps the *ne plus ultra* of disquiet.

Naturally, not all writers disturb our expectations in all of the ways noted above. Some, like Vergil in the *Aeneid*, intend to provide their public with a myth which will stabilize and celebrate the conventional glories of the society in which they dwell. However, even such writers use certain of the techniques that have been described here : there is no lack in Vergil of those textual oddnesses that arouse awareness of the concrete detail of experience. None the less, in view of the considerations listed at the start of this chapter, I wonder if the chief claim of literature (and of art in general) to our respect is not its capacity to disturb the expected, to make us feel and think again. It is not the ordered harmonies of literature that are its principal glory, but its aptness to disrupt our categories : not so much its presentation of apparent truth as its questioning of unnoticed falsity.

Some critics have spoken of a 'community of writer and audience' which (so legend has it) existed in the blissful golden age of Shakespearian England – a time when writer and audience 'spoke the same language', and no gulf of incomprehension lay between them (Daiches 1936, p. 145, for instance). I have often wondered whether this was really so. Perhaps in reality the form such a 'community' took was simply this : that in Shakespeare's time the public were more willing to be amazed : their horizons were those of an expanding world : they had courage to face this world : they were thirsty for the *new*.

5. Disrupting the Categories II

But if our own literature may teach us the lesson of disappointed expectation, so (even more effectively perhaps) may the literature of a foreign tongue. In the first place, the simple learning of the language carries this lesson with it. All those who know more than one language are well acquainted with the experience of their familiar categories failing them. Not that this experience is brutal or quintessential like contemplating the works of a Magritte. Rather, one language is subtly and constantly *betrayed* by the other. One cannot learn a second language without being brought immediately face to face with such things as the non-correspondence of the English 'girl' and the French 'fille', the English 'woman / wife' and the French 'femme', the English 'door / gate' and the French 'porte / portière'. A 'door' is of course a door into a building, a 'gate' into a space open to the key; French uses 'porte' for both of these, 'barrière' for farm gates, but employs 'portière' for doors into vehicles, a distinction which does not exist in English, and which, to judge by the grammar-school pupils I used to teach, is extraordinarily difficult for the average Anglophone to remember. There are countless traps lurking in our attempts to learn and use a foreign language. When Hunt and Hoffman explored the assimilation of Puerto Ricans into American society in Chicago, they reported that they had difficulty adopting American forms of committee democracy. The translation of 'chairman' in Spanish is 'presidente'. But this suggests a *directing leader* of a committee, not a neutral referee of procedure. Thus a Puerto Rican club which had been given an 'English' type constitution, was unhappy until 'the constitution was amended so that no vote could be taken until the president had delivered himself of a *pronunciamento*' – a word which itself does not quite correspond to the English 'opinion' (L. C. Hunt & N. von Hoffman in Hayakawa 1959, pp. 52–65).

The testimony of translators at international gatherings is interesting. As one might expect, disagreements are often due to the different connotations of translational 'equivalents' in different languages, and behind these disagreements there may lurk a whole political and social philosophy. Glenn for instance notes an intervention of the Australian delegate at the Security Council, in which there was an allusion made to the need of investigating 'the situation which is before us'.

> 'Which is before us' becomes 'qui nous est soumise' in French and 'rassmatrivayemym nami' in Russian. 'Which is before us' is neutral. 'Qui nous est soumise' means literally 'which is submitted to us' and implies the assumption of authority of a body of men – the Security Council – over a situation. The Russian expression means 'which is under consideration' but with the connotation of 'which is being taken apart' or 'in regard to which the precise category into which it falls has to be determined'.
>
> (Edmund S. Glenn in Hayakawa 1959, p. 27)

Hence, according to Glenn, the Russian phrase assumes in advance the existence of a fixed set of categories.

Similarly, Glenn recalls an argument between the U.S.S.R. and the U.S.A. at an international conference over the phrase 'expanding economy'. In Russian this suggests a naturally or intrinsically expanding economy, and since they hold that the economy of the West 'must' contract, they refused to accept the term (Ibid., pp. 15–17).

One cannot help feeling that there is something peculiarly valuable in the curious grammatical rule in English by which a singular collective noun (e.g. government, committee, group, party, ministry) may take a plural verb. Something peculiarly valuable, that is, to foreigners learning the language, since we ourselves hardly ever notice the phenomenon. We say, for instance, 'The government, *which has* decided on this measure . . .', but 'The government, *who have* decided on this measure . . .' In the first case, 'government' is treated as a singular neuter object; in the second as a plural assemblage of individuals. Once this is noticed, it reminds us that collective entities like 'nations' and 'governments' have no real existence except as the individuals of which they are composed.

The distinctions and suggestions conveyed by the 'same phrase' in different languages may be of amazing subtlety and complexity. Steiner (whose remarks as a tri-lingual especially sensitive to language, deserve the utmost respect) writes:

> *Das Kind ist unter die Räder gekommen.* Though it signifies violent, presumably sudden mishap and aims at instant communication, the

German phrase encodes a fairly elaborate gesture of fatality. 'The child has been run over', which is the equivalent offered by the 'teach yourself' manual, hardly reflects the cautionary dispassion of the original. In the German phrasing the wheels have a palpable right of way; somehow the child has interrupted their licit progress. The grammatical effect is undeniably apologetic and even accusing: the syntactic neutrality of *das Rad* together with the near-passivity of the verb form edges the onus of guilt towards the child. The wheels have not culpably 'gone over it'; it is the child which has 'come to be under them'. 'Undergo' would be inadmissible as translation, but it in fact conveys the accusatory hint. *L'enfant s'est fait écraser* is even stronger in implicit blame. Any attempt at giving a naïve equivalent in English would generate a sense of volition: 'the child has had itself run over'. The French idiom intends nothing so crass. But the nuance of indictment is there and more, perhaps, than a nuance. It results from the fact that *se faire* plus an infinitive can function as a kind of passive without losing altogether the substratum of purposeful action. For what may be obscurely historical or legislative reasons, both the German and the French expression suggest the stance of the coachman or driver. The English phrase is scrupulously equitable. Thus no exact transfer is available.   (Steiner 1975, pp. 305–6)

These subtleties seem to reflect the different flavours, the different attitudes, the different approaches, of different peoples to the business of living. If we can surpass our natural chauvinism, we can find such meditation invaluable. It is here that the translation of literary passages as a student exercise, hoary old butt though it is of educational iconoclasts, may in fact have its particular usefulness. The struggle for an exact equivalent – though often none can be found – should lead the student to attempt to feel exactly what is expressed by the phrase in another language, and exactly what might be expressed by various possible equivalents in his own. There will often be no 'right translation', no 'perfect equivalent'. But the impossibility of the task does not invalidate it; for its value lies not in the finding so much as in the effort to find.

Literary translation must therefore be defended against its modern critics. It is a valuable *practical* experience of the hidden implications of language, and should lead us too to an understanding of the relative artificiality of our categories. We cannot regard the constructs of our own language as having *coherent reality* or a *true definition* or a *reality independent of their content*, once we perceive that in other languages the 'same' construct has a rather different content which is there regarded as equally 'natural', equally 'self-evident'. Moreover, the principle of *reversibility*, the fact that the applicability of a construct always depends on its concrete instances, and the need to trace it back to those instances, is also brought home to us by one of the conditions of good translation : namely, the necessity of considering the concrete situation, the concrete context, of a form of words so as to be able to translate it properly. Thus the phrase 'l'horizon était bouché' could be translated as 'the horizon was overcast' or 'shrouded in fog' or 'blotted out'. It will depend on whether it is cloud or fog that prevents one seeing the horizon, which of the first two alternatives one uses; and if one wished to preserve the ambiguity, the third would be the one to select. Similarly, in the phrase 'un bois de chênes dévalait, ressautait sur deux ou trois plissements rébarbatifs', we should translate 'an oakwood fell away/sloped away, rose again over two or three ugly-looking ridges . . .' 'Was slipping away' would only be possible if the wood were actually moving in a landslide; and though 'ressauter' can in other contexts be used for 'jump up again' or 'jolt' or 'bounce', these English verbs cannot be used here where the wood appears frozen into the static shape of such a movement : they have to be used in contexts where an object actually does move. The translator has to be constantly aware of the *particular* state of affairs being described.

Now literature is a sort of foreign language within the language – or rather a range of such languages, since the styles of writers are as distinct from each other as they are from that of speech. Thus the literature of a foreign language will be *at two removes* from the native understanding of a reader. Let us take for instance some lines of Herrick, and analyse them first within English and secondly from the point of view of a French reader :

A sweet disorder in the dresse
Kindles in clothes a wantonesse;
A lawn about the shoulders thrown
Into a fine distraction;
An erring lace, which here and there
Enthralls the crimson stomacher . . .

In one style of critical practice, the precise sense of the images will be inspected, and be found to be multiple, not simple. 'Wantonness' for instance needs to be glossed by a whole series of terms such as 'undisciplined, rebellious, naughty, pert, skittish, lascivious, sexy, amorous, sportive, reckless of decorum, capricious, robust, unrestrained'. 'Erring' means 'wandering, straying, being careless', and may have a faint hint of 'sinning' in it. Thus the student is brought face to face with the content of the language : each word is a clenched bud of meaning, which opens up under our eyes. The verb 'enthralls' means literally 'holds in' (the stomacher is held in by the lace) and 'holds in thrall, as a lover is held by his mistress'. There is a half-paradox in the word : the lover is his mistress's slave; the corset hides and defends the woman's body from him, however – or rather pretends to do so. The sexual excitements of clothing and unclothing hover round this image as they do about the poem. In addition, our modern usage adds what is perhaps an anachronistic connotation : 'delights, as listeners are held spellbound by a story'. Is this connotation one intended by Herrick ? It is difficult for the modern reader to rid himself of the overtone, for it fits too well. And, at least from the point of view of the linguistic lesson given by the poem, no matter. For criticism is here furnishing invaluable testimony to the shifting, many-valued sense of words. We confront the interplay between reference and connotations, and cannot rest content with words' usual opaque pretence to be unitary realities.

The lesson is even clearer, however, if we give the poem to a French student. He may at first view it through the distorting glass of his own language, which might provide a picture like that of F. Delattre's translation :

> Un doux désordre en la toilette
> Rend une robe ensorceleuse ;
> Un linon autour des épaules
> Jeté dans un fol abandon ;
> Un lacet furtif qui, à peine,
> Enferme le rouge corset . . .

But this is simply not the same girl ! The physical energy, the charming sexiness of 'wantonness' has been quite lost ; and 'enthralls' has been diluted, separated into the two words *ensorceleuse* and *enferme*. *A peine* loses the casualness of 'here and there'. *La toilette* is much more deliberate than 'dress'. And the phrase *un fol abandon* is too much the cliché to suggest a real *abandon*. In French these lines suggest a more carefully calculated, less spontaneous disorder. The sexiness of Julia's dress has been subtly diminished : this French Julia has not quite the naturalness and gaiety of her English original.

Or let us look at French through English spectacles. Guillevic's poem about the essence of perfect roundness runs :

> *Rond*
> Qu'est-ce qu'il ya donc
> De plus rond que la pomme ?
>
> – Si lorsque tu dis : rond,
> Vraiment c'est rond que tu veux dire,
> Mais la boule à jouer
> Est plus ronde que la pomme.
>
> Mais si, quand tu dis : rond,
> C'est plein que tu veux dire,
> Plein de rondeur
> Et rond de plénitude,

Alors il n'ya rien
De plus rond que la pomme.

⌜Whatever can be rounder
Than an apple?

– If when you say : round,
It's really round you mean,
Then a bouncing ball   (literally, 'a bowl')
Is rounder than an apple.

But if when you say : round,
It's full you mean,
Full of roundness
And round with fullness,

Then there is nothing
Rounder than an apple.⌟

(Reprinted from Martin 1972)

Now what precisely is one to do about the word 'boule'? A French bowl
is made of metal, perfectly spherical, shining with a sort of sulky glossi-
ness. Is there anything that resembles it quite in English? I think not.
An English bowl is smooth, glossy and wooden, more gentle to the
hand than a *boule*; besides, it has 'bias' to make it run in a curve : psychologically, therefore, it is not quite round. There is the problem too of
the homonym 'bowl', meaning a sort of dish. What other alternatives
might one employ? A cannon-ball is menacing and deadly, and often
roughened by age and rust. A bed-knob belongs on the end of a bed,
and is not necessarily round. A football can be deflated, and is doubtless
too soft. And so on. In my own translation of this poem, I used the phrase
'bouncing ball', because such a ball is viewed in mid-air, in mid-leap, at
the perfection of its roundness. It seemed therefore another ideally
round object such as the *boule*, since one needs some such image of
perfect roundness to contrast with the even more perfect, living apple.
However, I must admit that the solution is not ideal : the bouncing ball
is too active, too joyous, too full of life to be a proper equivalent for the
heavy, sullen, glowering French *boule*.

As a final example, let us take another of Steiner's discussions, that
of Genesis 1 : 3 :

> *Fiat lux. Et facta est lux* has a memorable sequentiality. The
> phonetic and grammatical exterior proclaim a phenomenon at once
> stunning and perfectly self-evident . . . 'Let there be light: and
> there was light' in the Authorized Version . . . expand⌜s⌟ on the
> Latin. There are now eight words in the place of six. And the
> punctuation is lightened. The purpose, presumably, is to give a
> sense of instant consequence. But the omission of the full-stop

97

together with the lower-case 'and' sacrifice the Latin pedal-point. In the original the note of cosmic command is fully held while the division into two short sentences makes for a dynamic surge. This is exactly what is called for: an instant of pent breath above a ground-swell of complete certitude.

The French version is also eight words long and opts for a punctuation precisely medial between the two English variants. *Que la lumière soit; et la lumière fut.* But much has altered. Latin, Italian, German and English preserve the characteristically Hebraic repetition of the cardinal word 'light' at the climax of the sentence(s). In each of the four cases the word-order is powerfully imitative of the action expressed. 'Light' has its pride of place in God's order and realization. In the French text the drama of accomplishment, of shattering obviousness is that of the verb: it turns on the movement from the imperative subjunctive of *soit* to the perfectedness of *fut* . . . But the major difference comes with the use of the definite article. 'Let there be light, and the light was.' The diminution of impact is obvious . . . Neither Latin, Italian, German or English admit of the article when rendering God's fiat and its primal fulfilment. The difference from the French version is profound. The syntax of the Deity and of accomplishment make for an effect of balance, of equation rather than of tautological majesty. The definite article posits conceptual essence before phenomenality. *Que la lumière soit* has an 'intellectuality' altogether lacking from either the blank imperative of *Fiat lux* or the unforced immediacy of 'Let there be light' . . . In French, phenomenal appearance, epiphany are categorized and conceptually prepared-for as they are not necessarily in English. This is not a question of poorer means, but of metaphysical insistence.

(Steiner 1975, pp. 306–7)

The moral is clear. One way of becoming sensitively aware of the clash between reality and words, and the provisional and approximate, but powerfully suggestive, nature of the latter, is to study literature. And one even better way perhaps is to study the literature of a foreign language, or to compare translations of the same passage. Categories which, in ordinary language, and particularly in one's own, are mere stepping stones to be trodden rapidly as you pass from one side of the river to the other, have their content restored to them. Constructs flicker and half-fade: the object reappears.

The discussion in this section, then, constitutes a defence of certain traditional aspects of education, of the translation of literary passages,[16] of the study of literature, and in particular of the study of foreign literatures. These studies take further the process that Jerome Bruner (for I shall end the chapter, as I began it, with him) sees as a main function of education. Unschooled children, he claims, are unable to distinguish between their own thoughts or statements about a thing, and the thing itself: 'thought and the object of thought seemed to be one' (Bruner 1974*b*, p. 372). As schooling progresses, they are increasingly able to categorize the 'same' stimuli according to several different criteria or points of view, and increasingly able to differentiate between self and not-self.

School separates word and thing and destroys verbal realism by presenting for the first time a situation where words are systematically and continually there without their referents ... When names, or symbols in general, no longer inhere in their referents, they must go somewhere; and the logical place is the psyche of the language user. Thus, the separation of word and thing demands a notion that words are in people's heads, not in their referents ... The concepts 'thinker' and 'thought processes' thus become important in the shedding of nominal realism. Meaning is seen to vary with the particular speaker, and the notion of psychological relativity is born. Implicit in this notion is the distinctness of oneself and one's own point of view. Thus, the individual must conceptually separate himself from the group; he must become self-conscious, aware of having a particular slant on things, a certain individuality. (Ibid., pp. 389–90)

The stage is set for 'the real [to become] but a subset of the possible' (Ibid.).

But the process of education, the deepening of understanding, should continue as long as life continues. To learn more about any subject, more about any person, entails readjusting or rejecting the categories within which we previously imprisoned it or him.

Thus someone who has learned up a subject from an elementary textbook must break down these earlier ways of thinking as he progresses to a more advanced understanding of the subject. The same relationship is illustrated in the way book learning is broken down and enriched by practical experience; and conversely by the 'practical man's' achievement when he settles down to learn the basic principles of his craft. It is difficult to [objectively] define 'adequate' as [an adjective] qualifying 'understanding', but it seems to include such components as richness of associative interconnexions; ability to reformulate what one 'knows' in alternative terms; and ability to use it in one's own thoughts and actions. And perhaps also an emotional attitude involving a kind of intellectual humility – a concern with probabilities rather than certainty, and an awareness that problems get more complex rather than less complex the more one knows about them.

(McKellar 1957, p. 194)

These remarks rest upon the following propositions (which I take to be unassailable) : (1) that language does not fit reality as the glove fits the hand; (2) that even if it did so, the glove and the hand are not the same; (3) that this is shown unmistakeably by the disagreements between different languages; (4) that language, the awareness of reality and the fit between the two are operations that the individual in the last resort performs. And if the philosophical position that we are then driven to is a sort of 'individualism', then so be it. Any position which denied these basic facts would be untenable. Only if one is enclosed within the self-congratulatory world of a rigid society (or of some rigid-minded subgroup) where language, behaviour and reality are all quite unquestioned, can one have the delusion of a total fit between word and world. And indeed that is why so many prefer to live with such inflexible assumptions : they are comforting and comfortable : they provide the illusion of certainty and security. But the moment the question of words and reality arises, the doubt which prompts the question is seen to be justified.

If progress and movement are desirable, then an awareness of some degree of psychological relativity is also desirable. For we cannot change our views till we see that they are merely temporary and tentative, and till we can recognize that other views are possible. The real must indeed be seen to be a subset of the possible; and our *notion* of the real must be seen to be incomplete and imperfect.

Language is certainly invaluable to us in so far as it does 'in fact' reflect reality. But in so far as it does not, the most pernicious thing within language is those of its fictions which are taken to be facts; and the most valuable thing within language is those of its fictions which cannot be taken for anything *but* fictions. For, in these latter cases, the *décalage* (or inexact correspondence) between fiction and reality clearly reveals the *décalage* between language and reality in general, just as the *décalage* between the sculpture and the materials of which it is made, reflects the *décalage* between what we see things as, and what else they may be. Thus, by a curious irony, reality is better rendered by the inexact, than by the exact, copy. Or rather it is better rendered so long as one is aware of the inexactitude. This is why the modern painter flaunts his technique in our faces : we must see that Van Gogh's picture of the cherry-blossom is made of paint. It is not reality : it is a picture of it; and our accounts of reality are only pictures of it, not reality itself.

For those who are capable of facing such tiresome truths, the study of languages and literatures is invaluable. One must agree with George Steiner that the confounding of the tongues of man at the Tower of Babel was an event to be welcomed, not mourned. The loss of any of our human languages is a disaster, removing from humanity a special, irreplaceable viewpoint. And if ever, across the perilous uncertainties that mask our future from us, we were to reach a situation where all men spoke the same language, and all but that one language were to die, the human race would be sadly impoverished. A defining criterion of humanity is its variety; the differences between our languages express, therefore, something that is essentially human.

4. Evoking the Unsayable

Ces pensées que j'écris ne sont pas les vraies pensées que j'ai eues . . . ⌈These thoughts I write down are not the true thoughts I have had. . . .⌉   (Valéry, *Les Cahiers*, Vol. 7, p. 662)

La pensée abstraite demeure confinée aux alentours du réel; elle ne mord pas sur lui. Elle nous aide à le manier; elle ne nous fait pas le connaître. ⌈Abstract thought remains confined to the outskirts of reality; it has no purchase upon it. It helps us handle it; it does not provide knowledge of it.⌉
(Laporte, *Le Problème de L'abstraction*)

We shall understand neither thinking nor reading . . . until we can explain what more it is to entertain a proposition or to know a fact than to merely and silently recite so many words.
(Shepard, 'Cognitive Psychology')

Ma mémoire bat les cartes,
Les images pensent pour moi.
⌈My memory shuffles the cards,
The images think for me.⌉
(Eluard, *Oeuvres complètes*, Vol. 1)

1. The Incompleteness of Language

THE PREVIOUS chapter has demonstrated that language, as normally employed, conceals its true content from us : abstractions may be used without an awareness of the concrete realities for which they ultimately stand; but also quite ordinary concrete terms are customarily used as if they were opaque discs of meaning, solid symbols of solid objects; so that we tend to forget or to overlook the fact that each disc has a content of defining connotations, and that each refers to an object which has a content of criterial attributes. However, we may be reminded of these facts when we study a foreign language; for the denotations of two equivalent words in two languages never quite fit : they do not fit because the connotations are never quite the same. We may also be reminded of these facts when we study literature, and *a fortiori* a foreign literature. For literature forces on the words a set of new interpretations, which involve a change in their normal connotative pattern; it forces new connotations into our awareness. Thus the study of a foreign language and the study of our own or a foreign literature, are invaluable to us in breaking down our accepted categories, in sapping away at our presuppositions.

Now it may be objected (and rightly objected) that the problem of abstract word categories and that of concrete word categories are in fact two different problems. Abstractions don't fit in different languages because they are like slightly different machines, which have different parts, assembled in rather different ways. 'Democracy' in Russian normally means 'a system of government in which the people (defined as the working class) "rule", but rule only as incarnated in the persons of the ruling committee'; in English it means 'a system of government in which the people (defined as the whole people) "rule", but rule only by being able to confirm or replace their representatives every five years.' The parts, relationships and constituent referents of the two words are in most respects different.

The problem with concrete word categories is quite different. Concrete word categories do not fit in different languages because of their extensions; but the objects being designated are none the less in most cases the same. Thus the extensions of 'gate' and 'door' are different from those of 'porte', 'portière' and 'barrière'; but the objects described by these words in French and English are the same group of objects, and French and English speakers would agree about the features of all these objects.

However, French and English abstract different features from the objects in question when assigning categories to them. Thus in French you have to consider whether the 'door/gate' opens into a field or a vehicle, in English whether it opens onto a closed or an open space. This clash between the categories of different languages is valuable to us because it reveals that there is more to the concrete object than is 'represented' by any given language. And this chapter will be devoted to some aspects of the business of breaking down concrete word categories, so as to reveal the depth and sensory density of the referents themselves.

For is there not an even more radical reproach to be made to the categories of normal language, namely that, even if we make due allowance for the connotative richness hidden under the smooth and glossy surface of each denotation,[1] these connotations in their turn are merely surfaces? Surfaces which, it is true, lie at a greater depth, but still are merely tokens which cannot properly represent the richness of experience. Language gives us manipulative power over the world and over our own ideas; but it is still merely an abstraction. 'Stone' is not the stone we see and touch; and if we analyze the concept 'stone' into its connotations, we find that these too are just as perfunctory, arbitrary and schematic as the concept 'stone' itself. Thus we may define the connotations of 'stone' as 'hardness, opaqueness, impenetrability, roughness, a generally irregular shape' and so on. But all these verbal labels are merely general terms : they describe what the stone has in common with other stones : they are as general as the concept 'stone' itself. The *particular* hardness, opaqueness, roughness of the *particular* stone are still not communicated. For there are all sorts of degrees of hardness, even among stones; and all sorts and degrees of roughness. 'Hardness' and 'roughness' are abstractions and generalizations from all the different hardnesses and roughnesses which exist in nature; and all particular hardnesses and roughnesses have been left out of the word 'hardness' and 'roughness', in favour merely of a classification.

We might of course go further with our description of the stone : we might add any number of details to it, and we might define and redefine the connotations, giving the connotations of their connotations. But the process would be impossible to bring to a conclusion. Friedrich Waismann remarks on the

> *essential incompleteness* of an empirical description. To explain more fully : If I had to describe [this] right hand of mine which I am now holding up, I may say different things of it : I may state its size, its shape, its colour, its tissue, the chemical compound of its bones, its cells, and perhaps add some more particulars; but, however far I go, I shall never reach a point where my description will be completed : logically speaking, it is always possible to extend the description by adding some detail or other.
>
> (Waismann 1951, pp. 121–2)

There is always more that can be said of an object. In speaking of it we may be able to say *a*, *b* and *c*, leaving *d*, *e* and *f* unsaid. We may afterwards say *d*, *e* and *f* too, but we then become aware that we have left out *g*, *h* and *j*. We also become aware that *a*, *b* and *c* are imprecise, and could be made less so; and that these statements too are incomplete. And so on *ad infinitum*. For the alphabet of the phenomenal world has no final *z*.[2]

And if this is true of particular individual objects that we can touch, observe and examine, how much more true is it of particular individual feelings; and how much more true again of such complex and multifarious things as 'the attitude of the Germans' or 'the behaviour of French women'. For here we are not even dealing with one particular individual attitude or action, but with vast numbers of such particulars.

There are thus at least two kinds of incompleteness in language : the first is the fact that, even if we went on talking for ever, we should never come to the end of what can be said about real objects and events; the second is that what we say about them is in any case merely schematic, merely generalized. Wittgenstein writes :

> Compare *knowing* and *saying* :
> how many feet high Mont Blanc is –
> how the word 'game' is used –
> how a clarinet sounds.
>
> If you are surprised that one can know something and not know

how to say it, you are perhaps thinking of a case like the first. Certainly not of one like the third. (Wittgenstein 1967, §78) Describe the aroma of coffee. – Why can't it be done? Do we lack the words? (Ibid., §610)

Here we see that certain experiences, such as sounds and smells, are even harder to describe than stones. Sounds and smells are particularly good examples of the difficulty of describing things, because of the excessive generality of our vocabulary, and because this generality emphasizes what is lacking in our efforts to describe the experiences, namely any sort of precision or density. If we describe the sound of a clarinet, for instance, as 'rather high, piercing, but sweet', how many other sounds of a quite different quality could this description be applied to! The actual 'feel' of the sound has been completely lost. The description is neither precise nor explicit: it is imprecise because it does not unmistakeably specify the particular sensation; it is inexplicit because it does not express its quality.

The reason for this loss of the actual 'feel' is that language does not directly communicate actual subjective sensations. If thirty people, seeing a certain object, say 'It's blue', we say they are 'seeing the same colour'. But all that the repeated statement 'It's blue' guarantees is that they can all distinguish one segment of the colour spectrum from other segments in a consistent way. It is no guarantee that the *sensation* of seeing this particular segment is in all persons identical. And indeed it cannot in the nature of things be so, since language is interpersonal and records merely the elements of common agreement in an experience.

But unless people have a particular sensation which is consistently different from the other sensations they have when viewing other parts of the spectrum, they will not be able to distinguish this segment of the spectrum. So the *criterion* of saying 'It's blue' is an irreducibly subjective experience, whose content is not reproduced by the words 'It's blue'. 'It's blue' signifies merely a coincidence between the *segmentations* of the spectrum by different individuals, not a coincidence of their actual sensations.

The same argument can be extended to all perceptions. They all rest ultimately upon subjective sensations, and it is only coincidences in the *ordering* of those sensations which are expressed by language. Thus, colour-blind individuals can have no idea what it is for a normally sighted person to see red or green; and vice-versa. Thus again, if some people saw all the colours of the spectrum, but saw them in reverse order (indigo–blue–green–yellow–orange–red instead of red–orange–yellow–green–blue–indigo), we should never have any means of telling this, because the *relationships* between the colour sensations would be the same as ours, though the *actual* colour sensations would be different. Yet, as I said above, it is the *actual* sensations which enable us to distinguish between them and hence enable us to perceive relationships between them.[3]

Someone might interject at this point: 'Yes, but let's return to your stone. Perhaps language is not inadequate as far as *it* is concerned. Now you may be able to *say* of that stone lying in the centre of the beach only that "It has curious rough striations across it, of a rather whitish colour", and this *as a statement taken apart from my seeing the stone* is indeed only schematic, but my reference to it is clear, and you can see from the stone what I mean.' In other words, we may take 'reference' in more than one sense: in the first place it may mean only such features of the object as we state and imply in our sentence; in the second place we may say (in opposition to this first statement) that none the less our referent is the real stone in the outside world there; and that it is the whole of the stone we mean.

Now this is quite true. However, it does not alter the fact that, in the absence of the stone, only what is stated or implied (and understood to be stated or implied) by my sentence can be communicated. To that degree, at least, language is inadequate. And the problem of communicating experience is therefore *to manipulate language so that some of the things we apprehend, but which we cannot state, can be transmitted.*

But there is more even in our actual visible stone, present before us, than those unstated characteristics of it which we may assume are being referred to. For there is always more in it than we know. We may thus distinguish between three senses of 'reference': (1) the stated referent, just what is said or implied by language and no more; (2) the intended referent (i.e. whatever more we intend by our statements than is actually stated or implied by our words); (3) the real referent (i.e. the actual reality of the stone: whatever it is including what more there may be in it than we intend or know. For instance we never know what is inside the stone (until we break it open – and we cannot break open all the stones, all the trees, all the lakes that we meet), though we may make a good guess at it. We thus obtain the following picture of reference:

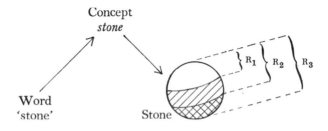

Referent 1 is what our words state and imply; referent 2 is that plus what more we intend; referent 3 is referents 1 and 2 plus what more is unknown.

2. Tacit knowing

This diagram, however, simplifies the situation, in that it appears to suggest a clear and determinate boundary between what we know and what we do not know of an object. Now it is far from being the case that such a clear boundary can be established. Moreover, if there were a completely abrupt cut-off between what we know and what we do not know, then (intuition would suggest) it might be impossible for us to know that there were things we do not know. This is much the same observation as Michael Polanyi's thoughts on Plato's problem in the *Meno*, which is approximately: How do we come to know something that we do not already know? Polanyi poses the problem as follows:

> Either you know what you are looking for, and then there is no problem; or you do not know what you are looking for, and then you are not looking for anything and cannot expect to find anything.[4]   (Polanyi 1964, p. 14; 1967, p. 22)

Doubtless there are cases where Polanyi's observation is not true; but there are also cases where it seems to apply. It does so in all those cases where we perceive that there is more to find out about an object, or where we are puzzled by its behaviour and seek to know more. For, if all there were to knowing was what we could explicitly state, how could we know that there was more to it than that? We have, in such cases, a sense of something lying hidden, awaiting our discovery. There is a sense of there being more in the object than we know of it or can say of it. And Polanyi sees scientific investigation as proceeding from an awareness of there being something more in the phenomenon than had previously been seen. We have, as it were, an anticipatory glimpse of something new in the object, an intuitive reaching out into the object, and with it, a sense that there is some further coherence in it that as yet escapes our conscious understanding, but can in some way be apprehended. Before we discover, we use our antennae; tacit knowing guides our path. And indeed, many scientists have borne witness to something of this kind. Einstein took up his own particular branch of study because he felt that his intuitions were stronger in that field.[5]

Polanyi's fundamental insight is: *we know more than we can tell.* Stated thus, it seems quite obvious; but, as Polanyi points out,

> It is not easy to say exactly what it means. Take an example. We know a person's face, and can recognize it among a thousand, indeed among a million. Yet we cannot usually tell how we recognize a face we know. So most of this knowledge cannot be put into words. But the police have recently introduced a method by which

we can communicate much of this knowledge. They have made a large collection of pictures showing a variety of noses, mouths, and other features. From these the witness selects the particulars of the face he knows, and the pieces can then be put together to form a reasonably good likeness of the face. This may suggest that we can communicate, after all, our knowledge of a physiognomy, provided we are given adequate means for expressing ourselves. But the application of the police method does not change the fact that previous to it we did know more than we could tell at the time. Moreover, we can use the police method only by knowing how to match the features we remember with those in the collection, and we cannot tell how we do this.   (Polanyi 1967, pp. 4–5)

Polanyi then goes on to list a number of similar examples of what he calls *tacit knowing*: our recognition of the moods of the human face; students at university who are trained to identify diseases and specimens of rocks; learning to play the piano or ride a bicycle; and so on. And he points out that although we can certainly be taught such activities, or learn them for ourselves, it is largely by example and imitation that they are taught, and by practice and intelligent cooperation that they are learnt, and not by words. Learning what a particular sort of rock looks like, for instance, involves not only being given a verbal description of it, but being shown examples of it. The verbal description is what Polanyi calls 'explicit knowledge'; the showing and seeing of the object communicate 'tacit knowledge'.

Before I proceed, I must make two comments on Polanyi's example drawn from the use of police 'identikit' pictures. In the first place, to the extent that this technique actually works, it shows clearly that tacit knowledge (the tacit knowledge of a face) can be made explicit: it shows the sceptic, in fact, that tacit knowledge does exist. However, this formerly tacit knowledge is only *pictorially* explicit; it still cannot be made *verbally* explicit. In the second place, the technique of identikit is notoriously chancy and unreliable; and, quite apart from the vagueness of people's memories of a face seen only once, this chanciness may have something to do with the fact that the pieces of the identikit, the selection of eyebrows, noses, cheekbones, mouths, chins, etc., which are its stock of symbols, are themselves only instances of the infinite variety of shapes which human features can adopt. Complete identity of shape between any of these features and the features of the suspect who is sought for questioning is of course never achieved. This is not quite the same thing as – but it is not very different from – the situation in language, where words (like 'hard', 'rough', 'coarse', etc.) are generalizations which correspond only schematically to the realities of any *particular* instance.

Polanyi's observation thus bears out my own remarks about the approximate and schematic nature of language. And indeed he himself asserts elsewhere that *nothing can be said precisely* (Polanyi 1958, pp. 87–88). For precision sacrifices content, since it involves formalization; and formalization is of course my 'abstraction' or 'generalization'.

Here, then, is one component of Polanyi's tacit knowing. Some knowing has to be tacit for the simple reason that language is not fitted to express it : there are things we cannot say about the objects we know, because the language cannot be made particular enough, and because the moment we use it something particular is lost from the object. But there are further insights that Polanyi treats under the general heading of tacit knowing. One very important one has to do with the phenomenon of *attention*. When we contemplate a face, for instance, we are aware of the face focally, and aware of the features which go to make it up only in a subsidiary way : we consciously notice the face, but half-consciously subsume the features into it. Or we may turn our attention to the beard on the face; we shall then be focally aware of the beard, but only subsidiarily aware of the hairs which make it up, of the dim shape of the mouth hidden under the moustache, and of the presence of the other features round it. There is, then, focal awareness and subsidiary awareness (which 'may vary over all degrees of consciousness' : Polanyi 1958, p. 92). It will be clear that this feature of perception is quite commonplace. Throughout our entire waking lives we are focally aware of certain of the things about us, marginally aware of others. As I type this chapter, I am focally aware (focally enough, I hope) of the meanings of what I am writing, somewhat less aware of the words I am using – though at times a particular choice of words will become focal too (focal awareness continually shifts about); and all the time I am marginally aware of my surroundings : the typewriter, the table with my papers on it, the open curtains, the view of Salisbury Crags through the window. There are other things too that I am still more dimly aware of, such as the door a few yards away over my right shoulder, the colour of the carpet, and so on. Awareness shades off steadily into unawareness, and to talk merely of focal and subsidiary awareness is a simplification. There is focal awareness, there are all sorts of degrees of subsidiary awareness (Ibid.), there is marginal awareness; and there are things of which, at any given time, we are totally unconscious.

The psychologist Ulric Neisser's remarks on 'focal attention' correspond quite well to these observations. He notes that there must be 'preattentive processes' which take in the 'whole scene' in front of us and grasp it 'globally' and 'wholistically' (sic). From this scene we are drawn to attend to certain elements of it, to structure it and see it as a scene of a particular kind. The preattentive processes make this selection for us. In addition, there are certain activities we engage in, such as 'walking, driving, visual tracking, etc.' which *are* normally preattentive. And Neisser notes that these preattentive processes have to be distinguished from our subliminal awareness (1967, p. 87ff).

We may sum up the insight which Polanyi's observation gives us, as follows: there is explicit knowing, there are various degrees of tacit knowing; there are also elements of reality of which we are totally unconscious. Even explicit knowing cannot, however, be *made* totally explicit *in language*, because no language is fitted to express everything we are aware of: as Polanyi says, 'nothing that we know can be said precisely'.[6] Some knowledge has to be tacit, on the other hand, because it is only present at the fringes of awareness. And language is an obstacle to our being aware of, or exploring, the tacit areas of perception, because it directs our attention to those features of things which are most generally known or habitually accepted.

Reality contains more than we can normally speak of, and more too than we can be aware of: 'perception has this inexhaustible profundity', it contains 'boundless undisclosed, perhaps yet unthinkable, experiences' (Polanyi 1967, p. 68). And language disguises both the unsayable and the unthinkable from us. What is to be done? We need to do something, for, useful as it is to manipulate old categories and old abstractions, we need also to be able to see what is missing from them.

Language is abstract: it is a representation of abstract thought. And abstract thought may be a representation of reality, certainly; but it is a schematic representation. It is like the symbols on a map: excellent for finding one's way around, but giving only a very general idea of the actual objects to be met with in the country one is walking through. Thus the symbols by which a map shows a church may be of two sorts: a church with a tower, or one with a spire. The words 'church with a tower', 'church with a spire', give no more idea of the concrete reality of any particular church than the symbols on the map. Or take the moment in *The Magic Flute* when Papageno checks Pamina's portrait against the real Pamina's face, but, as he is hiding the picture from her, keeps turning round to look at her. 'Eyes blue', he says, inspecting the portrait. 'Yes, right', he says as he gazes at her. 'Lips red'. Again he turns to look at her: 'Yes, right.' The audience laugh; for girls tend to have red lips; and a very large number of them have blue eyes. Yet what verbal description will ever be enough, to give us an idea of someone's face? Words, as we saw in the case of Polanyi's identikit pictures, are too general for the recognition of any individual. In language, the direct sensory reality of the objects disappears: we are working among schemata, mental diagrams, operations and relationships.

On the other hand, if I look at this rose: its branches and thorns are massed in a pattern that I can see but can not totally schematize; the complexion of its petals shades indescribably from one red to another; the edge of one petal has a brown curl to it; the bush is rooted in black earth of a particular quality and texture. I may make these observations consciously, but like the rose-bush in its earth, each is rooted in the actual data of perception. I can state what I see, but I cannot state all that I see, for each of my statements is an abstraction from dense sensory reality. My sense experience of the rose has a dense and solid reality which my words can only offer a crude map of. Or look at that child : he laughs and skips, but to say this neither communicates the quality of his laughter nor the exact motion of his body. To say his cheeks are red does not communicate their precise appearance; to say his hair tosses about his ears gives you no exact impression of its form and movement. What do we conclude? One of the tacit components that are left out of language and out of abstract thought, is our actual sense-impressions, the indescribable solid reality of the people and things in front of us. Abstract thought is a lattice of points and lines; sensory reality is a warm moving density, filling the world of the senses, and hence an extensive region of the mind.[7]

3. Mental Imagery

There is more in the mind than abstract thought. The notion of mental imagery has been much scoffed at by philosophers. But it seems to be intellectually respectable again, at least among those modern psychologists who are interested in 'information processing'. Common sense always thought it to be so. Most of us think we can perfectly well call up to the mind's eye a picture of a mountain that we know, or to the mind's ear the sound of the opening trumpet fanfare in the Christmas Oratorio. And I recall a story of children who were asked by their teacher whether they preferred radio or television drama. One wrote : 'Radio drama – because the seenery [sic] is better.' Of course there are problems : our internal representations of such things seem to vary considerably from person to person, and some philosophers report that they have no mental imagery at all.[8] But that some sort of *equivalent* of a mental image, though it may not always be introspectible in just those terms, is often present, seems proven by the evidence of the modern psychology of information processing. And this is important, because if there are certain kinds of language which can lead us to inspect our mental images of reality at some depth, then these kinds of language may be able to impel us to inspect some of the tacit and unsayable elements in our own experience.

Let us see, then, what the psychologists have to say about mental imagery. The most approachable recent account that I have found of this area of psychology is in Brown & Herrnstein's *Psychology* (1975, pp. 422–39).[9] They start with immediate sense-perception. Briefly, the findings are these. A visual scene can be presented to the eyes for as short a period as fifty milliseconds. The scene however lingers 'in the mind's eye' for some hundreds of milliseconds, and, despite the fact that it was impossible for eye movements to scan the whole scene during its original brief presentation, for a short time the subject can none the less inspect his own internal impression of it, answer questions about it, correctly identify which elements of it were letters and which shapes, and so forth. This ephemeral impression is termed an 'icon'.[10] An astonishing amount of detail is present in such icons, despite the brevity with which they are shown to the subject: experiment shows that fifty milliseconds give as good an icon of four characters as they do of one; that they give as good an icon of ten characters as they do of four; and Brown and Herrnstein write that no upward limit has yet been found to the amount of detail that can be retained in the icon during its brief life. 'The icon is a much more complete picture of the stimulus than a person's description of it would suggest. The question is, How complete is the icon? A limited amount of data leaves open the possibility that the icon is a virtual snapshot of the stimulus' (Brown & Herrnstein 1975, p. 424).[11] The icon thus contains a considerable amount of the tacit, unsayable elements in our perception.

Moreover, attention can be directed to different elements of the icon just as it can be directed to different elements of a visual scene that is still in front of the eyes. If, after the subject sees a set of characters presented in two lines, one above the other, he hears a brief note (as a signal to tell him to list the upper row, or the lower row as the case may be), he can follow this instruction. This experiment 'and the many others that have confirmed it, [suggest] that you might be able to tune in the violins *after* [hearing the music], out of the auditory *icon* instead of the auditory *stimulus*' (Brown & Herrnstein 1975, p. 424). The icon thus contains some of those tacit elements *to which we did not attend at the time*.

Now common sense would assert that we can call up, from our long-term memories, mental pictures which closely resemble these icons. For common sense has always believed in a 'mind's eye'. And common sense would be right: 'the research has just confirmed what people already knew' (Ibid., p. 427).

'People will for example say that a harp sounds more like a guitar than a bassoon. They do not need to be listening to the actual instruments when they make the judgment. It seems unlikely that everyone who can perform this simple mental judgment on request has at some time in his life made the judgment while listening to the actual instruments. The mental judgment seems to require some current representation/reproduction of the sounds, rather than a memory of an earlier judgment. Similarly, you can compare the tastes of steak and eggs, oranges and rice, etc., with no great strain and with nothing in your mouth. In short, some part, or reconstruction, of your past experience is always accessible, and the evidence suggests that what is reconstructed . . . corresponds to what we experience in the presence of an external stimulus . . . we cannot ever experience the objective stimulus itself, even when it is right there. We experience its transformation by our sensory and perceptual machinery . . . In that sense, we experience a similar world whether the stimulus is present or not.' None the less, the original and the reconstructed icon 'are not identical in every respect, for if they were, we would have no way to tell them apart' (Ibid., p. 435).[12]

There are two types of 'icon' involved in these statements, and we had better be quite clear about them before we go on. In the first place there is what may more properly be called an 'icon', namely the brief impression left in the 'mind's eye' after contemplating some scene, but which fades within fractions of a second. Secondly, there are the images we manage to reconstruct in our minds, either out of our short-term memories, or out of a lifetime of experience of sensory data.[13] These I have been terming the *reconstructed icon*. The important point here is that we can use both types of icon, in much the same way : we can inspect them, turn them round in our minds, direct our attention to different aspects of them; and both types of icon may contain a very considerable amount of fine detail (Brown & Herrnstein 1975, p. 433; see Cooper & Shepard 1973).

Thus people can be asked to mentally compare the shapes of American states, and say whether Colorado and Oregon are more similar in shape than Colorado and West Virginia (Shepard & Chipman 1970). And, as we all know perfectly well, we can mentally compare the texture of chalk and cheese, the smell of dung and roses, the sonority of trumpets and flutes. The evidence seems to suggest that icons and reconstructed icons are 'isomorphic', that is, they are experienced in a very similar way (Brown & Herrnstein 1975, pp. 433–6; Shepard & Chipman 1970). Tacit elements are present in both.

'Reconstructed icon' is a clumsy term and, besides, there is always the possibility of semantic confusion. 'Icon' is after all usually employed in literary studies in a different, though connected, sense : 'when poetry is iconic, its language *resembles* the objects being described'. Now it will be clear that, except for the special case of onomatopoeia, and except in some unusual cases of formal or even spatial representation of objects (such as Apollinaire's calligrams), the language of poetry cannot really be said to 'resemble' what it describes (cf. Martin 1975a, p. 241). For poetry is not composed of the objects which it evokes, nor of the material of which those objects are made, but of words. Except for onomatopoeia and a few other cases, poetry is iconic only in the sense in which I am using the word here : namely, that it evokes mental icons. The reconstructed icons which are evoked by poetry *do* resemble the external

113

events that poetry describes – or rather they resemble our sense-impressions of those events. However, so as to avoid possible confusion between (1) icons as immediate sense-impressions and reconstructed icons, and (2) these reconstructed icons and the 'iconic poetry' of literary criticism, it would seem that we need a new term. For the remainder of this chapter, I shall therefore call reconstructed icons, the mental images which we summon up out of our short-term or long-term memory, *isons*.[14] For such reconstructed images are 'isomorphic' to the sense-impressions we receive in minute-to-minute experience. I must apologize for this piece of jargon; but it has at least the *virtues* of jargon, in that it should promote clarity.

4. The Strength of Memory

Isons, then, are images of sense-data retrieved from our short-term or long-term memories. *In how much tacit detail?* And indeed, how much detail is there available in memory for retrieval? Strangely enough, there exists the possibility that everything we have ever experienced may still be stored somewhere in our memories, in full detail – and that we can call up very little of it, not because it is lost, but rather because it is just difficult to recover. The curious phenomenon of *age-regression* under hypnosis is sometimes quoted in support of this. It seems that, under hypnosis, a subject can be 'regressed in time', that is, taken backwards to specific dates in his earlier experience, and enabled to recall events and thoughts of a period in his life which he cannot normally remember. Parents can sometimes corroborate what he reports, and the subject may act as if he were ten years old, or five, or whatever age he has been regressed to. Explanations of age-regression are controversial, and more cautious writers suggest that these subjects are merely putting on an extremely convincing act; although it is none the less quite clear that unconscious and repressed thoughts can be retrieved in this way.[15]

Another equally strange phenomenon is the memories apparently induced by directly stimulating certain areas of the brain *electronically*. One of Penfield's subjects for instance reported : 'My mother is telling my brother he has got his coat on backwards. I can just hear them.' He was asked whether he remembered this happening, and when it had happened. 'Oh yes', he replied, 'just before I came here.' So detailed are these memories, exactly like replays of the actual experience, that Penfield supposes that no waking events may be forgotten, and that their whole detail is carried in the 'neuronal record' of the brain.[16] Needless to say, this interpretation has been questioned, notably by Ulric Neisser, who writes that even if some events are totally remembered, this 'hardly proves that no events are forgotten'. And he adds that 'what is surprising is only the *vividness* of the imagery, which is seen or heard as clearly as if real objects were being actually perceived' (Neisser 1967, pp. 168–9).

It will be seen that, despite Neisser's reservations about the hypothesis of a total record of past events (and despite, indeed, his other reservation, which is that the electronically evoked memories may not all have been *particular* memories, but sometimes amalgams of memory-data), he is in complete accord with the thesis I am putting forward here. For he accepts that electronically evoked memories may indeed have a tacit density and substance comparable with that of real perceptions. They are in fact extraordinarily like those strange *Proustian moments* of involuntary recall, when certain rare individuals may, perhaps once in a lifetime, have the impression that a whole fragment of the past, in all its reality, has for a moment been restored to them. Thus Judith Kerr, who had been brought up in pre-war Germany, had fled to England, and had forgotten more and more of her German over the years, writes:

on a recent visit to Germany a strange thing happened to me. I was on a bus, idly reading the signs above the shops in the street we were passing through, when I saw the word *Blumenladen*. Suddenly I was in a different world. I was conscious of being very close to the floor, surrounded by the legs and feet of people who towered above me. There were plants everywhere, as big as bushes and trees – thick green leaves and enormous coloured flowers. It was like a jungle, and I was in the middle of it, clutching a huge hand from which a huge arm stretched up into the distance above me.

And then I was back on the bus, a middle-aged woman on a visit from England.

I had found a bit of my childhood, pickled in a word that had lain unused for forty years until I had happened to come across it.

(Kerr 1975)

Paul Valéry records a similar experience:

J'entends des coups de marteau, ce 3 août 1920, qui sont, pendant un/n de seconde, les coups de marteau qui à Cette, vers 1880, bâtissaient les baraques de la foire vers le 15 août. Le choc d'aujourd'hui frappe sur le bois de 40 ans . . . Le choc a éveillé ces baraques de Cette; le rythme a agi. J'ai vu les platanes, les bois, les planches, l'Esplanade – l'ennui, le marché. J'y étais . . .

(Valéry 1957–61, Vol. 7, p. 569)

[I hear the blows of a mallet, this 3rd August 1920, which are, for an *n*th of a second, the mallet-blows at Sète, around 1880, constructing the hutments of the fair around the 15th August. Today's blow strikes on the wood of 40 years ago . . . The blow recreated those hutments in Sète: the rhythm acted. I could see the plane trees, the wood, the planks, the Esplanade – boredom, the market. I was there . . .]

And everyone is acquainted with the similar events in Proust's *A la recherche du temps perdu*, when the taste of a biscuit soaked in tea, or the sensation of the narrator's foot stumbling over an uneven paving-stone in the courtyard of the Guermantes' house, similarly replaced the present with a whole fragment of experience from the past.

Such experiences are extremely rare.[17] Most of us, indeed, never have them – unless the common experience of *déjà vu* is perhaps the beginnings of such a moment. And indeed, when Proust's narrator takes his first sip of the tea, and while the total experience of the past is still shut out behind the curtains of his memory, his description of this moment strongly resembles the strange questing sensation of *déjà vu*, our sense that something is hovering just out of reach, like a half-remembered phrase, 'on the tip of the tongue', but refusing to manifest itself in speech.

Further evidence of the possibility of total recall is provided by investigations of eidetic imagery. Thus Haber and Haber report for instance that an apparently 'complete' image of a picture can be retained by some children and a few adults for up to four minutes. The picture can still be 'seen' during this period in all its detail (Haber & Haber 1964). And a few exceptional individuals have the most amazing eidetic recall. The historian Macaulay is said to have been able, years later, to quote whole pages of books he had read only on one occasion. Another instance is the anonymous S described by Luria in his *Mind of a Mnemonist*, who could memorize whole tables of numerals, and read them off out of his memory, often years later. It seems he achieved such feats of recall by 'seeing' the tables in front of him, and Luria comments : 'it appeared that there was no limit either to the *capacity* of S's memory, or to the *durability of the [memory-] traces he retained*' (1969, p. 11). Indeed, his great difficulty was forgetting, and when there was an image that he wished to forget, he had to resort to devices such as imagining that he had drawn a curtain across the image. Moreover, his own internal images were so strong that they competed with S's living experience for his sense of reality. As a child he would wake in the morning, knowing that he had to be at school by 9 o'clock, would note that the hands of the clock stood at 7.30, and would continue to laze in bed till nearly nine – for he continued to 'see' the hands of the clock still standing at half-past seven! (Ibid., p. 144).

What are we to conclude? Do our minds indeed contain a complete recording of the stream of consciousness, as Penfield would have us believe? Is there a total record merely of some experiences among others? Or is such detailed recording possible only for some rare and unusual individuals? It seems difficult to prove either that all our memories remain for ever intact or that any of them can ever be lost (Wright *et al.* 1970, p. 375). Many psychologists are willing to hypothesize that memories are never lost once they are placed in the long-term store.[18] Even if we accept Neisser's rather sceptical view, that the 'permanent record of the stream of consciousness' is a fiction, there is still no doubt that our memories can store a great deal of information for very long periods of time (Neisser 1967, p. 169). And it seems to me that evidence proves, and proves conclusively, that there is sufficient detail in our memories for us to be able to reconstruct quasi-iconic reality out of them. For this is the very minimum explanation necessary to explain such phenomena as Proustian recall, or the apparent density and reality of electronically-induced mental imagery. And this indeed is Neisser's explanation of such phenomena.

It would seem, then, that there is a vast amount of sensory detail present in our memories, and available to be incorporated in our *isons*. And much of this detail is tacit; it is not merely verbal or formalized. Posner for instance shows that 'there is a visual component to Long Term Memory' (1969, p. 96).[19] Norman writes: 'How do people store information? The proper conclusion is that different forms of information are necessary for different purposes. Image-like information is used for some tasks. Categorization and semantic information seem necessary for other tasks' (Norman 1976, p. 195). Atkinson and Shiffrin write that 'long term memory exists in each of the sensory modalities: this is shown by subjects' recognition capacity for smells, tastes, and so on' (1968, pp. 103–4). And Reed writes: 'Current evidence suggests that recall or reproduction of a pattern depends upon a verbal description, but recognition depends more upon a visual image' (1973, p. 137).

It is clear that it may be extremely useful to be able to summon up a fairly exact image, say, of a friend's face (if we are trying to describe him to someone else), or of one of our own rooms painted in an imaginary colour scheme (if we are proposing to decorate it). But a caution must be given here. It would hardly be helpful to us if, on each occasion that we were required to visualize any dog, any clock, or any mother, our isons were so precise and detailed that they gave us the image of a particular dachshund called Fritz, or of the nursery clock fixed immutably at twenty-past eight, or our own mother's face looking over the side of the cot we slept in as a baby. Images so precise would usually fail to fit the context, and interfere perhaps with our understanding of it. And this is exactly what occurred with Luria's S. 'When S read a passage from a text, each word produced an image. As he put it, "Other people think as they read, but I see it all." As soon as he began a phrase, images would appear; as he read further, still more images were evoked, and so on' (Luria 1969, p. 112). On one occasion, he was asked to interpret the sentence: 'The work got under way normally.' S was immediately in difficulties. 'I read that "the work got under way normally." As for *work*, I see that work is going on . . . there's a factory . . . But there's that word *normally*. What I see is a big, ruddy-cheeked woman, a *normal* woman . . . Then the expression *get under way*. Who?

117

What is all this ? You have industry . . . that is, a factory, and this normal woman – but how does all this fit together ? How much I have to get rid of just to get the simple idea of the thing !' (Ibid., p. 128).

Faced with poetry, S fared even worse.

> S found that when he tried to read poetry the obstacles to his understanding were overwhelming : each expression gave rise to an image; this, in turn, would conflict with another image that had been evoked. How, then, to break through this chaos of images to the poetry itself. Note for example how difficult a poem like the following proved to be.

> An old man was standing in a grape trough,
> Clutching a pole, stamping grapes with his feet.
> But the worker in him, grown fierce with greed,
> Eyed that river of wine he so revered.

> Sunset came as usual, gigantic it rumbled,
> Rocking the grass, the wind pounding the old man's hut.
> He stepped out of that low wooden trough,
> Barefoot entering his hut, now such a jumble.

> N. Tikhonov, *from the Georgian poems*

> I saw the old man clearly. He was a little taller than average, had rags wrapped around his legs, and looked something like Leo Tolstoy. He was standing in a place that resembled a garden . . . As for the word *kupel* [here meaning 'grape trough'] that's a bunch of grapes. What first appeared was the brown polished barrel of a gun . . . I saw the old man. It seemed as if he were cursing the servant for something. Farther on I saw the river of wine, a dark river since wine [Russian : *vino*] is such a dark word. The river that appeared was one I know in Rezhitsa, near a place called the Mount of Bathsheba . . . Earlier there had been an old ruined castle on this mountain. Behind the mountain I could see some sort of glow – sunrise, apparently. Most likely it was coming up behind the sawmill in Rezhitsa . . . Then I saw some tall grass that began to sway . . . I didn't know what this signified – individual blades of grass, tall grass, sedge . . . I was standing at the shore and saw all this from a distance . . . Then the objects grew large. The figure of the old man, transparent, rushed past me, swept by like a zephyr. Through it I could see the grass and to the left, it seemed, a hut with a tightly fitting roof. The furniture inside was familiar to me – no doubt the furniture we had at home. No, I just don't understand this . . .

> The impression I got of the poem was rather like what you'd get if you accidentally overheard a conversation – fragments of images that made no sense . . . At first it seemed the old man was enraged

with the servant and was kicking him because the servant was rich, was wearing rope sandals. The servant doesn't protest, for he loves wine . . . Then the river appeared to me. After that I gave up trying to follow the poem. It was a nightmare . . .

(Record of March 1935 : Luria 1969, pp. 120–2)

Luria comments (Ibid., p. 120) that it thus seems as if poetry must give rise to ideas, not images. There is, however, another possibility, which is that poetry gives rise, in normal readers, to *only so much of the images* as is necessary for understanding. And it will be remembered that the unpractised reader of poetry does in fact quite often report having private images; and that some such readers say that they never agree with other readers about what the poems suggest, simply because their own images are so private. Their difficulty, though not so acute as S's, is of the same kind : they find it hard to rid themselves of irrelevant details.

The evidence of more ordinary uses of language, in real life, however, suggests that we can, most of us, (1) on the one hand visualize isons, but (2) on the other hand visualize only so much of them as we need for the particular context. It is not that there is no isonic element in our visualizing, it is merely that our isons can be flexibly combined with other isons, can be blended and compared with one another, a thing which S's particularly vivid and specific images were too strong to permit him to do.[20] And this is precisely what poetry requires of us : not to visualize isons in isolation, but in combination with each other in metaphor or simile, 'woman' with 'rose', 'moon' with 'skull', 'spiders' with an army on the march. As Brown and Herrnstein say of quite an ordinary use of language, 'If asked whether lemon is sour, you may call forth only a tiny fraction of the original sequence of responses. Less of the sequence, certainly, than if you have been asked to compare its flavour with that of lime' (Brown & Herrnstein 1975, p. 437). Then again, if you are asked to compare the flavour of one brand of beer with that of another, or of the beer drawn from the barrel in the pub you happen to be in, with that of the 'same' beer from another bar the evening before, much more precision is called for in the ison. Evidently, it is the degree of attention that we are exercizing which evokes less or more of the ison, as the case may be. 'It is *attention* that rehearses and analyzes some aspects of the [ison] and not others . . .' (Ibid., p. 439). I would say, therefore, that the example of Luria's S constitutes no objection to the theory I am advancing here : as someone who could not forget, he assists my argument in bearing witness to the (possibly) almost complete isonic *capacity* of the human memory; but he is not an instance of the isonic *process* in normal individuals, or in normal poetry-readers.

Sometimes, then, we compare two isons superficially : very little of their content is drawn upon; sometimes we explore them more deeply, and draw upon more of their content; and often our contemplation of them is of remembered sensory data which would be difficult, if not impossible, to reduce to words. We cannot specify the taste of Blogg's beer in words, except by using the imprecise and generalized classificatory devices we looked at in the first part of this chapter. We can fairly well imagine the aroma of coffee, but may find it impossible to describe, even if we have been on some lonely expedition for a couple of weeks, coffeeless, and suddenly its smell overcomes us with almost hallucinatory strength. Called upon to compare two different shades of red – blood and tomato ketchup – we are obliged to *visualize* the two shades of red in question : we contemplate isons *of the actual colours*; it is not two different *words* that we contemplate. Isons, in short, involve tacit elements, which cannot be reduced to mental abstractions or verbal classifications. Our deepest contemplation of our isons involves contemplating fragments of remembered experiences. My mental ison of the rose is doubtless never so dense or substantial, so full of tacit depth, as my immediate perception of the rose itself. But it is certainly more, much more, than a mere linguistic or intellectual abstraction.

What then is the role of language (and of literature) in evoking isons? Judith Kerr's experience with the German word for flowermarket is interesting : the sight of the word produced an experience of total sensory recall, as if the word were a string attached to the memory; one tug on the string, and the memory reappears, years later, in all its density and reality. This is suggestive : words are our filing system, they are (to use a metaphor that I have employed elsewhere) the labels on the drawers of memory : they enable us to file vast quantities of information in the mind, and, when we require it, to pull open the drawers of memory, and find the recollections we seek. They are mere signposts, but without them we should no doubt be unable to find our way about our memories with anything like the same ease, or to distinguish between our perceptions with the same precision.

DeLee Lantz describes an experiment in which she presented people with a set of colours.

> First a subject was allowed to look briefly at a single chip in a controlled exposure apparatus for just five seconds. The colour would be removed and, after an interval of five seconds, he would be asked to try to find, in the full array, the colour he had just seen . . . Some subjects were given a more difficult task of recognition : they saw four chips at once and then had to try to identify all four.
>
> How does one work at this task of delayed recognition? For myself, and for many subjects, it goes like this. When the colour initially appears you try to give it a distinctive name, not speaking aloud but verbalizing to yourself. When the colour is removed the name can be retained, even rehearsed. Somehow, names are responsive to volition in a way that images are not. Then you

search around the perimeter of the wheel of colours, testing each chip against the name to see whether the two belong together. When the chip is found which best deserves the name, that is recognition.[21]   (Brown 1965, pp. 333–4)

And of course, as Brown goes on to say, when you have not one but four colours to retain, *most* people find it necessary to utilize the linguistic code.

Language, in fact, stabilizes our concepts. As Linnaeus wrote, 'Nomina si nescis, perit et cognitio rerum.' (If you do not know their names, your knowledge of the things themselves perishes.) We all know how much easier it is to remember a telephone number if we say it aloud to ourselves, and do not simply try to visualize the figures.[22]

5. A Philosophical Objection

At this point, and before proceeding further, we might do well to consider briefly one common philosophical objection to the notion of mental imagery. In the face of the evidence quoted above, such an objection can scarcely carry great weight; but it would be just as well to show that, even in the absence of such evidence, the objection itself is still misconceived. It is often asserted that we cannot have mental images for the following reason. An image is always determinate : on a picture of a tiger we can always count the stripes. But how many stripes has my mental image of a tiger? I cannot say, and therefore (so runs the argument) I must be mistaken about having a mental image of one.

Thus Dennett argues :

> If seeing or imagining is having a mental image, then the image of the tiger must – obeying the rules of images in general – reveal a definite number of stripes showing, and one should be able to pin this down with such questions as 'more than 10 ?', 'less than 20 ?' If, however, seeing or imagining has a descriptive character, the questions need have no definite answer . . .

(Dennett 1969, pp. 136–7, quoted in Fodor 1976, pp. 187–8)

As Fodor says, 'a number of philosophers appear to hold that this sort of argument provides something like a demonstration that there aren't mental images' (Ibid.). It does, however, nothing of the kind. As Fodor points out, a *picture* is always determinate at some level or other, but this determinacy is often at such a level that many of the features of the *subject* remain indeterminate. (The reader might like to contemplate the picture of a spotted dog that appears on p. 14 of Gregory 1971.) In short, the portrayal of the subject may be blurred, as with those newspaper photographs which have a 'coarse screen', or with oil paintings where one cannot count the leaves on the trees. (There are in fact very few oil paintings where one can.) An image, in short, may perfectly well portray its subject in a vague and misty way. Thus, when people report (as they normally do) that their mental images are blurred and hazy, this does *not* prove that they cannot be image-like.

Indeed, it is rather the opposite. A picture of an object is never identical with the object, and always involves some blurring, some imprecision in detail as compared with the object. It would seem, therefore, that images are by their very nature imprecise – and they are so, of course, in varying degrees.

It is worth adding too that it is by no means clear whether even a very fine-grained photograph of a tiger would enable us to determine how many stripes it had. If one visits a zoo, one discovers that a tiger's stripes are made up of a large number of bands of varying width, of patches, dots, splotches and markings which branch out, ramify, converge, or come to a sudden stop. There is nothing so clear and definite as a set of precise and enumerable lines. It is plainly unreasonable to require a mental image to be more precise than the object itself is!

We may, I think, confidently dismiss this philosophical objection and proceed to our next business. If further argument is needed, readers might consult Fodor's *Language of Thought* (1976, pp. 187–91), which to my mind definitively settles the matter.

6. Metaphor

The psychological evidence I have quoted is in strikingly close agreement with the proposals about metaphor that I made in *Language, Truth and Poetry* (Martin 1975a, pp. 206–10). It is in this special psychologist's sense of the word 'icon' that poetry can be called 'iconic'. Or rather, I should say that poetry is not iconic, but *isonic*, for it calls up out of memory our recollections of experience. In Greek mythology, the mother of the Muses was Mnemosyné : Memory. Spender writes that

> all poets have this highly developed sensitive apparatus of memory ... I have a perfect memory for the sensation of certain experiences which are crystallized for me around certain associations ... A few fragments of unfinished poems enable me to enter immediately into the experience from which they were derived, the circumstances in which they were written, and unwritten feelings in the poem that were projected but never put into words ... It is perhaps true to say that memory is the faculty of poetry, because the imagination itself is an exercise of memory. There is nothing we imagine that we do not already know. And our ability to imagine is our ability to remember what we have already once experienced and to apply it to some different situation.
>
> (in Vernon 1970, pp. 70–2)

Poetry can demand of its readers precisely what Brown and Herrnstein demand of their subjects : namely to mentally compare the taste of lemons and lime, the sound of guitars and trombones, and thereby visualize both more clearly . . . or even come up with some strange new amalgam of the two. Let us consider what must be presumed to happen in the mind of the reader when he contemplates a metaphor.

Let us first take a simple case, a dead metaphor like 'the nose of an aeroplane'. Normally, we use this term without ever thinking why: we apprehend it literally, as we do such terms as 'aileron', 'cockpit' or 'strut'. There are, however, many first uses of the term. For every time the word is applied in the presence of a child who has never heard it before, this is a first use as far as he is concerned. Let us therefore perform what scientists call a thought experiment. Let us assume that a picture of the aeroplane is present – or the aeroplane itself – and that the speaker does not point to the nose but merely mentions it. The child, however, will (if he is not too young) understand the word, and will know to what part of the aeroplane it is being applied. But how, by what mental process, can he connect the word 'nose' with the object in question? The mental situation is as follows: the word 'nose' is heard, and interpreted as some area or extended sense of the concept *nose*; the front of the aeroplane is seen and mentally interpreted as the *front of the aeroplane*. Somehow, the mind conceptually identifies *nose* with *front of the aeroplane*, thus:

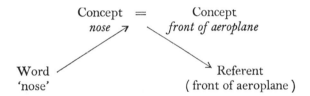

Now what happens inside the mind, in the area indicated by the equals sign? How can the idea *nose* be connected or equated with the idea *front of the aeroplane*? The only explanation must be that the latter is seen as being 'nose-like', in that it may be shaped something like some noses, and in that it is at the front. The concept *nose*, in fact, can be applied to the nose of the aeroplane in virtue of the connotations *nose-shape* and *frontness*. Our diagram of the mental process will therefore look something like this:

The two concepts *nose* and *front of aeroplane* are connected by means of the connotations that they both have in common. And *it is impossible to understand how the hearer could understand 'nose' at all* in this context, unless some mental process of this kind were operating. A mental connexion *must* be assumed; and it must be assumed on the basis of likeness of mentally perceived features between the two concepts *nose* and *front of aeroplane*.

With further uses of the word 'nose' of aeroplanes, the usage becomes quite familiar and normal. The connexion between 'nose' and the aeroplane's nose is felt to be quite direct. As we say, the metaphor dies:

(Connotations : *nose-shape, frontness*)

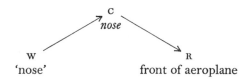

The hearer no longer has to go through the mental process of connecting *nose* to *front* by way of the semantic content of each concept. He knows now that aeroplane's fronts are always called 'noses', and that is how he thinks of them. The connotations (*nose-shape* and *frontness*) are submerged behind the concept's surface. The mental electricity no longer has to pass *through* them.

Connotations such as *nose-shape* and *frontness* are very easily grasped by the reason : they can be grasped in a very schematic, perhaps even in a purely linguistic way. The child is not being asked to mentally *compare* noses with the fronts of aeroplanes : he is merely being required to identify what part of the aeroplane is being spoken of. There is no need for him to look hard at the two concepts *nose* and *front of aeroplane*, and contemplate them mentally. The simplest and most uncomplicated of connexions can be made. It is rather like someone being asked if lemon is sour. Very little of the two isons *sourness* and *taste of lemons* needs to be brought into play.

There are clearly any number of degrees possible in this process. It is a question of (1) how many factors in the two isons have to be brought into play, and (2) how much of their tacit and non-abstractable elements are involved. Comparing lemons with limes is perhaps not too difficult, but involves a fairly distinct 'picturing' of the two tastes. The two isons have to be brought in contact, as it were, and compared. The process appears to be immediately much more conscious than the process involved in identifying the aeroplane's nose. For the latter involved rather schematic representations of the two isons in question. The former involves a rather fuller 'picturing'. It is only if we compare to some extent our mental images of their *tastes* that we can perform the operation of comparison at all.

This seems to show that the criterial connotations of some concepts *are* sensory data. For the ison of the taste of lemon or lime is our criterion for recognizing which sort of drink we are tasting. The same is true of sounds and colours. The criterion of something being called 'red' is that it appears red. The criterion of a sound's being identified as that of a clarinet is that it sounds like one. One criterion of coffee's being coffee is that it smells like coffee. In all these cases we have to inspect our isons to arrive at a decision; as Haber (1971, p. 7) writes, linguistic meaning may act upon our perceptual experience directly.[23]

Now I should not wish to assert that all poetic images work in this way. With many or perhaps even most of them, we may be presented with more, or denser, connotations than usual, without being actually forced to inspect our isons. But plenty of poetic images can none the less be found where it seems highly unlikely that isons are not involved. For in some lines of poetry, it would seem impossible to understand them, unless the process of understanding passes, as it were, *through* some part of the ison. Thus, I hope to have shown above that we can understand the mental link made between 'nose' and 'front of aeroplane' only if we assume that they link *through* certain connotations; and that we can identify lemon as 'lemon' and lime as 'lime' only by linking the present experience with the remembered word *through* the recalled experience.

In Sylvia Plath's 'Balloons',

> Brother is making
> His balloon squeak like a cat.
> Seeming to see
> A funny pink world he might eat on the other side of it,
>
> He bites,
> Then sits
> Back, fat jug
> Contemplating a world clear as water,
> A red
> Shred in his little fist.   (1965, p. 85)

to assent to the rightness of the comparison of the balloon's squeak with the cat's mew, we have to imagine these noises to some extent. And the rightness of the metaphor 'fat jug' can only be felt by referring to our experience of the bottom-heavy instability of squatting babies, and to the similar sense of the bottom-heavy stability of jugs, which is in part an experience of our muscles. The comparison is also valid because of jugs and babies both being filled with milk; and a further two isons that have to be put together and compared are the shapes, respectively, of baby and jug. For these shapes are not schematic like squares or triangles : they are visual and tactile.

As for the milk in Valéry's much-discussed image 'le lait plat' (flat milk), nothing in the usual usages of 'plat' prepares us for this. We have to visualize milk in a bowl before we can see that it is its surface which is flat, of a flat and smooth whiteness too; and mentally 'taste' its ison before we can see the aptness of the adjective to that too!

Or let us take Tennyson's little poem on 'The Eagle', which contains the line : 'The wrinkled sea beneath him crawls;' the aptness of 'crawls' has to be checked against some possible image of the sea's surface, however sketchy; when we imagine the steady serpentine movement of lines of crinkling waves towards the shore.

In Shelley's lines on the skylark,

> Keen as are the arrows
> Of that silver sphere,
> Whose intense lamp narrows
> In the white dawn clear
> Until we hardly see – we feel that it is there.

sharp points and sharp sounds have to be compared; and we can hardly understand the 'narrowing' of the 'intense lamp' until we summon up a mental picture of the moon becoming apparently paper-thin and transparent to the sky 'behind' it. Nor can we assent to the last line unless we can refer to our mental experience of the moon dimming into near-disappearance in the morning light.

Similarly, (though this is not a metaphor) we cannot either accept or reject MacCaig's image

> – like a trout
> A foot above the water it extravagantly
> Emerged from – you remember it
> A foot above the water, not coming out
> Or returning to it : a still.   (MacCaig, 1967, p. 36)

without inspecting our memories to check whether we have indeed had a similar visual impression.

Again, our conventional view of the thrush is so homely and sentimental that when Hughes writes

> Terrifying are the attent sleek thrushes on the lawn,
> More coiled steel than living – a poised
> Dark deadly eye, those delicate legs
> Triggered to stirrings beyond sense – with a start, a bounce, a stab
> Overtake the instant and drag out some writhing thing.
> (Hughes 1960, p. 52)

it would be hard to assent to his description of the bird's behaviour unless we had some mental image of birds catching worms. Finally, when Baudelaire writes

Il est des parfums frais comme des chairs d'enfants,
Doux comme les hautbois, verts comme les prairies
[There are perfumes fresh and cool as children's skin,
Sweet as oboes, green as meadows]   ('Correspondances')
to assent to his statement, requires us to compare certain odours,
textures, sounds and colours in the imagination.

These (and many others) seem to me cases where the proper understanding of the poem *demands* some reference to sensory isons. The
evidence of introspection suggests that, even when there is no demon-
strable *compulsion* to inspect such isons, we none the less quite frequently
do so. It is hard not to receive some image of the eyes of Lowell's
drowned sailor :

The corpse was bloodless, a botch of reds and whites,
Its open, staring eyes
Were lustreless dead-lights
Or cabin-windows on a stranded hulk
Heavy with sand.   (The Quaker Graveyard in Nantucket)
or of Plath's unShelleyan moon :

The moon has nothing to be sad about,
Staring from her hood of bone.   (1965, p. 85)
and in Hopkins's 'Inversnaid' again we are obliged to refer to our isons :

This darksome burn, horseback brown,
His rollrock highroad roaring down,
In coop and in comb the fleece of his foam
Flutes and low to the lake falls home.
'Horseback brown', 'fleece' and 'flutes', in particular seem to demand a
mental comparison of vehicle with tenor, the colours and shapes of water
being compared with things 'unlike' them.

7. Isonic Levels

Our memory stores, however, contain the records of more than sensory
data alone. They contain records of past emotions. One may presume
that emotional isons are there too to be drawn upon by poetry; but there
is no need to spend much time arguing this : it is a matter of experience.

Is not the ison of a particular form of awe evoked by Baudelaire's line
'Je t'adore à l'égal de la voûte nocturne'? For so strange is the comparison of the feeling of gazing up at the fearful vastness of the night sky,
with that of contemplating one's feeling for a woman, that these two
feelings have to be put together and allowed to interact.

Or take Webster's lines in the *Duchess of Malfi* :

One met the duke 'bout midnight in a lane
Behind St Mark's Church, with the leg of a man
Upon his shoulder; and he howled fearfully;
Said he was a wolf, only the difference

127

Was, a wolf's skin was hairy on the outside,
His on the inside . . .   (Act V, Scene 2)
The duke is a concealed wolf, a suppressed wolf; his evil is destroying
him from within; he is more dangerous than a mere werewolf, since he
does not visibly change his shape. We may well feel horror. But what is
the physical connotation of the last unpleasant image? Does it not echo
the sensation of the skin 'crawling' that we feel in the presence of the
unnatural? The emotional link, then, between this sensation and
Ferdinand's behaviour is horror : and it is evoked quite specifically.

The clearest cases, however, are probably the kind of image which
Archibald MacLeish makes such great play with in *Poetry and Experience*,
namely those juxtapositions of images or of situations which make
no rational sense, but which merely sit there on the page confronting
each other, and demand us to find a link between them.

> The sound of her silk skirt has stopped.
> On the marble pavement dust grows.
> Her empty room is cold and still.
> Fallen leaves are piled against the doors.
>   (Arthur Waley, quoted in MacLeish 1965, p. 51)

or

> O westron wind when wilt thou blow
> That the small rain can rain?
> Christ that my love were in my arms
> And I in my bed again.
>   (Traditional, quoted in MacLeish 1965, p. 63)

MacLeish's sensitive comments are singularly apt to the subject of this
chapter :

> The poem . . . is not a poem about weather. And neither is it a poem
> about making love. The emotion it holds is held between these two
> statements in the place where love and time cross each other. Here,
> as in those old Chinese poems, the emotion, somehow contained
> in the poem, is an emotion which words cannot come at directly –
> which no words as words can describe. *How* will you 'describe' in
> words the poignancy of the recognition of the *obstacle* of time . . . ?
> But if you cannot 'describe' it in words how then can the words
> contain it? . . . By *not* speaking of it. By *not* speaking of it at all. By
> speaking of something else . . . , of two things which, like paren-
> theses, can include between them what neither of them says. By
> leaving a space between one sensed image and another where what
> cannot be said can *be* . . .   (Ibid., pp. 63–4)

And this, doubtless, is what MacLeish meant, when he wrote in a
famous poem, that poetry 'should not mean, but *be*' (1952, p. 41).

Or consider another of MacLeish's examples : one of the most powerful and disturbing poems of all time, Baudelaire's 'Une Charogne' :

Rappelez-vous l'objet que nous vîmes, mon âme,
  Ce beau matin d'été si doux :
Au détour d'un sentier une charogne infâme
  Sur un lit semé de cailloux,

Les jambes en l'air, comme une femme lubrique,
  Brûlante et suant les poisons,
Ouvrait d'une façon nonchalante et cynique
  Son ventre plein d'exhalaisons.

[Do you remember the thing we saw, my soul,
  That fine warm summer's morning?
At the path's turning a foul corpse
  Lying on a bed of gravel,

Legs in the air like a lewd woman,
  Burning and oozing poisons,
Nonchalantly, cynically opening
  Its stinking belly.]

And so on through a dozen verses of painfully vivid descriptions :

Les mouches bourdonnaient sur ce ventre putride,
  D'où sortaient de noirs bataillons
De larves, qui coulaient comme un épais liquide
  Le long de ces vivants haillons.

Tout cela descendait, montait comme une vague,
  Ou s'élançait en pétillant;
On eût dit que le corps, enflé d'un souffle vague,
  Vivait en se multipliant.

Et se monde rendait une étrange musique,
  Comme l'eau courante et le vent,
Ou le grain qu'un vanneur d'un mouvement rythmique
  Agite et tourne dans son van.

[The flies buzzed on its putrid belly,
  From it crawled black battalions of larvae,
Like a thick fluid oozing
  Over the living rags of flesh.

It rose and fell like a wave,
  Foamed and seethed;
As if the corpse were softly breathing,
  Living and multiplying.

It was a world full of eerie music,
  Like running water or the wind,
Or the whispering grain the winnower's rhythmic swing
  Tosses and turns in the basket.]

Baudelaire ends, addressing his mistress:

> Oui! telle vous serez, ô la reine des grâces,
> Après les derniers sacrements,
> Quand vous irez, sous l'herbe et les floraisons grasses,
> Moisir parmi les ossements.

> [Yes, this will be you, O queen of graces,
> After the last sacraments,
> When you will go down under the grass and the lush flowers,
> To rot among the bones.]

As MacLeish writes, 'Death and sexuality are coupled in the incongruous congruity of panting lasciviousness and heaving putrescence' (1965, p. 70). And I use this example because the strength with which these conflicting feelings, sexual pleasure, the sense of beauty, the horrified recoil from filth and corruption, are stirred, roused and combined in a single intolerable image, can surely leave no doubt in the reader's mind that emotional isons are in fact evoked.

Thus it is not mere sensory data that may be evoked by poems, but (even more commonly) isons of feeling and emotion. And one may wonder if something more inaccessible, more fundamental and less rational even than our conscious feelings, may not, in poems like 'Une Charogne', be being called upon. After all, the impulse of recoil from this horrifying conflict of emotions is almost physical. Outside our conscious reach, a link is made between the images: the electricity passes through some subterranean cavern, along some submarine cable of the brain. The invisible isons of the unconscious are stirred, and the effect upon our conscious feelings is palpable.

Now it is true that we cannot inspect what is occurring in these areas of the mind. But certainly a very large number of poets have sought to effect such poetic connexions – have actually stated that it is their intention to do so: Jouve for instance, or the Surrealists, or Jean-Claude Renard (see Martin 1978, Introduction). And certainly, while reading poetry, one often does experience a curious sense of rightness and of profundity, as if such uninspectable processes were occurring. It is reasonable to suppose that poetry can evoke tacit experience at this depth too.[24]

It follows, therefore, that we might be able to set up a notional set of different isonic processes, which might occur at different 'levels' or in different regions of the mind. Poetic language may operate at (1) the sensory level, (2) the emotional level, and (3) the unconscious level. But I do not mean this in any rigid or doctrinaire fashion. These 'levels' are a more or less arbitrary division among various mental areas, and their justification would be merely on grounds of utility; for they might permit us to make distinctions between different sorts of poetry, and explain the different effects that these poetries seem to have. Thus, we might find that Keats's, Hopkins's and Hughes's poetry produces more sensory isons, and Bonnefoy's more emotional and unconscious ones, whereas Shakespeare might perhaps be found to work on all levels at once. And it may be that different languages operate on one or more of these levels more readily than on others. Bonnefoy's own remarks on French and English poetry would suggest for instance that French poetry works on levels 2 and 3, English on all three levels (see Martin 1980).

Two further points need to be made. First, if apparency can occur in poetry, if we can be made to contemplate isons, if some fragments of our remembered experience have to be drawn upon, and if we cannot reduce the contemplation of these images of reality to mere intellectual and verbal schemata, then we have made a considerable discovery: we have solved the age-old problem of *ut pictura poesis*.[25] Poetry can give us the impression that it 'shows' reality, because to understand it we have to evoke isons in our mind's eye; we have to contemplate tacit fragments of sensory and emotional experience – fragments which we cannot but contemplate, because we cannot reduce them to words.

Secondly, if what I have been saying throughout this chapter is at all persuasive, it will be clear that there are insoluble problems for the practice of criticism on all three of the isonic levels at which poetry may be assumed to act. For if poetry can produce apparency by evoking our isons and hence giving us some sort of simulacrum of recalled experience; if the isons contain irreducibly tacit elements; and if some of the levels on which poetry operates (and particularly that of the unconscious) cannot be drawn out totally into the light of explicit statement; then a great deal of what we *say* about a poem, when we criticize it, is merely an approximation, merely an abstraction. And this is no more than we might expect. For language, in its rational and discursive form, provides us merely with abstractions and generalizations *from* the actual solid sense-data that we perceive, and *from* the actual dense and stirring emotions that we feel. The language in which we talk of literature is no exception. Hence, all that I say about the connotations of an image, is merely an abstraction from those connotations. I may say that a rose resembles a girl in such and such a poem because they share the following connotations: 'youth, beauty, fragility, a petal-like bloom, ephemerality, being at the mercy of fate', and so on. But I have not thereby done any more than to classify the particular connotations which are aroused by the image; I have not evoked the isons in question, I have merely labelled them.

If we accept then that language is merely the labels on a set of drawers, literature's trick is to make us open the drawers themselves (in which the isons are kept) and take a brief glance inside (Martin 1975a, p. 127).

Listing connotations does not give us the isons themselves in all their density; it merely guides us in our exploration of them. But this in itself is the justification of this sort of criticism; and it is a double justification. In the first place, to list connotations is to reveal and to guide the reader; but in the second place, since I can do no more than that, I can rebut the charge that exploring the meanings and 'ambiguities' of poetry kills it. For my statements about the poem are not an equivalent for feeling and reliving the poem, for contemplating the isons it evokes. Criticism cannot kill poems by explaining them any more than sociology can abolish the individual by explaining the society in which he lives; for both criticism and sociology are merely abstract accounts of reality, and stand at some distance from it: they cannot be substituted for the concrete experience either of living or of reading.

8. The Sense of Newness

> To find out what our experience has, all along, been really like, is to remake experience.
>
> (C. S. Lewis in Lewis & Tillyard, *The Personal Heresy*, p. 148)

My speculations in this chapter may seem to imply a conclusion that many poetry-readers will find distasteful: they may appear to leave no room for the creative function of metaphor. For do we not feel, reading Plath's description of the baby – or Hughes' lines on thrushes – that we have been given a new experience, have seen something in a new light, more clearly than before? Yet, if the effect of metaphors is dependent on their touching some memory, evoking some past experience, or amalgam of past experiences, then where can the sense of freshness come from? In particular, can poetry provide us (as some have suggested) with the sense of a new reality?

What would such a new reality be like? David Kipp asks whether it is possible for the two halves of a poetic image to fuse in the mind in the same way as the colours yellow and blue fuse in vision to create green.[26] The point of the question is that green is experienced as a unity, quite unanalysable into its two elements. Does anything similar ever occur in poetry? Is seeing a baby as a jug a new reality of this kind? Is Baudelaire's combination of sexuality and repulsion such a new reality? Is Webster's werewolf image? If the blending of two isons created a new experience of this kind, we should be able to make a very strong assertion indeed about the capacity of metaphor to produce newness.

Perhaps the evidence of introspection may vary from reader to reader. My own belief is that the elements of a metaphor are always felt as combined but separate, a medley of blue and yellow, not a single unitary hue of green. But even if we agree with Kipp that such a radically new reality is unthinkable, we may make a weaker assertion. A poetic image is a medley of familiar experiences put in unfamiliar combination, like Lefebve's familiar building seen from an unfamiliar angle and hence seen afresh (see p. 77 above). We see a thing as something else and hence as more itself than ever. In forming this new combination, isons are evoked and elements of reality which we usually take for granted are brought back into consciousness – or to the fringes of consciousness. We see, indeed, what in a sense we already knew – but did not know that we knew it – or had forgotten we had ever perceived it. It should be remembered too that an icon can contain some of those tacit elements of an experience which we did not attend to at the time and thus which *were not*, in a sense, *part of the experience*, since, consciously, we did not notice them. We saw earlier that we can 'tune in the violins *after* [hearing the music]' (see p. 112 above; Brown & Herrnstein 1975, p. 424). Introspection suggests we can do this with isons too, so that Hughes's lines on the thrush can strike us with a sudden shock of recognition : 'Yes, of course, now you mention it, thrushes' beaks *are* like steel daggers, the birds *are* like steel springs. I'd never noticed that before.'

Our sense of metaphor's creative powers, therefore, may be due to the newness of the *combination*, its evocation of actual *isons*, and our surprise at seeing something, *again* perhaps, but more concretely than usual. But it may above all be due to those metaphors which reveal elements of the ison which lay dormant and unnoticed in the experience – so that we then undergo what is in effect *a new experience*.

There is a further possibility. If the isons that are stirred were hitherto unconscious, then the experience will be by definition a new one. Profound emotional impulses may be aroused by such poems as 'Une Charogne', and brought into the fringes of awareness for the first time. Plath's 'Daddy', the racialist excesses of *Les Nègres* (see Martin 1975*b*), the bleak landscape of 'Childe Roland', the voyage of the Ancient Mariner, the naggingly mysterious psychology of Hamlet : it may be because of this that we think we glimpse a half-understood revelation in such things. It may be that we do glimpse one.

In short, there are within us things that we did not know were there. It is no objection to the theory of isons that we find only what is already within ourselves; for as a matter of fact there are whole dark continents awaiting exploration within each and every one of us. Man is not so much a personage dressed in a dark suit; he is more like a bottomless pit.[27] And naturally I gasp with astonishment when the conjurer hauls some living rabbit out of the bottomless black box of my own unconscious.

9. Summary

The argument of this essay has been long and involved. I shall summarize it as follows. Experience contains more than we can say : it contains tacit

133

elements which we cannot reduce to verbal or other schemata. Moreover, as modern experimental psychology strongly suggests, our memories contain data of a precisely similar sort to our immediate experience. Many of these data too are tacit. This is borne out by some rare experiences such as eidetic recall, but also by our common knowledge that we can compare two scenes in the mind's eye, two tastes on the mind's tongue. Moreover, some of the connotations of words are remembered sense data. If these 'isons' (mental images) were always too static and specific, we should be unable to understand poetry. But normally we can use fragments of isonic imagery in flexible combination. It is this that allows us to say *ut pictura poesis*, or that poetry 'shows' us reality. We need not fear the critic's verbal analysis of poetry, for it is verbal, and therefore leaves the isonic element merely labelled, not exhaustively described. And finally, to be reminded of what we had not previously noticed is to see experience recreated.

5. Culture and 'Culture':
A Proposal for Redefining Them

The acquisition of such skills [as reading and writing] is ... very
much a circus trick ... Reading, writing and arithmetic are still
basic skills if you want to end up as a synthetic member of the
nineteenth century liberal middle class, ... but [they] no
longer represent 'the ruling class'; and the associated cultural
values ... are no longer the dominant cultural ideology.

(Sir Edmund Leach, Professor of Social Anthropology,
Provost of King's College, Cambridge[1])

Like sociologists, anthropologists do not recognize facts which
have not been written down, preferably in ritual language, by
those of their own totem.

(Anon., in Good, *The Scientist Speculates*)

'But I tell you, Winston, that reality is not external. Reality exists
in the human mind, and nowhere else. Not in the individual
mind, which can make mistakes, and in any case soon perishes:
only in the mind of the Party, which is collective and immortal.
Whatever the Party holds to be truth, *is* truth. It is impossible
to see reality except by looking through the eyes of the Party.
That is the fact that you have got to relearn, Winston. It needs
an act of self-destruction ...'   (George Orwell, *1984*)

MY CONCLUSION, then, is that art is not for art's sake alone. It
is *about* reality and it is *for* perception. It is awareness-enhancing and
consciousness-expanding.

There is a corollary to this conclusion: art is not the lace curtains at
the window of the mind, a parasite upon the social tree, a masturbatory
haven from reality. It may be a tower (for we can see further from a
tower), but it is not an *ivory* tower. Like science it mediates between
nature and society, between reality and human consciousness, it is a tool
of knowledge and understanding. It is thus misleading to regard it as
'merely a piece of human behaviour, merely a socio-cultural phenomenon'. It is this case that will be argued in the present chapter.

1. Socio-Culture and Value-Culture

Everyone knows that 'culture' has at least two definitions: (1) the
creative fine arts (including often some other intellectual disciplines),
and (2) the manners and customs of a people, their religious beliefs
and social organization, their technology, their explicit or implicit

attitudes and values. And writers on the subject of 'culture' almost always take pains to point out that they do not confuse these two definitions. Thus, we find such careful statements as these :

> Conventional definitions of human culture, which usually [confine] this term to the creative 'fine arts' are, to the sociologist, arbitrary and restricted . . . For sociological purposes he will regard as 'culture' *everything* acquired by human beings which is not physically inherited. (Worsley 1970, p. 24)

> The term 'culture' is often abused . . . A culture in the proper sense (that of the anthropologist) is a way of life in which the total activities of a society, including its arts and science and religion, are integrated and create for the participants a life of emotional significance as well as rational organization. (Downie 1971, p. 45)

Such conscientious *sorties* into definition are typical of most writers on sociological topics, and it is interesting to see that, despite all their sincere concern neither to be confused nor to confuse their readers, they none the less both promote and suffer from confusion. Worsley, by calling the usual sense of 'culture' 'arbitrary and restricted', implies that there are no criteria for distinguishing artistic culture from other human behaviour; Downie suffers from the delusion that words have 'proper senses' rather than accepted senses, or senses which it is more useful to use than others. Perhaps neither writer intended such an implication; but it is certainly the impression which the reader may receive.

Let us examine these two statements a little more closely. Downie talks as if 'culture' can be defined exactly as 'ostrich' is defined. We can ask 'What is an ostrich?' and all English speakers will agree in pointing to the same creature. The bird can then be looked at and described : 'A running bird as tall as a man, with rudimentary wings and an unselective appetite'. In other words, the word 'ostrich' has a single referent; and that referent is a phenomenal object : its connotations depend on the observable attributes of the referent. Given the general agreement in English that an ostrich is called an 'ostrich', we cannot choose or not choose to incorporate its gangling legs, its long flexible neck and its degenerate wings in the ostrich's definition; for they are there independently of our choice in the matter. But 'culture' does not have a single agreed referent : it is applied to at least two different human constructs, namely human social behaviour, and artistic and intellectual behaviour. Moreover, neither of these definitions applies to single well-defined phenomenal objects, but to assumed patterns of behaviour about which there can quite properly be a good deal of disagreement. The boundaries of patterns of behaviour are always difficult to establish. There will be disagreement about what is to go under the heading of social culture : are psychological sex differences socially determined, for instance, or are some of them physically determined; and to what extent? There will also be disagreement about what is to go under the heading of high culture : are certain kinds of popular music, jazz or folk-song for instance, art-forms or not ? Both because 'culture' has two different referents, and because these referents are human constructs with hazy and overlapping edges, we cannot be dogmatic about what culture 'is'; and complaints that culture 'is' not this, but 'really' that, should be addressed to the Muse of definitions and not to the literary and artistic critic, who is merely using a referent of 'culture' long hallowed by English usage.

I do not, of course, assume that Downie has actually committed this mistake. But he talks as if he has, and this in itself shows how easy it is to say misleading things about abstract constructs. The first quotation is not open to so much objection. None the less, it is not 'arbitrary and restricted' to define 'culture' as artistic culture. The artist or literary critic needs a term which refers to the artistic area of human activity; and the term 'culture' in this sense is sanctified in the only proper ways that sanctification can occur : namely, by usage and by usefulness. Moreover, to say that 'culture' defined as high culture is a restrictive definition, suggests that high culture is 'really' a part of social culture. Now the sociologist is obliged to talk about artistic culture only in sociological terms; his subject, sociology, defines itself as the relationship between society and human activities. Naturally, therefore, the only way in which he can approach art and literature is by looking at their function within society. To suggest that art and literature are hence no more than social phenomena, is the really 'arbitrary and restricted' thing; for it suggests that sociology can tell us all there is to know about art and literature, and that sociology is the complete human science; and this would be to make the definition of sociology the same as the definition of human knowledge itself. This is indeed the claim of some of the 'sociologists of knowledge', a claim which we should not accept till it has been properly investigated. And even if we find that social culture and artistic culture form a continuum, this is no argument against distinguishing them from each other : black for instance forms a continuum with white.

I think, therefore, that the confusion between the two definitions of 'culture' has not been and cannot be fully avoided even by writers who are completely aware of the confusion; and that we urgently need two separate terms. I shall accordingly propose 'value-culture' as the term for intellectual and artistic culture; and 'socio-culture' as the term for culture in the broad anthropological sense. We shall then, instead of assuming that the two are 'really' identical, or that value-culture is merely a limited area of socio-culture, be able to inquire whether they are the same or not, and whether value-culture has some special qualities which give it, precisely, value, *in addition* to the social norms that it to some extent reflects.

But, it will be asked, are the two really distinct? Does value-culture not arise out of a particular socio-culture, or else belong intrinsically to it? Thus the Gothic cathedrals of medieval Europe have been said to be elements of the social life of the time, shared by everyone from the archbishop to the penitent, from the mason to the child, from the noble to the pauper.[2] So were the religious dramas of Ancient Greece, the sculpture and architect of the Parthenon, and of the temple of Diana of Ephesus. In these areas of what we now call 'art' (usually with a capital A), the situation was more or less that obtaining in primitive societies, where the 'works of art' that a tiny intellectual public now go to admire in the art galleries of Paris, London and New York, were mysterious votive objects which had a definite function for members of the primitive community. This function was a double one: it was *utilitarian*, in that it created the magical assurance of the health of next year's crops (for instance); it was *social*, in that it promoted the social unity of the tribe, and its sense of identity.

The contrast with the situation in the modern world is striking. The appreciation of art, music, highbrow literature, painting and sculpture is confined to a tiny minority, who are often said to belong to the 'upper echelons' of society (see e.g. Baumol & Bowen 1973). Is highbrow art, then, not merely an aspect of the socio-culture of a certain sector of society, of the middle and upper classes to be precise? It could then be seen as performing a social function, in that it is a part of these classes' social world, an expression of solidarity among the individuals who share that world. In this it might resemble the social function of bingo, or, better, that of primitive art, which (among other things) promotes the tribal sense of identity. On the other hand, unlike primitive art, it has no apparent utility, because our modern upper classes do not worship God at the shrine of Velazquez' *Madonna and Child*, nor expect Beethoven's *Pastoral Symphony* to assist the grape harvest. Mind you, they perhaps worship Mammon at the shrine of Sotheby's, when they auction a Picasso self-portrait for over a quarter of a million pounds.

Art in the modern world (so it is argued) performs a purely class function. It is no longer an expression of social solidarity, but divides class from class. Now this proposition rests on a number of assumptions, and in particular on the following ones: (1) that art is totally determined by social system or social class; (2) that art, however caused, is in practice the culture of a particular group; and (3) that art has no value outside the world-view of the society or class to which it belongs. I would argue that there is no respectable evidence for the first two points; but that, even if they are accepted, the third point is untenable; so that, however art may be caused, and whoever it may reach, it has a value which it is our duty to propagate, as we should propagate all genuine values. If kindness were exclusively middle-class (which manifestly it is not!), it would be one of the benefits which the middle class confers on society : it is the same with art.

To take the first point : (1) is art totally determined by society or social class? Such writers as Arnold Hauser seem to think so; and this view is of course commonest of all among Marxists – because they adduce economic and social factors as the basic controls upon all human behaviour. Richard Wollheim, however, notes that

> despite the intensive study of the arts that has gone on in the last seventy or eighty years, no historian has produced any correlation between social conditions and art forms except on the most general, and therefore most trivial level. (Wollheim 1970)[3]

Thus it has been observed that nomadic societies build nothing monumental! The relationship between a society and its art is so variable that those who wish to assert one, have been led to say that art may *depict* society, or *idealize* it, or *compensate* for it. But then, if its relationship to society may be almost anything at all : if it may reflect it, distort it, or reflect its opposite; and if this is still explained as society's *causing* such reflections, distortions and their opposite, then the explanation explains nothing whatsoever! As Wollheim comments on the Marxist critic Plekhanov,

> he held that the role of art in society can be explained in terms of one or other of two principles : the principle of *imitation* . . . and the principle of *contradiction or antithesis* . . . It is difficult to see how this does not in practice amount to saying that works of art either copy social conditions or do not copy them. (Ibid., p. 576)[4]

Our first proposition, then, seems somewhat dubious and unscientific. But in any case, unless a *complete* explanation of art in social terms is available, we have to assume that other explanations are at least a part of the truth; and it then follows that art has values other than purely social ones. In effect, then, my case is already shown to be reasonable and tenable.

Let us turn none the less to the second proposition, (2) that art, however caused, is in practice the socio-culture of a particular group. Now there appear to be certain class differences in leisure pursuits : the middle class go to the theatre, listen to serious music, read highbrow novels, more than do the working class. But in fact a majority of the middle class rarely go to the theatre; and a number of the working class do. Is it proper to call value-culture 'middle-class' when a majority of that class do not engage in it? Just what degree of correspondence between class and theatre-going is to count as proof? The authorities who have studied the question simply do not agree about this. Baumol & Bowen (1973) seem to assert that class and value-culture correspond fairly well; Roberts (1970), McQuail (in Tunstall 1970) and Tunstall do not agree with that conclusion. One researcher reports that *all* leisure-activities, whether they be value-cultural or other, depend primarily on the age of the audience and the amount of money they have; and this is natural if one considers that time and money are needed to engage in any leisure-activity whatever (Birch 1976). Besides, most of the writers on this topic use the roughest of rules of thumb to decide to what classes their respondents belong, and to decide how value-cultural an activity is; nor do their criteria for determining class or value-culture always agree. Indeed, what precisely is to count as value-cultural? Attendance in evening dress at the Glyndebourne Opera may have purely socio-cultural motives: Mr and Mrs X-Y wish to be 'seen' there. Proust's aristocrats are usually philistines paying value-culture a merely token homage. The majority of the middle and upper classes do not appear to the intellectuals who live among them to be markedly cultured, and I should for my part be happiest to apply the term 'bourgeois' to that majority of the middle class who are as insensitive as the working class are often accused of being. I cannot think that art appeared to be a bourgeois activity to Verlaine, Rimbaud, Modigliani, Van Gogh, the Cubist Movement, the Surrealists, D. H. Lawrence, Antonin Artaud, Bela Bartok,[5] Henry Moore, or to Rembrandt and Turner in their old age. It is worth recalling Birch's poker-faced conclusion to his study of 'Leisure Patterns in Britain': 'most people prefer to derive their enjoyment from pursuits which are not too demanding of physical or mental effort' (Birch 1976, p. 21).

In any case, what is class? It seems to be one of those concepts which is as problematic as the phenomena it seeks to explain. Is it to be defined by the occupations of different sectors of the community? Then adoption of those occupations will inevitably go hand in hand with certain abilities and certain interests. Is it to be defined by income? Income within one 'social class' (in its normal definition) varies enormously, and overlaps with other 'social classes'. Is it to be defined by the class that people take themselves to belong to? Art is practised and appreciated by a multitude of people who issue from the working class, and still assert their allegiance to it.[6] Is it to be defined by the tastes and habits of a group of people? Then it is a self-referring definition, which does no more than provide a handy label for the people who have in fact those tastes and habits. It is a category; it is not an explanation. This is not of course to say that it is not a useful category, in that it allows us to study groups of people as a whole; but until very precise criteria can be established for (*a*) class, and (*b*) the genuine appreciation of value-culture as opposed to mere attendance at value-cultural activities, until the researchers agree about these criteria, and until certain clear relationships can be shown to hold good consistently, we can remain happy in our scepticism.

All these observations, of course, leave untouched the fact that the creators of value-culture, and its consumers, are a tiny minority of our socio-culture, But that only a tiny minority eat rabbit, does not disprove the value of rabbit as a food. That is a question for the science of the human digestion, not for a majority vote. Besides, if *some* are not sensitive to value-culture now, there is little hope that *many* will be later. Even if art were totally caused by social factors, and even if it were the actual preserve of one class rather than of all, this would still not affect the question of art's intrinsic value. The truth of Einstein's theory of relativity is not impugned, as the Nazis supposed, by the 'fact that he was a Jew', nor, as the Zhdanovites claimed, by the 'fact that he was a bourgeois intellectual'. It is rather the concern of Nazis and communists for truth that is impugned by their interest in such irrelevances; for a man is revealed, not as a seeker after truth, but as a believer in authority, if he judges by the provenance of an observation, and not by its content. Trusted friends are not always right, nor suspected foes always wrong. If a fact is a fact, it remains a fact, no matter who asserts it.

Thus, it is interesting that Hauser, despite his insistence on the total causation of art by social factors, none the less clearly believes in its value. For he ends his monumental work on *The Social History of Art* with the assertion that art should not be confined, but extended to a vaster public; and that it should not be simplified to suit the unsophisticated, but that the public should be educated up to it (Hauser 1951, pp. 958–9). None the less, among those whose marvellous vision of the unity of mankind, and of the unity of all groups within each single human society, leads them to think that the only proper form of art would be one that all individuals, from whatever class or background, could participate in as equals, there are those who would restrict both people and art, instead of expanding both.

2. The New Treason of the Clerks

No-one should be in any doubt about the attractiveness of this vision. It is sad that so many are shut out from the temple of art . . . though, since it is sad, it might be thought that the cure would be to open the doors of that temple as far as they will go. The sixties and seventies have seen the opposite reaction : instead of throwing wide the temple of art, some people would have it locked, and then burnt to the ground like the Library of Alexandria. Roger Taylor for instance writes :

> The 'cultural' life of our society is a confidence trick practised on the masses . . . Works of art . . . are identifiable as such simply because the social processes . . . have fixed onto them the label 'art' . . . Art, now, is nothing over and above what the bourgeoisie calls art.   (Taylor 1978, pp. 2, 49)

Jean Gimpel proposes that painting and sculpture, ballet, opera and the

141

theatre should be erased from the canon of the arts (1969, p. 158) and, to judge by other remarks of his, poetry and the novel will also be excluded (Ibid., pp. 135—41). 'It is time the Fine Arts made way for younger and more democratic arts,' he proclaims; and he recommends the film, photography, television, illuminated 'books' which can be replayed through television sets, and so forth. It seems to be on this basis too that John Blacking, professor of social anthropology at Queen's University, Belfast, writes :

> If more public money is to be spent on the arts, why can it not be directed towards making redundant 'the artist' as a special category of person, and recreating a society in which all men and women can participate fully in artistic activities ? This should surely be the aim of any truly 'socialist policy for music'. For instance, 'greater encouragement of talented musicians' may only serve to perpetuate the star system, which stifles creativity and artistic development in any society, because it also encourages the mistaken notion that some people are born more musical than others. The Labour Party's experts on music ought to be asking how it is that in the United Kingdom only some members of society appear to be musically talented, whereas in many pre-capitalist societies all members display musical talent, though not necessarily at every period of their lives.[7]

Now I am myself an ex-folk-singer (though not a very accomplished one), and a jazz enthusiast. I consider that both these are art forms, and an essential and too often despised part of value-culture. Francis Newton compares the masterpieces of jazz to Shakespearian soliloquies for their power and emotional effect; and it would be right to make the same remark of a great deal of folk-music. However, my love of folk-music and jazz does not entail a contempt for classical music. It should be quite clear what the implications are of Blacking's immoderate remarks : Western classical music (just like Indian classical music) is so technically difficult to play that it requires virtuosi who have gone through a lengthy and demanding training. If this training were to be abandoned, it would be impossible to ever perform Western classical music again. Gimpel and Blacking would have almost the whole of value-culture, from Bach to Britten, from Bosch to Picasso, from Donne to Dylan Thomas, consigned to the dustbin. To take the arts to the people, to have more people appreciate and participate in them, is an eminently desirable thing; but it will be self-defeating if it entails the total destruction of the finest products of the Western mind.

It may be objected at this point that Gimpel and Blacking's proposals are in any case outrageous and extreme, the view of a tiny and isolated minority; and that I am wrong to waste my time over them.[8] To this I should make two replies : first, however extreme the proposal may be, it will enable us at least to discuss the essential question : just what is it that is valuable, and intrinsically valuable, in value-culture ? There is nothing like a black and white contrast for producing clarity; and we should take extremism seriously in case we forget why we should *not* take it seriously. Secondly, I am not so sure that the minority in question is so tiny and isolated. As we shall see in a moment, there is an influential body of opinion among sociologists of knowledge and sociologists of education, who hold that value-culture has no value. It should be noted that such people wield a considerable amount of power in educational counsels; and that their influence over the young is not inconsiderable. A recent discussion in the correspondence columns of *The Times Higher Educational Supplement*[9] is evidence that it is not only financial pressures which threaten the place of literature within our universities, but also this current of sociological thinking. The value of literature was questioned by more than one correspondent; and we should remember that financial pressures are sometimes exercised by conscious human beings.

For instance S. H. Fiske wrote from his Department of Social Studies that the study of English literature sometimes fails to question

the role of essentially Victorian concepts in a mass democratic society [and to recognize] the changed role of literature in this society. It appears that most societies need some form of imaginative, creative activity, textual or oral . . . The root functions of this activity (let us call it literature) are firstly to structure and thus give significance to our response to [an inchoate] reality, and secondly to fit this structure into a cultural consensus and thus maintain the cultural cohesion necessary to any society . . . However, where our society seeks its cultural consensus, its symbolic structures that enable it to grasp reality, is not in Samuel Beckett but in *The Sweeney*, in *News at Ten*, in *Come Dancing*.[10] The role of highbrow authors in our cultural activity is now peripheral, not central. They explore the areas of imaginative activity that the mass media leave to them; they no longer define areas of central cultural concern.[11]

So when Professor Holloway admits ruefully that Arnold's idea of English studies 'has not caught on', he may well reflect that it is because of the nature of the discipline itself. Its emphasis on the word, the complexities and internal dynamism of the text, its direct links with past authors and its power to 'elevate' and 'deepen' the *individual's* response, are all at odds with a society where literacy is functional (of use for form filling) and not cultural.

The need is to cope not with the problem of the introspective alienated individual tortured by the unacceptable demands made upon him by society, but with the more common and socially more important problems of maintaining a cultural identity in the face of the multifarious global reality with which we are now faced . . . Central cultural needs are thus answered by the mass media, and if university departments brought to these the same academic rigour that they apply to historic written texts, the need to defend themselves [might] be diminished . . .

(*The Times Higher Educational Supplement*, 19 March 1976)

Fiske's remark about literature exploring 'the areas of imaginative activity that the mass media leave to [it]' proves the opposite of what he wishes it to prove. Literature and the arts are not interested in exploring those 'areas of imaginative activity' which the mass media engage in; for value-culture stands on the frontiers of discovery. It is precisely *not* concerned with the conventional, the acceptable and the universally accepted. It is concerned with fresh perceptions, with breaking down the system of routine categories, *not* with reinforcing them as the mass media so frequently do. And for this very reason art and literature are of more 'central cultural concern' than are the mass media.

Fiske's point about 'structuring an inchoate reality' is however an excellent one, as G. H. Bantock duly noted in his letter on 26 March. To Fiske's attack on the individual and insistence on the social collectivity, he replies that social changes in Western society have been comparatively superficial over the centuries, and that literature deals with

certain fundamental traits – capacities for love, hate, jealousy, fear, compassion, charitableness and so on . . . It is for this reason that great literature is always 'relevant' and the differences between the treatment of these matters by the great Victorians (or the Greeks, or Elizabethans, or what have you) and their manifestations in the trivialities of the media today raise fundamental questions of truth to human experience. To be specific, *Oedipus, Hamlet, King Lear* explore, as part of what they encompass, aspects of parent–offspring relationships which reveal truths about those relationships that make their treatment in a typical media product like *Steptoe and Son*[12] ludicrously inadequate.

Terence Hawkes then took a hand, claiming that *Oedipus, Hamlet* and *King Lear* were, none of them, 'as plays, . . . essentially a work of literature at all', and that the parent–offspring relationships mentioned by Bantock are a matter of 'relative triviality'. 'The sky is not falling', he concludes, 'we are simply constructing a different version of reality. Nature, after all, does not grow on trees' (9 April 1976).

I should be the first to agree with Hawkes's splendid remark that 'Nature does not grow on trees'; for indeed the works of art that we encounter help us to structure reality. On the other hand, it is at first sight hard to say what Hawkes means by asserting that *Oedipus, Hamlet* and *King Lear* are not works of literature. The explanation can be found in his book *Shakespeare's Talking Animals*, where he offers his own restrictive definition of 'literature'. He writes, 'Quite clearly, drama is not literature' (Hawkes 1973, p. 26). He emphasizes the 'talking' nature of man and of drama. Drama is language, he says. And its language is, in his mind, opposed to literature, which, he says, 'is not a "social" or "communal" medium. Writing and reading, the means by which literature communicates, are solitary activities . . . They demand skills which have to be laboriously acquired "against the grain", as it were . . .' (Ibid., pp. 218–9). He deprecates the modern theatre because it has not fulfilled its manifest destiny of appealing to the masses, and because it is kept alive by subsidy. 'Such a situation can only encourage lavish and ludicrous production for minority audiences who thereby indulge the unhealthy luxury of seeing themselves as upholders of a sacred tradition.' The theatre has been given artificial respiration, and its survival 'obstructs the rise of another kind of theatre which would inevitably take its place' (Ibid., pp. 228–9).

I am not clear exactly what Hawkes wants. Does he want, for instance, to see an end of the 'solitary activity' of reading? On the other hand, he clearly wishes to see an end to the production of plays in our traditional theatres, and their replacement by a new, truly communal, mass drama. Well, the latter would doubtless be admirable. But should we for that reason not also continue productions of Strindberg, Shakespeare, Pirandello and Beckett? We do not throw away peaches because they are less common than apples. We eat both.

As for Hawkes's remark on parent–offspring relationships being a matter of 'relative triviality', it is absurd. The individual's consciousness is invariably what mediates experience, and his individuality is conditioned and to some extent created by his childhood experiences, so that it is impossible to claim that parent–child relationships are trivial. They are indeed central; the family is responsible for a large part of social conditioning itself; nor can the individual members of the family be eliminated from this process, since it is their consciousnesses that mediate the conditioning and react to it.[13]

The argument, like all such arguments in periodicals, was sketchy, hasty, and indicative of moods and attitudes rather than of thought-out positions. But for that very reason, it is a useful clue to the prejudices which motivate opinions. In particular, Fiske's long letter illustrates precisely the Blacking–Gimpel point of view that I am assailing here (though it is more subtle than theirs in its recognition of the 'structuring' role of art). Fiske sees literature as performing a purely social function. It exists to structure reality for us, but only so as to harmonize that structure with the developing attitudes of society. It does not exist to open people's eyes to alternative structures, to clash them together, or to reveal the inadequacy of all structures. It is a part of the socializing process, a part of society's conspiracy against the specialness of the individual viewpoint; and he welcomes it as such. It follows that those works of art which conventionalize the individual, which enable him to conform to society's wishes, are those which Fiske favours, and whose study he would promote.

It is logical therefore that he should be contemptuous of the small élite who practise and enjoy highbrow literature. These people stand apart from society, and are defined as separate by their literature : which at once promotes alienation from the masses, and gives the alienated a common socio-cultural structure and a common identity. And indeed, *if* it is right to see nothing in value-culture but the socio-culture of a small and privileged class, *if* that is, it has no merits other than social merits, and *if* social merits are merely demerits when they distinguish man from man, privileging some and depriving others, then Gimpel, Blacking and Fiske must be correct : away with Beethoven, away with Turner, away with poetry! Ay, there's the rub. For there is a great deal more to art than that. Just as science is influenced by socio-cultural pressures, but not totally controlled by them; and just as science expresses new truths which are not the mere expression of socio-cultural wishful thinking, but revelations of a more accurate and dependable truth; so the arts may be on the one hand partly free of socio-cultural pressures, and on the other hand have intrinsically useful lessons to impart.

We may express these special qualities of the arts as follows : (1) Reality is disguised by the categories (of language and social custom) which we impose upon it. The arts perform a useful function in questioning and breaking down these categories, at least temporarily, so that we can be led to view experience in a novel and unexpected way. And indeed, this process of disrupting categories is the basic mechanism by which literature operates. We may then be led to a more flexible view of reality, one which is more open to its manifold possibilities. (2) Reality is disguised by any single unitary viewpoint which may be imposed upon it. As in the relative universe all viewpoints are equally valid, so in the artistic universe all individual viewpoints have their value. For it is not to be supposed that we know the whole truth already, that we have final and absolute certainty : conflicting viewpoints must therefore be permitted, for without them we should have no possibility of amending our opinions, and hence getting nearer to reality itself. This is the irrefutable argument for free inquiry in science; it is the equally irrefutable argument for the freedom of individual viewpoints in art. (3) Experience has tacit and personal elements. It is a falsification of reality, therefore, to assume that only its 'objective' aspect deserves attention. Art has value in drawing our attention to that element of experience which is not 'objective' but 'subjective', that is, particular to the individual; for to say that it is particular to the individual is not to deny its reality as a part of experience.

Summing up the qualities of value-culture so far, we may say therefore that it was perceptive of the late eighteenth and early nineteenth centuries to have introduced the term 'aesthetics' as a description of the study of art; for the Greek αἴσθησις (aisthêsis) means 'perception' or 'sensation'. It is precisely in its function as a refiner and revealer of our perceptions that art's prime value lies. An alternative term for 'value-culture' might have been 'perception-culture'. Socio-culture is a wall painted with conventional and formal murals, distorted images of the outside world; value-culture is the window through which we may glimpse fragments of reality.

But who have perceptions? Individuals, and individuals alone. Thus value-culture has value in (4) reminding us where the foundations of all knowledge lie, namely in individuals. It has value too in (5) demonstrating the variety and difference between individuals, in (6) contrasting individual perceptions with the clichés and conformities of the categories embedded in our socio-cultures, in discussing the relationship between an individual and his socio-culture, and finally in (7) discussing the relationship between an individual and other individuals. Socio-culture is an impersonal force; value-culture is the real and the personal.

Now, as we saw on p. 29, socio-culture is less real than individual consciousness, and parasitic on it. As we saw both there and in Chapter 2, values cannot be derived from social laws, for this would mean that the former were merely relative. These conclusions may be supported too by the following remarks : that, as with perceptions, so with values; both perceptions and moral judgments cannot be made save by conscious human beings. History and society, being insensate forces, do not utter moral opinions; and if I am reminded that 'the law' is sometimes said to do so, I shall reply that this is a mere manner of speaking : it is in fact those who administer, conduct or discuss the law who utter opinions for which *they* claim legal force. If, on the other hand, I am reminded of such 'moral authorities' as religious and political creeds, and am asked if the individual does not have (according to such creeds) a 'duty' to them, I shall reply that it is always an individual's decision whether he adopts such a belief or not; so that it is *he* who attributes the duty to himself and the authority to his creed. Moreover, such 'moral authorities' are always composed of, and their decisions proferred by, conscious individuals (sometimes by a single conscious individual, such as the Pope or the First Secretary of the Communist Party of Russia). This must be so, for history is not only blind, but dumb; society is an abstraction, and cannot hold a pen; and churches are defined theologically (and correctly) as their own human membership.

In short, (*a*) only conscious individuals make moral judgments and (*b*) such conscious individuals are always more real than the abstractions (such as society, history, communism, the church) among which they move.

Human beings are the source of values. But they are also the purpose of values, and for much the same reasons. For instance one cannot speak of 'doing good' to an insensate object like a stone. One speaks, it is true, of 'treating an allotment well', but this is either a metaphor, or else it is by virtue of the indirect good thus done to conscious human beings that we use the turn of phrase. More convincingly perhaps, it might be objected that we speak of 'conferring great benefits on France' or 'on the local miners' union'. But, as I have pointed out elsewhere in this book, such phrases are meaningless unless they signify 'on the French' and 'on the members of the local miners' union'.

Individual consciousnesses are thus both the source and the purpose of values. We must therefore conclude that the value of a socio-culture resides in the degree of benefit it confers upon the individuals who partake in it. The more it values individual consciousness, the more it will be led to defer to that value. And, since value-culture (as we have just seen) tends both to promote a more lucid and perceptive consciousness and to increase the value put upon consciousness in general, it follows that *one important index of the merit of a socio-culture will be the extent to which it prizes value-culture.*

We are thus now in a position to refute such a typical example of the modern educationist's philistinism as the following:

> It is misleading to equate 'culture' with 'high culture', i.e. the style, outlook, language uses, tastes and interests of particular groups, mainly those educated in the arts and humanities . . . Culture is essentially process. Its understanding requires us to examine the meanings which men develop in and through social interactions . . . Moreover, the use of the qualifier 'high' is a valuation: the culture in question is being rated higher than others. Are we entitled to make such a judgment?   (Reynolds & Skilbeck 1976, p. 71)

Yes, indeed, we are so entitled.[14]

Society is but an area of experience among others. It interacts with individuals, and it interacts with their knowledge of reality. But both the individual consciousness and Nature are logically prior to society. For society is *composed* of individual consciousnesses, and has to *submit* to Nature. It is misleading of writers on education to say things such as this:

> Education is only one part of a more general process which we call socialization. Socialization begins at birth and ends only with death. Education is primarily deliberate learning, which fits the individual for a highly specialized job in society.   (Worsley 1970, p. 159)

Certainly the sociologist of education can only treat the question of education from this point of view; for this approach is imposed upon him by the subject-matter of sociology itself. But then, to that extent, sociology is itself a misleading and falsificatory study. For education in facts, other than socially required, socially admitted, and socially 'useful' facts, has here been totally omitted. Should we learn merely what society would have us think, those patterns of behaviour and of understanding to which it would have us conform? There are other truths. Education should be a training in perception first and foremost, since we can only arrive at 'facts' about nature and about individuals by recognizing the difficulties inherent in our attempts to understand them, difficulties which are caused by the limitations of our perceptual faculties and of our socially imposed categories. It might be, then, that *education should be primarily a training in value-culture and in science*, as Whitehead, Herbert Read and many others have proposed.[15]

To treat value-culture, then, as a mere subdivision of socio-culture, is to make a grave, even a fundamental, mistake. Value-culture is not totally divorced from socio-culture, certainly : what human creation is? But it is something else as well, namely a technique of knowing and a mode of knowledge. As if they had foreseen this claim, *some sociologists have gone so far as to assert that knowledge itself is totally controlled by social factors*. According to the 'new direction' sociologists of 1971, all socio-cultures are relative : none can be said to be 'better' or 'worse' than any other. This must imply that there is no way of standing outside socio-cultures to compare them, since, though we may describe their differences, any implicit judgment that is present in such descriptions is itself conditioned by the socio-culture to which we owe allegiance. It would follow, therefore, that eighteenth-century Spain with its Inquisition must be as 'tolerant' a socio-culture as twentieth-century Sweden; and that Aztec society with its mass human sacrifices is as 'kindly' a socio-culture as the permissive Samoa. Morally, there can be no objection to *suttee*; or to the Khasis of Assam, who used to push two sharpened sticks up the noses of any little boy that they caught until the child, in the belief that the more he cried and screamed, the more delighted the Gods were. This is clearly as reasonable a belief as is our own in the rightness of giving presents to our children at Christmas! Similarly, according to relativist principles, the World Health Organization is grievously at fault in condemning (as it did recently) the operations of clitoridectomy and infibulation. (These involve respectively (1) excising the clitoris so as to destroy the equal partnership of women in sexual pleasure, and (2) slicing off the labia minora and sewing up the vagina at puberty so as to ensure that all brides must be virgins. The former practice is widespread in Black Africa, in Egypt, Syria and Iraq; both practices are *combined* in the Sudan, Ethiopia and Somalia.[16] It follows that a relativist cannot be a feminist.)

Relativists cannot possibly object to such practices. For if all societies are equally valid, all societies are equally utopian . . . or, for that matter, equally anti-utopian. For it is then impossible even to *compare* one society with another, and thus to express a moral preference for (say) modern Scotland as against that of John Knox, or for the modern English criminal code as against the eighteenth-century use of hanging as the punishment for over 100 crimes. Relativism therefore makes complete nonsense of the idea that any society can be either improved or impaired.[17]

One can thus operate a *reductio ad absurdum* on moral relativism – though there is a somewhat bitter irony involved in the fact that some people actually hold the absurd views that I have just lampooned. I find for instance a Christian apologist writing :

> If I hear that one of my neighbours has killed another neighbour's child, given that he is sane, my condemnation is immediate . . . But if I hear that some remote tribe practises child sacrifice, what then ? I do not know what sacrifice means for the tribe in question. What would it mean to say I condemned it when the 'it' refers to something I know nothing about ? If I did condemn it I would be condemning murder. But murder is not child sacrifice.
>
> (Phillips 1970, p. 237)

By the same token, 'there's nothing wrong with Hitler's extermination of the Jews. It was just the accepted Nazi way of doing things.' Phillips doesn't say this, but to be consistent he ought to. For if we define morality as custom, we destroy the very notion of morality. Which, I think, is what G.B.Shaw meant to suggest by defining custom as *immorality*. We should have no truck with people for whom the opposite of conformity is deformity.

I am not here misrepresenting the 'new direction' sociologists. Their views can be examined in Michael Young's *Knowledge and Control*, though it must be admitted that Young's own standpoint is particularly difficult to follow, since he affects an indigestible prose which might be intended either to give his views the cachet of 'scientific' jargon, or, by disguise, to protect them from attack. The clearest analysis of his standpoint that I have seen is Denis Lawton's, though I must caution the reader that Young does not present his views as necessarily correct : he offers them as worthy of consideration. Let us then by all means consider them. Lawton's analysis of *Knowledge and Control* produces the following five propositions : (1) that education in a capitalist society is a tool of ruling class interest, that is, that it is a way of keeping the poor poor; (2) that we should look with suspicion at what counts for knowledge in our society, and see what counts as the most important knowledge, for such definitions are arbitrary and their purpose is to preserve the social *status quo*; (3) 'that if the existence of subjects results in an unfair distribution of knowledge in society, then subjects should be abolished' (Lawton 1975, p. 62); (4) that there is no such thing as knowledge: it is socially constructed, and relative to the socio-culture; and (5) that rationality itself is merely a convention.[18]

Similar views are held by other writers. Most of the contributors to *Knowledge and Control* assent to some or all of these propositions. The first (that education's function is to keep the poor in their place) seems to be shared by the French theorist Pierre Bourdieu (in Brown 1973). Brian Jackson, Director of the Advisory Centre for Education, writes:

And who can doubt, seeing the evidence, that if – as individuals – the middle class wish for an open education system, as a group they shut the poor out partly in order to grease their own access to university opportunities?

Later in the same passage he says: 'Knowledge is dynamite, and schools have to see it is handled harmlessly', a remark which seems to mean, in its context, that knowledge is deliberately made irrelevant to poor children (Jackson 1973, p. 232). The influential educational sociologist Basil Bernstein writes that the organization, distribution and evaluation of knowledge is controlled by 'the social context' and by 'power relationships'; that the notion of 'educability' is also dependent on these (in Cosin *et al.* 1971, p. 65); and that to classify knowledge and experience is an act of social control (in Reynolds & Skilbeck 1976). Reynolds and Skilbeck put forward the view that the function of examinations is to 'maintain the present class structure of society' (1976, p. 33); and George Molnar says: 'There is no conclusion beyond the obvious one. Exams are a means of social control in an authoritarian sense.'[19] Ioan Davies writes that 'Institutional education, as much as politics or the mass media or religion, is an attempt to initiate students into the rituals of a dominant culture. As such, it is the prerogative of a controlling elite' (in Brown 1973, p. 334). As anyone who interests himself in education must be aware, these are but a handful of the writers from whom I might have quoted. A recent Open University textbook (which has a large number of contributors) has the following remarks on its back cover: 'Most of the authors represented [here] see education as a form of social reproduction or of social control' (Dale 1976).

As for Young's proposition (4), that knowledge is entirely relative, the well-known philosopher of science, Thomas Kuhn, is often quoted as claiming that the later of two scientific theories is not necessarily 'a better approximation to truth. I believe that nothing of that sort can be found' (in Lakatos & Musgrave 1970, p. 265). (I doubt, by the way, that Kuhn is in fact a relativist. But his statements are often quoted triumphantly by them.) Ioan Davies writes that 'All knowledge is shrouded in ideology' (in Hopper 1971, p. 129) and that ' "knowledge" is anything that "makes sense" to people in society' (Ibid., p. 130). Young himself criticizes two authors for 'drawing on a metaphysical "out there", in terms of which, they claim, we must check our theories against our practice' (1971, p. 43). Whatever can Davies and Young suppose? That there is no external reality? And that, in the north of England where folk-wisdom advises you to draw the curtains while you are lighting the fire, sunlight puts fires out, whereas in the south of England it does not? These writers should perhaps be called the Christian Scientists of sociology.

Along with this attack on knowledge there sometimes goes an assault on the fundamental medium by which knowledge is communicated, namely literacy. Skilbeck and Harris make the cryptic remark that one of the extracts they publish in their Open University textbook 'shows that the analysis of the place of reading in the curriculum provokes value-questions and provides plenty of scope for ideological thinking' (Skilbeck & Harris 1976, p. 16). One can only assume that their meaning is the same as Neil Postman's when he writes : 'Teachers of reading comprise a most sinister political group . . .' (1973, p. 86) or as Enzensberger's when he writes : 'Alienating factors cannot be eradicated from written literature . . . Learning to write forms an important part of authoritarian socialization by the school' (1970, p. 32). Sir Edmund Leach, the most eminent social anthropologist of his generation, has written a short attack on literacy in *The Observer*,[20] claiming that reading and writing are important only because our socio-culture has deemed them to be so – which, according to him, it no longer does. It is not clear how seriously one should take such an article; but, considered or not, it is at least evidence of a 'gut response', of the emotional reflex reaction of the provost of an ancient Cambridge college against the basic tools of knowledge, the basic medium of intelligent communication. This attitude may sadden us, but should not surprise us too much. For if one holds, first, that any activity whatever is given value by – and only by – its function in the social system; and if, secondly, one 'cannot accept quality distinctions between cultures' (as Donald Swift, a professor of education, writes in Richardson & Spears 1972, p. 156); then it necessarily follows that literacy is no more or less intrinsically valuable than crossing oneself, eating snakes, or practising human sacrifice.

For Young's proposition (5), that rationality is a convention peculiar to our socio-culture, one might quote Thomas Gladwin in his support.[21] The Wittgensteinian philosopher Peter Winch has also sought to assert that 'If *our* concept of rationality is a different one from [someone else's], then it makes no sense to say that anything either does or does not appear rational to *him* in *our* sense' (in Wilson 1970, pp. 97–8). (This, of course, might be true enough of the beginnings of communication between the two people in question; but can we rest content with such mutual incomprehension?) One must also add that some Marxists evidently find their own worship of the laws of history so easily refutable by the tools of reason, that they assert reason's relativity *to* history. Thus Milton Fisk writes: 'reason takes second place to history', and objects to the use of reason in establishing a political system.[22] The influential philosopher Marcuse asserts that, since science and the established political order are interrelated, if society were to change, scientific facts would have to change: 'science would arrive at essentially different concepts of nature and establish essentially different facts. The rational society subverts the idea of Reason' (Marcuse 1964, pp. 166–7). What an emphatic use of the word 'essentially'!

Now it is true that some of these writers affect to be putting forward such views merely as possible ones. However, there seems to be a reluctance on their part to examine precisely whether such views are tenable or not. Ioan Davies shelters behind the restricted field with which sociology must concern itself: he tells us that he is seeking 'to avoid the non-sociological position of looking at education in its own terms' (in Brown 1973, p. 318). Skilbeck and Harris mount what is to some extent a reasonable attack on the objectivity of science, but in such terms that the incautious reader might well take it that, since science is not totally objective, it could be totally subjective; and they then dismiss the topic with the words: 'However, it is not necessary for us to enter into this complex debate.'[23] But on the contrary, there is every need for us to enter into it, since Young's five propositions are all interdependent, and if one falls probably all must fall. We must investigate the objectivity of knowledge, because Jackson's assertion that the education system is a tool of social privilege *and nothing else*, rests ultimately on the question whether knowledge is or is not *totally* conditioned by society. We should therefore ask this question: are Young's five propositions tenable, or are they on the contrary either untenable or so dubious as to merit little serious attention?

Let us start with his fifth proposition. For if it is unreasonable to be reasonable, then I might as well stop writing this chapter, and the reader might as well stop reading it. Now Young neither states which rational principles he takes exception to, nor does he propose any others to put in their place. If, however, we take the basic principle of reason to be that we cannot hope to arrive at any common agreement save by discussion; and if discussion involves (as it always does) pointing out contradictions, either within a theory, or between the theory and experience; then an attack on reason involves an attack both on discussion and on the hope of agreement (cf. Popper 1966, Vol. 2, Ch. 23). It is difficult then to see what action those in disagreement could resort to, except to violence of one kind or another. Humanity's great gift of language would be dispensed with in favour of the fist and the bullet.

We can, however, be even more precise in our objections to Young. For to be able to apprehend each other's meanings at all, we need certain rational principles. Two of these principles are as follows: (1) the meaning of *statement A* is the same as *A*'s meaning; and (2) if *statement A* contradicts another *statement B, A* contradicts *B*. If Young's statement is not subject to these principles, it neither affirms nor denies anything.

Moreover, Young's statement also rests upon this further principle: (3) that whatever is true must have a sufficient reason why it is true. For he states that it is a sufficient reason for believing rationality to be dubious, that rationality is relative to our society. Now, as I say, Young neither states which rational principles he takes exception to, nor does he propose any other principles to replace them with. But that is neither here not there. For if, to make his statement, he needs these three principles, and if, by using them, I can refute his statement, then he is lost. For it is then clear that he cannot make this statement at all except by assuming the validity of the laws of reason.

Perhaps Young might reply that this only applies to his statement as it is couched in English, and that there is perhaps some other language belonging to some other socio-culture in which these laws do not apply. I must say that, if this is so, the onus is on him to prove it. For if, in any given language, the meaning of his statement were not the same as its meaning, or if it did not contradict what it purports to contradict, then it would mean something other than Young means, or contradict something other than reason. Alternatively, if his statement were true without there being a sufficient reason for it to be true, then the sense of 'true' would be different. If any of these three conditions is not observed, in any conceivable language, then the meaning of Young's statement would be different. In short, it is impossible for Young to mean what he means, unless he observes these three rules of rationality. His statement thus cannot refute these three rules; and since they are the foundations of reasonable argument, we can happily continue with reason in refuting his other propositions.

It may be said in passing that irrationalism probably entails self-destruction. For if someone were to take self-contradiction and disregard for sufficient cause, to be a possible mode of behaviour, then he would be not only intellectually, but physically, lost. For if it is not a sufficient cause of someone's death that he shoots himself through the heart, or that he immerses himself under water for an hour or so, or that he asphyxiates himself with cyanide gas, then he may by all means do any of these things. The proof of the pudding is in the eating, and we may appeal to the irrationalist to explain precisely why he does not in practice perform any of these acts. I suspect he would find it difficult unless he were to use the familiar mode of reasoning.[24]

Furthermore, it may be doubted whether reason can be questioned, save with the tools of reason. If we suppose even that reason is finally inadequate to describe the world, it remains true that only reason can tell us when reason has broken down. According to the mystical doctrines of Buddhism, the higher reality which is immanent in the appearances of this world, is ineffable : it cannot be talked about, only pointed to or hinted at, by for instance using the tools of reason to demonstrate that reason can take us only so far but no further. Mādhyamika philosophy for example rests upon this fundamental rational principle : namely that when our statements about the world contradict each other, it can be seen that our reasoning about the world is inadequate (see Murti 1955, passim). But, as I say, we are then beyond speech, because speech embodies rational principles, and is inadequate to express the super-rational. Young would thus be reduced to silence.

We may, then, with a clear conscience reject Young's fifth proposition, and use the tools of reason in attacking the other four. The fourth of these, on which the first three depend, states that knowledge is socially constructed, and is relative to the society in which the alleged 'knowers' find themselves. There is of course a kernel of truth in this proposition; but it is of a limited kind. It is true to this degree : that what we accept as true is conditioned by our experience, and this again is largely conditioned by society. It is true also in this respect : that the models which people propose and with which they seek to explain physical phenomena, are often drawn from other areas of understanding within the socio-culture. Thus Freud's theory of repression and sublimation has been (rather cynically) explained as the result of applying the model of the steam engine, with its pressures and its safety valves, to the human mind. However, (1) there is a distinction between on the one hand what is true and accepted as true, and on the other hand what is false but accepted as true; and (2) the provenance of a theory may perhaps suggest to us whether it is more or less likely or unlikely. But its correspondence to the facts has nothing to do with its provenance.

The sociologists of knowledge[25] seem to hold a Whorfian view of understanding, according to which people in different socio-cultures actually see reality in different ways. I have already discussed Whorf's theories elsewhere (Martin 1975a, Ch. 10), so I shall be brief here. To 'see reality in different ways' is ambiguous. The physical basis of perception is clearly the same in all peoples. If there are differences in perception, then these must be due to the different ways of categorizing experience, and perhaps to different underlying 'philosophies', present in different languages.

It is, however, difficult to set up experiments which test this theory. For, the moment two observers from different cultures are presented, in an experimental situation, with, say, a set of colours to distinguish, they are immediately put on their guard : their attention is aroused, and they will no longer be in their normal position of *automatically* classifying these colours according to the normal categories of their own language. Of course the facts are the same for both of them; and of course they are likely to be seeing these facts (as far as their eyesight is concerned) in the same way. In the circumstances it is . . . highly remarkable that the experiment related by Brown succeeded at all.[26]   (Ibid., p. 125)

This quotation illustrates the two planks of my own case in the present book : (1) that on the one hand perception is to some extent conditioned and limited by the language we use; but (2) that on the other hand these limitations can be at least partially overcome.[27] And indeed, sociologists must beware : if our perceptions are so controlled by our own socio-culture that we cannot understand the perceptions of another, different society, then social anthropology becomes quite simply impossible.

We must therefore assume that a person from one socio-culture may be given a considerable degree of understanding about the categories which operate in another one. For instance, an Eskimo who has numerous words for different sorts of snow, has at his disposal an extremely useful discriminatory tool. But a North American who lives long enough with the Eskimos can perfectly well gain some understanding of the necessary distinctions. Thus, when we visit France again and again, we may in time begin to understand exactly what differentiates the use of certain French words from their 'equivalents' in English; and we may begin to use them correctly. I do not necessarily assume that one will ever be able to use all of the necessary distinctions with the accuracy and subtlety of a native speaker. But this is not a perfect world; and the fact that we can make such considerable progress with a foreign language demonstrates that the distinctions we make are not totally conditioned by the language which our socio-culture imposed on us as children; that the individual human being can be more perceptive than his socio-culture; and that, in short, the interaction between the real world and our perceptions is the instrument which tests and judges the conventions of all socio-cultures. As Pring says,

one may give a sociological account of why we come to make the distinctions we do; but there must be something about the world which makes these distinctions possible. *That* we distinguish between cats and dogs may be due to certain social conditions; that we *can* so distinguish has something to do with cats and dogs.
                     (Pring 1972, p. 25)

And, I should add, the moment we can perceive a distinction that is not imposed upon us by our socio-culture, this proves that our perceptions are to that extent free of socio-cultural control.[28]

However, there is no need for further argument. As I above operated a kind of *reductio ad absurdum* on the notion that all societies are equal, so I shall do again here. The Trobriand Islanders, Malinowski tells us, do not posssss the concept of paternity: according to them, men have nothing to do with procreation, they think a spirit from the sea is responsible, and there is no word for 'father' in their language. Now, because our society and theirs take different views of procreation, is there no objective fact to discover here? Is there no way of telling whether fathers produce children or not?[29] Similarly, if knowledge is merely relative, how did it happen that when Columbus discovered the West Indies, he did not find himself standing alone on the shore, while the members of his crew had all fallen over the edge of the flat earth – since this is what their socio-culture had told them would be their fate? If knowledge is merely relative, then how did it come about that Japanese working people whose socio-culture knew nothing of atomic bombs, could be destroyed in their thousands at Hiroshima? Next time that one of our sociologists of knowledge falls ill, let him visit the Mongolian shamans, in the equal validity of whose knowledge he so evidently trusts.

Am I being unfair? I have already pointed out that Young claims only a partial relativity of knowledge. But if knowledge is partly, gradually and painfully arrived at, as I should myself agree; if it is a matter not of certainty but of approximation, this still means that there are better and worse approximations, and better or worse methods of arriving at them. If the history of science has taught us anything, it has taught us that. Those relativists who assert partial relativity, but talk and write as if it were complete, are in practice confusing two different propositions: they are confusing 'Most knowledge has some degree of unreliability' with 'All knowledge is equally unreliable'; and such confusion assorts ill with their often important reputations and positions.

But they are not even consistent with themselves. It is no good arguing that society is badly made if your very basis for so arguing is that there are no criteria for deciding whether a society is badly made or not. For, if all socio-cultures are equal, why ever seek to change one of them? If justice, truth and (presumably) happiness are relative to the society which gives them its own slanted definitions, then why should these educational sociologists be so eager to propose that schools should be actively used by the teachers in them, in an attempt to change society?[30] If everything is relative, no change can be asserted to be either for the better or for the worse. If all is relative, why agitate for reform? And equally, if all is relative, why be so eager that working-class socio-culture (for instance) should *not* be reformed?

For this is their view. According to them, there is no such thing as 'cultural deprivation' because no socio-culture is better than any other; hence, we should not try to educate working-class children, for that would be trying to alter their socio-culture.[31] To put such an attitude into practice would result for instance in our teaching only bingo, beer-drinking and brass-band playing in northern English working-class schools, on the grounds that these are the local 'cultural' (i.e. socio-cultural) activities. Now there is everything to be said for brass bands; but this is because they are in fact a value-cultural activity as well as a socio-cultural one, and consequently promote the intellectual and perceptual development of their members. Brian Jackson (who is typical of these writers) makes no such distinction. The list of 'cultural' activities which he gives in a *New Society* article runs as follows:

> Spend any time in a decaying back street, and you'll see how important television or football pools are. Or chalking on walls. Or pulling a motorbike to pieces. Or a group of girls dolling up each other's hair. Why isn't the education service there, putting on children's chalking competitions, building runnable cars out of junk, dress making, street theatre, 'Holiday at Home' weeks?
>
> (Jackson 1973, p. 230)[32]

From his book *Working Class Community* we could no doubt elicit certain aspects of television, brass bands, and the jazz club, as value-cultural. He himself makes no such distinction. And we may justifiably complain, not so much of the paucity of working-class value-culture nor of some of Jackson's own proposals (both of which on this evidence contain some excellent elements), but of his uninterest in distinguishing between valuable and not-so-valuable activities. Why does he not for example take someone like Billy Connolly as an instance of how a working-class socio-culture can develop its own value-culture into marvellous wit and verve? Why not instance the moving musical 'soliloquies' of any number of folk-singers?

And this is the crux. If no activity is better than any other, then we shall never be disposed to favour some more than others. Indeed, if working-class culture is so well justified in its own terms, one might wonder why Jackson is worried about it at all. But at least one knows why the rest of us should be worried. To confine working-class children to working-class cultural activities is to limit their intellectual and perceptual development. The object of training any child is to continually extend and expand the horizons of his perceptual life, not to confine them narrowly within the bounds of the socially permitted. Brass bands are excellent things; folk-songs are poetry and the musicalization of feeling. Learning to appreciate them is a never-ending process; and they also constitute two doors open on the whole world of poetry and music. I am not suggesting that they be used merely as stepping-stones to 'higher things'; for the values implicit in them are implicit too in the whole of poetry and the whole of music. I am merely saying that a child's acquaintance with such things must not be *restrictive*.[33]

If we restrict a child to his own value-culture, we are behaving no differently from Dr Verwoerd when he recommends :

The Bantu teacher must be integrated as an active agent in the process of the development of the Bantu community. He must learn not to feel above his community. He becomes frustrated and rebellious when this does not take place, and he tries to make his community dissatisfied because of such misdirected ambitions which are alien to his people.

(Quoted by Alan Watkins in *The Observer*, 8 August 1976) Such policies are an artificial constriction of the mind, and are intended as such.

To prevent a child from extending its horizons as far as its vision will permit, is an act of oppression. It is also unwise, even from society's own point of view. For the more of its citizens have more understanding, the greater the benefit to society. After all, this is the entire purpose of sociology itself: to make us more aware of what society is, and no longer take it so for granted that we did not even know we were taking it for granted, or else took it to be ordained by nature. To see society quite objectively is no doubt impossible; but to gain *some* degree of understanding of it is no doubt feasible. Anthropology will help in allowing us to compare one society with another; sociology will help in allowing us to question how society actually operates; science will help in showing us the biological and physical conditions of our existence; literature will help in reminding us of our primary nature as individuals, both of society and not of it. All these activities perform a function *vis-à-vis* society which is similar to the function performed by poetry within language : they reveal the hitherto accepted and hence the hitherto unknown – they attack the automatic conformism of the system in which we live.

It will be plain where the sociological viewpoint has gone astray. It has confused value-culture and socio-culture, by denying the former any function other than the social, and the class-social at that. It is easy to understand why it has done this : it is, in the first place, because the word 'culture' is used by sociologists in merely one of its two senses; in the second place, because, according to these sociologists, it looks as if it is not the working-class who go in for value-culture. However, it is equally easy to identify the mistake, and to clear it up : *socio-culturally*, and only in their *social* manifestations, the arts have sometimes been thought to be 'bourgeois' (though, as the reader will have seen, I think this is a mistake due to inadequate research and too crude analysis); but *value-culturally*, they are nothing of the kind : for they are nothing less than techniques for promoting individual awareness and for refreshing human perception.

3. In Praise of Value-Culture

No doubt we cannot be content with the situation as it is, since value-culture is appreciated only by a minority (although this minority has probably little to do with 'class'). But what should be done to improve this state of affairs? We do not restrict doctors to middle-class patients on the grounds that doctors 'belong to middle-class culture'. Similarly, value-culture exists for people, not to be defended from them. It is not value-culture that is the social disease, but people's general indifference to it, living as they do in a philistine socio-culture, taught (often) by philistine teachers. Clearly, we must civilize Philistia, or at least increase its level of civilization. But in this task, certain schools of sociology will be of no help at all.[34] For the definition of sociology as a subject is the study of human affairs in social, and not in any other, terms. There is a parable by Eddington which relates how a Greek philosopher (let us call him Ichthyon) set about studying marine biology. He let down into the sea a large net with a two-inch mesh. He then studied the creatures he had caught, laying them out systematically along the quay-side. His first conclusion? 'All fish are at least two inches long.'

Similarly, since sociology measures knowledge and value-culture as social phenomena, it cannot help but see them *only* as social phenomena. Like Ichthyon, we can none of us see further than the limitations of our tools.[35] There is a school of sociology, many of whom are particularly influential in education, which sees only social facts, and which can see only that aspect of scientific facts and that aspect of individuals which can be 'explained' by social facts. Certainly there are social scientists who are very different.[36] But one notes Wilding's view that social science normally tends to devalue the importance of the individual. And Mary Douglas writes that 'The first source of our troubles as cultural anthropologists is that we have no adequate conception of the individual.' She speaks of the danger of putting 'a mindless robot in place of an intelligent human being'. 'All too often', writes the editor of *New Society*, 'in current British sociology, the individual – who has choices, interests and an intelligence – vanishes' (Wilding 1976).[37] It follows that, if we are to improve our philistine education system, we need to have fewer sociologists in positions of power and influence; and we need to have more scientists, mathematicians and people who know what value-culture is about. Then perhaps the practice of the arts might be made a central part of education.

The shallow and unthinking egalitarianism[38] of the British mid-seventies is partly an effect of this underlying philistinism. It doubtless also has something to do with the 'counter-culture' celebrated by

Roszak, in whom justified horror at the aberrations of Western society has led to an unjustified but equal horror at most of its achievements. Young's denial of the value of reason could be attributed to this.[39] But the reader will recall the old proverb 'In the country of the blind the one-eyed man is king', and Wells's pessimistic commentary on it in 'The Country of the Blind'. A valley in the Andes has been cut off from all human contact for generations; a strange disease ensures that the whole population is blind, and that all the children born to them are blind. Into this isolated community a climber, Nuñez, comes. He at first thinks he might become their ruler; for he alone has sight. But it soon dawns upon him that there is no such possibility. He is regarded by the natives as their inferior, because he is different; and one of them discovers that what differentiates him from them is connected with his eyes, which cause his brain 'a constant irritation and distraction'. If he is to become equal and normal, he will evidently have to be blinded like everyone else. This, the natives propose to do. But Nuñez cannot bear the thought of losing his sight: he escapes, and lives to tell his tale to the outside world.

So runs the story. Its moral is ambiguous. In one sense, Nuñez's superiority over the blind natives of the valley is not real; for they are far more clever and dexterous than he . . . within their valley. In another sense, it is a tragic parable of the resentment of the majority against claims for special prescience which they can have no hope of understanding. In what follows, let us hold tight to both these interpretations.

Human beings are naturally inclined to differentiate themselves from groups to which they do not belong. It is hardly surprising that value-culture is, by most of the people within our socio-culture, regarded with puzzlement, hostility and contempt. They do not understand it, its prophets make absurd claims, it is not *theirs*. On the other hand, the advocates of value-culture are sometimes guilty of an unthinking *hubris*. After all, there are other things in life than Beethoven and Matisse, and I do not think we should have come very far without certain of the most widespread and basic human virtues. It behoves both sides to respect the other, and if necessary across the barrier of mutual incomprehension.

But, for this very reason, we should not accept the position of the egalitarian. Because value-culture is not appreciated by the majority is no reason for introducing an anti-cultural censorship. The nonconformist has his value. The man who invented fire was in a minority of one. (Or three, or four.) However ingenious the discovery of the plow, it was not invented by all peasants in all countries at five o'clock on the same afternoon. We do not argue that because everyone is not kind, we must destroy kindness. And this is because kindness is a good in itself. We might argue equally that because everyone is not cruel, therefore we should destroy cruelty; and this argument looks more plausible, because its conclusion is more acceptable. But logically it is equally fallacious. It is not because cruelty and kindness are not universally practised, that we admire the one and deprecate the other : it is because of their consequences. The test of worth is not how many people practise something : it is its usefulness.

We must therefore agree with Stuart Hampshire's complaint about the present British attitude to the arts, and with his analysis of what is wrong with it :

> The philistines still have the initiative, and both the major political parties encourage cant about 'the man in the street' and 'the plain man', and the need for 'democracy' in support of the arts. This is cant, partly because everyone, including the mythical man in the street, admires, studies and imitates the few supreme practitioners, and also the competent critics, in any pursuit that he takes seriously, whether it is an art, a craft, a game, a sport. No-one thinks that local connexions, earnest endeavour, and goodwill are any substitute for genius and talent in any pursuit in which they are really interested. But it is convenient for politicians to ingratiate themselves with this 'man of the people' style.
>
> (Hampshire 1977, discussing Minihan 1977)

In short, in any useful activity, it is the best that is sought; for the best is necessarily the most useful.

Equality or inequality has thus nothing whatever to do with the question. Nothing, at any rate, to do with the question of valuing any given activity. The only complaint that might be levelled against a given value-culture is that it is exclusive, that it excludes certain people from participating in it. But that is not a complaint about the *values* embodied in the value-culture; indeed, it would be a pointless complaint if it did not implicitly recognize that there *are* such values. Nobody minds being excluded from the Ik.[40]

Given, then, that the values embodied in our value-culture are real, the only question remains : how far and how fast is it practicable to spread them? The answer to this question depends on the will of politicians, on the capacities of artists, musicians, teachers and writers, on the capabilities of the population. Will, capacities and capabilities are all different in different individuals – or at least, I should like to be told of a society where this is not true. Egalitarians seem to believe that the innate capacities of all are exactly the same, that we are all born with precisely the same potential to become Beethovens, Shakespeares, Stalins, Henry Fords, Van Goghs, Buddhas and Rutherfords. However, the proposition does seem faintly improbable. As an adolescent, Bertrand Russell reports that he was so unhappy that he contemplated suicide, and was only prevented from committing it by his awakening interest in higher mathematics. As Gabor remarks, if you forced most adolescents to study higher mathematics, you might bring *them* fairly close to suicide. And the claim that the innate ability of all human beings is identical receives absolutely no support from those who have studied the question.[41] Certainly, we are doing very badly at the moment in our attempts to spread value-culture, and we should try to do better. But egalitarians should try to understand that, even if it is one day discovered that most people are born of different parents, in different places, and grow up into different individuals – even if (perish the thought) they are discovered to have different heredities – this is not a total disaster. The egalitarian dream, taken to any extreme, is in fact the disaster, expressed these days in parable form as the science fiction nightmare of the cloned human being, a tribe of absolutely identical people, all split off from the same germ plasm, in the utopian longing to become a race of identical machines. The themes of science fiction often reflect premonitions and forebodings about the real world. But I do not want to spend this life or any future one talking to myself, listening to myself, conversing with a hundred myselves, marrying myself, getting on the bus with myself, hearing political speeches by myself, and folksongs sung (invariably) by myself.

'Oh come now', the reasonable egalitarian will say, 'it won't be like that at all.' So he admits difference, does he? Let him be careful: any little difference is still a difference, and the moment I can distinguish between myself and another, I shall also be eager to say that I know more about X than he does, that he knows very little about Y, and that he has made astonishing progress since he thought Z. The solution to quality, equality and inequality must be sought elsewhere than in Procrustes's bed.

As Raymond Williams puts it,

> the only equality that is important, or indeed conceivable, is equality of being. Inequality in the various aspects of man is inevitable and even welcome; it is the basis of any rich and complex life. (1963, p. 304)

Now what is equality of being? It is of course the principle of the primacy of consciousness. We are each of us a universe unto ourselves. We do not all start from the same point, let alone reach it. Human beings begin at different points in mental space. There are then two judgments possible upon them. The first is this: the movement from the initial point that they achieve. My horizon may be limited by mountains, or enlarged by ocean. Let me therefore climb one of those mountains and expand my vision. Let me take a trip in a boat, and see the other side of the world. What is unforgiveable is to stand still. We shall all start from different points, move off at different speeds, end up at different destinations. On the way we shall need guides, for if some had not already gone part of the way, how little progress we ourselves would make! We can define the achievement of a society in terms of the complicated scatter of points reached by all the individuals within it; and we can define the progress of an individual in terms of his starting-point and the distance he has travelled. There are two principles, but progress lies behind both of them. And a man can be respected for the progress that he achieves, no matter how far on or how far back his starting point.

And from this we should take comfort. What would be the point of respecting other people if we respected them for being the same as ourselves? That would not be respecting other people, it would be congratulating ourselves. What would be the motive for requiring them to be like ourselves? The fact that we could not bear it when they were not, and that would be hating other people. To hate people so much for their differences from us that we insisted that all people were 'in fact' the same, would be a totalitarian reason for believing in democracy, for it would destroy the very reason for democracy by asserting that we ourselves know best.[42] Mistrust all those who assert equality while denying difference; for a man's liking for others is merely selfish unless he likes them for themselves, likes them (that is) for their *difference* from himself.

No people are uninteresting.
Their fate is like the chronicle of planets.

Nothing in them is not particular,
And planet is dissimilar from planet.

And if a man lived in obscurity
making his friends in that obscurity
obscurity is not uninteresting.

To each his world is private,
and in that world one excellent minute.

And in that world one tragic minute.
These are private.

. . .

Not people die but worlds die in them.[43]

Thus, however little I approve Michael F. D. Young's crude relativism, I cannot but agree with his namesake Michael Dunlop Young, when he writes wistfully of the 'classless society':

It would be one which both possessed and acted upon plural values. Were we to evaluate people, not only according to their intelligence and their education, their occupation, and their power, but according to their kindliness and their courage, their imagination and sensitivity, their sympathy and generosity, there could be no classes. Who would be able to say that the scientist was superior to the porter with admirable qualities as a father, the civil servant with unusual skill at gaining prizes superior to the lorry-driver with unusual skill at growing roses? The classless society would also be the tolerant society, in which individual differences were actively encouraged as well as passively tolerated, in which full meaning was at last given to the dignity of man. Every human being would then have equal opportunity, not to rise up in the world in the light of any mathematical measure, but to develop his own special capacities for leading a rich life.

(Young 1961, p. 169)

Young proceeds to quote from Matthew Arnold. The passage runs :

Culture works differently. It does not try to teach down to the level of inferior classes; it does not try to win them for this or that sect of its own, with ready-made judgments and watchwords. It seeks to do away with classes; to make the best that has been thought and known in the world current everywhere; to make all men live in an atmosphere of sweetness and light, where they may use ideas, as it uses them itself, freely, – nourished and not bound by them.

(Arnold 1932, p. 70)

This, I take it, is the moral of Young's satirical anti-utopia, though I am doubtful how sincere his expressed concern for intelligence and education is. For he apparently despises science as useless (all his instances of scientific endeavour are absurd or positively damaging);[44] and the arts fail to get more than a passing reference. He is, in short, quite probably as hostile to value-culture as his namesake; and my assent to the above quotation may be more honest than Young's, despite the fact that he happens to be its author. Young professes concern for multiple values; but his book subtly suggests that he disparages those of the arts and of the intellect. Whereas I should for my part willingly admit that there are different paths through life, and agree with Dennis Gabor when he stresses the importance of those individuals with a gift for morality and for kindness, or who can contribute to society through their capacity for communicating happiness to others[45] . . . or whose wisdom is not of a cerebral kind. We need *all* admirable human qualities. And is it not precisely in literature that the qualities of the ordinary man are most powerfully expressed? Value-culture is that civilizing element of society which reminds us that there is not simply one way of being human, of being good, useful or admirable; that the sage and the workman, the housewife and the technician are all individuals with a singular value of their own. I think of Sandburg's poems, of the characters of Dickens, of the harsh sympathy of R. S. Thomas for his Welsh peasants. I think of the wisdom that is to be found in Tolstoy's Platon Karatayev and, still better, in the courtesan Hermine in *Steppenwolf*.

Physically we are almost blind. Our eyes see only a tiny segment of the whole range of electro-magnetic radiation. We have two alternatives : to close our eyes, or to use what we have while trying to supplement our deficiencies. One does not recommend people to bandage their eyes in broad daylight and step off the pavement across the street; one recommends white sticks, guide-dogs and Braille. We must draw the logical conclusion for our minds too. Anything that enlarges our vision of the world is valuable. Socio-culture is a curtain drawn across reality, a *status quo* that filters but also blocks the light; value-culture is one of those activities that can tug open a few inches of oppressive curtain. Let us side with dispellers of illusion and purveyors of light : let us side with our artists and our scientists.

Appendix:
Consciousness and Meaning

In Chapter 1, I noted some (apparent) denials of the reality of consciousness. A still more recent attack on consciousness has been made by certain French structuralists. Culler briefly discusses their attitude, and remarks that 'once the conscious subject is deprived of his role as source of meaning . . . the self can no longer be identified with consciousness' (Culler 1975, p. 28). And he reminds us that indeed the sources of meaning include unconscious processes within the subject and social processes outside him. More and more of the self, he claims, can be explained as the result of such processes; more and more of it can be seen as the product of conventions.

No twentieth-century man is going to deny this; but it does not affect the issue of the reality of consciousness, for the self and consciousness must not be confused. The self is doubtless in part constructed by social influences, but *the fact of being conscious* is independent of them. Our perceptions too are to some extent free from such influences. All men may be presumed to see, feel, taste, smell and hear in basically the same way. Their more abstract deductions from this evidence may vary, certainly, but it seems probable that concrete perception is relatively free from, and categorization relatively subject to, social influences (see pp. 155–6). And the whole point of this book is to show how we may achieve some degree of freedom from these conventional categories. We may therefore attribute to the 'essential individual' the characteristics of consciousness and concrete or direct perception.

We have not thereby disposed of the structuralist argument completely, however, since if meaning is not bestowed by the individual but by a combination of linguistic, social and unconscious forces, it is outside the control of the conscious individual. Structuralists speak of this denial of primacy to consciousness as the 'deconstruction' of the individual; for he is seen as being entirely analysable into what caused his delusive individuality. Analysable in principle, that is; for the deconstruction of the individual must remain unproven, because in the case of any particular individual, little of the alleged influencing and controlling processes is available for inspection.

A further difficulty for the theory of deconstruction is that, if social factors are asserted to entirely produce the individual's meanings, then the individuals who assert this are claiming that their assertion is itself produced by those social factors. Needless to say, this casts doubt upon the assertion, which can only be valid if it is based on observations that are *not* controlled by social factors; but if there are such observations, then the assertion itself is invalidated. At the very least, the assertion must depend on the evidence of the senses; so that the evidence of the senses is not assailable (cf. the epigraph to Chapter 1 by Democritus).

It must also be pointed out that the test of reference is consciousness. By this I mean that we can only know by observation whether an alleged event actually occurred or not. A fiction cannot be identified as a fiction except by observing that it did not occur, and a fact can only be known to be a fact by observing that it did (cf. pp. 9–10). In addition, the assignment of an object to a particular category involves an act of judgment which can be performed only by a conscious individual. Admittedly, the category and its criteria may be 'given' by the linguistic community; but a conscious individual is required (1) for the perception of the object and (2) to judge that it belongs to a certain category.[1]

We have therefore saved some elements of the individual from the structuralists' sweeping denial : namely consciousness, concrete perception, and judgments about truth and about appurtenance to categories. The outer fringes of individuality, however, might perhaps come under the structuralist ban. It might in theory be possible to deconstruct the personality into social and unconscious forces. However (to take social forces first) it is equally possible to deconstruct them into individual perceptions and actions. We would then have the situation of the individual being influenced by other individuals. But in that case the individual is not merely passive, but an actor in a process of mutual influence and interaction.

As for unconscious influences, these come from within each individual separately, and although the underlying unconscious processes in all human beings may be similar, nothing permits us to assert that they are in all cases identical, and still less allows us to deny that different individuals react in different ways to them. We may again assert, therefore, the difference between individuals.

Furthermore, when a language system contains the term 'tree' to denote tree, this means in fact that the individuals within that language community are in the habit of so calling it. The language-system does not exist except within the individual minds of its users. As Culler says, 'Structures and relations . . . emerge only in a structuring process. And though the individual may not originate or even control this process – he assimilates its rules as part of his culture – it takes place through him, and one can gain evidence about it only by considering his judgments and intuitions' (1975, p. 30). Now what happens when one does inquire of individuals about the meanings of words in their personal language-system? One discovers that each speaker's system is broadly similar, but that there are always some small differences. An 'ear of wheat' is seen differently by an expert in cereal crops, a farmer and a townsman. They will agree about the reference, and they will agree about some of the connotations. But other connotations will be different from all three, for the meaning of a word varies with different individuals' experience of it and of its referent. Now this observation can be extended to *all individuals*, since all individuals' experience is subtly different in some respects, so that connotations will on occasion vary (cf. Martin 1975a, pp. 43–4). Whatever the reasons for this variation (and doubtless they are largely outside the control of the individual), it occurs within the individual, and it is therefore *individuals who mean* different things by their words. *The focus of meaning is thus the individual.*

If this conclusion is doubted, let us consider the evidence we can obtain from linguistics itself, of a common type of change in word-meaning:

> Leonard Palmer has a passage on the semantic change that took place in the meaning of the word *beads*. He has just been discussing its shift from the meaning 'prayers', metonymically to that of 'a rosary', and from thence to 'small round pierced objects usually strung together to form a necklace'. Either some hearer, on seeing rosary beads, had taken the word in the third sense given rather than the correct second one; or some inventive utterer had, consciously or unconsciously, made the semantic transfer. He considers the situation where rosary beads are being handed from one agent to another, but one is taking them merely to be 'small round objects, etc.' while for the other they are a rosary: 'What is important is that the speaker cannot correct this misapprehension in the hearer *because he does not know of it*; for it is only from the behaviour of the hearer that the speaker can know whether he has been successful in conveying this meaning or not. Since in this case the behaviour evoked is precisely what the speaker intended, the hearer exhibiting awareness of the indicated situation, there is nothing to show that, though the answer is right, the "arithmetic" is wrong.' One has 'divided through' and 'cancelled out', but the arithmetic is wrong. In another context with slightly different demands the answer might be wrong too for *one* of the agents. Imagine a monastery that has just received a bequest in the form of some jewels, including a necklace; the abbot asks a monk to bring the *beads*, and the necklace is brought. Not until that moment did the abbot know that the monk had, throughout years of communication with this word, been applying a different rule.
>
> (Wright 1977a, pp. 45–6)[2]

Edmond L. Wright (the author of this passage) has an elegant theory of the way two people achieve a common and reciprocal meaning out of their personal meanings. But, as he insists, the *basis* for this common and reciprocal meaning is the personal meanings involved. For it is only in so far as the two individuals are able to *use* their meanings in the same way that we may speak of a 'shared meaning'. There is always the logical possibility that the *rest* of their personal meanings are not shared.

But, to tell the truth, for personal meanings not to coincide is a common enough phenomenon. Wright instances a parliamentarian calling for the death penalty for I.R.A. terrorists because 'they are *making war* on the state'. As he says, 'Not everyone that heard him would agree with the correctness of his reference via the term *making war*, nor further to the deduction that he made based on his semantic criteria' (Wright 1976, p. 520). And indeed much of the present book testifies to the disagreements that can quite commonly arise over different people's different interpretations of words. It is in all cases *people* who apply words, and they do so according to criteria which may be more or less personal to them. That in general we tend to agree does not refute those cases where we evidently disagree.

It may clinch the whole issue if we consider it as follows. Structuralism claims that the 'source of meaning' is the system and not the individual. But is it possible to say and mean something that has never been said and meant before? Was it possible for Darwin to enunciate the theory of evolution, Marx to write the communist manifesto, Einstein to propose the theory of relativity, or even for myself to write Chapter 3 of this book? We know that it was. Now who or what is the 'source of meaning' in these cases? The system or the person using it? Language is a pre-existent tool which is used by people for their own purposes, which very frequently limits those purposes, but which sometimes can be adapted to new ones. Because a spade was not invented by me, it does not mean I am not using it. Nor that I cannot use it for some other purpose (as a lever, for instance, or a weapon). Nor that I cannot improvise some new object for a new purpose.

It matters little, therefore, whether we accept that the individual can theoretically be 'deconstructed'. For, influenced or uninfluenced, his experience still remains different from that of all other individuals; his meanings are therefore in some respects different too; he may institute new ones; and the only evidence we can obtain about these different meanings is *via* his consciousness. Consciousness retains its worth as ultimately the sole window upon language, as it is the sole window upon the world.

Besides, what is the purpose of consciousness? It is precisely to enable us to be aware of the forces, both exterior and interior, which act upon us, and so to select our own reactions to them. What defines the arts and sciences is precisely that they seek to discover and make conscious continually *more* of what had been hitherto unconscious. What other purpose could the effort towards 'deconstruction' itself have, but to prise open the tiny space of consciousness and freedom? 'Deconstruction' is thus a partial cure for the malady it itself diagnoses : once shown new areas of unfreedom, the space of freedom is enlarged.

Notes

Chapter One

1. Democritus of Abdera, Diels frg. 125; quoted in Schrödinger (1958, p. 103).
2. See Evans (1970, pp. 38-9) for a succinct statement of James's view. Polanyi & Prosch (1975) quote 'three authoritative voices denying the existence of human consciousness: (1) ". . . the existence of something called consciousness is a venerable *hypothesis* : not a datum, not directly observable . . ."; (2) ". . . although we cannot get along without the concept of consciousness, actually there is no such thing"; (3) "The knower as an entity is an unnecessary postulate." These three statements were made, respectively, by Hebb, Kubie and Lashley at a symposium on brain mechanisms and consciousness in 1954. It is not that these distinguished scientists really believe that consciousness does not exist. They know, for example, that pain exists. But they feel obliged to deny the existence of consciousness, for it eludes explanation in terms of science.' (pp. 25-6) My reaction is the same as Polanyi's : 'They don't mean it!' But I would add that, if by any chance they do mean it, they are denying that they know what they mean; so that their statements are self-contradictory.
3. Cf. Eddington (1928, pp. 51-2) : 'We have intimate acquaintance with the nature of time and so it baffles our comprehension.' Cf. also Whitrow (1961) who holds that 'the idea of time cannot be derived from prior concepts which involve no implicit appeal to it' (p. 288) and cites the mathematician L. E. J. Brouwer for whom 'the psychological fact that our minds operate by successive acts of attention . . . was the fundamental phenomenon of the human intellect . . .' (p. 119).
4. I wish to make no unnecessary exclusions, such as to preclude the possibility of stepping out of consciousness, or rather deepening its nature, that seems to be offered by the extraordinary agreement between mystics in the world's major religions. However, I do not wish to appeal to non-ordinary experience; and what I have written here about the locking of individual consciousness within itself, seems to be the universally normal experience.
5. The phenomenologist's point of view is that consciousness does not exist except as consciousness *of* something; that the perceiving subject and the perceived object can be 'in principle' separated, but not in practice. But as I say, whether this statement is correct or not does not matter at all in the present context.
6. Wigner (1967, pp. 187-8), somewhat condensed.
7. Cf. the epigraph to this chapter by Democritus.

8. If this passage is taken seriously as a model of the emergence of consciousness, and then of consciousness of the world, it has certain implications. It will be observed that the sense-data are present before the awareness of self. Does this suggest that consciousness is a construct *out of* sense-data; and therefore that our consciousness is dependent entirely on the presence of sense-data, and that they are primary? Actually, this statement is inexact: we can be conscious also of dreams; but this does not affect the issue. For we are still left with the suggestion that consciousness comes into existence only as an effect of certain mental processes.

   However, we should note that the initial sense-data are *conscious*, despite the fact that the self which is conscious of them has not yet been identified. The sense-data do not exist without consciousness, nor (in this passage) the consciousness without the sense-data. We might equally well suggest therefore that *located consciousness* is primary, located because it is attached to a particular point in space and time. The absence of an identified self is thus irrelevant; and this absence would fit in well with the speculations of child psychologists as we shall see below, since they believe that the self is gradually constructed by the child.

   Longer discussion of this point would not be in order here. I will merely observe that it does not affect my central point, that consciousness-*of* is prior to understanding the outside world. Huxley's description at least bears witness to this.

9. Evans (1970, pp. 60-2) mentions various philosophers such as Mill, S. H. Hodgson and William James, who have held the same view. It seems that Piaget and various psychologists of both Jungian and Freudian persuasions, also hold this opinion.

10. There is an ancient philosophical controversy about the relationship between knowledge, sensations and reality, but such statements as this by Gregory agree fairly well with Ayer's remark: 'in referring as we do to physical objects we are elaborating a theory with respect to the evidence of our senses' (1956, p. 147).

11. For accounts of this process, see for instance Mitchell (1975, p. 42); Piaget (1955, pp. 247-52, 318); and Winnicott (1967).

12. Huxley (1937, p. 253), where he bases himself on the views of Emile Meyerson.

13. See the refutation of Anglin (1970) by E. V. Clark in Moore (1973).

14. Margenau (1950, pp. 49-65); discussed in Martin (1975*a*, pp. 128-30).

15. For 'reversibility', see below, p. 22.

16. Margenau (1950, pp. 75-6); see Martin (1975*a*, pp. 133-4).

17. Hadrons: the strongly interacting nuclear particles.

18. Cf. the story of the discovery of Neptune and the supposed discovery of Vulcan (Martin 1975*a*, pp. 131-2).

19. The case could be made even stronger: the universe has a hazy and ambiguous quality at its base (cf. Martin 1975*a*,

pp. 58, 156-7). 'Absolutism' might perhaps best be defined
negatively, as follows: '"Liberty . . . is the possibility of
doubting, the possibility of making a mistake, the possibility of searching and experimenting, the possibility of
saying no to any authority – literary, artistic, philosophic,
religious, social, and even political." "But that," murmured
this eminent functionary of Soviet culture in horror, "that
is counter-revolution."' (Silone, in Crossman 1950,
p. 107).

20. Asymptote: 'a line which approaches continually nearer to
a given curve, but which does not meet it within a finite
distance'. The line meets the curve only at infinity, i.e. in
the mathematician's never-never land. ἀσύμπτωτος means
'not-together-falling'.

21. It would be relevant to cite Hume and Popper here.

22. A particularly clear and elegant statement of one of the
consequences of relativity theory can be found in Capra
(1975, p. 177). He is explaining that the length of an
object depends on its motion relative to the observer. 'It is
important to realize that it makes no sense to ask which is
the "real" length of an object, just as it makes no sense in
our everyday life to ask for the real length of somebody's
shadow. The shadow is a projection of points in three-
dimensional space onto a two-dimensional plane, and its
length will be different for different angles of projection.
Similarly, the length of a moving object is the projection of
points in four-dimensional space–time onto three-dimen-
sional space, and its length is different in different frames
of reference.'

23. Popper's account of scientific objectivity is identical. He
writes: 'ironically enough, objectivity is closely bound up
with the *social aspect of scientific method*, with the fact that
science and scientific objectivity do not (and cannot) result
from the attempts of an individual scientist to be "objective", but from the *friendly-hostile cooperation of many
scientists*. Scientific objectivity can be described as the
intersubjectivity of scientific method.' (Popper 1966,
vol. 2, p. 217, his italics.) He even goes so far as to say
that a Robinson Crusoe, alone on his island, using a method
and arriving at a result similar to normal science, would
not be acting scientifically. Perhaps this view might be
attacked by saying that Crusoe could try to treat his own
findings as critically as other scientists might. However,
that is neither here nor there.

At this point I had better defend myself against the
charge of relativism, particularly as I myself shall be
mounting a brutal attack on it later in the book. Unfortunately it is inadvisable to hold up the argument by a
lengthy excursus into the theory of knowledge. I shall
therefore make the briefest of statements.

Truth is *correspondence* between what we believe and
what is the case. It will be evident from what I have said
that no total correspondence can be achieved, but we may
hope for partial correspondence. How are we to arrive at

it, however? This is the real problem: what *shows* correspondence? I shall say that perceptual evidence *plus* coherence does so. Perceptual evidence tends to carry its own conviction for most of us most of the time: nothing is more real than pleasure, than the sight and smell of roses, than the taste of whisky, than the enfolding grasp of the sea, than (above all, I regret to say) pain. However, some of our (apparently) sensory experiences are hallucinations. So in problematic cases we need the additional check of one sense against another (as on p. 6 of this book), and the additional check of other people's perceptions against our own. These checks provide us with *coherence*.

As for more abstract theories of the nature of things, we proceed in an exactly similar way. We check the coherence of theory with theory, the coherence of sensory report against sensory report. The ultimate goal is to construct a world-picture in which all theory and all perceptual evidence are mutually coherent. This is the nearest we can get to correspondence.

If it is objected that, *logically*, this still does not *show* correspondence, I shall agree; but add that no other procedure will do as well; and if we seek an exit from our ignorant darkness, we have to take the most plausible way out. A man lost in a maze and confronted by five doorways may toss a coin if he has no better reason for choosing between them. But if one of them offers him his consciousness, his senses, his mind, and the consciousnesses of other living beings, he has reason to select that doorway. To do otherwise would be a rejection of his own nature, and also a rejection of the very way he proceeds and *must* proceed in the everyday business of life. It would be a self-destructive act.

24. Peirce (1931-5, vol. 6, pp. 264, 268). His argument seems to depend on the difficulty of thinking that consciousness could emerge as a totally novel and dissimilar phenomenon from the combination of unconscious chemicals. Consciousness *qua* consciousness cannot be broken down to these constituents: so how can they be its constituents? This is indeed a problem; and it is in no way resolved by the common way of treating it, which is simply to assert or hypothesize that it is so.

25. See *Nature*, 25 April 1964. Mentioned in Firsoff (1967, p. 102).

26. Schrödinger (1958). Cf. perhaps Ernst Haeckel's 'psychoplasm'.

27. They refer to Dicke (1961), who argues in effect that one can either ask: 'Here is the universe, so what must man be?' or: 'Here is man, so what must the universe be?' They claim that, out of all the possible structures and sizes that the universe might have had, it has precisely those which enable life, and hence consciousness, to exist. The universe is, as it were, inconceivably more finely tuned than one might have expected; and this fine tuning is precisely what enables consciousness to have emerged.

They therefore hazard the guess that it is because of consciousness that the universe is tuned as it is; and that consciousness does not merely observe, but *participates in*, the universe.

The argument, of course, is fallacious; for it is circular: if the universe had not been so finely tuned, we should not be here to observe the absence of fine tuning. Circular arguments are usually objectionable. But, in this particular case, that is in this special case of dealing with the ultimate 'Why' of the universe, it may be wondered if they are any more objectionable than the complete dead-end which noncircular argument produces: namely: 'Why is consciousness?' – 'Because of life.' – 'Why is life?' – Because the universe is as it is.' – 'Why is the universe as it is?' – 'Because it is as it is.' In other words one may have to end up in circularity, even though using circularity on the way there is thoroughly inadmissible.

But I am merely speculating so as to suggest the importance of these problems. And whether or not consciousness is necessary to the universe, is not strictly relevant to my basic argument, which takes it simply as an unavoidable axiom of human thought.

28. Natanson (1970, p. 72), but the legend is well known.
29. My admission that society 'exists' is perhaps slightly more cautious than this author's.

For instances of and reference to further discussions of the issue of holism versus individualism in social theory, see Brodbeck (1968, pp. 239-335).
30. *Passim* in the newspapers of early 1977.

Chapter Two
1. Because, if all societies are equally valid in their own terms, and if their own terms are the only scale of measurement, then none can be worse than any other (or better, for that matter!).
2. She and her girl-friend had been sunbathing naked.

Chapter Three
1. Ornstein (1975, pp. 31-2), referring to Bruner 'On perceptual readiness' in Bruner (1974*a*). The other authorities cited are Adelbert Ames and George Kelly.
2. C.S.Lewis puts this nicely when he remarks: 'Abstraction is very like money. Neither gold nor paper is real wealth, but it is more convenient than real wealth for the purposes of exchange. Poetry has the real wealth which the abstractions represent, but this is too cumbersome for the commerce of thought.' (Lewis & Tillyard 1939, p. 110)

Bruner's views on categorization are in accord with Berger & Luckmann (1971, pp. 70-1), who write: 'All human activity is subject to habitualization. Any action that is repeated frequently becomes cast into a pattern, which can then be reproduced with an economy of effort and which, *ipso facto*, is apprehended by its performer *as* that pattern. Habitualization further implies that the action in question may be performed again in the future in the same manner and with the same economical effort . . . Habitualization carries with it the important psychological gain that choices are narrowed . . . This frees the individual from the burden of "all those decisions" . . . Habitualization provides the direction and the specialization of activity that is lacking man's biological equipment . . . And by providing a stable background in which human activity may proceed with a minimum of decision-making most of the time, it frees energy for such decisions as may be necessary on certain occasions.'

Peter Marris's *Loss and Change* (1974) also utilizes the same profound insight, emphasizing particularly the interdependence of 'conservatism and adaptability'.

3. Cf. the errors of categorization noted in Martin (1975a, pp. 117-22). And see Chapter 4 in the present volume for deepening our more normal experience.
4. Bruner *et al.* (1956, p. 228), apropos of Tolman's views (1951). Reference to Frenkel-Brunswik, Bartlett and Adorno can be found in the same passage.
5. Cf. Adorno *et al.* (1950, pp. 461ff, p. 481).
6. Both this and the following two examples of belief-patterns were originally found in Polanyi (1958, pp. 287-8).
7. Cf. Berger & Luckmann's account of face-to-face contact (1971, pp. 44ff). 'The reality of everyday life contains typificatory schemes in terms of which others are apprehended and "dealt with" in face-to-face encounters. Thus I apprehend the other as "a man", "a European", "a buyer" "a jovial type", and so on.' They point out that such typifications become increasingly 'anonymous as they are removed from the "here and now" of the face-to-face situation'. And they point to the value of the face-to-face situation, i.e. of concrete and direct experience of others, because it is much easier for people to ignore the realities of the other so long as they do not meet him face-to-face (p. 44). This again is in complete harmony with the case I am making.
8. No doubt it is useful for many purposes to distinguish 'referent' from 'predicate'. But we need a term which will cover *all* those aspects of the world which are referred to by language, and I therefore define 'referent' thus. See my brief discussion of this point (Martin 1975a, pp. 70-1).
9. Cf. Wittgenstein's 'family resemblance', where for instance we might have four items containing features *a* to *f* as follows :

    1. *a* *b* *c*
    2.   *b* *c* *d*
    3.   *c* *d* *e*
    4.   *d* *e* *f*

so that item 1 contains none of the features of item 4. The only cure for confusion in such cases is to be clear about the actual features.

10. Sartre relates this anecdote in the film *Sartre par lui-même*.
11. *The Observer*, 12 February 1978. Parity here means equal pay for equal work.
12. The latter instance is British, the former Russian (see *New Society*, 9 February 1978).
13. Since writing these paragraphs, I have noticed that very similar analyses of the meaning of 'tolerance' are offered by Rawls (1972, §35), and Popper (1966, vol. i, ch. 7, n. 4).
14. Consult Brittan (1968, ch. 5), for a number of alternative models. No model would ever be totally satisfactory, of course, because every model is a simplification; but any would be preferable to our present uni-dimensional one. It should be noted that Brittan rightly attacks Eysenck's two-dimensional model for the counter-intuitive way in which he classifies views as 'tough-minded' or 'tender-minded'. I might add that Raymond Williams's *Keywords* (1976) contains neither the entry 'left' nor 'right', but that some of his other entries bear interesting witness to the sorts of confusion I am criticizing here.
15. i.e. Social Security.
16. I do not mean, by the way, to assert that literary passages are the *only* ones that should be translated, but simply that they should have some place in translation because, in them, the problems of linguistic equivalence are particularly evident and important.

Chapter Four
1. I define 'denotation', as in Martin (1975a, p. 40), as the concept considered as a counter or surface, without regard to its content or connotations. I was asked at the time whether I regarded 'denotation' thus defined to be a 'real linguistic entity'. The answer is that it is real when and to the extent that a concept is treated by a speaker or listener as being a mere counter or surface.
2. Popper (1976) remarks that 'there is an infinity of unforeseeable nontrivial statements belonging to the informative content of any theory, and an exactly corresponding infinity of statements belonging to its logical content' (p. 26). The insight seems rather similar.
3. Logical positivists would object at this point that my last sentence but one is meaningless because there is no way of testing it. But I should inquire whether they can understand the sentence or not. Besides, to say that the sentence is meaningless amounts to saying that talk of having sensations is meaningless because every sensation is irreducibly subjective. But (1) we know that we have sensations if only because the relationship between them is usually agreed on, and because the relationship between them is sometimes disagreed on – by colour-blind persons for instance; (2) sensations can be distinguished from the relationships between those sensations, just as two towns can be distinguished from the distance between them. If there were not two towns, one could not speak of the

distance between them. Hence (3) one cannot talk of the relationships between two things unless the two things exist. And sensations therefore exist.

Also, what would logical positivists before 1794 (had there been any) have said of the suggestion that some people saw colours differently from others? Yet before John Dalton's description of colour-blindness in that year, the phenomenon had never been noticed.

4. Plato's solution of this problem is given in his doctrine of recollection, namely that learning is being reminded of something, i.e. of some truth that we had lost. The modern world does not in general find this solution acceptable, and Polanyi's theory of tacit knowing may be thought to solve the problem. Plato, *Meno* 82eff, *Euthydemus* 275dff.

5. Einstein (1951, pp. 15-17), quoted in Martin (1975a, pp. 319-20).

6. Polanyi (1958, pp. 87-8). The proposition that explicit knowing cannot be made totally explicit in language, is not always explicit in Polanyi! But it is clearly implicit!

7. Black (1972, pp. 160-5) and Ambrose (1972) discuss the inadequacy of language to reproduce experience, and conclude that to complain of this is to utter a 'pseudo-complaint'. Ambrose says in effect that if you can remedy the complaint, it exists; if not, then it doesn't. (However, because there is no remedy for death, it doesn't follow that death does not occur, or that people don't regret it occurring.) Similarly, Black writes: 'In any intelligible sense, a barrier is an obstacle that can be imagined removed, as a fence or a wall may be removed to facilitate entry ... A "barrier" that it is logically impossible to remove is not, in any interesting sense, a barrier at all.' (p. 165) Black and Ambrose must not, however, be misunderstood: they are not denying that tacit elements in experience are by definition inaccessible to language; on the contrary, they strongly affirm this. They are merely pointing out that it is futile to lament this fact. Black puts my case most persuasively: 'Look attentively at any common object, say an oak leaf, and you may easily be seized with an intense conviction of the irremediable poverty of language. That quite particular green, with the light reflecting and modifying the hue; the contrast between the colour of the veins and the stalk; the sharply etched, plainly perceived, yet indescribable outline; the special feel of the surface and the contrasting roughness of the underside; the earthy (what a poor word!) yet faintly aromatic scent; and so on and so on. How on earth is one to reproduce all this in language?' (p. 162)

Besides, this chapter will show that something can after all be done about linguistic inadequacy.

8. Aldous Huxley says in *The Doors of Perception* (1954, p. 10) that he has always been a poor visualizer, and McKellar (1957) provides a short list of other eminent men who claimed to have little or no mental imagery.

9. Other fairly full accounts may be found in Haber & Hershenson (1974), Neisser (1967) and Reed (1973, pp. 87-153).
10. By some authorities at least. This term was apparently first applied by Ulric Neisser (1967).
11. Atkinson & Shiffrin (1968, p. 95) say it is a 'more or less photographic trace'. Cf. Haber & Hershenson (1974, p. 169) : 'It appears as if all the information in the retinal projection is available in this iconic storage, since the perceiver can extract whatever part is asked for.'
12. Cf. Shepard (1968, p. 287), for our ability to compare reconstructed icons in the imagination. As Shepard & Chipman (1970) point out, we do not need to become bogged down in philosophical difficulties about the meaning of 'I am imagining a green square'. When someone says this, 'he is not telling us there is anything that is literally either green or square going on in his head. What he is really telling us is that whatever is going on is functionally similar to what usually goes on when he is confronted with the kind of external object to which we have all associated the words "green" and "square".' (p. 16)
13. Psychologists usually assume there are three separate stores of memory, namely iconic memory, short-term memory (or primary memory), and long-term memory. Cf. Haber & Hershenson (1974, pp. 164-5).
14. Greek ἴσος : equal, equivalent, like.
15. See LeCron (1965, pp. 152-74), for some interesting but perhaps limited evidence. Barber (1969) takes a sceptical view of this matter, for similarly people can be projected forward to a time when they would be much older. This is indeed difficult to accept, and suggests they may be play-acting. Barber however does not deny that unconscious material can be recovered by age-regression. And, though I cannot adjudicate in such matters, Reiff & Scheerer's (1959) evidence is often highly persuasive.
16. Penfield (1954, pp. 179-83). See also Penfield & Roberts (1959) for further discussion.
17. It is not difficult to see why. Such recollections of the past totally erase, for a moment, all awareness of the present. It is clear that, if such experiences were at all common, the business of living in the here and now would become difficult if not impossible. Imagine for instance such a moment of total recall overcoming an African native escaping from a wild beast, or a man driving a car down the motorway, or simply someone doing something so ordinary as going down a flight of stairs. Disaster would ensue. It follows that, if total recall is possible, and if our continuous awareness of the present is to be safeguarded, an efficient mental censor is essential. If we accept the possibility of total recall, we must assume that evolution developed such a mental censor to ensure our very survival.
18. See e.g. Shiffrin & Atkinson (1969). Norman (1969) says that the difficulty is retrieval, not storing (p. 118).

19. Cf. Reed (1973, p. 137) : 'Visual images exist in long-term memory but are less detailed and less specific than the original patterns.'

20. Luria perhaps would not agree; but a careful reading of his evidence (1969, pp. 113-28) suggests that this is just as good an explanation. S's isons were almost totally rigid : he found it impossible either to combine one with another in sequence, or to blend one with another at the same moment.

21. For the original experiment, see Lantz (1963).

22. Cf. Brown & Herrnstein (1975, p. 437), for our habit of converting visual and other sensory experience into 'auditory icons' so that we can afterwards recall them more easily.

23. Cf. Anderson & Ortony (1975) for further evidence that context and existing knowledge of the world are essential in understanding language.

24. After writing this chapter I came across Katz & Sharma (1977), who discuss the aesthetic theory of the great Indian tenth-century writer, Abhinavagupta. He believed that poetry could evoke *vāsanā* or 'unconscious impressions left in our minds by events, which endure from life to life in the course of transmigration. When a play or poem revives some of these unconscious impressions it is possible for a spectator to identify with experiences he has never had in his present life . . . In terms of modern psycho-analysis, the real explanation of *rasa* [aesthetic or imaginative experience] is that unconscious elements, timeless and universal, have been exposed. As in mystical experience, the self has somehow been attained.' (p. 263)

25. See Martin (1975a, p. 210), where I had not yet discovered the 'icon' of information processing.
    I should add a qualification to my remarks in this chapter. Some people claim that they rarely if ever are aware of mental images. But the isonic process is doubtless less conscious, or more conscious, in some individuals than in others. With Luria's 'S.' it was excessively conscious; with poor visualizers like Huxley, highly unconscious.

26. Kipp (1975, p. 75). Though I regard some of Kipp's final conclusions as regrettable, the argument which gets him there, and the observations he makes on the way, deserve the most serious attention.

27. Paraphrased from Jouve; see Martin (1975a, p. 223).

Chapter Five

1. In *The Observer*, 20 February 1977.

2. See e.g. Gimpel (1969, p. 164). Is this view a modern form of the myth of the Golden Age ? It has certainly been questioned (see e.g. Goodridge 1975). But I am not concerned here to examine its truth, but merely to mention the view as part-explanation of the tendency of some (including Gimpel) to subordinate art to society.

3. He draws attention also to Schapiro (1953, pp. 310-11).

4. See Plekhanov (1953, pp. 31-50).

5. I refer here as much to his experiences as a refugee in the U.S.A. as to his interest in folk-music.

6. A writer in *Le Monde*, 1 April 1977, p. 21, concludes that 'Poetry reviews are not, like other cultural domains, the privilege of the intellectual class', and cites fourteen names of poets whose jobs would be defined as 'working-class' by those who care about such things.

7. From a letter in *The Times Higher Educational Supplement*, 26 September 1975, p. 22. See *THES*, 10 September 1976, for a fuller account of his views. Blacking's opinion in part depends on his belief that there are no 'gifted children' : 'if one normal human being can be taught these tricks, all human beings should be able to learn them' (1972, p. 15). This can only mean that he thinks that all human beings are biologically identical. But even if this were true, it would not affect my point here : namely that an immense and very specialized training is necessary for a Western (or Indian) classical musician. The explanation for all members of some primitive societies being competent in music is the relative lack of complexity and technical difficulty of their music.

   It suggests, however, that a reasonable level of musical achievement could be fairly universal, and that everyone might be encouraged to become musical to some degree. This is an excellent suggestion, and indeed it is precisely the lack of value-cultural training in our schools which is one of the things I most regret about them. But promoting the practice of the recorder and the guitar does not entail chopping up the concert grand.

8. A recent study of philistinism in Sweden (a country in which some profess to find our own future reflected) provides alarming evidence of the anti-cultural movement in modern Western society. One Professor Linde is quoted as saying : 'If mass culture . . . is called the opium of the people, then we should acknowledge in the same breath that high culture functions as the opium of the bourgeoisie, an escape from social and political realities.' And the Swedish Social Democratic Party's Cultural Committee proclaimed in 1969 that it did not see 'a lack of activity in the theatre, art, music or exhibitions as a sufficient sign of so-called "cultural impoverishment" . . . To describe people who are active in politics and trade unions, who fish, hunt and go berry-picking, with a high degree of unity and interaction, as "culturally impoverished"' is to be guilty of 'a gross underestimation of the value of these people's lives.' (Gedin 1977; cf. Brockbank 1977) Once again, we see the customary confusion of socio-culture and value-culture, and the consequent devaluation of the latter.

9. On 20 February, 5, 19, 26 March and 9, 23 April 1976. The discussion was started by a pessimistic John Holloway. Mine was one of the last two letters published.

10. Popular television programmes of the time.

11. 'Central cultural concern' needs to be translated into

English : a thing not of central cultural concern is something that doesn't matter very much because not very many people do it.

12. Another popular television programme, perhaps not entirely remote from *Oedipus*.

13. In case the reader objects that I have already ridiculed the theory of the social causation of art, because it cannot tell us why art should reflect or reject social experience, I must point out that the answer lies in the individual : his psychology is at least a part of that answer; and this is what is left out of the social theorist's account.

14. Particularly as I put no narrow interpretation on value-culture. The lenses of perception are polished also by jazz and folk-song, by oral tradition.

15. Whitehead (1926, p. 279). Read (1955, p. 139) : 'Education should be conceived as primarily . . . *aesthetic* education. Such a concept of education has often been proposed by philosophers and poets, and if we find it difficult to accept, it is no doubt because our sensibilities are no longer responsive to the original sources of human vitality and vision.'

16. See e.g. Zwang (1967). A propos of the latter practice he writes : 'La "fermeture" de la femme était ainsi si efficace que le mâle acquéreur devait, au soir de ses noces, s'ouvrir le chemin avec un poignard; ces ignominies salissent l'espèce humaine.' Relativists who disagree with his judgment should please sign here.

17. I am aware of course that the assumption of relativity as between different socio-cultures has been an invaluable working hypothesis in social anthropology. But we must discriminate. To describe another society in terms of our own is evidently most misleading; for then we shall never see how it functions in its own terms, nor where its values lie. We must therefore, in studying a society, 'accept it on its own terms' *initially*. This is, however, only the first stage. If we wish to compare societies with each other, we shall have to take them once again on their own terms, but use overriding principles which apply to both. If there are no such overriding principles, there can be no grounds for comparison. And finally may come evaluation. For it is simply not possible for the student of social anthropology to learn about the different ways in which different societies deal with (for example) adolescent sex without his making a covert comparison with his own society. He is inevitably led to wonder if it is better or worse, even in terms of his own society, than the behaviour of others. And indeed, there is no point in social anthropology other than (*a*) to teach us respect for other socio-cultures, hence a critical view upon our own, and thus (*b*) to teach us to seek more universal human principles to apply to the judgment of all human cultures. The lesson of social anthropology is the reverse of the relativist's message : it is, by learning more about the variety of human possibilities, to move *away* from the relativism of our own culture.

18. Lawton (1975, pp. 85ff). I have paraphrased him. The reader might also care to consult Kathryn Morgan (1975) for a lucid account of this kind of point of view, and Flew (1976, chs. 2, 3 and 4) for a conclusive critique.

    Cf. A. F. Blum, in Young (1971, p. 131): 'Thus, it is not an objectively discernible, purely existing external world which accounts for sociology; it is the methods and procedures of sociology which create and sustain that world.'

19. In *Radical Philosophy* no. 8, Summer 1974, p. 5. Cf. also Daniels and Houghton in Richardson & Spears (1972, p. 72).

20. 'Literacy be damned', *The Observer*, 20 February 1977, p. 12.

21. In Keddie (1973), his opening statement.

22. Daniels (1975, p. 80 and p. 79): '. . . one will not rely on analytic reason to construct and legitimate a conception that will then become the basis for an enduring [social] agreement'.

23. Skilbeck & Harris (1976, p. 22). It is of course irrational to insinuate that if A is not entirely B, it must be entirely not-B. I should perhaps add here, to clarify my own position further, that, as I am opposed to those who admit only total certainty, so I am opposed to those who admit only total ignorance. We exist *between* knowing and not knowing; and we constantly tend towards the former, though perfect knowledge is an ultimate which will always evade us. I have even suggested that all language is metaphor. But it would be impossible to do so if there was nothing for it to be a metaphor *of*.

24. The argument I use in this paragraph is in effect the argument which Kekes (1976, pp. 118-32) uses as the 'external' foundation of rationality. 'Internal' foundations for rationality are not, according to him, sufficient to refute the relativist's position, since the norms of rationality can be regarded by the relativist as mere conventions. If, however, we can show that the problems we have to face, both of a cognitive and an experiential nature, can best be solved by the use of rational principles; and if we can show that those who fly in the face of such principles will endanger their own existence, then it is evident that the standards of rationality are imposed upon us by the nature of the world itself and of our own human nature. 'A framework is rational, *inter alia*, if it contributes a possible solution to a problem of life. Since problems of life are independent of theoretical frameworks, so is the standard based upon them.' (Ibid., p. 125)

25. The sociology of knowledge seems to originate with K. Mannheim, M. Scheler, and perhaps ultimately Hegel. Popper operates a devastating *tu quoque* argument on their position (1966, vol. 2, p. 216). The position of the sociologists of knowledge is the result of a confusion between the (admitted) relativity of knowledge and the (not admissible) relativity of truth; and from the refusal to admit that there may be degrees in the relativity of know-

ledge, so that one theory may be (although not perhaps completely true) still closer to the truth or less subject to error than another.

26. See Brown (1970, pp.235ff). The experiment presented Zuñi and English speakers with colours, which they were asked to categorize; they seemed to do so in slightly different ways. There is an absence, however, of really *strong* evidence; but this may be explicable by the considerations mentioned in this quotation.

27. Cf. the remarks in Dreske's (1969) interesting *Seeing and Knowing* on 'perceptual relativity'. Subject to the normality of their vision, all human beings in all socio-cultures will see, non-epistemically (i.e. tacitly) the same objects and events (p. 77). It is our different linguistic or socio-cultural categories that may interfere with our agreement about what we see. Later in his book Dreske invents a little green man called Tobakee (pp. 190-201) who does not share our human views of motion and rest, and who substitutes for them two concepts, 'stationing' and 'mosing', which relate perfectly well to observational facts, but which do not correspond to our 'rest' and 'motion' at all. Two interesting points emerge, and both are in agreement with my own viewpoint. (1) We must admit that where people have learnt to categorize things differently, they will tend to see them differently, and to overlook those features of them which do not conform to their own expectations. (2) None the less, we have nothing to lose but our prejudices : it is clear from Dreske's careful description of what 'stationing' and 'mosing' are, that by analysing their perceptions and their categories, Tobakee and a human being could arrive at an accord. Perhaps they will not; but with sufficient good will on both sides, they could. An objective solution to this disagreement is therefore possible.

28. It might be argued that, since poetry is untranslatable, one language's set of categories cannot be grasped by people who belong to a different language. Now it is true that poetry is relatively (but only relatively) untranslatable. But this is because the particular complex of meanings embedded in the particular sounds of words in the particular order and effect in which they occur in any given poem, cannot be transferred into another language while conserving exactly those meanings and that effect. It does *not*, however, mean that this particular complex of meanings, etc. cannot be *understood* by a foreigner who has learnt the language. And all we need for the sake of my argument is to admit that a person from language A can learn to *understand* language B and its literature. No human language cannot be learnt by human beings. There must therefore be an enormous area of common understanding even between people of different native languages.

29. Though I do not wish to pursue Michael Young's first three propositions in detail here, it is evident that some knowledge is fairly reliable; and this being so, it deserves

to figure in educational curricula. We have to ensure that
what is known is known *by* somebody – and preferably by
as many as possible!

30. A very popular and widely-canvassed view among modern
educationists. See for instance Reynolds & Skilbeck (1976,
pp. 31, 119) or Skilbeck & Harris (1976, pp. 38, 40).

31. Such statements are baldly made in Keddie (1973, Introduction) and Simon (1974).

32. Readers might also like to consult Jackson's brief article in
The Times, 27 February 1973, where he says that working-
class culture is not 'better than any other', but 'is as valid
as any', and lists 'the pith and vivacity of working-class
speech, the traditions of mutuality in the industrial North,
qualities of emotional directness, and that intricate kaleido-
scope of brass bands, humour, pigeon fancying, family network, working-men's clubs, children's games and so much
else that makes its unique pattern.' All admirable things,
of course. But science and value-culture are conspicuous by
their absence from Jackson's view of the purposes of education. We may diagnose : (1) cultural relativism; and (2)
a definition of 'culture' purely as socio-culture.

33. Braden (1978), an account of 'Community art' in Britain,
suffers at one point from an apparently philistine attitude
to the value-culture of the past, when she writes : 'the so-
called cultural *heritage* which made Europe great – the
Bachs and Beethovens, the Shakespeares and Dantes, the
Constables and Titians – is no longer communicating anything to the vast majority of Europe's population . . . It is
not that these cultural forms are "above people's heads"
but that it is a *bourgeois* culture and therefore only immediately meaningful to that group.' (p. 153) And I should in
any case deny that the term 'bourgeois' can be meaning-
fully applied to value-culture. However, I welcome with
enthusiasm the participation in art that she wants for
people as a whole. And she takes an entirely healthy view
of the arts when she writes : 'the coexistence of the *two*
sets of values' (that is, of community art and of highbrow
art) 'should be seen as an enrichment – and the challenge,
if there is one, should act as a stimulus for future development' (p. 169).

34. We must not be too sweeping. The viewpoints expressed in
Albrecht (1970) for instance are, on the contrary, of
immense value.

35. I am no exception. But the *effort* towards understanding
more than one standpoint is itself the beginnings of a cure
for narrow-sightedness. We need, like the blind men and
the elephant, to see phenomena from more than one angle.

36. Berger or Kelvin for instance.

37. Mary Douglas (1978) and Aaron Cicourel quoted in *New
Society*, 6 April 1978.

38. The egalitarianism to which I am objecting is that which
preaches equality of outcome and relativity of values; not
that which used to teach equality of opportunity and of
individuals.

39. It fits indeed with certain linguistic usages of his own and of his fellows, such as 'indoctrination', meaning 'the teaching of facts' and 'teaching that there is more than one valid opinion'; and 'ideology', meaning 'a distrust of ideologies'.
40. A primitive society whom endemic scarcity has made brutal.
41. See the overview by Brown & Herrnstein (1975, pp. 520-3) where it appears that the consensus of opinion assigns 75-80% of I.Q. variation to heredity.
42. For we ourselves are 'always right'; so that if someone who is the same as us disagrees with us, it must be, not because he is different, but because he is wrong.
43. Yevgeny Yevtushenko, 'People' in *Selected Poems*, Penguin 1962. Ivan Illich quotes from the same poem at the end of his *Deschooling Society*.
44. Or at least so regarded by himself (Young 1961, p. 55).
45. Gabor (1972, pp. 75ff). On p. 85: 'The most valuable people in a mature society will not be the most productive, perhaps not even the most creative, but those men and women who are themselves happy and can spread goodwill and happiness around them.' For if there is anything more difficult than being contented despite one's good reasons for malcontent, it is being contented despite one's good reasons for contentment.

Appendix
1. Cf. Polanyi (1958, p. 80): 'identifying manifestly different situations in respect to some particular feature . . . requires a series of personal judgments'. Cf. also Miller & Johnson-Laird (1976, p. 692): ' . . . in order to make a discriminative response to stimulation one has to attend to and make judgments of various properties and relations offered by the perceived situation . . . [It is] the outcome of such attentional-judgmental abstractions from perception, not the particular percept itself, that provide[s] a basis for learning [linguistic] labels.' And, I should add, for *applying* them.
2. Edmond L. Wright's essays (see Bibliography) are to be highly recommended for his original and profound rethinking of the problems involved in meaning. In the above passage he quotes from Palmer (1972, p. 321).

Bibliography

Adorno, Theodore W. (1976) ed. *The Positivist Dispute in German Sociology*, London.

Adorno, Theodore W. *et al.* (1950) *The Authoritarian Personality*, New York.

Albrecht, Milton C. *et al.* (1970) ed. *The Sociology of Art and Literature*, London.

Allport, Gordon W. (1954) *The Nature of Prejudice*, Cambridge, Mass.

Althusser, Louis (1970) 'Philosophy as a revolutionary weapon', *New Left Review 64*, 10.

Ambrose, Alice (1972) 'The problem of linguistic adequacy' in *Philosophical Analysis*, ed. Max Black, pp. 14-35, Ithaca and New York.

Andersen, Hans Christian (1950) *Fairy Tales*, trans. R.P. Keigwin, Leicester.

Anderson, Richard C. & Andrew Ortony (1975) 'On putting apples into bottles', *Cognitive Psychology 7*, 167-80.

Anglin, J.M. (1970) *The Growth of Word Meaning*, Cambridge, Mass.

Arnold, Matthew (1932) *Culture and Anarchy*, Cambridge.

Asch, S.E. (1952) *Social Psychology*, Englewood Cliffs.

Atkinson, R.C. & R.M.Shiffrin (1968) 'Human memory: a proposed system and its control processes' in *The Psychology of Learning and Motivation*, Vol. 2, ed. K.W.Spence (G.H.Bower) & J.T.Spence, New York.

Ayer, A.J. (1956) *The Problem of Knowledge*, London and New York.

Barber, Theodore Xenophon (1969) *Hypnotism: A Scientific Approach*, New York.

Barnes, Barry (1974) *Scientific Knowledge and Social Theory*, London and Boston.

Bartlett, F.C. (1932) *Remembering*, Cambridge.

Baumol, W.J. & W.G.Bowen (1973) 'Audiences: some face-sheet data' in *Sociology of Literature and Drama*, ed. E. Burns & T.Burns, (Penguin) London, pp. 445-70.

Beichman, Arnold (1975) 'An angry fancy', *Lugano Review 2*, 18-24.

Berger, Joseph (1971) *Shipwreck of a Generation*, London.

Berger, Peter L. & Thomas Luckmann (1971) *The Social Construction of Reality*, (Penguin) London.

Berger, Peter L. & S.Pullberg (1964) 'Reification and the sociological critique of consciousness', *History and Theory 4* (no. 2), 196-211.

Bhaskar, Roy (1978) 'On the possibility of social scientific knowledge', *Journal of the Theory of Social Behaviour 8* (no. 1), 1-28.

Bibliography

Birch, Francis (1976) 'Leisure patterns in Britain', *Population Trends 3* (Spring), H.M.S.O.

Black, Max (1972) *The Labyrinth of Language*, (Penguin) London.

Blackburn, Robin (1972) ed. *Ideology in Social Science*, London.

Blackburn, Robin & Alexander Cockburn (1969) *Student Power*, (Penguin) London.

Blacking, John (1972) *Man and Fellowman*, Belfast.

Bowie, Malcolm (1978) *Mallarmé and the Art of Being Difficult*, Cambridge.

Braden, Su (1978) *Artists and People*, London.

Bradley, Francis Herbert (1876) *Ethical Studies*, London.

Brittan, Samuel (1968) *Left or Right: The Bogus Dilemma*, London.

Brockbank, Philip (1977) 'Culture and nullity', *Times Literary Supplement* 14 October (review of Gedin 1977).

Brodbeck, May (1968) *Readings in the Philosophy of the Social Sciences*, London and New York.

Brown, Richard (1973) *Knowledge, Education and Cultural Change*, London.

Brown, Roger (1965) *Social Psychology*, New York and London.

(1970) *Psycholinguistics*, New York.

Brown, Roger & R. J. Herrnstein (1975) *Psychology*, London.

Bruner, Jerome S. (1974*a*) *Beyond the Information Given*, London.

(1974*b*) 'Culture and cognitive growth' in *Studies in Cognitive Growth*, ed. J. S. Bruner, R. R. Olver, P. M. Greenfield, pp. 368-93.

Bruner, Jerome, J. J. Goodnow & G. A. Austin (1956) *A Study of Thinking*, London and New York.

Burma, B. H. & E. Mayr (1949) 'The species concept: a discussion', *Evolution 3* (no. 4), 369-73.

Caillois, Roger (1948) *Babel*, Paris.

Capra, Fritjof (1975) *The Tao of Physics*, London.

Chattopadhyaya, Debiprasad (1975) *Individuals and Societies*, Calcutta.

Cherry, Colin (1955) 'Communication theory and human behaviour' in *Studies in Communication*, ed. A. J. Ayer, J. B. S. Haldane *et al.*, London, pp. 45-67.

(1961) *On Human Communication*, New York.

Chew, Geoffrey F. (1968) 'Bootstrap: a scientific idea?', *Science 161*, 762-5.

Cohen, John (1974) 'Reflections on the structure of mind', *Scientia 5*, pp. 1-23.

Cooper, L. A. & R. N. Shepard (1973) 'Chronometric studies of the rotation of mental images' in *Visual Information Processing*, ed. W. G. Chase, New York, pp. 75-176.

Cosin, B. R., I. R. Dale *et al.* (1971) ed. *School and Society*, (Open University) London.

Crossman, Richard H. S. (1950) ed. *The God that Failed*, London.

Culler, Jonathan (1975) *Structuralist Poetics*, London.

189

Bibliography

Dahrendorf, Ralf (1973) *Homo Sociologicus*, London.
Daiches, David (1936) *New Literary Values*, Edinburgh.
Dale, Roger *et al.* (1976) ed. *Schooling and Capitalism*, London.
Daniels, Norman (1975) ed. *Reading Rawls*, Oxford.
Dennett, D.C. (1969) *Content and Consciousness*, New York.
Dicke, R.H. (1961) *Nature 192*, 440-1.
Douglas, Mary (1978) *Cultural Bias*, London.
Downie, R.S. (1971) *Roles and Values*, London.
Dreske, Fred I. (1969) *Seeing and Knowing*, London.

Eddington, Sir Arthur S. (1928) *The Nature of the Physical
    World*, Cambridge.
Einstein, Albert (1951) 'Autobiographical notes' in *Albert
    Einstein*, ed. Paul A.Schilpp, New York, pp. 1-95.
Eluard, Paul (1968) *Oeuvres complètes*, Pléiade, Paris.
Enzensberger, Hans Magnus (1970) 'Constituents of a theory
    of the media', *New Left Review 64*.
Erikson, Erik H. (1963) *Childhood and Society*, 2nd edn, New
    York.
Erlich, Victor (1954) *Russian Formalism: History – Doctrine*,
    The Hague.
Esland, Geoffrey M. (1972) *The Social Organization of Teach-
    ing and Language*, Bletchley.
Evans, C.O. (1970) *The Subject of Consciousness*, London and
    New York.
Evans-Pritchard, E.E. (1937) *Witchcraft, Oracles and Magic
    among the Azande*, Oxford.

Firsoff, V.Axel (1967) *Life, Mind and Galaxies*, Edinburgh
    and London.
Flew, Antony (1976) *Sociology, Equality and Education*, London.
Fodor, Jerry (1976) *The Language of Thought*, New York and
    Hassocks.
Fowles, John (1970) *The French Lieutenant's Woman*, London.
    (1974) *The Ebony Tower*, London.
Frenkel-Brunswik, Else (1949) 'Intolerance of ambiguity as an
    emotional and perceptual personality variable' in *Perception
    and Personality*, ed. J.S.Bruner & D.Krech, Durham, N.C.,
    pp. 108-44.
Furst, Charles (1971) 'Automatizing of visual attention',
    Perception and Psychophysics 10 (no. 2), 65-9.

Gabor, Dennis (1972) *The Mature Society*, London.
Geach, Peter (1957) *Mental Acts: Their Content and their
    Objects*, London.
Gedin, Per (1977) *Literature in the Market Place*, London.
Gibson, Quentin (1960) *The Logic of Social Inquiry*, London.
Gimpel, Jean (1969) *The Cult of Art*, London.
Glucksmann, André (1975) *La Cuisinière et le mangeur
    d'hommes*, Paris.
Gombrich, E.H. (1968) *Art and Illusion*, 3rd edn, London.
Good, I.J. (1961) ed. *The Scientist Speculates – An Anthology
    of Half-Baked Ideas*, London.
Goodridge, R.Martin (1975) 'The ages of faith – romance or

reality', *Sociological Review 23* (no. 2), 381-96.
Gouldner, Alvin W. (1971) *The Coming Crisis of Western Sociology*, London.
Gregory, R. L. (1971) *The Intelligent Eye*, 2nd edn, London. (1972) *Eye and Brain*, 2nd edn, London.

Haber, Ralph N. (1971) ed. *Information Processing Approaches to Visual Perception*, London.
Haber, Ralph N. & R.B.Haber (1964) 'Eidetic imagery: I. Frequency', *Perceptual Motor Skills 19*, 131-8.
Haber, Ralph N. & M.Hershenson (1974) *The Psychology of Visual Perception*, New York and London.
Habermas, Jürgen (1972) *Knowledge and Human Interests*, London.
Hampshire, Stuart (1977) 'Private pleasures and the public purse', *Times Literary Supplement*, 13 May, pp. 578-9.
Hauser, Arnold (1951) *The Social History of Art*, London.
Hawkes, Terence (1973) *Shakespeare's Talking Animals*, London.
Hayakawa, S.I. (1959) ed. *Our Language and Our World*, New York.
Hintikka, Jaakko (1970) 'On semantic information' in *Information and Inference*, ed. J.Hintikka & P.Suppes, Dordrecht, pp. 3-27.
Hopper, Earl (1971) *Readings in the Theory of Educational Systems*, London.
Horney, Karen (1939) *New Ways of Psychoanalysis*, London.
Howe, Irving (1971) *The Decline of the New*, London.
Hughes, Ted (1960) *Lupercal*, London.
Huxley, Aldous (1937) *Ends and Means*, London.
(1943) *The Art of Seeing*, London.
(1954) *The Doors of Perception*, London.

Idries Shah (1974) *Thinkers of the East*, (Penguin) London.

Jabès, Edmond (1976) *Le Livre des ressemblances*, Paris.
Jackson, Brian (1968) *Working Class Community*, London.
(1973) 'How the poorest live: education', *New Society 23*, 229-32.
Jameson, Fredric (1971) *Marxism and Form*, Princeton.
Jammer, Max (1975) *The Philosophy of Quantum Mechanics*, New York.

Katz, Ruth & Arvind Sharma (1977) 'The aesthetics of Abhinavagupta', *British Journal of Aesthetics 17*, 259-65.
Keddie, Nell (1973) ed. *Tinker, Tailor . . . The Myth of Cultural Deprivation*, (Penguin) London.
Kekes, John (1976) *A Justification of Rationality*, Albany.
Kelvin, Peter (1970) *The Bases of Social Behaviour*, London and New York.
Kerr, Judith (1975) 'Writing with borrowed words', *Times Literary Supplement* 4 April, p. 398.
Kipp, David (1975) *Poetic Truth: A Theoretical Inquiry*, Perth, W.Australia (obtainable from author, School of Social

Inquiry, Murdoch University, Murdoch, W. Australia).

Koestler, Arthur (1974) *The Heel of Achilles*, London.

Krech, D., R.S.Crutchfield & E.L.Ballochey (1962) *The Individual in Society*, New York and London.

Kuhn, Thomas S. (1970) *The Structure of Scientific Revolutions*, 2nd edn, Chicago and London.

Läkatos, I. & A.Musgrave (1970) ed. *Criticism and the Growth of Knowledge*, Cambridge.

Lally, A.J. (1976) 'Positivism and its Critics' in *New Directions in Sociology*, ed. D.C.Thorns, London and Vancouver, pp. 55-75.

Lantz, DeLee (1963) 'Colour naming and colour recognition', Unpublished Doctoral Dissertation, Harvard University.

Laporte, Jean (1940) *Le Problème de l'abstraction*, Paris.

Lawrence, D.H. (1936) *Phoenix*, London.

Lawton, Denis (1975) *Class, Culture and the Curriculum*, London.

Leavis, Q.D. (1979) *Fiction and the Reading Public*, (Penguin) London.

LeCron, Leslie M. (1965) ed. *Experimental Hypnosis*, New York.

Lefebve, Maurice-Jean (1965) *L'Image fascinante et le surréel*, Paris.

　(1970) 'Discours poétique et discours du récit', *Nouvelle Revue Française* 1 February, pp. 269-78.

　(1971) *Structure du discours de la poésie et du récit*, Neuchâtel, La Bâconnière.

Lewis, C.S. & E.M.W.Tillyard (1939) *The Personal Heresy*, Oxford.

Lin, Nan (1973) *The Study of Human Communication*, Indianapolis and New York.

Lukes, Steven (1973) 'Methodological individualism reconsidered' in *The Philosophy of Social Explanation*, ed. Alan Ryan, Oxford, pp. 119-29.

Luria (Luriya), Aleksandr R. (1969) *The Mind of a Mnemonist*, London.

　(1973) *The Working Brain*, (Penguin) London.

Lyons, John (1968) *Introduction to Theoretical Linguistics*, Cambridge.

MacCaig, Norman (1967) *Surroundings*, London.

MacKay, Donald M. (1969) *Information, Mechanism and Meaning*, Cambridge (Mass.) and London.

McKellar, Peter (1957) *Imagination and Thinking*, London.

MacLeish, Archibald (1952) *Collected Poems, 1917-52*, Cambridge, Mass.

　(1965) *Poetry and Experience*, (Penguin) London.

Marcuse, Herbert (1964) *One-Dimensional Man*, London.

Margenau, Henry (1950) *The Nature of Physical Reality*, New York.

　(1964) *Ethics and Science*, Princeton and London.

Marris, Peter (1974) *Loss and Change*, London.

Martin, Graham Dunstan (1972) ed. *Anthology of Contemporary*

French Poetry, Edinburgh.

(1975a) *Language, Truth and Poetry*, Edinburgh.

(1975b) 'Racism in Genet's *Les Nègres*', *Modern Language Review* 70, 517-25.

(1978) ed. Jean-Claude Renard *Selected Poems*, London.

(1980) 'Evoking the *objet profond:* The poetry of Y. Bonnefoy' in *The Language of Poetry, Crisis and Solution*, ed. Michael Bishop, Amsterdam, pp. 69-92.

Miliband, Ralph (1969) *The State in Capitalist Society*, London.

Miller, George A. & P.N. Johnson-Laird (1976) *Language and Perception*, Cambridge.

Minihan, Janet (1977) *The Nationalization of Culture*, London.

Misner, Charles W., K.S. Thorne & J.A. Wheeler (1973) *Gravitation*, San Francisco.

Mitchell, Juliet (1975) *Psychoanalysis and Feminism*, (Penguin) London.

Monod, Jacques (1970) *Le Hasard et la nécessité*, Paris.

Moore, Timothy E. (1973) ed. *Cognitive Development and the Acquisition of Language*, New York.

Morgan, Kathryn (1975) 'Socialization, social models, and the open education movement' in *The Philosophy of Open Education*, ed. David Nyberg, London and Boston, pp. 110-45.

Murti, T.R.V. (1955) *The Central Philosophy of Buddhism*, London.

Natanson, Maurice (1970) *The Journeying Self*, Reading (Mass.) and London.

Neisser, Ulric (1967) *Cognitive Psychology*, New York.

Newton, Francis (1961) *The Jazz Scene*, (Penguin) London.

Norman, Donald A. (1969) *Memory and Attention*, New York and London.

(1976) *Memory and Attention*, 2nd edn, New York and London.

Ornstein, Robert (1975) *The Psychology of Consciousness*, London.

Palmer, Leonard (1972) *Descriptive and Comparative Linguistics*, London.

Palmer, Richard E. (1969) *Hermeneutics*, Evanston.

Peirce, Charles Sanders (1931-5) *Collected Papers*, ed. C. Hartshorne & P. Weiss, Cambridge, Mass.

Penfield, Wilder (1954) 'The permanent record of the stream of consciousness' in *Proceedings of the 14th International Congress of Psychology*, Montreal Neurological Institute, Report no. 486.

(1966) 'Speech, perception and the cortex' in *Brain and Conscious Experience*, ed. John C. Eccles, New York.

Penfield, Wilder & L. Roberts (1959) *Speech and Brain Mechanisms*, Princeton.

Phillips, Dewi Zephaniah (1970) *Faith and Philosophical Inquiry*, London.

Piaget, Jean (1950) *The Psychology of Intelligence*, London.

(1955) *The Child's Construction of Reality*, London.
(1970) *Psychologie et Epistémologie*, Paris.
(1974) *The Child and Reality*, London.
Plath, Sylvia (1965) *Ariel*, London.
Plekhanov, G. V. (1953) *Art and Social Life*, London.
Polanyi, Michael (1958) *Personal Knowledge*, London.
(1959) *The Study of Man*, London.
(1964) *Science, Faith and Society*, Chicago and London.
(1967) *The Tacit Dimension*, London.
Polanyi, Michael & Harry Prosch (1975) *Meaning*, Chicago and London.
Ponge, Francis & Philippe Sollers (1970) *Entretiens*, Paris.
Popper, Karl (1949) 'Naturgesetze und theoretische Systeme' in *Theorie und Realität*, 2nd edn (1972), ed. Hans Albert, Tübingen, pp. 43-59.
(1961) *The Poverty of Historicism*, London.
(1966) *The Open Society and Its Enemies*, Vols. 1 and 2, 5th edn, London.
(1976) *Unended Quest: An Intellectual Autobiography*, revised paperback edn, London.
Posner, Michael I. (1969) 'Abstraction and the Process of Recognition' in *The Psychology of Learning and Motivation*, ed. K. W. Spence (G. H. Bower) & J. T. Spence, Vol. 3, New York.
Postman, Neil (1973) 'The politics of reading' in Keddie 1973, pp. 86-95.
Pribram, Karl H. (1969) 'The neurophysiology of remembering', *Scientific American* January, pp. 73-86 (offprint no. 520).
Pring, Richard (1972) 'Knowledge out of control', *Education for Today* Autumn, pp. 19-28.
Proust, Marcel (1965-7) *A la recherche du temps perdu*, (Livre de Poche) Paris.

Radhakrishnan, S. (1940) *Eastern Religions and Western Thought*, 2nd edn, London.
Rawls, John (1972) *A Theory of Justice*, Oxford.
Rawson, Philip (1978) *The Art of Tantra*, revised edn, London.
Read, Herbert (1955) *Icon and Idea*, London.
Reed, Stephen K. (1973) *Psychological Processes in Pattern Recognition*, New York and London.
Reiff, Robert & Martin Scheerer (1959) *Memory and Hypnotic Age Regression*, New York.
Reynolds, John & Malcolm Skilbeck (1976) *Culture and the Classroom*, London.
Richardson, K. & D. Spears (1972) ed. *Race, Culture and Intelligence*, (Penguin) London.
Roberts, K. (1970) *Leisure*, London.
Rosenthal, R. & K. L. Fode (1963) 'The effect of experimenter bias on the performance of the albino rat', *Behavioural Science* 8 (no. 3), 183-9.

Sachs, Mendel (1969) 'Space time and elementary interactions in relativity', *Physics Today* 22 (Feb.).

Sartre, Jean-Paul (1972) *Plaidoyer pour les intellectuels*, Paris.
Saussure, Ferdinand de (1966) *Course in General Linguistics*, New York.
Schapiro, Meyer (1953) 'Style' in *Anthropology Today*, ed. A. L. Kroeber, Chicago.
Schilpp, P. A. (1949) ed. *Albert Einstein: Philosopher-Scientist*, Evanston.
Schrödinger, Erwin (1958) *Mind and Matter*, Cambridge.
Shannon, Claude E. & Warren Weaver (1949) *The Mathematical Theory of Communication*, Urbana.
Shepard, Roger N. (1968) 'Cognitive psychology', *American Journal of Psychology 81*, 285-9 (review of Neisser 1967).
Shepard, Roger N. & S. Chipman (1970) 'Second-order isomorphism of internal representations', *Cognitive Psychology 1*, 1-17.
Shiffrin, R. M. & R. C. Atkinson (1969) 'Storage and retrieval processes in long-term memory', *Psychological Review 76*, 179-93.
Shiffrin, R. M. & G. T. Gardner (1972) 'Visual processing capacity and attentional control', *Journal of Experimental Psychology 93*, 72-82.
Simon, Joan (1974) '"New direction" sociology and comprehensive schooling', *Forum for Discussion of New Trends in Education 17* (no. 1), Autumn.
Skilbeck, M. & A. Harris (1976) *Culture, Ideology and Knowledge*, (Open University) London.
Sperling, G. (1967) 'Successive approximation to a model for short-term memory', *Acta Psychologica 27*, 285-92.
Steiner, George (1975) *After Babel*, Oxford.
Sturrock, John (1969) *The French New Novel*, Oxford.

Taylor, Roger (1978) *Art, An Enemy of the People*, Hassacks.
Tolman, E. C. (1951) 'A psychological model' in *Towards a General Theory of Action*, ed. T. Parsons & E. A. Shils, Cambridge, Mass., pp. 279-361.
Trilling, Lionel (1961) *The Liberal Imagination*, 2nd edn, London.
Tunstall, J. (1970) ed. *Media Sociology*, London.
Turnbull, C. M. (1973) *The Mountain People*, London.

Valéry, Paul (1957-61) *Les Cahiers*, Vols. 1-29, c.n.r.s., Paris.
Vernon, M. D. (1971) *The Psychology of Perception*, 2nd edn, (Penguin) London.
Vernon, P. E. (1970) ed. *Creativity*, (Penguin) London.
Vinacke, W. E. (1952) *The Psychology of Thinking*, New York and London.

Waismann, Freidrich (1951) 'Verifiability' in Flew 1951.
Walsh, David (1972) 'Sociology and the social world' in *New Directions in Sociological Theory*, ed. Paul Filmer *et al.*, London.
Watkins, J. W. N. (1959) 'Historical explanation in the social sciences' in *Theories of History*, ed. Patrick L. Gardiner, Glencoe (Ill.) and London, pp. 503-15.

Bibliography

Whitehead, Alfred North (1926) *Science and the Modern World*, Cambridge.

Whitrow, G.J. (1961) *The Natural Philosophy of Time*, London and Edinburgh.

Whyte, William H. (1960) *The Organization Man*, (Penguin) London.

Wigner, Eugene P. (1967) *Symmetries and Reflections*, Bloomington and London.

Wilding, Paul (1976) 'Objections to social science', *New Society 36* (no. 705), 72-3.

Williams, Raymond (1963) *Culture and Society 1780-1950*, (Penguin) London.

(1976) *Keywords*, London.

Wilson, Bryan (1970) ed. *Rationality*, Oxford.

Winch, Peter (1972) *Ethics and Action*, London.

Winnicott, D.W. (1967) 'Mirror-role of mother and family in child development' in *The Predicament of the Family*, ed. P.Lomas, London, pp. 26-33.

Wittgenstein, Ludwig (1967) *Philosophical Investigations*, 3rd edn, Oxford.

Wollheim, Richard (1970) 'Sociological explanation of the arts' in Albrecht 1970, pp. 574-81.

Worsley, Peter (1970) ed. *Introducing Sociology*, (Penguin) London.

Wright, D.S. *et al.* (1970) *Introducing Psychology*, (Penguin) London.

Wright, Edmond L. (1976) 'Arbitrariness and motivation', *Foundations of Language 14*, 505-23.

(1977*a*) 'Words and intentions', *Philosophy 52*, 45-62.

(1977*b*) 'Perception: a new theory', *American Philosophical Quarterly 14* (no. 4), 273-86.

(1978) 'Sociology and the irony model', *Sociology 12*, 523-43.

Young, Bob (1977) 'Science *is* social relations', *Radical Science Journal 5*, 65-129.

Young, Michael Dunlop (1961) *The Rise of the Meritocracy*, (Penguin) London.

Young, Michael Francis Dykes (1971) ed. *Knowledge and Control*, London.

Zwang, Gérard (1967) *Le Sexe de la femme*, Paris.

Indexes

Subjects

DATE DUE

GAYLORD			PRINTED IN U.S.A.

Hitler Youth

Michael H. Kater

HARVARD UNIVERSITY PRESS
Cambridge, Massachusetts
London, England
2004

For my daughter Anja

Contents

Hitler Youth

"Make Way, You Old Ones!"

In 1992 a former Hitler Youth or Hitler-Junge, now a respected historian, sat down to reflect upon his childhood and early adolescence in Nazi Germany. Hermann Graml, who was born in 1928, concluded that there were many aspects of his life as a member of the Hitler Youth (HJ) that had appealed to him. Most important was that he, along with his friends, was "wooed and flattered beyond limits" by the powerful political system of the Third Reich, and thus he was proud to be a part of the largest ever youth organization that it had created. He was attracted by the spiritual and national hymns they sang and by the cult-like activities that initiated young people into the movement, such as swearing an oath of fealty to Adolf Hitler, the supreme leader. In the struggle for ultimate authority over the children that sometimes took place among the church, schools, parents, and Hitler Youth, Graml and his friends enjoyed being the center of attention and the object of adult desires. However, they tended to side with the Hitler Youth more often than not because it seemed to be "more modern" and forward-looking than any of the other institutions. Indeed, they found that the Nazi regime appeared to be more supportive of youth in terms of granting autonomy from parents and allowing liberal relations with girls of their age. Unlike family, church, and school, the HJ was not weighed down by tradition and taboos and seemed to offer an exciting opportunity for young people to be respected and responsible.

When Graml's time came to be drafted as a young soldier, he and his friends accepted the incipient war as a given because of the paramilitary training he had received in the HJ. He, and other youth, had been preparing for war's eventuality for years and were not frightened by the prospect of active combat at the front. On the contrary, Graml remembers being motivated by a "lust for adventure, daring, and risk," a love of flirting with danger. Not everything in the Hitler Youth appealed to him, however, and some of the training went against the grain of his experience. Lessons in "biological racism" and ideas of a "Germanic world empire" seemed abstract and far-fetched to a young boy. National Socialist visions of enlarged living space could not stir his interest, nor could the concept of a German "master race." Despite his training, he remembered contravening Nazi dogma by making friends with Soviet prisoners of war forced to work in local factories, and when serving as a flak cannoneer he continued such friendships with Soviet mercenaries fighting alongside him and members of his platoon. Thus, in retrospect, he saw himself as having resisted total submission to the HJ despite his positive reaction to its spirit and activities.[1]

Margarete Hannsmann, a German actress and novelist born in 1921, recently composed a memoir entitled "The Sun is Rising: A Child Becomes Nazi." In the book she tells about slowly emancipating herself from her parents, especially her authoritarian father, with the help of the Hitler Youth, and how, as a girl in her mid-teens, she felt like a responsible adult when helping a farmer in the fields during a special HJ agricultural program. She describes being flattered by the attentions of an older, handsome Hitler Youth leader and her sense of liberation in a subsequent affair with him, her first. The highlight of her years in the Hitler Youth was her appointment to an intermediate leadership post and the assumption of responsibility toward other, younger girls. But she reports being deeply disillusioned by the Hitler Youth leader's callous, coldly controlling treatment of her when the affair ended, and she was incensed when comrades wrongly accused her of having stolen money from a communal locker room. Growing up in the HJ had its humiliations as well as its pleasures.[2]

Bittersweet experiences of joy and suffering may have characterized the life of younger, ordinary Hitler Youths such as Graml and Hannsmann, at least according to their post-1945 recollections. However, the extant memoirs of more highly elevated HJ leaders, apart from all the post-1945 self-criticism they contain, are suffused with a scarcely veiled sense of pride in their former power, and are graphic in their description of the type and extent of this power. They demonstrate that the very authoritarian nature of the Nazi regime, coupled with its merciless ideology of the survival of the fittest as it was eugenically implemented, constituted a major point of attraction for adolescents who were searching for certitudes in a swiftly changing and newly structured world, however harshly regimented. According to a well-defined Nazi leadership creed, this authority made them strong vis-à-vis a multitude of younger, weaker juveniles who were their charges, and it gave them an incomparable sense of superiority over average German citizens of any age, even when they were Nazis, and nearly absolute power over those who were not.[3]

These observations raise a number of questions about the complicity of members of the Hitler Youth, both the young ones and the older ones, in the consolidation and, by extension, the breakdown of the Third Reich. These questions must be asked, even if they cannot all be answered. For example, can children of ages ten to eighteen (the usual range for membership in the HJ), who usually are not culpable in a court of law, be held responsible for having participated in the activities of a dictatorship's youth organization, even when those activities were criminal? Or were they culpable at a somewhat more advanced stage of their life, when they were either drafted or volunteered to wage war against innocent neighboring states? Many youth were inducted into the HJ as children and had little choice in the matter. Either they were placed in the movement by their parents or teachers, who thought this offered the best opportunity for mobility in the state before HJ membership was made compulsory, or it was difficult to escape the pressure of peers for uniformity and solidarity. Furthermore, one can understand young people's attraction to spiffy uniforms and to the paraphernalia of premilitary drill, such as air guns. Similarly, it is not hard to understand the appeal and satisfaction of belonging to a large, dominant, and protective community and participating in their communal singing, marching, and camping. Above all, there was the omniscient and omnipotent father, Adolf Hitler, who provided immense guarantees of safety at a time shaken by continued economic depression and recurrent fears of war. As much as authority overawes children and instills fear in them if they are disobedient, it also provides security as long as the children agree to conform to prescribed standards of behavior that do not strike them as too odious. It was one of the great propaganda achievements of the Nazi rulers that they were able to offer a political and ideological world view that granted status, certainty, and power to young people, so much so that teenagers of both genders could accept and abide by the prescribed behaviors with hardly any qualms. Through the elaborate propaganda process and its propagation of racial theory and the superiority of the *Volk,* Hitler was able to shape private and public behavior as well as reinforce public support of the Nazi regime and the people's intimate ties to him, their Führer. Young people, with their ideals and energies, would have been especially vulnerable to such values in their own search for identity and meaning.[4]

The issue of complicity changes as one focuses on Hitler's youths in their transition from juveniles to young adults. It is necessary to determine at which stage a youth would have had the option either to accept or to reject an opportunity for advancement to higher leadership responsibilities. Members' compliance with such advancement from the lower HJ ranks was voluntary and necessitated a fair amount of ideological conviction in the Nazi cause, something that a youth from age sixteen to eighteen could evince as persuasively and sometimes even as eloquently as a diehard Nazi in his early thirties. It is fair to say that seventeen-year-old HJ leaders with a few hundred charges under their command, in contrast to the ten-year-old underlings, made themselves culpable, to the extent that they knowingly imparted Nazi values to these underlings, inciting them to racial hatred and warfare against Poles, Russians, and Jews. As they got older, preconditioned, brainwashed children would swap air guns for machine guns and willingly be drafted to use them against Hitler's foes.

The issue becomes even more difficult as young people made the transition from mature Hitler Youth membership to tours of duty in the armed forces or associated branches such as the Reich Labor Service. Even if such duty was the consequence of general conscription, the subsequent behavior of a former Hitler Youth in war could depend on how seriously he had taken the paramilitary routines he had practiced throughout his youth, and the catechism of beliefs he had been taught. These would influence his comportment in war: whether he would kill his adversary or make him a prisoner of war; whether he would shoot when ordered to kill civilians. The certainty which the Nazi regime had provided to a Hitler Youth in peacetime through a tightly structured totalitarian dictatorship would be continued in the armed forces, albeit slightly changed: instead of a chain of command dominated by National Socialist ideology, it would now be one determined by the Wehrmacht's tried-and-true rules of war. As it turned out, Nazi rules and Wehrmacht rules often coincided after 1938 to create conditions under which a German soldier, as a former Hitler Youth member or leader, would find it difficult to be guided by a humane conscience. The pattern of order and authority that a Wehrmacht soldier was able to cling to during war was his strength to a great extent but, ultimately, his weakness as well. It canceled out all gray areas and made choices simple by reference to what the Führer thought best— but that only lasted as long as the Führer did.

The seemingly coherent world view offered by the Third Reich was a far cry from the atmosphere of a disintegrating democratic republic in the waning years of the Weimar state and society. The pluralistic public arena was filled with competing ideologies and plans. Few among the young had confidence in the government to provide jobs, security, or national stature. The suicide rate among university students, beset with uncertainty and poor morale, was three times as high as in the general population—a phenomenon not seen before or after in modern German history.[5] As Peter Loewenberg has shown, the youth cohort born between approximately 1903 and 1915 was afflicted with various economic, social, physical, and psychological problems. This group of young men and women were between the ages of eighteen and thirty in 1933, when they constituted nearly one-third of the German population.[6] Brought up as children during World War I, they and their mothers were abandoned as the fathers fought in the trenches. Malnutrition, inadequate shelter, and deficient heating resulted in hunger, illnesses, and deaths well into the post-1918 Allied blockade period. The children's pain was prolonged when the fathers returned from the war as losers who had been thrashed. Many were nominal fathers who did not understand their children anymore and were often regarded by them as rivals for the affection of their mothers.[7] Others never returned: two million men had been killed in the war, leaving war widows alone with their children.[8] The disastrous results of the postwar runaway inflation, which lasted until 1924, left many children feeling frightened, dreading real or potential impoverishment—a feeling exacerbated by the high unemployment and wage loss during the Great Depression starting in late 1929. This deflationary recession was still in full swing when Hitler assumed power.[9] As this generation of young people became apprentices, journeymen, young merchants, or university students, and hence prospective full-fledged members of the nation's workforce (or, as females, future wives of putative breadwinners), their sense of economic uncertainty led to profound doubts about their social station. Those from the middle to the lower strata accustomed to moving up in society experienced barriers in their path; those from the middle to the upper strata despaired over unsuccessful attempts to stave off downward social mobility. Many if not most of the youth cohort for the period of the 1920s and very early 1930s felt cheated out of whatever chances they had thought were theirs and increasingly looked to radical alternatives. The time was ripe for a new source of promise and support for young people, a source that gave them hope for themselves and their state in the future.[10]

These multiple difficulties were complicated by extraordinary tensions between this young generation and their elders. Indeed, intergenerational conflict was a dominating theme in Germany from the beginning of the twentieth century up to Hitler's attainment of power.[11] This conflict found expression not only in day-to-day socioeconomic and political relations but also in the arts and literature; it became a subject for many plays and novels and was starkly evident in graphic art and even music.[12] It was a determining factor in the German youth movement, in which youth sought refuge to escape from some of their difficulties, including problems with their elders. Some young people were members of the *Antifaschistische Junge Garde* (*Antifa*), the youth wing of the Communist *Rotfrontkämpferbund,* and at the close of the Weimar Republic battled Nazi storm troopers in the streets of the large cities. Others, on the other end of the ideological scale, belonged to the *Jungnationaler Bund,* a group patronized by the piously Lutheran and national-conservative establishment.[13]

The German youth movement had been founded in 1901 in Steglitz, then a thoroughly middle-class suburb of Berlin in a semirural setting, by Protestant male adolescents who were reacting against the materialism and bourgeois complacency that characterized the new German Empire's rapid industrialization in the late nineteenth century. Calling themselves *Wandervögel,* or hiking birds, they became suspicious of and bored with what the British historian Walter Laqueur, a former member of a Silesian youth group of the 1920s, has labeled a "world of growing plenty and rapid technical advance." Laqueur writes that the incipient youth movement was "an unpolitical form of opposition to a civilization that had little to offer the young generation, a protest against its lack of vitality, warmth, emotion and ideals." These young people, boys as well as girls, stressed individualism; inspired by cultural pessimists like Lagarde, Schopenhauer, and Nietzsche, they wanted to lead their own lives beyond urban confines, away from homes, parents, and teachers. They roamed the countryside, following their own rules of simplicity and honesty, dressed in makeshift garb, singing rediscovered folksongs, eating simple food by the campfire, and espousing a sexually clean life. They were in search of a romantic absolute, what since the nineteenth century had been called the "Blue Flower." They became enthralled by mysticism, whose sources they found in Cossacks of the Russian steppes or Buddhist priests in Far Eastern temples. Most of this was alien to their parents' experience and barely understood by them. Thus the theme of intergenerational conflict was already built into the very first chapter of German youth-movement history. Although the youths' activities were apolitical, they occurred within the wider framework of pre-liberal, romantic, and in some respect resurrected medieval social and political values. In conscious opposition to the ideals of the Enlightenment, they eschewed rationality in favor of emotion.[14]

With its professed contempt for society, politics, and the state, the early German youth movement did not hesitate to wholeheartedly embrace the Empire's entry into World War I. War was viewed as highly idealized combat, and struggle in battle as natural and organic. The concept of the nation, too, had never been forsaken. As an idea unrealized, it had played a role in medieval times, as it did in the early-nineteenth-century Romantic movement and then again in the post-1848 restorative era. World War I was therefore welcomed as the catalyst in a huge cleansing process that would purge European nations, especially the new modern German nation-state, of their materialism and would resurrect archaic values. (A similarly idealistic goal was upheld by young French and English fighters for their countries, though in different ways, as their letters and diaries illustrate.)[15] In a battle near the Belgian village of Langemarck on November 10, 1914, thousands of voluntarily enlisted *Wandervögel* threw themselves against the British and were mowed down. They were regarded by their surviving peers as symbols of a tremendous sacrifice for the nation as well as for their own cohort and the youth of future German generations.[16] Henceforth, celebrations eulogizing Langemarck became a characteristic part of the developing youth movement.[17]

After November 1918, when it was realized that not even half of the 12,000 *Wandervögel* who had rushed into battle had returned,[18] the center of gravity of the German youth movement shifted. While it had always been elitist and anti-modernist, it now became increasingly martial, hierarchical, attached to discipline, uniforms, and drill, racist, and suspicious of girls in its midst—all of which was a departure from the days of the Empire. As such, the youth movement was alienated from the new republican system of Weimar, whose essence was equality as expressed in parliamentary democracy and whose representatives had signed the humiliating Treaty of Versailles (1919). In fact, the movement became downright hostile. The successors to the *Wandervögel* were the ascetic *Bünde* (leagues—because of their mystical connotations, most of these terms defy translation), who wanted nothing to do with Weimar party politics.[19] They always maintained that they were above political parties, but in fact they were ideologically right of center. Soon, however, dedicated political youth wings of the Weimar parties also came into being, as well as Protestant and Catholic youth leagues. Inasmuch as they all overlapped with the core *Bünde*, they shared the defining characteristic of the postwar German youth movement, namely its anti-democratic stance and concomitant rejection of all that Weimar stood for, in particular its modernism. A tiny minority of republican-inspired youth leagues arose that supported the new political order, but they were only a drop in the bucket.[20] On the overtly political side, there were offshoots of the parties such as the *Bismarckbund* (aligned with the German National People's Party—DNVP) and the *Antifa,* which had evolved from an earlier Communist youth league. On the extreme right, there was a youth league called the Hitler Youth, after the Führer of the Nazi Party.[21]

Because of countless disagreements on means and objectives among the multiplicity of youth leagues, serious structural weaknesses developed, resulting in flux. As typified by the Communist youth groups, change was becoming the only constant in the youth movement, giving it a notorious volatility at a time when the Weimar regime itself was becoming increasingly unstable. From 1918 to 1933 the history of the youth movement was one of an "uninterrupted chain of unions, splits and reunions."[22] Adding to this instability was the fact that the

intergenerational conflict that had once defined the archetypal youth
movement of 1901 itself became a problem for the youth leagues. By
the end of the 1920s, members who refused to leave when reaching
adulthood often took charge of new generations of members and
increasingly were resented by them.[23]

In the years from 1929 to 1933, a faltering political regime, pressing
economic hardship with little hope for the future, non-sympathetic
parents, and self-serving and static youth groups left many young men
and women with few places to turn to. This was the opportunity that
some leaders of the National Socialist movement under Hitler had
been waiting for. One of their war cries in those years, which could not
help but impress Germany's alienated youth, was "Make Way, You Old
Ones!"[24] Many Nazi leaders drove home the point that the government of the Weimar Republic was leaving young people in the lurch,
providing no agencies to care for them and leaving their problems in
the hands of the disparate youth leagues. They skillfully exacerbated
the existing generational tensions to their own ends.[25] Aware of the
joblessness that stigmatized the young, ancillary organizations of the
Nazi Party sought to help in job creation and tried to broker gainful
work. The HJ was one of these organizations, appealing, in particular,
to the lower strata of society, for which the elitist *Bünde* had not been
created.[26]

While Hitler appeared to many young people as the father or older
brother they had never had or had already lost, the Nazi movement,
with all its factions, was coming across to many as a party made for
youth. Its visible formations in the street seemed to be young—the SA,
the SS, and the National Socialist Student League, which from bastions in the universities had acted as a vanguard of Nazism in Germany's educated middle class since the mid-1920s.[27] Above all, the
members of the Nazi Party themselves were visibly young, with a mean
age of approximately thirty-one for all new joiners in the period from
1925 to 1932. This compared favorably to any other Weimar party
except for the KPD.[28] Moreover, during national elections toward the
end of the Republic, the support of youthful voters for the NSDAP

tended to be stronger, at least within the urban electorate, than that of older voters, because it was in the towns that economic problems were greatest.[29]

If disenchanted young men and women at the end of the Weimar Republic put stock in the growing Nazi movement with a view to their own future, the Nazi leaders in turn regarded youth as companions on their immediate road to success and as indispensable in the realization of their planned millennium. Although a uniform Nazi policy on youth did not exist from 1919 to 1933, the words and deeds of individual Nazi officials at certain points in time reflect an exalted view of youth. At first Hitler had been oblivious to the problems of youth, since adolescents were too young to vote or attain Party membership. Thus he could not understand why anyone among his followers would want to found, during the mid-1920s, a Nazi Students' League.[30] But once he had been persuaded by his supporters of the importance of young people, and when he realized that adolescents over sixteen were useful in big-city street fights, he acquiesced and made overtures to the youth. No doubt influenced by more astute tacticians such as Joseph Goebbels and Gregor Strasser, Hitler acknowledged by 1930 that young people were needed as recruits and guarantors of the longevity of the movement. And so he said to Munich students in the summer of that year, when their social and economic situation was becoming acute, that they should "acquire rich knowledge, in order to assume leadership positions in a coming Reich."[31] Albert Speer's later statement that Hitler was always particularly interested in youthful enrollments for the survival of his regime is true only for the post-1930 era; this was an interest forever in need of shoring up by Hitler's advisers.[32] The Führer's ambivalence toward youth helps explain why his circle of associates aged without younger reinforcements until the end of the Third Reich, and why the Nazi Party itself suffered from senescence.[33] This ambivalence and the central problem of structural ossification to which it led are connected to fundamental weaknesses in the organization of the Hitler Youth and the training it sought to provide for its members.

Apart from Hitler, there were astute Nazi lieutenants who realized early on the importance of leadership issues and how these related to the timely enlistment of youth, but their pronouncements and decisions never possessed the authority of those made by the Führer himself. In the period after World War I, when it was known that the birth rate in Germany was declining,[34] Goebbels, whose intelligent insights into policy matters were second to none in Hitler's entourage, stated precisely: "True leaders are born. Leadership cadres, however, may be trained. To engage in politics one must be called, yet to function administratively it suffices to be instructed, drilled, trained, and bred."[35] Two years after that 1930 dictum, Strasser, the chief of the Party's bureaucracy, decreed that it would be incumbent on the young generation, together with the front soldiers, to be "the sole bearers of future politics."[36]

By 1933, the young generation whom Strasser addressed consisted of those born after 1915. The common denominator of the members of this young cohort was their incorporation in the Hitler Youth between the start of Hitler's reign and its termination, that is, between 1933 and 1944, the year when the last batch of youths was initiated. By this criterion, the "Nazi Regime Youth Cohort" was not a "generation" in the classic sense, but in the sense of a group that shared a major experience within a relatively short time span.[37] Hitler Youths usually were between the ages of ten and eighteen, and thus the oldest members of the "Nazi Regime Youth Cohort" were born in 1916, and the youngest in 1934. They all "grew into the Nazi state," as the German parliamentarian Erhard Eppler, a former HJ boy, has described it in his memoirs. It is to their collective experience that we now turn.[38]

Serving in the Hitler Youth

In 1938, a story by Hitler Youth Hans Wolf, entitled "Comradeship," was published as part of a public-school primer. This is how it began: "It was a hot day and we had far to march. The sun was burning down on the heath, which was bereft of trees. The sand was glistening, I was tired. My feet were hurting in those new walking shoes, every step was hurting and all I could think about was rest, water, and shade. I clenched my teeth to keep walking. I was the youngest, and this was my first outing. In front of me strode Rudolf, the leader. He was tall and strong. His backpack was heavy and pressed down on his shoulders. Rudolf carried the bread for us six boys, the cooking pot, and a pile of books, from which he would read us wonderfully thrilling stories, at night in the hostel. My backpack only contained a shirt, a couple of sneakers, washing utensils, and some cooking gear, apart from a tarpaulin for rainy days and straw beds. And yet I thought I could not lug this backpack any longer. My comrades all were somewhat older and had camping experience. They hardly felt the heat and hardship of the march. Every now and then they would sigh and drink lukewarm coffee from their canteens. More and more, I remained behind, even though I tried to make up for my slack by running. Suddenly Rudolf turned around. He stopped and watched me crawling up to him from a distance, while our comrades continued in the direction of a few trees on the horizon. 'Tired?' Rudolf asked me, kindly.

Ashamed, I had to say yes. Slowly, we walked side by side. I was limp-
ing. But I did not want to let on to Rudolf. When we got to a juniper
bush, the leader sat down and said: 'For a little rest!' Relieved, I threw
myself down. I did not want to talk, for I was shy. Rudolf gave me
something to drink. I thanked him and leaned back comfortably, glad
to be able to stretch my aching feet, and before I knew it I was sleeping
. . . When we resumed our march, my feet hurt much less and my
backpack did not press down on me so. I was very glad about that."[1]

Hans Wolf's story encapsulates the essence of the communal Hitler
Youth experience. In exemplary fashion, it illustrates why the Hitler
Youth was so attractive and worked so well for millions of boys and
girls, certainly in the early years of the Nazi regime. Because it demonstrated key Nazi values, this story was thought fit to be distributed as
primary reading material to school children in their early teens. The
very title conjures up the important sense of belonging, as one small
individual, to a larger community, the organic *Volksgemeinschaft*. The
shared experience of marching, as the youngest of a group, in a difficult
environment reminds the young pupils of how small and weak they are
by themselves and how important it is to be supported by a group of
stronger friends. The leader of these friends is Rudolf, the strongest of
them all, who not only looks after the physical needs of his charges—
he carries the bread for them—but also acts as their spiritual mentor,
through stories he reads to them. In the larger Hitler Youth, too, the
strong members would support their weaker pals, and knowledgeable
leaders would be at hand for physical as well as mental direction. If
physical activity—much like the march in the scorching heat of the
treeless heath—however unbearable, would steel the boys' muscles and
sinews, readings and discussions in the evenings would train their
minds in Germanic lore and Nazi ideology, part of which was the
Führer cult. As a Führer in the heath, Rudolf himself is a shining
example. Sacrifice and fealty are important to him, especially in adversity, yet in the end he will save his troop, as he saves little Hans from
fatigue and total breakdown.

In 1938, as that story was being read in German classrooms, the

Third Reich was not far removed from a time of much longer marches, in territories of even more heat and fewer trees than in the story's scenario, yet undertaken for the ultimate Nazi goal of winning new living space in foreign lands. To condition German youth to serve such a goal was the principal purpose of the Hitler Youth, just as it was the purpose of Hans's story to remind all boys and girls of eligible age how important it was for them to join.

To be sure, like many institutions of the Third Reich, the Hitler Youth did not originate as a result of systematic planning and was not always an expression of monolithic cohesiveness as might have been expected in a totalitarian dictatorship such as Adolf Hitler's. Indeed, this dictatorship itself was less streamlined and much more heterogeneous than the Führer and his lieutenants would have preferred.[2] To that extent, then, Hans Wolf's depiction of comradeship, harmony, and sacrifice under the authority of a strong and omniscient leader might have overstated the actual efficiency and inner workings of the *Volksgemeinschaft* and its political agencies, if not the Hitler Youth itself. However, there is no denying that most Hitler Youths in the fold loved its program of activities and did feel looked after, knowing that they would graduate to become bearers of the new Reich. From their subjective point of view, the sentiments of belonging, of sharing, of being willing to follow orders from tough but caring leaders, were very real. It is against this backdrop of a broad and general consensus among youth in Nazi Germany that exceptions and inconsistencies must be judged.

In Search of Monopoly and Uniformity

The Hitler Youth emerged from the highly polarized pattern of youth leagues in the Weimar Republic. It had been a group of young people tied to the National Socialist German Workers' Party (NSDAP, or Nazi Party). Its origins go back to early 1925 when Adolf Hitler, just out of Landsberg prison after the abortive Beer Hall Putsch of November 1923, was rebuilding his Nazi Party. The youth group was initiated by

Kurt Gruber, a law student and admirer of Hitler from Plauen in Saxony, home to many blue-collar workers. Thus the beginnings of the Nazi youth affiliate were in the proletarian realm, and at least until Hitler's takeover in January 1933, the groups emphasized their working-class mystique. However, the proletarian image became more and more threadbare over time, as more middle-class youths joined. The groups were first called Hitler-Jugend (or HJ as a short form) in July 1926, when they were placed under the command of Hitler's SA; Hitler himself did not take a great interest in them at that time because he focused only on adults old enough to vote for his Party.[3]

Until 1930, in comparison with the *Bündische Jugend*, the HJ remained insignificant. Politically, the *Bündische* were right-wing (including anti-Semitic) enough to attract the majority of German youths who detested the Weimar Republic. The difference was that they were not fixated upon a single leader, as was the HJ, and their social composition was much more middle- to upper-class. There were about 50,000 *Bündische* when the Nazis became the second-largest national party after the Reichstag elections of September 14, 1930. By this time the HJ membership had increased to 18,000, and their social base was broadening from working-class members to middle-class youths from secondary schools, or Gymnasien, concerned about career mobility in industry, state administration, and the academic professions. It was at this time that the HJ instituted a female section, the Bund Deutscher Mädel (League of German Girls or BDM), to be part of the larger HJ organization. In addition, a Jungvolk was created for teenagers from ten to fourteen (later these would be known as Pimpfe). By the end of 1930, the age range for the HJ of both genders was from ten to eighteen.[4]

In October 1931, Baldur von Schirach was appointed by Hitler as chief of all the youth activities for the NSDAP. Schirach had led the Nazi University Student League since 1928, as well as the Nazi Pupils' League. He would soon give up both, to devote himself entirely to the Hitler-Jugend. (The Student League lived on, whereas the Pupils merged with the HJ.) In 1931 the HJ already had close to 35,000 members, which still comprised about 69 percent young workers, 12 percent pupils, and 10 percent white-collar shop clerks. It was assumed that during this time of the Great Depression, about half of the parents of these adolescents were unemployed.[5]

Baldur von Schirach, a handsome man although always on the flabby side, was three-quarters American and one-quarter German. His great-grandfather, Karl Benedikt von Schirach, once a German judge, had emigrated to the United States in 1855, where his son Karl Friedrich fought in the Civil War, on the Union side as a Major. Having lost a leg in the Battle of Bull Run, Karl Friedrich von Schirach was an honor guard at President Lincoln's funeral in 1865. Major von Schirach, Baldur's grandfather, married Elizabeth Baily Norris from a patrician Philadelphia family, but his son Karl Norris von Schirach, Baldur's father, was born back in Berlin, and eventually he too wed an American, Emma Tillou, from another good Phildelphia family. Karl Norris von Schirach was an American citizen until he joined the Prussian Army, from which he retired as a Colonel to become Generalintendant of the Weimar court theater in 1908. From this position he was ousted—unjustly, he claimed—by the revolutionary currents after World War I. Until that time, between the hallowed aura of Goethe and Schiller on the one side and the visionary modernism of the Bauhaus on the other, the Grand Duchy of Weimar was marked by mostly mediocre artistic achievements, including those in the theater directed by Karl Norris von Schirach.[6]

Into this moderately well-off family with high but frustrated cultural ambitions, Baldur von Schirach was born in 1907, in Berlin. Since his family had strong monarchist and nationalistic leanings and hated the revolution and its republican aftermath, Baldur was predisposed to the radical right even as a child. Adolf Hitler passed through Weimar one day in March of 1925, and Hans Severus Ziegler, a local right-wing culture broker close to the Schirach family, introduced Baldur and a friend to him. "Hitler pressed our hands for a long time, looking us deeply in the eyes . . . Running home, I composed one of my many bad poems: 'You stand a thousand strong behind me / And you are me, and I am you / I have not lived a single thought / Which did not quiver in your hearts.'" Hitler visited the Schirach home in the fall of that year, whereupon Baldur's American mother exclaimed: "At last a German patriot!"[7]

By the spring of 1927 Schirach had moved to Munich University to take up the study of German and English literature as well as art history; already fluently bilingual, he fancied himself a budding poet and wanted to lead the stimulating life of an artist and intellectual. As he became involved in the machinations of the Nazi Student League, he participated in its ongoing boycott of Jewish students. Again he met Hitler, who made him leader of the League in July 1928. At the same time the Führer reminded him: "Schirach, you are studying with me!"[8]

After Hitler appointed him the Party's youth chief in October 1931, Schirach nominally became a subordinate of Ernst Röhm, who now, for the second time, was the leader of the SA, or storm troopers. In 1932, Hitler elevated Schirach to the same Party status that Röhm himself enjoyed, and the HJ was set free. To emphasize his new position as a leader much closer to Hitler, Schirach organized his first youth mass rally on October 1 and 2, 1932, at Potsdam, near Berlin. There were marches, speeches, drills, and fanfares, and, naturally, both Schirach and Hitler addressed the crowd. The occasion appears to have attracted an impressive 70,000 boys and girls from all over Germany, all of whom had paid for the journey themselves.[9] December 1932 capped a period of turmoil for socially insecure people in large cities, with the radical left fighting the radical right in the streets. On the Nazi end, the SA and Hitler Youth were the main participants. In Kiel, one day in 1932, when the Party and its affiliates had been forbidden to wear Nazi uniforms by the Papen Cabinet, a clutch of HJ butcher apprentices walked down the street in their white butcher aprons, with everyone afraid that they were hiding huge butcher knives underneath.[10] By the end of the Republic, the HJ had lost twenty-two comrades in these fights, the most glorified of whom was Herbert Norkus, son of an SA man from the lower-class Moabit district of Berlin, who was hounded down by Communist youths and stabbed to death in late January of 1932.[11]

As soon as Hitler became Chancellor of the German Reich on January 30, 1933, Schirach tried to consolidate all of Germany's youth. His aim was to take over as many as possible of the diffuse youth leagues, large and small, that existed by then and turn them into Hitler Youths. On June 17, Hitler appointed Schirach Youth Leader of the German Reich. Schirach would remain in this position until August 1940, when he would be promoted to regional chief or Gauleiter of Vienna; Artur Axmann, the twenty-seven-year-old head of the Berlin social services office of the HJ, would replace him as Reich Youth Leader. Axmann's loyalty could not be doubted; born in Westphalian Hagen, he had become active in a Berlin HJ cell in 1928. But Schirach always maintained his grip on German youth: in October of 1940 Hitler appointed him Reich HJ Inspector and Plenipotentiary for Youth Education of the NSDAP, charging him with the responsibility for KLV, a program for children to be moved to the safety of the countryside, under the guidance of the HJ.[12]

By any standards, the growth figures of the Hitler-Jugend are impressive: over 100,000 by the time of Hitler's assumption of power, over 2 million at the end of 1933, and 5.4 million by December 1936. At that time Schirach, who had just been granted additional powers by the Führer, claimed to have the allegiance of 60 percent of all young people from ages ten to eighteen. While this was truly remarkable, demonstrating the attraction of the authoritarian Nazi system for young Germans, it still did not constitute the 100 percent that Schirach craved.[13]

In early 1933, the Hitler Youth showed much promise for development but was still based on a relatively small, voluntary membership. Because it prided itself on the voluntarist principle, the HJ depended during the first years of the Third Reich on the voluntary flow of new members. In order to fill the comparatively small membership rolls more quickly, Baldur von Schirach tried soon after January 1933 to manipulate the wholesale takeover of the entrenched youth leagues.

This was not too difficult, since many of their leaders sympathized with the HJ and could be lured with promises of instant leadership positions, as had been done before 1933. What these groups had in common with the Hitler Youth was a generic hatred of the Weimar republican system, its parliament and democracy; they preferred authoritarian leadership structures. What had to be overcome was individual allegiances to many single chiefs, in exchange for a unitary commitment to one national leader and his deputy.[14] Those of the republican youth groups that had derived from Weimar political parties such as the *Jungnationaler Bund* became amalgamated first because the presidential Emergency Ordinance for the Protection of People and State of February 28 paved the way for the banning of all political parties and their ancillary organizations. As the former West German Chancellor Helmut Schmidt, who was fifteen in 1933, recalls, this provoked non-organized teenagers like himself to join the HJ, so as not to be left out in the cold.[15] Schmidt speaks for many who were then under considerable peer pressure to join. Stigmatized groups, like the Communist youth league, KJVD (*Kommunistischer Jugendverband Deutschlands*), were simply dissolved and their leaders sent to a concentration camp; residual Marxist splinter groups who attempted resistance were all but snuffed out by 1935.[16]

The bourgeois and politicized youth groups who were known under the overarching label of *Bündische Jugend,* including such groups as the *Wandervögel* and *Deutsche Freischar,* whose members were given to hiking in the countryside to get away from their elders and tended to be suspicious of the Republic, had all officially been neutralized by 1936. This Nazi victory had been achieved by totalitarian methods: the terror and wounds of street fights, generally initiated by Hitler Youths despite Schirach's official ban on such confrontations.[17] But doubtless, Schirach had issued his order only perfunctorily, and it was gleefully ignored by his followers. In southwest German Baden in the summer of 1934, for example, where the *Deutscher Pfadfinderbund* (German Boy Scouts) had so far gone unmolested, forty Hitler Youths attacked two of their members without apparent cause, sending one to the hospital.[18] In another instance the charismatic Eberhard Koebel, whom his followers in the *Deutsche Jungenschaft* knew as "Tusk," after flirting with Communism had made overtures to the HJ in the autumn of 1933. However, in January 1934 the Gestapo arrested Koebel, who then slit his wrists and was sent to the hospital, where he jumped out of a window and suffered a concussion. After his release a few days later, he fled to England via Sweden.[19] Other bourgeois youth leaders were murdered outright. A typical incident occurred in June 1934, when in Plauen the former leader of the *Deutsche Freischar*, Karl Lämmermann, was killed by a frenzied HJ mob. Lämmermann had already come over to the HJ as leader in 1928; after January 1933 he continued to indoctrinate his charges in the spirit of individual freedom which had typified most of the pro-republican youth leagues, and thus he reached a violent end at Nazi hands.[20] By 1935, the Hitler Youth leadership calculated that youth groups with a total membership of almost 3.5 million remained outside its influence.[21] On February 8, 1936, the Gestapo forbade all those bourgeois youth leagues to exist or meet, using again the emergency decree of February 28, 1933.[22] This order had to be repeated several times because problems persisted with some *bündisch* youth formations, especially with the markedly Catholic ones among them.

The Hitler Youth faced less of a challenge in trying to incorporate the Protestant leagues. Many Protestant youths and their leadership had already declared their sympathy with the HJ before 1933, as had their parents, disproportionately, with Hitler and his Nazi movement.[23] To the extent that Protestant youth leagues wished to preserve their independence after January 1933, it was on account of claims for their institutional freedom rather than religious beliefs. To the racist Nazi "German Christians" in the Protestant Church, who thought that the Jewish Jesus really was a blond "Aryan," Hitler appeared as having been directly sent by God in order to save Germany. But even their rivals in the church, the Confessional Christians led by Pastor Martin Niemöller, believed in ceding to Caesar what they thought was Caesar's. And so easily enough, Schirach and the Protestant Youth leadership arrived at an agreement in December 1933 that merged Protestant youth groups seamlessly with the Hitler Youth.[24] A positive feature for the church leaders, or so they thought, was that Bible study could be continued in groups beyond the ranks of the HJ. But within a few months those who did so were regarded with open suspicion by local HJ leaders and harassed to the point of suppression or absorption.[25]

Catholics had been more skeptical toward the Nazis from the beginning, not least because since the Wilhelmian Empire they had had their own Catholic Center Party. The situation for Catholic youth groups, with over a million members, seemed ambiguous, but then in July 1933 the Concordat between Berlin and the Vatican was concluded, guaranteeing the Catholic Church in Germany sovereignty over all religious matters, but proscribing any sort of political activity and closing down the Center Party itself.[26] Organized Catholic youths now thought they could coexist with the Hitler Youth, but Schirach would have none of this. He accused them of being political even when they were not. There were many fracases especially in heavily Catholic regions between HJ and Catholic groups, involving notably the largest, the *Katholischer Jungmännerverband,* and the athletic organization *Deutsche Jugendkraft.*[27] Symptomatic of Nazi brute force was an incident in the Bavarian countryside near Berchtesgaden, where in May 1934 Hitler Youths accosted young Catholic churchgoers and ripped their *Jugendkraft* club signs from their clothes.[28] The shutting down of the Catholic youth leagues occurred in stages between 1935 and 1939; even youth groups with harmless names, such as "Franciscan Youth" or "Catholic Young Men's Association," could not convince the HJ leadership of an absence of political intentions.[29]

Thus the growth of the Hitler Youth from January 1933 to the beginning of World War II was in large part contingent on the forced incorporations of previously organized leagues and less on voluntary memberships, as Schirach and his minions had claimed.[30] Indeed, of three statutory provisions concerning the HJ before September 1939, only the last one called for compulsory membership of boys and girls aged ten to eighteen. The first of these provisions was Schirach's formal appointment by Hitler as Reich Youth Leader of Germany on June 17, 1933, which gave his office of youth supervision high priority without elevating it to the status of a Reich ministry.[31] Schirach could issue patriotic appeals and use psychological ploys such as invoking peer pressure, which would serve as a powerful incentive for non-organized German youths to join, but he could not force them outright. The second provision, the Hitler Youth Law of December 1, 1936, stated that "the entire German youth within the territory of the Reich is coordinated in the Hitler Youth." This was wishful thinking in the guise of a decree, but it had not actually been accomplished, even though it created a strong illusion in Germany that Schirach was right, thus adding more power to peer pressure.[32] The third provision, on March 25, 1939, specified that "all adolescents from age 10 to 18 are obligated to put in service in the Hitler Youth."[33] With war in the offing, Hitler now thought it prudent to fashion the HJ more strictly as a training cadre for the Wehrmacht, and this could not be accomplished without coercion. These three consecutive administrative measures are reflected in the Hitler Youth's growth statistics. According to the HJ's own figures, at the end of 1933 there were 2.3 million young people, or 30.5 percent of the total age cohort, in its ranks. This figure had climbed to 64 percent at the end of 1937, and by early 1939, undoubtedly because of the March decree, membership briefly reached a respectable 98.1 percent.[34] To all intents and purposes, Schirach with his carrot-and-stick policy—a typical governing ploy in the formative years of the Third Reich—had been resoundingly successful.

German locales were affected unevenly by these developments. Of 137 elementary schools in the region of Vechta in northern Germany, 80 had co-opted all students in the last four grades by July 1934, meaning those from ten to fourteen years old; the rest claimed a success rate of at least 80 percent.[35] By contrast, schools somewhat further south in the area of Lippe at about the same time could barely win half of the students for the Hitler Youth.[36] In June 1935 in a trade-school class in Hamburg only seven of twenty students were in the HJ, and thus the Party representatives were handing out questionnaires asking: "Why are you not a member?"[37] Students of trade schools throughout southwest German Baden in October of that year managed an HJ membership of less than 80 percent, whereas Gymnasien were higher than 90 percent, and elementary schools just under 90 percent.[38] Eight Gymnasien in the vicinity of north German Brunswick (always a Nazi stronghold) in February 1936 boasted HJ membership figures from 94 to 99 percent, but in Catholic Bavaria, in elementary and trade schools, merely 44 percent followed Schirach's call.[39] In all of Württemberg, to the northwest of Bavaria, less than a year before the compulsory order of March 1939, 89.7 percent of students in all schools had joined, with those in Gymnasien at the highest rate, those in trade-oriented schools the lowest, and elementary pupils somewhere in between.[40]

Although these figures are respectable, they also show that not all schools attracted HJ recruits equally and that religious and regional factors had something to do with a teenager's willingness to join. As individual case histories bear out, the membership rate in a Gymnasium tended to be high because, contrary to its pre-1933 lower-class motto, the HJ leadership now wooed older and socially well-placed students who could lead youths two or three years younger than themselves. This incentive was absent in elementary schools, from which students graduated at age fourteen with apprenticeships or jobs in mind that allowed little room for HJ interests. And that situation was even more pronounced in designated trade schools, some of whose students were already engaged in a job.[41]

Wherever it existed, the porousness of the HJ membership structure until March 1939 still allowed some flux. Obviously, when young Germans chose not to join, they were challenging the societal or labor-market sanctions that such an attitude would evoke. One of these Germans was the budding Nobel Prize novelist Heinrich Böll in Cologne, sixteen years old in 1933: "I just *could not* go to the HJ and I did not go, and that was that."[42] Local HJ pressure to join was often overcome with the help of parents, more precisely the mother, and in

Catholic regions the local priest could strengthen any anti-HJ resolve.[43] In the summer of 1936 country girls in the Bavarian village of Weildorf refused to attend BDM evenings, citing lack of parental permission, church obligations, and fatigue after a hard day's work in the fields.[44] Once they were members, some boys and girls played hooky because they were bored, did not like the songs, found exercising and marching too strenuous, or did not get along with the (scarcely older) group leaders.[45] One Nazi publication hints at something more sinister: in the story of Hitler Girl Ursel and her friends, a BDM newcomer, Marga, refuses to fit in. She does not abide by the BDM cleanliness code and is interested only in silly pranks. She sticks her tongue out when told to behave, all to no avail, until the leader, Ursel, strips Marga of her uniform and insignia. Marga turns on her heel, slams the door shut, storms out, and is never seen again.[46] The willingness of well-conditioned Hitler Youth teens to brand outsiders as enemies of the Nazi community, even in those early years, was effective then and foretold of things to come.

Because members could leave at will if they were disgruntled, social and political sanctions were brought to bear. At least in theory, Gymnasium students absent from the HJ were not permitted to pass the Abitur, the mandatory entrance examination for university. Working youths were to be denied apprenticeships in trades or factories, and could not become hereditary farmers (*Erbhofbauern*). The political consequence of non-participation was to be barred from the Nazi Party or any of its affiliates forever. This was supposed to amount to "political ostracism and a ban from all public life."[47] But already in 1936, with a dearth of workers for the incipient war economy, these stipulations were rendered meaningless, and for those who hated the HJ enough to avoid it, public office in a Nazi state would have been loathsome in any case.

Even after the Youth Ordinance of March 1939 the constancy of HJ attendance was still not what it should have been, as too many teenagers came and went or did not enroll at all.[48] The HJ leadership got some help in November 1939 when it was decreed that it could use the state bureaucracy to enforce its rulings. This meant notifications to local and regional government agencies, such as county heads (Landräte) and, subsequently, the police.[49] Henceforth the HJ aimed to solve the truancy problem at two levels. If, for example, boys or girls had missed three meetings, the local gendarme could put them behind bars for an entire Sunday (so they would not miss school), on a diet of water and bread. Once parents were held responsible, Nazi Kreisleiter or district chiefs could threaten them with the withholding of social benefits until their children became faithful members.[50]

In the following months many HJ outposts tried this route, but with mixed results.[51] Indeed, government agencies such as the judiciary doubted the efficacy of currently available sanctions, not least because of the red tape involved.[52] Everyday practice bore this out. In Biberbach near Ulm on a Sunday in April 1941, several HJ members chose to go to church rather than attend a specially scheduled morning drill. They were supported in this not only by their parents but also by virtually the entire village population, of which it was said that "it holds the position that the boys belong in church, as there is enough time during the afternoon for drills."[53] Only in rare cases did young repeat offenders appear to have been actually arrested, tried, and punished.[54] And so throughout the Reich, not much improvement was seen. In some places, such as the Bavarian district of Landsberg, by the middle of 1942 "there had not been any Hitler Youth activity for 2–3 years."[55]

Although at the national level, these incidents appear not to have had great importance, they still irked the Hitler Youth leadership. Thus the HJ leaders decided to solicit Heinrich Himmler's aid in his capacity as Chief of SS and Police, including the Gestapo, in order to enforce total service in the HJ. Through the Youth Service Compulsion Decree of November 24, 1942, Himmler laid down much tougher laws that did not require bureaucratic channels to implement. The police were empowered to move quickly against a culprit's parents, who could be fined or imprisoned. Alternatively, the youths themselves could be held accountable. They, too, could receive a fine, be incarcerated on the express order of the Hitler Youth, or be taken into special custody by the criminal police or, worse, the Gestapo, as asocial aliens and unre-constructible criminals.[56] Subsequently, this regulation served as the basis for much more rigorous attempts to stamp out absenteeism, espe-cially when combined with the ultimate social punishment meted out by the HJ, expulsion.[57] However, all this could not change the fact that Hitler Youth attendance even at the height of the war was not perfect.[58]

Young Germans who mustered the courage to resist HJ incorpora-tion often did so not just out of boredom or dislike of annoying rou-tines and drills. Many were individualistic enough to reject, on their own behalf, the stereotypical mold into which the Hitler Youth leader-ship wished to press all of its members, thereby allowing for no devia-tions from the norm, no idiosyncrasies whatsoever. The HJ's idealized self-image was stiflingly uniform and militantly exclusive at the same time—in keeping with the vision of a future Nazi elite, in which many ruthless political führers were needed for every governmental eche-lon.[59] This uniformity was manifested not just by the required cloth-ing—black shorts or trousers and khaki shirts for the boys, and dark-blue skirts with white blouses for the girls—but also by the mili-tary short cut (with hair the length of matches) for the boys, and long braids or rolls for girls.[60] Within specifically German frameworks, the ideologically racist Hitler Youth defined itself for practical purposes through folk songs, life in the outdoors, and physical exercise—said to be the opposite of international decadent Jewry, American-style films and jazz, and modern international art forms.[61]

Thus, even during times of (officially) universal HJ membership, when most members, like Hermann Graml and Margarete Hanns-mann, loved the daily cult and sports routines, there were always some reflective adolescents of both sexes who were different. They protested against the stifling rigor by refusing the state's youth conscription. In this they were mostly acting alone and only sometimes with the back-ing of parents or friends. One boy in northern German Rendsburg, supported by his father, risked total confrontation with his leaders

simply by growing his hair long.[62] Another, Max von der Grün, later a
writer, resented the demanding HJ because his father was incarcerated.
Peter Wapnewski, later a professor of German literature, as a youth was
hypnotized by American jazz and swing and thus forged a doctor's letter to stay away.[63] A Frankfurt boy who skipped the Hitler Youth meetings in favor of the movies altered his HJ identity card in order to view
the adult-only films.[64] A particularly sensitive girl in Hamburg risked
expulsion from the BDM because she found its views to be drivel, after
she had seen paintings by Emil Nolde, George Grosz, and members of
the Bauhaus school which were displayed as deterrents at the 1937
Exhibition of Degenerate Art.[65] Karma Rauhut, too, was a Hollywood
film and jazz aficionado, who exchanged her meetings with BDM pals
for ones with Eleanor Powell and Clark Gable. Like Wapnewski, Rosemarie Heise, socialized by Social Democratic parents, forged a medical
certificate in order to stay home and listen clandestinely to the BBC.[66]
The noted Hitler biographer Joachim C. Fest, who even at seventeen
was a critic of the Führer and his Nazi regime, had never bothered to
join the HJ. After he carved a small caricature of Hitler on his wooden
desk in 1941, he faced expulsion from school as well as political
recriminations from the Hitler Youth. Without hesitation, his sympathetic father took Joachim out of the Berlin Leibnitz-Gymnasium and
quietly moved the family to Freiburg.[67]

Although these exceptions were quite rare, they still contradicted,
from the hopeful beginnings in 1933 to the catastrophic finale in 1945,
the image of a uniform monopoly by the Hitler Youth that its leaders
consistently projected. And few as they might have been, they constituted the basis for several of the HJ's growing problems. Yet there is no
denying that the Hitler Youth, beginning with Schirach's watch and
continuing under Axmann, managed to gather by far the greater part of
German youth between the ages of ten and eighteen into its fold.

Authoritarianism, Militarism, Imperialism

Although this was always denied by Hitler Youth leaders after 1945,[68]
the hallmark of HJ socialization was militarization, with a view to a

war of territorial expansion and, as its predetermined goal, the neutralization of Europe's Jews. To be sure, matters of military import had
already played a role in the late Weimar republican youth movement,
but, because of post–World War I disarmament, they were never as
central or as significant. This situation had already begun to change
with the rhetoric of Nazi leaders after January 1933, and it did change
in April of 1935, after the introduction of universal conscription on
March 16. Armed Forces Minister Werner von Blomberg announced:
"Service in the Wehrmacht is the last and highest step in the general
educational process of any young German, from the home to the
school, to the HJ and Labor Service."[69] At the same time, the youngest
HJ boys of ages ten to fourteen were officially quoted as saying: "What
are we now? Pimpfe. What do we want to be? Soldiers!" In 1937 Lieutenant Colonel Erwin Rommel, destined to be famous as Hitler's
Desert Fox in the North African campaign, was appointed by the German Army High Command as the first liaison officer to the Hitler
Youth leadership.[70] During World War II, the connection between
premilitary training in the HJ and actual combat in the field was of
course made much more explicit, as one became a precondition for the
other.[71]

Even before the beginning of the global conflict in September 1939,
the most ingenuous Hitler Youths found this trend quite normal: they
had been told in school and at home—to say nothing of the HJ
itself—that Germany was preparing for an "unavoidable war."[72] The
most common Hitler Youth activities involving premilitary training
were camp and hiking exercises, practiced in a far more rigorous way
than the Weimar youths or the Boy Scouts in England had done. Local
HJ groups enthusiastically played "war games" against each other, during which boys could be roughed up badly in order to steel themselves
for greater adventures.[73] Local camp events often took place in tents,
with mandatory overnight stays; the game plan included many military features, such as roll calls during flag ceremonies, military trumpet
fanfares, and rifle practice, all controlled by a strictly hierarchical command rule.[74] Much importance was given to the study of maps and the
spotting of imaginary or designated enemies (usually an opposing HJ

posse, perhaps from an adjacent city district). In the guise of games and play, constant vigilance and discipline were practiced.[75] This applied as well to the regional and national hikes, which would take the Hitler Youth on strenuous marches to historically important sites, preferably near the borders of countries to be conquered later, such as Schleswig (Denmark) and East Prussia (Poland).[76] Once the war had begun, these routines were well in place and were continued with the express purpose of immediately transferring eighteen-year-old youths into the armed forces.[77]

A large part of this premilitary training consisted of sports, in keeping with Hitler's own tenets in *Mein Kampf*, where he had singled out boxing as his favorite.[78] Indeed, boxing was one of the preferred sports in the Hitler Youth.[79] Programmatically and in accordance with the biopolitical principles underlying the Nazis' *völkisch* community, it was held that sport was not a matter of individual relaxation, but a "necessity for keeping the *Volk* healthy"—hence to be entrusted exclusively to the national monopolist youth organization.[80] From 1933 until well into the war, the Hitler Youth leadership organized large-scale regional and national competitions among its members, after having attained a state monopoly in the organization, administration, and conduct of all types of sport.[81] Again, the connection with war was obvious: through sport the body was trained for combat, and certain sportsmen were needed for special tasks, such as skiers in the spring of 1940 after Germany had invaded Norway under General Eduard Dietl.[82]

Whether they were aware of the military implications or not, most Hitler Youth members liked the sports, since there was plenty of variety. There were calisthenics, swimming, fencing, ball games, and the nationally beloved soccer, which was said to further a mutual feeling of community.[83] The writer Siegfried Lenz reports that he was fond of spear throwing, preferring it even to handball and the high jump.[84]

But not all Hitler Youths were so happy with the sports and drill because much of it overextended them physically. Although this was not unusual in premilitary groups of any day or age, the Nazis perfected sports and drill techniques so as to humiliate their young

charges to the point were they lost their self-respect, becoming deper-
sonalized and totally malleable. "We had to run for hours," writes one,
"crawl through filth, and hop up and down." "Did we feel degraded,
drilled, demeaned, or caught?" writes another, in retrospect claiming
not to have known that he was being readied "for a war."[85] The HJ,
explicitly honoring the Social Darwinist principle of the superiority of
the fittest, encouraged individual and group sadism, physical and mental torture, and peer-group hazing, more than any republican youth
league would have done. There were forced tests of courage such as
making youths jump from five-meter boards into water, often when
they could not swim, making them climb up the side of ravines without proper support, and forcing them to perform endless knee-bends.
In one camp, a non-swimmer drowned in the deep end of a swimming
pool.[86]

Learning how to shoot was a key element in premilitary training and
a regular part of the agenda early on for all boys, from ages ten to eighteen. Those up to fourteen years practiced with air guns, while the
older boys were taught how to use small-caliber rifles. The instruction
was theoretical as well as practical.[87] On the whole, these exercises were
understandably very popular with the HJ membership, who for some
years could not foresee but only guess to what uses their skills would be
put one day.[88] But their enthusiasm did not diminish after the war
began and the need for gun training became wholly transparent. If
anything, more frequent and elaborate shooting matches such as those
prescribed by an ordinance of October 15, 1939, sharpened the boys'
appetite for real-life combat, since they had already been sufficiently
conditioned in a martially attuned society.[89] Frequently, the increased
familiarity with and casual handling of guns led to accidents, as in February 1941 in Munich, when a sixteen-year-old Gymnasium student
shot his friend to death with a handgun during play-acting. The
revolver was a Browning, which at the time was routinely handed out
to Hitler Youths by their superiors.[90]

Although gun sports were prevalent throughout the Hitler Youth,
they may have mattered less in some branches and more in others,

depending on their specialization. Apart from the general HJ, there were some specialized units that were regarded as more elite than others, such as those with gliders, then turning into the Fliers' HJ. In these units, experience in the air was paramount, often after courses in model-plane construction, and playing with handguns or rifles took second place.[91] It is obvious that these eager young pilots were coveted by Göring's Luftwaffe when the war was on, just as the ground forces would claim experienced members from special details for motorcycles and even automobiles (Motor HJ). In the Motor HJ, some of the vehicles were owned by senior HJ members or their well-to-do fathers; others could train on the HJ's own vehicles, which again incited much enthusiasm in the boys.[92] In the North, the Marine HJ was sought-after, since many youths in Hamburg, Bremen, or Kiel were already familiar with sailboats and kayaks.[93] After 1938 these young men easily found their way into the Navy, which most of them joined just as will-ingly as others did the Luftwaffe. Like the motor branches, members of the Equestrian HJ and the Communications HJ, which trained with the telephone and Morse code, would also merge with conventional ground troops.[94]

There also was a music division in the Hitler Youth. The boys and girls who flocked to it were artistically inclined and, because of their sensitivity, less interested in physical activities and therefore more subject to harassment by their peers than was the norm.[95] The music cadres usually were attached to radio stations (HJ-Rundfunk-Spielscharen), where HJ choirs or small orchestral ensembles per-formed alongside other offerings, frequently political ones, broadcast live from the studios. These HJ musical groups also performed at pub-lic recitals, and whenever the Hitler Youth leadership needed them for inspiration at its own political and disciplinary exercises, such as regional camp meetings or occasions when the HJ had to reinforce Nazi Party rallies.[96] At drill time the repetitious use of a song helped in the numbing of young minds, as part of the Nazi educational canon.[97] Such music could be turned exclusively to serving ideological ends, aided by a plethora of ideologically charged texts. Fully aware of this, the HJ leadership maintained music academies and chairs at universities to help in the forming of politicized musical Nazi servants. Some respectable German composers, including Heinrich Spitta and Wolfgang Fortner, contributed their talents to this effort, and Carl Orff wanted to put together at least one songbook for HJ mass consumption in 1933.[98] Indeed, most of the songs that the Hitler Youths were encouraged to chant, in the manner of soldiers on the march, were clearly martial in character, related to Fatherland, duty, honor, blood and soil, and above all fighting and death.[99] A prime example of this is "Our Flag Is Showing Us the Way," with lyrics by the would-be poet Schirach himself, used for HJ propaganda as early as 1933 in the Ufa film *Hitlerjunge Quex,* which glorified the 1932 Nazi martyrdom of Herbert Norkus. The song conjures up a battleground, speaks of defying danger, of a glowing Germany, of possible doom, of Hitler the Führer ("We are marching for Hitler through night and dread / With the banner of youth for freedom and bread"), and reassures the enraptured singers that "we are the soldiers of the future."[100]

As one might expect, even in peacetime the Hitler Youth boys and girls spent a good many hours per week in HJ-owned houses, after school or work and regularly on weekends. Here indoctrination took place and plans were made for extracurricular outdoor activities, such as bivouacs, sports, and drill. In the early years of the Third Reich, existing Weimar youth movement hostels were confiscated and new HJ clubhouses were built from scratch or by renovating rudimentary structures such as stables and tool sheds. During this construction and the meetings following it, the beloved HJ hymns were intoned.[101] These clubhouses (HJ-Heime) became much more important in the winter time, when the teenagers could not be sent away to rural areas to do some practical work for the nation. For the regime, the most valuable of these tasks, especially during summer school vacations, turned out to be the work of aiding the peasants on the farms. Such field activity helped serve the purpose of keeping the youths physically fit, while at the same time honoring the Nazi dogma of "Blood and Soil," which tried to put a stop to the current exodus from the land to the cities. Not least, such work was good for the overall economy and was, once again, an important preparatory step toward premilitary recruitment and, eventually, the deployment of young people in battle, the occupied territories, and for war emergencies at home.[102]

From the beginning of organized agricultural service, around 1934, the Nazis targeted eastern territories in particular, first German ones adjoining the Polish border such as Pomerania and Silesia, with a view to occupying them in a sweep of conquest behind the German Wehrmacht.[103] Thus helping on the farms and in the fields, whether this involved harvesting, cutting wood, or milking cows, was complementary to the barely disguised imperialistic hikes by Hitler Youths to the coveted borders.[104] When the time came, these youths would know those territories and how to exploit them. HJ-Landdienst, or agricultural service, was always characterized by an imperialist quality. Its ideology was based on that of the racist *Artamanen,* a pre-1933 youth league on the extreme right of would-be eastern settlers, to which leading National Socialists had once belonged, among them Heinrich Himmler, Reich Peasant Leader Richard Walther Darré, and the future commandant of Auschwitz, Rudolf Hoess. It is telling that the *Artamanen* were among the few Weimar republican youth groups to blend easily with Schirach's budding Nazi youth movement, when it absorbed them in 1933.[105]

It was during the war that the agricultural youth service revealed its true predatory character. Teenagers were sent to the newly conquered western areas of Poland where many Germans lived in the countryside, most of them adhering to a standard of nutrition and hygiene typical of their Polish neighbors, which the Germans in the Reich despised. The mission of German youth was to re-educate those ethnic Germans, or *Volksdeutsche,* and lead them back to the proper ways of the life and livelihood of their forefathers. Eventually, such Nazi hubris even extended to Germans living in the western borderlands such as Eupen and Malmédy, which had been reconquered from Belgium, and Alsace-Lorraine, reconquered from France. In the Southeast adjacent to annexed Austria, Lower Styria, too, once part of Yugoslavia, was targeted.[106]

In 1940 this HJ service was still voluntary, and tens of thousands of teenagers moved to the borderlands. Not only did they willingly toil on the farms, in the forests, and in the fields, but they also gave German lessons to ethnic Germans who had lost or adulterated their language.[107] Nazi-specific culture, such as that derived from traditional German music or folk dance, and ideological issues also became part of the broader catechism.[108] Many of the Germans from Poland were to be resettled in the Reich, and this number was greatly increased after 1941, when approximately 350,000 emigrants from rural areas of the Soviet Union, mostly the so-called Volga Germans, had to be cared for as well, in large resettlement camps.[109] By 1942 this colonization work had become mandatory for members of the Hitler Youth, and they were typically deployed during the summer or fall for a period of six weeks, when entire classes were taken out of school and sent on the job.[110] During such sojourns German youths were also commanded to guard the youth of conquered nations in special camps, in particular Polish youth, and in this way were taught the techniques of subjugation, which not all of the Reich's teenagers were immediately comfortable with.[111] Now more than ever the Hitler Youth leaders—as did Himmler's SS—worked with the concept of *Wehrbauerntum,* or fortified farmsteads, as border bastions in an incrementally conquered East, where young German families would be settled, plow in one hand and gun in the other. The goal, originally projected by the *Artamanen* in the 1920s, was to subjugate the indigenous populations and use them as slaves on the land that had been taken from them, with the Germans as sole beneficiaries and absolute masters.[112]

On the home front during the war, the Hitler Youth went from door to door collecting valuable raw materials, such as rags, paper, and scraps of metal for recycling, an activity that was essential for the war economy. HJ members also had to participate in the search for mushrooms and for herbs, used for tea and medicinal purposes, as well as helping out in town and country in various auxiliary positions, such as tram conductor, ersatz-coffee dispenser at train stations, or letter carrier.[113]

But the ultimate trial for the Hitler Youth came during direct contact with the effects of the war itself, on the home front as the tide turned against the Germans. HJ members had to assist soldiers who were home on furlough or sick leave, many exhausted or disabled, some of them maimed beyond recognition. The boys and girls helped in the building of fortifications in the streets or close to the fronts and were on call for emergencies and war-triggered catastrophes such as flooding.[114] Teenagers functioned as air raid wardens and helped to fight fires, often at lethal risk to themselves. One former Hitler Youth, sixteen years old in 1940, remembers what he saw: "People under shock, with burns and singed hair, old women who had gone insane, mothers with an injured toddler in a blanket, momentarily blinded people, men weeping quietly. Pictures which carried me into many nightmares."[115] The worst such experience occurred after half of Hamburg had been leveled by British phosphor bombs, in July and August of 1943. The Nazi regime praised those youngsters as heroes—twelve, thirteen, or fourteen years old—who had saved civilians from burning ruins, even as some were themselves consumed by flames. One of those who made it through the inferno, which killed 42,000, writes that "we didn't have any sun at all for three or four days; it was completely dark out. We only saw a blood-red ball in the distance, which didn't penetrate the dark cloud that hovered over Hamburg for days: smoke, cinders, and ashes. The dead were piled in the entrances of houses. And when you went by you just saw a heap of feet, some barefoot, some with burned soles. The corpses were beyond identification. We would dig entire families out of their basements, sometimes two, three weeks later; they'd fit into a bathtub. Even the adults were very small. They were completely mummified, burned, and melted together by the heat."[116]

One might think that youth cohorts thus conditioned by a totalitarian regime were, like Sparta's young, toughened by removal from their primary environments of nurture and formal education, whether parental homes or schools. This was undoubtedly the ideal of the Nazi state in recruiting suitable leaders and followers, to keep the millennial Reich on track. However, Nazi socialization of the young in the long run was difficult because in Germany it had to contend with traditionally strong mainstays of society, namely parents and teachers and in some cases employers, with whom Hitler Youths might be apprenticing. Although the employers became less of a problem because the primacy of a war economy was recognized early and shops might make fewer demands on a youth's available time, ties to home and school posed difficulties which the HJ leadership took pains to overcome. In this struggle, the HJ leaders knew they could count on Hitler himself, who in the 1920s had declared in *Mein Kampf* (a book that few Germans bothered to read or take seriously) that developing a fit body was paramount, and anything else, including "the development of intellectual acumen," took second place.[117] In December 1938, after the Sudeten crisis, Hitler made clear his concept of the total politicization of youth when he announced publicly: "After these youths have entered our organizations at age ten and there experienced, for the first time, some fresh air . . . we shall under no circumstances return them into the hands of our old champions of class and social standing, but instead place them immediately in the Party or the Labor Front, the SA or SS . . . And then the Wehrmacht will take them over for further treatment . . . And thus they will never be free again, for the rest of their lives."[118]

To be sure, in the beginning the Hitler Youth leadership, with its revolutionary self-image, paid lip service to the institutions of old, but only to trick them into submission and subsequently to defeat them. Pronouncing on a three-pillar theory of home, school, and HJ, Baldur von Schirach early on attempted to assure parents that their traditional role as nurturers would not be interfered with, and educators that they would remain role models in the classrooms. But even then he left no doubt that the HJ's task of indoctrinating the young with the Nazi weltanschauung and developing their physical and martial prowess

took precedence over any traditional grooming.[119] Still, to pacify especially the teachers, Schirach in conjunction with the Reich Education
Ministry allowed for a Staatsjugendtag or State Youth Day in June
1934. This meant that much of the weekly HJ service encroaching on
school time would be concentrated outside of school on Saturdays,
during which those teenagers of ages ten to fourteen not yet organized
in the HJ were allowed to remain in regular school attendance. Wednes-
day evenings were to belong to the HJ.[120] To placate parents, Sundays
were to be reserved for them, and Schirach made a special point
in 1937 that Christmas, now as ever, was "the festival of the German
family."[121] Even in 1940, after the HJ had achieved unassailable state
monopoly status, the three-pillar theory was still upheld, with the family being singled out as the avatar of pre-school socialization.[122] By this
time, however, the HJ leadership had not only made service in its ranks
a national obligation, but was also able to use the exigencies of war as a
rationale to step up its battle against parents and teachers alike.

In *Fear*, a play from 1944, Bertolt Brecht depicts the situation of a
couple fearing they will be denounced by their son, Klaus-Heinrich, as
he steps out of their flat for a short period to buy himself some candy.
Even after his return home, they have no way of knowing whether or
not he has turned them in to the Gestapo. They are certain that Klaus-
Heinrich has overheard anti-regime remarks, and they know that he is
a member of the Hitler Youth.[123] This fictionalized scenario was a very
real one for many parents of Hitler Youths who could not hold their
tongues, certainly in the period before the beginning of the war when
the official status of the HJ often seemed arbitrary and parents still
assumed their traditional educational prerogative. Indeed, there are
documented cases where children turned in their parents to the police,
for whatever reason—such as a certain Herr Hess, once a Communist,
who had called the Führer "a blood-crazed maniac." Reported by his
son, a mid-level HJ leader, he was arrested on the very night of the
remark and sent to Dachau, where he died at age forty of a sudden
"heart failure."[124] There are other instances where brazen HJ leaders,
callow youths of sixteen or seventeen in uniform, confronted the

fathers of sons in their cadres and threatened them en masse.[125] Girls
did the same to mothers.[126] Much more numerous, however, were
those cases in which, as Brecht describes, parents *thought* some anti-
regime remark had been made or where the HJ child *knew* of their former political affiliation, such as Communism, Social Democracy, or
membership in a religious sect like the anti-Nazi Jehovah's Witnesses.[127] Nor were political or ideological factors the only reason for a
denunciation. Normal intergenerational conflict may have somehow
been resolved in the democracy before 1933. But in Hitler's totalitarian *Volksgemeinschaft*, which often pitted son against father or daughter
against mother as a matter of tactics, such conflict was being politicized, to be exploited subsequently by Schirach's HJ in order to keep
the adults in check.[128] Thus perhaps unwittingly, children often became pawns in a fundamental confrontation between the regime and
its less than pliant subjects.

Without a doubt, regime leaders knew and took advantage of the
fact that for many youngsters the parental atmosphere was too narrow,
or that they could not abide a family's religious practices, now frowned
upon in the Hitler Youth.[129] Melita Maschmann, later an influential
BDM leader, once met a young sympathizer who disliked his father, a
professor of psychology, because he was a devotee of Freud.[130] Aesthetic reasons, such as a distaste for the plebeian Nazi uniforms, motivated many parents to try to keep their children from joining the HJ
when this was still not compulsory, and this provoked resentment in
their children.[131] National Socialism as celebrated in the Hitler Youth
symbolized something new. The "revolution" that Schirach liked to
invoke was seen as genuine by adolescents who often thought their
old-fashioned parents were behind the times. Many young people
wanted novelty and change and perceived the HJ as offering it.

Still, there is no denying that tension between the HJ and parents
constituted only one side of the coin, for on the other was the huge
reservoir of sympathy that a plurality of parents harbored for the Nazi
cause. HJ leaders could always count on Nazi parents, some of whom
had been Old Fighters in Hitler's Time of Struggle in the 1920s, to win

over the lukewarm or resistant ones. These parents frequently went to great lengths, for example organizing "Parent Friends of the HJ," a lobby that was formed in early 1936 in Hanover.[132]

The situation was more complicated in the case of schools and teachers: whereas the HJ was an institution of Party and State, educational institutions nominally were its equal because they came under the time-hallowed State Ministry of Education. By contrast, the family was traditionally in the private, not public, sphere. Hence Schirach had a freer hand whenever the Ministry elected to cooperate with him on behalf of its teachers, but he got exercised whenever the Ministry or teachers attempted to restrain him. Fortunately for him, Schirach was a much more dynamic, and certainly much younger, Nazi official than the former secondary-school teacher Bernhard Rust, the Minister of Education, whose love of the bottle was the stuff of Nazi gossip.

In his struggle with the schools Schirach was indirectly able to claim victory after the proclamation of the Law for the Reconstitution of the Civil Service on April 7, 1933, whereby unreliable teachers, such as Social Democrats and Communists (to say nothing of the Jews), were summarily dismissed. What followed were screening routines of the remaining teaching staff by the police, which, as irreversible actions, could only work in the future interest of the HJ leadership.[133] Thus when the Staatsjugendtag was introduced in May 1934, it looked like a concession by Schirach to the teachers, but its concept and practice were still so much to the disadvantage of the schools that it was abandoned in December 1936—significantly, at just the time when Schirach claimed to have united all of Germany's youth under his leadership. One telling sign that the Staatsjugendtag had been a shabby compromise for teachers was that although on Saturdays it had kept non-HJ pupils under fourteen in the classrooms, about a quarter of youths over fourteen had been missing class on Saturdays because, as HJ leaders, they had to supervise the younger HJ pupils in the field.[134] By May of 1938 Schirach felt strong enough to launch a massive public attack on the school system, claiming that it was hopelessly out of date, counter-revolutionary, and statically tied to the civil-service tenure of its teachers. Schirach echoed Hitler's sentiment in *Mein Kampf* when he asked: "Why is it that almost all the men our nation takes pride in have advanced themselves not because of their school education, but in spite of it?"[135]

With some good will, Schirach could have found common ground with the teachers, for the majority were neither Nazis nor anti-Nazis but German national conservatives, who despite the defeat of 1918 had adapted themselves in the Weimar Republic and did not find it too difficult to acquiesce in the post-1933 order. In 1980 Alfred Andersch drew a portrait of this type: a Gymnasium teacher with a pot belly, always smartly dressed in suit and tie, smug, a believer in law and order who would vacillate between dispensing favors and picking on students for the sake of maintaining absolute power, and, inevitably, proud of his World War I record. This particular teacher, under whom Andersch studied Greek and history at the Wittelsbacher Gymnasium in Munich in 1928, was the principal of that well-regarded school. His name was Secret Counselor Gebhard Himmler, at that time sixty-three years old and the well-respected father of Heinrich.[136]

The authoritarian and militaristic persona of teachers like the older Himmler eventually blended easily with the ideal of totalitarian educators which the Third Reich espoused, even before the pressure of the second war. Indeed, constant classroom references to personal war experience between 1914 and 1918 bolstered the self-esteem of teachers and—this Schirach could appreciate—kept most of the students spellbound. The teachers were able to accommodate Goethe, Beethoven, Nietzsche, and Schopenhauer, as they lauded the demise of modernism which they had experienced during the Republic. As called for, the moribund monarchic idea of the Hohenzollerns was easily supplanted by the notion of a National Socialist Reich, and for the teachers, too, Fatherland turned into *Volksgemeinschaft*. The concentration in Nazi-style history classes on figures of the Germanic past, such as Arminius the Cheruscan, Luther, Frederick the Great, and Bismarck, was little different from that in the schools in the decades after German Unification in 1871.[137]

Even within this conservative yet adaptable set, there were those who embraced Hitler and Nazism fully only in the aftermath of the threatening Law of April 1933.[138] This law was much more on the minds of that minority of anti-Nazi teachers who were forced to hide their opposition to the regime under various guises. They had to walk a tightrope between internal rejection of the Hitlerites and postures of approval. Many had been lucky not to have been caught by the law, for once found out and denounced—by malevolent colleagues or fanatical HJ pupils—they could not only be dismissed but also arrested and incarcerated, especially if they had already once been demoted.[139]

The courage of those teachers often bordered on the miraculous, and their ruses in cheating Nazi superiors were nothing short of ingenious. One teacher called Krättge, "a young man with thick glasses, a high forehead, and unkempt hair," taught German literature in Berlin. He was hated by many and beloved by few. He emphasized themes of peace where everyone spoke of struggle, exposing the cruelty in a poem about a soldier lying mortally wounded at the front for two days without anyone tending to him. The torture ballad "Feet in the Fire," from the Huguenot Wars in France, was subtly twisted to point at the Nazis' victims.[140] Heinrich Böll reports that Herr Schmitz, his German teacher in Cologne, used *Mein Kampf* as a mandatory text, by way of a bad example, to teach his pupils concision.[141] There is a touching story of a teacher who clandestinely approached Max von der Grün as a young boy, whose father, a Jehovah's Witness, was then languishing in Flossenbürg concentration camp and whose hatred of the Nazis was ferocious. The teacher removed newspaper wrappings, produced the Jewish author Stefan Zweig's *Decisive Moments in History*, and implored his student not to show it to anybody. "For me, this was the hour of destiny in my life," writes von der Grün. "I began to read with awareness. I began to develop an interest in history, and the history I read was very different from what we were taught at school." In short, says von der Grün, he began to read "the history of the vanquished rather than that of the victors."[142]

Predictably, the Nazi concept of the superior Aryan race constituted the framework for subjects such as biology, history, and geography, and some teachers adapted neutral subjects like those in the hard sciences or mathematics to ideology by dwelling on military examples, as could be done with ballistics. In music, Beethoven and Wagner were stressed and Jewish composers like Mendelssohn ignored.[143] Invariably, such teachers humiliated pupils who were wholly or partially Jewish for as long as they were allowed to be in the classrooms.[144] The comportment of these teachers conformed closely to Nazi etiquette: some of them arrived in mustard-colored Party uniforms, barked in a tone of military command, offered the Hitler salute, or boasted of honorary positions in the regime.[145]

Not least because of the growing cooperation of many of those teachers, Schirach was slowly but steadily winning his campaign against the schools. Until the outbreak of the war, more and more teachers complied with his demands that they act as recruiting agents for his youth groups, and more and more of the younger ones donned HJ uniforms, thus symbolizing the increasing subservience of formal education to Nazi indoctrination.[146] Building on earlier efforts, Schirach by February 1938 had succeeded in creating the category of "liaison teachers" (*Vertrauenslehrer*), educators as mere stooges of the Hitler Youth.[147] Pupils themselves eagerly arrived in their classrooms dressed in HJ outfits; as Manfred Rommel, son of the general and a future lord mayor of Stuttgart, described it, "we tended to be against the school and in our HJ uniforms felt like grown-ups and strong in a group."[148]

By 1937 it had become obvious that the mounting politicization of the teachers combined with the growing neglect of school matters in favor of HJ service by many students was leading to a dilution of conventional pedagogical standards; students were learning less. Schirach seized the moment in early 1938 by once again ridiculing teaching as a profession and insisting on the superiority of ideological and character training, HJ-style, over the acquisition of formal knowledge. In a gesture of defeat, Minister Rust then shortened secondary education by a year, with the dire consequence that even fewer young men and women were willing to enter the teaching profession than before. This was on the eve of the war, when the teachers' collective strength was already being sapped by countless individual conscriptions.[149]

The war years served merely to demonstrate further the capitulation of the conventional school system to the HJ, against the background of continuing powerlessness in parental homes. Teachers, no less than parents, in the spring of 1940 and again in the fall of 1942, complained about the broken relationship between schools and families on the one side, and the Hitler Youth on the other, despite the necessities of a global war that was ideologically sanctioned.[150] The HJ leadership remained unmoved; it had further disparaged the family with impunity, and it knew that millions of its charges had been weaned from the schools and were now putting in service in the armed forces or in the Party echelons.[151] Denunciations of dissident teachers on the indictment of defeatism had become easier and more frequent; moreover, large numbers of the younger and more fanatical teachers who were at the fronts returned to the classrooms on furlough, in order to incite an already militarized student body further.[152] The school curriculum itself had become less substantive, shortened and progressively corrupted by ideology or applied war-related arts.[153] Isolated protests by school principals against the widespread alienation of students from the classrooms, because of services required for Party and State, remained unheard, as exemplified by a particularly urgent letter from a secondary-school official in Goslar, in September 1942.[154] As one schoolboy, Hitler Youth, and soldier, not without cynicism, later recorded in his memoirs: "Learning was postponed to the period after the Final Victory."[155]

Early in the war the Hitler Youth was provided with an additional opportunity to strengthen its powers over both parents and teachers. By September 27, 1940, Hitler had decided to create a program called Kinderlandverschickung (KLV), or "Save the Children in the Country," with the HJ in charge. Its purpose was to protect children old enough to be separated from their parents, from about age four to the early teens, from the bombs increasingly falling on German towns and cities, by removing them to out-of-the-way, non-urban places. Children could be sent away for six months at a time, and once installed in specially prepared HJ living quarters, they were subject to rigorous disciplinary controls beyond the purview of their parents. While children up to age ten were sent to live with Nazi families by state social workers, those between ten and fourteen were in HJ-controlled locations. Usually themselves members of the HJ, these children came to be supervised by somewhat older Hitler Youths. Thus, the parental home appears to have been totally eclipsed.[156]

This expansion of HJ jurisdiction over the nation's young posed new problems for parents and teachers alike. The main question for the parents was whether they should allow their children to leave at all. But while that decision was indeed their own, most of them had little choice because the Nazis' argument that children should be protected from bombs was a sensible one; moreover, since pupils were removed from schools by grades as class units, peer pressure made it virtually impossible for a single child to stay behind.[157]

The boys and girls were carried by special trains to rural locations all over Germany, but also—and here the imperialism of the Nazi regime was the underlying factor—to villages in Axis countries such as Romania, Hungary, Bulgaria, and Slovakia, and more significantly, to conquered areas, such as Luxembourg, the Protectorate of Bohemia and Moravia, Denmark, and western Poland. Depending on their luck, the children and their warders might be quartered in the shabbiest of surroundings, such as run-down hospitals or school buildings in poverty-stricken parts of Bohemia, or in luxury hotels and even beach resorts and castles, as in Tirol and Luxembourg. The camps in Poland were almost always wretched, while the ones in South Germany tended to be in swank little pensions in alpine resorts with names like Garmisch-Partenkirchen and Berchtesgaden. If the statistics are reliable, 200,000 special trains transported approximately five million German children to as many as 12,000 camps by early 1945, at which time the actions were officially called off.[158]

More often than not, the fear among parents was great, for however much they trusted this program in their heads, they were suspicious of it in their hearts—unless they were the sturdiest of Nazis. The HJ knew this and therefore discouraged visits by parents to their camp sites wherever they could, even though they were not always successful.[159] Children found it difficult to communicate with their mother or father because their letters home were censored; sometimes they were even ordered by their HJ supervisors to write that they were doing well, homesickness and illnesses notwithstanding.[160] However, the regulations were still on the parents' side; so if they really wanted to have their children back home, there was nothing that could be done to stop them.[161] Usually it was sufficient for children to convince the HJ or their parents that they were quite ill, so that they could be brought home.[162]

Not only was it clear that the HJ was winning more victories over parents through the KLV program, but the HJ also found ways to further aggravate the teachers. The regime had fiendishly made use of its scheme of multiple responsibilities by which no agency knew who was ultimately in charge of public administration, and representatives of the Party, symbolizing the Nazi revolution, usually prevailed over the State's civil servants. In the case of KLV, the teachers who were transplanted from the classrooms to the HJ camps were supposedly responsible for a continuation of the pedagogical process and were even told to exercise supervision, whereas in fact the much younger Hitler Youth leaders who controlled the logistics of the camps were the true bosses. Even though the regime saw to it that most of the teachers sent out were trusted members of the National Socialist Teachers' League (NSLB), this arrangement turned into a true humiliation of the educators and a triumph for Baldur von Schirach and his successor, Artur Axmann.[163]

To settle the control issue, altercations between teachers and HJ camp leaders were common; these ended with an academic victory for the former and an actual one for the latter.[164] The HJ leaders enjoyed the added advantage of easy recourse to local Party powers, such as regional Hitler Youth chiefs or, as in the Protectorate, a regent such as the egregious Karl Hermann Frank.[165] To a greater extent than earlier in the Reich, normal school routines were reduced and sacrificed to HJ exercise and drill, often led by thoroughly corrupt young chieftains, with the result that the evacuated pupils were reading even fewer school texts than before.[166] The ultimate affront to the teaching profession occurred after a low point of the war in early 1943, when many more of the younger teachers were conscripted for the trenches, while the remaining older ones came under the command of ever younger Hitler Youths, because the older HJ members were at the fronts.[167]

At the KLV sites, in total disregard of the encumbered teaching personnel, the HJ extended its proven drill regimen from the home bases, again with calculated attention paid to premilitary training. Children were bullied, especially if they were found to be bed wetting—a frequent occurrence in the camps and indicative of the sense of loss they generally must have felt.[168] "Often they were simply beaten up," recounts one-time inmate Ralf Dahrendorf, today a British subject and member of the House of Lords.[169] In some places, ten- or twelve-year-olds who were starting to masturbate had their hands covered with thick gloves and then tied to the bed frames. But in other sites there were masturbation contests, and the entire practice became part of the entrenched hazing regimen.[170] Regular HJ announcements at roll calls about the air-raid death of close relatives, designed to toughen the charges' character, often broke the spirits of the stunned youths.[171] Unsanitary conditions and inferior nutrition frequently caused diseases that could not be cured because of lack of medications and medical staff, although the HJ did not hesitate to use medical students.[172]

The darkest aspect of this entire exercise, in keeping with the racist-imperialistic aims of the Nazis, was that they purposely planted their youth in surroundings known to be hostile to them. This afforded the HJ ample opportunity to point out the difference between HJ children as heirs of the master race on the one side, and those slaves who had already been vanquished, on the other. This was not without danger to the youngsters, who in Occupied Poland and the Protectorate in particular were always regarded with unmitigated hostility in the streets, to the point where it was dangerous for them to be alone or in small groups without the protection of firearms held at the ready by accompanying senior Hitler Youths.[173] Children were being taught to hate in the field, as it were; they would have to use this skill later at the extended fronts, to defend their status as members of the German ruling caste.

Problems of Training, Discipline, and Leadership

To liberate itself completely from the conventional school system, the Hitler Youth attempted to create educational institutions of its own. These were the Adolf-Hitler-Schulen (AHS), which Baldur von Schirach, behind Reich Minister Rust's back, in early 1937 conceived in an alliance with Robert Ley, the leader of the German Labor Front (DAF) and a fellow Party dignitary. Not surprisingly, Rust was furious when he found out. Hitler, however, was on the side of Schirach and the schools that would bear his name.

The first of these schools was opened on April 20, 1937, the Führer's forty-eighth birthday, in Pomeranian Crössinsee, at one of Ley's own training establishments. The projection was for about fifty such schools, at least one for each Nazi Gau or region, with a projected enrollment of 15,000 altogether. By 1941, however, there were only ten schools, and at the end of 1943, a mere 2,027 pupils attended. One reason was lack of money, for the Party's purse was notoriously tight as the war progressed. Upon graduation, after six years of schooling (subsequent to their initial six in a primary school), AHS students were supposed to enter one of Ley's own "order castles" for further Party training. Thereafter, a special Nazi university, the Hohe Schule, under chief Party ideologue Alfred Rosenberg, was to take over as a political-elite finishing school.[174]

As a new type of secondary school, the Adolf-Hitler-Schulen were Nazi Party–specific, and therein lay their early promise for Party leaders like Schirach and Ley. Beginning with the process of recruitment, the schools' entire structure rejected previous educational ideals:

they were anti-traditional, anti-knowledge, anti-Gymnasium, and anti-parent. The schools' charter was supposed to be inspired by a revolutionary dynamic, which would motivate its pupils always to put Nazi dogma first. The selection of AHS pupils was to be made by HJ leaders in conjunction with regional representatives of the Party, a certain contingent of them being assigned annually to each Gau. Although the sons of proven Nazi parents were to be preferred, the parents themselves could not apply for their children's admission and later were forbidden to take their offspring out of an AHS school. Selection criteria focused on Hitler Youth boys at least twelve years old, racially attractive, fit for sports and drill—hence with already outstanding pro-Nazi dispositions and what was called "character," a quality deemed superior to intellect and based on Nazi notions of honor, bravery, and devotion to the Führer. The ultimate career objectives for AHS students, as far as the regime was concerned, were jobs in the Party hierarchy, such as HJ leader or Gau administrator, and, as a second choice, jobs as conventional civil servants.[175]

Because of the lack of synchronization of curricula with ordinary secondary schools, the pattern of continuing education beyond primary school, and the very restricted role of parents during initial selection, the prescribed quotas for these new institutions were never attained. It was not at all surprising, Albert Speer pointed out in his postwar memoirs, that "the top functionaries did not send their children to those schools themselves."[176] When toward the end of the war the Party officials saw the error of their ways, they decided to allow intelligence more weight than "character," and to create, upon graduation, the formal learning prerequisites for entry to the Reich's universities. But it was already far too late; the damage had been done.[177]

The inferior quality of instruction was a result of the collective profile of the teachers handpicked by the HJ leadership. Whereas the older teachers tended to be staunch Party cronies, the younger ones, still in their twenties, were HJ liaison teachers, for whom Nazi politics and ideology ranked above scholarship. Shunning the time-honored school books, they worked with study aids manufactured by the social engineers of the Hitler Youth.[178] A specially dedicated Educators' Academy in Sonthofen was on the drawing board as early as 1938, in order to mold the AHS instructors of the future, but by 1943 these plans still had not been realized.[179] One and all, those teachers were "good comrades," concedes former AHS student Harald Grundmann, "they strove admirably, but they did not know enough."[180]

This lack of teaching qualifications was reflected in the curriculum. Although Schirach himself maintained in 1938 that in his new schools the substance would remain the same and only the teaching methods would change, the reality was different.[181] To a large degree, AHS instruction consisted of an intensification of the physical and mental exercises favored during regular HJ service. Among conventional school subjects, those which emphasized the German past and racial superiority were stressed, as in history, geography, and biology; foreign languages were to be studied for the sole purpose of communicating orders to future subject peoples.[182] Still, on any given school day, only an hour and a half was to be dedicated to such academic pursuits, while five hours were given over to sports.[183] Subsumed under sports were the old drill and physical tests and trials, again with the ultimate goal of warfare. "Love of war and the readiness to embrace a hero's death" was the didactic motto.[184] Since Nazi character was deemed superior to intellect, ideological indoctrination was at the top of the list. AHS students were taken to concentration camps to get to know the internal enemy. A professor of medicine explained to them the "euthanasia" program, the killing of the handicapped and infirm. And there were "combative discussions" revolving around questions of Nazi weltanschauung, politics, and novel Nazi doctrines, such as why the Aryan race was thought to be superior to any others.[185] During his school years he was always challenged physically, Grundmann remembers, but "never intellectually."[186]

The Hitler Youth had hoped that extensive school enrollment would further the Nazis' overall aim of a social revolution which would give opportunity to all classes, an ideal the HJ had held high before 1933 and still paid lip service to. Hitler himself said in 1942 that the

Adolf Hitler Schools should enable "even the poorest boy to rise to any position for which he is potentially suited."[187] Therefore almost no fees were charged to the students, either for class instruction or for room and board.[188] Nonetheless, even though the children of the lower classes turned out to be somewhat more heavily represented in AHS schools than in traditional ones, their number was insufficient to change the middle-class character of the entire student body in the Reich.[189] Proclaiming social equality had done nothing to heighten the schools' prestige.

Yet another reason for the schools' lack of success as training grounds for a future Party elite lay in the unsuccessful promise of follow-up institutions. Ley's Ordensburgen or "Order Castles"—Crössinsee and one more each in West and South Germany—which AHS graduates were to enter around age eighteen, were conceived neither as traditional universities, which some of these young men would ordinarily have preferred for an academic career, nor as military academies such as those offered by the Wehrmacht. Their didactic concepts were shrouded in racist mysticism, and with only a small number of students and an insufficient staff, they never reached even a rudimentary stage of functionality.[190] Nor was the final plateau in this hierarchy, Rosenberg's Party university Hohe Schule, ever realized—it remained a chimera for the time after the Final Victory.[191]

Yet another Party high school, the partially subsidized NS-Deutsche Oberschule in Feldafing on Lake Starnberg, was not considered as competition for the AHS by HJ leaders. This school, housed in no less than forty villas, was more for sybarites than ascetics (often the off-spring of self-important Party leaders); students played golf there or went sailing after a minimum of formal lessons. No one ever received a grade, and no one ever failed a course. The school, for pupils from twelve to eighteen, had been founded as a recruitment instrument by SA chief Ernst Röhm in 1933, and was maintained, after his execution in July 1934, by Deputy Führer Rudolf Hess. It posed hardly any competition to the HJ because it was comparatively small, and its instruction staff was no more qualified than Schirach's or Ley's.[192]

But if this multiplicity of Nazi training institutes was not yet a threat to the HJ's own pedagogical ambitions and its goal of monopolistic control, the threat from the SS-run former military cadet academies was real. For these Nationalpolitische Erziehungsanstalten (NPEA) did everything the Adolf-Hitler-Schulen were attempting to do; only they did it much better and with tangible results. Three NPEA had been established under Schirach's old rival, Minister Rust, in April 1933. By 1940, there were twenty-one.[193] Himmler's SS, in connivance with Rust, assumed control over them in 1936, when SS General August Heissmeyer became their chief inspector. His teaching staff were not only academically schooled in the traditional manner, but also, for the most part, genuine SS members.[194] Generally, more boys from the upper-middle and upper classes—with merely nominal ties to the HJ—attended the NPEA.[195] The complete submersion of their egos through inhuman drill and calculated psychological torture eventually led these graduates, who had flocked in large numbers to the SS by September 1939, to commit killings as "political soldiers" without the slightest qualms.[196] And yet their academic achievements were quite respectable, hardly below the average in the Reich's Gymnasien.[197]

One striking indication that the Hitler Youth's own schools fared badly in their attempt to replace the conventional education system is that problems of discipline arose with the first of these institutions and escalated after the start of World War II. Even beyond the schools, lack of discipline permeated the entire HJ. The Hitler Youths were "a chaotic bunch," writes Heinz W. Kämmer, who joined in 1933 in Thuringian Erfurt.[198] As early as 1933, Hitler told Schirach that Reich President Paul von Hindenburg was cross with him because "the young people did not show the necessary respect to old officers, teachers, and ministers of the church."[199] Later in the Third Reich, HJ miscreants in their early teens were known for committing petty theft, obstructing railroad tracks, and accosting civilians in the streets.[200] As for the older ones, traffic violations such as racing with staff cars became a serious problem, sometimes resulting in the injury of innocent bystanders. HJ leaders were habitually driving their cars with such speed that often "they cannot be brought to a necessary stop," according to an official complaint.[201] Homosexuality and sadism became rampant among HJ members.[202] In one notorious case in the summer of 1938, a mid-level teenage leader inflicted long-lasting torture on his charges by tying their wrists and ankles during an outing and then beating them with his steel-studded belt.[203]

The public, no less than other Party agencies, blamed the older HJ supervisory personnel, who did not appear capable of assuming the responsibilities of leadership that Schirach had envisioned. Indeed, arrogant HJ members went out of their way to seek altercations with representatives of the SA, the police, the Party and, after the spring of 1935, even the Wehrmacht.[204] Thus the problems continued to mount.

Even though soldiering inspired greater discipline among the Hitler Youth rank and file, especially after 1938, these difficulties did not go away. During the war years boys and girls continued to engage in crimes like theft, impersonation, or gross acts of vandalism. As a result, clashes between the police and other agencies of the regime and the HJ multiplied.[205] "Our HJ is being hoodlumized," charged one Swabian Party leader in January 1943, two weeks before the catastrophe of Stalingrad.[206] Nazi character training notwithstanding, homosexuality could not be curbed, and more women were being sexually molested than had been the case in peacetime.[207]

The root causes of this situation were the Hitler Youth's leadership structure and the principles by which it was governed. Schirach had taken an adage from the Weimar youth movement culture, which had prided itself on independence from an older generation, real or imagined: "Youth must be led by youth."[208] Of course, Schirach himself was barely twenty-six when Hitler appointed him Reich Youth Leader in June 1933, and his policy was to have boys (or girls) of any given age lead those who were perhaps only a couple of years younger. This conformed to his anti-intellectual view that shaping a person's character through experience was superior to a formal schooling of the mind.[209] However, in accordance with the National Socialist leadership principle—and often in contrast with Weimar youth movement practice—these leaders and sub-leaders were appointed from above and never held responsible for their actions toward their subordinates.[210] As alluring as this may have seemed to German teenagers at the time, it opened the floodgates to incompetence, abuse, and corruption.[211]

Schirach and, after August 1940, his twenty-seven-year-old successor Artur Axmann tried to establish checks and balances on abuses by setting up their own leadership courses, seminars, and academies for an ever-growing number of ever-younger HJ leaders. The first of such schools opened, even before Schirach's formal appointment, in April 1933 in Weyarn, south of Munich, under the direction of a police lieutenant. Not surprisingly, more attention was paid here to matters of discipline, as a "soldier's posture" was said to be paramount.[212] Soon there was a Reich Leadership School in Potsdam as the HJ's principal training institution, and later several smaller ones all across the Reich, offering individual weeks of command training as well as ideological instruction, for example in race science and German history. By January 1935 Schirach boasted that some fifty thousand youth leaders of both genders and all ranks had been trained.[213] This number grew to 78,000 in 1936, but since at that time there were 496,000 leaders of one sort or another (part of a total membership of approximately five million), it meant that only 16 percent of them were actually trained.[214]

And even by HJ standards, there were doubts concerning the value of the instruction offered. In a speech of January 1935, Schirach himself had alluded to the difficulty of securing adequate staff.[215] Two years later, one of his regional commanders criticized the deplorable quality of HJ training thus far and the subsequent reliance on inferior trainers. One could not adequately educate one's own trainers, he grumbled during a Berlin staff meeting, because educators in the HJ were too badly paid for anyone to choose that occupation.[216] A few months after that, in Tübingen, senior instructor Oskar Riegraf wrote that he had recently completed teaching fifty-six courses only as a favor to Stuttgart's Gauleiter Wilhelm Murr, and that now he was "finished with the HJ."[217]

Especially during the war, when staff was at a premium, the instructional standard for tens of thousands of presumptive Hitler Youth leaders of both genders appears to have sunk quite low. One young trainee in March 1943, who actually liked physical drill under duress (similar to the way some twenty-first-century youngsters like extreme sports), told of indoctrination sessions that featured themes from *Mein Kampf,* the history of the Nazi movement, and the subsequent rise of the Third Reich since 1933. In the afternoons, he wrote, they discussed Göring, Himmler, and Goebbels.[218] One of his more mature comrades, an Austrian, was sent to the training camp in Thuringian Eichsfeld, after he had already fought at the front. "I was supposed to be reacquainted with Nazi weltanschauung and brought up to date. But to my surprise I did not quite get it. I soon noticed what the difference was: the candor of the soldier was missing." This combat-experienced warrior deplored the bureaucratization of home-based HJ functionaries who had forgotten how to be leaders. "They had settled into many spots and made themselves indispensable . . . They allowed no one to speak who had something else, something better to say." Moreover, "They felt they had a monopoly on heroism."[219]

Early on, the HJ heads had thought that help was on its way in the form of a so-called Academy of Youth Leadership in Brunswick. Schirach declared in October 1935 that he had reached an agreement regarding real estate with the town of Brunswick. In 1936 it was announced that the institution would be commencing its work by the end of the following year.[220] But it took until April of 1939 for the newly constructed Academy to open, with an allegedly demanding course of studies. Even then, the first semester had to begin at a sports site in Berlin; the move to Brunswick did not take place until August, when the building was finally completed. Requirements for the Academy included graduation from Gymnasium, strict pre-selection, four months of apprenticeship in a HJ region, and eight weeks at the leadership school in Potsdam, to be followed by twelve months of residency at the Academy. Thereafter candidates had to work for three weeks in some war-related industry and undergo six months of training abroad.

Successful graduates were to be officially designated as "Youth Leaders of the German Reich," but had to sign on for full-time service for at least twelve years with the Hitler Youth. In those positions, they would enjoy the status of one of Schirach's virtual generals.[221]

As it turned out, the Academy could not live up to its promises. Even though its quarters were sumptuous, it was quickly hampered by the war's manpower needs and its makeshift courses lasted barely five months instead of the required twelve. The Academy's "thorough training" was deceptive at best, for it could not even come close to the level of what today would be called a community college.[222] The "famous scholars and university teachers" whom Axmann invented for his 1995 memoirs in reality were third-rate guest lecturers—Nazified faculty from outlying universities. The students attending that first summer semester stayed only a few weeks, after which they rode off to the front lines. Those who arrived after September 1939 were mostly mid-level youth leaders who had been wounded in the war and had combat experience under their belts. There was little the Academy could now teach them.[223]

How ill-suited the academy was for the the average HJ member is illustrated by two postwar reports. One veteran wrote that life in Brunswick was the equivalent of "a comfortable vacation"—cynically noted by those who had already fought at the fronts. Drill consisted of relaxed marches through the picturesque town of Brunswick. Nothing from the lectures by the visiting university teachers made any impression at all: "nothing really stuck, the metaphysically argued ideology remained incomprehensible to us." And when Schirach himself deigned to address these students, "one after the other fell asleep."[224] Another former student spoke of the visit of a high HJ leader who had received the Knight's Cross in the war—in other words, a nationally admired paragon for all future leaders. But he chose to display only arrogance during his inspection. The student, an apprentice with the Stollwerk chocolate company in Cologne, "intellectually could not follow the arcane training program" at Brunswick although, in 1942, he was already among the highest ranks of the HJ. In his memoirs of 1994 he admitted to dozing off during what were advertised as intellectually challenging lectures.[225] Summing up his overall impression up to 1945, this onetime regional HJ chief wrote that as "the leaders became younger, their training became shorter."[226]

Chronically inadequate leadership recruitment and training inevitably contributed to systemic faults in the HJ leadership structure, as a result of the lack of capable chiefs. Whether in the Palatinate, Brunswick, or Bavaria, the HJ had to accept as leaders just about anybody who showed interest, with predictably distastrous results.[227] This was true especially in the countryside, where boys and girls tended to pass up the HJ for work on the farms, during weekends and after school.[228] Meanwhile, Schirach tried to mollify his critics by claiming that youth leaders were not born "ready-made" and that, after all, leaders still had to be found for this, "the largest youth movement in the world."[229]

The beginning of World War II exacerbated these difficulties because now the older set of leaders, aged seventeen and up, were incrementally conscripted. On October 1, 1939, of the very top full-time chiefs in Schirach's administration, 273 had been called to fight, out of a total of 424; by January 1, 1940, 25 percent of all leaders were at the fronts. Not yet two years later, this rate had swelled to 60 percent.[230] The war intensified what had already been a problem in peacetime: as older leaders vanished, they had to be replaced by ever younger ones who lacked expertise for any HJ governance.[231] By 1944, boys in their mid-teens were commanding comrades of equal age, and during the last two years of the war, many youths could not believe that suddenly they had been promoted to what in the Wehrmacht was the equivalent of Major or higher.[232] Lina Heydrich, the widow of the SD chief, was beside herself when in July 1944 she had to inform Himmler that because sixteen-year-olds were guiding the HJ, her little son Heider was being unduly neglected. Himmler granted her wish that henceforth Heider be relieved from all HJ duty.[233]

Constant personnel changes in individual locales made the teenagers nervous, as well as their parents, teachers and, not least, the Party brass.[234] In some places, HJ posts disappeared altogether because there was no staff.[235] The Party Chancellery, under Martin Bormann, intervened as early as March 1940 in an effort to shift local youth chief authority to its own representatives, but since this amounted to an ill-disguised attempt by Bormann to make the HJ subservient to him, Schirach did not even deign to respond. In November 1942 the Reich Interior Ministry once again insisted on this change, also with no result. Right up to early 1945, the Party tried to exert an influence on the personnel department of the HJ leadership, from regional leaders to the highest levels. But until the end, Schirach and Axmann remained impervious to external intervention and retained sole control.[236]

To insiders, as well as many on the outside, the HJ appeared corrupt and diseased to the core. As early as 1934, lower-down leaders were embezzling money through bullying and double book-keeping.[237] Local HJ officials often appeared vain and arrogant.[238] "You probably know," wrote the high-placed Riegraf to a former comrade in November 1938 from Nürtingen, "what kind of an outfit the HJ currently is. Things are going on which no decent person can possibly tolerate any longer."[239] Others observed "HJ leaders who were smoking, lewd BDM maidens, and drunken youth chiefs," and, inevitably, Hitler Youth personnel of both genders having sex in their offices.[240] By 1943 Axmann was socializing with Goebbels, who was well known for his habit of procuring film starlets for intimate parties at his various Berlin hideaways. Axmann helped Goebbels chauffeur these young women and himself held some parties on the side, to which he invited those starlets and pretty BDM maidens.[241] Instead of causing the reins to be tightened, Schirach, too, appeared to be acting irresponsibly. In early 1945, for instance, as Gauleiter charged with the defense of Vienna against the Red Army, he donned a red-and-gray "sort of general's uniform" in the mode of Göring and invited his lieutenants, a group of higher HJ leaders, for a dinner of chicken with rice and polite conversation. They had been expecting stern direction in their fight against the Russians. Earlier, after putting in some weeks of nominal service at the western front in 1940, Schirach appeared with a huge bandage around his head which, he pretended, stemmed from action at the front. In reality, he had only had a car accident.[242]

Hess and Bormann had tried to interfere with Schirach's erratic recruitment and training policies because, understandably, they had an interest in a regular, orderly replenishment of Nazi Party personnel. As early as the spring of 1934, Schirach had agreed to the wishes of Party executives that more senior HJ leaders should serve as adjutants to local and regional Party bosses, down to the level of Ortsgruppenleiter, or local chapter leader.[243] How popular this arrangement was with the HJ rank and file is shown by the fact that it was never put into place. Nonetheless, Hess and Bormann persisted with their demands, so that subsequent ordinances were drawn up. But especially after the beginning of the war, when the Party and its affiliates needed fresh leaders because military conscription had taken the older ones away, the HJ leadership countered that they too lacked leaders for the very same reason and thus they could not comply with the Party's request.[244] In any event, Hitler and Goebbels continued to depend on the reserves they believed the HJ could furnish. Goebbels remarked in August 1941 that recruits in his propaganda sector were "very thinly planted" and that he was looking forward to an agreement with the HJ administration for a deployment of "a large contingent of seasoned HJ leaders."[245] This was half a year before he had occasion to bemoan the fact that "the first generation" of old Nazi Party fighters was beginning to die out.[246] In May 1942 Hitler complained to his inner circle that for leadership functions, he had to remain dependent "on the same old people."[247] A year later, after tens of thousands of German men in their prime had died on the battleground in Stalingrad and large numbers of youth leaders were on the verge of taking their places on the eastern front, Bormann quoted Hitler as saying that the Nazi Party could "rejuvenate itself only from the ranks of youth and the ranks of soldiers."[248]

As before, the youths themselves regarded the Party's plans far more skeptically. In the period from 1941 to 1944, the number of HJ volunteers for Party office was minimal, so that by the fall of 1943 the Party had to concede that its echelons had been staffed by HJ leaders only "to a certain degree."[249] And in early 1945, when the war was all but over, a revealing conversation took place between Melita Maschmann, a high BDM leader, and her colleagues. One of them had said that now they had proof that Party Chancellery chief Bormann was leading Germany into the abyss, by systematically misinforming Hitler. Wishing to pursue the point, Maschmann asked her comrade why he and his companions did not cause Bormann to disappear. "For what other reason are you lugging around your large handguns? I only know one answer to this question: you are too cowardly to sacrifice yourselves for such an act, as important as you think it might be." Maschmann was assured that after the Final Victory, youth together with the front soldiers would ally themselves with Hitler in order to send the old Party bosses to the devil.[250]

Such sentiment was indicative not only of the naïveté of many in the upper youth echelons, but also of the common belief of most Germans during the entire reign of the Third Reich that however much the Nazi bureaucracy was wanting, Hitler himself could do no wrong.[251] Some Hitler Youths were even willing to exempt from their criticism that branch of the Nazi movement known to be closest to the Führer, namely the SS. To the extent that the Hitler Youths regarded themselves as the young elite of the movement, they knew that by current standards the SS represented its mature elite. The SS, too, knew of this real or imagined affinity, and early on attempted to exploit it.

This became apparent on June 27, 1934, when Hitler made his wish known to reinforce his SS elite unit "Leibstandarte Adolf Hitler" with seventeen-year-old Hitler Youths, who had to be at least five feet ten inches tall (the SS norm then was five feet seven inches). The date is significant, for at that time Hitler knew he would quell what he said was a budding revolt within the disobedient SA under Röhm. Hitler also knew that in 1931–32 Schirach had resented being formally under Röhm's command, with the HJ an affiliate of the SA. When the purge actually occurred on June 30, it was the Leibstandarte that was the executioner.[252] Hitler Youths may indeed have been proud to be recruited by such a unit (albeit too late to participate in the purge), but in

December of that year Schirach's headquarters had to caution the SS to stop wooing and admitting to its ranks mere youths of seventeen. He feared they would be lost prematurely to the HJ's own designs.[253]

Himmler pushed the issue of HJ recruitment further when in May of 1936 he addressed Schirach's youths on the Brocken mountain in the Harz range, not far from Brunswick where the SS had just opened its leadership school. In his speech, he explained the essence and the task of the typical SS leader and then invited the HJ up to Brunswick— the town where Schirach was planning, at that very time, to erect a leadership academy of his own.[254] Exchanges of this kind between the SS and the HJ were intensified through 1937 until August 1938, when increased conscription into the Wehrmacht posed a real threat to SS recruitment and Himmler started using the HJ-Streifendienst (SRD) as a convenient feeder mechanism for his units. From its founding in July 1934, the Streifendienst was to consist of male Hitler Youths between sixteen and eighteen, who in close cooperation with the Gestapo and other SS branches were charged with the policing of, first, wayward members of the entire uniformed HJ and, second (and especially important for the war), any suspicious members of the Reich's youth as a whole. For the SS, the deployment of the Streifendienst, which would have comprised the most enthusiastic Hitler Youths, possessed two major advantages: it conditioned already convinced young Nazis as potential policemen and hence readied them for serious enforcement duties inside and beyond the Reich later, such as subjugating conquered peoples and killing civilians; it also attracted an elite-conscious youth group eager to step far over conventional boundaries at the very site of their HJ commands. Because of close personal and organizational liaisons, transfer protocols were set up, bringing into line, for putative converts, the HJ ranks with SS ranks.[255]

By the end of 1938 Himmler was, in addition to the SRD, recruiting from the agricultural service of the HJ (Landdienst), whose imperialist ideology was akin to that of the 1920s *Artamanen,* in whose ranks Himmler himself had served. At this point—the Sudetenland was being occupied—Himmler and Schirach jointly made mention not only of the general black-shirted SS, but also the SS-Verfügungstruppen (which after the beginning of the war were to turn into the Waffen-SS), and the SS Death Head's Squads that already guarded concentration camps.[256]

Two years later Himmler showed himself pleased with the performance of the Streifendienst as a youthful vanguard of the SS; there were 50,000 members, and he was aiming for 80,000.[257] Regional reports asserted that HJ candidates who had applied had to be turned away for lack of qualifications. Individual testimonials from HJ boys who made it into the SRD mention the advantages of superior boxing and jujitsu instruction, to say nothing of pride in "the duties of the police." They suggest that for the HJ boys, these adventurous sojourns were vastly attractive—exercises which they knew could lead to politically more important tasks.[258] But if indeed SRD service was as popular with the boys as the sources suggest, this could not have been so without prior training in Nazi racist ideology.

Such training meant acquaintance, from an early age, with the dogma of German racial superiority and, conversely, the inferiority of other peoples, especially Slavs, Sinti and Roma (colloquially known as Gypsies), and Jews. That such indoctrination went on more or less systematically in HJ ranks from age ten and up has characteristically been denied by post-1945 apologists of the Nazi youth culture.[259] Of particular significance in this connection is the assertion that there was no HJ participation in the signally anti-Jewish pogrom of Kristallnacht in November 1938.[260] The truth is that participation did occur, even though HJ boys and girls were not generally dispatched to these actions in any organized fashion. While a few took an active part, the great majority became involved by way of being forced to watch and digest the experience and learn the required racial lessons from it. However, in Alzey in Rhenish Hesse the SA, who had been commissioned for these schemes by the regional Party leaders, co-opted the local HJ group and led them to the apartment of a Jewish family, where, with the frightened victims looking on, the boys proceeded to demolish all the furniture with an ax.[261] In Munich the HJ drove around in ostentatious staff cars to the residences of Jews who were known to be rich, taking money from some and intimidating others into deserting their villas.[262]

More important to the HJ leadership was exposing its charges directly to the mêlées of Kristallnacht, which were to serve as an example of how to treat the Jews—a first or second step in an ever-escalating sequence leading up to the Holocaust. Many boys and girls, already ideologically formed, found the spectacles as fascinating as they found them justified.[263] Some Hitler Youths struggled with it all, attempting an argument or seeking an explanation from their leaders, particularly after soul-searching discussions with parents.[264] Others were disturbed, choosing nevertheless to close their eyes and then to accept what they thought to be unavoidable after all.[265]

For the HJ command, the Jews appeared at the center of a carefully constructed profile of aliens that was to be conveyed to the foot soldiers through daily propaganda and well-scheduled training sessions. These were intended to dispel doubts that teenagers might still harbor, especially in the early years of the regime, about how to identify a Jew, or why Jews were different, or why indeed they were considered evil.[266] After all, significant questions revolved around the physical appearance of a role model like Goebbels: he was dark-haired, "very small and narrow," and walked with a limp because of a clubfoot. Did this correspond with the antipodal Aryan stereotype conjured up during ideological schooling?[267]

This schooling had both a theoretical and a practical side. The theory of the Jew as subhuman was taught by older HJ leaders during routine camp and chapter meetings, with the help of special training materials (*Schulungshefte*) or Julius Streicher's semi-pornographic rag *Der Stürmer*. The latter depicted ugly Jews with curly hair and fleshy noses in the shape of a 6, always on the lookout for blond German maidens to seduce.[268] At one of those gatherings during the war, a local Berlin HJ chief, Stammführer Karl-Heinz Wirzberger, warned that "world Jewry had decided to fight the Germanic race."[269] Boys and girls were assembled to listen to special addresses such as the one by Reich Economics Minister Walther Funk in May 1938, who explained to them why German Jews had to be expropriated. After taking from them their businesses and their wealth, Funk declared, one could grant them a kind of inferior leaseholder status, "so long as we do not have the capability to move them completely out of Germany."[270] HJ teenagers sang anti-Semitic songs with texts that sanctioned "Jewish blood dripping from the knife," and in 1943 they were dispatched en masse to watch Veit Harlan's film *Jud Süss* (Jew Sweet), by all accounts the most anti-Semitic feature film ever made in Nazi Germany.[271] One HJ boy who during the war was living in Nazi-occupied Lódz (then called Litzmannstadt) was taken for a car ride by a German policeman who told him, when passing the large Jewish getto, that "we should fire into this vermin on a daily basis." Thinking back to this incident in 1998, the writer remembers he agreed because it was the right thing to do.[272]

Hitler Youths were told to seek out practical experience in dealing with Jews. In Vienna during the Anschluss, uniformed boys were commandeered to supervise the chicanery inflicted upon bearded orthodox Jews in their characteristic caftans, as they were shoved into synagogues or ordered to clean the pavement with toothbrushes or, in some cases, their bare hands.[273] (Later it would be Schirach who, as Gauleiter of Vienna, would stand out from among his colleagues by impressing upon Hitler the necessity of cleansing the city of its Jews—60,000 of them that might easily be sent to, say, Occupied Poland.)[274] In 1941 a contingent of Hitler Youth was taken to Theresienstadt concentration camp in the Protectorate, to view the Jewish enemy first-hand. They were confronted with one of them who, they were told, had to stand upright for twenty-four hours on end. "And if he faints?" asked an incredulous visitor. "Then he gets a bucket of water over his pelt," replied the swaggering HJ leader, with a laugh. "And then you will see how quickly he will get on his feet!" And he continued: "Of course these are no ordinary criminals, they are depraved creatures, detritus, you understand?" An SS guard hastened to add: "The Jews are our most repulsive cases. One has to approach them like a disease, like an epidemic."[275]

Victor Klemperer, a Jewish retired professor of French literature with a gentile wife who was precariously tolerated in a so-called privileged marriage, has recounted the regimen of indignities that Dresden Hitler Youths subjected him and his coreligionists to during the height of the war when ever younger HJ chiefs were called up for special home front duty. During a roundup of Jews for transport to concentration camps, Hitler Youths would officiate. Others were told, on marches, to turn their heads and "eye the Jew, so you will know what the Jews are all about." In 1944 Hitler Youths appeared, in lieu of Gestapo or SS, to organize "privileged Jews" such as Klemperer for Sunday cleanup in enemy-bombed houses.[276]

Undoubtedly, some of the anti-Semitic currents the youths were exposed to originated in their homes and schools, to the extent that Jew-hating parents and teachers were vocal there. It is clear that the hatred of Jews was an integral and critical factor in the rise and coming to power of Nazism and that such sentiment pervaded people's homes after January 1933. Inevitably, those in the younger generation were steeped in this attitude and were socialized as little anti-Semites—who were not so little any more when they were called to fight in the war at age seventeen or less in 1944.[277]

The situation in the schools was similar, if one considers that it did not necessarily take a teacher of finely distilled Nazi convictions to spout anti-Semitic slogans. There were far too many German nationalists on the staff of schools, some of them front soldiers from World War I and ex-*Freikorps,* for whom the hatred of Jews, who allegedly had sold Germany down the river in 1918, was an article of faith.[278] Add to this the fact that some of the younger teachers were coming to the Hitler Youth as liaison personnel, that some read *Der Stürmer* on a regular basis and drew caricatures of Jewish noses on the blackboard, rejoiced in telling anti-Semitic jokes, and enthusiastically used anti-Jewish teaching aids in their profession, and one has a lethal combination.[279] Even a mathematics instruction book read as follows: "In Germany the people of foreign race are the Jews. In 1933 the German Reich had 66,060,000 inhabitants. Of those, 499,682 were practicing Jews. How much is that in percent?"[280]

The children of many of these practicing Jews still went to school with their gentile fellows during the period 1933–1936, until, one by one, they were forced out. The Nuremberg race laws of September 15, 1935, legally defined Jews as persons having at least three Jewish grandparents; thereafter *Mischlinge* of the first degree (those with two Jewish grandparents) and of the second degree (those with one) were still allowed in German schools, but always at their own risk. This risk was evident when they became victims of vicious teachers or their applauding Aryan flocks. The situation was worse, of course, for the full Jews, as long as they were in the classrooms. Not everybody was as fortunate as the historian Peter Gay, born in 1923, whose name in Berlin was Peter Fröhlich when he attended the Goethe-Gymnasium in the early years of the regime. "Our teachers were on the whole free of bigotry and did not set out to make their Jewish pupils' lives harder than those of our gentile classmates," he writes.[281] Most tell a different story. The class in another Berlin school shortly before the war was told by its teacher that "all Jews are bad," and, as he pointed to the dark, curly-haired Esau, who had done nothing wrong, "even Esau and the other two Jewish students in this class."[282] Ineluctably, school children were overwhelmed by the pervasive anti-Semitism in their classrooms, where it would take merely one of several potentially anti-Semitic teachers to push the whole class toward hatred against Jews. As one former student remembers a Jewish classmate: "I did not want to have anything to do with him. Of course I ignored him, but then I did not hurt him either. Somehow he had fleas, I did not like him. Not because he was personally unpleasant, I did not relate to him in any way, it's just that he was a Jew, and therefore I could not stand him."[283]

It is not surprising that such sophistry, in this case driving perhaps one of the duller German pupils, could also propel the marginalization of mere *Mischlinge,* be they of the first or second degree, for only the Nazi law books were at pains to make such specious distinctions. There are many examples of how these partly Jewish pupils were degraded by fellow students and teachers alike. One "Aryan"-looking girl, whose gentile father enjoyed that rarefied German status of having fought in the front lines of the Great War but who had a Jewish mother, was ostracized by the entire class as soon as her pedigree became known. Former friends would touch her and then cry: "Ouch, I have come into contact with Steinbrecher, and now I smell of garlic."[284] She was then taken to a Jewish school where pupils had to sit at some distance from the windows lest they be hurt by rocks hurled by German passersby. The Tübingen neurologist Jürgen Peiffer, born in 1922, recalls that in Stuttgart in the early 1940s the two *Mischlinge* in his class had to wear white shirts during school ceremonies, when everybody else wore their uniforms. And of course after October 1941 they had to wear the Yellow Star. A "half-Jew" named Hanns-Peter Herz reports: "We had a tough, hard-core Nazi as a physical education and swimming teacher. The first day we had to put on our bathing trunks and stand alongside the pool. When we were all lined up, he said: 'Herz, step forward. And you stay there. We won't go into the pool with a half-Jew.' From then on I spent swimming class, two hours every week, standing at the edge of the pool in my trunks. I didn't learn to swim until 1963."[285]

One former Nazi remembers that while in the Hitler Youth he had always heard that the Jews were Germany's destroyers and that the Führer had described them as a race that was parasitical and reponsible for Germany's defeat in 1918.[286] In this statement the first archetypal cliché about Germany and the Jews was matched exactly by the second regarding Hitler's infallibility as the ultimate bearer of truth. From 1933 to 1945, belief in the Führer was the bedrock of any Nazi education as carried out by diehard Nazi parents, teachers, and HJ leaders alike. It was the anchor of Nazi conviction, and it sank into even the most doubting of these young acolytes.

Führer worship was at the center of all HJ and school activities, and in the average German dwelling there hung at least one portrait of Hitler.[287] The schools made Hitler's personal and political biography part of history or German lessons; the *Schulungshefte* of the HJ did the same. The two holiest of Nazi holidays, Hitler's birthday on April 20 and November 9—the approximate time of Germany's World War I defeat, of Hitler's Munich Beer Hall Putsch of 1923, and, not coincidentally, of Kristallnacht in 1938—were punctiliously observed; the April date was the time of official Hitler Youth initiation. (For the SS, including its promotions, both dates were used.)[288] Young people of both genders were ecstatic whenever they had the opportunity to see and hear Hitler in person, as happened more often during the beginning of his regime. And if they were not so fortunate, they collected small Hitler pictures made by cigarette manufacturers like Reemtsma for trading and putting in albums on the model of American sports heroes.[289]

The most satisfying way for the youths to experience the Führer vicariously was during broadcasts of his many speeches or, even better, to be able to witness his speech and gestures during mass meetings such as those held at the Olympic Games in the summer of 1936.[290] One of the most effective of these, because it happened early and was brilliantly orchestrated by Speer and Leni Riefenstahl, was during the Nuremberg Reich Party rally in September 1934. In her classic masterpiece *Triumph of the Will,* Riefenstahl recorded this event both graphically and sympathetically: on September 8, 60,000 Hitler Youths marched into the stadium to salute the Führer. The cries of "Heil" resounded for seemingly endless minutes. Fanfares rang out. A Hitler Youth band played "We Boys." Then Schirach spoke, introducing the Führer. "Twelve months ago," Hitler shouted, "the struggle for power granted us success. And since then our movement, whose young vanguard you are and whose standard bearers you will be, has repossessed one position after the other in this state and thus returned to the German people . . . We know, nothing in the life of the world's peoples is for free. Everything has to be fought for and conquered . . . You have to learn to be tough, to accept sacrifices without ever succumbing . . . Within yourselves, Germany will live on, and when we are long gone, you will be clutching the flag in your fists which once we pulled up from nowhere!" As he finished, a storm of applause filled the stadium, and then the 60,000 boys belted out their signature song, "Our Flag Is Showing Us the Way."[291] "It was the most fascinating thing I could imagine," remembers Bertram Otto, who was ten years old at the time and saw Riefenstahl's film repeatedly at the theater. "He was illuminated and revered: the Führer, *my* Führer."[292]

All of this demagoguery was well engineered, and for a higher purpose. The Third Reich needed its young generation to continue what it now was molding as tradition, to ensure a fresh reservoir of leaders for the most ambitious—and of obedient followers for the more complacent. Above all, it needed young Germans to fight, sooner rather than later, against foes who had long been excoriated by propaganda. Continued allegiance to Hitler, of the kind Schirach had shown since 1925, was key in this effort. The Reich Youth Leader expressed it succinctly when he said, in 1939: "We are marching to the Führer—and if he wants us to, we shall also march for him!"[293]

German Girls for Matrimony and Motherhood

In the 1920s and early 1930s, Irma Grese was growing up in the village of Wrechen in Mecklenburg, not far from Berlin. She was in her early teens when she joined the Hitler Youth as the daughter of a farm laborer. The blond girl, who had lost her mother early, was beautiful if not delicate. She was "a frightened young girl," as she later admitted, predestined to be bullied by her classmates. She wanted to excel, but her schoolwork left something to be desired. However, service in Hitler's youth squads, of which her father disapproved, pleased her. Soon she was a fanatical member of the HJ organization for females, the BDM. First a nursing assistant, then a dairy helper, Irma was merely eighteen in 1942, when she was somehow persuaded to enter the SS Female Helpers' training base at the nearby women's concentration camp of Ravensbrück. In that camp, these helpers, or SS-Helferinnen, were subjected to tough routines. Nazi-style discipline was to be learned by watching and practicing cruelty on inmates and engaging in promiscuous sex with male SS guards. Such discipline was designed to rob the girls of any vestiges of conventional morality.

Her SS training completed, Irma was transferred to Auschwitz in March of 1943. Here she became notorious as the Beautiful Beast. "She was one of the most beautiful women I have ever seen," recalls former inmate Gisella Perl. "Her body was perfect in every line, her face clear and angelic and her blue eyes the gayest, the most innocent eyes one can imagine." Conscious of her stunning looks to the point where she became obsessed with the idea of becoming a film star after the war, Grese, in a tight-fitting uniform, her golden hair carefully coiffured, and always carrying a whip, was feared because of her sadism toward women inmates. A prosecutor later accused her of beating "women until they fell to the ground" and then kicking them "as hard as you could with your heavy boots." Grese acquired the reputation of a nymphomaniac who would coerce male or female prisoners into sex as well as taking Nazi lovers, among them camp physician Josef Mengele and commandant Josef Kramer. In Auschwitz, she was the youngest female guard and also the most cruel, in charge of 30,000 women inmates. Because of a liaison with an SS guard who was transferred to Bergen-Belsen camp in the spring of 1945, around the time that Anne Frank was succumbing to typhus there, Grese moved to that camp as well. Here British soldiers encountered her when they liberated the gruesome site. Along with other SS-Helferinnen, Grese became a defendant in the Bergen-Belsen Trial conducted by the British Military Government in Lüneburg. Her case was highly publicized in the German press, and Hitler's former subjects could not believe that such a lovely young woman would be capable of evil. Grese was convicted of war crimes and hanged at Hamelin prison on December 13, 1945. Together with two other condemned SS women, she had stayed up the night before, laughing and singing non-stop the well-known Nazi hymns. Her face showed no remorse when she told the hangman: "Quick, get it over," as he was placing the noose around her neck. At the hour of her death, Irma Grese was twenty-two years old.[1]

Grese's career was hardly typical of those pursued by other girls who had also been trained in the BDM. Yet her story raises the important question not only of what girls did after graduation from the Hitler Youth, but also how active they were in the shaping of the Nazi Reich. To date, there have been two main theories regarding the latter point. One holds that women were just as responsible as men for the rise of Hitler before 1933 and for what happened in the Third Reich thereafter. Even though women could not fight at the fronts and usually did not murder Jews, they supported their men in these actions, either directly, by sharing their Nazi beliefs and giving the men active moral support, or indirectly, by remaining silent yet giving tacit approval to anything political or military their men might be up to.[2] The second view is that by Nazi ideological definition, women were a subordinate group ruled by the exponents of male supremacy, and they were forced by biology and circumstances into roles they did not want to play and even into the status of victims, which was especially obvious as the war neared its terrible finish.[3]

It would seem that young girls in Nazi Germany between the ages of ten and eighteen who were forced by parents, teachers, or peer pressure to join the BDM were more passive participants than malefactors. Just as in the case of boys, however, as young girls became older they were charged with more responsibility, got used to it, and liked it, so that with increasing age they also became more culpable. This is true despite the fact that girls and women in Nazi society never attained positions of supreme responsibility, for even the Reich Women's Leader, Gertrud Scholtz-Klink, had as her superior a man.[4] Girls did not possess the same degree of herd instinct that characterized the males, which motivated them to join groups, gang up on others, and eventually made them complicit in crimes such as assault and murder. Girls had constituted only one-third of the total membership in the Weimar youth movement,[5] which suggests a greater tendency to maintain their individuality rather than submerging it in a mass group. Many young women, as former members of nationalist Weimar youth groups such as the *Jungnationaler Bund,* were too old to join the BDM after 1933, but neither did they join the Nazi Women's League of Scholtz-Klink. Their only political commitment might have consisted of hanging a Hitler portrait in their living rooms and having husbands who eventually joined the Nazi Party.[6]

Girls could attain their share of power, and could exhibit a measure of cruelty. However, it was never quite as extensive as that exhibited by the boys or young men.[7] Two factors should be kept in mind when considering the fate of girls and young women in Hitler's youth organizations. First, girls were integrated into the larger Nazi youth movement in a manner similar to the way boys were treated, with little planning from above to account for gender difference. Nominally, Hitler boys and Hitler girls were coequals, in terms of the leadership structure, the basic psychological and ideological schooling, and many of the daily tasks to be performed. It never occurred to the Nazi authorities that perceived mental and physical attributes of females, based on their lower rank in the Nazi hierarchy of the human species, made a political mass organization unsuitable for them. Consequently, Hitler boys and Hitler girls, pressed into one organizational mold, often behaved dysfunctionally. Second, as the entire purpose of the Hitler Youth changed after September 1939, girls not used to martial regimens were much more severely shaken than the boys. The conversion from folk dancing and hikes to outright political tasks and military postures was more radical and traumatic for girls, as more of them suddenly were needed for the war effort. Consequently, in the phase of actual warfare, especially toward the end, however much boys were exploited as children required to be soldiers, young girls suffered even more in an environment that was, by definition, anathema to the German notion of girlhood and female virtue to which they had been conditioned.

The Bund Deutscher Mädel in Peacetime

The Bund Deutscher Mädel (BDM) or League of German Girls originated in the late years of the Weimar Republic, as a part of Nazi organizations for women. The development of these organizations occurred within a specific value system consistent with Nazi ideology and practice. In a patriarchal movement based on the biological-eugenic tenets of Adolf Hitler, women had three important interrelated functions: to serve as helpmates to the men, to bear them children and rear them according to Nazi values, and to be faithful homemakers.

These functions were reflected in the earliest Nazi pronouncements, which were aimed at a conservative group of followers who championed what they regarded as a naturally determined sexual division of labor.[8] In Hitler's mind, the biologically defined *völkisch* state was ruled by laws of male supremacy and was in need of women "who could again give birth to men." Educating women would be tantamount to grooming future mothers.[9] Hitler's Gauleiter for Bayreuth, Hans Schemm, enlarged on this theme when he declared that to be a mother of Germans meant being a devoted woman, a conjugal mate to a German man.[10]

Such emphasis on women's secondary role vis-à-vis that of men translated into relative passivity for women and a constant state of subordination. Early Nazi women themselves posited the superiority of men, especially as embodied in Hitler. Women tended to shy away from the male-dominated Nazi Party; only about 5 percent of females had joined by early 1933.[11] When in the Nazi movement's Time of Struggle Nazi women began to organize themselves locally in order to serve the menfolk better, they did so on their own accord without any substantial help or sanction by the Nazi men, and in a haphazard fashion. A national Nazi Womens' League (NS-Frauenschaft or NSF) did not come into being until 1931 and was regarded with suspicion by husbands as well as fathers, brothers, and boyfriends.[12] As much as women might busy themselves in the service of Hitler's movement, the popular consensus was that politics was a man's game and they had better stay out of it. Thus conditioned, they acquiesced when Deputy Führer Rudolf Hess told comrades at the Nuremberg Party rally of 1938: "Talk to your wives only about such matters which are expressly designated for public discussion."[13]

In the late years of the Weimar Republic, Nazi women supported the members of a political party that was often small, dispersed, and illegal. At that time the Nazi Party, being on the right-radical fringe, was held in contempt by a plurality of Germans, especially the truly dedicated citizens of the Weimar Republic. In such adversity, women's service to their men's cause often assumed victim if not martyr status.

Not the least of such female ministrations consisted in presenting themselves at public meetings, to achieve a respectable Nazi body count and to cheer on male speakers through their sheer physical presence. In March 1925, many women attended a Nazi convention in Nuremberg, at which Hitler and the city's Gauleiter, Julius Streicher, spoke. The Party had barely been reborn with Hitler's release from Landsberg prison. Streicher later praised the fact that "so many women" were in the movement.[14] In August of 1927, Streicher's Nuremberg was host to the third annual Nazi Party rally, which drew up to 20,000 visitors from all over the country. A local police report commented that "among the participants many were youthful and female persons. Several women and girls were wearing Hitler dress and even joined the SA march through the town, although they were prevented from parading before Hitler."[15] Among these women at Nazi meetings, the younger ones often were fanatical, and even more so the closer they found themselves to the Führer. As Baldur von Schirach's father-in-law Heinrich Hoffmann, Hitler's personal photographer, recounted, young girls frequently interrupted the leader enthusiastically with "frantic applause." The wealthy and sophisticated Ernst ("Putzi") Hanfstaengl, a Hitler acolyte and Harvard-educated art publisher in Munich, whose sister Erna had hidden Hitler in her villa after the 1923 putsch, wrote after a Nazi rally: "Only a few yards away there was a young woman, her eyes fastened on the speaker. Transfigured as though in some devotional ecstasy, she had ceased to be herself, and was completely under the spell of Hitler's despotic faith in Germany's future greatness."[16] Susceptible to the leader's charisma, some young girls found an idol to be adored.

Apart from flocking to meetings for the sake of full attendance and a sense of communal belonging, women performed the kind of household and nurturing work for their men that was expected in a Nazi home. The early Nazi movement considered young women's Party obligations as preliminary practice for the properly run Nazi family, once Hitler had come to power. Local organizations of women as caregiver groups to the Nazi Party and its affiliates are documented for the period before the Munich Beer Hall Putsch in November 1923, such as the one in Saxony which included Henriette Mutschmann, mother of the future Saxon Gauleiter Martin Mutschmann.[17] When Hitler was in prison in 1924, many women undertook pilgrimages to Landsberg to visit and console him, and some sent care packages. To one women's group Hitler wrote, in November of that year, that the package had arrived undamaged "and provided much joy to all of us, on the anniversary of the uprising."[18] (Hitler continued to collect bric-a-brac from admiring women during the republican period, which later he exhibited in his *Berghof* above Berchtesgaden, as he could not part with it for emotional reasons.)[19] Times were difficult for a largely lower-middle-class and proletarian Nazi following, even in the so-called Golden Twenties of the Weimar Republic, and women had to help their men, whose jobs were often at risk as they tried to revive the frequently illegal NSDAP. Women darned socks and mended trousers, collected money from door to door, and helped to distribute flyers. In February of 1927, for instance, Joseph Goebbels, then the propaganda chief of the Party, received some money from groups of women to help men recently wounded in street fights. Goebbels wrote back with "many cordial thanks for the sacrifice."[20]

A new phase of Nazi women's work began in 1929, at the beginning of the Great Depression, when conditions for Nazi fighter families worsened while Nazi membership numbers were rising. This was the time when the SA, Hitler's brown-shirted storm troopers, held sway in the proletarian sectors of large towns, where they were battling the Communists.[21] Women's groups organized soup kitchens for the SA and shelters for wounded comrades, often harboring men who were wanted by the republican police.[22] Earlier work such as providing clothes and collecting money continued unabated.[23] Since 1928 Party comrade Frau Thieme in Halle, for example, had been known for her large Open House with a swastika flag on the roof. It served as a generous SA kitchen for those in need, despite having its windows broken every day and being under constant police surveillance.[24]

One factor motivating Nazi women was a virulent hatred of Jews. It was not a hatred derived from abstract anti-Semitic theory, although undoubtedly Nazi ideology fanned fires that had been set long before. Rather, it was a feeling based on the women's everyday experience, in their encounters with the Jewish store owners and professionals on whom they depended for goods and services. Nazi women focused on the well-worn, gender-specific stereotypes of Jewish physicians, especially gynecologists, as documented around Heidelberg in 1927, or Jews as perpetrators of cosmopolitan, "un-German" fashion in 1930 Königsberg, or Jews as the owners of chain stores in 1932 Berlin, where women were accustomed to shop daily.[25] Nazi men augmented these racist dispositions with eugenic arguments to the effect that pure German women, as future mothers of heroic males, must not allow themselves to be defiled through sexual congress with Jews.[26] The caricature of the male Jew as sexual predator, no less than the derogatory economic and religious images, corresponded to the same kind of anti-Semitism on which Nazi women would thrive after Hitler's assumption of power. And it was this racism of the adult females that was passed on to their daughters who eventually made their way into the BDM.

The earliest gatherings of Nazi girls came about as offshoots of local women's associations. They originated haphazardly, locally and regionally, and were different from one another; some, the Party chronicle alleges, began as early as 1923. The affinity with the women's groups was clear. From the beginning, the girls' chores were "to help, where they were needed . . . to stitch flags and brown shirts, cook meals, lend medical first aid and post guard at some political demonstrations and pass along warnings," underlining a similarly servile role vis-à-vis the men.[27] In 1931 the Hitler Youth leadership claimed central control of the disparate girls' groups with a view to merging them with its own fledgling girls' league, in existence since 1930 and now called Bund Deutscher Mädel. In July 1932, Schirach succeeded in neutralizing the cloying interference of the NS-Frauenschaft, the Party's organization for adult women, which thereafter would become a permanent, if ultimately unsuccessful, rival for supervision of young girls.[28] Nazi concern with teenage females was evident in the choice of a "uniform." Initially, drab and frumpy uniforms had little appeal for fashion-conscious teenagers even of the Nazi persuasion. However, in 1932, Hitler himself seems to have had a hand in commissioning professional designers to come up with a costume which would appeal to the girls and which eligible young men would find attractive. This was another signal by Nazi leaders that the female's biological goal in life was to attract the male for future procreation.[29]

The theme of subordination to men's needs and desires characterized the subsequent history of the BDM. The BDM never acquired an independent leader directly responsible to Hitler, as was the case with Schirach as leader of the boys. Instead, after an interregnum lasting until June 1934 when no particular woman was consistently in charge, a so-called BDM-Reichsreferentin (Reich Deputy) was appointed, reporting directly to Schirach. She was Trude Mohr, formerly of the German youth movement, who had lately been head of the BDM's division in the East. Thirty-two years old, from a middle-class family, she was suitably undereducated; never having completed Gymnasium, she had worked in the lower echelons of the national postal service. Her motto for the BDM was in keeping with the tradition of the past and aptly pointed the way for the future: "Don't talk, don't debate, live a National Socialist life in discipline, composure, and comradeship!"[30]

After her marriage, which disqualified her from this position, Mohr was succeeded in November 1937 by Jutta Rüdiger, a twenty-seven-year-old woman with a doctorate in psychology, who had belonged to the pre-regime Nazi Student League. Rüdiger would serve under Schirach and later Axmann in that role until the end of the Third Reich.[31] It is unclear why a woman with a Ph.D. was chosen at that time—Rüdiger was far better educated than both Mohr and Schirach himself. Apparently a northern regional leader, Lisa Husfeld, had been the first choice, but this young woman had declined, pointing to Rüdiger as one who "can do this better than I can."[32] There are two possible explanations. Perhaps the HJ leadership, displeased with the fact that Mohr married and left the BDM, reasoned that highly educated women would scare away potential husbands, and thus Rüdiger was perceived as having a fairly good chance of remaining dedicated only to her girls. As it turned out, she did stay single. Another possible reason for the choice of Rüdiger is that Schirach, a man with some university education, may have realized that psychological understanding of girls would be helpful in a difficult-to-supervise mass organization like the BDM. Even in the macho Nazi Reich, there were paths that no marching boots could tread. However anti-academic the Nazis were, they exploited the applied arts and sciences for their own purpose. In this case, they believed that the use of "organic" (as opposed to "Jewish" Freudian) psychiatry and psychology to get inside the minds of German girls would make it easier to rule them.[33]

The BDM, with its members from ages ten to eighteen, grew somewhat more slowly than its male HJ counterpart. After March 1939, the Third Reich made membership in the HJ obligatory for both girls and boys. Earlier there had been a gap in the post-fourteen-year cohort in the BDM, probably because more girls would join the work force after primary school at age fourteen than boys. There was also less job-site pressure on girls to join the BDM, at least until the policy of compulsory HJ membership by the summer of 1939.[34]

The BDM was built on a command structure analogous to that of the male HJ. The female leaders in the more responsible positions would be schooled in special training centers, especially as those with the highest authority became full-time salaried staff.[35] However, there were significant differences in the schooling and treatment of these young women which set them apart and actually demeaned them in relation to boys and young men. Apart from the leadership structure as such, most other factors were identical, and leadership shortage problems plagued both the female and the male HJ.[36]

What set the girls' BDM division apart from the boys' division in the wider Hitler Youth? To answer this question one can explore further the rudimentary service routines of these girls, which had been pre-charted by Nazi women as early as 1923. In keeping with an officially projected feminine image, the BDM's approach to young recruitable girls was softer and gentler than that employed for boys, although this was primarily true during the period of voluntary membership until 1939. It was especially so with the youngest and most impressionable age cohort from ten to fourteen, a group called Young Girls, or Jungmädel, the female equivalent of the Pimpfe. The BDM's approach was designed to emphasize the ideal of physical passivity (vis-à-vis boys and men) and lack of activism, which were commensurate with the hoped-for future eugenic role of girls as Nazi childbearers.

Accordingly, the memoirs of former BDM inductees reflect the published propaganda of the organization itself, with an emphasis on pleasure, friendship, the warmth and charisma of somewhat older leaders, communal fun, and play rather than physical exertion in drills, athletics, and competition. Many young recruits of those days typically recall the joys of joining the BDM and being welcomed by sympathetic leaders and groups of like-minded friends.[37] Since Schirach openly condoned "the games of young girls" (1934), including much of the outright romanticism of the late-Weimar youth movement, these activities, such as watching a full moon and then spending the night in a barn, were self-consciously continued, whereas in the case of the boys, they had been discouraged.[38] Military aspects of BDM service could easily be disguised as innocent contests and games; anything that might look like a military exercise or that presaged war was played down.[39]

Much as with the boys, the girls were given the very positive experiences of going on hikes in the country, roasting sausages over campfires, communal singing, enacting fairy tales and theatrical plays, and performing puppet shows, folk dances, and recorder trios. "The weekends were crammed full with outings, campings, and marches when we carried heavy packs on our backs. It was all fun in a way and we certainly got plenty of exercise . . . These young BDM leaders taught us songs and tried desperately to maintain a certain amount of discipline without ever really succeeding."[40] In winter, handicrafts and needlework shops in the BDM clubhouse were very popular.[41] Whatever political message the HJ leadership wanted to convey to the girls, it was imparted subliminally. In the early years of the regime, and certainly for the younger groups, political indoctrination was practiced lightly and hardly noticed by the (admittedly innocent) target group. Play and games, however, were decoys for sterner things to come.[42]

One clever bait for the girls was the aesthetic appeal of fashion. The early attention paid by leading Nazis to the BDM's attire bore fruit. It is true that the standard costume—dark blue skirt, white blouse (both reminiscent of the youth movement), and black kerchief with a knotted tie of leather strips—made girls look alike. Judged singly, however, the garments were generally thought to be attractive, especially the spiffy tie. A mustard-yellow vest (*Kletterweste*) was not so popular with most, but a few found it especially fashionable.[43] Fashion here catered to a remarkable blend of impulses, and the Nazis knew how to exploit that. On one hand, there was a sort of lemming effect, where peer group pressure motivated girls to belong by imitating. "I thought this was really chic and I just had to have this too," said one former member in explaining her feelings at the time.[44] On the other hand, girls wishing to express their individual personalities through the style in which they dressed still felt they had leeway to do so, for instance by making slight modifications or by ignoring (or emphasizing) the somewhat controversial yellow vest, wearing different knee socks, or paying attention to the hairdo—mostly braids for the youngest girls, but they could be of different lengths, and hairstyles could change with increasing age.[45] Indeed, as the girls got older and developed a sense of adult fashion, the uniforms too were invariably altered, as they were for the leaders: universally admired insignia were added, such as the green leadership cord, or fashionable overcoats were worn. There were other opportunities to dress up in different clothes, for instance the white dresses with colorful aprons and ribbons that were worn for the public performances of folk dance—a very satisfying experience for the girls involved.[46] To the boys, attire mattered much less; their vanity would be satisfied in other ways.

The various sports offerings for the girls were also attractive, particularly since they were treated more as group play than individual competitions. Usually, rhythmical gymnastics took the place of athletic strain. This kind of exercise emphasized harmony and the sense of resting within one's own physical body as well as the collective body of the group. Thus the girls practiced organic *Volksgemeinschaft.* At the same time, the flow of gymnastic movements was closely related to the feminine anatomy and the future role of women as childbearers. Where boys had to be forceful, girls had to show grace. And while there were opportunities for female competitive sports such as swimming for points or Nazi honor badges,[47] the overall emphasis was not on individual performance but on collective movement, not unlike women's aerobics of a later era, but less driving and challenging even than those.[48] Games with softballs were popular, and during the 1936 Berlin Olympics more than a thousand BDM girls gyrated simultaneously, in a synchronized show of unity—a symbol of totalitarian strength that was later successfully imitated by other dictatorships such as the People's Republic of China.[49] Such scenes were brilliantly captured in the films of Leni Riefenstahl.[50]

Communal, synchronized sport was a technique to ensure what, according to Schirach, was the duty of young women, "to correspond with the beauty ideal of male adolescents and grown-ups."[51] Officially, this ideal was of a woman who did not use lipstick or makeup, did not arrange or dye her hair—all the denigrated attributes of slick Weimar-republican city girls or French seductresses.[52] The perfect German woman did not wear pants, nor did she smoke.[53] For women in German society generally, and older girls in the BDM in particular, the Nazis projected the paragon of a Nazi female as a woman who tied her hair in a bun and dressed tastefully yet simply. In the BDM, the white and blue uniform was considered feminine enough without even a touch of elegance or sensual suggestiveness, and except for a ring and a watch, no jewelry was allowed. High-heeled shoes and silk stockings were off limits.[54] As BDM members became older and obtained leadership positions, however, especially during the war, those rules were relaxed, although too stark a transgression could still raise eyebrows in public.[55]

The regime dictate of a well-groomed and well-dressed young woman was designed to attract a German man for breeding and child-rearing. Hence the ideal of a healthy mother was always proclaimed, and so were her typical chores as a homemaker. Hitler himself made certain that training in the BDM did not stray too far from the domestic path when he reiterated at the 1936 Nuremberg Party rally that "motherhood was woman's supreme function, and that a woman could make no greater contribution to the nation than the birth of several children."[56] Toward that end, special BDM physicians constantly watched over the health of their young charges, in particular with a view to preventing physical overexertion (for instance, after sports), and monitoring prenatal potential.[57]

Many of the things that BDM girls did while hiking or congregating in the clubhouse amounted to practical exercises in preparation for wifehood and motherhood. Certain activities were thought to appeal to the girls because of their gender-specific nature: the door-to-door selling of trinkets for welfare purposes, or the household collections of toys and clothes for the needy.[58] Girls were valued as servants of the muses when the BDM performed in choirs, played in amateur orchestras, or told stories for the little ones during "Children's Hour" on the radio.[59] As early as 1934 *Mädel im Dienst,* an official manual for the Jungmädel cohort between ages ten and fourteen, listed their goals as the "warmth of the homey hearth fire," needlework, proper cooking practices, and how to outfit and furnish a home.[60] Considerable space was apportioned to family celebrations, such as Mother's Day, which had been celebrated in the Weimar Republic but which the Nazis elevated to a state holiday and used as an instrument of propaganda for women.[61] Ultimately, of course, there was much talk and writing about giving birth and bringing up children, the high duty of every German woman.[62]

It was also thought in the BDM that two excellent ways for young women to prepare to be future housewives and mothers were learning to help out as maids in households and working in the country as farm hands, or in the farmer's house. These were both accomplished in various programs under the labels of Pflichtjahr, or Duty Year, or the Landdienst or Landjahr, these latter two simply denoting service in the country.

The farm programs lasted anywhere from a few months in the summer to two solid years, and until early 1938, they were voluntary. They arose from a combination of ideological motives, grounded in the racist *Artamanen* doctrine of the 1920s, which aimed at rooting more young Germans in the soil and further developing the infrastructure of the rural East. This formula would provide the basis for recolonization of the non-German East once the war against the Third Reich's eastern neighbors commenced. Beginning in early 1934 the BDM took care of employment for fourteen-year-old girls just released from school, who were looking for jobs in industry. On the one hand, the Nazis discouraged the gainful employment of women, as there was still unemployment in the cities because of the lingering Depression.[63] On the other hand, farm jobs were not popular, and this labor shortage had to be filled for the sake of the economy. Here, the BDM's program satisfied ideological as well as economic objectives. In 1934, 7,000 German girls started farm work; by 1937, 43,000 had been sent out—mostly to farmsteads in the East, in Silesia, Pomerania, or East Prussia. The girls lived and worked with the farmers and in the evenings mingled socially with the youths of the village. Nazi social engineers such as demographic planners looked upon this as creatively molding the *Volksgemeinschaft*.[64]

Between 1936 and 1939, this farm program was expanded. Retraining and schooling facilities were established to help as many city girls become farm girls as possible. Rural farm labor was seen as developing feminine qualities and readying a girl for marriage and motherhood all the more effectively. With the girls kept away from urban ills and corruption, it was hoped that young women would be more likely to choose an occupation consonant with the Nazi agenda for females: nurse, social worker, teacher, or—in the rarest cases and at a higher plane—pediatrician.[65] The girls' farm service became compulsory after January 5, 1938, when Schirach, now in complete control of the BDM, decreed it as such.[66] But because membership was still voluntary and the need for farm workers great, Hitler's Economic Plenipotentiary, Hermann Göring, weighed in a few weeks later with a decree that established the Pflichtjahr within his Four-Year Plan for all teenage girls, whether in the BDM or not.[67] This Pflichtjahr was for a full year, so that before a young woman could accept a permanent position in the work force, she had to complete her service either on a farm or in city homes as a maid—another unpopular job category. Thus by 1940, there were 157,728 German girls starting Pflichtjahr work in agriculture, and another 178,244 in domestic service.[68] In addition to the agricultural training centers, already existing *Haushaltsschulen,* or household schools for domestic service, were built up and new ones founded.[69] Girls' memoirs of those years in either work branch tell varying stories of happiness and woe; what was evident in all the girls' experiences, however, whether they realized it then or not, was a ruthless exploitation of unpaid menial labor, in the country as much as the city households.[70]

Conveniently, these two interrelated programs, the farm service and the household aid, would be followed and amplified by the Reich Labor Service for young women, the Reichsarbeitsdienst (RAD). It observed the same triple goals of ideological indoctrination, discipline, and national economic improvement as did the BDM. Even though the RAD had been around for some years as a voluntary institution, its real mission and force would only emerge in wartime.

The Challenges of World War II

As the Pflichtjahr continued to be mandatory for younger BDM members during the war, the Reich Labor Service came to the fore for older girls, as part of the general Labor Service. That service had already been established in the Weimar Republic on a voluntary basis. It was made compulsory for young men in 1935, as a prerequisite for the newly introduced general conscription, whereas it became a duty for the girls only with the beginning of hostilities in 1939. Female volunteer work camps had existed since 1935. They were expanded to receive all girls from ages seventeen to twenty-five who were single, not yet employed, or not in some formal training or educational institution.[71] In 1938, there had been about 25,000 "Reich Labor Maidens," as they were officially called. By April 1940 more than twice that number were concentrated in over two thousand camps all around Germany, and shortly thereafter in annexed and occupied territories such as the Protectorate, Alsace, and Denmark.[72]

The original term of service was six months, and the work was very similar to (and often merged with) that delineated by the Pflichtjahr— in households or farmers' homes and in the fields. Things were much less carefree in the RAD, however. The girls in these camps were ruled by a different regimen from the one they had experienced in the regular BDM. Paramilitary drill replaced communal gymnastics, and an atmosphere of compulsory service supplanted the genial, voluntary spirit. The changed atmosphere manifested itself in a change of attire: unflattering navy or olive-green work dresses and a plain hat replaced the stylish BDM costumes; roll calls demanding quick changes in uniform, interrupted only by tasteless meals and noxious sports and drill, became the daily routine. The girls' labors took up thirteen hours of the day, and they were free only every second Sunday.[73] Such extended BDM service resembled the much tougher HJ obligation for the boys from the age of ten on. However, young men of around seventeen were drafted into a separate two-year RAD service which immediately took them closer to the fronts—something that these early RAD Maidens never experienced.[74]

But the situation changed after June 1941, when Reich Munitions Minister Fritz Todt convinced Hitler that he needed more man- and womanpower toiling in war-related industries, specifically the processing of mass ammunition. As far as the women were concerned, they were supposed to take the place of industrial workers who had recently been conscripted by the Wehrmacht. By October 1, 1941, to aid the newly opened campaign against the Soviet Union, those RAD Maidens who were just due to be released were ordered to serve an additional six months, for a total of twelve, in what was called Kriegs-hilfsdienst, or Auxiliary War Service. From then on, every RAD co-hort, upon its release, had to do secondary duty in the war industry. For this work, each of the girls was paid 45 marks a month (in contrast to unpaid regular RAD service), which was still a pittance in relation to what they were commissioned to do. Although farm labor or house-work was to be continued in some of these cases—for instance, work-ing in a bakery in Alsace or herding cattle in Posen (Poznan)—work in the Reich's munitions factories became the norm. This could mean sorting and crating ammunition like grenades, gluing together rubber gas masks for horses, or sewing up Army uniforms. Many young women were trained as radio and telephone operators, telegraphers, and stenographers.[75] Toward the end of the war, when the situation for the government was becoming desperate, hundreds of young women were earmarked for the construction of anti-tank obstacles and anti-aircraft artillery aid, and some were actually deployed.[76] This meant that large numbers of women were, at one time or another between October 1941 and May 1945, moved to the proximity of the fronts, though still behind the lines. Yet especially in early 1945, facing the advancing Russians, this became a frightening experience for many. A smaller proportion of these girls still labored in households or in fields, as well as in hospitals, particularly military ones. While most found themselves far from home, a few were fortunate enough to be placed in venues close to their parents' residences.[77] Because of the large number of personnel involved, the lack of adequate supervision and organiza-tion, and the fact that the Maidens had neither sufficient experience nor on-the-job training, the efficiency rate of the overall work in both the regular RAD and its Kriegshilfsdienst ancillary turned out to be dismally low.[78]

For the younger girls in the BDM, those who had not yet reached the RAD stage, the tone changed also, as did their tasks, after September 1939. One of these tasks was taking charge of ethnic German peasants

in conquered Poland, in a caregiving role. The program was named
Osteinsatz, or Eastern Service; its work could also be shared by the
older girls in the RAD.[79] The BDM had already had a similar experience in peacetime with Polish-Germans in the traditional eastern
provinces. Either as part of their obligatory Pflichtjahr or on a volunteer basis, girls usually aged sixteen and older would assist Polish-
Germans and German resettlers from eastern Europe in the arts of
keeping a house, using the mother language properly, and bringing up
their children in accordance with Nazi hygienic standards.

Their work took place mostly in the so-called Wartheland (the Nazis
preferred the term "Warthegau"), which was Polish territory around
Posen, and in the southern tip of Upper Silesia, which had been German until the outcome of World War I had forced its cession to Poland. After Poland was conquered by Hitler in 1939, it was divided into
the Wartheland (now again considered a German province) and Poland
proper, which was militarily occupied and governed as the Generalgouvernement under Hitler's old Munich lawyer, Hans Frank. The situation was very confused ethnically and culturally in the Wartheland:
there were ethnic Poles with German names speaking mostly German,
and Germans with Polish names speaking mostly Polish. Many other
combinations between these two extremes were possible, and the problem for Heinrich Himmler, as Hitler's newly minted Reich Commissar
for Ethnic Resettlement, was to distinguish and separate the ethnic
populations from each other and settle them accordingly. The grand
scheme was to drive the Poles out of Wartheland and into Occupied
Poland, leaving the ethnic Germans behind on much larger home-
steads. As the war in the East progressed, other ethnic Germans from
the Baltics, Bukovina, Volynia, and Bessarabia, eventually even from
the Soviet Volga Basin, were supposed to join them. In this scheme of
things, the crucial task for the regime demographers was to establish
beyond a doubt who was truly German and who was Polish.[80]

Once the distinctions had been made, however haphazardly, by the
specialists of the SS, Schirach, Axmann, and Rüdiger's girls were supposed to help settle the ethnic Germans. The population transfer of

Poles and Germans was massive and complicated. It has been estimated that approximately one million Poles were removed from Wartheland to the Generalgouvernement, to make room for 350,000 ethnic Germans from outside Poland, including up to 200,000 juveniles. This does not include the tens of thousands of ethnic Germans who were already in Poland. To facilitate Nazi resocialization, 19,000 of the Reich's BDM girls and their youthful leaders were called in and billeted in 160 special camps, for an average stay of four to six weeks at a time. The girls were ordered to work in teams of up to fifteen, each team being responsible for four or five Polish villages, often in collaboration with the SS who had just finished driving out the Poles.[81]

The girls usually found their chores distasteful throughout because, according to their inculcated dogmatism, the Poles were dirty people and kept a filthy house. One report talks about having to hack away at layers of caked dirt in a former Polish dwelling, to make room for cleaner ethnic Germans.[82] What surprised and shocked these girls even more, however, was that the Germans they then had to help resettle were hardly cleaner than the Poles, and few of them knew how to speak their mother tongue. "Romantic illusions" were being destroyed after confrontation with reality, wrote one intermediate BDM chief; it was clear that "good Germans" could not easily be made out of "half Poles" within a short time.[83] Although most ethnic Germans were very friendly with their "liberators" and dreamed of a Golden Age under Nazi rule after the Final Victory, for the time being they continued speaking Polish with the remaining Poles in the village "and viewed them as their total equal." They often slept in a bed with them, ate from a common bowl, and shared the same fleas, lice, and scabies. Frequently illiterate, these ethnic Germans had an extremely high infant mortality rate, incest was rampant, and some could not be weaned from their wood alcohol. Above all, they could not understand why German girls like the BDM zealots would want to work so hard on their behalf.[84]

Such impressions of ethnic Germans caused them to be ranked a notch or two beneath the racial benchmark of the BDM themselves.

One former BDM leader recalls that she was forced to tell Polish-reared German colleagues in the Warthegau that they were to be replaced by young women from the Reich, because in the end they were not seen as fit to lead.[85] This leader's action was in accord with official ideology: in the Nazi racial hierarchy, Germans ranked at the very top, followed by the ethnic cousins of dubious quality, then the alien Poles, and finally, insofar as one could be aware of them there, the Jews.[86]

The prejudices against Poles were reinforced by tales of Polish suppression and even murder of ethnic Germans, which were bruited about by the surviving relatives of the slain from before World War II.[87] The BDM had been instructed at home by their leaders and were reminded again and again that Poles were a people "worthy of disgust, genuine sub-humans, who deserved to be ruled by a master race. Any shyness or even politeness on the part of Nazi representatives would be tantamount to a betrayal of the ethnic Germans."[88] Back home, one girl had been lectured by a family friend that finding a place to live in Poland was not a problem at all. "You can look at all the apartments of rich Poles and can then select the ones you want. All you have to say is: Get out, you pigs!"[89] Finally placed in a Polish village in the Ostein-satz, the same girl was asked by an ethnic German woman to venture out into the field and beat up the small Polish boy who failed to mind the cows: "With Polacks you cannot be squeamish; you have to hit them, or they will not obey." The frightened girl actually did go out to confront and then to hit the undernourished little lad, symbolically, with a stick. She felt terrible about it and could not help noticing his eyes, "wild with rage and hatred," the memory of which then pursued her day and night.[90]

Another girl, in Cracow, saw the bloodied corpses of two German policemen who had been assassinated by the Polish Underground. The next day at the same site, she discovered forty Poles lying side by side on the grass, shot in retaliation by the Germans. An SS soldier was keeping watch. Poles, this girl took note, had to keep their distance from the Germans in all public places. Fully recognizing their subjugated status, the Poles viewed their conquerors with hate.[91] BDM girls were recipients of this hatred, as when a girl, Carola, on the way to contact future German settlers in Volynia, entered a train compartment in her BDM uniform. She saw that all civilians were immediately forced to vacate her compartment, only to threaten her, through the window of the adjacent one, with clenched fists.[92]

After stressful weeks of work in Poland, important new duties awaited the BDM girls back in the Reich as part of their regular service. Although they were still expected to prepare to be model wives and mothers, the war's exigencies temporarily put the national economy and war-related matters first. This meant fewer drills and sports, and almost no hiking, camps, or cookouts in the peacetime mode. By 1941, bombing raids were already making these activities impossible.[93] What was required instead was the equivalent of man-hours, tangible work for the benefit of civilians and soldiers. There was a plethora of chores on an almost daily basis, with the effect that school or occupational instruction suffered markedly. Many of those chores were gender-specific or at least gender-neutral, as HJ boys of similar ages were drawn to warrior-like tasks in the war effort, some in paramilitary postings and increasing numbers close to or at the fronts.[94]

Apart from the continuation of household or farm labor service within the Pflichtjahr or, for the older girls, the RAD, other girls were increasingly involved in the collection of medicinal herbs—some for ersatz tea—in the countryside. In the entire Reich in the period 1939–1940, over a million BDM members spent 6.5 million work hours on the collection of various herbs and tea. In Mecklenburg in the Northeast, the BDM's collection of herbs more than doubled from 1939 to 1941, but then fell off again somewhat in 1942 because of increasing air raids.[95] In the countryside, additional jobs were done within the KLV program, where somewhat older BDM teens with some intermediate leadership rank were called upon to supervise younger children in the HJ evacuation camps. Thus Hildegard Morgenthal, from a workers' family in Berlin, at the age of sixteen became the HJ camp director in Steinseifersdorf, Lower Silesia, in March of

1941. There she was to function alongside four female teachers and
three junior BDM leaders, to manage 130 girls from ages ten to thirteen. She and other camp directors of comparable age and rank were
joined by representatives of the BDM health corps, who had been
trained by and were deployed in conjunction with the German Red
Cross.[96] More mundane services had to be rendered in towns and
cities, where BDM girls replaced tram conductors, postal employees,
and sales personnel in corner stores—presumably filling in for all the
conscripted males or the older girls now staffing the RAD. Already in
the first year of the war, more than eleven thousand girls were performing clerical work in police stations and fifteen hundred of them were
with emergency fire departments.[97] Some girls were minding municipal day-care centers, while others designed toys for toddlers.[98]

As the war progressed, it became more important to aid those
immediately affected. In the civilian sector, BDM members were regularly found at train stations, where they assisted mothers with children
or handed out sandwiches and hot drinks to hungry passengers; this
work became ever more significant as the conflict wound down and
fugitives, mostly from the East, were crisscrossing the Reich in search
of an elusive safety.[99] Collection of herbs tended to be replaced by collection of those items needed quickly by the air-raid-stricken: emergency utensils for personal hygiene such as combs, toothpaste, towels,
and brushes.[100]

Of paramount importance was assistance to the afflicted themselves,
immediately after air-raid hits. A program described as Katastropheneinsatz, Action in Catastrophe, employed teenagers for grueling
tasks which were far removed from the dreams of eleven-year-old
Hitler Girls in 1934. The larger and more strategic the German city,
the greater were its chances of being attacked. Hence in Bremen, a
major northern port, scores of BDM girls were toiling in kitchens trying to feed 1,500 suddenly homeless people three times a day—and
the girls themselves were always on the run from the next bomb
attack.[101] How such an event could shape up is told by thirteen-year-
old Ilse Koehn. In the capital she was preparing sandwiches with com-

rades, who were cooking soup, in 1942. Then the sirens sounded. "The lights go out, tumult and screams. 'Take cover, everyone take cover! Into the cellar!' Flashlights shine on these masses of people, pushing and screaming and screeching." And then: "All the noise is drowned out in the rush of the falling bombs. The walls tremble, and the horrified screams almost tear apart my ear drums . . . Fearful eyes glance at the ceiling. Will it hold?"[102] It was always worse when the raids were over and the dead had to be hauled up from below. A year later in Berlin, a BDM girl was helping survivors surface from the ruins when she herself was hit and, "in order to save herself, cut off her own leg, which had been caught in the rubble."[103]

Many of the girls' first-aid tasks were shifting from the field to the hospitals, for civilians and soldiers alike. Already in the first year of the war more than 60,000 BDM girls were lending a hand in sickrooms.[104] In early 1945 in Ulm, northwest of Munich, when the personnel shortage was most acute, one schoolgirl was supervising four patients in a local hospice. These were not strictly medical tasks, but nonetheless, such nursing took the place of school work, regular BDM duty, and any free time she would otherwise have had—until the next Katastropheneinsatz occurred, and then she had to be in the shelters to help those hurt by air raids.[105]

Increasingly, such patients turned out to be soldiers. More immediately and symbolically, the girls were finding themselves back in the service of German men, for whom they had been said to be destined. Many of those soldiers had already received care packages and morale-supporting letters at the fronts from the BDM girls, or group entertainment like folk singing during furlough. In the former cases, the names of the front soldiers had been pulled out of a hat by the girls' leaders, who then urged their charges to write comforting letters to the soldiers.[106] But with the wounded in the hospitals, it was disturbingly different. Certainly, the girls would bring flowers and gifts to the wounded men and would serenade them to cheer them up.[107] But increasingly, they would attend to the soldiers' wounds, and often the sight of these maimed young men was too much for them to bear. In one bed a BDM veteran found a "barely living wreckage, in it lies what is left of a very young man, his face suffused with a translucent pallor and his head attached to what appears to be a rectangular package under the sheets—the first quadruple amputee we have seen."[108] Maria Eisenecker, another nurse's helper, wrote that she just could not get over the fact that "young men without legs, with bullet wounds were lying there, who could neither live nor die."[109]

Such was the service of girls on behalf of the Reich and the young men who served it in the Army. However, there was also service to the SS. Some three thousand young girls, coming straight out of the BDM, allowed themselves to be recruited as assistants to the SS, and several became concentration camp guards. This meant complete subservience to the dictates of brute force and male domination associated with Himmler's Black Shirts. Many of these young women were caught up in the brutal practices around them and became cruel themselves, thus moving far away from the feminine ideal of nurturance which the BDM leadership had preached to them earlier. Girls like Irma Grese succumbed completely to the abandonment of all humanity and indulged in grossly criminal behavior without a backward glance. Others could do so only with major doses of cigarettes and cognac. One of the female SS assistants was a stenographer behind the lines at the eastern front. She took minutes during the SS interrogations of suspected saboteurs and was part of a process during which some victims went mad during torture and were "screaming like wild animals." For a few like Grese, such sadism became addictive. Evidence shows that a few others who could tolerate it no longer eventually were allowed to make arrangements to return home.[110]

Eugenics and Race

In a more developed stage, the Bund Deutscher Mädel strove to cultivate an elite group to serve as a test object in the Nazis' wider racial-eugenic planning. Much of this occurred in close cooperation with the SS, which, of course, ultimately groomed the male elite, the incarnation of male supremacy in the Third Reich. The program, announced by Baldur von Schirach on January 19, 1938, ran under the trademark "Glaube und Schönheit," or Faith and Beauty.[111] This was an emblematic designation inspired by aesthetic ideals promoted by Albert Speer, the architect, and Leni Riefenstahl, the filmmaker. Not coincidentally, Speer and Riefenstahl, who were themselves unusually attractive, collaborated on cultural projects such as the filming of Party rallies and the Olympics, with heightened concentration on beautiful young bodies in synchronized motion.[112]

With the SS in the background, "Glaube und Schönheit" was a model blueprint for eugenically perfect propagation of Germans in the National Socialist interest and therefore of the highest significance to Nazi social engineers. At first glance the program seemed to be out of line with other Nazi phenomena. Its first leader was a veritable Countess, Clementine zu Castell (formerly the Nuremberg regional BDM chief). She remained at her post until she got married to another Count in 1939 and resigned. However, her title had already served its purpose of attracting aspiring young women.[113] "Glaube und Schönheit" recruited young women from seventeen to twenty-one and older, some of whom could still have been regular members of the BDM while others, the older ones, might have been in the process of being claimed by different (mass-oriented) Nazi Party affiliates. The program made a point of appealing to especially beautiful and Nordic-looking young women who were already physically mature. These women had to be unmarried and could be gainfully employed; their course of duty would be for four years, and normally they would meet once a week. Membership was entirely voluntary, even in wartime, as if there were no dictatorship and women were free to make their own decisions.

As with the early BDM, fashion—this time glamorous apparel for women with film-starlet figures—was a major enticement. The young women were encouraged to peruse fashion magazines in an attempt to create well-fitting attire for themselves; during the summer they were clad in tight teeshirt-like tops and well-cut, pleated, very short skirts, all in suggestively innocent white. Photographs show leggy blond beauties with medium-length hair, not tied in the usual Nazi-type bun, presumably without makeup and casually playing with hoops. By any standards, they were sexually alluring.[114]

These girls were to congregate for workshops where they could engage in all the leisure and sports activities open to the pre-war BDM during a typical month, such as swimming, needlework and shop work, or running and softball. They had to register for courses that were optional; group gymnastics, however, was mandatory at least once.[115] There were modeling shows at which the girls put themselves on display like professionals, either publicly or for a more select Nazi male audience. Moreover, three very elite sports were offered that the ordinary BDM girls never had access to: tennis, horse riding, and fencing.[116] Another activity was home design, but of a more sophisticated and elaborate kind than in the common BDM program. These young women were to help create a Nazi-specific home-decoration and furniture aesthetic, the capstone for an elite Nazi family.[117]

In the official literature the description of these goals was embellished with phrases betraying the true eugenic nature of this venture in the Nazis' demographic blueprint. "We know that especially the beautiful girls will embrace these activities enthusiastically," wrote Schirach's top lieutenant, Günter Kaufmann, in 1938.[118] And "the themes of these workshops demonstrate that all issues which concern girls and women in our *völkisch* life are covered here." In straight biological terms it was explained why a girl would ideally have to be around twenty years old in order to join this program. "It is only when they are about twenty-one that German girls outgrow their girlhood and, as women and mothers, move into the great German *Volksgemeinschaft*. Therefore, we want to use this time of adolescence, as the developmental stage of our Nordic race between childhood and womanhood, to learn as many pedagogical lessons as is possible for us in our *völkisch* existence." The most revealing statement regarding the ultimate mission of this program was made in 1943, when it was written that "the ideal of the lovely, beautiful, and proud girl" was equal to the ideal of the "courageous, chivalrous boy."[119]

And herein lay the key to the whole enterprise. It was Himmler, that inspiring mentor to Schirach and Axmann in the business of human recruitment, who had very distinct notions about Nordifying the German people and already was on record for coveting superior Hitler Youths for his SS. In addition, he was interested in outstanding young women as future mates for his prized warriors, as was common knowledge throughout the BDM.[120] As he explained to his masseur Felix Kersten early in 1941, when the "Glaube und Schönheit" program was fully implemented, Himmler wished to see blond, blue-eyed girls molded according to German racial and eugenic criteria. By the time they were no older than twenty-eight, they would be ready to assume the title of *Hohe Frau,* or High Woman. (Himmler also thought that ordinary Party leaders should divorce their wives for the sake of marriage with a *Hohe Frau.*)[121]

Himmler, a former chicken farmer and south German *Artamanen* chief, was ruled by very strong beliefs regarding the application of breeding theories to humans—by way of positive selection for the "Aryans" and negative selection for their natural enemies, the Slavs, Gypsies, and Jews. Positive selection, as he was attempting to prove within his SS and as was routinely discussed in the higher BDM echelons, meant that biologically superior males should be allowed to sire as many children as possible, consensually with a eugenically appropriate partner, out of wedlock.[122] These children would then be brought up in special SS homes, the Lebensborne or Founts of Life, which were being erected all over Germany (although never quite the breeding institutes that popular belief imagined, where strapping SS inseminated eager blondes).[123] To that effect, Himmler issued a "Procreation Order" to his men in November 1939, and he barred SS officers from promotion if they did not marry and, if married, did not beget offspring, ideally sons.[124] In the SS view of cohabitation, libido or eros per se was not allowed to matter, only as a vehicle to national biological fulfillment; hence the sex act was merely a technicality, a clinical necessity. This was stated unmistakably by J. Mayerhofer in the summer of 1943, in an article entitled "Love and Marriage" in Himmler's internal publication *SS-Leitheft*.[125] It was for this reason that Himmler, who obviously underestimated his men's basic sex drive, had to issue an SS ordinance in June 1942, prohibiting the seduction of innocent girls for the sake of mere carnal pleasure.[126]

Hohe Frauen were supposed to be beautiful and expert in everything the "Glaube und Schönheit" curriculum taught its candidates. The young women were expected to be of above-average intelligence and to have mastered gymnastics and superior modern skills such as driving a car, using a handgun, riding a horse, and, especially, fencing, which Himmler considered an "intellectual exercise." In this he was no doubt encouraged by his top aide, Reinhard Heydrich, himself a champion fencer. Eugenically, these young women were expected to be fit to bear children, at least three in their lifetime, in accordance with the assumed feminine ideal of the Germanic tribes of two thousand years ago, who, Himmler said, were "racially outstanding."[127] This corresponded with the genetic assumption underlying the "Glaube and Schönheit" program, which emphasized that all Germanic women, like the current students, espoused the Aryan "union of body and soul."[128] Thus it followed that for practical purposes both Himmler's SS and the BDM grooming program would pay close attention to a girl's more immediate Aryan ancestry, traceable, in church records, through two or three centuries.[129]

With eligible young SS leaders in view as breeding partners, "Glaube und Schönheit" placed a remarkable emphasis on the virtues of race, particularly the uniqueness of the German race in contrast with that of "foreign peoples," especially in the East.[130] It helps explain Himmler's *Wehrbauern* scheme in which elite women were viewed as the ideal biological mates for SS leaders who, for "hundreds of kilometers," would farm and stand guard in a conquered European East with no more Jews and with Slavs as slaves.[131] It was suggested that some SS leaders should even have two women, and perhaps some high Party brass too. Himmler's friend Martin Bormann was already practicing such a policy officially, with a wife and many children in Berlin, and his mistress Manja Behrens, a beautiful actress, constantly at his side.[132] Himmler heartily aided and abetted such attitudes, if more discreetly. In addition to his dour wife Marga (with whom he had his daughter Gudrun), he too had a mistress—his attractive secretary, Hedwig Potthast. With her he sired a boy, Helge, and a girl, Nanette Dorothea.[133] Indeed, if things went according to Bormann and Himmler, bigamy was to become universal in the *Volksgemeinschaft* after the war.[134] These ideas were further rationalized by the bloodletting at the fronts, which meant that the Third Reich, for a generation at least, would be left with a surplus of women over men, and hence the biological survival of the *Volk* would be imperiled.[135]

The racial bias of "Glaube und Schönheit," especially as it was implicitly endorsed by Himmler's SS, was reflected in instruction on "circumstances conditioned by race" and "Questions of *völkisch* Life."[136] This racial ideology was mirrored on a much more massive scale in the general BDM. It was anchored in four particular conditions: early Nazi women's hostility against Jews, especially physicians, viewed as dangerous predators; the ongoing racial indoctrination in the BDM, starting with the younger cohorts and accelerating with the older girls; the BDM's imperative to its members, as future childbearing mates to German males, to keep themselves racially pure; and the first-hand experience of mature female teenagers with Poles and, by extension, Jews, in Poland after September 1939. These experiences and their implicit racial indoctrination constituted the single significant exception to an otherwise largely non-political socialization for girls in the Bund Deutscher Mädel after 1933. It was their racial identity which was central to the Nazi agenda.

In the Third Reich, enduring images of racial aliens as biological foes, with Jews in the first rank, followed by Gypsies and Slavs, underlay much instruction. Such views were routinely imparted through teach-in sessions in the BDM clubhouses, for instance under the label "Race and Volk." Here, the basic principles of what Nazi scholars understood by "race science" were carefully taught.[137] The governing anti-Semitic canon spawned malicious commonplaces about the necessity for a "racial rebirth" of the German people, on the model of a

racially pure German *Volksgemeinschaft.*[138] German girls were to be the
guardians of "German blood, German culture, German way of life and
customs, physical and spiritual health and correctness."[139] One former
BDM girl remembers that she and her comrades were lectured about
being the better people in this world, and aesthetically the more perfect. "And the Jews were the opposite—this is how they interpreted it
to us."[140] At the height of the war, an intermediate BDM leader repeated Hitler's mantra to her charges: "By destroying the Jews, I am
doing the work of the Lord."[141]

Lectures, films, and history books taught these girls about a political
and biological danger posed by Jews in recent history, particularly as
far as women were concerned. BDM instructors and manuals spoke of
the "Oriental" origins of the Jews, how they deviously made their way
into German lands and in 1812 even received civil rights.[142] That was a
result of a "false" doctrine, said *Mädel im Dienst,* namely "that all men
are equal."[143] Jews were said to be responsible for the shameful outcome of World War I, the predominance of a gutter culture in the subsequent Weimar Republic, and questionable practices during that
period, such as fraudulent cattle-vending in the countryside and cheating through chain stores in the cities.[144] All told, there was "racial
degeneration" during the Republic resulting from the presence and
dominance of Jews. Since his time in Palestine, the Jew was said to have
absorbed Negro blood and to have a particular affinity to those French
colonial Negroes who terrorized the German population under the
French occupation of the Rhineland in the early 1920s, notably
through their compulsive rape of women. And then, the story went,
Jews already settled in Germany facilitated the entry of hordes of eastern Jews, who were easily recognized by "a stocky, short figure, the
short head with the flat back cranium, somewhat protruding eyes, the
Jewish nose in the shape of a 6, and the chin set back."[145] The Nazi
stereotypes of Jews abounded and were conspicuously directed at the
core of German womanhood. Such propaganda fell on fertile soil. As
one eighteen-year-old noted in her diary in early 1940: "We just had
political training, for an hour and a half. The origins of the Great War,

the mood in Germany, and the consequences of Jewry. I like this training very much and I am glad to be able to keep my knowledge up to date."[146]

In 1940, Veit Harlan's feature film *Jud Süss*, with his wife, the Swedish blond actress Kristina Söderbaum, playing the innocent German girl Dorothea who is raped by the Württemberg court Jew Süss in the eighteenth century, was shown to large numbers of girls.[147] It was designed to serve as a timely warning to them about the sexual devastation Jews had wrought in the past, and also as a reminder of the Nuremberg Race Laws of September 1935, which had prohibited such alleged crimes and which were constantly under discussion.[148] The eugenic purity of German virgins vis-à-vis the predatory designs of Jewish infiltrators was a primary theme in the instruction of girls. It was elaborated upon with graphic clarity by Julius Streicher's semi-pornographic rag *Der Stürmer*, in the most coarse and virulent terms. In one story, in 1935, Streicher depicts a slender young girl reclining on a doctor's couch, with the bald and fat physician, his 6-shaped nose prominently displayed, leering at her with a salacious grin. Underneath the prominent caricature, the story reads: "Inge is sitting in the waiting room of the Jew doctor. She has to wait for a long time. She leafs through the journals on the table. But she is much too restless to read even a few sentences. She constantly has to think about the warnings of her BDM section leader: 'No Germans can go to a Jew doctor! And especially not German girls! Many a girl who sought treatment from a Jew doctor found only decrepitude and shame.'" The story about Inge continues, as she waits and then hears a girl crying in the physician's office and a man laughing viciously. She again thinks of what her BDM superior had told her. "And then the door opens. The Jew appears. A scream escapes from Inge's mouth. Terrified, she drops the journal. Mortified, she jumps up. Her eyes stare into the face of the Jewish doctor. And that face is the face of the Devil. In the middle of that Devil's face there sits a huge hooked nose. Behind the glasses glisten the eyes of a criminal. The bulging lips are contorted in an insolent smirk. A smirk that says: 'Finally I've got you, little German girl!' And

then the Jew approaches her. His fleshy fingers grope her."[149] Such stories terrified young girls and their mothers and bred revulsion toward
Jews.

Anti-Semitism attained even more currency when framed by theories about German superiority and the contemptible inferiority of
others. The concept of the strong, virile Germans as the master race
provided a particularly protective feeling for a German teenage girl. "I
always was under the impression," said one girl born in 1929, "that we
alone were the great rulers of the world and nothing could ever go
wrong for us. And all the others were, well, something like lower subjects."[150] Most Germans traditionally despised the "others" in their
midst, such as Gypsies who, unlike Jews, were not known to ravish
German girls—rather, the lore was about promiscuous Gypsy women
seducing German men.[151] The point about French colonial blacks was
driven home repeatedly, for France, though defeated by 1940, was still
the arch-enemy, and "from France we are threatened by the Black Danger, the bastardization through Negroes and Negro mongrels."[152] And
in southern Austria, now called Ostmark, visiting BDM girls working
on the land were made aware of local disdain for *Windische,* or half-
assimilated Slovenians, "whom one must now get rid of."[153] These ethnic groups threatened the purity of the *Volk,* and young girls who were
potential vehicles of such infection needed to be taught to loathe the
"alien."

Next to the Jews, of course, came the Slavs in Eastern Europe and,
farther afield, even the Mongols, regarding all of whom the Party as
late as spring 1944 exclaimed in terror that they "multiplied like rab-
bits," hence the need for a German "victory of the cradles."[154] Even in
1934, *Mädel im Dienst* taught that the Poles and other eastern peoples
were extremely fertile, and therefore it was possible to figure out by
what year Poland would be overpopulated.[155] It was in 1938, a year
before Hitler's premeditated attack on Poland, that the BMD's primary
song book, *Wir Mädel singen,* published songs with insidious verses to
be chanted communally, such as "Let's ride against the eastern land"
and "Into the east wind throw your banners / For the east wind makes

them wide / Over yonder we shall start building / Which will defy the rules of time."[156]

Thus it was maintained that, with the eugenic tasks to be solved for the preservation of the *Volksgemeinschaft*, the German girl was "the racial conscience of the nation." Every German girl, whose prototype was firmly planted in the BDM, had to be a "guardian for the purity of the blood and the people, in order to bring up heroes from among the sons of the *Volk*."[157] This defined the mutual relationship between German girls and German boys, as future biological partners who in the HJ and BDM were being conditioned for their reproductive missions. Their roles were stereotyped in line with Nazi ideology, which, it is true, took cues from German conservative thinking, but with the biological functions vastly exaggerated. A Hitler Youth boy had to be chivalrous and protective toward a Hitler Youth girl; the girl would not be his "to play with," but his "comrade." Such ethics sprang from the Nazi theory of the reciprocation of the sexes in that both were considered equal, albeit with different pursuits, duties, and goals. The differentiation derived from the naturally assumed biological variance, as in the cliché of the boy being strong and protective and the girl meek and dependent; yet each, in his or her own way, was conceived of as a fighter.[158] As the historian Jill Stephenson has observed: "The 'difference' lay in both their contrasting natures and their complementary functions. In essence, this confirmed the traditional division of labor, with men dominating the public sphere and women controlling the private sphere."[159] What this amounted to in everyday life, and what made it uniquely Nazi, was that "women, like men, were to serve their 'ethnic community' [*Volksgemeinschaft*] in the manner decreed by their political masters, for goals over which only these masters had jurisdiction."[160] None other than Hitler himself underwrote this view, when at the 1934 Party rally he conjured up the curative tasks of the women of the Time of Struggle and then went on to say, at the top of his voice: "The emotional capacity of women has, since time immemorial, corresponded to the intellect of man . . . and this then is the miraculous effect of Providence, that no conflict between the two genders is possible, as long as each part observes whatever is its specific requirement by nature."[161]

Thus the rhetoric about the equality between the sexes translated in practice into an unqualified subordination of the female to the male, as could be seen within the Hitler-Jugend and Bund Deutscher Mädel, as well as in all other Party affiliates and Nazi society at large. There are telling examples of true inequality for the girls. Political training did not exist in any form, with girls generally shying away from discussing the politics of the day because they knew they would be laughed at or censored by their HJ peers.[162] Cadre schooling of any kind, in comparison to that for the males, was deficient, so that there were no Adolf Hitler elite schools and only two Nationalpolitische Erziehungsanstalten for the girls (compared with ninety-three NPEAs for the boys). And not only was the BDM formally a branch of the male-dominated HJ as a matter of course, but the Brunswick leadership academy, which opened in spring 1939, was accessible to girls only for a very brief period because of the lack of males to fill its spaces.[163] Even a higher BDM leader could never issue an order to the lowest HJ boy.[164] On many occasions, despite the chivalrous reputation that theoretically preceded them, HJ male leaders were gratuitously condescending or downright offensive to their female comrades.[165] Girls were reminded, especially before and during the war, that they were not made of the stuff that could fight in the trenches or that they could not share in the "tough, masculine romanticism" and camaraderie which allowed boys to sing the old fighting songs of storm troopers.[166] Several of the more ambitious BDM members suffered from this attitude. "I thought it was an unkind fate that had caused me to be born a female," remembers Gudrun Pausewang, "for I could not offer my life to the Fatherland."[167]

Some women thought they had broken through to that hallowed goal when in the course of the war the personnel shortage manifested itself, especially at leadership levels. All of Nazi society was afflicted with manpower shortages, so that women physicians, for instance, who earlier had not been allowed to practice, were called into service to stand in for colleagues at the fronts. But there were disadvantages: the women were always in dependent postings, they were ill-paid, and they were on notice to return to civilian life as soon as the men came back to reclaim their rightful, prestigious positions.[168] However, just as the male HJ had to be led by ever younger boys, ever younger girls moved up to take the place of older BDM female leaders who were called up to assume some of the functions of male leaders now in the Wehrmacht or SS.[169] Thus, service on the farms by girls increased by a ratio of 2 to 1 vis-à-vis boys in 1940, and 6 to 1 by 1944.[170] But it could not have helped their egos: many a full-time BDM leader, around age twenty or so, was unable to easily master the new and ambitious tasks thrust upon her.[171] Trained for the home more than the field, these young women often found the adjustment difficult and dangerous.

The uppermost figure in the male-supremacist hierarchy was of course Hitler. Despite the myth that the Nazi Party attained power because in pre-1933 elections the women's vote had tipped the scale, there is little doubt that women of all ages were captivated by Hitler's persona, and at mass rallies often reacted to his presence with complete hysteria. It cannot be overemphasized that this hysterical adulation continued well into the Third Reich.[172] Hitler exuded a sexual magnetism for German females which today can only be compared with the mass appeal of an international rock star. Hitler understood his intense appeal to women and used it strategically. His rationale for remaining a bachelor (until the day before his suicide) was that of a seasoned demagogue: if he were married, he would be seen as having been spoken for and would lose the support of many German girls and women. He wanted to be indelibly imprinted in their hearts as an eligible bachelor and potential spouse. Not unlike a nun's marriage to Christ, the female Aryan would always be joined to her Führer.

In the BDM, Hitler may have been a kind of father figure for many of the younger girls, although in Freudian terms even this image has serious sexual overtones.[173] As the girls became older, that sense of sexuality escalated, and the BDM leadership itself reinforced this disposition. Hitler's persona as a virtually omnipotent male was held up in training sessions at all levels, where one talked about "the life of our

Führer," and joined in the "Song of the New Era" which proclaimed: "Across the streets the columns march / A Führer strides ahead / He opens the path to freedom / Huge shouts from everywhere / Hitler leads the way!"[174]

Girls loved their Führer as a father and a god.[175] And they were erotically enraptured when they were fortunate enough to see him in person. "I have seen our great Führer," wrote Lore Walb in her diary in October 1933, "twice! On the way to the Niederwald Monument and back. So solemn, yet so strong and great he stood there, with his raised right arm in his car! At that moment, tears welled up in my eyes."[176] Doris K. also saw him twice, first in 1934, during Thanksgiving on the Bückeberg mountain near Hamelin. "I still remember the eyes this man had. Eyes, in which you could almost drown. Dark-blue eyes, some say they were black, but I saw them as blue. And this man gave me his hand, and thereafter I did not wash my hand for three days." Four years later Doris saw him again in Stuttgart; this time she was fourteen. "Everybody screamed like crazy. Mass suggestiveness! The scream became a roar . . . Especially the women were fascinated. Their emotions were strongly touched and so were, without a doubt, unfulfilled sexual wishes and desires."[177] Helga Giessel was fourteen as well when she fell totally in love with Hitler. She was old enough to wish strongly to travel to Berlin to give a child to the Führer, although she had not quite figured out how, technically, this was to be done.[178]

"Giving a child to the Führer" was a favorite, ritualized rationale for sexually active teenage girls before, as much as during, the war, and this alone gave the lie to Baldur von Schirach's affirmation that a "sexual problem of youth" did not exist in the Hitler Youth.[179] Indeed, against the intentions of the regime, Nazi racial-eugenic policy provided an alibi of sorts for its young protagonists, causing its originally clinical-biological function to be extremely sexualized. The chief consequence of this was a constant release of libidinal energies among HJ adolescents of both genders who would have been constrained under more traditional sexual mores. Once fully recognized, unabashed sexual promiscuity among youth turned out to be a slap in the Nazis' face, but, seemingly paradoxically, it played to the prurience of men like Bormann and Streicher and quietly amused outright philanderers like Goebbels.

It is characteristic of male-supremacist Nazi society that in most contemporary accounts it was the girls, rather than the boys, who were singled out as sexually abnormal or seduction-driven culprits. However, it is likely that boys and girls were equally responsible, acting on their own accord (for they both welcomed the new revolutionary freedom of being out of reach of traditional homes). But because girls had previously lacked the opportunity for this sexual freedom, being well guarded by their parents, the change was viewed primarily as an emancipation for girls and young women, who thus posed a threat to males.[180] For it is generally true in any authoritarian polity that by "all those who see military discipline, self-sacrifice, austerity, and worship of the Leader as the highest social ideals, the power of female sexuality will be seen as a dire threat."[181] And misogynist Nazi males steadfastly subscribed to the traditional German view that where there was sexual seduction, women were doing the seducing, and if anyone was to be blamed, it had to be them.[182]

Rumors about sexual indecency filtered through to various Party headquarters, including the HJ's own, as early as 1934. From Saxon Bärenstein it was reported in March that a BDM leader and her HJ counterpart were found alone in a HJ home and then were spied upon to see what they were up to. Unambiguous reputations preceded BDM girls, so that in neighboring Frohnau, HJ boys invited recent BDM recruits over in order to accost them sexually. As a result, the Frohnau BDM chapter never materialized.[183] Matters progressed in a similar vein elsewhere. In Mannheim in the following year, twenty-five BDM girls were confirmed in a Protestant church; fifteen and sixteen years old, every one was pregnant. In Saxon Heidenau, parents complained about "the sexual depravity in the Hitler Youth and in the League of German Girls." During this time in nearby Chemnitz a BDM girl, after giving birth to a baby and being asked who its father was, answered that it could have been any one of thirteen boys.[184] In 1936 young girls serving in the Landdienst often camped out near a corresponding boys' camp, and then became pregnant by the dozens.[185] During the Reich Party rally of that year, nine hundred BDM girls returned home from Nuremberg carrying a child; in only half of the cases was the father known.[186] As a result, to curb the worst excesses, camping out was prohibited for the BDM in 1937.[187] As far as the girls were concerned, the escalation of sexual libertinage during the war was mainly a result of two factors: the general sexual frustration of girls and women left without men on the home front and on the farmsteads, and the steady escalation and indoctrination to induce what the German historian Adelheid von Saldern has defined as the "pronatalist racial welfare state," as exemplified in the "Glaube und Schönheit" program, among others.[188]

Mature German women left behind by their men after September 1939 at first accepted their fate of loneliness and sexual deprivation with equanimity and then increasingly turned to lovers, such as prisoners-of-war or, less frequently, other German soldiers returning from the fronts on furlough. Their affairs with POWs or, more commonly in the countryside, with conscripted foreigners working as farm hands, became widespread. Among these men, Poles were the most ubiquitous and also the most dangerous to be caught with (the men were always hanged after the act); Frenchmen were sought after for what was considered a refined sexual technique, and Italians were only slightly less popular.[189] A German woman, married or not, who was convicted of an affair with a foreigner usually was imprisoned, often in a concentration camp such as Ravensbrück, while in villages, according to medieval custom, many had their heads publicly shaved.[190] Extramarital affairs with soldiers, mostly in cities, were looked upon less harshly and often depended, for a solution, on the attitude of the duped husband (if he returned from the war alive). Nonetheless, marriages were breaking down at a record rate.[191] It reflects the male-chauvinist character of the Nazi Reich that German men caught sleeping with Polish servant girls received incomparably milder treatment: males could receive a reprimand, while the Polish girls landed in concentration camps.[192]

Many of these sexually experienced women—sometimes sisters or even mothers—were models for BDM girls. It is not hard to imagine how sexual desire and experience would be rife among girls' groups in wartime Germany. By 1940, BDM members in the Ermland area preferred affairs with conscripted Polish laborers and prisoners of war; in the Upper Danube region, work-drafted Czechs, Poles, and Bulgarians were the chosen paramours. In the Thuringian countryside near Halle a sixteen-year-old girl, together with her girlfriend, had herself locked into a Polish POW camp. "She did nude dancing and had sexual intercourse with several men."[193] By early 1942, after the Wehrmacht had attacked Russia and the first Soviet prisoners were brought into the Reich, they were preferred for sex around Berlin, second only to the Poles; all Slavs were thought to be exotic.[194] Two sixteen-year-old girls in a small town near Munich entertained French POWs, who were employed in shops next to their own; the trysting place was a wooden shack near the prisoners' camp.[195] For much of 1942, another Bavarian eighteen-year-old had sex regularly with a French POW who was helping out on a farm; this girl had been sexually active since she was fourteen and well into the BDM.[196] There was mounting evidence for such incidents until 1944, when a subordinate of Bormann's exclaimed, probably in mock surprise, that "even BDM girls had carried on with aliens."[197]

Often these girls had earlier been sexual partners of German soldiers, or had been in multiple relationships, and knew how to play foreigners against Germans for best advantage. In 1943 one seventeen-year-old, working off her mandatory year in a household, was told by a Wehrmacht soldier wooing her that German men were just as good in bed as Frenchmen. But she stunned him with the reply that her Frenchman knew exactly where to touch her all over and that she had come to expect "full satisfaction."[198] If foreign men were exotic and ravishing especially to simpler country girls, philandering German soldiers appealed to the more sophisticated, patriotic maidens, particularly in the large cities, and the dashing officers among them were often seen as nothing less than gods. Hitler Youths attending Gymnasium at the time recall that especially in more well-to-do circles, comely girls dreamed of handsome officers in uniform and more often than not became their prizes, leaving their jealous comrades with short pants in the dust.[199] Many of these casual sexual encounters were the result of those comfort letters that BDM girls had been exhorted to write to the men at the fronts; the girls then became "comfort women" as the men visited on furlough in hotels.[200] Soldiers as well as anyone in Germany knew about the changing reputation of the Bund Deutscher Mädel, whose acronym, BDM, popularly came to stand for *Bund Deutscher Matratzen* (League of German Mattresses) or *Bubi Drück Mich* (Come on Boy, Press Me Hard).

If BDM teenagers did not meet their soldier lovers through prior correspondence, they encountered them daily among civilians on the home front. In early 1940, after she had seen an older man platonically a few times before he became a candidate for officer training, one girl confided to her diary: "When he bid me goodbye by kissing my hand, he said—and I am sure he was sincere—that he enjoyed having met me and that he was hoping to see me again. Momentarily, that is my greatest wish as well. Being so much in love perhaps may be terrible, but I don't care that he is married (that is: I am actually sorry that he is). Still, this does not render him 'taboo' for me. He could have kissed me, I was longing for that."[201] Deprived of many of the more usual pleasures and satisfactions of peacetime life, young girls were susceptible to the attentions and desires of lonely men.

More daring girls went to the local train station to be picked up by a soldier for a one-night stand. This widespread phenomenon all across Germany became a social problem of the highest order as the war dragged on and fewer men were available to sexually satisfy a growing contingent of women left alone at home. BDM girls knew they had an advantage over older and, particularly, married women, because they were young and unattached, and in their uniform they could move about quite freely under the guise of official duties. Soldiers got to know this situation well and ruthlessly took advantage of it, to the point where authorities were charging them with gross irresponsibility, indecency, and rape. Wehrmacht personnel quartered in youth hostels across the country for longer terms, apart from the regular barracks, exacerbated the situation. Girls as young as twelve hung around these residences and threw themselves at the soldiers, using lines such as: "Don't worry, you can go with me, I am already sixteen." In some places such as the town of Dachau, park benches and adjoining lawns were notoriously occupied by soldiers and their teenage consorts, and every spot was littered with condoms. As a result of such promiscuity, illegal pregnancies increased further, and so did cases of venereal disease.[202] Because the BDM, as well as somewhat older RAD girls, often accepted small gifts and even money from men, authorities were inclined to speak of "covert prostitution."[203] Indeed, reports from Berlin as early as 1941 indicated that the red-light districts were disappearing, as professional whores were being pushed out of their jobs by BDM amateurs.[204] All this constituted a particularly unseemly aspect of the Nazi militarization of German society, the ideals of which had been preached at length to the boys in the HJ.

As the more perceptive girls would have been able to tell, sexual exploitation pervaded the HJ itself. A report from the summer of 1940 tells about a HJ-Bannführer, high up in the hierarchy, whose Streifendienst was raiding a small hotel: "There are two beds in the room, each containing a couple. Naked . . . In the other rooms the situation is very similar. Everywhere the SRD has surprised young couples. In one room there are even twelve straw mattresses."[205] RAD maidens kept in work camps were especially susceptible to sexual temptations by HJ boys stationed in surrounding, similar establishments.[206] However, all BDM girls were easy prey for boys in the HJ, with the females frequently taking the initiative.[207]

During the second half of the war, young women appear to have suffered the highest incidence of venereal disease in the entire civilian population.[208] At that time, the proverbially loose morals of the BDM in the Third Reich made all of its members into obvious targets, even for Party officials, who thought the girls were theirs for the taking.[209] Rather than emancipation vis-à-vis males, which can either precede or follow sexual freedom, this exploitation symbolized the subjugation of young females to the twisted value system of the male-supremacist Nazi rulers. There were only a very few girls who were strong enough to resist what they experienced in the Hitler Youth in a serious way, and one of them known to have done so paid for her courage with her life. She was a former BDM leader from Ulm, and her name was Sophie Scholl.

Dissidents and Rebels

Dissidence in Hitler's Germany was the exception. Despite an occasional lack of structural cohesiveness, an extremely well organized Hitler Youth mobilized the great majority of Hitler's young subjects toward Nazi ends. It is against the background of this all-encompassing youth recruitment that rebellious actions, mostly on the part of courageous individuals and groups, appear so dramatic.

The story of the German resistance to Hitler has often been told, beginning with a classic account by Hans Rothfels, printed by H. Regnery, a right-wing American publisher, in 1948. Rothfels was a converted Jew who had to emigrate to England and then the United States from Germany in August 1939, two weeks before the war broke out. Until his return to Tübingen in 1951, he taught at Brown and the University of Chicago. Significantly, he had included for treatment in his original volume only groups and individuals he deemed to be worthy traitors of the Third Reich, ideally conservatives and those associated with the attempt on Hitler's life on July 20, 1944. The Bielefeld historian Hans-Ulrich Wehler, who as a German youth was almost killed by Allied bombers during the final months of the war, observed that in Rothfels's view "the resistance was dominated by members of the old upper stratum—the officer corps, senior civil servants, and the clergy." Rothfels himself, who had lost a leg during patriotic service in World War I, was politically a reactionary. Before his forced emigration he had condemned the Peace of Versailles, and, as a conservative, had been a staunch enemy of the Weimar Republic. He had advocated *völkisch* expansion in the East and had in fact hoped that he could stay in Nazi Germany after some kind of accommodation to the new regime. Thus in his 1948 book, which served as self-justification and legitimation for the German ultra-conservative establishment, marginal groups that resisted Hitler were not mentioned. These would have included high-minded but unorganized individuals, adherents to religious sects such as the Jehovah's Witnesses, members of the political left, and a large number of young people. It is significant that Hans and Sophie Scholl of the White Rose resistance group in Munich made their appearance only on one page of his book, even though they quickly attained the status of icons in the historiography of resistance to the Third Reich, in the judgment of more progressive authors.[1]

Rothfels's original argument in 1948 was that the Third Reich had been such an evil monolith that resistance was well-nigh impossible, and where it did occur, it was tantamount to the highest form of heroism. Such an undifferentiated view put no stock in the possibility that more modest figures might have attempted resistance, that their resistance might sometimes have been on a smaller scale than political or military opposition, and that the everyday dysfunctionality of Hitler's regime invited attitudes and acts along a broad spectrum from disagreement to implacable defiance. This is not to deny the difficulties inherent in non-Nazi-aligned behavior. As the Canadian historian Robert Gellately has persuasively shown, even though the police apparatus of the Third Reich may have been deficient or too small, there were plenty of ordinary Nazis ready to turn in their neighbors on a daily basis and for the slightest of infractions—to the point where a Gestapo was hardly necessary.[2] That ever-present danger is underscored by a recent recollection of George Wittenstein, once a close friend of Hans Scholl and himself a member of the White Rose in Munich, who writes: "I witnessed an illustrative incident in a movie theater: During the newsreel—which always showed Hitler—the Gestapo suddenly arrived and arrested a man two rows ahead of me.

He likely had made a derogatory remark about Hitler, which was overheard by someone who instantly reported him . . . There simply was
no way of communicating safely."[3]

And yet there were youth in the Third Reich who decided to break
ranks. Some were members of the Hitler Youth, but others never even
bothered to join and instead opted for nonconformity or sabotage of
one kind or another. Some were members of the White Rose, and
some were paracriminal juveniles. Did the latter act in opposition to
the regime because they had a criminal disposition, or were they crimi-
nalized by a regime that chose to define deviant behavior in such a way
as to entrap them? That the Nazis simply labeled them deviant is suggested by the savagery with which the leadership struck at them in the
final years of the war. However, this savagery could equally have been a
manifestation of furious despair, after the regime's leaders realized that
their claim to the total control of youth was harder to achieve than
they had at first imagined. The youth who were to be the next generation's Nazi elite were not a monolithic cadre committed to the Führer.
There were some who dissented.

The Varieties of Dissidence

Individual withdrawal from the Hitler Youth in peace or war constituted an important form of dissidence in the Third Reich, although it
hardly ever endangered the institution's monopoly. However, loosely
organized groups of dissenters caused the HJ to worry that the spirit of
opposition could be spread far and wide. On the one hand, the HJ had
reason to fear organizations that were remnants of the republican past,
which it thought it had neutralized, but which were reappearing again.
On the other, there were signs of new group formations that tended to
move beyond the HJ's control. Adherents to such dissenting groups
might still be formally incorporated in the Hitler Youth, but they
tended to miss meetings often. Others had already been expelled, and
some had never joined.

The first category of officially suppressed youth consisted of those who belonged to groups that had for the most part surrendered their existence to the state monopoly early on, but who continued to maintain illegal offshoots. Nostalgic for the individual liberties they had enjoyed before Hitler came to power, they bore names invoking the Weimar period and usually harkened back to the traditions and practices of the *Bündische Jugend,* or Eberhard Koebel's Communist-inspired *Deutsche Jungenschaft,* or Catholic youth leagues, or a romanticized and fuzzy combination of some or all of these. The main thing was that to varying degrees they had been and continued to be anti-Nazi. In June 1935 an athletic association, calling itself *Turnverein Burg-Lesum,* was detected by the police near Bremen. During the Whitsunday weekend they had gone camping dressed in garb typical of the *Bündische Jugend,* such as blue shirts, white stockings, blue pants, and blue jackets. Clashes with the HJ were feared, and so the police and Hitler Youth collaborated in disbanding this group.[4]

Similar groups, including some with female members, were maintained all over Germany; some persisted even into the war years. In Leipzig and Berlin a *Jungenschaft* chapter coalesced around Horst Vanja and lasted until 1942. They, too, planned hiking weekends; they wore characteristic hiking dress and took along mandolins to accompany songs by Bertolt Brecht and Russian Cossack melodies, and books to read by censored authors such as Ricarda Huch and the early Weimar youth movement mentor, Stefan George. Politically, the spectrum of youth groups ranged from Communism to liberal democracy to the Catholic Center of Heinrich Brüning, one of the Republic's last chancellors. Another clique that had originated around Frankfurt, the *Orden der Pachanten,* had no less than fifty members. Its tradition was that of the *Nerother Bund,* which had long been forbidden by the Nazis.[5] This group and another Frankfurt group named *Bündischer Selbstschutz* hiked to secret camp sites as far away as Berlin, Bremen, and Nuremberg in defiance of Nazi rules. They were kept alive by apprentices, many from the graphics trade, who supported and joined their activities. The Don Cossack male choir, which gave concerts across Europe to some of these youths, symbolized freedom of expres-

sion and spirit against the totalitarianism of the Third Reich and the
Soviet Union. Yet another group that stood outside the HJ was the
Schwarze Schar in Berlin, which managed to hold a camp meeting on
the Baltic island of Rügen in 1938 and whose male members kept in
contact with one another even while serving in the Wehrmacht.[6] In
spring 1939 the Gestapo spotted similar groups around Munich,
which they could not name but were able to identify by their strange
outfits, often with "laughable headdress"; without a moment's hesitation, the policemen earmarked these groups "as a danger for the state
youth."[7] Even in Vienna in 1940 and thereafter, several hundred
bündische youths rapturously attended Don Cossack choir concerts
before they were interrogated and imprisoned by the secret police.[8]

On the Roman Catholic side, the oppositional *Graue Orden* (Gray
Order) was founded in 1934, at a time when Catholic youth organizations were already heavily under fire. The group seems to have had at
least 150 members in 1936, mostly from West and Southwest Germany. In 1934 they hiked to Lapland, and in 1936 to Montenegro.
Although they behaved like the *bündisch* youth, and carried similar
paraphernalia such as the peaked *Kote* tent which had been proscribed
by the HJ, they were much more interested in spiritual content. They
read texts by the Catholic theologian Romano Guardini and the Jewish
philosopher Martin Buber. In January 1938, eighteen of their members were arrested by the Gestapo, but during their subsequent trial for
subversion they were freed because of a general amnesty in celebration
of the Anschluss with Austria.[9]

Considerably more risky was the behavior in Bruchsal in the Baden
region of a Catholic Gymnasium student group named *Christopher,*
which in May 1941 was being led by Wilhelm Eckert. On the twelfth
of that month the Gestapo caught him red-handed in his parents'
house with a copying machine, used for the manufacture of a pro-
Catholic, anti-Nazi group letter intended for soldiers at the front. This
was after Baldur von Schirach's compulsory Youth Ordinance of
March 1939, and so the members of Eckert's group, who had avoided
the HJ, were expelled from Gymnasium and their parents punished.

Franz Schmitt, a mentoring priest to the group, was apprehended and later executed in the aftermath of the anti-Hitler July 1944 putsch. Eckert himself received a comparatively mild sentence of eight months in prison. Upon his release he was to be conscripted for work in Occupied Ukraine, but he preferred to join the Wehrmacht, and there he died as a soldier during a battle in Sicily in July 1943.[10]

Walter Klingenbeck, a Munich mechanic's apprentice, age sixteen in May 1940, fared worse. Over the radio he had heard about the massive destruction of Rotterdam at the hands of German troops invading Holland. By 1941, he had gathered around him a number of equally outraged young Catholics, formerly from Catholic youth groups like his own, *St. Ludwig*. At first they listened to enemy radio stations, which could have cost them their lives even then, but later they printed and duplicated flyers with slogans such as "Down with Hitler," and they painted the British victory symbol "V" on Munich residences. In 1941 and 1942, they assembled three radio transmitters and did a trial broadcasting of anti-Nazi propaganda. The police got to Klingenbeck and two of his friends in early 1942. The friends were sent to the penitentiary, but Klingenbeck was beheaded in Munich's Stadelheim prison in August of 1943.[11]

Given the irreconcilable differences between Nazis and Catholics on core issues of dogma and ideology, it is not surprising to find the remnants of Catholic youth groups so persistent even after official proscription. The Protestant youth tended to be much more tame and accommodating. But even among the Protestant youths there were some who dared to stray from the official path. In February 1939 in Rothenburg ob der Tauber, Protestant HJ and BDM members organized themselves, with the help of their church, in an illegal group, which local Nazi officials urged be disbanded.[12] And in November 1940 Augsburg's HJ leadership criticized get-togethers of Protestant youths in church-owned buildings in nearby Lechhausen for more than two hours every Saturday, a prime time during which the HJ itself would schedule major events.[13]

The last of the former youth leagues who attempted independence or considered resistance to the Third Reich were the Marxist ones. In addition to illegal hiking trips, they discussed Karl Marx, Communism, the Soviet Union, and possibly active resistance in secret meetings.[14] A *Schwarze Schar,* or Black Band, originated illegally in Berlin in January 1934. Its leader was Heinz Steurich, "Jonny" to his friends. Steurich offered a roof for other "red leagues" to congregate under: *Rote Pfadfinder, Rote Jungpioniere, Turnverein Mariendorf.* Until many of their members were caught in 1937, these leagues organized hikes and, during the Olympic Games in summer 1936, attempted to make contact with foreign youth representatives. The *Schwarze Schar* even conducted rifle training at a shooting range, although it does not seem to have been overtly conspiratorial. Nevertheless, one leader, Rudolf Wernicke, or "Ajax," committed suicide during the Gestapo raids of 1937. Some members of this group survived in a loose network until May of 1945.[15] A similar group of fifteen young Marxists, previously tied to the *Sozialistische Arbeiterjugend,* was broken up in Bremen in November of 1938 and their members, two of them girls, were put behind bars.

Some dissenting youths in the German Reich had not been organized earlier, but had found each other and then collaborated in the interest of a common goal, which was hatred of the Nazi system and its large, odious youth cohorts. One such group existed in Vienna, led by the Gymnasium student Josef Landgraf. He was only fourteen when the Anschluss occurred in March 1938, and even though we do not know how he had been socialized as a child in the Austrofascist system of Engelbert Dollfuss and Kurt von Schuschnigg, it is certain that it did not take him long to develop a dislike of the new regime. At first a member of the Hitler Youth, he soon avoided its meetings and drills altogether. Unusually mature for his age, he gathered around him other students, three of whom were put on trial alongside Landgraf for treason in late summer 1942.

Landgraf and his friends had been listening to the BBC even before the war and had collected newspaper clippings about Churchill, Roosevelt, and Anthony Eden because they saw them as guarantors of world peace. By autumn 1941 they were authoring anti-Nazi texts and distributing them in flyers. Hitler, "The Bloody," and his paladins were depicted as rapacious world conquerors, bent on subjugating other nations, including of course Austria. Adverse military news from enemy broadcasts and anti-Hitler jokes completed Landgraf's leaflets. In one of these, directed toward Austrian farmers, he wrote: "Do you want to deliver your crops to market so that Göring and his cronies can become even fatter?" Another said: "Copy this flyer and help us enlighten the others! Turn only to good and reliable friends! You must convince the undecided by handing them the flyer in such a way that they cannot recognize it was you!" The sheets were sent to others by mail or were distributed in the streets or near buildings. A fellow student and a suspicious teacher, who later testified against him, betrayed Landgraf and his friends to the Gestapo. He was apprehended on September 20, 1941.[16] Landgraf was condemned to death but later was pardoned.

These activities demonstrated a great deal of courage and idealism, especially for so young a fighter. Helmuth Hübener, a Hamburg youth from a Mormon family, was similarly motivated. Only seventeen years old, he was a clerk in the civil service when he was executed after a trial by the infamous People's Court on October 27, 1942. Even though he was a Mormon, it is not certain how much his religion had to do with his anti-Nazi attitude, because Mormons in Germany were law-and-order people who were generally pro-Hitler.[17] Hübener, too, got together with three friends, listened to enemy broadcasts, and distributed what he had heard through leaflets. Among these was one with a message to the HJ: "German Boys! Do you know the country without freedom, the land of terror and tyranny? Well, you know what it is all right, it's just that you do not wish to say it. They have already oppressed you to the point where you don't dare any more, for fear of punishment. Yes, you are right, it is Germany, Hitler-Germany."[18]

In a similar manner the Berlin publisher Wolf Jobst Siedler, at age seventeen, got together with Ernst Jünger, the son of the famous novelist of the same name, whose trench novels from the Great War were then studied in Nazi elite schools.[19] Jünger and Siedler had long been friends in a Gymnasium class in Berlin, where Siedler's father, critical of Hitler, moved in industrialist circles. Ernst Jünger Sr. was posted to the Wehrmacht in Occupied Paris; a self-professed non-Nazi of dubious fascist distinction, he still adhered to elitist ideas of a handpicked Spartan caste.[20] His son and Wolf Jobst in November 1943 were part of a group of auxiliary cannoneers (Flakhelfer), all Berlin classmates, at an airport on the North Sea island of Spiekeroog. "The two of us founded a group to oppose the Hitler Youth at our boarding school," Siedler recalls. "We also discussed what would happen if the war was lost." Young Ernst, who according to Siedler shared his father's dislike of vulgar mob rule, wrote, for others to read: "This war will never be ended unless an assassination attempt on Hitler succeeds. As long as Hitler is alive, there will never be an armistice." And: "When Hitler is hanged, I will personally walk barefoot from Berlin to Potsdam to help pull on the rope." Siedler and Jünger listened to enemy radio stations and then disseminated what they heard. The group was exposed by a spy in their midst, and Siedler and Jünger had to stand trial in January 1944. A military court sentenced them to a term in prison, but eventually both ended up as soldiers at the Italian front. Here Ernst was deliberately put at risk by his superiors, and he was killed by a bullet to his head, near Carrara, early in January 1945. Siedler suffered a kinder fate: an explosion that injured his left hand resulted in a lengthy stay in the hospital, which undoubtedly saved his life.[21]

Jünger and Siedler had derived much of their resentment against the Third Reich and its youth movement through first-hand experience with Hitler's military machine. This was also the case with the male members of the Munich-based White Rose resistance group; at the same time its female members had to accept at face value alarming stories about the Wehrmacht and SS which they heard from their brothers and boyfriends. Of these young women, Sophie Scholl was by far the most important. But as a teenager, Sophie too had been in the Hitler Youth. "Sophie at that time was very enthusiastic, very fanatically in favor of National Socialism." So reports Eva Amann, who at the age of twelve was in the BDM of Ulm when Sophie, the sister of Hans, Inge, Werner, and Elisabeth Scholl, was a leader of the Jungmädel, the BDM cadre under Jutta Rüdiger consisting of girls aged ten to fourteen. Back then, in 1936, Sophie was fifteen. Although in most respects she was an enthusiastic BDM girl like the others, in some ways she was different from the other girl leaders; she wore her hair short and took the socialism in Nazism seriously by distributing the food rations during BDM hikes painstakingly evenly. "Sophie always liked to sing ballads, very heroic ballads. They dealt with Siegfried, who carried the gold from the heath." She accompanied herself on the guitar, and the atmosphere was romantic, with a campfire. "Yes, Sophie was very romantic and idealistic and also fanatic." She loved exercising her girls while marching: "Left, two, three . . . that was really dashing."[22]

The graphic artist Otl Aicher, then a classmate of Sophie's younger brother Werner, remembers Sophie from their shared adolescence in Ulm. "She leaned her head back a bit, blinked against the disappearing sun and walked with her hip a tad forward, her feet somewhat apart." In contrast to her sister Inge, tall and four years her senior, Sophie was diffident and indulged an almost extreme physical and mental rigorousness. "She had a straight intellect and could catch up quickly," says Aicher. Sophie was certain the invasion of the Western Allies was imminent when she talked with Aicher at the end of 1942; Aicher was a soldier home on furlough, and they both anticipated a catastrophe at Stalingrad.[23] By that time Sophie was receiving letters from her boyfriend, twenty-five-year-old Wehrmacht Captain Fritz Hartnagel, who informed her of the desperate situation around the doomed city before he was flown out. He wrote about "thousands of fugitives, women and small children and old men without shelter or food," and that he had assisted one old man, scarcely able to walk, as well as a young woman.[24] Already in April 1940 Sophie, nineteen years old and in her last year at the Ulm Gymnasium, had written: "Sometimes I shudder because of the war, and all hope for a better future is leaving me. I just do not wish to think about it, but soon there will be nothing more than politics, and as long as that is so confounded and so evil, it would be cowardly to turn one's back on it." Sophie was at that time still a leader in the BDM.[25]

Sophie's brother Hans, born in 1918, was tall and handsome in a manner more immediately striking than his pretty, inner-directed sister. Aicher admired him deeply, although some of Hans's friends, while not denying his charisma, thought him "self-serving, filled with a sense of his own importance" and manipulative of people.[26] "He thought when he talked," remembers Aicher. "His was a rhetorical existence, dialogue as well as dialectics. Insights came to him as to a constantly turning spotlight on a beacon." He was "always radiating, always receptive. This technique invariably placed him in the center, even when he did not wish it." Like Inge, whom some remember as a much tougher BDM superior than Sophie, Hans was seen as a born leader, with an aura of natural authority for his friends.[27]

Like Sophie and Inge, Hans had been a junior chief in the Ulm HJ. When he joined the Hitler Youth in 1933, he did so, at the time, in protest against his father's thoroughly democratic convictions. Hans was then calling his father, Robert Scholl, a former Swabian small-town mayor and civic administrator, a "reactionary." Soon Hans became "an enthusiastic standard bearer." He carried the flag, representing 4,000 Ulm Hitler Youths, at the nearby Nuremberg Party rally in September 1935—the one at which the noxious Race Laws were promulgated. Significantly, this marked Hans's departure from Nazi ideals. He began to resent the pronounced militarism, the overt racism, the victimization of the weak. When a higher HJ leader was bullying a younger lad who could not hold the banner straight, Hans boiled over and hit the older boy in the face. In 1937 Hans joined one of the forbidden resurgent *bündische* groups, the *d.j.1.11* with secret ties to the exiled Eberhard Koebel.[28] At the end of the year he was arrested, in the wake of the police ordinances prohibiting such gatherings. Even Inge and Hans's younger brother Werner came under suspicion and spent weeks as a guest of the Gestapo, while Sophie was screened and quickly released. As a fresh volunteer for the Wehrmacht, Hans too won his freedom before long. In April 1939 he began to study medicine in

Munich, and in 1940 he was in a medical student company as an orderly with the advancing troops in France. By that time his opposition to the regime had clearly crystallized.[29]

The four other members of what was to become the active core of the White Rose resistance group were Willi Graf (b. 1918), Alexander Schmorell (b. 1917), Christoph Probst (b. 1919), and Jürgen (later George) Wittenstein (b. 1919), all of them friends and colleagues of Hans Scholl as university students of medicine. Wittenstein's rich industrialist mother had already smuggled a Jewish woman into Switzerland, from her country estate on Lake Constance.[30] Originally from Saarbrücken, Graf had been in the Catholic youth movement of the Republic and after 1933 was one of those German boys who steadfastly refused to join the Hitler Youth. Instead, in 1936 he became a member of the Gray Order, until it was extinguished in 1938. Graf was then studying medicine in Bonn, but he remained equally interested in history, philosophy, and theology. From June 1941 to April 1942 he served at the Russian front. After witnessing German war crimes at first hand, he wrote: "The war, especially here in the East, leads me to see things which are so terrible as I could never have thought possible." He was posted to Munich in spring 1942 to enable a completion of his medical course of studies.[31]

Schmorell had a German physician father, who was born in Russia and returned to Germany after the October Revolution, and a Russian mother who was the daughter of an Orthodox priest. After his mother died, his father began practicing medicine in Munich. Alexander learned fluent Russian from his nanny, Nanja, and was raised in the Russian Orthodox faith. When the group of *bündisch* youth he belonged to was conflated with the HJ, Schmorell withdrew immediately. He was something of a roamer, wandering around by himself and seeking new and strange friendships, often communing over jugs of wine with vagrants. Much like Hans Scholl, Schmorell was what the Hitler Youth coveted as "leadership material": he was a first-rate swimmer and fencer who also played the piano and sketched and turned into an expert sculptor. Wittenstein today calls him "a multifaceted and multigifted artist at heart."[32] But such an individualist had problems subordinating himself to the Wehrmacht, which he tried to leave once drafted, in 1938. While still in training he met up with the medical student Jürgen Wittenstein, one of the few White Rose survivors and today a distinguished thoracic surgeon in southern California. Schmorell himself began his medical studies in 1939, and in the fall of 1940 was a medical student at the University of Munich.

Christoph Probst's father was a passionate private scholar of Sanskrit with ample money and time, who lived in Zell near Berchtesgaden. Eventually Christoph was sent to a Gymnasium in Munich, where he met Schmorell. He too remained aloof from the HJ but, like Scholl and Graf, showed no interest in any of the illegal or secret groups. Probst tried to overcome his revulsion against the Reich's labor and military service by immersing himself in art, literature, and music. He began his medical studies in Munich out of a general love of humankind, and specifically out of hostility to the euthanasia program of the Nazis, to which, as many Germans were becoming aware, the mentally and physically infirm were increasingly falling victim after 1939. He was the only one of the five main principals in the White Rose who, at the time of their arrest in February 1943, was married and had children.[33]

In the fall of 1941 Otl Aicher informed Hans Scholl of the written protests by Clemens Graf Galen, the Catholic Bishop of Münster, against Hitler's euthanasia campaign. Letters and flyers with such contents had been dropped into people's mailboxes in Ulm, which was in the vicinity of the killing centers at Grafeneck and Kaufbeuren. They originated with three Gymnasium students, one of whom, Hans Hirzel, knew the Scholls. This was the first time that Hans Scholl commented on the expediency of owning a print duplication machine.[34] By early 1942, in Munich, the medical students were already active, preparing their resistance flyers. Hans reluctantly initiated his sister Sophie into his circle only after her urging, when she joined him in

Munich in May to take up the study of biology and philosophy. Between June and July, the first four of a total of six *Weisse Rose* flyers were sent out to the students in the university.[35]

Soon afterward, the medical student company with Hans Scholl and his friends was ordered to leave for the eastern front, to work as auxiliary physicians right behind the lines. Passing through Poland, they were appalled by the treatment of the population and what they saw of the abuse of the Jews. Utterly shocked, Wittenstein photographed the victims of the Warsaw Ghetto. These German medical students were impressed by Russia because of the simplicity of the peasants, the nostalgia of their folk songs (just as the Cossacks had impressed the Weimar youth movement), and the expansive landscape in which they sensed the Russian soul. Dostoyevsky became their quintessential author, as he had been for earlier generations of pro-Russian Germans. Schmorell, who with his knowledge of the language and of the mentality of the people was able to arrange meetings with the peasants, further advanced this idealization of Russia. This romance with Russia was in stark contrast to the human tragedies of pain and death which the medical students had to cope with in the field hospitals. At the end of August, Scholl wrote that he could hear the moaning of his wounded patients day and night, and neither music, nor Dostoyevsky, could help him get over it. Small, simple acts of kindness, whenever possible, helped to ease the young men's own pain from day to day. When Scholl met an old, suffering Jew in a work detail, he handed him his entire tobacco rations, and Schmorell risked court-martial after he chided a Wehrmacht soldier who had beaten a Soviet prisoner to a pulp. Wittenstein took pictures of "some of the horrors: shot-down Russian planes, willfully desecrated churches and icons." And he saw "trucks crowded with people disappear into a forest, heard rifle shots, and saw the trucks return empty." In a train on their way back home, the group of medical students sang anti-Nazi songs, unmolested. Their mood was one of invincibility and soaring hope as they returned to Munich in November 1942.[36]

By that time, there existed a loose circle of more mature friends who were supporting the Scholl group spiritually and psychologically. Probably the most important of these was Professor Carl Muth, a left-leaning Catholic writer and scholar whose journal *Hochland* had been prohibited by the Nazis in 1941. Although Hans Scholl himself was Protestant, Graf and Probst and a few others in the outer circle were Catholics. During the summer of 1942, Scholl catalogued Muth's extensive library and had many heart-to-heart conversations with the older man. In spring 1942 Scholl met the architect Manfred Eicke-meyer, who confided in him what he had seen in Occupied Poland, where he had supervised construction work. Eickemeyer told Scholl of "shootings by the SS of Poles and Russians," and, since he had gotten around quite a bit, of "how the Germans had carried on there." Another influential mentor was the philosopher Theodor Haecker, who had written about human nature and had been silenced by the authorities in 1935. Haecker conveyed to Scholl that the current suffering of the Jews was due to Germans in their capacity as Christians and represented true evil—perhaps not a strikingly original hypothesis, but one which impressed Hans deeply.[37]

And then there was Kurt Huber. Born in 1893, he taught psychology at the university, but his formal training was in musicology and he was also very interested in philosophy. His specialty was Bavarian musical folklore. This had probably made him fall in line with the Nazis easily after their assumption of power. In 1935–36 Huber wanted to help found a "German School of Folk Music and Dance" in Munich, to counter "the champions of Marxist tendencies and Jewish products." He was interested in music to be played by laymen and folk dance "in the spirit of National Socialist weltanschauung." Toward that end, he wished to enlist the aid of the Hitler Youth.[38] At that time Huber believed in musicianship that was "rooted in the soil," to retain the "purity of German folk art," in the song of the fathers, "whose *völkisch* race was congenitally tied to our own."[39] Huber had moved to Berlin in 1938 to assume the direction of the newly created folk song archive, but had to return to Munich when he clashed with Nazi authorities over his professional future. As late as 1940 he had joined the Nazi Party, probably to increase his chances for a full chair at the university, where he was teaching as a poorly paid adjunct professor. His ingrained Catholicism, his treatment at the hands of the authorities, and possibly a growing concern over what he cumulatively witnessed in the dictatorship slowly turned him into an enemy of the Third Reich. He certainly was opposed to the regime when he met the Scholls for the first time in July 1942, although it is still unclear exactly how altruistic his motives were then.[40] An indication of his state of mind during this phase can be gathered from a lecture that Wittenstein heard him give on Spinoza. The seventeenth-century philosopher Benedict Spinoza was a Jew, and it was forbidden to teach his ideas. "But Professor Huber managed his lecture so brilliantly that it became evident that this 'despised, decadent Jew' was one of Germany's most important philosophers."[41]

In December of that year there was another important meeting between Huber and the White Rose group. The emblem of the White Rose was now on the flyers that were circulating. It had been taken from writings by the nineteenth-century romantic Clemens Brentano, who had composed songs of liberty against Napoleon, and it symbolized freedom of thought and expression. In January 1943, the most active month for the White Rose, Huber was an integral member of the group. More leaflets were prepared; they were sent off in the hundreds by mail and distributed in people's mailboxes in the towns surrounding Munich, some as far away as Frankfurt and Vienna. Several thousand leaflets were placed in Munich itself. On the fourteenth of the month, Munich's Gauleiter, Paul Giesler, asserted in a speech at the university that women were useless as students and thus "had better give a child to the Führer"; they could easily produce academic credentials in the form of one son a year. Those girls not attractive enough to find a boyfriend might be taken care of by his own adjutants. The crude import of his speech first provoked a riot among those students who had heard him in the lecture hall and then caused a larger disturbance among the entire student body. The Gestapo arrested a few students but let them go after several days.[42]

Then came news of the German defeat at Stalingrad on February 2, 1943. Against the background of the recent altercation with Giesler and the demonstration of student dissent, White Rose members felt certain that their own victory was not far away, and they became foolhardy. For several nights they engaged in dangerous actions, painting slogans such as "Freedom," "Down with Hitler," and "Hitler mass murderer" as well as crossed-out swastikas on university walls and free spaces in the streets surrounding the massive main building.[43] One incensed observer reported that they had used red paint to print those slogans on the sidewalks of the major thoroughfare, Ludwigstrasse.[44] Wittenstein wrote similar graffiti in the restrooms of the university.[45] The group then mass-manufactured a sixth flyer, which Huber actually conceived and wrote for them, in which he cleverly capitalized on the disaster of Stalingrad. On February 18, nearly two thousand copies of this flyer were distributed by Hans and Sophie Scholl in broad daylight throughout the university building on Ludwigstrasse and were thrown over the balcony of the inner, glass-covered light well. They were observed by a caretaker, who immediately took them to the university rector, Professor Walther Wüst, a Colonel in the SS and an intimate of Himmler's. Wüst held the two in his office until the Gestapo came to take them away.[46] Hans and Sophie Scholl together with Christoph Probst were tried before the People's Court on February 22. Graf, Schmorell, and Huber followed a few months later. (Schmorell had tried to flee to Switzerland, but had been hindered by deep snow. A former girlfriend, Gisela Schertling, allegedly betrayed him after recognizing him in a Munich air raid shelter.)[47] The sentence for all was death by guillotine.[48] When Hans put his head on the block, he shouted: "Long live freedom!" Sophie said to her parents, who had come to say good-bye from Ulm: "This will make waves."[49] But as courageous as her remarks were at the time, they were not prescient.

The leaflets distributed by the White Rose in 1942 and early 1943 are characterized by a mixture of high idealism and crass naïveté. But the contents of these flyers and the consequences of their fearless distribution made these young Germans, most of whom had barely graduated from the Hitler Youth, into the few true heroes of the unevenly organized resistance movement against the Nazi regime, from beginning to end.[50] What stands out most clearly from the White Rose group's proclamations is the clear characterization and condemnation of tyranny, abhorred by civilized societies since the Enlightenment. "Nothing is less worthy of a cultured nation," began the first flyer, "than to allow it to be 'governed' without protest by a clique of rulers who are dependent on irresponsible and dark drives." In the second flyer it is astutely observed that, from the beginning, the Nazi movement was predicated on a need to defraud the citizens; always rotten to the bone, it was built on lies. This assertion was at odds with the widespread German belief, until about January 1945, that with all its faults, the Nazi movement was always salvageable because it had the virtuous Hitler at its center.[51] Hans Scholl and his friends showed a healthy democratic sense when they urged, in the fifth flyer, that in the future, a viable Germany could only be based on a federal system as an integral part of a rejuvenated Europe.

Also notable in the White Rose leaflets is the frequent allusion to German classical and romantic ideals and icons—in particular Goethe, Schiller, and Novalis, but also the universally adopted Aristotle and Lao-tzu. Such references are characteristically couched in the jargon of the German *Bildungsbürgertum,* the humanistically educated intellectual elite, of which these young men and women would have been future members. In that spirit, the second flyer began: "It is impossible to take on National Socialism intellectually, because it is itself anti-intellectual." In their last leaflet the group's members identified themselves shrewdly, using the National Socialists' own terminology, as "workers of the brain," and condemned the Hitler Youth, the SA, and the SS as primitives who for years had tried to anesthetize "the most formative educational years of our lives."

Alongside the western-humanist commitment, a strong religious conviction shines through these pages. "Christian and Occidental culture" is a phrase that appears early in the first leaflet and is echoed throughout. The idea of a cleansing through suffering, the concept of "guilt" or "shared guilt," and that of "punishment" are key Christian notions. The Nazi state is identified as "the dictatorship of evil" and Hitler is likened to Satan, the fallen angel, and his mouth to "the stinking pharynx of hell." A reference to "the fight against the demon, against the messenger of the anti-Christ" reflects the deep Catholic beliefs of approximately half of the White Rose core group.

What renders the six leaflets ultimately persuasive are the succinct references to past and current crimes of the regime, those things that for all Germans were unspeakable, if they were known at all. The White Rose states that "since the conquest of Poland three hundred thousand Jews in that country have been murdered in the most bestial manner." There is reference to the wholesale liquidation of the Polish intelligentsia and to the gruesomely onerous advance of the Wehrmacht on the eastern front, requiring the death of many German soldiers. This is in contrast to the "hero's death" of a husband, brother, or fiancé usually celebrated in the daily press, and for most Germans long a bitter cliché. In this regard, the leaflet of February 1943 is the most strongly worded, as it makes cutting allusions not only to the recent insult of the female university students by the prurient Giesler, but also, and more significantly, to the catastrophe at Stalingrad: "Thoroughly shaken, our people is witnessing the destruction of the men of Stalingrad. Three-hundred-and-thirty thousand German men have been senselessly and irresponsibly hounded, to die and perish, on account of the brilliant strategy of that World War I corporal. Führer, we thank you!"

These observations and analyses cannot be outweighed by the few misconceptions or wrong judgments contained in those leaflets. Their authors might have been aware that it would be senseless, even counterproductive, to conjure up Goethe at a time when this quintessential German genius was appropriated (as was Beethoven)[52] to be cited when needed by Nazi ideologues and propagandists. (This was not so true of Goethe's friend Schiller, to whose universal cries for freedom, for instance in *Wilhelm Tell,* the Nazis could react phobically.)[53] The White Rose conspirators were correct in describing the plight of the

Polish intelligentsia, but their claim that noble Polish girls had been shipped to Norwegian brothels for the SS was unsubstantiated. They also assumed incorrectly that the Nazis were financing their war economy largely by printing paper money as needed, and they overestimated the slave-like labor of German industrial workers, who in fact were earning higher wages from increased armaments production. Scholl and his friends printed entreaties for "passive resistance" on the part of the entire population at a time when such resistance would be identified as active opposition punishable by death. Most naïve, and at the same time most touching, was the repeated assurance that the Third Reich was near its end, that "the war is approaching its certain finale," even that "the war is already lost." Nothing could have been further from the truth, as several more German offensives against the Allies, and a second, more diffuse and morally much less credible resistance attempt against the regime in July 1944, were yet to show.

The Munich White Rose had its support roots in Ulm, and sympathetic friends as far away as Hamburg, Freiburg, Saarbrücken, and Berlin. Otl Aicher, born in 1922 like his friend Werner Scholl, belonged to Ulm's subversive subculture. Aicher had been idiosyncratic enough never to join the Hitler Youth (and consequently had been prevented from completing Gymnasium); as a teenager, he had been repeatedly nabbed by the police on charges of vagrancy.[54] Then there was the older Inge Scholl, who had chosen not to be a student in Munich and therefore, like Werner and Otl, was not implicated in the activities of early 1943.[55] But all three were interrogated at the time by the Gestapo, although later released. Werner was reported as missing on the eastern front by that summer.[56] Sophie's close friend Susanne Hirzel, who moved between Ulm and Stuttgart, was also interrogated, and she and her brother Hans Hirzel, aged eighteen in summer 1943, were jailed for several months.[57] At the University of Hamburg, Hans Leipelt, who had a Jewish mother and who had been in 1942–43 a chemistry student in Munich, spread White Rose ideas and planned acts of sabotage in Hamburg. He acted together with his friends Traute Lafrenz, a former girlfriend of Hans Scholl, Heinz Kucharski, and

Greta Rothe, even after the death of the Scholl siblings. Lafrenz eluded the Gestapo, as did Wittenstein and Kucharski. Leipelt was executed in 1945; Rothe died in transit between prisons.[58] In Saarbrücken, Willi Bollinger, a friend of Graf, had just enough time to remove printing gear and leftover flyers before the Gestapo caught up with him, sentencing him to three months in jail in April 1943.[59] And in Berlin, university students who had received flyers in March 1943 from Wittenstein, who had smuggled them there from Munich by train, proceeded to duplicate them for shipment to Switzerland, Sweden, and England, to alert the world.[60]

At the height of the war the authorities identified other groups of youthful opponents to the regime. Most lacked the altruism of the White Rose but shared with its members important concerns on other counts. Chief among those concerns was a hatred of the monopolistic control exerted over them by the Hitler Youth. In an attempt to categorize this opposition, the judiciary, the police, and the HJ leadership came up with a range of rebellious attributes, from criminal activities to sexual promiscuity to Communism, but also including loyalty to traditional *bündische* ideals and preferences for Anglo-American values. Nevertheless, the authorities themselves realized that despite substantial distinctions between opposition groups, the Nazis had to blur these differences and pathologize and criminalize all their members, irrespective of their offenses, in order to resist and defeat them.[61]

The first of these groups, and surely the least idealistic and politically sensitive, were the cliques, bands, and gangs dispersed all over the Reich, some of whom, particularly in South Germany, liked to call themselves *Blasen,* or Bubbles. They tended to be workers or tradeshop apprentices of proletarian or lower-middle-class backgrounds, with spotty or non-existent Hitler Youth membership records and a marked predilection for petty crime. They were not particularly unique to the Third Reich; similar groups had existed in the Weimar Republic and even before then, with comparable resistance to authority. In the post-1933 context, however, anti-authority had changed to anti-authoritarian, and the cliques' transgressions assumed at least partially the dimensions of political protest. The young boys and their girl-friends of the Munich *Blasen* and similar gangs in the rest of Germany resisted the limits on their personal freedom as dictated by the Hitler Youth, and they expressed their anger not only by staying away from HJ events but also by committing acts of sabotage, theft, and some-times gross sexual indecency to protest against the society that har-bored the HJ.

It is significant that these groups, irrespective of their time of origin, became an acute threat to the regime only after the introduction of mandatory Hitler Youth service in March 1939. This was in the sum-mer before the war, when young men were being drafted in larger numbers. What the authorities characterized as unruly misfits were spotted in Breslau, Chemnitz, Hamburg, and parts of East Prussia and the Lower Danube region. In Vienna, where they had a sense of fash-ion reminiscent of the demimonde, these youths were called *Schlurfe,* or Slouches. "They let their hair grow and groomed it carefully, wore especially long jackets and long, wide pants and thin, very long neck-ties and they picked up super girls," recalls the author Ernst Jandl, "and they had switchblades and knuckledusters, and no one in HJ uniform could go to the Prater at night without the risk of being stabbed," as had been known to happen.[62] In Munich in the fall of 1941, appren-tices who belonged to an *Auerblase* (named after local wetlands) com-mitted petty theft of bicycle parts and somebody's military boots, and tried to break into telephone booths and people's homes; they were in competition with a Munich *Lidoblase* and a *Spitzblase.* Disdain for the HJ among all was de rigueur.[63]

In Hamburg, too, with its large proletarian subculture especially in suburban Harburg and Altona, attacks on HJ groups and their quar-ters were reported as early as the fall of 1939.[64] The Hamburg gang members also wore their hair long and showed off their adventurous clothes, sometimes embellished with white scarves. Their cliques, staffed with apprentices and pupils of the less exclusive schools, had names like "Jumbo Band" and "Bismarck Band" and "Death Head's Band." Petty theft, often of goods from air-raid-damaged stores, alternated with physical attacks on the Hitler Youth, particularly its police division, the universally hated Streifendienst (SRD).[65] These boys and their girlfriends were sexually active; moreover, the boys might sexually molest young women in the streets as well as carry their ill-gotten loot to the brothels of Hamburg's red-light district.[66] Even by January 1945 this phenomenon had not abated; the German youth gangs now directed their lawless activities against foreign workers, who in the face of certain Nazi defeat were moving about more defiantly and were envied for their black-market connections.[67]

Relatives of the Munich *Blasen* conducted their criminal activities also in the Bavarian hinterland, as in the provincial town of Landshut in the north. In early 1943 an "Al Capone Gang" operated in Hanover, whose prey were mostly civilians on downtown streets, and in the Pomeranian Treptow region American-gangster-style hoodlums stole goods after several break-ins; they were disenchanted apostates from the Hitler Youth.[68] In 1943 and 1944 gang activities were reported for Cottbus, Erfurt, Magdeburg, and Königsberg in East Germany, for Alfeld in central Germany, as well as for Berlin. Railway stations were favorite targets. In the capital, youths in their middle teens specialized in breaking into bakeries and grocery stores, and again stole bicycles to get around the bomb craters. National Socialist symbols such as the Hitler greeting were ignored; they counted as little for these gangs as the Hitler Youth itself.[69] In Stettin on the Baltic Sea, cliques with names such as "Violet Blue" and "Fifth Column," some fifty teenagers strong, made trouble for the HJ by loitering en masse near the post office, stealing from tobacco stores, and grabbing radios from exposed basements. Seven automobiles were stolen, and female hangers-on were forced into sex. Under the cover of darkness, the Hitler Youth's SRD suffered badly. When these fifteen- to sixteen-year-old rebels were caught, however, it was found that several were themselves leaders in the Hitler Youth.[70]

Cliques with a similar social background but with stronger ideological ties to what had once been the German political left operated in East and West Germany. In the East they were concentrated in Leipzig and known as *Meuten,* or Mobs; in the West they operated out of Cologne and Düsseldorf and cities of the industrialized Ruhr such as Duisburg, Dortmund, and Essen. The names of the western groups varied, but they were mostly known as *Edelweisspiraten* (Edelweiss Pirates). The groups' locations in East and West explain the leanings to the left, for Saxony, the Rhineland, and the Ruhr Valley had, at various times before 1933, been strongholds of Communism. But vestiges of the *bündische* groups were also visible in the clothes they wore, the songs they sang, and the names that subgroups often bore. This was especially true in the West: if the authorities tended not to criminalize the *Edelweisspiraten* as much as the *Meuten,* it was because the former were able to trace deeper roots in the comparatively less dangerous *bündisch* tradition, in contrast to the Communist roots of the *Meuten.*[71]

The *Meuten* became active around Leipzig in 1937, when military conscription was well under way and the Hitler Youth was applying greater pressure to German boys and girls to join, albeit not yet by law. Like members of the *Blasen,* they were blue-collar workers, apprentices, and shop clerks. When the *Meuten* were not congregating in cinemas, public swimming pools, or formerly Communist neighborhood pubs, where card games and talking politics were popular, they liked to hike in groups, usually with their girlfriends, who were discouraged from participating in the beer hall discussions. These discussions, innocuous as they might have been, were not surprising, since some of the older ringleaders had been active in Communist youth groups of the late republican era; a smaller number came from the youth movement camp. These not always congruent traditions were reflected in the youths' motley clothes: plaid shirts, white socks, and lederhosen in summer, slalom shirts and ski pants in winter. The girls wore the long blue skirts of the traditional youth movement. Red kerchiefs as tokens of pro-left sympathies were very popular. The *Meuten* listened to Radio Moscow and, stretching the customary *bündisch* bias for everything Russian, romanticized conditions in the Soviet Union without really knowing much about them. A vulgarized Russian greeting, "bud cadoff," a fantasy name, was used instead of "Heil Hitler." The *Meuten* were not as sexually promiscuous as the less organized petty-criminal gangs, but they were certainly no prudes. Outright criminal activity even as a form of sabotage of the regime did not interest them. The overriding concern for all was, once again, the official power and sanction of the Hitler Youth (to which some of the *Meuten* members nominally belonged); therefore they sought open confrontations with its squads. HJ members were despised as prigs and snobs, as juveniles out of touch with the lower-class society and culture of which the *Meuten* were proud. One of their slogans was: "Beat the HJ wherever you come across them!" At the height of World War II, the Leipzig *Meuten* were estimated to be about 1,500 strong.[72]

That there were *Meuten* in Dresden and other Saxon towns is certain, for they roamed even in neighboring Thuringia. But the records on this activity are scarce, probably because those *Meuten* never gave the authorities sufficient cause for prosecution, as did the large original group in Leipzig. One of the tangible grounds for prosecution by the judiciary was Marxism.[73] However, Marxist ideology was less pronounced as a motivating force behind the actions of the western German *Edelweisspiraten,* if not entirely absent. There were even fewer former Communist youth leaders in these groups than in the East. While it is true that a similar proletarian subculture served as a breeding ground for these young blue-collar workers and apprentices, influencing their self-conception, attitudes, and actions, Communism was tempered in the West by middle-of-the-road Social Democracy. Hence a workers' song, passed down through Marxist tradition, could at times be heard, but this was not necessarily evidence of doctrinaire Communism;[74] it could have been filtered through the sieve of more bourgeois Social Democracy. Most of the Edelweiss Pirates had a journeyman's pride. They were fully employed and earning their keep. They were neither Communists nor scum, as they were regarded by their contemporaries, above all those in the Hitler Youth.[75] One former HJ leader even in the 1990s described them as "from the lowest circles . . . from a milieu, in which law and order were not known," and as people whom "one did not wish to touch with a ten-foot pole."[76] The only recorded example of a direct translation of orthodox proletarian loyalties into revolutionary violence stems from the summer and fall of 1944, when six boys aged sixteen to eighteen, members of an *Edelweiss* branch in Cologne-Ehrenfeld, assisted German desperadoes who were conspiring with East European foreign workers. These teens, related to or acquainted with former KPD members, distributed antiwar flyers and derailed freight trains. Then they got themselves handguns and became involved in the illegal procurement of ration cards, as well as robberies and the killings of a guard and a local Nazi leader. They were even planning to blow up Gestapo headquarters in Cologne when they were caught and executed, along with their accomplices, in a public hanging.[77]

These western groups had several things in common with the *Meuten:* their time of origin, their intense hatred of the control exercised by the Hitler Youth even if they were members, the adventurous semi-*bündisch* outfit, the hanging-out and roaming within local and regional boundaries, and the liberal sense of sexuality.[78] What set them apart, however, were four factors: their idiosyncratic romanticism, their desire for mobility vis-à-vis the state and society, their view of girls as inferior (apart from women's sexual usefulness), and their geographic dispersion.

The romanticism of the *Edelweisspiraten* was reflected in their name alone: "Edelweiss Pirates," some of whom actually wore little Edelweiss pins. Some branches called themselves Navajos, after the North American Indian tribe; others were Kittelbach Pirates, named after a stream running north of Düsseldorf. These designations as well as the songs they favored and the nicknames they used were handed down from traditional youth movement lore. The proximity to Germany's western borders may have inspired them with fantasies connected to the United States, Mexico, and other Latin American countries. In addition to the obligatory "Cossacks," their songs featured buffalos bellowing across the prairies, where Bobby was throwing his lasso and his girl never said no, after whiskey had made the rounds with the boys. If there was no explicit political meaning in those lines, there were other ditties warning the Hitler Youth's SRD of imminent destruction: "Edelweiss is marching, watch out, clear the way!"[79] The conjuring-up of America as a representation of unlimited opportunities implicitly criticized a totalitarian society that increasingly fettered its young, and the express mention of the Hitler Youth targeted the aggressor.

The *Edelweisspiraten* disliked the HJ not so much for ideological reasons, such as its racialist world view, as for the fact that it denied them mechanisms for social advancement. They were acutely aware that the many lower and middle-level leaders in the monopolistic youth organization were usually chosen from among Gymnasium students whose parents were members of the social elite. Young Rhenish apprentices or skilled and unskilled workers with an elementary-school education felt ill at ease in a hierarchy that preserved the old order by precluding social mobility within HJ ranks. Despite Schirach's and his successor Axmann's perennial slogans in which they tried to connect to the HJ's pre-1933 lower-class tradition, such practices persisted. Thus these young workers at first avoided, then collided with the HJ, then kept to themselves. At seventeen or eighteen they preferred to join the Wehrmacht, often volunteering, which would open conventional paths of advancement.[80] In the case of the *Meuten* it was their more manifest leftist persuasion which prevented them from taking that voluntary step, even though they, too, would not resist conscription in the end. Ultimately, this implied a tacit recognition of the Hitler state by these "pirates," if never of the Hitler Youth, with whom they sought altercations whenever possible.

As a rule the *Edelweisspiraten* took the principle of exclusion of women from their private meeting places farther even than the *Meuten,* because their lower-middle-class (not Communist) understanding of society was that women were inferior to men and had to be kept in their place.[81] Ironically, this paralleled both the practices of the Hitler Youth in its placement and treatment of the BDM, and the ideology and real world of Nazi Germany, where a male-supremacist Party ruled and egocentric men took advantage of virtually all the women in their midst.

Starting from the proletarian/lower-class subculture tied to industrial structures in the greater Ruhr area from Cologne in the Southwest to Dortmund in the Northeast, the *Edelweisspiraten* spread from their core bases to locales as far south as Frankfurt, and places as far north as Minden. Moreover, because of demographic changes resulting from the bombings, such as huge evacuations from city to country and region to region, but also as a consequence of the HJ's Kinderlandverschickung program, some *Edelweisspiraten* were swept away from western Germany entirely. In early 1945, when everything was in chaos, some of these youths could be seen huddling together in the train station bunker of Hanover, hundreds of miles east from the Rhine and the Ruhr.[82]

It is on record that Düsseldorf's *Edelweisspiraten* provoked clashes with members of the Swing Youth whenever they encountered them, although both groups shared an opposition to the HJ.[83] But the Swings were different from the Edelweiss Pirates and the *Meuten* in more ways than one. Most important was that, like the members of the White Rose, the Swing Youth came from a higher social background—upper-middle-class with more than a smattering of lower-middle-class members, but no workers. Commensurate with their superior social position, the Swings tended to be at the Gymnasien from which the Hitler Youth recruited its local and regional leaders and which were anathema to the less formally educated gangs in Saxony and the Rhineland. The Swings, both boys and girls, ritualized their aesthetic and economic differences from the HJ through a predilection for Anglo-American swing and Dixieland jazz music, indulgence in the so-called swing dance, trendy fashions, and the consumption of refined liquors. True to their self-image as potential elites, there was not a trace of left-wing ideology motivating them, not even in the somewhat nominal mode of the Pirates, let alone the quasi-Communist conviction of most *Meuten*. One symbol of opposition, however, which the Swings certainly shared with the more primitive, petty-criminal gangs such as the South German *Blasen* was self-indulgence, whereas members of the *Edelweisspiraten,* the *Meuten,* and especially the White Rose were more idealistic and practiced self-denial.

It is characteristic of whatever German political opposition to Hitler and the Nazi regime existed that it was divided into several factions from beginning to end. Not the least of these divisions was social. For all their commonalities, the divisions between the dissenting youth groups, albeit at separate levels, were similar to divisions characterizing the older and more experienced intellectuals, politicians, and military leaders of the classical resistance. Such parallels help to explain why the youthful dissenters ultimately had to be defeated by an unforgiving regime, as were the older resisters.

Like the other dissenting youth groups, the Swings had originated around 1938, in the wealthy northern port of Hamburg, and assuredly for the same reasons. Socially privileged boys and girls who knew one another from Gymnasien, some of them very exclusive, and from elite sports clubs, would gather together at a major downtown skating rink. In the words of one Hitler Youth critic, "they visited certain cafés in droves, wore conspicuous clothes, and enthusiastically embraced English music and English dances."[84] There were smaller groups in Frankfurt, Kiel, Breslau, Brunswick, and Berlin, probably transplanted there from Hamburg, although Frankfurt's swing and jazz subculture arose independently.[85]

The Hamburg Swings came to the attention of regional authorities in early 1940, a few months after the Hitler Youth leadership had been authorized to utilize state agencies for the enforcement of compulsory HJ attendance in accordance with the decree of March 1939. The well-heeled sons and daughters of some, if by no means all, of Hamburg's patricians rejected such force either by quitting the HJ service altogether or by attending irregularly; a few tried to sit on both sides of the fence. In the following months until 1942–43, when the group was suppressed, the authorities became aware of various performances and personal practices, more or less visible to outsiders, which the Swings of Hamburg decided to engage in. These included swing dance, based on the American Lindy Hop of the 1920s and '30s, which was practiced at a number of semi-private and carefully chosen public venues. The musical accompaniment was provided by indigenous German bands playing American Benny Goodman-type swing, sometimes of questionable amateur quality, but also by Dutch and Belgian professionals such as the John Kristel or Fud Candrix orchestras. Regarding one large open Swing party at Hamburg's Curio-Haus in March 1940, for which printed invitations had been sent to the cognoscenti, the patroling HJ reported as follows: "An emcee announced the numbers in English. English hit songs were played and crooned. Almost entirely they were dancing swing, from the tamest to the wildest. They shoved their upper torsos forward while shaking their lower bodies. Moreover, many times 4–6 people danced and hopped around in circles, knocking their hands together and even rolling their heads against each other."[86]

In addition to the dance and swing music, the Hitler Youth officials and their colleagues from the Gestapo took note of the peculiar dress, hairstyles, and makeup of these individuals: "The male participants were legitimized by their long hair, often reaching to their collars (hair length up to 27 centimeters). Predominantly they wore long, frequently plaid British jackets, shoes with thick, light-colored crepe rubber soles, eye-catching scarves, diplomats' hats on their heads, an umbrella over the arm in every kind of weather." And, about the girls: "They preferred their hair very long. Eyebrows were penciled in and lips painted, and the fingernails were lacquered."[87]

The Nazis also noted the Swings' penchant for English and especially American films. Disapprovingly, they wrote: "The laid-back attitude shown in those films appealed so much to these adolescents that, by their own admission, they consciously tried to make a derelict impression. The 'American' element in their attitude and comportment to them constituted an ideal." Moreover, the inquisitors were aware of the Swings' heavy trade in current swing and Dixieland records, which allegedly were hot commodities demanding the highest prices. Some of these records were reported to have been copied with special appliances, changing hands for even more money. "The more fantastic and louder the disk, and the more bizarre and crazy the rhythm, the greater was the demand." The censors wrote down that non-"Aryan" members belonged to the clique, and that certain cafés and nightclubs were frequented with regularity, such as the Schiff Ahoi.[88]

More than anything, the HJ and Gestapo were intrigued by what they described in their reports as sexual practices, vibrant as they were refined, involving even fully Jewish girls between fifteen and eighteen. They observed such activity by the Swings in the nightclubs, in private homes, and during special outings in the environs of Hamburg. Alcohol was mentioned as an ever-ready stimulus. "Personal devotion usually played less of a role than the calculated choice of a partner for sexual intercourse," they quoted one of the arrested Swings as saying. "The girls kept moving around in our circle, with those partners being favored who possessed rooms safe from outside interference." At private parties in the wealthy parents' villas, it was reported that lots were drawn, "after which all participants lost their garments to the point of complete nakedness." Thereupon the boys would take turns with the girls in the available bedrooms. What was known as "French" practices would occur, pruriently described by the Nazi stenographers as "sexual deviance."[89]

Much of what the authorities took down on paper was exaggerated, but sometimes they had to fill in the gaps. Regarding the social background of the Swings, Propaganda Minister Joseph Goebbels in August 1941 spoke of Hamburg's "plutocratic youth," whose only goal was to avoid the Reich Labor Service and military conscription.[90] Although most of the fathers of the Swings were either well-off merchants or professionals such as physicians and lawyers, with residences in high-end areas like Blankenese and Harvestehude, some were master craftsmen or lower civil servants or office clerks, for example from Altona. The occupations of the Swings themselves reflected this, with probably no more than 70 percent attending Gymnasien and the rest in some practical training. And while the students received generous allowances from home, the employed white-collar workers were already earning money of their own. Girls belonged in disproportionately greater numbers to the latter group; they were accepted by the original skating-rink clique if they were attractive, showed some sense of refinement, especially in fashion, and embraced swing music and swing dance. As Robert Vogel, then the young heir to a shipping fortune, recalls: "Surely it was easier for girls to be upwardly mobile. I remember one whose father had a welding business, hence was a master tradesman. It is important to know that girls of the kind we preferred were rare. Yet girls of lower social status who were all right, meaning who were good-looking, were welcome in our midst." One such girl was Helga Rönn, a statuesque beauty whose father was a clerk and whose mother worked as a streetcar conductor; she herself was training in various shops but thought she would get into films. Another was Hanne-Lore Evers, with a retail grocer for a father, who was a trainee in the textile industry. As a result she had exquisite taste; she was pretty as well as artistic. Soon she was in the company of key members of the Swings.[91]

The elite background of the leading Swings like Vogel was determined by the social origins of the skating-rink crowd, who were members of exclusive sports clubs, especially clubs for water sports, in that world port on the Elbe River with its central Alster waterways. The Norddeutscher Regatta-Verein, for instance, produced national sailing champions and owned facilities for socializing, as did similarly exclusive clubs. Until 1940 these clubs had a rarefied atmosphere with afternoon teas, English-style, at which Dixieland or swing records would be played or live bands might perform. After spending hours of relaxation and leisure there, these privileged sons and daughters would then repair to one of several expensive cafés or nightclubs, most likely to continue their dancing to the swing of German and also foreign combos; this and the consumption of alcohol on those occasions were never questioned. In the cafés and nightclubs the boys would meet up with their (frequently lower-class) girlfriends. Hans Engel, the son of a business executive who had represented the Deutsche Reichsbahn in

New York, recalls that in the Café L'Arronge, the musicians performed "the newest American hits." Engel, whom his admirers called "Jaeggi" (in a vain attempt to pronounce "Jackie"), was knowledgeable about this music; in addition to excelling at tennis, field hockey, and ice hockey, he spoke fluent American slang and knew his Louis Armstrongs and Fats Wallers first-hand. Helga Rönn, too, went with friends to L'Arronge, but also to the Alsterpavillon (where Kristel and Candrix played), the Ex-Bar, and the less reputable Faun-Casino.[92]

A few of these watering holes were near the Dammtor railway station not far from the Alster, where the Swing crowd liked to hang out in the afternoons. Next to it was the Waterloo Cinema, which was progressive in that it featured Hollywood movies as long as that was possible, and whatever German films the Swings would deem acceptable, such as Theo Lingen's *Frau Luna* (1941).[93] Among the U.S. films was Hal Roach's sophisticated comedy *Topper* (1937) with Cary Grant and Constance Bennett, who played two wealthy, freewheeling socialites who appealed to the tastes of these young Hamburg sybarites.[94] Much loved were films with American popular music in them, preferably swing, such as the *Broadway Melody* flicks of 1936 and 1938 with Eleanor Powell, a dancer who was alluringly attractive to the Swings.[95] In *Broadway Melody* (1936) Powell impressed the lower-middle-class girls like Evers and Rönn because she got her rich and famous man in a Hollywood-type happy ending, and even more important, her character, Irene Foster, came from provincial Albany to rise to stardom in New York City. This double leitmotif of professional and social advancement was both American and modern, something which intelligent and anti-HJ teenagers in Nazi Germany could identify with.[96] Standards from Powell's films such as "You Are My Lucky Star" and "I've Got a Feelin' You're Foolin'," sung by Powell herself or by co-stars Frances Langford and a very young Judy Garland, were marketed in Germany by Brunswick and Electrola and cherished by those teenage girls, as well as their boyfriends.[97] After the German declaration of war on the United States on December 11, 1941, the Nazis wanted to alter that pro-American image by exposing American vices in a propaganda film, *Rund um die Freiheitsstatue* (Round the Statue of Liberty). They denigrated, successfully they thought, swing, sexy fashions, jazz, and other alleged American addictions. Goebbels screened this film privately for Hitler, who showed himself pleased.[98] But large numbers of young German men and women in big cities, especially in Hamburg, viewed the film as an unusual opportunity to catch those precious snippets from the glamorous American way of life.[99]

The Swings showed themselves in public in those cafés, nightclubs, and cinemas, but also on extended strolls on Hamburg's main thoroughfares and on special outings, appearing in their characteristic attire and makeup, which were diametrically opposed to the humdrum uniforms of the Hitler Youth and its BDM. And they wore those outfits conspicuously during their swing-dance fests, both in public and at private parties. They dressed expensively and ostentatiously, with much of their fashion reminiscent of American styles in the movies, but with English accents as well. The girls appeared with long, shiny hair, lipstick, painted fingernails, silk stockings, and tightly fitting short skirts or pants to show off hourglass figures: this was how Hollywood actresses looked. Often a carefully draped trench coat was the finishing touch to a casually elegant appearance. The boys, too, sported long hair and trench coats along with their thick crepe-soled shoes, and often wore a star-spangled-banner or union jack pin on their glen-plaid jackets.[100]

The image of an Anglo-American life-style was reinforced by German and foreign recordings, such as those by Electrola featuring tunes from the music films, but mostly those with swing and Dixieland jazz. Even if illegal, the recordings were brought into the Reich increasingly after 1938 by soldiers from occupied countries like Holland and Denmark. The most urbane of the Swings, like Robert Vogel, had bought them on trips to New York. The Swings collected these recordings not as connoisseurs of art but mostly to dance and schmooze to. If they could not be purchased secretly or bartered, they were duplicated. One Swing girl had the audacity to suggest in school that English jazz records be played on the occasion of the 9th of November, the annual

Nazi commemoration of Hitler's Beer Hall Putsch and one of the Holy Days of the Hitler Youth.[101]

The authorities observed that the Swings were likely to go on excursions to Hamburg's outlying areas, taking records, alcohol, and portable gramophones along. Those outings might be to the banks of the Elbe, to nearby lakes, or, better, to the pricey Timmendorf resort on the Baltic Sea. The Nazis were suspicious of these customs because they resembled the roaming of the *Edelweisspiraten* or *Meuten* and, earlier, the bourgeois youth of times gone by. And even though the Swings never sought physical altercations with members of the Hitler Youth but rather haughtily ignored them, the authorities knew that whatever the Swings liked doing best was potentially contagious and could infect the State Youth where they were vulnerable. This was especially true in view of the sexual activities which were known to take place among the Swings, when they stayed overnight in small hotels or empty Army barracks or in the proverbial farmer's hay, as did Helga Rönn in June of 1941 with her clique in the lake area of Trittau.[102]

But mostly the shellac records were needed at the so-called house parties, a hallmark of the Swings, to provide the backdrop for their swing dance. These ritualized events took place at the homes of the more affluent members, sometimes when parents were nearby. When they were not, the consumption of alcohol could get out of hand, as would the sexual activities which so tantalized the Hitler Youth and Gestapo. Here anything was possible, from rather innocent affairs, where between dances the lights went out and couples were merely kissing, to group sex in the available bedrooms, although orgies seem to have been few and far between.[103]

Inga Madlung remembers that parties at the lavish flat of the Persian Oromutchi brothers on the sumptuous Bellevue promenade near the Alster featured mirrors, especially on the ceilings. She was there with blond Helga Rönn: "We young things naturally loved it."[104] This points to a characteristic of the Swings: their absolute tolerance of non-Germans and what the Nazis would define as non-Aryans. Inga and her older sister Jutta themselves had a Jewish grandparent; the cosmopolitan seaport of Hamburg had always attracted foreign export-import traders, and there was that traditional Hamburg hankering for anything British. At least two very rich young Greeks, whose fathers were in wholesale tobacco, were members of the Swing cliques; there were Swings of Dutch and Belgian origin and, until deportations began in earnest in 1942, there were Jews.[105] Hans-Joachim ("Tommie") Scheel remembers riding with his gang in a commuter train when SS men entered and chatted up two of the girls, who had their hair dyed blond. These were Jewish girls, and at the time Scheel thought it hilarious.[106]

Friendship with what were officially regarded as non-Germans or racial aliens was essential to the Swings; their life-style was a major reason why they had to dissent from the Hitler Youth to the point of neglect or withdrawal. And thus early on they denied themselves to the totalitarian regime—or they were perceived as doing so by the authorities, who sequestered and punished them. Those who escaped such a fate quietly changed over to the armed services or their affiliates such as the RAD, as did members of the *Meuten* and the *Edelweisspiraten,* volunteering or joining as soon as their number was called. But others did not escape.

The Empire Strikes Back

In order to rein in its insubordinate young, the Nazi regime employed three agencies, with their overall effectiveness in ascending order. The first of these was the Hitler Youth itself, with its various disciplinary devices. But its success was limited, because measures were directed mostly against its own HJ members, with whom the wayward youths to be targeted were not always identical. The second agency was the judiciary, which could reach beyond Hitler Youth membership, but which was still hampered by a comparatively humane legal heritage from the Weimar Republic. The judiciary sharpened its approach to wayward youth only under constant pressure from the police and SS, both of which attempted to neutralize it entirely. The third agency was Himmler's police apparatus with all its branches, which viewed itself as extra-legal and supreme and whose encroachment on the judiciary was becoming more successful with each passing year of the war. It is significant that the relatively feeble Hitler Youth profited from an early tactical alliance with the police organizations, which increasingly used inside knowledge of Schirach and Axmann's groups to insinuate themselves into the cohorts of the young. On the other hand, the judiciary, too, acquired more teeth over time, by expanding the category of youthful offenders, inventing new crimes, instituting more special political courts, and pronouncing longer and more draconian sentences. In this scenario, adolescents who were resolved to withhold their support from the Nazi regime unreservedly, not to mention those opposing it, stood little chance of escaping unscathed by the end of the Third Reich in May 1945.

These developments have to be viewed against the incidence of youth crime from 1933 to 1945. Using a yardstick of indictments and convictions from January 1933 to about 1937, at which time the authorities granted an amnesty for certain transgressions, the Nazis prided themselves on a decrease of crime in general, and of juvenile delinquency in particular. They correctly attributed this positive trend to a return to socioeconomic normalcy after the upheavals of the Great Depression (1929–1935).[107] But what they did not say was that the police presence was very much more in evidence after 1933, acting, directly or indirectly, as a powerful deterrent to social deviance.[108] After the start of the war on September 1, 1939, crimes by youths were on the increase as compared to 1937, with a brief break in convictions owing only to a short-lived amnesty issued by Hitler on the 9th of that month. This contrasted negatively with a slower increase in crimes committed by adults in the same period, as well as with a weaker pattern of youth crime for the beginning years of World War I.[109] What stood out in this statistic was a disproportionately high incidence of crimes committed by young females from 1937 to 1944. By implication, Nazi record keepers correlated such transgressions with a greater incidence of sexually motivated crimes among (male) juveniles already beginning in 1933, as if sex offenses committed by young men were the inevitable result of female promiscuity preceding them—a clear case of blaming the victims.[110] Another variable of this situation was the widening of the definition of "crime" through the creation of novel types of punishment such as Youth Arrest (*Jugendarrest*) and the promulgation of decrees like the Police Ordinance of March 9, 1940.[111] The latter identified new groups of juvenile delinquents, such as teenagers under eighteen who were seen smoking and drinking in public, those who did not heed a stringent night curfew, and those who appeared in questionable nightclubs or dance halls.[112] Now "any leisure time for youth was practically declared as hanging around the streets" and thus was punishable.[113]

Disciplinary procedures in place for the Hitler Youth could be invoked whenever any of the aberrant youths were members and proved to have absented themselves from HJ service.[114] Hence in early March 1940, when the Swing celebrations in the Hamburg Curio-Haus were uncovered, 102 of the male suspects indicted actually were HJ members, of a total of 237 culprits; 52 had left the HJ and 58 had never joined. Similar ratios obtained for the BDM.[115] In cases of individual HJ Swings, the Hamburg Hitler Youth was able to help other authorities with its judgments, as in the case of sixteen-year-old Christa Broders, who in February 1944 was said to have missed several BDM meetings, but nonetheless was judged by her local leader to be "not essentially of bad character, even though she is somewhat flighty; rather, she has suffered from a bad education."[116] At that time the Hitler Youth leadership was using Burg Stahleck, one of its service camps, to keep in line male members in the Rhineland with potentially deviant behavior.[117]

Since the lines between HJ membership and non-membership were often blurred, the Hitler Youth frequently erred on the side of injustice simply to go after its quarry successfully. In the case of Hamburg's "Tommie" Scheel, who was a Hitler Youth turned Swing and who at seventeen was grabbed by the Gestapo in 1940, even his school teachers could not say whether he was in the HJ or not.[118] Near Essen in the Ruhr, a Hitler Youth leader spotted some twenty-odd Edelweiss

Pirates wandering about in their adventurous costumes in October 1939; they were deemed to be under the jurisdiction of the HJ by virtue of illegal *bündisch* regrouping and were dispatched to a police station for questioning. These kinds of control occurred repeatedly during the war, with the HJ beating bands of Pirates into submission, pending further legal action.[119]

Because of the Reich Youth leadership's quasi-legal claim, expressed in the law of December 1936, to be responsible for *all* the youths in Germany under eighteen, Schirach and later Axmann groomed the internal surveillance service called HJ-Streifendienst or SRD for this disciplinary task. It had been established in July 1934, initially to combat "juvenile crime, delinquency, and undisciplined behavior" within the Hitler Youth itself.[120] SRD members were specially selected youths whom the HJ leadership had reliably indoctrinated. Wearing armbands resembling those of the Sicherheitsdienst (SD) of the SS, they would roam public places such as movie theaters, railroad stations, and neighborhood pubs, but also HJ youth hostels, in search of misbehaving members. With the help of the police or the SS, these youths would then be apprehended, to be disciplined inside the ranks or, in more serious cases, handed over for prosecution by the judiciary.[121] But strengthened by tighter legislation, the HJ leadership was using the SRD increasingly against lapsed or non-HJ members especially by the time of the appearance of the cliques and gangs around 1937.[122] The SRD was superfluous in the countryside, where local hostile gangs did not lurk.[123] But more often than not, in large cities the SRD tended to be outnumbered by stronger groups such as the militant *Meuten* and *Edelweisspiraten*. There were inside complaints that the Hitler Youth boys selected for the SRD (there were no girls), apart from their fanaticism, were ill suited for policing tasks, and since they could carry no handguns, they were laughed at as powerless by their often foolhardy opponents.[124] In August of 1943, with a questionable record of success, the SRD in its original form was disbanded.[125]

The very fact that the SRD, composed entirely of teenagers, was always forbidden to make arrests on its own was symptomatic of the growing dependence of Hitler Youth discipline enforcement on the police and SS on the one hand, and, to a lesser extent, on the bureaucracy and judiciary on the other.[126] Regional governments would consult the HJ or vice versa, and after November 1941 the HJ nominally chaired a Reich Workshop for Youth Support, to which representatives of State, Party, and Wehrmacht also subscribed.[127] Inevitably, the discussion at such meetings would turn to the pressing issue of an increase in youth delinquency because of the large number of fathers conscripted for the war, and a corresponding dearth of HJ leaders of Wehrmacht age who were also at the fronts.

At the height of the war, in their persecution of rival cliques, the HJ leadership collaborated incrementally but to dubious effect with the judiciary. Several higher HJ leaders now possessed law degrees, serving as *Rechtsreferenten* (legal experts); and courts of law, especially youth courts, maintained liaisons with the HJ on a routine basis.[128] But how weak the HJ leadership really was in suppressing disobedient youth is demonstrated by its failure to deal with the Swing Youth phenomenon when it was in full bloom. On January 8, 1942, HJ boss Axmann directed the following message to Himmler, as chief of the police forces, Gestapo, and SS: "In the upper schools of Hamburg or in the young affluent merchant class a so-called 'Swing Youth' has developed, which largely displays an Anglophile proclivity . . . Since the activities of this 'Swing Youth' at the home front cause a reduction in German national capacities, I think it essential that these people be immediately taken to a work camp . . . I would very much appreciate an order to your Hamburg offices to the effect that the 'Swing Youth' will be proceeded against as severely as possible."[129] Himmler subsequently employed the concentration camp system against dissident adolescents in Nazi Germany in such a harsh manner that Axmann, shortly before his death in 1996, regretted ever having alerted the police chief.[130]

Although the judiciary eventually surrendered much of its power to the police executive authorities, thereby severely afflicting German youth, it had been on a course of radicalization of its own since the last, authoritarian, years of the Weimar Republic. In general, this amounted to an undoing of liberal changes wrought by a reformation of the justice system under the auspices of the Weimar constitution, with the key year being 1923.[131] Some of the manifestations of this gradual regression, behind which Hitler's own hand was clearly visible, were an enlargement in the number of criminal offenses, a heightened use of the death penalty, the reduction of judges, attorneys, and especially defense lawyers to mere puppets of a totalitarian regime that eschewed due legal process, a hasty resort to "preventive police custody" (*vorbeugende Polizeihaft*), and the mutation of criminal offenses into political ones.[132] This last change brought with it the appointment and cumulative use of special political courts, where conventional courts were deemed inappropriately normative, called *Sondergerichte*. At the highest level, the Berlin-based Volksgerichtshof or People's Court, particularly under its bloodthirsty president Roland Freisler after 1941, incrementally adopted a penal philosophy of retribution rather than one of social integration.[133] This entire development was helped along by two interrelated factors. One was that three Reich Ministers of Justice, Franz Gürtner (held over from Franz von Papen's pre-fascist chancellorship of 1932), Franz Schlegelberger (Acting Minister since 1941), and Otto Georg Thierack (since 1942), showed themselves to be progressively ruthless officials at the helm of the judiciary, with Hitler's obvious approval. (It was significant that Gürtner as Bavarian Justice Minister had treated Hitler leniently after the Munich Beer Hall Putsch of 1923.)[134] The second factor was that because of the polymorphous character of the law in Germany after 1933—some pre-1933 legislation had been retained, much of it had been repealed or overridden by new ordinances and pronouncements by the Führer, and some had simply been voided by police decrees—the law was becoming ineffective as an administrative tool. Plans to reform it entirely, advanced by Hans Frank, Hitler's former lawyer, Reich Law Leader, and, as Governor General of Occupied Poland, no friend of the SS and police, never got off the ground.[135]

All of this affected German youth mainly in three ways: by making larger groups of them liable for prosecution, by creating new misdemeanors, and by introducing a greater variety and tougher forms of punishment. For example, the law reform of 1923 had "raised the age of criminal responsibility from twelve to fourteen and promoted the use of correctional education instead of punishment for juvenile offenders between the ages of fourteen and eighteen."[136] But in October 1939 correctional education in the case of capital crimes was abrogated for youths aged sixteen to eighteen, who could now be tried in adult court again and were no longer immune from judgments of indefinite detention for dangerous offenders (*Sicherungsverwahrung*), life behind bars, and even the death penalty.[137] In the autumn of 1942, the Party Chancellery under Martin Bormann, doubtless at the behest of Hitler and supported in this by the Wehrmacht, proposed to a largely pliable Justice Ministry the lowering of the limit of adult liability, in particularly severe cases, to the age of twelve.[138] Then there were the new infractions as defined by the Police Ordinance of March 1940. Not coincidentally, a few months later a novel form of Youth Arrest was instituted, placing young offenders in solitary confinement on a diet of bread and water, and under obligation of total silence, for up to four weeks. In 1941 it was observed that this form of punishment had turned out to be much more severe "than that provided by jail"; it was supposed to shock into immediate submission boys and girls who in the large majority were HJ shirkers.[139] With smirking satisfaction, HJ Leader Hische remarked in November of 1943 that up to 90 percent of all accused youths could now be sentenced, compared with a success rate of only 75 percent before the introduction of that measure.[140] And in September 1942 the Reich Justice Ministry, after particular consideration of the cliques and gangs, decided on the reintroduction of caning, which was subsequently implemented in special youth concentration camps.[141]

Insofar as the judiciary still attempted recourse to existing laws, it was most successful in cases where young Germans had committed breaches of a criminal nature. That was most evident in the case of the petty-criminal gangs like the *Blasen* in Munich, where indictments could be reached on the basis of theft or destruction of public property. The punishment would be jail or terms in youth detention centers.[142] Youth Arrest was also meted out to *Edelweisspiraten* who stole bicycles and pilfered mailboxes, and to those who beat up Hitler Youths, with resulting injuries. For all these infractions, there were paragraphs of conventional law on the books. As for "loitering in the street after 9:00 P.M.," the 1940 Police Ordinance could be invoked.[143]

But because of the shortcomings of existing criminal law in the prosecution of a greatly enlarged class of transgressions, regarded as political by Nazi standards, specially adopted political jurisprudence was resorted to. The original basis for this was the Emergency Ordinance of February 28, 1933, which was predicated on Article 48 of the Weimar constitution, the Republic's emergency law invoking presidential fiat in an assumed state of national emergency, and favored for everyday governance by the anti-democratic pre-Nazi chancellors. Subsequently, the February 1933 ordinance was combined with repeated injunctions such as the decrees of February 8, 1936, and June 20, 1939, against the *Bündische Jugend* or any of its reincarnations. In this way, members of nonspecified illegal youth groups who had even vague ties to the former *bündisch* youth could be hauled before Nazi special courts and dispatched to jail, for periods of a few months or even years.[144]

More easily recognizable gangs, like the *Edelweisspiraten* and *Meuten,* were similarly dealt with. In the case of the former, some *bündische* legacies seemed obvious, as were Communist proclivities in the case of the latter. Hence comparatively moderate court judgments against Navajos, *Edelweisspiraten,* and *Kittelbachpiraten* are documented for various parts of the Rhineland and Ruhr from 1937 well into the war.[145] The *Meuten* could be more harshly treated within the existing legislation forbidding the resurrection of any of the Weimar political parties, because being a Communist was a serious political offense.[146] At the same time, because the *Meuten*'s connection to Communism was at best tenuous, sentences against them on a charge of high treason could only be based on suspicion or conspiracy to commit this crime (sometimes bolstered by the charge of having listened to Radio Moscow), but never on its successful execution.[147] Thus a group of Leipzig *Meuten* was convicted in October 1938 and sentenced to between one and five years of incarceration.[148] Understandably, because of the more serious situation posed by the war, such sentences tended to be significantly longer after 1939.[149]

The most unequivocal and at the same time the most political jurisdiction occurred in cases where high treason against the Nazi state was actually proved. Invariably, these propagandistically useful trials were conducted before the People's Court, which could be moved from Berlin to other cities if necessary. Since Nazis viewed the accused as criminals in a time of national crisis, the death penalty was a foregone conclusion. This alone demonstrated the willingness of the judiciary after 1939 to acknowledge the stranglehold of the police and the highest Party authorities. What aided the merciless judges in their pronouncements against Josef Landgraf, Walter Klingenbeck, Helmuth Hübener, and the members of the White Rose was that charges of defeatism in wartime could also be adduced and bolstered by the fact that the defendants had listened to news from enemy stations such as Radio Moscow and the BBC and subsequently disseminated it.[150]

Against the Swing Youth, the judiciary was least successful, for lack of suitable paragraphs in the statutes to indict them.[151] And thus what ultimately proved to be abject impotence on the part of the justice administrators turned out to be a triumph for the State police, as the circumstances of the Swings well demonstrate. As a police spokesman said in 1943: "If there is no law or if it does not suffice because, due to its origins, it perhaps does not express National Socialist convictions, then the security police may, nay must, step in."[152] However, the police were in cahoots with the SS, and Himmler's racist ideology ruled both. Therefore, racialist indictments were applied against those wayward youths whose misdemeanors eluded the judicial norms.

This development had begun as early as November 1933, when preventive police custody provisions allowed all police organs to intern suspects in concentration camps without being authorized by the courts. Because the legal liability age had just been lowered, teenagers were potentially at risk.[153] In December of 1937 Reich Interior Minister Wilhelm Frick, the nominal superior of Himmler and his law enforcers, announced that the criminal police now had the right to take into preventive custody entirely new population groups defined as racially undesirable asocials, who would include vagrants, beggars, prostitutes, and chronic alcoholics—this at a time when cliques and gangs had begun to surface.[154] After the beginning of the war, at the turn of 1940, jurists came to agree with representatives of the police that the judiciary should hand over youths to them in cases where it was obvious "that it was not worth the effort at socialization."[155] Hitler himself re-emphasized the prerogative of the police when he decided in August of 1941 that unruly juveniles, incapable of reform by the justice system at the age of nineteen, should not be allowed to go free, but should be committed to a concentration camp, guarded by Himmler's SS.[156] In November 1943 the deliberations of 1940–41 were formalized when the Ordinance Regarding the Simplification of Youth Penalization stipulated that any recalcitrant youth while in indefinite detention as decreed by the courts could be transferred to the police for further treatment, to so-called youth protection camps.[157]

These youth protection camps or *Jugendschutzlager* were special concentration camps for juveniles and were the original creation and exclusive domain of Himmler's police and SS. They came to symbolize the supremacy assumed by the police apparatus in all matters of youth discipline. Ideologically, they were rooted in a key interest on the part of principal police administrators, in particular Himmler, in race biology, especially eugenics. This interest led to the establishment of a Criminal-Biological Office in Berlin police headquarters by December 1941. Institutionally, the youth protection camps represented a further triumph of the police executive in its overall struggle for total autonomy in matters of jurisprudence and the penal system; ideologically, they signified the supremacy of Nazi racist dogma in the country's educational processes.

The Police Ordinance to combat cliques of March 1940 had come about after a consensus between Hermann Göring, Goebbels, Frick, and Himmler that "very tough youth laws" would be needed, as Goebbels laconically put it in early February.[158] Thereafter SS General Arthur Nebe, the head of the criminal police under Himmler's police superintendent Reinhard Heydrich, took steps to interpret the Ordinance entirely in accordance with the law-enforcement visions of the police and SS, without any heed to the judiciary.[159] As a first result, male Swings in Hamburg considered to be racially degenerate ringleaders were arrested by the Gestapo, in collaboration with their school directors, in the fall of 1940. The Swings were brutally interrogated in the local Stadthaus jail and were sent, without intercession by the judiciary, to the municipal penal camp of Fuhlsbüttel.[160] Similar autonomous police action was initiated against the Swings of Frankfurt, the so-called Harlem Gang, shortly thereafter.[161] Subsequently, whenever a member of the Swings was not released after three weeks in investigative police custody, Heydrich's police headquarters in Berlin automatically pronounced it "protective custody," meaning arbitrary detention at the whim of the police captors.[162] As for the Edelweiss Pirates, some who had not yet been tried and sentenced by a law court were single-handedly committed by the Gestapo to a special "work and education camp" in 1941–42, one that outsiders, because of its appearance and rigorous drill routines, took to be a sort of concentration camp.[163] Socially and racially suspect offenders like Fritz Molden from Vienna were snatched from the courts and stuck into punitive SS battalions; in Molden's case it was a unit that had to explore dangerous moors on the eastern front to test their safety in partisan warfare, a mission during which several of these involuntary young scouts were sucked down to their deaths.[164]

Meanwhile, in early January 1942 Axmann had issued his plea to Himmler to make an example of the most offensive Swing members. Himmler replied on January 26 that he agreed to the need to act ruthlessly and that he had given the necessary orders. Indeed, he had already written to Heydrich that all previous actions by the police had so far constituted "half measures"—an unmistakable reference to what he considered to be the limitations dictated by the Police Ordinance of March 1940. He now wanted Heydrich to send the obvious kingpins, the most depraved boys and girls, to concentration camps for a minimum of two to three years.[165] Thus beginning in 1942, Swings over age twenty were incarcerated without trial in the camps of Auschwitz, Buchenwald, Neuengamme, Theresienstadt, Nordhausen, Bergen-Belsen, and Sachsenhausen.[166] Among them were the Madlung sisters and Helga Rönn's future sister-in-law, Ursula Nielsen.[167] Nor was Himmler only thinking of the Swings. In December 1942 the Gestapo caught 320 *Edelweisspiraten* in a dragnet, all in Düsseldorf, Duisburg, Essen, and Wuppertal, and detained 130 of them.[168] Two years later the Pirates of Cologne-Ehrenfeld, collaborators of "racially inferior" Slavic conscript workers, would be strung up by Gestapo agents without ever having been tried in a court of law.[169]

The youth protection camps of Moringen, for younger boys, and Uckermark, for teenage girls, were the brainchild of SS and Police Colonel Paul Werner; they were shaped by and became race-eugenic experimental sites for the psychiatrist Robert Ritter. Werner influenced his boss, General Nebe, and Nebe then prevailed upon Heydrich and Himmler to organize these camps. It is virtually certain that Werner himself had already been influenced by the eugenically obsessed Ritter, with whom the one-time chicken farmer Himmler saw eye to eye.[170] Born in 1901 and socialized in the fiercely nationalistic and anti-Semitic *Freikorps,* Ritter had obtained a Ph.D. with a dissertation on pedagogy at the University of Munich in 1927. His thesis, "The Sexual Problem in Education," showed an early interest in procreation and racially oriented eugenics; throughout his career the family man Ritter, who kept Eva Justin, his blond female assistant, as his mistress, was obsessed with sex and promiscuity among young women. In May 1930 Ritter's eugenic focus led him to a medical doctorate in Heidelberg, where his dissertation concentrated on heredity. Thereafter, he performed a postdoctoral practicum at the racist-oriented Burghölzli psychiatric institution near Zurich, and later in August 1932 he worked as an assistant in the psychiatric wing of the university hospital in Tübingen, where he was concerned with hereditary factors in the development of "asocial youths."[171]

By the mid-1930s Ritter, now a senior university physician grooming himself for an academic chair, had singled out Sinti and Roma and related vagrants, the so-called *Jenische,* as his new objects of study. As he laid out in his book, *Ein Menschenschlag,* the *Jenische* in Germany had historically been asocial, the "refuse of bourgeois society." Because they were congenitally of bad blood, which led to a variety of social misbehaviors, they were racial misfits and could not be reformed. Ritter intimated that sterilization of the current descendants of these groups—whom he alleged to be seeing daily as adolescents in his medical practice—by the sterilization law of July 1933 was the only solution to an obvious social evil, particularly since young *jenische* women had always exhibited an extraordinary degree of sexual promiscuity.[172] In 1936 Ritter was appointed director of the newly created Research Institute for Eugenics and Population Biology (Rassenhygienische und Bevölkerungspolitische Forschungsstelle) within the Reich Health Office under Interior Minister Frick, to research and take stock of the entire asocial, vagrant, and criminal population of the Reich. Thus Ritter became the Reich's foremost expert on the group popularly known as Gypsies and Gypsy-related bands. During the war he created what amateur eugenicist Himmler and the police would view as the scientific basis for the concentration and extermination of tens of thousands of Sinti and Roma, mostly in Auschwitz.[173]

In his capacity as a race-hygiene-oriented physician of increasing importance, Ritter became acquainted and soon collaborated with other physicians of the same scientific persuasion, as well as with criminal biologists, lawyers, and representatives of the police. All of these believed, like him, that physical or psychological disorders in certain groups of people in the Reich occurred independently of the environment, but instead were genetic and therefore irreparable. This nature-versus-nurture debate had of course been going on universally since

Darwin, but in Germany it had increasingly defined the medical *Zeitgeist* as racist, a view that held sway over all the leading National Socialists.[174]

While in Berlin, Ritter came into close contact with Professor Ferdinand von Neureiter, who was then the director of the Criminal-Biological Research Office in the Reich Health Office. Neureiter defined "criminal biology" as serving the aims of both the criminal law and hereditary race science, as Germans now understood it. The aim of criminal-biological research was to devise punitive programs, with the dual purpose of "atonement for the misdeed and removal or neutralization of criminal dispositions and tendencies." Hence this respected scholar helped to furnish the biological foundations for the retributive justice of the Nazis, which sought to protect the racial community rather than resocialize the wrongdoers. "Born criminals" were to be detected and permanently isolated from the healthy *Volksgemeinschaft*.[175] Ritter also got to know Heinrich Wilhelm Kranz, a less than credible ophthalmologist posing as a race hygienist at Giessen University. Kranz was working on a law for the permanent marginalization and isolation of *Gemeinschaftsunfähige*, or community aliens, meaning over a million persons deemed race-biologically unfit to be members of Nazi society, and suggesting their eventual liquidation.[176] Ritter's views at the time corresponded with those of an established Kiel University jurist, Professor Friedrich Schaffstein, a man much worried about the Swings, who held that while perhaps not all juvenile criminals were "biologically inferior," it was without question that "the tremendous significance of genetic factors in the criminality of youth has been corroborated by the more recent hereditary-biological research." The factor of punishment in the criminal justice system for the young, Schaffstein stated, had the important function of "removing the unworthy youths from the community."[177]

One of the higher-placed policemen in the capital who was following Ritter's exploits closely at the time and came to admire them to the point of emulation was Colonel Paul Werner, Nebe's delegate for the fight against youth crime in the Reich. Inspired by the eugenist-racist atmosphere, Werner developed into a racially motivated police extremist. Thus he came to believe that a future law for the treatment of *Gemeinschaftsunfähige* would aid the police leadership decisively in its long-standing quest for power over defendants without the cumbersome recourse to the judiciary.[178] Moreover, his extremist ideas regarding the prevention of crime before it was allowed to happen meshed with extremist views regarding the prevention of disease by some of Ritter's radical colleagues. For them, to be healthy was a duty and to be sick a crime: both concepts shared the same race-biological underpinnings.[179] In analogy to those Nazi physicians who would have liked to kill their patients in order to extinguish all diseases, Werner, who was convinced that most youth crimes were the consequence of hereditary predispositions, wished to eradicate crime by eliminating the criminals.[180] This accorded with the theories of Dr. Ritter in regard to *Jenische,* Gypsies, and wayward youth, and gained Himmler's wholehearted approval. Thus in the summer of 1941, Werner and Nebe agreed to appoint Ritter to the newly established Criminal-Biological Office in Himmler's police bureaucracy.[181]

At that time, the youth protection camp for boys in Moringen near Göttingen had already been set up. It had been established in August 1940 at the site of a former concentration camp under the guard of Death Head's units of the Waffen-SS. Male adolescents from thirteen to twenty-one could be sent there after arrest by the police, having bypassed judicial procedures. As in adult concentration camps, their stay was for an indefinite period; releases to the front lines, or, on reaching twenty-one, to regular concentration camps, were the norm; "a genuine conditional discharge is not usual." Inmates were to be tended to by "Educators," school teachers incorporated in the SS. But there was little for them to learn, for they had to slave in nearby war-related industries, including an underground munitions factory, seven days a week, with one Sunday off every month. They were subjected to a regimen of brutal punishments, including solitary confinement for extended periods as well as beatings.[182]

Of nearly 1,400 boys who were in Moringen until March 1945, close to a hundred died, many of hunger and tuberculosis. Several damaged their feet because of inadequate footwear. In August 1942 even the SS physician in charge, who had been trying to treat all kinds of infections, warned that less work would be performed and more boys would die "unless the diet is immediately improved." A number of boys were shot while trying to escape, and at least one was beaten to death during a public caning ritual. Bed wetters were concentrated in one barracks and were awakened first every two hours, then every hour during the night; they were forced to wear "penis clamps." Everyone got up at 5:00 A.M. and then worked for eleven hours. Mail could be sent out and received only twice a month.[183]

The camp for "fallen girls" was established at Uckermark in June of 1942, a stone's throw from Ravensbrück, northeast of Berlin, Himmler's concentration camp for women, where the terrible Irma Grese was then being trained. Again the guards were SS men, and the SS physician-on-duty came from Ravensbrück. Living and work conditions in Uckermark were very similar to those in Moringen, as were the hours. Some work details tried to convert swamps into meadows, while others were assisting farmers in the fields. Nutrition was so bad that some girls ate leaves from the trees; dysentery was common. Vicious guard dogs posed a particular danger here, maiming more than one girl. As one inmate remembers: "The camp commander was even worse than the Devil, this was Satan incarnate . . . I also was in Auschwitz, but for me, Uckermark was worse."[184] It was emphasized by the authorities that the main reason for the girls' incarceration was their uncontrolled sexuality, which led to immorality and endangered the biological integrity of the *Volk*.[185]

This reference provides an important clue as to why Police Colonel Werner's friend, the race- and sex-obsessed Robert Ritter, was constantly present in both camps and why in fact he helped define the various categories of inmates, of whom, altogether, less than 8 percent could ever hope to be freed.[186] Ritter was classifying youths according to the criteria of heredity versus milieu, which in the great majority of cases meant that the suspects were judged to be socially incorrigible on genetic grounds. On the basis of the biopolitical philosophy of the proposed law against community aliens—a law constantly reconceived yet never enacted—these renegades were preordained for a lifetime of incarceration, or death. Thus they were viewed in close analogy to the Sinti and Roma whom Ritter had been studying previously and continued to examine, effectively marking them for genocide. Indeed, in Moringen Ritter was keeping "Gypsies and part-Gypsies, a few partially Jewish and even two Negro bastards." A few Sinti were also in Uckermark. The issue of sexuality was crucial, because by Ritter's reasoning it provided both the explanation for disobedient behavior among juveniles within Nazi society and the potential for those juveniles' misbegotten progeny. Once the full range of community-alien Germans from the asocial to the criminal had been defined using race-scientific techniques in the Nazi mold, criminal biology, as it was currently anchored within Himmler's police, would assist in keeping the Nazi master race wholesome and pure.[187]

Thus it is not surprising that among the individual unreformable "misfits" who were inmates in Moringen and Uckermark, such as those notoriously contemptuous of HJ membership, there also were clutches of those *Blasen* and *Edelweisspiraten* whose asocial behavior had not been legally felonious and who, by default, became prey for the police. Moreover, Swings in their teens were conspicuous in these camps after 1941, as hardly any of their crimes were legally indictable—they had not, for instance, stolen property or beaten up Hitler Youths. The Swings' sexual profligacy predestined them as candidates for detention for the sake of the racially pure community, but also as subjects for eugenic-experimental scrutiny, to serve Ritter and his expert team.[188]

The girls eventually disgorged by Uckermark would spend the rest of their lives trying to adjust to a society of Germans still ruled by views such as Schaffstein's; for decades people refused to acknowledge the evil of an institution whose mission they mistakenly understood to have been social correction. The once beautiful Helga Rönn, for instance, who like Irma Grese had wanted to become an actress,

emerged from Uckermark broken in spirit and in body. Unable to remain in Hamburg facing ordinary Germans, she married a British soldier and became a housewife in England, never realizing her dreams.[189]
Boys conscripted to the front lines from Moringen usually were exposed to direct enemy fire and did not survive for long. Ironically, that
fate in war was shared by many of their contemporaries who, until induction into the armed forces, had tried, as best they could, to live up
to the ideals of the Hitler Youth.

In retrospect, one can view the dissent and resistance of these youth,
individuals, and groups, as diverse as they were, in terms of their social
background, the effectiveness of their actions, their political motivation, and their readiness for ultimate self-sacrifice. Socially, they came
from all strata of German society—the *Blasen* from the lumpen proletariat, the *Meuten* and *Edelweisspiraten* from the proletariat and lower
middle class, and the Swings and White Rose members mostly from
the upper classes. Some individuals, like Ernst Jünger Jr., might be
elite; others, like Helmuth Hübener and Walter Klingenbeck, came
from the lower rungs of society. In that sense these dissidents reflected
the social structure of the all-inclusive Hitler Youth they were trying to
avoid. The efficacy of their activities was null, no matter what their
means of opposition—whether they only tried to elude the control of
the HJ by staying away, as did the Swings, or were more proactive like
the *Blasen,* who tried to sabotage HJ property, or whether they sought
to engage the HJ in skirmishes, a favorite pastime of the *Edelweisspiraten.* Even the mass distribution of anti-regime flyers by the White
Rose merely established a post-1945 legacy of heroism for this group,
but did not change the regime. Differences in political motivation
reflect on the moral quality of these individuals and groups and provide a better premise for historical judgments of the HJ: the higher
such a motive, the starker the relief in which the fundamentally criminal character of Hitler's youth bands would appear—as criminal as the
dictatorship that had spawned them. This issue is related to the larger
one of self-sacrifice, for the more noble the motive, the more prepared
the dissidents would be to give their own lives. In this arena, the

Swings and *Blasen* obviously have no place, for they lived by the pleasure principle and just viewed HJ members as obstacles to their desires. It was only the members of the White Rose group who undertook their disruptive actions against Nazi society with the clear prior knowledge that they might not survive. Because most of them once had been loyal HJ members, their very existence amounts to a devastating commentary on the Hitler Youth, the first Nazi body to disappoint them; the HJ was unable to retain the loyalty of what were racially exemplary young Germans, in its relentless quest to generate the Third Reich's future elite.

Hitler's Youth at War

Historical records acquaint us with the life histories of two contemporaries, Herbert Taege and Claus von Amsberg, who were HJ members and subsequently fought in the war. Herbert Taege was born in Magdeburg, a mid-size town in Saxe-Anhalt, in September 1921, the son of a minor postal official. He joined the Hitler Youth as a Gymnasium student in March 1933, six weeks after Hitler's coming to power. Before that he had been in the German Boy Scouts, under the *bündisch* label. In the Hitler Youth Taege rose through the ranks, until on the first day of World War II he became a Nazi Party member at the age of eighteen. Simultaneously, he volunteered for the field-gray Waffen-SS, the armed branch of the general, black-shirted SS. Wounded at the front in 1940, he was transferred to the SS Death Head's unit at Dachau concentration camp, where he served as a guard. By 1943 he was in an SS tank division in Warsaw, at the time when the Warsaw Ghetto was being liquidated. In December of that year, an internal review characterized the young lieutenant as "physically very able, of honest character and open, and capable of good judgment." His knowledge of tank armor was judged sufficient and his acquaintance with Nazi ideology "far above average." This verdict was reinforced in the summer of 1944, when his superiors stated that "as a leader in the Hitler Youth, SS-Untersturmführer Taege showed particularly good ideological direction. One of his strong points was to represent National

Socialist military values with candor and conviction."[1] After the war
Taege settled in West Germany and founded Ascania, a neo-Nazi publishing firm, in which he printed his outpourings about the glory of the
former Hitler Youth, as well as other Hitler-friendly literature.[2]

Claus von Amsberg was born in September 1926 on his parents'
estate near Hamburg. Ten years later, upon entering Gymnasium, he
too, like most of his peers, joined the Hitler Youth. Then in 1943,
when he was sixteen, he was drafted into the ranks of the Flakhelfer,
juveniles who were forced to serve as cannoneers in artillery emplacements. His artillery setup was with a Navy unit near the strategically
important seaport of Kiel. Von Amsberg was fortunate not to be hit by
enemy bombs, and in the summer of 1944 he was drafted into the
Wehrmacht. He was trained for tank service, and from March to May
1945 fought with a panzer division in Merano, northern Italy. There
the U.S. Army captured him, and he spent time as a POW in Brescia
and England. By December 1945 he was a free man; as a former Hitler
Youth, he had to undergo formal denazification in order to attend university. Having repeated his *Abitur,* the final Gymnasium examination,
in 1947, von Amsberg studied law in Hamburg, and after graduation
in 1956 he joined the West German Foreign Service. After stays in the
United States, Central America, and Africa he was posted to Bonn,
where in 1964 he met the Dutch Crown Princess Beatrix. They fell in
love and were married in March of 1966, whereby von Amsberg
became Prince Claus of the Netherlands. When his wife inherited the
throne in 1980, Claus became, officially, her Prince Consort. At first
the new prince had not been welcome in Holland because of his Nazi
past, although the authorities had smoothed his path. Two things are
noteworthy about Amsberg's new career in Holland. He dedicated all
of his energies to furthering international peace and, especially, health
and economic improvements in the Third World. Although this
together with his personal modesty and charm soon endeared him to
the Dutch public, he fell victim to severe depression. This got worse
with age, and for long stretches he had to be hospitalized. Toward the
end of his life, Amsberg developed heart trouble, Alzheimer's disease,

and cancer. He died of pneumonia on October 6, 2002, much mourned by the people.[3]

What Herbert Taege and Claus von Amsberg have in common is their service in the Hitler Youth as teenagers and, subsequently, extended military training and active duty in the field. But what sets them apart, not counting birth and social station, is the quality of moral judgment governing their respective Nazi careers. Taege turned out to be a fanatical follower of the National Socialist creed and consequently, as a Holocaust denier, became an evil person. Von Amsberg, on the other hand, suffered from his involvement with Nazism and attempted to atone for it through his engagement with underdeveloped countries; a credible medical diagnosis at the time held that feelings of personal guilt contributed significantly to his steadily worsening melancholia.

The question of responsibility and even guilt looms large in a study of Hitler Youths, who, after years of military training, some of it initially camouflaged, were being asked to fight and kill in a real war. It is difficult to assess the individual moral guilt of young men like Taege and Amsberg and the millions of their comrades who served in the Wehrmacht and Waffen-SS. But questions of complicity do arise, and to make the task of dealing with them easier, it is helpful to have information about these youths' ideological motivations or absence thereof for war, their attitudes when training in pre-combat HJ formations, voluntarily or not, the nature of their actions and reactions when in the field, and their reflections, if any, when defeated. Taken together, these questions assume significance against the backdrop of historians' depictions of the role of German soldiers especially in the European East, and in particular where conventional military history touches on, and becomes intertwined with, the newer history of the Holocaust.

A related question is the issue of a conceptual division between the Wehrmacht and the SS, on which there have been two schools of thought. An earlier view maintained that the Waffen-SS fighting at the eastern front was almost exclusively responsible for any and all of the atrocities one heard about, against Jews or Soviet partisans, and that the Wehrmacht was not. A second, more recent school has held that such a distinction is specious, in that—as one American historian maintains—virtually every young German was brought up through premilitary training to view Slavs and Jews as subhumans to be mercilessly killed, and this was the one thing that propelled them at the fronts.[4]

With qualifications, there is much to be said for the arguments of this second school. Today we know that the Wehrmacht was considerably more in accord with the SS's lethal objectives toward Jews than its postwar representatives cared to acknowledge for years, and that its cruel treatment of partisans, prisoners of war, or hostages was dictated by contempt for, if not abject hatred of, humans other than those of "Nordic" blood.[5] Only recently, the German public was again reminded that in September 1943 ordinary German troops executed approximately 5,000 Italians who had been cornered on the Greek island of Kephallenia. This was a Nazi reprisal after Mussolini's fall in July of that year and the refusal by Italian General Antonio Gandin to follow German orders to disarm his troops.[6]

On the other hand, despite the millions who cheered on their armies' advance, there is evidence that young German soldiers, even in the SS, were horrified by what they saw and what they were ordered to do. And indeed, in the Wehrmacht, it is unlikely that *every* recruit fought with enthusiasm for the Nazi goals the way he had been instructed beforehand in the Hitler Youth. Especially in the later years of mounting defeat, many soldiers fought desperately, once they were at the front, because in the face of disaster all around them, they became afraid for their lives; they just wanted to get out and survive. "We have to meet again, I just cannot imagine that I will have to die so soon," wrote a desperate ex-HJ leader to his girlfriend from the Hungarian front.[7] That did not necessarily make their fight more humane or their responsibility less grave.[8] Still, even in view of the enthusiasm of all their dyed-in-the-wool Nazi comrades, a number of factors warn us not to engage in quick generalizations regarding trigger-happy post-HJ youths. One is that a horror of being sent to the eastern front evidently caused an increase in suicides among young soldiers after 1941.[9] Second, Himmler and his staff, in a progressively uncoordinated Nazi administration, experienced ever greater difficulties in the recruitment of Hitler Youth candidates for service in the Waffen-SS, a service that was becoming less popular as the war dragged on. Third, in order to embed National Socialist dogma more deeply in the Wehrmacht at the fronts, special Nazi indoctrination officers (NS-Führungsoffiziere) had to be employed—mirror images of the Red Army political commissars.[10] Finally, there were young Wehrmacht officers who attempted to stem the tide, as did the members of the White Rose on the home front. One officer who tried and eventually remained in Russian captivity was Wilm Hosenfeld, the Wehrmacht captain who allowed Jewish Warsaw Ghetto escapee Wladyslaw Szpilman to go free after hearing him play Chopin's Nocturne in C-sharp minor, as Roman Polanski's film *The Pianist* so movingly portrays.[11]

The corollary to an over-reporting of the criminality of young soldiers at the fronts is an under-exposure of the suffering of civilian young people back home in the Reich, as the war theater closed in on them and many were expelled from Germany's eastern provinces. In the shadow of the Holocaust, such suffering is a delicate subject, especially because reactionary postwar German historians used it as a counterweight to the pain inflicted on the Jews, thus attempting to exonerate Germans.[12] But in 2002 when Nobel laureate Günter Grass, himself a HJ Pimpf at ten, a Flakhelfer at fifteen, and a tank gunner at seventeen, memorialized thousands of German casualties resulting from the advance of the Russians, the majority of them young people, in East Prussia in early 1945, he had a different purpose in mind. Because he wished to help in "documenting these terrible, barbaric expulsions," he wrote about the torpedoing and sinking of the *Wilhelm Gustloff* by Russians near Gotenhafen (Gdynia) on January 30, 1945, with a loss of approximately 8,000 lives. Among the fatalities were hundreds of young Wehrmacht female helpers (Wehrmachtshelferinnen) and a thousand young sailors en route to Kiel for new submarine duty.[13] As the judicious South African J. M. Coetzee, a more recent

Nobel Prize winner, has observed, the Social Democrat Grass, long a critic of Nazism, felt freer than most to enter the ongoing debate about silence and silencing. For Grass was assuming, "in a characteristically cautious and nuanced way, a position that until recently only the radical right has dared to champion in public: that ordinary Germans—not just those who perished in the camps or died opposing Hitler—have a claim to be numbered among the victims of World War II."[14] In agreement with this, John Updike has written that Grass laudably called attention "to assaults on the reeling Third Reich that neither the victors nor the defeated victims were motivated to publicize."[15]

Elation and Disenchantment

When war broke out in early September 1939, former Hitler Youths aged eighteen or older found themselves as members of the Wehrmacht, helping to advance the German front against Poland. Their attitude was characterized by a boundless optimism that Germany would achieve quick victory, the view of an external enemy deserving of defeat as inferiors—as ideology in the Hitler Youth had dictated for years—and a sense of attachment to the younger HJ comrades whom they had left behind. This initial enthusiasm was so powerful as to stifle a sense of their own loss—the sudden death of a comrade or their own war injuries. The long-held images of the enemy were corroborated for these young soldiers—in the case of the Poles as slovenly and cruel, often civilians caught red-handed and shot as the accused prewar killers of ethnic Germans on Polish soil, and in the case of Jews as subhuman, with their beards and caftans and their dwellings in cramped, unsightly *shtetl* or large-town ghettos.[16] As Karl Kreutzer, a corporal and former local HJ leader from Heidelberg, wrote home in November to a friend, then still serving in the Hitler Youth and aching to rush to the front: "I am overjoyed that you believe in the proud Wehrmacht." For "a soldier's faith in victory is always fortified whenever he sees that

the loved ones at home believe in him, he who is out there day and
night in order to protect us all."[17]

This pattern was repeated during the campaigns in Norway and
Denmark in April and May of 1940, although the enemy here, with
their blond and "Germanic" appearance, was thought to be so respectable as to be worthy of assimilation.[18] The darker-haired French,
however, uprooted by the Wehrmacht a few weeks later, fared worse by
the Germans' racial standards, if still better than the eastern foes.
Young soldiers conditioned in the HJ as recently as a few months earlier were apt to describe the French as a derelict people, "indifferent,
deferential and dumb" in the countryside, yet morally decadent and
sexually depraved in the cities, especially Paris.[19] In the capital, the
epitome of corruption was observed, for example "Negroes who walk
arm-in-arm with white French women and who sit with them in the
street cafés," to the point where, as one enlisted youth insisted, he
couldn't "approve of that!"[20] To a greater or lesser degree, such self-
righteousness extended to other areas and populations, giving these
adolescents the certitude of being masters of a vanquished land,
whether it be Denmark or France, let alone Poland. They felt organi-
cally bonded to a master race and, in the occupied countries and after
intermittent bursts of fighting, thought they were entitled to a "master's life."[21] In this Manichean world view, they were at the summit,
and at the nadir were the Jews, who were said to have no right to life:
"As one watches these people one gets the impression that they really
have no justification whatsoever to exist on God's earth."[22]

Fueled by easy Blitzkrieg victories and agreeable occupation tasks in
northern and western Europe during 1939–40, the German euphoria
continued after the Nazi surprise attack on the Soviet Union on June
22, 1941. As more than three million Wehrmacht soldiers moved rapidly into Russia on three broad fronts—a northern, a central, and a
southern one—the dynamics of easy conquest during the summer and
autumn heightened the sense of superiority even of Hitler's youngest
soldiers. In these naïve young men's minds, fighting for an early "Final

Victory" in what was originally conceived as yet another lightning war was an article of faith.[23] "Since 2 o'clock in the morning we are at war with the Russians," wrote former Hitler Youth Hellmut to his parents on June 22, "and I am proud to be a part of this."[24]

Certain obstacles tended to dampen this conqueror mentality, but they were either suppressed in a state of denial or compensated for with the simple yet tangible rewards that war booty afforded. The most common palliatives were satisfying food and drink obtained from farmsteads or occupied estates, at a time when feasts were rare, but also clothing, especially as the Russians were discovered to have the more effective winter gear.[25]

By far the most serious impediment to an optimistic soldier's fortune was the figure of the Russian fighter himself, whose vitality and supremacy in numbers had not been expected but were soon palpable. In defeating this peril, psychological crutches helped. Hitler publicly called the Russians "swamp humans."[26] The HJ's own inbred stereotype of the racially inferior, primitive "Iwans," said to be Slavs mixed with Jewish and Asiatic elements (the Germans soon learned to conflate anything Russian with "Mongol"), helped to temper the fear of the enemy. This was reinforced by the wretched-looking Red Army POWs the Germans encountered early in the campaign; more than three million of them were captured already in the fall.[27] Even dead Russians spotted in a ditch presented a picture of "most miserable soldiers," wrote one of the former HJ boys in June; they reminded him of "croaked cattle." Another one observed about the Russian POWs, "Hardly ever do you see the face of a person who seems rational and intelligent. They all look emaciated and the wild, half-crazy look in their eyes makes them appear like imbeciles."[28] A young officer seeing starving, thirsty prisoners trying to lap up rainwater from the street pavement viewed this as proof of some lower form of life.[29] Almost from the start of "Operation Barbarossa"—the Nazi code name for the Russian campaign—many of the youthful soldiers would guard thousands of these Slavs at a time, cooped up in vast prisoner-of-war camps, where the Russians were left to themselves to die, usually of hunger and thirst and sometimes after acts of cannibalism.[30] (During the entire eastern campaign, the Wehrmacht would capture 5.7 million Red Army soldiers, of whom 3.3 million perished.)[31] Hence the very comparison of the lives of the Russian adversaries with their own convinced young German soldiers of their superiority and furnished them with a raison d'être for continued conquest. They adhered to the official mantra "that one German infantry soldier was worth ten or twelve Russians," or that Russians expected to be treated brutally because they were the product of a brutal environment.[32] The alleged brutality of Russians was typically substantiated after German comrades had been found mutilated, "hands tied, their ears, tongues, noses and genitalia cut off," as was observed in Tarnopol.[33] Members of a cultured, morally superior nation like Germany, it was implied after such gruesome finds, would not stoop to commit such deeds. Indeed, for most young men this belief was a fantasy they preferred to uphold even after they had witnessed and perhaps participated in the torture and murder of partisans and Jews.

Jews could be Soviet soldiers, and at the beginning of the Russian campaign Hitler proclaimed the "Commissar Order," stipulating that any Red Army political commissar, all of whom were automatically assumed to be Jews, should be summarily shot when captured.[34] But Jews could also be cunning partisans, in keeping with the image of the racial enemy par excellence, who were chased and killed by the SS-Einsatzgruppen, often with the regular Army's cooperation and as a weirdly attractive spectacle for young conscripted soldiers. Eyewitnesses have reported some form of "execution tourism," where enlisted men would congregate to watch and sometimes ask to be allowed to assist in the murder of Jewish men, women, and children.[35] Among the Jewish men (but also some women), many were suspected of partisan activity, and since Stalin relied heavily on them in his defense of the motherland, it gave ex-Hitler Youth warriors great satisfaction in helping to destroy them.[36] This spurred their ideas about eventually assuming high German office in the vanquished East, in particular becoming the lords of expansive *Wehrbauern* settlements.[37]

But despite all the success and satisfaction in the first campaigns—including one in North Africa and another in the Balkans—things were beginning to become undone for Germany's young soldiers, as new cohorts from the Hitler Youth entered the armed forces until early 1945, some as young as sixteen.[38] One source of discontent was a duplication of the pre-combat drill they had experienced in the HJ and had engaged in again for years during regular service as well as in specialty institutions such as the Adolf Hitler Schools. The premilitary training in the armed forces endured until the very end of the Third Reich, even though the HJ had stepped up its own training after 1935, with the introduction of conscription, and in 1938, several months before the war. During all this time there was no coordination between HJ leaders and Army officers as to which military exercises would make sense at the HJ level up to age eighteen, thereafter to be intensified and complemented by Army trainers prior to actual war duty. Moreover, apart from the necessary technical routines, such as learning how to scale walls and to use various firearms, the HJ recruits were unhappy with the psychological torture drills indulged in by Army sergeants and the nasty peer hazing for the sake of "character building"; they had already come to resent these insults under Schirach and Axmann. Such experiences began to erode morale in the Wehrmacht, apart from incrementally discrediting the legacy of the Hitler Youth in these young men's minds.

Wehrmacht inductees like the eighteen-year-old Erich Albertsen, who had already had more than his share of a punishing regimen in the Hitler Youth, had to march for long stretches in a heavy uniform, often wearing a gas mask as well. He and others had to scrub the barracks floors with toothbrushes and clean up lockers repeatedly, after they had been soiled with ashes by their drill sergeants. Any small oversight would lead to punitive exercises.[39] Jürgen Peiffer had to climb up trees with his gas mask on, and then sing, "It is so nice to be a Soldier." Often these chores had to be senselessly repeated when the men were on sick leave.[40] As had been the practice in the HJ, Ralf Roland

Ringler, training to become an officer, was forced to jump into the water from a 10-meter board; others who could not swim, rather than being taught that skill, were ousted in disgrace.[41] Hermann Melcher remembers the "Masked Ball," when for an hour or so Army recruits had to appear for roll call, only to be dismissed and told to reappear in a different outfit, always within three minutes.[42] In a drill as vicious as it was senseless, young soldiers had to dig holes in the ground to hide in, minutes before tanks would move over them, liable to crush them if the holes were dug badly. That was a form of chicanery not in the HJ's training arsenal.[43] Some of these exercises continued for weeks, even months on end, for soldiers who were eager to get to the fronts to defend their country.[44]

Moreover, the fortunes of war itself were changing, starting with September of 1941. It was then that the Wehrmacht's advances in Russia were slowed by an unexpectedly early rainfall, followed by a harsh and sudden winter, which created mud and then ice and snow for which the German soldiers and their armor were ill prepared. Now the numerical and technical inferiority of the German tanks as opposed to the Soviet ones was acutely felt.[45] In November, the German troops were stopped some thirty miles outside of Moscow. By December it was clear that the Red Army was able to hold its own and actually launch a counter-offensive. Whereas Hitler's allies—Romania, Hungary, Italy—remained impotent, the United States, foolishly challenged by Hitler after Pearl Harbor, became an ally to the British and the Free French, strengthening them militarily and morally. On December 16, Britain itself forged a difficult but tactically effective alliance agreement with the Soviet Union. Three days later Hitler accepted the resignation of his commander-in-chief of the Army, General Walther von Brauchitsch, and assumed this role himself, to his ultimate detriment. One month earlier, General Erwin Rommel had been defeated for the first time by the British near Tobruk, North Africa, despite the fact that the Germans had diverted two hundred extra bombers to the African theater in 1940. As Gerhard L. Weinberg, the foremost expert on the subject, has judged, by January 1942 the Germans' martial specialty, "the whole concept of a Blitzkrieg, a lightning war, had failed"— irrevocably as it turned out, and on all fronts.[46]

These setbacks and the ensuing more serious defeats had severe consequences for all of Nazi Germany's soldiers and caused particularly grave harm and disillusionment for the younger ones among them, who almost without exception had come from the Hitler Youth, where the tone had been nothing but optimistic right into the high war years. Even while marching into battle, the young soldiers were extraordinarily taxed. One former Hitler Youth wrote of marching forty-five miles every day from Finland toward the northern Russian front, for several days on end: "Day and night. No sleep. Hardly a crust of bread." This occurred during July with its short nights, "in wilderness, jungle, swamp and desert sand, under a scorching sun."[47] Food was frequently scarce, so that soldiers soon ate nearly everything, including potatoes fried in motor oil, which led to dysentery.[48] Other scourges were mosquitoes, especially in eastern and southeast Europe, and blood-sucking lice, which never disappeared.[49] Helmut Nielsen from Kiel noted in May of 1940, advancing into Russia: "We are tired to the point of falling down. The only things keeping us awake are alcohol, nicotine and the never-ceasing, ear-shattering rage and roar of the flak." All this had a numbing effect: "You can only act mechanically, you can't think any more."[50] Shell shock and battle horror reduced many young soldiers to automatons, and this got worse as the war progressed. One of them wrote home about a friend who had been in North Africa for twenty-three months without leave, always in the desert. During this time, his parents were killed in an air raid, his bride had betrayed him, and his brother had fallen at the eastern front.[51]

Actual battle for many former Hitler Youths, even with grueling war games behind them, turned out to be a rude awakening. When Friedrich Grupe had to join a dangerous advance detail in Russia in June 1941, he realized that this experience was rather different from the stories of World War I which he had read to his charges around the campfire; this was now "tough reality." His commander had sent him on a mission to find out whether the enemy was at the edge of the forest and what weapons they possessed. During this mission, many men were lost.[52] Also at the Russian front from 1942 to 1944 was Kurt Meyer-Grell, a pilot in a Luftwaffe Special Operations Wing which dropped agents over enemy territory. "Every time I was shot down behind Russian lines I was prepared to shoot myself," he recalls; "I had seen the remains of *Stuka* fliers who had been massacred by Russian soldiers, their stomachs slit open, and so on."[53] His comrade Hans-Ulrich Greffrath, who was wounded for the fourth time in the spring of 1944 fighting Russian tanks hand-to-hand, had come across mutilated Wehrmacht soldiers captured by the Russians, "without ears, without noses, without eyes. One of them was a very good friend of mine."[54]

Indeed, no Hitler Youth war games could have prepared these young soldiers for the death and destruction they would now help to cause on a daily basis and would often fall victim to themselves. When Hitler spoke in his Reichstag address of October 6, 1939, of 10,572 men who had fallen during the Polish campaign, 314 of these had been full-time HJ leaders.[55] Seeing the first dead or wounded of one's own battalion was always a major jolt, until one became inured, although that only occurred after a multitude of terrors. A former Hitler Youth assigned to a tank division still has stark memories from the Russian front: "We are lying flat on the ground. All around us is a raging inferno. Those who have already been wounded once are being hit a second and third time. You can hear their whimpering. The commander of the tank in front of me has taken a bullet in the head, and his brains are running down his face. He's running around in grotesque circles crying, 'mother, mother.' Finally, and almost mercifully, he is hit again by shrapnel and falls to the ground."[56] The lack of anonymity for these soldiers, fighting alongside their own friends, only increased the horror; this is what made partisan warfare so threatening, for it was always small bands of German soldiers who would be lured into an ambush, to be killed in the most gruesome manner, and then to be discovered by close comrades. The feeling of complete impotence in the face of omnipresent partisans was all-pervasive. Horst Lange tells of an incident near Gshatsk on the south Russian front in November 1941, when five partisans were caught and hanged. The next morning, a German soldier was found hanging right beside them.[57] Nor was the carnage limited to Russia. In Greece, partisans specialized in killing members of the Wehrmacht occupation forces by throttling them from behind with steel wire.[58] And such experiences were happening to ever-younger Hitler Youths who were drafted by 1944. When the invasion of Normandy by the western Allies occurred in June of that year, it was the tanks of the Hitler Youth division "Hitlerjugend" that tried to stop them; these tanks then became coffins for thousands of young soldiers, often after they had been burned alive.[59]

Apart from physical injuries and death, there were psychological factors that compounded the misery of these young soldiers and threatened to reduce their efficacy as cogs in Hitler's war machine. As is true of soldiers at all times, worries about young wives and girlfriends back home did much to undermine front-line morale. With young German women feeling lonely and deserted, and sexually tempted by the conscripted laborers at home, their fidelity could be in doubt. Thus young Hermann wrote to his sweetheart Rosl to ask whether she, too, was betraying him. "Dear Rosl, you have to love me. If I were with you I would have no fear, for then I could fight for you to the last, but this way I am far away from you and cannot see you."[60] Another soldier wrote to his girlfriend Herta that, surely, she had not forgotten him— or did she now have another lover?[61] Some of these doubts led to tragic results. One young conscripted man, suspecting that his wife had betrayed him, asked the opinion of a sergeant, who was renowned as a sage. The sage took the wedding band, fixed it to a human hair and, as it swung slowly across the photograph of the woman, divined that she was unfaithful. Desperate, the soldier sought death the next day.[62]

Entirely different, but equally damaging to the morale, were rising doubts about the truth of the Nazis' image of the enemy, especially in regard to the Russians. After several months the former Hitler Youths found that many of the Russian soldiers were open and valiant fighters, rather than the beastly cowards that Nazi propaganda had projected. "The Russians are extraordinarily tough soldiers," wrote one, "and if you call them subhuman, that's nonsense. Some who were captured looked as if they could easily have been in the HJ."[63] Already in the fall of 1941, the superiority of Soviet air power was conspicuous; after an early Nazi rout in June 1941, the Red Army once again had more planes than the Wehrmacht.[64] The partisans were, on the whole, deemed effective, and German soldiers had to admit grudgingly that their Soviet counterparts were humans like themselves.[65] Not surprisingly, many young German soldiers fell in love with Russian girls, who, contrary to the teachings of Schirach and Goebbels, were often found to be blond and blue-eyed.[66]

For the Germans, the defeat at Stalingrad on February 2, 1943, turned out to be a watershed in more ways than one, and it significantly affected Schirach and Axmann's erstwhile charges. Within his larger strategic scheme, Hitler needed this industrial city on the Volga River in the Southeast of Russia because it was to be instrumental in salvaging the area already conquered beyond the Crimea and was a key post for further expansion in the East. It was in this entire region and further east into the Donets Basin and the Caucasus that the German armed *Wehrbauern* settlement would be started, so that agricultural staples, heavy industry, and valuable oil would be secured. Beyond these immediate goals, Hitler was hoping to move his armies into Iraq and Iran for the control of oil in those regions. Thereafter, joining up with Rommel's forces who would push east from North Africa, the aim was to unite with the Japanese and expel the British from South Asia.[67]

After the Wehrmacht's setback on three extended Russian fronts in late 1941, Hitler's Army groups in the South were making headway again in the new year, conquering Sevastopol on the southern Crimea in early July, 1942. By the end of that month three German armies were moving east and southeast, and in early August they occupied the first of several rich oil fields near Maikop in the northern Caucasus. Further to the northeast, General Friedrich Paulus ordered the attack on Stalingrad on August 19. Paulus was assisted by Luftwaffe General

Wolfram von Richthofen, who flew 1,600 attacks against the city, bombing it into a field of ruins. Forty thousand civilians died. "Stalingrad was important not only as a major industrial center and as a place where the Germans could halt all shipping on the Volga but as the major connecting point to any operations in the Caucasus," writes Weinberg. It also possessed valuable armament factories. However, it soon became obvious that the city would be hard to conquer completely, in the face of continuing Soviet resistance. Until November, there was house-to-house combat. "Streams of blood in the streets," noted Nobel laureate Thomas Mann in his diary, who from his exile in Los Angeles was keenly following the war, "much of it German." When the Germans finally controlled most of the nearly destroyed city, their army had suffered huge losses. Having regrouped, the Russians began a concerted attack on the Wehrmacht in Stalingrad on November 19, and three days later, after a successful pincer operation by three Russian Army groups, Stalingrad was encircled. This came on the heels of the Soviet relief of Leningrad in the North, which had been besieged by the Germans for seventeen months. By January 1943, after three months of winter fighting, the Wehrmacht in southern Russia had lost more than half a million men in killed and wounded. Hitler, who refused General Paulus and his 6th Army permission to break out of the city, was still building on Göring's promise that Stalingrad could be well supplied from the air, with 300 tons of provisions per day, but the enfeebled Luftwaffe managed merely a third of that. And even then the Führer could not make good on his promise to send relief troops under General Erich von Manstein, but still he forbade Paulus to capitulate. The Soviets started to invade the city on January 10, 1943, and the German forces inside were split in two. On February 2 Paulus, having just been promoted to field marshal, capitulated of his own volition, surrendering 90,000 men to the Russians, of an army originally up to 250,000 strong. The rest had fallen or died of disease and hunger. Of those taken prisoner, most perished soon after; only 5,000 eventually made it back to Germany.[68]

The disillusionment and desperation experienced by the young soldiers before their certain doom is evident from their diaries and letters, as well as from the memoirs of the few wounded soldiers who were flown out by the Luftwaffe or those who eventually returned from captivity. They stand in grotesque contrast to Hitler's and Goebbels's decision to recast what was a major disaster for the nation as a giant heroic sacrifice. Instead of owning up to egregious military blunders and a deplorable defeat culminating in dishonorable unconditional surrender, as Paulus himself had been too cowardly to stand up to Hitler, Nazi propaganda proclaimed the event to have been a valiant action, in which every single German soldier in the cauldron of Stalingrad willingly laid down his life for Germany and its Führer.[69]

As part of this larger deception, German families on Christmas 1942 were linked to a radio broadcast from Stalingrad, so that they could join the soldiers in singing "Silent Night." Those families did not know that the link-up was a fake; 1,280 soldiers died in Stalingrad on Christmas Day alone.[70] Two separate reports on Christmas in and around Stalingrad tell us that one group of German soldiers had to dig themselves a new hole with a makeshift roof on Holy Night, during a snowstorm at minus 30 degrees Celsius. Lacking bread or potatoes, they made hamburgers out of horsemeat; there were no parcels or letters from home. The other group huddled nearby did have a bit of chocolate and candy, a few pieces of meat and bread. They consumed this an hour after Russian artillery had torn a comrade to shreds.[71]

Although there was hope against hope to the very day of surrender, a growing sense of despair had begun during the advance on the city in the late fall of 1942, especially among the young soldiers just out of the HJ and still dependent on home. The lack of mail delivery seemed incomprehensible to the younger men, particularly at Christmas.[72] And then there was hunger. Because of constant air-supply interruptions, rations of bread and meat had to be incrementally decreased, until by Christmas Eve sixty-four soldiers had died of undernourishment. Around this time, meat from the dying horses and the stray cats, dogs, and rats was becoming the sole staple, with minuscule portions at that. The men made soup from sawdust. Because of the lack of fresh water,

thirst added to the agony of famine. Göring's planes were still drop-
ping supply bags, but they often missed their targets, falling to the
enemy instead. During January the German soldiers were drinking
machine oil and cannibalizing dead comrades. Many of those taken
prisoner on February 2 had not eaten anything for about a week.[73]

The infamous Russian cold, setting in by early November, compounded the nutrition problem. The steppe in front of Stalingrad contained no wood for burning, and inside the city's walls combustible
material was scarce, as was gasoline. Garments were deemed to be sufficiently warm only after several dead soldiers had been stripped of their
uniforms; even then hypothermia proved endemic.[74]

The cold did not destroy lice and fleas, which carried diseases such
as typhus. One of the most common causes of death in the Stalingrad
area apart from malnutrition was freezing. Sheer exhaustion after days
and nights of sleeplessness was also widespread, weakening a soldier's
will to live. Having been wounded would prolong his agony, unless he
was lucky enough to be flown out of the encircled area. At one of two
functioning airports, the lightly wounded kept stepping over more
serious cases in an effort to reach a plane; they had to be restrained
with pistols. A doctor reported in January that on the roads around
Stalingrad lay the wounded, as well as those frozen to death and still
freezing, who were blocking his car with their bodies. "Their screams
begging to be run over or be rescued repeated themselves with variations over the entire route. Many were lifting their hands entreatingly,
hidden in soaked bandages, some were shaking their fists, and others
did not stir at all." By the end of the month approximately 40,000
wounded German soldiers were staggering from one field hospital to
the next, never finding entry and finally collapsing in the city's ruins.
The Russians bombed one of the central sickbays, resulting in 3,000
patients being burned to death.[75]

In both the civilian population and the armed forces, when the scale
of the catastrophe became apparent, the results were dread and discouragement. Contemporaries were not good judges of the past, nor
could they divine the future. Therefore, they could not adequately

gauge the significance of the defeat at Stalingrad as a turning point in the fortunes of Nazi Germany. As we now know, a string of serious reversals ensued: German manpower much reduced in the East; the tide of war turning in North Africa; the landing of the western Allies in Sicily; Mussolini's deposition; Hamburg's fire-bombing; D-Day in June and the attempt on Hitler's life in July 1944—all of these represented a major chain of disasters leading up to German capitulation in May 1945, virtually a mirror image of the string of successes the Nazis had taken for granted from September 1939 to February 1943. In hindsight, Stalingrad symbolizes the false security in which Hitler's young warriors had lived since the beginning of the war. To prescient minds even then, Stalingrad appeared as just punishment for past follies and as a bad omen for the future of generations younger than the ones who had moved into battle in September 1939. Among those who harbored such sobering thoughts were the Wehrmacht soldiers Hans Scholl, Alexander Schmorell, and Willi Graf of the Munich White Rose resistance cell, who would pay for voicing their conscience with their lives.

Problems encountered by young German soldiers even before Stalingrad led to doubts about their function in the Nazi regime and its expanding war in particular. For many, they also led to questions regarding the value of the Hitler Youth, insofar as it had been instrumental in landing them in what more often than not turned out to be physically and morally compromising situations. By the nature of the police state they were serving, any criticism had to remain muted—of the regime, the Army, the Party and its affiliates, including the HJ, if not of Hitler himself, whose charisma consistently rendered him immune to criticism; instead Germans generally thought he was being deceived by his entourage.[76] These widespread negative feelings belie the optimism that Goebbels displayed publicly when in December 1941 he visited more than a hundred men blinded during the recent campaigns, the oldest of whom was just twenty-four. After he had given each of them a radio set, "they were overjoyed like children," he claimed, "as they were already starting to pick up their lives again."

Goebbels was fooling himself and others when he concluded that from this field hospital, "doom and gloom" had been banished.[77]

Memoirs and even diaries and letters from the front, though censored by the Nazi authorities, suggest that some young soldiers, despite their indoctrination in the HJ regarding the enemy, were beginning to watch certain practices by their superiors with misgivings. They felt ill at ease when SS and police squads accompanying their units burned down whole villages or employed Wehrmacht comrades in the execution of prisoners.[78] Disillusionment could also set in whenever the Army ordered young men barely out of their teens to officiate at or participate in the ceremonial execution of deserters.[79] Not surprisingly, by late 1941 as the war was starting to go badly, more and more young soldiers developed doubts about it, and questions about the competence of the higher leadership arose. Such feelings intensified at the time of the assassination attempt on the Führer in July 1944; even diehard young Nazis were wondering what it was that could motivate Prussian officers to murder their commander-in-chief, whose inviolability was still being taken for granted.[80]

Seeing comrades around them die and be maimed, but also watching with barely concealed horror a similar fate befalling their adversaries at the front, young soldiers became more introspective, starting to think about their lives as a very expendable commodity. Despite the many Hitler Youth idealists, whose unchanging fanaticism remained a mystery to some of the more seasoned officers such as Army physician Curt Emmrich, who thought their idealism totally distorted, pessimism among some was palpable.[81] A few of these young men resolved to seek action at the front lines, looking for a speedy death; others kept bullets for a suicide in reserve, full of doubts that this war could ever be won.[82]

Another source of disenchantment especially in the last phases of the war was an increasing distance between conscripted soldiers and their commissioned officers, who, in order to drown out their own frustrations, were often observed amusing themselves at the expense of their subordinates. These amusements were sexual as well as involving all sorts of corruption such as hoarding and squandering liquor. In early 1944 the SD, the security service of the SS, reported that behind the lines officers were organizing parties with various women, for whose enjoyment the rank and file had to provide live entertainment. While the common soldiers were suffering from hunger, officers were feasting and even sending packets home. "The higher the rank, the better the good life," the SD cited one disappointed soldier as saying.[83] The longer the war lasted, the more frequently even married officers were taking French or Russian girls as lovers and unabashedly display-ing them in their company even during official functions, to the dis-gruntlement of the lower ranks. Even as promiscuous a man as Goebbels was complaining about this—presumably not the fact as such, but rather the lack of discretion with which it occurred.[84] "Almost all of us, the veteran youth leaders, experienced an inner cleansing process," recalls Ralf Roland Ringler for the period after 1943, "in that progres-sively we damned this war, although we did not have a clue how to carry on ourselves once it was over."[85]

Today one may doubt the intensity of this "cleansing process," since most former HJ leaders possessed neither the maturity nor any guid-ance other than the horrors of the war to recognize the fundamental wrongs. They had also been too thoroughly conditioned in the HJ ranks. But under the impact of this awful conflict, many were gradu-ally impelled to doubt its rationale, their own role in carrying out its aims, and the overall integrity of their superiors. It was dawning on them that unheard-of injustices were being perpetrated. After Warsaw had been bombed to bits in October 1939, one eighteen-year-old sol-dier wrote home that "the population is terribly starved and without shelter . . . we often share our own modest provisions, because the mis-ery of the children and women touches our hearts."[86] Fraternization with, even sympathy for the enemy was of course forbidden, but espe-cially during the murderous Russian advance some compassionate German soldiers tried to alleviate needless suffering by preventing acts of arson and calming down the peasants. Others visibly distanced themselves from the indiscriminate looting.[87] "The barbarism is becoming obvious," observed one young German soldier at the Russian front in the late summer of 1941, while another thought nothing of helping out wounded POWs with drinks of water.[88] In November 1941 a former Hitler Youth was devastated by the execution of some twenty Soviet female soldiers: they had to lie down in the dirt next to each other and then were flattened by panzers.[89] The moral indignation of many of his comrades increased after witnessing the front-line shooting of Jews; in one case a woman fell on her knees begging for her life, while the soldier could not help her.[90] Even at the risk of court-martial, by 1944 criticism of the regime voiced in the censored letters from the front became louder and more frequent; the war itself and the July attempt on Hitler were openly discussed.[91] Increasingly, as the war was drawing to a close, German soldiers refused to kill the enemy, especially in hand-to-hand combat, and one of them tells of defying an order to execute Italian partisans, thereby risking his own life.[92] The Hitler Youth was no moral compass in such situations; hence it was out of mind for many of these soldiers at that time. "I do not feel drawn to the HJ," stated one former member from a mountain division in 1943, for it "does not give a hoot about me any more."[93]

This comportment, however infrequent, approached not heroism but decency, as these soldiers watched the majority of their former comrades in the HJ continuing the vicious treatment of the enemy or participating without qualms in the killing of innocent civilians, partisans, and Jews. Others, however, were driven not by desperation motivated by high-mindedness, but by selfishness. They had concern merely for their own suffering, and thus they sought suicide or self-inflicted battle death, self-mutilation for the sake of being sent home, or outright desertion. How many desperate young men killed themselves or willingly tried to end their lives in the front lines is not known, because every casualty of this kind was officially declared a hero's death. (Attempted suicide was treated as self-mutilation.)[94] But desertions were accelerating, especially after Stalingrad, with various ordinances from 1934, 1938, and 1940 providing for incremental punishment.[95] More and more, prison sentences were replaced by the death penalty, the most honorable of which was death by shooting, which, after Stalingrad, had to be done as a deterring ritual, in public view of the troops.[96] In March 1943 Hitler as the new commander-in-chief of the Army stipulated that military and civil courts should carefully weigh the type of death penalty to be meted out. Next to shooting, dishonorable guillotining and, worse, hanging were to be decreed for especially shameful behavior, such as repeat offenses or having caused harm to others.[97] The staggering statistics pertaining to desertions between 1939 and 1945, with a steep increase from 1943 to 1945, reflect the worsening erosion of the Wehrmacht's morale. Whereas during World War I merely 150 German soldiers had been condemned to death and only 50 actually executed, during World War II nearly 23,000 death sentences were pronounced, of which up to 16,000 were also carried out. These death verdicts do not include the smaller number of cases in which deserters were successful or those where they tried and then gave up in the middle of the act.[98]

Today it is chilling to read the stories of those young German soldiers who actually made it. In early 1945 Horst Krüger along with a buddy crossed the Dortmund-Ems-Kanal at night to the American lines. When the GIs detected them at dawn, the Americans at first held up their hands in a gesture of surrender, believing the two to be part of a German advance platoon.[99] Twenty-year-old Heinz Brenner planned his escape meticulously. Wearing his old HJ outfit underneath the Wehrmacht uniform, in October 1944 he absented himself from his barracks, still in Germany, changed his clothes in the forest, and then boarded the train as the youth leader he had once been. Until the end of the war he hid with friends in a remote rural area near Ulm.[100] Albert R., an eighteen-year-old soldier, deserted from the elite "Grossdeutschland" division after only three weeks in early 1945. He was caught and sentenced to death, but during an air raid he managed to escape. Initially trying to reach the Russians, he then gradually drifted westward until he met up with U.S. troops.[101]

More disturbing is the fate of those who were killed. The military court procedures were juridically correct, punishing even brief unexcused absences from the troops but still allowing for pardons at an appeals court. Most often, these were denied.[102] A nineteen-year-old deserter from Berlin, blond, the picture of a Hitler Youth and German soldier, was executed in December 1942. A comrade remembers: "He stood straight like a candle and looked directly at the rifles. He did not scream, nothing. They aimed at his heart, toward his chest. And then there was a bang. He had been shackled, his hands tied behind him. Now his entire chest was ripped open, because eight soldiers shot at it. The poor fellow got the full load into his chest and then slumped down, but he was still alive. He was alive. And moaning terribly. We could hear this fifteen meters away. Finally the master sergeant appeared with his 08, approached him and—this was the most terrible thing—knocked two, three bullets into his head."[103] Indeed, even after several shots, some delinquents were still stirring and then had to be finished off with a coup de grâce.[104] At the end of the war, in early May, many German soldiers were tried, sentenced, and shot even when they had assumed—often correctly—that the Third Reich had surrendered and they just wanted to avoid falling into the hands of the enemy. In a particularly tragic case, two sailors, Bruno Dörfer and Rainer Beck, who while in Holland had deserted and joined the Dutch resistance, were delivered to a Canadian POW camp, where the captured Wehrmacht sub-commandant, who still had internal jurisdiction, tried them for treason. The Canadians thereupon delivered rifles to the Germans, so that both men could be executed, a week after capitulation.[105]

These executions degenerated to veritable lynchings in the last desperate German retreats of the war. Because desertion had become endemic, and the more so the younger a soldier was, the military police and SS exercised what was cynically termed "emergency justice" on the spot and hanged, on trees, lamp posts, or anything that could support a rope, any man who could not produce proper marching papers. Hitler Youth boys as young as fifteen and just drafted became ensnared in these actions because, children that they were, their nerves were giving out; they started crying and just wanted to go home to their mother. Some were thrown from the balconies of houses where they had sought shelter, with ropes around their necks. Others were given enough time to write big letters on a piece of cardboard, which was then fixed to their bodies. As the German film actress Ingrid van Bergen recalls it, fleeing East Prussia as a child of thirteen, one such sign read: "I am a deserter. I was a coward in the face of the enemy."[106]

Self-mutilation, which was defined as a punishable offense in the law of 1938, was somewhat less dangerous than desertion.[107] If done properly, it could go totally undetected by Army physicians and the "war-wounded" man might then be sent home, out of fighting commission for the balance of the war. The fact that what officially was an act of cowardice often worked as a ruse was due not least to sympathetic physicians who decided to shield the patients by not reporting them and nursing them back to health.[108] Still, at the eastern front, where soldiers were particularly prone to inflict wounds on themselves, the Army maintained special institutions in which suspicious candidates were subject to expert examinations and legal proof of defeatism could be collected.[109] Even if proved, however, self-mutilation led to fewer arrests than those for desertion, because in practice it was deemed less serious than running away from the war zone.[110] Nonetheless, there were no guarantees. These soldiers could still be shot, hanged, or guillotined, as was the case with twenty-five-year-old Berlin draftsman Heinrich Pryswitt in Brandenburg penitentiary in June of 1944, who was decapitated.[111]

The most common type of mutilation, sometimes with the help of comrades, who also were liable to punishment, was damaging a part of one's body, usually with a shot through the hand or by hacking off parts of a limb. One might also induce commonly recognized sickness symptoms by ingesting some chemical, or, especially at the eastern front and notably at Stalingrad, purposely freezing one's extremities.[112] Some of these war shirkers endured odysseys of self-injury. Josef Sch. from Bavaria was seventeen when in June of 1943 he injured his left foot with an ax, after having been called up to fight. Recovered, he was conscripted again in November, and this time he severed his left index finger. He was tried in July of 1944 and received eight years in penitentiary.[113] Also faced with conscription in 1944, Claus B. from Munich simulated abdominal pain, getting nowhere with physicians. He then smoked aspirin all night until he trembled, but the hoped-for neurological inflammation failed to appear. Finally he injected himself with turpentine, which destroyed the tendons in his arm. The doctor treating him saw through the ruse but kept his composure, and Claus then survived the end of the war by rubbing salt into his wound to keep it open.[114]

Hamburg's Wolfgang Borchert was able to combine the effects of a self-inflicted wound with true illness in order to survive, albeit in a pitiable state, beyond 1945. A sensitive young man and former reluctant Hitler Youth, at the age of twenty and just having seen action at the eastern front in 1942, he too cut one of his fingers off, claiming later, most implausibly, that he had lost it in close combat with a Russian. With the help of a skilled defense lawyer Borchert was sentenced to only six weeks' incarceration and subsequent probation at the front, during which he contracted a terminal liver disease. He returned to Hamburg a wreck; until he died in 1947, his life was a constant balancing act between mental exhaustion and illness, the terribly persistent memories of war, and unpleasant reactions to an unsettled postwar society.[115]

Detours, Duplications, and Alternatives

Subsequent to entering the armed forces by September 1939 and fighting at the fronts, German adolescents reared in the Hitler Youth experienced several changes, most often in close correlation with Germany's fortunes in war. As time went on, this had the effect of robbing many of them of their former faith in the Hitler Youth as a disciplinary and ideological training opportunity. But it could also render them less effective as soldiers: the duplication of training and drill in the Wehrmacht, vis-à-vis the HJ, seemed thoughtless and demeaning. Such counter-productive measures, apart from hurting the efficacy of the Wehrmacht in battle as well as the legacy of the Hitler Youth, ultimately caused much frustration and anger among the young soldiers, who saw their acquired skills ignored or treated contemptuously by non-HJ-related NCOs and officers alike.

The redundancy of training in the transition from Hitler Youth to Wehrmacht was repeated in other instances, resulting in additional duties and multiple chains of command, which further demoralized Germany's fighting youth, in addition to detracting from their effectiveness in the Third Reich's war machine. The first experience of this kind occurred through the Reichsarbeitsdienst (RAD), or Reich Labor Service, which most veteran Hitler Youths were enrolled in after 1935 as RAD Workmen, a step between HJ and Wehrmacht. It was one of the many rival organizations of Party and State clamoring for the total control of Hitler's subjects at various age, occupation, and gender levels after January 1933, in which institutional Darwinism determined the ultimate winners—often, but not always, with the Führer's final judgment weighing in.[116]

The RAD resulted from the Freiwilliger Arbeitsdienst (FAD), or voluntary labor service, which was created during the austere Brüning regime of the Great Depression in July 1931. It was the long-term product of conservative planners within right-of-center political parties, including the NSDAP, several Weimar youth leagues such as the *Artamanen,* and the national universities' student bodies, which by that time had been largely right-radicalized. Chancellor Heinrich Brüning had adopted the labor service as part of a national policy to get unemployed youths off the streets and provide them with minimum wages for performing public works such as draining swamps and building roads, but there was also a nationalistic pedagogical agenda.

When Hitler took over the government, there was a multitude of FAD groups, often involved in internecine fights against each other. The Nazis, interpreting this situation as just another sign of the hated pluralistic system of Weimar, consolidated these groups in 1933 under retired Army Colonel Konstantin Hierl, a dependable follower of Hitler, and created the state-monopolist Reichsarbeitsdienst. Its membership remained voluntary (although the consolidation of diverse groups had not been) until the introduction of re-armament and two-year conscription after March 1935, when it became obligatory for each young man past age eighteen to serve in it for six months. A variation of this service, which fit more appropriately into their educational program, was prescribed for adolescent females.[117] For young male Nazis, the Reichsarbeitsdienst became mandatory after service in the HJ. At all times the RAD was considered a stepping-stone to conscription. When the war broke out, RAD duty remained compulsory, wedged between HJ and the armed-forces branches, but now that service in the Wehrmacht was indefinite, the RAD duty came with a reduced term of three months.[118]

The RAD was not an ancillary to the Party, as was the Hitler Youth, nor of the Wehrmacht, which first reported to the War Ministry and after February 1938 directly to Hitler; instead, it came under the Reich Minister of the Interior, with its own disciplinary jurisdiction.[119] As such, the RAD existed in a separate space beyond the HJ and Wehrmacht and was not coordinated with the duties of either in any practical way. Since the RAD's original economic purpose had been fulfilled by the time Germany had conquered joblessness and had in fact reached under-employment in 1937, it had only two major objectives until the end of the Third Reich, either of which could have been, or actually was, assumed by the Hitler Youth and armed forces as well. In the prewar years both objectives were symbolized by the spade, which as the emblem of the RAD had to be obsessively polished by its bearers until it looked like a mirror.[120] This was demanded by RAD personnel, often unsophisticated men shunned by the Wehrmacht and SS, who erected a small empire of their own within which they were free to torment their Arbeitsmänner (Workmen) at will. The first of these objectives was National Socialist indoctrination in the tradition of "Blood and Soil," which the *Artamanen* youth league had held high, with its aggressive vision of eventually settling in armed camps in a conquered

East. Indeed, RAD leaders expressly acknowledged the ideologically grounded imperialist settlement aims of the *Artamanen* with their reference to Blood and Soil.[121] The spade, as the chief instrument for working the soil, was supposed to point the way to such a future. The second objective was military training, in which the spade, with its sharp blade and the heft of its long wooden handle, was a substitute rifle. Indeed, it would be presented like a rifle, repeatedly during endless roll calls, on the order of the RAD leaders, who were responsible neither to the HJ, from which their young charges had just emerged, nor to the Wehrmacht, where they were headed. But the spade signified humiliation in those camps where spadework was employed solely for Sisyphean tasks, such as building a camp road for a camp that was then dissolved.[122] The cult of the spade persisted until well into the war. After the introduction of rifle, revolver, and grenade training, RAD exercises anticipated those in the Wehrmacht.

In most ways, war-preparation activities and their accompanying circumstances in the RAD resembled those either in the Hitler-Jugend or the Wehrmacht, or both. RAD Workmen wore simple uniforms of a drab brown color and were housed in far-off barracks. Their basic training, involving first the spade and then increasingly firearms, was exacting but often redundant in relation to earlier courses in the HJ and subsequent ones in the Wehrmacht. Nutrition was substandard, often based on tripe and other offal. Freezing temperatures afflicted recruits in winter as much as excessive heat stifled them in summer; the mass latrines were humiliating and conducive to ailments. These consisted of rheumatism and scurvy, along with high fever, as well as the occasional frozen limb. The repetitive communal singing was unnerving, as were the various spade and flag rituals. The schadenfreude of the tormenting staff was ubiquitous. Apart from occasional real work such as reconstruction jobs in Occupied Poland, draining swamps, digging ditches, or helping farmers with the harvest, the primitive staff's designs for mindless drill ruled the work days, with the Nazi-specific purpose of numbing the Arbeitsmänner into a state of physical and mental submission, the better for them to function in the killing fields. More often than not, veteran Hitler Youths found these redundant drills demeaning and complained about them. Discouraged and disappointed, they would leave the RAD after three arduous months to join the Wehrmacht, hopeful that conditions would improve.[123]

The system of Wehrertüchtigungslager (WE), or armed-preparedness camps, existed alongside the RAD and operated on the same theme. The Hitler Youth, Wehrmacht, and sometimes also the SS organized these camps jointly. The WE camps were a new form of what had been the HJ's own paramilitary training for senior members, those from sixteen to eighteen, involving more rigorous, concentrated training exercises after 1941. Those of age fifteen and younger continued to receive junior military instruction locally, in the HJ's own ranks. This new idea for condensed stationary exercises, from initially three weeks to twelve in the end, was Artur Axmann's. It enjoyed a closeness to the military that the would-be poet Schirach never understood. When Axmann, in collaboration with Army General Hans Friessner, approached Hitler about this plan at the Berchtesgaden *Berghof* in April 1942, the Führer agreed to the founding of boot camps for older Hitler Youths, generally at installations owned by the Wehrmacht, RAD, or HJ.[124] It is likely that Axmann, who had lost an arm in 1941 while intermittently fighting on the eastern front, was hoping for a revaluation of his office in a more military mold, perhaps with a promotion to General for himself. He knew that many former HJ leaders were now front-line officers, and some intermittently returned from combat to continue in the Hitler Youth leadership as well. If they enjoyed dual status, why couldn't he? Indeed, when the camps were established by the summer of 1942, their commandants were always HJ leaders with Wehrmacht officer ranks, with the military coaching being done by seasoned NCOs who had been wounded in the field.[125] By the end of 1943, 226 WE sites had been set up, servicing almost 515,000 Hitler Youths aged sixteen and up; in 1944–45, with longer training terms to accommodate, fifteen-year-olds were also called up.[126] Among the boys, this service was deeply unpopular, because those already gainfully employed had to sacrifice their vacation time to attend, and secondary-school pupils, who were drafted as class units, had to forgo summer or fall holidays.[127]

In a positive description of the WE camps, one American historian has recently characterized them as "a successful way to implement universal paramilitary training for Germany's adolescent population."[128] However, this service represented yet another duplication of the training which youths had received in the HJ, and which would be experienced again in the RAD and then in the Wehrmacht recruitment drill. The WE camps complicated further the entire premilitary exercise regimen, exacerbating difficulties resulting from overlaps of organization or gaps in logistics, resource allocation, personnel deployment, and institutional jurisdiction. As was typical of his governmental style, Hitler had probably authorized the project with the knowledge that, so long as it did not threaten the center of his universe, the more chaos developed around him and the more decisively he could act as the final arbiter, the stronger he would emerge. Holding out promises to underlings that might never be fulfilled or doling out empty honors was a favorite personnel ploy of his (as in his futile promotion of Paulus to field marshal at Stalingrad); in this case he could rely on the venal Axmann's bolstered loyalty, at a time when Vienna Gauleiter Schirach's allegiance to the Berlin political leadership was already very much in doubt.[129] As for the type and quality of training in the WE camps, it differed only by degree from that of the HJ, or of the RAD and the Wehrmacht itself, with the same brutal terrain and mindless weapons drill.[130] All told, the forces of counterproduction triumphed, to the further detriment of overall military efficiency and the erosion of the will of the recruits.

Both factors were even more in evidence after the establishment of the Flakhelfer or auxiliary anti-aircraft emplacement program in early 1943. This was the direct consequence of the events surrounding the defeat at Stalingrad, which had cost the regime several hundred thousand men, and the stepped-up bombardments of German cities and industrial or strategic sites, by British planes at night and American ones during the day. Throughout 1940 and 1941, the Luftwaffe had still been able to ward off most air attacks, although British bombs, for example, had hit Berlin as early as August 1940.[131] In 1942 it became obvious that the industrial centers of the Ruhr were prime targets, followed by Berlin and the strategic northern ports. Three weeks after Germany's humiliation at Stalingrad, Air Marshal Arthur Harris took over the RAF bomber command and introduced "areal bombing." That meant the intensive shelling of densely settled urban areas and concentrated industrial sites, such as those between the Rhine and Ruhr rivers.[132] As a trial target with many flammable wood-frame houses, one of them Thomas Mann's paternal home, the Baltic port of Lübeck was pounded at the end of March. Rostock was next a month later, and at the end of May one thousand planes rained 1,455 tons of bombs on Cologne for ninety minutes, at a loss of only thirty-nine RAF planes.[133] After this bombing, there were 480 people dead, 5,000 wounded, and 3,300 buildings destroyed.[134] Yet while this called for stronger German air defenses, by the fall of 1942 the necessity of diverting more planes to the eastern front had become equally obvious. This meant fortifying artillery emplacements to be manned by soldiers rather than using fighter planes. However, those soldiers were also increasingly needed for combat. Thus in September Hitler ordered 120,000 ground specialists of the Luftwaffe to be redeployed in active fighting, at the same time authorizing the use of flak personnel to be drawn from civilians. Later in the year, to reinforce the replacement measures, Göring asked the Reich Education Ministry for permission to recruit teenagers from the schools. Reich Education Minister Bernhard Rust's bureaucracy, already weakened by much regime infighting, agreed to the measures after perfunctory protests, and they were implemented early in 1943.[135]

On January 26, 1943, one week before Paulus's surrender at Stalingrad and after Rust's and Nazi Party chief Bormann's grudging acquiescence, Göring conspired with Axmann to conscript male pupils in secondary schools from age fifteen up to and including age seventeen as auxiliary artillery personnel, or flak helpers in colloquial language. The pupils were to be stationed in bunkers near their flak emplacements, and since virtually all of them belonged to the Hitler Youth, they nominally were under its supervision, with their regular teachers giving them eighteen hours of instruction per week. Those attending occupational schools and employed in industry, now all considered to be war-related and controlled by Göring, were to be exempt at first, but they too were drafted by 1944. From early 1943 to the end of the Third Reich, then, a total of 200,000 teenagers came to serve as cannoneers. After a stretch of indeterminate duration, they were to join the RAD, and subsequently the regular armed forces. They were spared the trying weeks in the WE camps.[136]

Once on duty, these youngsters were ordered to assist in the destruction of a variety of enemy planes: the heavy British Lancaster and Halifax bombers, as well as the nimble fighter and reconnaissance Mosquito aircraft. Increasingly in 1943, the American B-24 Liberators and the B-17 Flying Fortresses became a target as well. In its time, the B-17 was the most advanced bomber in the world. Although it was susceptible to catching fire after shelling, it managed the farthest distances and could take a maximum of two thousand hits per mission, some planes returning to their English bases with only one of their four engines intact.[137]

From the middle of February 1943, in order to turn these children into soldiers—the youngest of World War II—the Luftwaffe gave them four weeks of training near their artillery sites, before they actually manned the guns. At first, these were situated as close as possible to their hometowns, schools, and original HJ commands. In 1944–45 some boys were sent farther afield, for instance from Bavaria to East Prussia or the northern coast, as the moving-front situation required and as new emplacements were established.[138] The boys' trainers and immediate supervisors were NCOs who would instruct them in the use of varied-gauge ground-implanted guns, from the lightest 2.2 to the heaviest 12.8-centimeter type, and then fight alongside them. The artillery with the 2.2 and 8.8-cm gauges soon became the norm. Flak helpers had to learn how to lug around the heavy ammunition, to load the guns, and then to fire. They had to detect enemy aircraft with a form of radar less developed than that of the Allies,[139] and had to shine huge searchlights on approaching aircraft at night so these could be targeted. They memorized complicated codes and were taught to service the equipment, which, even when inactive, could be dangerous. Usually an artillery battery consisted of four standard cannon systems known as Emil, Dora, Caesar, and Würzburg; later there were six. Not surprisingly, the Ruhr area in striking distance from the Channel and with Münster as the Luftwaffe command, along with the capital of Berlin, usually received the largest contingent of flak helpers, followed by Hamburg for the northern flank. There were special marine flak emplacements, for instance in Kiel and Heligoland, staffed by the naval HJ.[140]

The Flakhelfer experience beginning in February 1943 represented the first time in the history of the Third Reich that boys as young as fifteen were fighting as soldiers in active combat. Helping to shoot down enemy planes was a harrowing task for them and marked them psychologically in their development to adulthood, aside from the fact that it killed hundreds of them and wounded thousands.[141] Although the boy soldiers fought valiantly, the Reich-stationed artillery did not have a chance from the start because of enemy air superiority, which turned this venture into a considerable tragedy by the spring of 1945.[142] "To hit anything up there was like a lottery," as Ottmar Mantz, today an internist, sums it up; "not to be hit ourselves was sheer luck."[143]

One reason the flak helpers did not have better luck was that, young as they were, they never received the hours of sleep they needed even under normal circumstances. Frequently they had to fight at night and then again the following day. To compound the effects of sleeplessness, they were haunted by fright and became prone to nervous breakdowns on the eve of an attack.[144] They refrained from putting cotton in their ears, to protect them from the deafening raids, because they did not want to be despised as weaklings.[145] One flak helper remembers indelible impressions of these assaults. "Bombs were whistling and howling down on us. After crashing with a thump and a screaming explosion, bomb splinters whirred into the walls of our barracks and the earthwork of our embankments. We tried to claw ourselves into the ground, but were constantly thrown into the air, with every new bomb impact. Some were praying aloud. And then came the air mines . . . they made no noise and caused no shocks, but almost unbearable air pressure, which threatened to destroy eardrums and lungs . . . the pressure was followed by suction that appeared to pull us out of the embankment. About a meter into the air, we were thrown from one corner into another, hurting our heads and backs on the tubing."[146]

Casualties were severe. As early as March 1, 1943, six flak helpers died in Berlin; four days later, four were killed in Essen.[147] A few months after that a 1,000-kilogram bomb swept an entire team of seven students and their corporal off their platform in Berlin; no one survived.[148] Often the boys attempted to dig out their comrades trapped by earth and debris, as in April 1944 near Brunswick. "Here a body, there an arm and over here another limb. A terrible chore! After two hours we give up. Total casualties for our battery tonight: two dead, four critically injured, and six lightly wounded."[149] Time and again these boys, who had been drafted, about a dozen per battery, straight from the school benches, found that their best friends had died.[150] This was especially traumatic when they were forced to search for them, holding body bags with which to retrieve severed limbs.[151] These searches also occurred whenever a cannon malfunctioned and exploded—every flak helper's nightmare—tearing everyone around to shreds.[152] Probably the worst mishap in Falkhelfer history occurred toward the end of the war, on the North Sea island of Heligoland, when on April 18, 1945, the British dropped 1,000 bombs on what was considered a strategic platform to the German mainland. A hundred and fifty pupils from as far away as East Prussia and Silesia had been stationed at several emplacements. The concerted bombing lasted for two hours and killed at least a third of the boys. Entire batteries were seen sliding from the rocks into the sea, taking everybody with them.[153]

Apart from the ineffectiveness of their military prowess, the adolescent Flakhelfer soon found themselves in an uncertain situation, between the Hitler Youth on the one side and the armed forces on the other. More precisely, they were escaping the HJ's purview before they had been properly received into the Wehrmacht. Whereas this anomalous position tended to undermine their self-confidence, which they compensated for by overemphasizing military paraphernalia and comportment, it further weakened the authority of the Hitler Youth toward the end of the war as the national keeper of youth, while burdening the Wehrmacht with the responsibility for not having properly integrated Hitler's youngest soldiers into the armed forces.

As they were summoned to serve in the flak positions, the teenagers were proud to be able to leave behind the Hitler Youth, which they associated more with boyhood than manhood, and instead to link their fate to the Wehrmacht's, which, they thought, brought them closer to manhood and to serving the Third Reich. This started with the uniform they were ordered to wear—one that was vaguely gray-blue in color like the Luftwaffe's, but cut in the HJ style.[154] Even though it resembled Wehrmacht attire on the street, it was still marred in the view of the boys by two of the HJ's insignia: HJ regalia affixed to the cap, and the HJ armband. So, in order to bolster their self-esteem as soldiers, the Flakhelfer, at a safe distance from their emplacements, would hide the armband and fold away the cap emblem.[155] Although this was forbidden, it gave them advantages in the nearby towns such as attending adult-only films, staying up late in pubs, smoking and drinking alcohol—all against the Police Ordinance of March 1940, but guaranteed to impress the girls. Fortunately, such recreation could now be financed by military, albeit modest, pay.[156] The Flakhelfer justified such liberties to senior HJ critics with the argument that if they were old enough to give up their lives, they should also be ceded soldiers' rights. The HJ was an impediment on a fast road to adult status, which service in the artillery teams seemed to guarantee. To further prop up their self-esteem and new status, the flak helpers would avoid greeting HJ leaders outside their compounds. They chanted soldiers' rather than Hitler Youth songs, and in some locales they took delight in beating HJ teams in competitive sports such as soccer.[157]

After 1945, former flak helpers went to great lengths to emphasize that they rejected the Hitler Youth not because it was more National Socialist than the Wehrmacht, but because it stood for infancy and immaturity, despite all the war games and premilitary training they had undergone as boys there since age ten.[158] Indeed, forced into pseudo-adulthood by a totalitarian regime early on, these juveniles felt that living a Flakhelfer life was a logical next step; they seized on it as a way to speed up the growing-up process and to achieve a more significant status in the Nazi hierarchy. Still, by denying themselves natural steps in the development from childhood to adolescence and artificially forcing rites of passage, which, for their age cohort, were decidedly premature, they suffered an aborted youth.

This became apparent to them as soon as the flak helpers experienced the arrogant welcome they received from the entrenched Wehrmacht soldiers. This took the form of several weeks of preliminary exercise and drill, similar to what they had gone through in the Hitler Youth and anticipating what they would endure again in the RAD and in regular Wehrmacht front duty. "All of us, since the age of ten, had not only learned and executed all orders but many of us had taught and supervised basic training routines for more than four years," complains one veteran flak helper in retrospect. Now the familiar indignities were exacerbated.[159] One aspect of Flakhelfer basic training was especially distasteful as the boys, still not grown to their full height, had to wear adult uniforms (until they received their specially made outfits); their heads disappeared under helmets that were too large, and oversized underwear had to be tucked into ill-fitting Army boots. Some of them looked like scarecrows.[160] To add insult to injury, insensitive non-commissioned officers refused to give them shaving cream, because only a few of them displayed what could at best be described as downy facial hair.[161]

Those corporals wanted to deny these youths the very symbols of maturity for which they had embraced the Wehrmacht after turning their backs on the HJ. But in this case the age difference between the corporals and the flak helpers was significant, in contrast to veteran Hitler Youths over eighteen who had already been through the RAD and now were regular soldiers. These NCOs were rough and resented the superior education, dexterity, and often higher social backgrounds of the young draftees, most of whom later opted for officer training. In the words of Field Marshal Rommel's son Manfred, sixteen at the time, the best one could do was learning to "endure their insults." The NCOs reveled in off-color jokes that disturbed the mostly sexually innocent boys, and being themselves rather low in the military hierarchy, they delighted in bullying youngsters who sometimes could have been their sons. Nor was there any more sympathy expressed by the (often younger) commanding officers. As a rule, they were haughty, frequently as a result of rivalry for the affection of local girls, and, what was worse, they were slow to protect the flak helpers against encroaching HJ leaders who wished to reassert their authority.[162]

Although this was incomprehensible from a practical point of view, it was officially stipulated that Flakhelfer should continue to come under the jurisdiction of the HJ, and that one HJ leader per emplacement should act as "corps leader." There was even talk of regular Hitler Youth service to be maintained within the framework of the old formations, as if the new and all-consuming objectives did not matter.[163] Not surprisingly, however, even the former HJ leaders in the ranks of the flak helpers not only could not care less about their former functions, but also simply paid no heed to any call for HJ duty.[164] (Because of an overall lack of communication, they did not know that a particular regulation of the Luftwaffe backed them in this.)[165] Consequently, whenever a higher Hitler-Jugend functionary put in an appearance at a flak battery, he was resented and ignored by boys who now considered themselves above the HJ. In some cases, flak helpers threw their nominal bosses out of the compound, lest they show up a second time.[166] In September 1944, the Hitler Youth leadership urged its regional chiefs to visit the emplacements more regularly and pay more attention to ideological training, as well as insisting on the execution of HJ service, including, unrealistically, sports and rifle drill. "The guidance of the

Air Force and Navy helpers must take place much more strongly and more intensively than has previously been the case," the HJ leadership insisted, only to add: "Hitler-Jugend service has to be conducted in such a way that the Air Force and Navy helpers look forward to it, rather than rejecting it as a nuisance."[167]

In addition to manning the batteries, dealing with their Wehrmacht superiors, and trying to ward off HJ interference, the flak helpers still had to see their families, who usually lived in the nearby towns they were defending, as well as some teachers from their old schools. This applied only to Gymnasium students, for instruction in lesser secondary schools such as Mittelschulen had ceased.[168] Unlikely as it may sound, the Flakhelfer still had to undergo schooling of eighteen hours a week, instead of the regular thirty-six, in a reduced number of subjects, usually not more than four, with German and History topping the curriculum.[169] These exercises had very little benefit for anyone involved. Because only a small number of teachers, never more than three per week, were able to visit the flak compounds to teach their charges irregularly (after visits by the students to the school buildings had become impossible), the quality of instruction was minimal. The teachers themselves were old and often uninspired, generally over sixty-five and recalled after normal retirement. Having made these arduous trips to the emplacements, they found no proper teaching facilities there and felt that they were needlessly endangering themselves.[170] At the end of term, all classmates received indifferent, uniform grades; some passed a final examination or were handed school-leaving certificates, which later were not worth the paper they were printed on.[171] With most of the regular school instruction truncated, and what was left of it militarized, "the period spent as a flak helper was as good as lost for school study," recalls former cannoneer Rolf Schörken.[172] What was worse, and ultimately detrimental in civilian life, was that the wastes and losses incurred in formal education were not even regretted at the time by most pupils, either because of sheer exhaustion or because excitement now derived from weapons rather than the pen.[173]

Flakhelfer service also changed the relationship between the boy soldiers and their homes, and usually for the worse. The same insecurity
was at play here as when facing other authority figures: these teenagers wanted to be adults but had not yet mastered necessary hurdles
in their ongoing adolescence. To the same degree that they admired
soldiers and their officers—sometimes an experience that resembled
unrequited love—they somewhat unsuccessfully dismissed traditional
schoolteachers and regime-sanctioned youth leaders, thinking themselves almost adults. This mentality entered into their relationship with
older members of their families as well. With fathers or older brothers
mostly at the fronts or already killed, it was easy to ignore the authority
of concerned mothers, aunts, or grandparents.[174] While the boys, frequently close to their towns, were allowed home leave several times a
month, they used this opportunity to get home-cooked meals and a
good night's rest and for posturing, but hardly to return to the bosom
of the family. The boys felt uneasy at home, as a result of doubts about
their newly acquired status; they knew that something was out of
sync.[175] They especially resented it when mothers came to visit them in
their compounds, because this gave the older soldiers more grounds for
sarcasm.[176] Because of their ambivalence about maternal affection,
another childhood support was torn away from these teenagers.

The entire Flakhelfer interlude resulted in changes in these boys'
collective persona that set them apart from the world around them,
alienating them from their conventional peers and superiors, while not
yet amalgamating them with the new soldier class they craved to belong to. This gave them a strange new sense of identity as a group unto
itself; they developed their own rituals and taboos, where feelings of
negativity and self-doubt, but also the tremendous fear of instant
death, were turned into a subjective sense of being part of an elite. And
that brought with it certain entitlements. Because it just was not done,
Flakhelfer would enter into conversations with Soviet POWs who had
been commandeered to assist in artillery service, finding them quite
human (contrary to what Nazi propaganda made them out to be).[177]
While hardly wavering from the standard belief in Germany's "Final

Victory," they would also interest themselves in some of the enemy soldiers they shot down—British, Canadian, and particularly American
pilots and their crews—whose uniforms or haircuts intrigued them
and inspired their own budding sense of fashion.[178] America was, after
all, an interesting phenomenon despite being the enemy; the flak
helpers were impressed by the power of their superior planes. And
Allied Forces pilots were held in awe, even in Nazi Germany, where in
the worst of cases angry crowds in the country might lynch them as
"terror fliers."[179] But fleeting encounters with these western enemies,
as they were observed falling from the skies suspended from parachutes
or found as casualties in crashed planes, also led to curiosity about their
life-style and popular culture as gleaned through enemy radio stations,
which those elderly teachers did not talk about. Therefore, like the
Swings of Hamburg or Frankfurt, flak helpers soon took to listening to
Dixieland jazz and swing, though clandestinely, trying to heat up the
HJ hymns and wearing their hair a bit longer, as signs of mutual recognition among themselves and symbols of being different from the
world around them.[180]

It is important to emphasize that the Flakhelfers' unusual situation—wanting to outgrow the HJ and being ill served by teachers, yet
not accepted as full-fledged soldiers and hence developing certain idiosyncrasies like wearing their hair longer—did not translate for them
into a rejection of the Nazi system. On the contrary: whatever had
been abstract dogma or preliminary drill and training in the Hitler
Youth, could now be put to the test of hands-on practice in the flak
emplacements. The memoirs of former Flakhelfer attest to the fact that
differences between them and the HJ were not over ideology, but over
their status as juveniles or adults. The war itself, during which they
were attempting to shoot down enemy planes, for most of them reinforced pre-existing notions that they were fighting a justified war for
Adolf Hitler and his Third Reich.

The final factor that interfered with a smooth transition from the
Hitler Youth to the armed forces was the SS. Its armed wing, the
Waffen-SS, had been in existence since August 1938. Always beyond

the Wehrmacht but ideologically and institutionally tied to Himmler, it was routinely staffed by conscripting members of the black-shirted General SS, by Death Head's squads from the concentration camps, and by regular police units, as well as by enticing volunteers from the HJ.[181] The HJ youth were drawn to it for several reasons: the SS's reputation for hardness, its well-tailored uniforms, the prestige that Hitler's Praetorian Guards enjoyed among all of the Party cadres, and, not least, its status as the personification and embodiment of Nazi ideology and superiority. The SS claimed to be the elite of the renewed German nation, and as such was idolized by many young people. As soon as fighting began in September 1939, the standing of the field-gray-uniformed Waffen-SS was enhanced by its emphasis on the toughest discipline and order as well as resourcefulness and resilience in battle; it was said to be supported by superior apparatus such as fully motorized battalions. The fact that within its officer ranks the SS paid much less attention to social class than did the traditional formations of the Wehrmacht worked to its benefit. The truly fanatical members of the HJ who had embraced the racialist ideology revolving around the German master race, and especially the role of males in guarding core values, regarded the Waffen-SS with high enthusiasm, feeling that incorporation in its ranks was a natural complement to a fulfilling HJ tour of duty.[182]

Ideally, from the vantage point of Himmler and his insiders, every year starting from 1938 the top graduates of the HJ at age eighteen were to enter the Waffen-SS as volunteers. This claim was supported by a well-functioning relationship between the HJ and SS dating back to 1933, especially after the creation of the youth police, the HJ-Streifendienst (SRD), in 1934.[183] If anything, Axmann's relationship with high SS leaders such as Himmler and Reinhard Heydrich was even closer than that of his predecessor, von Schirach. But as time was to show, there were limits to the number of recruits the Waffen-SS could claim for itself from the ranks of senior HJ members, despite various ruses that Himmler and the deferential Axmann employed to get around the difficulties.

Primary among these limitations was the statutory advantage the traditional Wehrmacht branches held over the SS in that the Wehrmacht High Command had been assigned an official ratio for its forces, which it had to fill by conscription or through volunteers. With slight variations from year to year, until 1942, this consisted of 66 percent for the Army, 9 for the Navy, and 25 for the Air Force. The Waffen-SS, of whom the Wehrmacht had been suspicious as an upstart since its inception, was too small to be specifically included in this distribution scheme. Hitler had granted it a few armed divisions, leaving the details to be worked out by the Wehrmacht and SS.[184] Thus the Führer had once again seen to it that a potentially chaotic situation could be resolved ultimately only by himself. In effect, this meant that Himmler was permitted to induct a generous contingent of men from his General SS for his Waffen-SS, but that the number of volunteers he could court for the Waffen-SS from other sources would be limited. The Wehrmacht thus exercised a recruiting monopoly until the second half of 1942, when Himmler, too, was permitted to conscript recruits because Hitler wanted more and younger troops.

Another limitation on SS recruiting was that the Wehrmacht— apart from its official liaison with the HJ since 1935—made full use of its privilege of visiting the Reich's Gymnasien for the sake of courting future officers from among the pupils, who were of course also Hitler Youth. This was based on the rationale that when candidates joined the Wehrmacht as volunteers before being drafted, they could elect whatever armed branch suited their taste. On the other hand, if they waited until their name was called, they would be assigned to a branch they might not like.[185] Aiding the Wehrmacht in this quest was the fact that in the youths' eyes, the conventional military was legitimized by German history. Moreover, as a result of general conscription from March 1935 to 1938, the Wehrmacht was ahead of the SS by a full three years in actually possessing operational combat units. It reflects on the HJ as a prime conveyor of Nazi ideology that it could not motivate a critical mass of its graduates to choose the Waffen-SS over the Wehrmacht, despite the fact that originally both the HJ and SS were creations of the

Nazi Party. When faced with the choice, unlike their more enthusiastic comrades, many HJ leaders and ordinary members tended to pass up Himmler's revolutionary corps in favor of the Army, Air Force, or Navy.

This was the predominant trend from 1938 until capitulation in spring 1945. Within its limits, the SS was determined to recruit as many HJ youths as possible, by trying to outwit the Wehrmacht and availing itself of its good relations with Axmann. At first it was taken for granted that enough pressure could be exerted on veteran SRD members, with the result that they would join the Waffen-SS to a man, perhaps after first having joined the General SS. But despite constant exhortations, even those youths who were awed by the SS often did not feel up to it; it was precisely the elitist reputation of physical toughness and ideological rigor in the SS that induced them to consider the Wehrmacht's safer and less demanding alternatives.[186] It is true that there were SRD members who did join the Waffen-SS, accompanied by fellows from the general HJ, many of them flocking to Himmler's troops in their early stages.[187] Before long, however, quite a few of them, when home on furlough, warned their younger comrades not only of the excessive harshness in these Nazi elite troops, whose standards were much tougher than those in the Wehrmacht, but also of SS pressure to shed Christian church ties. As well, they told of atrocities against partisans, POWs, and Jews by the SS that they had witnessed in the field, often as accomplices.[188] Nor was the higher casualty rate among the Waffen-SS lost on HJ teenagers.[189] Although many were intrigued by it, others were repulsed by the blood-group tattoo that every SS man received near his armpit, for they saw it as a stigma betraying its bearers as a sworn group, a group whose purpose was dubious.[190]

As soon as the Waffen-SS recruiting teams realized that adverse news from the fronts was beginning to dampen the enthusiasm of potential SS candidates, they began to operate with a mixture of flattery and pressure. By 1941, recruiters were approaching senior Hitler Youths, complimenting them on their looks ("You two tall fellows, what are you looking for in the Navy? Come to the SS! That's an honor!") and then prompting them to sign their names. It took strength of will not to be seduced by the SS aura of power and virility.[191] Soon the Waffen-SS perfected a tactic that critics from the Wehrmacht termed "the categorical demand to join voluntarily," with the HJ leadership abetting. It instructed its local leaders to call in the boys for regular service, there to meet SS recruiters, but "without telling them what it is all about."[192]

During 1942, the SS was complaining about how little headway it was making in comparison with Wehrmacht recruiters.[193] Meanwhile, Hitler was approaching his manpower impasse in the months before the fall of Stalingrad. Impressed by the brutality and military successes of Himmler's squads thus far, Hitler allowed him to modify in his favor the recruitment allotment ratio set earlier, thereby facilitating enlargement of the Waffen-SS by conscription. The Führer did this duplicitously in order not to upset the Wehrmacht, and Himmler wisely commenced the SS draft not in the German Reich, but among ethnic Germans in the Balkans.[194] At the same time, the Waffen-SS intensified its recruitment efforts in local HJ stations by stepping up its pressure; sixteen-year-old Hitler Youths like Erhard Eppler could barely escape through quick pre-registration with one of the Wehrmacht's proprietary enlistment offices.[195] Wehrmacht pre-enlistment also became a favorite line of defense for Flakhelfer after the capitulation at Stalingrad in February 1943, because even in the face of the daily friction with superiors in the battery emplacements they had immediate recourse to a traditional armed-forces branch.[196]

By 1942, then, the SS was concentrating its efforts to recruit youth in three areas: in the newly established WE camps, the RAD camps, and the regular HJ stomping grounds. The WE camps offered great potential because out of 120 of them, about 40 were run by the SS, to which 90,000 HJ members were assigned. Here the SS was grossly over-represented, given that its stake in the combined Nazi armed forces was merely 3 percent. But the problem was that although the SS furnished 700 trainers for the WE centers, the great majority of their charges, including promising SRD veterans, still opted for Wehrmacht service, not least because of the cruelty of their SS warders. Ironically, of those who did apply, many had to be rejected because they did not meet Himmler's elite racial standards, as they were either too short or their skull measurements were not right.[197]

Himmler's next chance arrived when after the Stalingrad debacle Hitler relaxed the stern conscription rules for SS recruitment within Germany, to be initially attempted in the RAD camps.[198] But trying to press already discouraged RAD trainees into the Waffen-SS, a process during which SS recruiters would use all the physical and psychological force at their disposal, proved disastrous. Since there was still no official SS draft ordinance, only a tacit understanding between Hitler and Himmler, the RAD draftees resisted the bullying. This was not easy; the SS worked on some candidates for many hours without interruption, while others were physically assaulted. In at least one Reich Labor Service camp the SS pretended to sign up candidates only generally, specifically crossing out, in pencil, the name of the Waffen-SS. Only later did the HJ boys learn that the pencil lines had been erased.[199]

Understandably, Himmler was not too happy with the overall results. Even among those who had signed up, whether by the carrot or the stick, many were either physically unacceptable or mentally not ready, for example if they refused to renounce their Christian faith. Blaming the HJ, Himmler found many of the inductees to be afraid. "It was reported that the candidates were crying and that those who did not pass muster were rejoicing," he complained to Bormann in May 1943.[200] But until the spring of 1945, the pied pipers from the Waffen-SS had no choice but to continue their fiendish combination of persuasion and terror in every part of the HJ leadership's realm. By paying lip service to the principle of voluntarism, the SS extorted more signatures, sometimes after the visit of a dashing SS officer showing off his Iron Cross, on other occasions after screening a fascinating SS film from the front. But tricks and traps still abounded. In one case the boys were X-rayed for tuberculosis by Himmler's mobile radiation unit headed by an SS Colonel, Professor Hans Holfelder. When they confirmed the examination in writing, they also confirmed the small print, containing their consent to be drafted. As late as March 1945 in the countryside east of Munich, the SS was still using scare tactics: exploding grenades behind sixteen-year-old boys to shock them (they instantly wet their pants), or threatening others with handguns.[201] These dubious methods brought few rewards. The SS's own quotas could never be met, since juveniles from the Hitler Youth kept showing a marked predilection for "tank divisions, Navy, mountain troops, motorized units," but not those of the SS.[202]

It was in collaboration with Axmann that the Waffen-SS eventually attained a triumph, short-lived as it was, with a tank division manned almost entirely by Hitler Youths—the highlight of the laborious collusion between the HJ and SS. Overly ambitious and in craven devotion to Himmler, Axmann in early February of 1943 exploited the defeat at Stalingrad and, in search of a military legacy for himself, approached the highest SS echelons with a plan of creating HJ panzer troops. He knew this might be successful because he was familiar with the penchant of his charges for military rolling stock, especially tanks, which so far HJ trainees had only admired from a distance. Axmann used to his advantage the instinct for play in every Hitler Youth, who in the case of action in the field would be between sixteen and eighteen years old. In many ways they were still children, "in love with their vehicles," as one of their field commanders, SS General Hubert Meyer, remembers.[203] It is both significant and touching that when they were trained for combat in 1943 and early 1944, the panzer recruits did not receive cigarettes like mature soldiers, but candy.[204] Yet as with the Flakhelfer, in the acute situations of warfare, the fight was no game.

Himmler, backed in this by Hitler, was immediately attracted to the idea and decided that a HJ tank division, to be modeled on the classic "SS-Panzerdivision Leibstandarte Adolf Hitler," the first of several SS tank units, had to have around 20,000 men and 4,000 leaders. They were to be screened from among 30,000 current Hitler Youths as well as seasoned veterans of other SS divisions, but also from former HJ already in the Wehrmacht as NCOs and officers.[205] Nevertheless, Axmann soon had to concede that it would be difficult to recruit a youth contingent of that strength, especially since he did not have sufficient experts to train them.[206] The redoubled recruiting efforts of the SS especially in RAD camps that so bothered the HJ boys after 1942 was being done with these tank divisions in mind.[207] In the end, large numbers of youths were trained for many months in Wehrertüchtigungslager staffed by the SS as well as in Beverloo in Belgium, until they were ready for battle on the western front in the early summer of 1944.[208]

Their first encounter with the enemy was a day after D-Day, on June 7, 1944, near Caen, just off the beach in Normandy, as they faced Canadian, American, and British assault craft. There appear to have been close to 20,000 boys, and during one of their first attacks they promptly knocked out twenty-eight Canadian tanks.[209] A former HJ, in retrospect, has said, "our division fought valiantly."[210] With the ingenuousness and resilience of youth, but also fully conscious of being in an SS division known for murderous onslaught, the boys battled so tenaciously that by the middle of July they had lost 3,000 soldiers, and Himmler and Axmann were desperate for replacements.[211] Some of these youthful soldiers engaged in suicide missions that seasoned Wehrmacht soldiers would never have dared to attempt, such as allowing tanks to roll over them and then detonating a grenade.[212] German Army commanders like Rommel and Heinz Guderian got to be as much in awe of them as their enemies were.[213] Their fanatical faith in their cause and in themselves led them to commit war crimes, however; in the late summer of 1944 they shot sixty-four British and Canadian prisoners-of-war, for which their commanding officer, Kurt Meyer, was eventually sentenced to death by a Canadian court.[214] In keeping with the character of this tank division, Meyer had been the youngest divisional commander in the entire Nazi forces at the time of his appointment. Meyer was already the second commander after the first one had fallen during the invasion, and after his capture, he was followed by two more leaders.[215] Effective leadership could not be depended upon.

After many cataclysmic events at the fronts, the most disastrous for the HJ panzer division and also the most sobering for its survivors in the end was its defeat of September 1944. Faced with insuperable enemy forces and never-ceasing Allied air attacks, the 12th SS Panzer Division "Hitlerjugend" got caught in the encircled area near Falaise, some twenty miles south of Caen (which it had taken on July 9). With only 600 men remaining and no tanks breaking free and returning to the Reich, they regrouped as part of the 6th SS-Panzer Army under Hitler's favorite warrior Sepp Dietrich, a butcher's apprentice turned SS general, known for his desperate but unsuccessful attempt to save the regime.[216]

The Final Victory

When the ultimate defeat began to descend upon Nazi Germany in late 1944, its leaders had no choice but to husband their last resources in both manpower and materials. By this time the Allied air forces had attained total control of the skies, and the German Navy was losing its grip in the Atlantic, the North Sea, and the Baltic, the last of which had been crucial for the safe conduct of Swedish iron ore to German shores. Vital industrial installations in the Ruhr Valley were bombarded decisively in early 1944, as were the Schweinfurt ball-bearing works in northern Bavaria. The German synthetic oil industry was being knocked out, and Romanian crude oil was no longer available to the Nazis after successful British and U.S. long-range planes had staged their last raid on Ploesti in August 1944.[217]

All the while, after the successful invasion of Sicily in July 1943 and Normandy in June 1944, the western Allies were inching up to the Reich from the edges of Europe in the South and West, and the Soviets were preparing to take the capital of Berlin from the East. In September 1944 the U.S. First Army crossed over the German frontier for the first time, near Eupen in Belgium, occupying Reich territory north of Trier. By early February 1945, the western armies, consisting altogether of two million Americans, British, Canadians, and Free French, were poised to move from France into Germany. They reached the area west of the Upper Rhine on February 9. By the beginning of March the entire left bank of the Rhine River was in Allied hands, and on March 7 U.S. troops crossed the last remaining bridge over the Rhine at Remagen, some fifteen miles south of Bonn. The northern part of the heavily industrialized Ruhr area was subdued at the end of that month, as the Allies were now advancing toward the North Sea and Baltic coasts. Bremen and Lübeck fell to Field Marshall Bernard Montgomery's Army just before the Americans were able to take Hamburg on May 3. By early April the entire Ruhr had surrendered to the American Ninth Army, with over 300,000 German prisoners being taken. At that point Hitler's formerly unflinching vassal, Field Marshall Walter Model, put a bullet through his head.[218]

Having collected soldiers who had lost contact with their units, flak emplacement personnel as well as inmates of officer training schools and WE camps, Field Marshall Albert Kesselring had formed an Army Group South for the defense of southern Germany. Despite his efforts, General Alexander Patch's American tanks entered Nuremberg, an important shrine of Nazidom, which was theirs on April 20. Ironically, it was Hitler's birthday and the traditional day of initiation for new Hitler Youth recruits. Patch and his colleague George Patton continued into the Alpine region, Patton eventually to meet up with the Red Army, which had invaded Vienna on April 6th, conquering it on the 13th.[219] This happened after Budapest had been taken by the Russians in February, with a loss of almost 30,000 German men.[220]

Meanwhile, in the East, the White Russian Front of General Ivan Tscherniakovsky had plunged into East Prussia in October 1944, touching Gumbinnen, not far from Königsberg or, for that matter, Rastenburg, home to the Führer's command post Wolf's Lair. Even though the Soviet general had to beat a retreat for the time being, huge numbers of Wehrmacht soldiers had already been surrendering to the Red Army for some time. The conquest of East Prussia, bordering on the Baltic Sea, was essential for the march on Berlin from the North; in January 1945 Stalin knew the capital would be included in the future Soviet occupation zone. By the end of that month Königsberg was surrounded, with German forces driven onto Pillau, the Baltic peninsula somewhat northwest of the East Prussian capital. Further to the south, the Oder River—the last major impediment before Berlin—had been crossed and almost all of Silesia to the east of it occupied. February saw the Soviets pushing fiercely westward in a broad front from East Prussia and Pomerania down to Silesia. Small German counter-offensives such as the one at Pomeranian Pyritz-Stargard were soon quelled. The Russian advance was indirectly helped by a series of Anglo-American air raids against the Saxon capital of Dresden, a strategically important railway hub, on February 14–15. The death toll there of "tens of thousands" of civilians who were fire-bombed, many of them fugitives en route from the East, had a similarly devastating effect on German morale as the fire-bombing of Hamburg had had in the summer of 1943. From West Prussian Danzig (Gdańsk), a great many fugitives could still escape from the Russians by sea, until at the end of March that port too fell to the Red Army. As the Battle of Berlin was beginning by mid-April, Lower Silesian Breslau was still holding out and did so until early May, and so was Prague in the Protectorate, until on May 5 it was captured by Czech resistance fighters, who, however, had to surrender control to the Russians later in the month. By that time, countless "inhuman acts of cruelty," in the words of the German historian Lothar Gruchmann, had already been perpetrated on Prague's remaining Sudeten and Reich German population.[221]

The Russians could have captured Hitler earlier when he was at Wolf's Lair in October 1944, but by January 16, 1945, he had repaired to his bunker below the Berlin Reich Chancellery. By the middle of April Marshal Georgi Zhukov with his 1st Belorussian Front was moving against the northern outskirts of Berlin from the Oder River, while Marshal Ivan Koniev's Ukrainian forces were closing in on the city's southern environs, after having traversed the Neisse, a tributary of the Oder. Hitler briefly considered opening up a new German front under SS General Felix Steiner and Wehrmacht General Walther Wenck; Wenck's 12th Army division stationed near Wittenberge in Brandenburg on the Elbe and Stepenitz rivers, like Kesselring's to the southwest, was staffed by an assortment of young, inexperienced soldiers, including hastily drafted RAD Workmen and members of the Hitler Youth. Parts of these contingents were then set in motion to march eastward on Berlin, but were unable to get there before the end of April. U.S. forces too were moving east during this last month in the Third Reich's history, encountering heavy German opposition in the Harz Mountains east of Brunswick, where Himmler had addressed the Hitler Youth nine years earlier. On April 25, when the capital was completely encircled by Zhukov's and Koniev's armies, the Americans met up with Russian troops near Saxon Torgau on the Elbe, tentatively celebrating their hard-won victory. For seven days thereafter, until Berlin as a city surrendered on May 2, Russian tanks and foot soldiers waged ferocious street and house-to-house battles, winning territory inch by inch against disorganized squads of straggling Wehrmacht soldiers, motley Waffen-SS crews, and clutches of poorly armed Hitler Youths. Those desperate boys did not know they were defending a moribund tyrant who, shielded in his bunker by his cronies, married his mistress, Eva Braun, on April 29, only to commit suicide a day later.[222]

The increasing demands on men and matériel were raising important questions regarding ever-greater deficits in the Third Reich's overall resources. There had been problems ever since the invasion of the Soviet Union in June 1941, but after the disaster of Stalingrad in February 1943 and with enemy invasions looming, it had become clear that the Nazi regime had to redouble its efforts in the marshaling of economic and manpower potential. On the matériel side, the new Reich Armaments Minister Albert Speer, along with Reich Marshal Göring and Plenipotentiary for the Work Force Fritz Sauckel, took firmer control.[223] On the personnel side, Sauckel had insisted, a week before the fall of Stalingrad, that he needed all males from age sixteen to sixty-five to join the war economy.[224] However, as was typical of the confusion that had already infected all bureaucracies in the Third Reich, this would conflict with Goebbels's widely publicized Sportpalast speech of February 18, 1943, in which the Propaganda Minister asked the German people to agree to the new extraordinary demands of total war. Goebbels required "operative reserves," meaning the military deployment of hitherto non-draftable men, including adolescents.[225] Potential contradictions between the needs of the economy and those of the military were not removed when Goebbels became Plenipotentiary for the Total War Effort (yet another grandiose title signifying a parasitical office) on July 25, 1944, in which capacity he could scout for manpower additions to the war economy, thus assisting Speer and Sauckel, while at the same time helping to find new soldiers, in this way counteracting them.[226]

Hitler himself, as usual trying to have the last word in situations of disorder, appeared to cast his lot with the advocates of armed forces expansion when he decreed the establishment of the Volkssturm, a sort of last-ditch people's militia for the defense of the home front, to be recruited from among men aged sixteen to sixty, on September 25, 1944. Civilians by the Geneva conventions, and therefore in danger of being treated as partisans when caught, they would wear armbands over mufti to indicate combatant status and would be instructed in the use of whatever arms could be found.[227] In early October Himmler, freshly installed as Supreme Commander of the Replacement Army, decided that a new batch of fighters could be made available by declaring younger cohorts of Hitler Youths eligible for this service than had been the rule before: all those of age sixteen were to be trained in WE camps of six weeks' duration, and those of age fifteen in camps of four weeks' duration. A few days later, in conjunction with Bormann, Himmler ruled that anyone now in RAD camps—the stage just prior to Wehrmacht induction—could also be sent into immediate combat, within the framework of the Volkssturm. Newly organized HJ training courses would acquaint the youthful warriors with high-power weapons, such as machine guns, bazookas, and carbines, in only four days. Specifically mentioned were future encounters with enemy tanks.[228]

As the Allied invasions proceeded that year, it became clear how important the tank was as a weapon. Tanks were the land armament of choice for the Americans and the Russians, as they had been, indeed, for the only regular division ever set up under the banner of the Hitler Youth. To be conquered by Americans may have been bad enough, but there existed a mortal fear of the Russians among the German civilians living close to the eastern borders and among the Wehrmacht and Waffen-SS fighting near the Soviet lines. It dawned increasingly on the Germans that "as an incentive for the soldiers of the Red Army, now that the prewar territory of the U.S.S.R. had been freed of German occupation, the internal propaganda was concentrated on the theme of vengeance as a replacement for the earlier theme of defending the homeland."[229]

Hence by January 1945 at the latest, anti-tank weapons became part of the munitions arsenal of every HJ branch of the Volkssturm that was now organized and lying in wait, especially for Russians about to tread on German soil.[230] At that time Reich Youth Leader Axmann asked Hitler for permission to create special HJ anti-tank brigades, to prevent the Soviets from crossing the Oder. After some hesitation, Hitler, grasping at every last straw, welcomed the idea. From January on, the enrollment of fifteen-year-old boys for active combat, through special Hitler Youth, WE, or RAD camps, was further encouraged. Beginning in February, the possibility of combat for fourteen-year-olds (those born in late 1930) was not excluded.[231] And if until March the lines between voluntarism and compulsion in the various forms of the armed service by these youths—all under nineteen—had still been blurred, that uncertainty was removed when on the third of that month Hitler's Wehrmacht Chief of Staff, Field Marshal Wilhelm Keitel, ordered conscription for any male born in 1929 or earlier.[232] Moreover, Hitler planned to pull out all those born in 1928 from the Volkssturm and have them thrown in with troops at the regular fronts, however close those fronts may already have been to German towns and cities.[233] Those boys born in 1929 and 1930 were to serve in Volkssturm brigades or in Axmann's special anti-tank divisions, stationed in or near endangered German settlements.[234]

By the end of March those brigades were often staffed by boys who had already done much fighting elsewhere and, exhausted and sometimes wounded, represented reserves of the last resort. "Here they are," wrote Vienna HJ leader Ringler in his diary on March 28, "Willi with his artificial lower leg, Hubert with his shot-off thigh, Hannes with his damaged foot, Schorschi with a prosthesis and head bandage, Karl with his empty sleeve, and all the others, those already recuperated or barely so."[235] At the beginning of April, there were similar troops all over Hitler's Reich—Munich, Nuremberg, Berlin.[236]

Already in the fall of 1944 Goebbels was full of admiration for HJ squads that were rushing to the western front to help with heavy fortifications.[237] Later in the year and in early 1945, Hitler Youth troops of various sizes and provenance were specializing in halting the tanks of Americans pushing to the Northwest and South of Germany. In some locations, such as Nuremberg until April 20, the HJ troops also carried anti-tank rockets and rifles, typically older French and Italian models, because new ordnance was scarce. Usually, these HJ formations, whatever their size, were fighting in conjunction with the Wehrmacht or Waffen-SS.[238] Sometimes they informally attached themselves to individual officers, content to follow their orders, thereby sealing their own fates. Near Einbeck, between Göttingen and Hanover, four local Hitler Youths met up with Heinz Neupert, a fanatical Luftwaffe lieutenant, who was recuperating from a war injury. On Sunday, April 8, as American troops were moving east across the northern half of Germany, the four schoolboys loaded their bazookas into a small Opel car and under Neupert's guidance drove to the village of Lüthorst, close to the U.S. line of fire. They hid behind a pile of boulders and recklessly began to shoot at the Americans. According to a local witness, "one tank positioned itself in front of the village and shelled the quarry until nothing was moving any more. The boys were hit mostly in the abdomen. They were still screaming, but nobody dared to go in there."[239]

In the East, by the middle of January 1945 Königsberg had become the first important target of the Red Army. There were Hitler Youth troops on the East Prussian front, in defense of that one-time bastion of the Teutonic Knights. One squad consisted of the cadets of a glider school that had been transferred there from the West, sixteen and seventeen years old, who were now manning machine guns. However, some of them had only old rifles that froze and kept stalling in the cold. The Russians got dangerously close and totally overran this group. As Joe Volkmar later recalled, "out of 90 proud glider pilots, we lost 20 killed or missing in our four-hour combat experience that fateful morning of January 25th."[240] Hitler Youths were everywhere in the defense of Königsberg and its surroundings, but no sooner did Soviet soldiers come across them than they treated them brutally, often by beheading them with bayonets.[241]

Whereas Königsberg held out until April 10, Danzig in West Prussia had already surrendered on March 27.[242] In the spring of 1945 the entire eastern front, now being pushed steadily to the West, was sustained in large part by those newly created Hitler Youth battalions, with some interruptions, right down to Vienna.[243] In Pyritz, south of Pomeranian Stettin, there were many who had been trucked there as part of the last-ditch Volkssturm, holding the German lines against the assaults of the Soviet 9th Guard Tank Corps moving in from eastern Lippehne. Among them were former flak helpers who had been rushed there from elsewhere in the Reich and granted the status of soldiers (their dream of former months) to protect them under the Geneva conventions. When recalling this time, Rolf Noll can name comrades as young as thirteen, and he remembers how Russian tank drivers specialized in spotting youths in hastily created dugouts, then moving their vehicles over them and turning on the spot, thus crushing the boys underneath.[244] Further south in provincial Brandenburg, on the Oder River near Frankfurt and Küstrin, a specially called-up Hitler Youth regiment "Frankfurt/Oder" was fighting under HJ commander Kiesgen, trying to halt the Russian onslaught on the capital.[245] And in Silesia, too, there were such regiments, in particular one in Breslau called "Regimentsgruppe Hitlerjugend," under HJ leader Herbert Hirsch and several Wehrmacht NCOs. Altogether, 1,000 boys were fighting there in two battalions, as they retook from the Russians a railway station and a factory, mostly with hand grenades. At least half of those child soldiers perished.[246] Breslau fell in early May, as did Prague, where armed Hitler Youths had also been holding their ground. When the Czech insurgents took control of the city center, they—who were now drowning, hanging, and burning German civilians by the hundreds—singled out these boys. "Approximately forty Hitler Youths, blood-stained and with swollen, beat-up faces, were driven into the human square. In front of the assembled prisoners, after unspeakable cruelties, they were finished off with knives and clubs."[247]

Many if not most of these young German soldiers, out of desperation but also because they had been brainwashed in prior training sessions to show no mercy especially to Slavic enemy soldiers, were equally cruel. In order to boost their morale, but also for Goebbels's newsreels, Hitler received a contingent of twenty of them in his Reich Chancellery bunker on March 19. They had been brought in from Pomerania and Silesia, and each of them was presented as a little hero, having knocked out a tank single-handedly or having taken Russian prisoners. The youngest of them was Alfred Czech, twelve years old and from Upper-Silesian Oppeln, who had been decorated for rescuing twelve wounded Wehrmacht soldiers and catching a "Soviet spy." Some had knocked out tanks with bazookas; others served as couriers. All wore the Iron Cross. "You already know what battle is like from your own experience," said the gray, hunched-over Führer, "and you know that this struggle is for the German people, to be or not to be. In spite of all the hardships of our times, I am completely convinced that we shall emerge victorious from this battle, especially as I am looking at German youth and at you, my boys." Hitler could not have expressed it better in his *Mein Kampf.* "Heil, mein Führer!" shouted the boys, with their eyes agleam.[248]

By the end of March more and more Hitler Youths were being concentrated in clusters around Berlin, moved from places like Brandenburg an der Havel, Luckenwalde, and Oranienburg to locations inside the capital's suburbs, such as Spandau and Tegel in the North, and from there closer to the center. In mid-April nearly 6,000 of them were in the city, under the nominal command of Reich Youth Leader Axmann and his deputy, WE inspector Ernst Schlünder, awaiting the invasion of the Soviet troops. The youths were only supposed to assist regular Wehrmacht and Waffen-SS detachments, as well as firemen,

police, and the old men of the Volkssturm. But as it turned out, when
the Russians got inside Berlin on April 25, the older fighters, under
town commandant General Helmuth Weidling, were sadly deficient
and totally dependent on the reserves of Wenck, which were never to
materialize.[249]

Axmann himself was safe in the bunker, next to his Führer, "one of
those devoted believers, a blind idealist," as Hitler's private secretary
Traudl Junge remembers him.[250] The young fighters, on the other
hand, temporarily buoyed by prospects of fame and glory, took positions in dangerous places not immediately accessible to the invading
Soviets, many of whom were relatively immobile in tanks and trucks.
But they came, of course, in huge numbers. Armed mostly with
bazookas, hand grenades, and some firearms, and now with only rudimentary training, the HJ bands proved to be flexible and fleet-footed.
Especially for the younger ones, it was like playing cops and robbers, as
they moved around in underground passageways and subway tunnels,
hid behind ruins, and lay in wait in basements, cellars, and bombed-
out shops. Their specialty was holding still until a tank was only a few
yards away and then hurling their grenades. Some would lie on the
sidewalk playing dead until a tank arrived, and then they would fire. As
the Russians became more ubiquitous, engaging in house-to-house
combat with soldiers, Hitler Youths jumped onto rooftops, sneaking
up behind Red Army snipers and pushing them into the street.[251]

For lack of regular troops, thousands of Hitler Youths were charged
by Hitler's and Axmann's orders with securing strategic bridges, particularly those across the Havel River, to safeguard the Wenck Army's
crossing. (For his part in this, the "incitement of youth for war,"
Axmann was later to be condemned by a West German denazification
court.)[252] About six hundred of them were at the Havel Pichelsdorf
Bridge in Berlin-Spandau. Not only did Hitler expect Wenck in just
that area, but high-placed Nazis themselves used that bridge to facilitate their escape from the capital.[253] When the Russians took the bastion, however, almost all the Hitler Youths were killed. The same fate
befell those holed up in the Olympia stadium and those sniping from

bunkers in the Tiergarten, the large zoo in the middle of town.[254] In the end, after Hitler had committed suicide on April 30, Axmann in the company of Bormann made his own getaway, passing hundreds of dead HJ boys as he did so. Bormann was killed by Soviet gunfire, but Axmann was able to reach safety in South Germany. He had abused mere children in order to save his own skin.[255]

There can be no doubt that the few Hitler Youths received by the Führer on March 19, 1945, were ecstatic. Inspired by their personal successes against the enemy, they were being upheld as the paragons of a picture-book HJ career as it had been advertised by Nazi propaganda since 1933. And to meet Hitler in person was the fulfillment of a dream that virtually all HJ boys and girls had harbored (as did most German adults until late 1944), no matter how many reasons they may have had to complain about the conditions of their political and paramilitary socialization, especially in recent times. But the exigencies of this critical last phase of the war, which had truly turned into the struggle of survival their political leadership had always conjured up, made these young boys, who like their older peers had routinely been told that they would be male warriors and protectors of the Reich, particularly fanatical. In 1945 they were too young to have had the opportunity to evaluate the situation in the Reich in general, and their own, potentially highly perilous circumstances in particular. Hastily drafted and with superficial military training, they were thrown into the fighting by leaders spouting slogans of easy victory, which their older and more mature peers might have treated much more skeptically. Looking back, a fifteen-year-old with a bazooka on his shoulder fighting Russian tanks at close range on the Oder River in late 1944 probably would have been aghast, had he been told as a ten-year-old HJ novice at the war's beginning that he would end up at the front while still a teenager. In the face of imminent defeat, the majority of young boys who were forced to take up arms during the last phase of the Third Reich were demoralized, disillusioned, and scared for their lives, no matter what youthful ambitions and energies were still driving them. They had become desperate. In terrible skirmishes they had seen their comrades fall to the left and right of them and were hoping only to be lucky enough to survive. All they really wanted to do now was go home.

It is not surprising that with the radicalization of warfare, accompanied by an intensified Nazi indoctrination of youth in the last years of the war, there was, in its final weeks, a very small number of Hitler Youths who engaged in extreme activities unquestionably condemned by the Geneva conventions. First, there were some boys who were driven to commit crimes against humanity which at the beginning of the war they would only have committed as young adults, for example as concentration camp guards or as members of SS or Army death squads. Second, there were Hitler Youths who volunteered as members of what in postwar sensationalist literature has sometimes been falsely romanticized as the "Werewolves," a Nazi resistance movement.[256]

In order to inure HJ adolescents to inhuman acts, to make them complicit in the crimes of the Third Reich, and to bond them to its murderous reputation, its leaders ordered them to commit atrocities. For example, in mid-March 1945 a seventeen-year-old serving in a Volkssturm batallion was told to execute a Ukrainian conscript worker found guilty of looting. The Soviet lad was fetched from a bunker, and when attempting to flee he was gunned down by the HJ rifleman at close range.[257] Later that month a HJ-Bannführer commanded seven subordinates aged sixteen and seventeen near Austrian Deutsch-Schützen to escort sixty Jews into the woods. They then had to close off the area before two SS men executed the Jews. The HJ members had to bury them, only to notice that in one of the shallow graves a mortally wounded man was still stirring. After the SS had fired into the head of the victim, his burial began anew.[258] Also in Austria, fourteen-to seventeen-year-old Hitler Youths had to execute a deserter, one of their own from a flak emplacement. Barely over five feet tall and afraid of the advancing Russians, he had wanted to go home.[259] Further north near Soltau and close to Bergen-Belsen concentration camp, some fifty Hitler Youths were ordered to catch dozens of inmates who had fled. The hapless victims were lined up at dusk on the edge of town and then shot by the boys who had hunted them. One of them who witnessed this scene, but was spared the shooting, broke down in the face of such evil. His father took him to the local Party office, asking why children had to perform these traumatizing tasks. Characteristically, two high-placed functionaries answered: "We wish to educate the young people so that they become even tougher and will not shrink from any cruelty."[260] Still, whether on orders or not, Hitler's youths served and perpetrated the deadly racial ideology of the Third Reich. The issue of culpability is made exceedingly difficult by their youth, but the issue of complicity remains.

The Werewolves, by the more narrow and technically correct definition, were small suicide commandos of boys and sometimes even girls who were dropped behind enemy lines on what was already foreign-occupied German soil, to reverse the conquest—in itself an insane task. But in a wider sense the HJ leadership would have liked every one of its charges to become saboteurs, causing destruction among occupation forces in every way possible, in a casual rather than organized manner. This is apparent from a flyer dropped over North Germany in April with a request to "pass it on." It would not take much schooling or mechanical know-how to harm the enemy—merely a hammer, a pair of pliers, a knife, a screwdriver, and some basic skills could be enough to stall the enemy's war machine significantly. The flyer also contained suggestions for destroying army vehicles by throwing sugar into gas tanks or suspending invisible wires across roads, to cause decapitation. Instructions for derailing trains looked as foolproof as they were simple. And telephone lines could be rendered obsolete using heavy stones.[261]

The few Werewolf commandos of the HJ were organized and trained in conjunction with the SS. In fact, these activities signaled the finale in the unsavory collaboration between Himmler's and Schirach's formations since 1935. In the most notorious case, the new German anti-Nazi lord mayor of Aachen, Franz Oppenhoff, after having been installed by U.S. Forces, was successfully assassinated by an SS man, two HJ boys, and a BDM girl in March 1945. (After the Allied armies had penetrated Germany west of the Rhine, Aachen was the first major city to fall to them, in late October 1944.) The sworn group of young killers landed on Belgian territory near the Dutch border, having been dropped from the skies by a captured B-17 Flying Fortress. They immediately killed Josef Saive, a Dutch border guard. They then made their way into Aachen, shot Oppenhoff in his own house, and managed to flee, with the Americans in hot pursuit. In the end, they all perished on their way back to German-held territory, after having stepped on land mines.[262]

The event was played up in the German media for the best possible effect, but there were no others like this one. Armed with weapons and in possession of cyanide capsules for quick suicide, Werewolves tried to wreak havoc in Vienna during April but got nowhere.[263] In one instance a posse of Berlin Hitler Youths, again joined by the SS, were dropped behind Russian lines for suicide missions, but at least one of them gave up and made his way back to the capital, in good enough shape to tell about it.[264] Three days before the Reich's capitulation, two Hitler Youths were again parachuted behind American lines in the West, only to be caught. They were taken to Brunswick, put on trial as spies, and condemned to death. Sixteen and seventeen years old, they were executed on June 1.[265] The last Werewolves to make any impression at all were inmates of a WE camp who, when caught by the Russians in Berlin, were found to have signed their names on a list, promising to become active after the occupation of the Fatherland. Although they allowed the occasion to lapse, this did not help them much. Only one of them seems to have been immediately released; the others were taken prisoner. They lingered in Soviet camps for years, except for one who went missing.[266]

The march into captivity constituted the last episode in the history of Hitler's youths from 1933 to 1945. The figures vary; according to one account, at the end of World War II close to 12 million Germans were in the custody of the victor nations, which would represent more than 10 percent of the Reich's total population in 1933. We can estimate that of those captured, at least half had been in the Hitler Youth at one time or another, and that would include females.[267] The most credible sources maintain that over 3 million men had been captured by the Red Army. Of those in Soviet captivity, nearly 2 million were sent home by 1950, but an unknown number remained in Stalin's camps. Even in 1955, almost one-third of the German population was affected by this state of affairs. When Konrad Adenauer, the Chancellor of the Federal Republic, traveled to Moscow in June of that year, he was promised the release of 10,000 prisoners. By January 1956, after holding back some prisoners, the Soviet Union had returned the remaining 4,150 POWs still alive.[268]

More German soldiers suffered and died in Soviet captivity than under the supervision of any of the other Allies. One aggravating circumstance here was that in 1949 the Soviet Union, not bound by the Hague Laws of Land Warfare nor the Geneva conventions specific to POWs, sentenced 30,000 prisoners, randomly and after mock trials, to twenty-five years of hard labor for supposed war crimes, thus removing them from the comparatively privileged category of war prisoners to that of common (native) criminals and launching them into the notorious Gulag. This was predicated on Stalin's decision that Russia needed laborers.[269] Predictably, life even in the POW camps was onerous, marked by dangerous chores, starvation, pests, and disease, among which hunger edemas and dysentery were endemic. There was cruelty on the part of the guards and Soviet-appointed German capos. Hitler Youths who had been pressed into the Waffen-SS and received the blood-group tattoo were singled out for special treatment, as were voluntary members of the SS (hence they often tried to remove the stigma by burning or cutting it out, but the scar gave them away like a mark of Cain).[270] All told, however, these hardships scarcely measured up to the levels of sadistic abuse and murder which the SS had inflicted on their victims in the concentration camps, or which the Wehrmacht, for that matter, had practiced in camps for Soviet POWs. Indeed, bad as they were, the conditions in the Soviet POW camps were perhaps not unexpected in view of the Nazis' long-time propaganda against the allegedly subhuman Russians and their vicious campaign of material and human exploitation after June 1941, to say nothing of the outright destruction of Soviet Jews. However demoralized and ineffective they became, German soldiers had anticipated long before the final catastrophe that falling into Soviet hands would be tantamount to a life sentence or death, and had therefore tried to get moved away from the eastern front as soon and as far as possible. But especially in the final weeks of the war, anybody caught by the SS or military police attempting this on their own without proper identification would be shot on the spot or strung up on the nearest pole.

The United States was the other major Allied nation responsible for German POWs. The Americans kept prisoners on occupied German soil and in Belgium, France, and Britain, as well as state-side. Experiences in those camps varied widely. Those Germans who were eventually brought to America fared best, being fed on normal American rations.[271] The most devastating conditions obtained, for hundreds of thousands of German soldiers, in camps near the Rhine River, all of them in the open. In Worms across from a U.S. Army base in picturesque Heidelberg, there was a former Wehrmacht barracks where up to 40,000 men were fenced in at any one time. For the majority, little food was on hand, and the latrine for all of them consisted of a huge square dug into the ground, where some men would drown during the night.[272] When inmates from this camp, which was not far from the French border, were handed over to camps in the south of France, the German POWs, fearing French revenge, despaired and many mutilated or killed themselves. (Whereas the Free French had not captured even a quarter of a million Germans, under the command of Charles de Gaulle they came to guard over a million of them.) In those camps POWs tried to survive in open cages in situations as bad as the worst American ones.[273] Meanwhile, the U.S. Forces had established unsheltered camps on the swampy banks of the Lower Rhine, the so-called *Rheinwiesen-Lager,* which acquired a terrible reputation for the way inmates were treated there. Especially notorious were the camps near Wickrath, Rheinberg, and Remagen. During the spring and summer of 1945, left virtually to themselves, the German men vegetated in earth pits under open skies. Scores suffocated in water and mud after heavy rainfalls, while others starved to death on meager rations; some had only tree bark and clover to eat.[274] It was clear that the Final Victory had eluded them.

Hitler's Young Women Deceived

From the beginning of the Nazi regime, girls and young women were told by the political leadership that they were eugenically valuable because they were the biological complement to men whose helpmates in the home they would be, as well as the mothers of their children, in order to perpetuate the German master race. They were conditioned in this manner by parents of Nazi persuasion, in most schools, and, unequivocally, in the Bund Deutscher Mädel of the Hitler Youth, after age ten and often far into their twenties. They were trained for female-specific occupations—caregiving and homemaking—while being discouraged from politics, male-centered activities, intellectual pursuits, and large-scale decision-making. They would have to submit to males without question in every respect, in particular sexually, and in return, they were told, men would protect them. All this meant that young women did not have to shoulder important responsibilities in the industrial and agricultural processes of the nation; above all, it meant that they would never have to bear arms.

However, because at many levels Hitler's dictatorship was dysfunctional and, as such, ultimately not able to defend itself against the external foes it had conjured up, beginning in the mid-1930s, young women were gradually compromised to the same extent that the Nazis were compelled to compromise their ideology, in order to survive. In both farming and industry all women had to assume ever-heavier work loads (although without the attendant benefits in status or earnings that usually accrued to men in comparable positions), until during the war they were standing in for males in stop-gap, transitory capacities.[275] After 1938, the girls were engaged more and more with war-related work, in theory and practice, through the Hitler Youth and its affiliates such as the RAD and, less commonly, the elite racist program

"Glaube und Schönheit." At the height of the war, tens of thousands of women were serving in semi-military circumstances, which became more life-threatening to them as more of the menfolk perished and Hitler's inevitable military defeat drew near. Even after the Reich's capitulation on May 8, 1945, German adolescent females continued to be victimized as the wrath of the conquerors turned against them especially in the eastern provinces, where they were raped, mutilated, killed, or deported to long terms of captivity.

However, insofar as many young and older women had assisted their male superiors in creating a system that facilitated ever-greater human abuses, including their own continuous exploitation, German women were by no means without blame. Although they may have lived after 1933 in a male-supremacist society in which policy decisions affecting them were made largely above their heads, still their own responsibility for their misfortune by 1945 was hardly negligible. After all, some women like Gertrud Scholtz-Klink, the Nazi women's leader, and Jutta Rüdiger, the BDM leader, even while under the supreme control of males had wielded power and perpetrated cruelty on others. In the BDM, many had accepted the racial theories constantly propounded to them, and a few, like Irma Grese, had taken these to their farthest terrible extreme. The adage concerning the survival of the fittest had influenced the behavior of girls who bore down on the minority of those in their ranks who showed little enthusiasm for sports, who were physically weaker or in appearance did not conform to the Aryan ideal, or who tended to stay away from Hitler Youth functions. Older girls in the "Glaube und Schönheit" program were willing participants as their immaculate racial countenance was complimented by the regime leaders; they knew they would be coveted as wives by the highest Nazis and thus would rule over Slavs in eastern European zones that had been cleansed of Jews.[276]

The Nazi leadership called up young females to serve in auxiliary military situations by 1940, when clerical personnel were increasingly needed in the occupied countries. Senior graduates of the BDM and members of the female RAD were at first voluntarily called and later seconded or conscripted to do tours of duty as "helpers" (Helferinnen) for the various branches of the armed forces, including the Waffen-SS. Thus there were staff helpers, Navy helpers, nurses, and Luftwaffe helpers, as well as communication (telegraph or telephone operator) helpers for the Army, who were known as Nachrichtenhelferinnen. While so-called staff helpers, usually for the Army, took care of clerical work, interpreting, accounting, and some chauffeuring and horse-handling, Luftwaffe helpers assisted in running alarm and warning systems and in measurements and other technical tasks. Some men had also been carrying out these functions, but when more of them were sent into combat with the attack on the Soviet Union in June 1941, more girls were called up to replace them. This became a recurring theme for the rest of the war, as—with the Blitzkrieg concept abandoned—increasing numbers of men were needed to face the enemy in action rather than for occupation and home-front duties. The ages of these girls ranged at the beginning of the war from eighteen to about twenty-two, but toward the end of the conflict it widened to between sixteen and well into the mid-twenties. More young women had been newly inducted after Stalingrad, so that by the spring of 1945, when the armed forces comprised approximately 10 million male soldiers, there were nearly half a million Wehrmachtshelferinnen.[277]

How close were these young women to combat, injury, capture, and death, and, as auxiliaries to soldiers, how much harm did they inflict themselves? Until the end, at least theoretically, the government held fast to its dogma that women should not bear arms. Reichsreferentin Jutta Rüdiger of the BDM after 1945 prided herself on the fact that her girls, having been forbidden, never had to fight like soldiers.[278] But the reality was quite different. The armed-forces helpers were exposed to partisan attacks in the occupied territories, and even on the home front they could undergo air raids and then, after the multiple invasions, near-combat situations, for instance in heavy bunkers, as the fronts were being pushed inward. When they were surprised, along with the male soldiers they were serving, by the furious onslaught of the Red Army in the East, they often took up arms and joined in battle, fighting quite ferociously and undoubtedly killing many. This alone made them complicit in Hitler's aggressive warfare since 1939. Some of them received decorations for this fighting, such as the Iron Cross. These women all came under German military jurisdiction and in case of capture were theoretically protected by formal combatant status according to the Hague (1907) and Geneva (1929) conventions.[279]

But even though toward the end of the war the Wehrmacht had special orders to see to the timely evacuation of these young women from front zones in the face of imminent danger, many were captured by the Allies, especially in the East. Nobody knows how many were ultimately lost; some 25,000 German women are said to have been carted off to Stalin's Gulag—not as POWs, which would have eased their lot, but as civilians, who could be more brutally treated and held indefinitely. The Czechs and Yugoslavs acted particularly viciously against those who had not been able to save themselves in time; in Prague, during the mêlées of early May 1945, many nurses were shot point-blank, while other helpers were stripped naked, and, with their tendons cut, were forced to crawl across Wenzel's Square, with an enraged crowd kicking them, until they all succumbed.[280]

In colloquial German the armed forces helpers were called *Blitzmädel*, or lightning girls. This term was ambivalent. Originally it derived from "Blitzkrieg," lightning war, for the first helpers had been sent to assist in the occupation of countries conquered by lightning warfare, such as France. The second meaning was derogatory, for *Blitzmädel* soon became known as adventure-loving girls who were quick in dispensing sexual favors.[281] Since they were usually over eighteen, this was undoubtedly an extension of the culture of sexual license that had characterized the over-fifteen echelons of the Hitler Youth in all of Germany since the mid-1930s, and from which, of course, these girls had graduated.[282] In the armed forces they got to know men who were often older and more experienced than themselves; bent on seduction, these soldiers were generous with flattery, money, and unambiguous presents such as lingerie, perfume, and liquor, particularly in France. As one soldier wrote home from Rennes: "Recently this has been all we care about: what do you eat, who do you lay, where do you go on Sundays?"[283] Officers in handsome uniforms especially knew how to take advantage of these circumstances, although officially liaisons were discouraged.[284] The girls themselves often were eager for pleasure and love affairs, since fraternization with the enemy was forbidden, whereas German Wehrmacht soldiers took ample advantage from their superior positions in starting relationships with young women in the occupied countries.[285] To the extent that these foreign women became rivals to the *Blitzmädel,* the German girls often found themselves in situations where they practically had to offer themselves to soldiers, even for the sake of normal social intercourse.[286] These scenarios in 1940–41 in France, Scandinavia, and to a lesser degree Poland and Greece foreshadowed what would happen at much lower ranks of the BDM and with distinctly younger girls toward the end of the war in most German towns and cities.[287] On the one hand, therefore, one might say that the exigencies of the war themselves created conditions in which girls lost decorum and self-discipline beyond what sexual mores would have allowed in peacetime back home. On the other hand, these were additional signs of victimization of young females in situations where, vis-à-vis more powerful males sanctioned by the Nazi system, they were coerced into settings in which sex became unavoidable, whether the official excuse of "giving a child to the Führer" or plain libido was a factor.[288]

When the fronts moved closer and the *Blitzmädel* were on longer tours of duty with less time off, such sexual activity ceased. This became the rule for all the other groups of young women militarily employed after Stalingrad, when the mood was more somber and defensive chores multiplied. In 1944, for example, many of the female helpers who had worked for the Luftwaffe were deployed to artillery emplacements, for service alongside male Flakhelfer. No sooner had they arrived on the scene than they were augmented by members of the female RAD and even the BDM, some of them as young as sixteen.[289] Hitler, in conjunction with Luftwaffe generals, had authorized the use of female adolescents in this way in July 1943, and Göring had supported it that fall.[290] After the defeat of Stalingrad this had become necessary, as the conscription age of male Flakhelfer for service in the Wehrmacht was gradually being lowered and large numbers of them were removed to the fronts. In their stead, by the spring of 1945 tens of thousands of female Flakhelfer were stationed in approximately 350 artillery emplacements at the key strategic centers of the Reich— chiefly the Rhineland, the northern coasts, and Berlin. Before being sent there, they had been specially trained not on site by rough NCOs, as the boys had been, but, for four weeks and more sparingly, in a unique facility in Rendsburg, close to the North German entry zone for many Allied airplanes.[291]

In 1943, when they were first assigned, it had been expressly stated that female flak helpers were not to be engaged with the actual use of firing equipment aimed at aircraft. However, even having to put young women close to armory bothered the Nazi leaders. They betrayed their uneasy conscience when they declared, in November 1944, that "the question whether such a service for women is fitting is moot. Assuredly we would like to see our girls performing other tasks."[292] In fact, during 1944, these girls were also employed as anti-aircraft gunners, as the boys had been from the beginning.[293] In addition to learning how to fire the cannons, some were instructed in the use of machine guns, grenades, and small firearms. One troop of female Flakhelfer who had been assigned to a Waffen-SS artillery unit in the center of Prague shot their way out of town, pursued by Czech snipers, until they landed, west of the city, in U.S. captivity. As handmaidens of the SS, they knowingly killed Czech civilians who might have been merciless in trying to recapture Prague, but who as patriots had moral justice on their side.[294] The fact that girls were now firing weapons proved even more embarrassing to the Nazi leadership. "The Nazis were hiding from the German public the fact that women were being used to shoot down planes," former flak helper Erna Tietz told an American author in the 1980s, adding that she was given a special identification, *z.b.V.*, short for *zur besonderen Verwendung* or "for special use." This meant that "maybe I could have been active in news gathering for the Wehrmacht, or in the secretarial pool, or distribution of clothing, or so on. One wanted to avoid that the public learn that women were assigned to weapons."[295]

In the pursuit of these non-feminine tasks, the flak girls, who like the boys used their skills to down enemy planes, came to much harm. Totally exposed to air raids and especially targeted by enemy aircraft in the emplacements, many lost their lives, although complete statistics are not available.[296] Some girls saw others die and were unable to cope with the calamity. Lisa was a sixteen-year-old BDM girl when in January 1945 her battery took a hit from an RAF plane. "I felt the blood on my face, it came from my left temple. My thigh was full of grenade splinters." That was bad enough. "But the corporal had his stomach ripped open, so that his guts were hanging out. I stood in front of him without being able to move. 'Lisa, take the pistol, kill me!' I could not do it."[297] Others were bombed on treks, in an attempt to flee.[298] Elisabeth Zimmer witnessed how a group of girls cracked under the strain; those who had run for cover without expressly being told to do so were later pulled out and shot for cowardice.[299] At the very end of the war, under reasonably compassionate superiors, female flak helpers were allowed to disband, but many ended up in captivity—American or British if they were lucky, or Russian if they had been stationed too far east.[300]

At the beginning of November 1944 Bormann conveyed a final decision by Hitler that German females, flak helpers or otherwise, were not to be utilized in any organized combat.[301] But—another contradiction in a regime full of paradoxes—exactly one month later Jutta Rüdiger, the chief of the BDM, linked up with Reich Women's Leader Gertrud Scholtz-Klink in a general call for arms. "German women and girls" aged eighteen and over were implored to join the armed forces anywhere in the Reich and "render the kind of service which they may be asked to undertake within these ranks in accordance with their aptitude, in lieu of soldiers."[302]

Although Axmann later argued that this did not constitute an order since any such assignment was voluntary, the pressure even on BDM girls was great, because that appeal also affected girls under the age of eighteen.[303] In fact, from December 1944 to May 1945, BDM girls as young as fourteen joined the Volkssturm and other military facilities that provided instruction in the use of hand grenades, bazookas, machine guns, and lesser firearms.[304] Forthwith, in small detachments, they integrated themselves into whatever regional front was battling the invading enemy, mostly in the East and the capital. At the Oder front they fought with anti-tank weapons and some, freshly inducted from the RAD, in hand-to-hand skirmishes, wielding spades against the bayonets of Russians.[305] In the defense of Berlin they specialized, like their male cohorts, in hurling anti-tank grenades from short distances.[306] There was also a "death squad" of young girls commanded by the Waffen-SS, who had red-painted lips and fought with abandon, but the documentation about what exactly they did is missing. Since the SS was involved, it is likely that by the terms of the Geneva conventions they overstepped their bounds.[307] After all, there were SS-directed female Werewolves, like the BDM girl in Aachen, who from Berlin were dropped behind the Russian lines, each with a poison pill.[308] It may be assumed that those girls who fought alongside the SS were sufficiently faithful to fit the Nazi ideal for boys, but as young girls transformed into Amazons they were the most extreme embodiment of Hitler's ideological sellout. For the average BDM girl in those final months, it was a combination of love for the Führer and hatred of the noxious invaders that motivated her actions. Doris Schmid-Gewinner, who, fourteen in 1945, was trained in Stuttgart on bazookas and was waiting for the Americans, wrote later: "I don't believe I thought: I am dying for Hitler. No, we have to go against those who are hurting us so. Just imagine how much I hated the bomb throwers at that time—and now they were supposed to come to Stuttgart. I would have fired any number of bazookas against them."[309] It is likely that in her memoirs Schmid-Gewinner suppressed the fact that she had also been prepared to die for her Führer, because over the years she had invested too much in him to see his world, and her own with it, tumble down in the end.

While many German teenage girls were exposed to the enemy in large numbers, to the point of being embroiled in active and perhaps morally questionable combat in the last four months of the "Thousand-Year Reich," a much greater number of them were placed in harm's way as non-combatants. Their fate was to become entrapped by invading troops, especially in the East, and to have a very uncertain future to look forward to. All girls over ten years old were nominally members of either the BDM or the female RAD until Germany's capitulation on May 8, 1945.

The events in East Prussia in October 1944 were a foreshadowing of what was to follow. The Red Army had advanced to a line east of Königsberg, including Gumbinnen, Nemmersdorf, and Goldap, towns that were easily captured. Until the Wehrmacht retook the area, atrocities were committed by Russians against the civilian population, just as atrocities had been committed by German troops in Russia, which prompted an exodus to the West, swelling to a flood in early 1945.[310] By January, large numbers of women, children, and old men were departing from East Prussia, some on ships supplied by the Wehrmacht. One of these, the *Wilhelm Gustloff,* was sunk by Russian torpedos off Gotenhafen on January 30 with its 8,000 passengers, among them 400 female flak helpers. To this day, this remains the greatest disaster in maritime history.[311] Many other civilians from the countryside fled by wagon treks, the last express train having pulled out of Königsberg's main station on January 23. On that day the Red Army was in Elbing, down the Baltic coast halfway between Königsberg and Danzig (which was not occupied until March 27), attempting to block all roads and rail traffic. By public loudspeakers, the Wehrmacht under General Otto Lasch urged Königsberg's citizens to leave the city on January 27, and the flood of fugitives increased.[312]

More refugees tried to flee East and West Prussia, Pomerania, and Silesia during the winter and spring until May of 1945, "plagued by icy cold and hunger, pursued by the enemy, shot at, sometimes overtaken and leaving countless victims on the way." Historians have counted these episodes among "the most terrible tragedies that Hitler's war visited upon the German people."[313] Eventually, a total of more than 10 million Germans managed to escape from the Russians.[314] During these harrowing journeys, the young girls suffered more than most, and for the least of reasons. Thirteen-year-old BDM trooper Ingrid van Bergen, her father killed at the front, fled with her mother and their new baby from Danzig west to Oliva, but then turned around. They reached a refugee ship that was supposed to take them to Holstein. Clambering onto it, soldiers with passes tried to push past them. "For the first time I was being confronted with the cowardice and recklessness of men," notes the actress; "if they could find a better spot they brutally shoved women and children aside." The vessel was bombed by Russian planes, but without consequences. However, a neighboring ship carrying wounded soldiers was hit. Van Bergen remembers seeing the boat listing to one side, and "how the stretchers with the wounded on them slid from the deck into the ice-cold sea. The terrifying thing was that from where we were, you could not hear a sound."[315] How many veterans of the Hitler Youth were on that Red Cross carrier, we shall never know. Hannelore Sch., finally released from the RAD, moved west to fetch her siblings in Mecklenburg and continued on foot to Holstein, where she learned of the suicide of her parents, who had stayed behind.[316] Others were trying to abandon the Protectorate. Ingeborg P., like Hannelore Sch. not yet twenty, fled with her mother, sister, and twelve-year-old brother, but lost both mother and brother to Czech violence just before reaching East German soil. What followed were months of pillage and much worse under Red Army occupation, until the Poles took over.[317]

There were other and worse forms of suffering for young German females during this period: rape, torture, and murder. To be sure, the injuries suffered even by blameless young people during the Nazi period are often overlooked or downplayed, in light of the towering injustices perpetrated by the Nazis on their foreign enemies. However, the chronicle of this suffering must also find its place in the history of youth under Hitler.

Many details regarding the rape of girls and women by Red Army soldiers in the eastern provinces of the Reich, as the Russians were advancing, and especially in Berlin, as they occupied the city between April 24 and May 5, have already surfaced. But in order to see the whole picture, some considerations have to be kept in mind. Although the total number of injured can hardly be doubted—up to half a million in Berlin alone (which would mean every third female)—this treatment of women, as Atina Grossmann has said, was in some ways like a self-fulfilling prophecy in that Hitler and Goebbels had for years excoriated the evil image of the "Mongols" who, beast-like, were on the prowl for rape and murder.[318] The fact that not just the Russians did the raping, although they certainly stood out, provides further perspective: all the victor armies engaged in it, as triumphant armies throughout history have always done. In the Stuttgart region, for example, over a thousand cases of rape of women by invading French troops, involving females from ages fourteen to seventy-four, were placed on record.[319] In the village of Merklingen alone, on the road to Ulm, by the end of April, 152 girls and women needed medical attention, some with pregnancies, the youngest twelve years old.[320] Indeed, rapes by French occupation soldiers, in addition to the Russians, were notorious, whereas in American and British zones of influence the borderline between rape and consensual sex became blurred, since the use of chocolate, lingerie, and cigarettes as barter encouraged covert prostitution.[321]

When the Red Army had first invaded East Prussia in the fall of 1944, its soldiers raped and murdered many women who were subsequently discovered by the Wehrmacht when they arrived to reclaim the territory.[322] The Germans charged that the Russians were following repeated exhortations by the Soviet writer Ilya Ehrenburg, sanctioned by Stalin, that to exact revenge on German fascists by killing every man and raping every woman was a Red Army soldier's duty.[323] It is true that in almost daily articles for its newspaper Ehrenburg had aimed to teach the Army "how to hate," urging it to kill as many German soldiers as possible. But he never called for raping German women. This was a lie, planted personally by Goebbels.[324] On the contrary, during the entire invasion of the Reich, Russian officers kept insisting that the

Red Army was forbidden to abuse women (which did not stop them from actually doing it themselves); Ehrenburg himself reinforced the official position against rape when visiting with Red Army troops in East Prussia in the spring of 1945.[325]

In any event, after December 1944 no order could stop sexually frustrated Russian soldiers from going on a furious rampage against the women whose men had killed thousands in Stalingrad, had besieged Leningrad for over a year, and had conquered the suburbs of Moscow.[326] In 1945, at the end of January, the Russians were back in the hinterland of Königsberg and close to the coast northwest of it, where they occupied the villages of Metgethen and Gross Heydekrug. Here they raped every female in sight, no matter what age, and killed some with bayonets or rifle butts. Teenage girls, all rightly suspected of being in the BDM, were crucified on barn doors after their violation or dragged behind Army trucks until dead. When the Germans briefly recovered the area in February, they found not only every former inhabitant killed, but two piles of bodies, close to three thousand adults, children, and infants—all female.[327] In Fuchsberg, fifteen miles southeast of Königsberg, the Soviet artillery officer Yuri Uspanski noted in his diary: "In the house of the divisional staff, evacuated women and children stayed overnight. Then came the drunken soldiers, one after the other, to select their women, to take them aside and abuse them. Several men to one woman. The soldiers said that 13–15-year-old girls were also abused. Oh, how they fought it!"[328]

On April 10 Königsberg itself was surrendered to the Russians, who now began to lead General Lasch's Wehrmacht soldiers away to captivity, but not without committing cruelties against the civilian population. One German POW on his way out later reported seeing "girls and women, being pulled into houses protesting and crying, children calling out for their parents . . . The ditches were filled with bodies, which showed the traces of unimaginable maltreatment and rape. Dead youngsters were lying around in masses, there were people hanging from the trees, their ears cut off, their eyes gouged out, German women were being led in both directions, drunk Russians were fighting for a German nurse, with an old woman sitting near a tree, both her legs squeezed off by vehicles."[329]

As the Russians swooped down on East Prussia, and thereafter adjoining West Prussia and Mecklenburg, as well as, to the south, Pomerania, Silesia, and then Brandenburg surrounding Berlin, an orgy of destruction, rape, torture, and killings swept over these provinces. Among potential victims, females were in the majority, because many males were gone or fighting somewhere else; the younger and more attractive the girls, the more endangered they were. In one village in Pomerania, all the young women were gathered together, and after being forced to shed their clothes, they were driven into a barn to be gang-raped.[330] Girls scarcely in their teens were being violated, with their mothers having to watch and even to assist the Russians.[331] No matter what assurances had been given, Russian officers often hand-picked the most attractive teenagers for their own use, then handing them down to the men. Suicides, including those of many girls, multiplied.[332] Using ashes and old sackcloth to make oneself look older seldom worked, but because Russians were extremely afraid of contagious diseases, pretending that some girls had typhoid fever sometimes helped, as it did in the village of Eichenau, Upper Silesia, in early May.[333] In Berlin, young women sometimes had the chance to say "I syphilis" when asked, by Russians, "you healthy?"[334] Others painted their inner thighs red, in order to feign menstruation.[335] But often even this did nothing to stop the rapes. The Russians would enter hospital wards looking for nurses, and after finishing with them (as they did in one clinic every night) would search patients' beds for more girls.[336]

There are hardly any known cases of teenagers who were not raped by Red Army troops after the invasion of Greater Berlin on April 25, especially during the first terrible week lasting to about May 3.[337] Those who escaped this fate must have been completely hidden, crippled, or otherwise been perceived as ill.[338] When the fighting was over and they were finally victorious, Russian soldiers went about Berlin with four pleasures in their mind: stealing watches, consuming food and alcohol, joy-riding on bicycles, and having sex with women.

They would stuff their pockets with watches no matter how many they had already. They would requisition food and especially wine and schnapps and would feast in people's homes to the limit. When drunk, they would try to get on bicycles and, unaccustomed to their use, would usually wreck them quickly. Then they would look for women, and although they preferred young ones, neither old age nor lack of physical attraction was protection for this particular prey.[339]

Acts of rape occurred during any time of day or night and in full private or public view; the rape victims were often infected with venereal disease. If girls refused, they could be killed outright, as were two acting students, whose torsos had been sliced open.[340] Often girls were murdered after multiple rapes (if they had not died from them already), and as news of this spread around, the fear of being violated became endemic.[341]

In some cases, virtually entire families perished. In the outskirts of the capital a mother had lost one of her daughters and had made a pact with the remaining one to shoot the daughter once the Russians approached her. When the Russians arrived, she fired at her daughter twice and missed, only to be shot by the soldiers in turn.[342] In the upper-class section of Dahlem, a drunken Russian violated two women and five daughters, aged eight to fourteen, in a basement. He had killed them all during the sex act and then hung them from the walls.[343] Of course, there were no longer any men to shield these unfortunates, except perhaps for a liberated, compassionate Jew or a lone courageous cleric. The Lutheran pastor Heinrich Grüber, for example, who had had ties to the Resistance, had helped Jews and been in Nazi concentration camps. When young girls were in his care he locked them into a room, blocked the threshold with his body, and then used his holy office to some effect. If the common soldiers did not understand him, the commandants, who frequently spoke German, might listen. But his was an isolated stand.[344]

The ultimate humiliation for young women was deportation to the camps of eastern Russia. They were not alone in this; any German deemed able to perform hard work was chosen, sometimes even children under ten, but often the choice was made arbitrarily. These measures, which also involved German POWs, occurred as part of the grand scheme by Stalin to secure cheap labor for the Soviet economy, after the land had suffered from German invasion, occupation, and the extraordinary exertions by Soviet citizens for home defense. Tens of thousands of civilians had been driven out of Stalingrad alone by the marauding Wehrmacht.[345] The Russians selected for these actions the provinces immediately adjacent to them (and those where they would not be interfered with by western Allies), the first of which, East Prussia, was scheduled to become theirs by annexation and hence had to be totally depopulated. "East Prussia," wrote Ehrenburg, was "the most reactionary part of Germany."[346] West Prussia, Pomerania, East Brandenburg, and Silesia, next to the Generalgouvernement and Wartheland, were to be claimed by the Poles and thus could also be emptied of Germans, with many being deported to the Soviet Union and others expelled by the Poles to Germany later.[347] Major collection points for evacuation were Insterburg in East Prussia and Beuthen in Upper Silesia, where more indignities were suffered. Altogether, the entire German territory east of the rivers Oder and Neisse was at risk. How many girls disappeared in these population transfers is not exactly known, but the figure is in the tens of thousands.[348]

The transportation of girls and young women by the Russians to the East, by forced marches, trucks, and cattle trains, was always preceded and accompanied by beatings and rapes at the hands of guards—Red Army soldiers or members of the Soviet secret service NKVD—of the kind already described. Rape and sometimes pregnancies—in a further ironic twist of Nazi eugenics—were also a part of the daily lives of the captured women in the camps, albeit less frequently.[349]

During transport, teenagers were routinely asked whether they belonged to the BDM or RAD. Most of them did and admitted it, which is what the Russians wanted to hear. Those who were still too young or had really not been members were threatened and beaten until they signed something in Cyrillic, which they could not read, and that sealed their fate.[350] The journey to a Soviet camp—civilians were sent to the Gulag—took many weeks; there was little food or water and an absence of sanitary facilities. "Almost all of us had diarrhea," remembers Erna B., who was twenty-four when she was carted out of Pomerania; "the truck convoy stopped only once a day. And then there was the thirst, so that in the mornings we licked the dew from the truck walls."[351] On one rail transport, the dead were collected every day from the cattle wagons and stacked on top of the coal piles in the fuel car behind the engine.[352]

The names of the Gulag camps have not all been recorded. One was Karpinsk in western Siberia; another was Chelyabinsk, further to the southeast. Two others were Nogatka in the Urals and Anthrazyd in the Don River region, where coal was mined. Here typhoid fever broke out already in May.[353] The food was unmentionable, sometimes consisting only of strongly salted herring or a horse's head boiled in water.[354] Young women had to do dangerous work, some being crushed by huge logs or perishing in unsafe coal mines; there was dysentery; and many went insane or died of malnutrition or other ailments. But there were fewer rapes, no systematic beatings, no medical experiments, and no mass liquidations; on the whole, conditions were much better than they had ever been in Nazi concentration camps.[355]

In the end, it is impossible to weigh the inhumanities perpetrated by Nazis on the one side and Soviets on the other. Both of them were murderous regimes. However, there is an element of bitter irony in this, the unintended finale of Adolf Hitler's youth policy, for it turned out to be the inversion of his original goals. The Führer had wanted to see his young men and women as masters in an expansive foreign land to colonize it: tilling its soil, reaping its fruits, harvesting its mineral wealth, all the while lording it over the indigenous population, who were to be the slaves. Now the young Germans were there, but they had become the slaves. While some returned to the land of their birth decades later, most of them never came back.

6
The Responsibility of Youth

In the play *The Man Outside* Sergeant Beckmann, having returned in tatters from the lost war, tries to find acceptance from the people he encounters in his home town of Hamburg. He has just found his wife in bed with another man. With his unshaven face and haggard look, his gas-mask eye goggles held together by a rubber band, and his shabby Wehrmacht coat, he makes a terrible impression. The young woman who finds him near the Elbe River, where Beckmann has attempted suicide, takes him to her room, but Beckmann has to leave in a hurry when her husband suddenly returns from the front. Next Beckmann visits his former Colonel, a jolly schnapps-drinking fellow who does not even remember him. "What do you want from me?" he asks. "I am returning it to you," says Beckmann. "Returning what?" the Colonel wants to know. Quietly, Beckmann says: "Responsibility. I am returning the responsibility to you." Beckmann reminds the Colonel that near Gorodok on the Russian front, on February 14 in subzero temperatures, the Colonel had given him responsibility for twenty men. This was for reconnaissance purposes, and to take a few prisoners. And then they had moved on and there was shooting in the night. "And when we returned to our position, eleven men were missing. And I had the responsibility. Yes, this is all, Colonel. But now the war is over and I want to get some sleep and I am returning the responsibility, Colonel, I don't want it any more, I am giving it back to you, Colonel."[1]

This haunting scene from what became the first successful German postwar play depicts its author, Wolfgang Borchert, who himself is Beckmann. He is the former reluctant Hitler Youth who as a soldier at the Russian front tried to maim himself so he could get away from the horrors of the war, and who escaped from the Nazi courts only with difficulty.[2] Borchert had returned from the front a sick and injured man. During the first few years after the German catastrophe he had found some work with Hamburg theater groups and moved in the newly reviving literary circles. But his liver disease was incurable, and he became more and more emaciated until he died in a sanatorium in Basel, one day before his play was premiered, on November 21, 1947. He was twenty-five.[3]

Beginning in May 1945, there were many Beckmanns who made their way back from the fronts, equally desperate and equally confused.[4] What they found in post-Hitlerian Germany was a devastated land under foreign occupation, in which even the most obvious survival techniques often could not save a person's life. Family members were dead or displaced, dwellings destroyed, food scarce or nonexistent and, during the dreadful winters of 1945–46 and especially 1946–47, the cold lethal. People's health was at risk, and work was hard to find in an economy that was barely functioning. Black Market conditions ruled; the fertility rate decreased. Cologne had lost 75 percent of its housing. In Hamburg in 1946, twelve men, women, and children were dying of malnutrition every ten days. As in the period before the Third Reich, young people were again disproportionately represented among the growing mass of unemployed.[5] One factor contributing to this, in the U.S. Zone of occupation for instance, was an employment embargo by the summer of 1945 against anybody who had ever held a leadership position in the Hitler Youth (as had most), no matter how nominal or inferior.[6]

The question is whether in all of this chaos young HJ and war veterans like Borchert really had any responsibility to return, responsibility for subordinates they had commanded, or responsibility for the crimes committed by the Third Reich. Among the many records and testimonials of the postwar era, there are only a few from individuals who admit to any responsibility or even guilt for Hitler's regime or who promise to atone for it.[7] By far the majority of young people claim to have been victims, in the sense of having been seduced by the Nazi regime, then used and thrown away, and thus having been cheated out of youth. They admit to a feeling of shock shortly after capitulation on May 8, 1945, when it became clear that they had been deceived by a criminal regime whose nature they had been unable to comprehend.[8] One young person cried that he could not bear to watch his ideals "sink into the mud"; another claimed that he had "lost my belief in humankind."[9] Nine out of ten juveniles had been in the Hitler Youth, and most expressed relief about having made it through the final hostilities alive. Apart from acute peril to life and limb, they claimed to have hated the increasing militarization in all Nazi formations most, with its attendant reduction of personal freedom. But such hatred had been balanced by promises of future leadership in the Third Reich.[10]

Resocialization of youths was first attempted in the Allied prisoner-of-war camps. The Free French were the least active in this effort because they had not had enough time to work on political re-education concepts, and there were not enough French POW camps to begin with. They also subscribed to the cynical belief that according to past experience, German nature was immutably fascist unless there was forced "degermanization," and that in daily life it was better to deal with Germans on an ad hoc basis.[11] As for the Soviets, they had distributed an appeal by 250 captured former Hitler Youths as early as October 1942, which attempted to make youths in the Reich aware of certain facts: Before conscription, they had been trained in special skills, yet this was not for the sake of jobs but for the military use of handguns, tanks, and planes. As Hitler Youths, they had been sent camping not for the enjoyment of nature but to learn how to march. They had engaged in sports not to strengthen their health but to train for even longer marches.[12] Because quick releases from Soviet POW camps were not forthcoming, German soldiers there were never aware of the preparations for citizenship in a newly reconstructed Germany.

Instead, once in the eastern Soviet-occupied Zone, if they ever got there, boys and girls were brought under the control of the FDJ, the Free German Youth, which, totalitarian in its own right, was Communist-controlled and anything but free. Others, deemed recalcitrant by the Soviet occupiers, were held in special youth internment camps; girls and young women were always at risk of being raped.[13]

The Americans and British, schooled in democracy, were much more conscientious. Great Britain began broadcasting messages to German soldiers during the war about the value of democracy as opposed to the scourge of tyranny. On the BBC, one of Thomas Mann's pre-recorded addresses from Los Angeles ridiculed Baldur von Schirach in October 1942 as a "poetry-dabbling fat-boy of advanced age" and belittled his claim to lead a united youth front in Europe.[14] "Re-education" became a formulaic answer to the problem of eradicating the Nazi weltanschauung in British POW camps; the British were careful to introduce new ideas about democracy and tolerance slowly and tactfully. They co-opted captured Germans who had high levels of education and ideals beyond suspicion to help them in the educational process, thereby attempting to dispel doubts and resistance among the fenced-in troops. Still, as Chancellor Emeritus Helmut Schmidt remembers from his own POW camp, there were always those, especially among the younger Wehrmacht officers, who thought that, in collaborating with the former enemy, they had "fouled their own nest."[15]

The British extended these efforts, less successfully, in special internment camps on German soil, and later carried "re-education" into Germany's youth population by way of "youth officers." They arranged orientation and cultural meetings and organized social clubs, where reconciliation was to be preached and practiced. Here, too, the results were mixed, if only because the target groups were from the higher German social classes: Gymnasium and university students. Willy Schumann, who would end up teaching German literature at Smith College, recalls an instance of kindness that must have done more than all the theoretical lectures put together. In the British Zone near Hamburg, on a very hot summer day when he and his friends were working in the field trying to harvest some produce, they noticed a small group of British soldiers passing by, who stopped to put something on the edge of the field, waved, and walked on. Because of non-fraternization orders, speaking was forbidden. As it turned out, they had left their lunch boxes for the emaciated-looking Germans. "This small human gesture," writes Schumann, "made an enormous, positive impression on all of us, even on my father, who was not an Anglophile."[16]

Once in Germany, American re-educators were just as likely to engage in such acts of mercy, as they would prove with their care packages under the Marshall Plan.[17] But they had much larger groups of POWs, and later, youths on German soil to deal with. Early on, their re-education policy was guided by theorists who were often exiled German Jews and knew the enemy country's background well, but were not always on the mark. Kurt Lewin, who had been a professor of psychology at the University of Berlin and in 1943 was teaching at the University of Iowa, held that Nazism was "deeply rooted, particularly in the youth on whom the future depends." Contrary to the evidence, he believed that a streamlined Nazi educational system had made an egoistic, uninhibitedly aggressive and destructive individual out of every German juvenile. He thought it absolutely necessary to change "a group atmosphere from autocracy toward democracy through a democratic leadership," by turning autocratic followers into democratic ones. But Lewin was pessimistic about the ability of German youths to do this, for he also believed that they, as a "lost generation," had the potential to go underground and "prepare the next world war."[18]

After German capitulation, further position papers were published by representatives of the Pentagon and the U.S. State Department, aided by other Central European emigrants. In 1946 German teenagers located in camps in Hesse and Bavaria were questioned, as were groups of POWs around the age of seventeen, held in northern France. It was concluded that they were "still totalitarian youth in search of leadership," who now echo "what they consider to be the official views of their current masters," thereby revealing "their totalitarian attitude of implicit and uncritical submission to authority, ingrained by Nazi education and German tradition." Untrained in democratic procedures, "German youth appear to presume that the American leaders will now solve their problems in an authoritarian fashion just as the Nazi leaders proposed to do."[19] Around the same time, Department of State Research Analyst Henry J. Kellermann concluded, more affirmatively and realistically, that the current nihilism of German youth was "largely the result of the breakdown of the Nazi system." Under arms-length American supervision and with German authorities more directly in control, indigenous youth organizations should be created for the purposes of recreation, culture, and religion, "as instrumental to democratic education."[20]

In the months that followed, many other American control officers would work along such positive lines. They could make use of the information they had gathered in their POW camps, located in the United States years before the war was over, and later also in England, France, and western Germany. It is true that often German resistance to re-education was considerable, grounded not only in a persistent idealization of the Führer, but also in clumsy indoctrination methods by the victors.[21] The initial lack of depth in reschooling methodology, however, in time gave way to more effective persuasion, and this was particularly true with regard to youth. By the summer of 1945, for example, approximately 7,000 German boys aged twelve to seventeen were "taught democracy" by Americans in a camp at Attichy in France. They were all captured soldiers and had been purposely separated from their more hardened older comrades. In the camp they studied trades and farming and took commercial courses. School subjects they had long ago been forced to give up were reintroduced to them, with geography by far the most popular. Their instructors were 144 carefully screened non-Nazi prisoners of war. In order to stamp out behavioral patterns of militarism, the boys did not salute, but tipped their caps. Instead of bugle calls, there was Brahms's Lullaby. Military band music was prohibited in favor of orchestral concerts.[22] The Americans were less successful when they mistook groups of former opponents to the Hitler Youth, such as the *Edelweisspiraten,* for hoodlums, dismissing them or placing them in camps without giving them the hearing they deserved. Out of ignorance or spite, local German administrators did nothing to correct this injustice. One such administrator was Professor Friedrich Schaffstein, who continued in a position of juridical authority, inveighing against *Edelweisspiraten* and other Nazi-incriminated groups as he had done before 1945.[23]

General Dwight D. Eisenhower had nullified the Hitler Youth Law of March 25, 1939, requiring total membership in the HJ, on September 28, 1944.[24] This constituted the beginning of political re-education as a program for the Americans, which continued later within the tight occupational framework of OMGUS (Office of Military Government of the United States for Germany). Until the late 1940s even for young people this took place against the intimidating backdrop of the Nuremberg Trials, which were often experienced as an undeserved manifestation of "the right of the victor."[25] The consequences of those trials for Germans from all walks of life were interrogations, endless questionnaires, internment, and regional denazification proceedings. These caused more resentment, for instance when politically suspect students were prevented from registering in the universities.[26] But "re-education" was soon overlapping with and then superseded by "re-orientation," which had been facilitated by a general youth amnesty for political infractions, as early as August 1946 for the U.S. Zone (to be emulated shortly by the British and in May 1947 also by the French authorities, for their respective jurisdictions).[27] In pronouncing their amnesty, the Americans admitted that they wished to concentrate on prosecuting older Nazis, for whom it was easier to prove that they were guilty for the crimes of the Third Reich.[28]

During the process of re-orientation, at the end of which Americans visualized re-integration into a Western value system and full democratization on the parliamentary model, German youths were able to benefit from cultural stimuli which were coming their way through various media.[29] One was the phenomenon of the *Amerika-Häuser,* institutes sponsored by the State Department where young people could go to read in libraries, view films, listen to recordings and the occasional lecture, and take in exhibitions. Although there was an elitist quality to these activities, because ideally the young people had to know English and thus probably came from from the higher social strata, the administrative staff were Germans and one-quarter of the literature was in German. In 1946 the first *Amerika-Haus* was established in Frankfurt; by early 1951 there were already twenty-seven in the largest towns, most of them in the American Zone.[30] The one in Kaiserslautern, founded in 1952 and featuring a bookmobile for the outlying country, sponsored 2,560 events in that city in its first year alone, when close to 300,000 German locals from all walks of life attended.[31]

Since music knows no language barriers, American radio stations became even more important. First and foremost there was the American Forces Network (AFN) run by the Pentagon, which broadcast in English for the military only, delivering U.S.-generated news and programs reflecting American culture. But precisely because the network was not specifically directed toward Germans, they became interested in it like forbidden fruit, and eventually they formed a huge "shadow audience." AFN turned into a cult vehicle for introducing the American way of life all over Europe (wherever GIs were stationed), but particularly in Germany, which already had a strong pre-1933 history of adopting American popular culture. AFN featured cowboy music (which in the 1950s was to evolve into the genre of country and western music) and items from the American hit parade, and these were increasingly cherished by ordinary Germans in their teens and twenties.[32] The more educated and eclectic among them would listen to late-night jazz shows—programs which the British emulated in their region with their own BFN.[33] New German stations influenced by American culture, especially popular-culture programming, were Radio Frankfurt, Radio Stuttgart, Radio Munich, and RIAS Berlin, all in the American Sector.[34] These stations were also obliged to rebroadcast programs from the Voice of America in Washington, D.C., which sponsored overtly political content, and therefore, despite Willis Conover's jazz offerings, they were less frequently listened to, particularly with the commencement of the Cold War in 1947, by which time German youth in the western half of the country was fully on the way to re-orientation.[35]

But things were different at the beginning of the occupation period. The relatively early amnesty for the politically tainted among the youth in the three western zones in 1946–47 could have been viewed as an olive branch extended by former enemies willing to forgive. Yet not all adolescents wished to see it this way. Right after the war, many still professed their admiration for the Führer. National Socialism had not been such a bad idea, if only it had been executed right.[36] Denazification and the Nuremberg Trials caused much resentment. Many remained impervious to the idea, as did Manfred Rommel, the ex-Flakhelfer, that democracy of the Western type could work with Germans.[37] In the first few postwar years, an appreciable number of adolescents were still exhibiting racist patterns of prejudice, as when a boy with a KLV background found himself spitting at a displaced Polish worker in Hanover, a captured nurse resented having to work side by side with American Jews, and the physical proximity of black soldiers was reported as being offensive.[38] Abject hatred was reserved for the Soviets, who were thought to have murdered Polish officers in a forest near Katyn—a crime for which many Western occupiers still held the Nazis responsible, wrongly as it later turned out.[39] With cynicism, German boys and girls in the so-called Tri-Zone looked across the unfortified border with eastern Germany, where the blue-shirted FDJ was being built up, so it seemed, on the fascist model of the Hitler Youth. They had merely changed their shirts.[40] Others smarted under the stigma of former SS incorporation, especially when, toward the end of the war, they had been conscripted against their will.[41]

Unreconstructed university students were a special problem, for they could use sophistry in anti-West arguments. In Bonn, still in 1945, Stephen Spender encountered Herr Haecker, a student who claimed to be not a Nazi, but a nationalist. Although Hitler's anti-Semitism was a great mistake, he said, there was no denying that the Jews were an "inferior section of the population." Haecker rushed to explain: "Race is real. We Germans really do belong to a Nordic stock which is different from and superior to the Southern and, especially, the Eastern peoples."[42] In Heidelberg, lectures given by the philosopher Karl Jaspers on German collective guilt were greeted with hostile responses, and when a medical professor mentioned a disease affecting only Jews and said that one could not observe this disease any more, he was interrupted by raucous laughter and the pounding of feet.[43] In 1946 U.S. Research Analyst Kellermann, too, found that there were hotbeds of student chauvinism in the universities of Erlangen, Hamburg, Jena, Göttingen, and Aachen—largely senior HJ graduates and frustrated veterans of the armed forces.[44] It was in Göttingen that a fascist Wiking Youth group was started in 1947, as an adjunct to the neo-Nazi Deutsche Reichspartei led by Adolf von Thadden, because here the British had allowed the re-establishment of new youth groups, politically oriented ones included. But other, democratic-minded youth leaders were alarmed, and on their urging the British authorities had the Wiking Youth dissolved.[45]

Since these events occurred at the very beginning of the military occupation phase and had no lasting consequences, it is fair to conclude that the resurgence of Nazism was not a major problem in the country at least during the second half of the 1940s, and certainly as far as German youth was concerned. By 1951, when the newly charted Federal Republic was set on its democratic course, an American-conducted opinion poll of the population found that in the new polity, only 10 percent would applaud the rise of a new Nazi Party, while 4 percent would actively support it. Even though youths appear to have been pushing these percentages upward, they still did not constitute a danger to the new democratic order.[46]

In 1945, the youngest members of the "Nazi Regime Youth Cohort" were eleven years old, and the oldest twenty-nine. In 1950, when conditions in Germany were settling down and these youths along with them, they were sixteen and thirty-four respectively.[47] Within this crucial five-year period, these children and young adults, shattered morale aside, adjusted to a German society which was initially shaken by the effects of destruction, the loss of loved ones, unsteady political governance, economic disruptions, and a breakdown in the public healthcare system. In the late 1940s and throughout the 1950s, a number of American and German social scientists held that youths in Germany were apathetic and, in regard to society and politics, "passive and usually still uninterested."[48] Dismissing the community around them completely, they maintained an interest only in themselves, in their immediate "personal and economic problems."[49] Because they had been misled and disappointed by an older generation, they mistrusted any authority other than their own, even if they knew that to be shaky. "The great majority is still waiting and watching—not so much out of indecision as because of the fact that they don't want to be 'wrong' again in three, five or ten years. German youth is still in the transient stage between yesterday and tomorrow."[50]

One German scholar who pursued this thesis relentlessly was the sociologist Helmut Schelsky. To describe youths well into the 1960s, he coined the catchy phrase "The Skeptical Generation," popularized in articles, lectures, and a book with that title published originally in 1957.[51] Schelsky wrote that this skepticism of youth was paired with a crass egotism that was practical, realistic, and totally centered on materialism. These youths were not interested in community, although they constantly worked out and revised clever schemes of social adaptation for the sake of everyday survival. Taking a cue from the Flakhelfer generation included in his target group, Schelsky denied these young Germans maturity, which, he alleged, they had lost by being forced to grow into adulthood too fast. According to him, there reigned a "skepticism against and repudiation of the politics of the past as well as the present, a distrust of political ideologies and theories, a 'without us' attitude toward all public and societal demands, so as to be able to concentrate on the private and professional, on areas manageable in terms of one's own powers of judgment and responsibility."[52] In writing this, Schelsky had his own ax to grind, for as a former Nazi Party member (1937) who once officiated at the SS University in Strasbourg, he viewed the Third Reich in retrospect as the structural monolith the

Nazi leadership had claimed it to be, implying the highest degree of totalitarian pressure on youth. The result, he held fatalistically, was that they as a group were stultified and stunned.[53]

To a certain extent, contemporary examples seem to prove Schelsky right.[54] In its first issue, on February 21, 1946, the soon-to-be-prominent German weekly *Die Zeit* printed a statement authored by Ernst Samhaber, which contained a collective vote of non-confidence in the newly founded United Nations: "We do not trust the powers which constitute the U.N. They have faced us in war for six years . . . Neither do we trust the men who represent the U.N. They are human beings who are subject to human weaknesses, to fear, suspicion, passions, and to error."[55] At a political forum at Munich University shortly thereafter, attended by outside observers such as André Gide and the historian Walter L. Dorn of OMGUS, students voiced their ongoing pessimism. One in particular, the fine arts major Annemarie Krapp, who claimed to have left the BDM voluntarily, was so outspoken that she incurred the anger of many in the audience. She said, "I would gladly say to you that I believe in democracy, but I would be lying. It is not that I reject democratic ideas; on the contrary, not only do I have the best intentions, but I even wish to be convinced." But how could she form an opinion? "Are we sure today that perhaps in a few years we will not again be called criminals, because we are now supporting one of the existing political parties?"[56] These sentiments were shared by many other students, one of whom, Jost Hermand, now at the University of Wisconsin, admits to never tuning in to the radio for news or reading political commentaries in the papers at the time because of his total mistrust of politics.[57] But young people outside of Gymnasien and universities were equally guarded. Subjects of indifference ranged from politics to the military to moral guilt to human rights; some downplayed the media, others shunned social bonds; man was assumed to be evil.[58]

Concurring with Schelsky in 1958, a female observer from Hamburg agreed that German young people were "indolent, superficial, weary of government and materialistic."[59] However, beyond an otherwise pessimistic verdict, this analyst was one of the few who attempted to differentiate, in this case in terms of a division of the generational cohorts. She argued that those youths born before 1930, having been exposed to National Socialism the longest, were the ones most likely to have been drawn into the line of fire at the front, or used in dangerous home defenses. Hence their level of consciousness about social or political matters was thought to be higher than that of the generation born after 1930, who had also been infected by National Socialism, but, since they were still children, not as seminally.[60]

Such a qualifying view was supported by others, notably Helmut Schmidt, who maintained that all those who had been children before the Third Reich were, of necessity, lacking "any education toward democracy."[61] Some pointed out that one reason this older HJ cohort seemed so indifferent to the world around it was that unlike the members of the younger HJ cohort, who were still or again being taken care of by parents and teachers, they had had to fend for themselves in largely adverse circumstances, to the point where nothing else could matter.[62] In the immediate aftermath of May 1945, the older HJ cohort's attitude was based not on global disinterest, but, as many were claiming, on feelings of shock which had rendered them furtive and jaded. However, as young people found their way back into a society that was being newly anchored in democracy and, eventually, economic stability, they began to find time and opportunity to make up for the losses and disruptions of their adolescence, and in time they became mature citizens.[63]

Moreover, when questioned further, young veterans admitted to being disinterested not so much in matters of politics in the widest sense as in anything having to do with *party* politics, as in the Nazi Party. Having grown up mostly in a one-party system, they regarded politics as synonymous with the rule of a single autocratic party, and they had to be taught the values of multi-party pluralism. That of course was the essence of parliamentary democracy of the Western type, something which had been tried in the Weimar Republic and which, as some of the oldest ex-Hitler Youths might still remember, had often been vilified in Hitler's speeches.[64]

One interesting barometer of this gradual change toward normal social and political awareness among youth was membership in new post-1945 youth organizations, at least in the western zones, as they were gradually authorized by the Allied Forces. Even in the short period from April 1946, when youth clubs were again permitted, to February 1948, when the founding of the Federal Republic was near, membership in them increased six-fold, reaching just under a million and a half in the U.S. Zone. Sports clubs drew the majority of young people, even more than religious ones; trade union groups were next; and the *Falken,* hiking groups supported by the reborn Social Democratic Party (SPD), constituted the largest outright political formation.[65] That a left-wing youth group would be the foremost political band in a West German landscape gradually dominated by Konrad Adenauer's home-grown conservatives, spoke well for former Hitler Youths as future guarantors of democracy.

Yet contrary to what the new Federal German President, Theodor Heuss, said publicly in 1950, the overwhelming majority of the newly constituted youth leagues held no connections to the moribund Weimar youth groups, which had been largely anti-democratic and thus had sold out so easily to Schirach.[66] Baldur von Schirach, Artur Axmann, and Adolf Hitler played critical roles in what happened to German youth between 1933 and 1950. Even though they could not convince all youths, they had made a credible start in generating a functional elite for a totalitarian Reich of a thousand years, despite many inconsistencies in their regime structure. The regime's lethal power was proved during a war of aggression of nearly six years, when it was obvious that without the recruits that Schirach, Axmann, Rommel, and Himmler had trained, however haphazardly, they would not have had an army of many millions of men and hundreds of thousands of women to subjugate and kill persons they considered aliens on a grand scale. No lack of prior planning, no contradictions in a heterogeneous governing structure could prevent those crimes from being instigated or stop them once they were under way. And the increasing discomfort of a youth generation that was placed inside this structure and, on the whole, performed as expected almost to the end, likewise could do nothing to stop those crimes.

In the end, Hitler made short shrift of youth. One day before he killed himself, despite the fulsome words of praise for youth he had spoken many times before, he wrote simply in his political testament that he was about to die happy with the thought of youth on his mind, a youth that had carried his name and had not shied away from action.[67] Axmann did not even bother with such a commonplace before or during his selfish retreat from Berlin, which was shielded by hundreds of his charges. Instead, he went into hiding, only to start one of the earliest neo-Nazi groups by 1946.[68] The BDM's chief, Jutta Rüdiger, also remained an unreconstructed Nazi after internment.[69] Hitler neglected to mention either Axmann or Rüdiger in his will.

Nor did he mention Baldur von Schirach. The pompous founder of the Nazi youth organizations, and their mentor until the end, at first wanted to defend Vienna as its Gauleiter. But unlike many of his young lieutenants he despaired early and, disguised with glasses and a moustache, fled to Schwaz in the Austrian Tyrol. He called himself Richard Falk, pretending to be an author. Always a spinner of phrases, he was now working on a novel called "The Mysteries of Mira Loy." But in early June he thought better of this and surrendered to the Americans, whom he addressed in a southern drawl.[70]

It was at the Nuremberg Trials in 1946 where Schirach, as one of the main Nazi defendants, decided to do what the Colonel in Wolfgang Borchert's play had trouble comprehending: to accept the sole responsibility. "It is my fault to have educated youth in the service of a man who was a murderer of millions," he confessed. "I believed in this man. This is all I can say in my defense, or to explain my actions. I bore the responsibility for youth, I held it in my charge, and hence I alone bear the guilt for these juveniles. The young generation is guiltless."[71] Schirach's rhetoric was disingenuous, calculated to persuade the High

Court to decide not to condemn him on charges of having misled German youth, because he appeared to be contrite. His calculation bore fruit, for he did not suffer the death sentence. Instead he received twenty years of incarceration, not for any crimes against or on behalf of youth, but for having assisted in the deportation of Jews from Vienna.[72] His words, however, only compounded the central problem regarding the responsibility or guilt of German youth from 1933 to 1945. The responsibility that Schirach wanted to claim for himself to exonerate youth did not exist as the kind of moral issue he made it out to be. Schirach had his own responsibility, which he could never shed; there was no way for him to assume the collective responsibility of his charges.

For Schirach's underlings were answerable on their own behalf. In the case of the younger and older generations of Hitler Youth and the young armed forces veterans who now found themselves adrift, however, guilt could not be apportioned that easily. This is not to say that most of them were not complicit in the tragedies they helped to cause as members of the Hitler Youth and Hitler's armies, including the SS. Even if they were merely small cogs in the huge war machinery, or in the intricate system of persecution and mass liquidation, they had become a part of these systems, helping to guarantee their terrible functionality. That most of them knew this after May 1945 is demonstrated by their attitudes of shock and their refusal, at least at first, to become engaged in any civic matters. Their own discussion, insofar as it happened, of their possible status as "victims" was strongly indicative of a bad conscience, of wishing to explain away any part of their biographies dating from before the Nazis' humiliating surrender.

While the issue of complicity for all youth in the Third Reich is one the historian can have little doubt about, the question of moral guilt is harder to come to grips with. The degree of guilt that any Hitler Youths possessed, whether boys or girls in HJ camps, whether young men or women fighting at the fronts, depended on their age, their hierarchical position in Nazi governance, and, ultimately, on the sum total of activities of a criminal nature they became engaged in. These activities would have included the Nazi indoctrination of their peers for imperialistic ends or what later would be subsumed under war crimes, or, with reference to Hitler's specific annihilation warfare, "crimes against humanity": serving in concentration camps; setting Polish villages ablaze; guarding Soviet prisoners in starvation camps; undue cruelty against enemies in hand-to-hand combat; and, the worst atrocity of all, assisting in the genocide of Gypsies and Jews. It is clear that many actions in this category could not have been undertaken by some, as they were still too young or were physically removed from the scenes of crime—for example, a sixteen-year-old Hitler Youth who was drafted in 1944 and never saw combat, or a young woman who served as an auxiliary telegrapher in her home town. But in a martial society where the entire youth culture was systematically contaminated with concepts of intolerance and oppression of the physically weak and hatred against those who were of a different "race," there could hardly have been a Hitler Youth who had not learned to adopt notions of power over those below him, since he was emulating those above him powerful enough to have taught him. Such was the chain of command, militarily, mentally, and morally. Hence there was many an eleven-year-old Pimpf who in 1934, after only one year in the Hitler Youth, had learned to humiliate the ten-year-olds who had just joined, and there were large numbers of flak helpers of both genders at the fronts who in the spring of 1945 made sure to take no prisoners. In 1943, there existed tens of thousands of Waffen-SS soldiers who were breaking universal laws of humanity; they had been indoctrinated in the Hitler Youth as juveniles and, through its racist tenets, now became guilty. And there were many HJ judges who officiated while still in their twenties, after having moved through the HJ ranks and then obtained a law degree; they used as their yardstick the perverted legal code of a criminal regime, for example when they were condemning youthful dissenters to solitary confinement, and thus they themselves became criminal. By 1945, among the surviving youths, Nazi ideology often was still so prevalent that, as in the encounter between Spender and the Bonn student Haecker, a sense of German racial superiority was unshakable. For others, like the Munich student Annemarie Krapp, it was the knowledge of having been misled not without their own complicity that caused them to experience a feeling of guilt, while cautioning, at the same time, against any further commitment to future German politics.

Thus Wolfgang Borchert, who knew about these liabilities, was portraying a psychological truth when he pictured the Colonel in his play as a man who just did not understand. According to the Colonel, by the military as well as the Nazi leadership principle, responsibility toward subordinates or for actions taken was something that everyone in the hierarchy had to bear for himself; it could not be passed back. This is why Borchert himself, through his play's character Sergeant Beckmann, in the final analysis could not shake off his own responsibility or perhaps even his guilt for the death of the men he had led in a sortie against the Russians (or for other deeds he might have committed in war). He himself bore this burden. As Borchert rightly saw, all of this had been the consequence of children not having been taught to ask the right questions beforehand, and of their superiors, including parents, teachers, and politicians, not ever feeling motivated to offer appropriate answers.[73] Indeed, some of those questions were at least as old as the Weimar Republic, which in its last stages had caused young people to wonder about their own and their parents' role in the midst of psychological tension, political turmoil, and economic misery, many of these generated by the First World War.

Eventually, German youth, partly guilt-ridden and partly disenchanted but hardly innocent, resolved to help in the reconstruction of democracy in West Germany, thereby also building a sound new economic base for the state and for themselves. The mechanisms by which this happened within a relatively short time span still call for more explanation. What is clear, however, is that much of the democratic government under Konrad Adenauer, himself a former sufferer under the Nazi regime yet a politial reactionary, was compromised, since not only his own party, the Christian Democratic Union (CDU), but also the so-called Free Democrats (FDP) and, especially, smaller right-wing groupings harbored many old Nazis. It goes without saying that Hitler Youth veterans and one-time Wehrmacht soldiers constituted majorities in all of these parties, even the oppositional SPD.[74] Possibly because questions about complicity or guilt were just too vexing and detracted from the path of economic progress, but also because they wanted to erase the memory of often joyful, but later more bitter, days under Nazi rule, middle-aged Germans in the 1960s not only became successful at their jobs but even helped to maintain a viable democracy on the British, French, or American model.

In the early postwar phase, the silence of the younger generation about the past had served an anesthetizing purpose. But by the late 1970s, when these former Hitler boys and Hitler girls were becoming grandparents and their past appeared less threatening, they started to recollect, and many sat down to write their memoirs—a process that is still ongoing. It was the trauma of their knowledge, about the rule of force and the intolerance engendered by a totalitarian dictatorship, that had kept them from remembering earlier, when they had still been much too close to shame and disaster. As they grew older and looked back, they found it easier to face the memories of their place in this dictatorship, including the contributions that they themselves had made—a dictatorship which oppressed, maimed, and killed millions, and, if they were honest enough to admit it, had damaged their own souls.

Abbreviations

ADJ	Archiv der Deutschen Jugendbewegung, Burg Ludwigstein
AFN	American Forces Network
AHS	Adolf-Hitler-Schulen
Antifa	*Antifaschistische Junge Garde*
APA	Author's Private Archive
ARL	Institut für Rechtswissenschaften, Arbeitsgruppe Jugend und Strafrecht, Universität Lüneburg
BA	Bundesarchiv Koblenz
BAB	Bundesarchiv Berlin (records from the former Berlin Document Center)
BAF	Bundesarchiv Freiburg—Militärarchiv
BBC	British Broadcasting Corporation
BDM	Bund Deutscher Mädel (League of German Girls in the HJ)
BFN	British Forces Network
BHSAM	Bayerisches Hauptstaatsarchiv München
CDU	Christlich-Demokratische Union (Christian Democratic Union)
CM	Allgemeine Korrespondenz, Carl Orff-Zentrum, München
DAF	Deutsche Arbeitsfront (German Labor Front)
DAOW	Dokumentationsstelle des Österreichischen Widerstandes, Wien
DNVP	Deutschnationale Volkspartei (German National People's Party)
FAD	Freiwilliger Arbeitsdienst (Voluntary Labor Service)

FDJ	Freie Deutsche Jugend (Free German Youth)
FDP	Freie Demokratische Partei (Free Democratic Party)
Gestapo	Geheime Staatspolizei (Secret State Police)
GStAM	Geheimes Staatsarchiv München
HHSAW	Hessisches Hauptstaatsarchiv Wiesbaden
HIS	Hoover Institution, Stanford
Hiwis	*Hilfswillige*
HJ	Hitler-Jugend (Hitler Youth)
IfZ	Institut für Zeitgeschichte München
KJVD	*Kommunistischer Jugendverband Deutschlands* (German Communist Youth League)
KLV	Kinderlandverschickung (Save the Children in the Country program)
KPD	Kommunistische Partei Deutschlands (German Communist Party)
NHSA	Niedersächsisches Hauptstaatsarchiv Hannover
NPEA	Nationalpolitische Erziehungsanstalten (National Political Educational Institutions)
NS	*Nationalsozialistisch* (National Socialist)
NSAO	Niedersächsisches Staatsarchiv Oldenburg
NSAW	Niedersächsisches Staatsarchiv Wolfenbüttel
NSDAP	Nationalsozialistische Deutsche Arbeiterpartei (Nazi Party)
NSF	Nationalsozialistische Frauenschaft (Nazi Women's League)
NSKK	Nationalsozialistisches Kraftfahrkorps (Nazi Motor League)
NSLB	Nationalsozialistischer Lehrerbund (Nazi Teachers' League)
OLA	Oberösterreichisches Landesarchiv Linz
OMGUS	Office of Military Government of the United States for Germany
RAD	Reichsarbeitsdienst (Reich Labor Service)
RIAS	Radio im Amerikanischen Sektor [Berlin]
SA	Sturmabteilungen (storm troopers/Brown Shirts)
SAB	Staatsarchiv Bremen
SAF	Staatsarchiv Freiburg
SAG	Staatliches Archivlager Göttingen, Gauarchiv Ostpreussen (Niedersächsisches Staatsarchiv Bückeburg)

SAH	Staatsarchiv Hamburg
SAL	Staatsarchiv Ludwigsburg
SAM	Staatsarchiv München
SAMs	Staatsarchiv Münster
SAN	Staatsarchiv Nürnberg
SAND	Staatsarchiv Neuburg an der Donau
SD	Sicherheitsdienst (Security Service of the SS)
SPD	Sozialdemokratische Partei Deutschlands (German Social Democratic Party)
SRD	HJ-Streifendienst (Security Service of the HJ)
SS	Schutzstaffel (Black Shirts)
StAM	Stadtarchiv München
Stuka	*Sturzkampf-Flugzeug*
TGI	Elke Föhlich, ed., *Die Tagebücher von Joseph Goebbels: Sämtliche Fragmente,* 5 vols. (Munich, 1987)
TGII	Elke Fröhlich, ed., *Die Tagebücher von Joseph Goebbels, Teil II: Diktate, 1941–1945,* 16 vols. (Munich, 1993–1996)
Ufa	Universum Film-Aktiengesellschaft
U.N.	United Nations
WE	Wehrertüchtigungslager

Notes

1. "Make Way, You Old Ones!"

1. Hermann Graml, "Integration und Entfremdung: Inanspruchnahme durch Staatsjugend und Dienstpflicht," in Ute Benz and Wolfgang Benz, eds., *Sozialisation und Traumatisierung: Kinder in der Zeit des Nationalsozialismus* (Frankfurt am Main, 1992), 74–79. (All translations from German-language sources are those of the author.)
2. Margarete Hannsmann, *Der helle Tag bricht an: Ein Kind wird Nazi* (Munich, 1984).
3. Melita Maschmann, *Fazit: Kein Rechtfertigungsversuch,* 5th ed. (Stuttgart, 1964); Edgar Gielsdorf, *Vom Christkind eine Landsknechtstrommel* (Cologne, 1994); Renate Finckh, *Mit uns zieht die neue Zeit* (Baden-Baden, 1979).
4. Ian Kershaw, *Popular Opinion and Political Dissent in the Third Reich: Bavaria, 1933–1945* (Oxford, 1983); Kershaw, *The "Hitler Myth": Image and Reality in the Third Reich* (Oxford, 1987).
5. Michael H. Kater, *Studentenschaft und Rechtsradikalismus in Deutschland, 1918–1933: Eine sozialgeschichtliche Studie zur Bildungskrise in der Weimarer Republik* (Hamburg, 1975), 108; Ursula Baumann, *Vom Recht auf den eigenen Tod: Die Geschichte des Suizids vom 18. bis zum 20. Jahrhundert* (Weimar, 2001), 326, 330; Reinhold Schairer, *Die akademische Berufsnot: Tatsachen und Auswege* (Jena, [1932]), 6.
6. Peter Loewenberg, *Decoding the Past: The Psychohistorical Approach* (Berkeley, 1985), 251.
7. For an example involving a very young child, toward the end of the Republic, see Hildegard Morgenthal, *"Rotkopf, die Ecke brennt, Feuerwehr kommt angerennt": Leben in der NS-Zeit und zwei Leben danach* (Frankfurt am Main, 2000), 88.

8. Ute Frevert, *Women in German History: From Bourgeois Emancipation to Sexual Liberation* (New York, 1989), 198.

9. On the economic upheavals, see Gerald D. Feldman, *The Great Disorder: Politics, Economics, and Society in the German Inflation, 1914–1924* (New York, 1997); Harold James, *The German Slump: Politics and Economics, 1924–1936* (New York, 1986); and the articles in Ian Kershaw, ed., *Weimar: Why Did German Democracy Fail?* (London, 1990). On unemployment especially among youth, see Manfred Hermanns, *Jugendarbeitslosigkeit seit der Weimarer Republik: Ein sozialgeschichtlicher und soziologischer Vergleich* (Opladen, 1990), 16–21, 77–80, and the report of social worker Albert Lamm, *Betrogene Jugend: Aus einem Erwerbslosenheim* (Berlin, 1932).

10. Loewenberg, 249, 254–62, 268, 270, 278–79; Kater, 43–73; Kater, "Generationskonflikt als Entwicklungsfaktor in der NS-Bewegung vor 1933," *Geschichte und Gesellschaft* 11 (1985): 224–229. See also a contemporary source, Leopold Dingräve, *Wo steht die junge Generation?* (Jena, 1931).

11. See Peter Suhrkamp, "Söhne ohne Väter und Lehrer: Die Situation der bürgerlichen Jugend," *Neue Rundschau* 43 (1932): 681–696.

12. Peter Gay, *Weimar Culture: The Outsider as Insider* (New York, 1968). See also Werner Hasenclever, *Der Sohn: Ein Drama in fünf Akten* (Leipzig, 1914); Franz Werfel, *Nicht der Mörder, der Ermordete ist schuldig: Eine Novelle* (Munich, 1920); Ernst Glaeser, *Jahrgang 1902* (Potsdam, 1928). Otto Dix and George Grosz caricatured many of the power mongers of the older generations who were blocking the path to progress for the younger ones. See M. Kay Flavell, *George Grosz: A Biography* (New Haven, 1988). For this theme in the music establishment of the Weimar Republic, see my article "The Revenge of the Fathers: The Demise of Modern Music at the End of the Weimar Republic," *German Studies Review* 15 (1992): 295–315.

13. Rudolf Kneip, *Jugend der Weimarer Zeit: Handbuch der Jugendverbände, 1919–1938* (Frankfurt am Main, 1974), 157–158, 215; Peter D. Stachura, *The German Youth Movement, 1900–1945: An Interpretative and Documentary History* (London, 1981), 64, 111.

14. Walter Z. Laqueur, *Young Germany: A History of the German Youth Movement* (New York, 1962), 10–83 (quotes, 3–4).

15. See Modris Eksteins's trenchant analyses in *Rites of Spring: The Great War and the Birth of the Modern Age* (Boston, 1989), 95–207. On England, see also Paul Fussell, *The Great War and Modern Memory* (London, 1977).

16. Laqueur, 87–98; Stachura, 34–37.

17. Karl Unruh, *Langemarck: Legende und Wirklichkeit* (Koblenz, 1986); Werner Kindt, ed., *Die deutsche Jugendbewegung, 1920 bis 1933: Die bündische Zeit* (Düsseldorf, 1974), 74–75, 139–144, 159, 288, 352, 423–424.

18. Bernhard Schneider, *Daten zur Geschichte der Jugendbewegung* (Bad Godesberg, 1965), 36.

19. An excellent overview can be found in Felix Raabe, *Die Bündische Jugend: Ein Beitrag zur Geschichte der Weimarer Republik* (Stuttgart, 1961).

20. Stachura, 40, 42, 105–108.

21. Kneip, 39, 136–137.

22. Laqueur, 144.

23. Howard Becker, *Vom Barette schwankt die Feder: Die Geschichte der deutschen Jugendbewegung* (Wiesbaden, 1949), 109; Michael H. Kater, "Bürgerliche Jugendbewegung und Hitlerjugend in Deutschland von 1926 bis 1939," *Archiv für Sozialgeschichte* 17 (1977): 149–150.

24. Gregor Strasser quoted in Loewenberg, 250.

25. Gottfried Neesse, "Der Jugendführer des Deutschen Reiches," *Archiv des öffentlichen Rechts* 26 (1935): 203; *Hitler-Jugend, 1933–1943: Die Chronik eines Jahrzehnts* (Berlin, [1943]), 13–14; Kater, "Generationskonflikt," 239–240.

26. Peter D. Stachura, *Nazi Youth in the Weimar Republic* (Santa Barbara, Calif., 1975); Kater, "Jugendbewegung," 146–148; Kater, "Generationskonflikt," 237.

27. Loewenberg, 478–479; Kater, "Generationskonflikt," 232, 240; Kater, *Studentenschaft*, 111–205.

28. Hans Gerth, "The Nazi Party: Its Leadership and Composition," *American Journal of Sociology* 45 (1940): 529–530; Michael H. Kater, *The Nazi Party: A Social Profile of Members and Leaders, 1919–1945* (Cambridge, Mass., 1983), 139–144, 230–231, 233–236.

29. Jürgen Falter, *Hitlers Wähler* (Munich, 1991), 152–154.

30. The detailed explanation of Hitler's entire pre-1933 political strategy is still unsurpassed in Dietrich Orlow, *The History of the Nazi Party: 1919–1933* (Pittsburgh, 1969). Also see Michael H. Kater, "Der NS-Studentenbund von 1926 bis 1928: Randgruppe zwischen Hitler und Strasser," *Vierteljahrshefte für Zeitgeschichte* 22 (1974): 173–174.

31. Hitler cited in Kater, *Studentenschaft*, 118.

32. Albert Speer, *Erinnerungen*, 8th ed. (Berlin, 1970), 137. For September 1933, see Dietrich Orlow, *The History of the Nazi Party: 1933–1945* (Pittsburgh, 1973), 81.

33. Kater, *Nazi Party,* 235; Martin Broszat, *Der Staat Hitlers: Grundlegung und Entwicklung seiner inneren Verfassung* (Munich, 1969), 56; Peter Hüttenberger, *Die Gauleiter: Studie zum Wandel des Machtgefüges in der NSDAP* (Stuttgart, 1969), 200–201. For Nazi dread of this, see entry for May 24, 1942, *TGII,* vol. 4, 354; and for April 19, 1943, *TGII,* vol. 8, 131.

34. For a Nazi voice, see Hans Spethmann, ed., *Die Stadt Essen: Das Werden und Wirken einer Grossstadt an der Ruhr* (Berlin, 1938), 312. Critically: John E. Knodel, *The Decline of Fertility in Germany, 1871–1939* (Princeton, 1974).

35. Joseph Goebbels, "Erziehung und Führerschicht," *Nationalsozialistisches Jahrbuch* (1930): 179.

36. Gregor Strasser cited in Jürgen Reulecke, "Jugendprotest—Ein Kennzeichen des 20. Jahrhunderts?" in Dieter Dowe, ed., *Jugendprotest und Generationenkonflikt in Europa im 20. Jahrhundert: Deutschland, England, Frankreich und Italien im Vergleich* (Bonn, 1986), 2.

37. Karl Mannheim, "Das Problem der Generationen," *Kölner Vierteljahrshefte für Soziologie* 7 (1928): 157–185, 309–330. Cf. Alan B. Spitzer, "The Historical Problem of Generations," *American Historical Review* 78 (1973): 1353–1385; Walter Jaide, *Eine neue Generation? Eine Untersuchung über Werthaltungen und Leitbilder der Jugendlichen* (Munich, 1961); Michael Mitterauer, *Sozialgeschichte der Jugend* (Frankfurt am Main, 1986), 48–50, 247; Christopher Hausmann, "Heranwachsen im 'Dritten Reich': Möglichkeiten und Besonderheiten jugendlicher Sozialisation im Spiegel autobiographischer Zeugnisse," *Geschichte in Wissenschaft und Unterricht* 13 (1990): 607–618.

38. Erhard Eppler, *Als Wahrheit verordnet wurde: Briefe an meine Enkelin,* 3rd ed. (Frankfurt am Main, 1995), 104.

2. Serving in the Hitler Youth

1. *Deutsches Lesebuch für Volksschulen: 3. und 4. Schuljahr,* 2nd ed. (Lahr, 1938), 264–265.

2. For improvisation as a rule of governance in the Third Reich, see the representative essays in Christian Leitz, ed., *The Third Reich: The Essential Readings* (Oxford, 1999).

3. Peter D. Stachura, *Nazi Youth in the Weimar Republic* (Santa Barbara, Calif., 1975); Heinz Boberach, *Jugend unter Hitler* (Düsseldorf, 1982), 19.

4. Stachura; Baldur von Schirach, *Ich glaubte an Hitler* (Hamburg, 1967), 101–102, 153.

5. Von Schirach, 153; Arno Klönne, *Hitlerjugend: Die Jugend und ihre Organisation im Dritten Reich* (Hanover, 1960), 11.

6. Von Schirach, 7–8, 11–12. On Weimar at the turn of the century, see Laird M. Easton, *The Red Count: The Life and Times of Harry Kessler* (Berkeley, 2002), 145–156.

7. Von Schirach, 18–22, 28 (quotes).

8. Ibid., 33, 40–61 (quote, 59).

9. Ibid., 101–102; 159; Boberach, 21. In Nuremberg Schirach mentioned 100,000 youths (Schirach cited for May 23, 1946, in *Der Prozess gegen die Hauptkriegsverbrecher vor dem Internationalen Militärgerichtshof Nürnberg, 14. November 1945 – 1. Oktober 1946* [Munich, 1984], vol. 13, 412).

10. Werner Klose, *Generation im Gleichschritt: Ein Dokumentarbericht* (Oldenburg, 1964), 19.

11. Boberach, 21; Jay W. Baird, *To Die for Germany: Heroes in the Nazi Pantheon* (Bloomington, 1990), 108–129.

12. Von Schirach, 190, 264–265, 269–271; Harald Scholtz, *NS-Ausleseschulen: Internatsschulen als Herrschaftsmittel des Führerstaates* (Göttingen, 1973), 285. On Axmann, see Robert Wistrich, *Who's Who in Nazi Germany* (New York, 1982), 7.

13. Klönne, 15; Von Schirach, 193, 232; Matthias von Hellfeld and Arno Klönne, *Die betrogene Generation: Jugend in Deutschland unter dem Faschismus* (Cologne, 1985), 35.

14. Harry Pross, *Vor und nach Hitler: Zur deutschen Sozialpathologie* (Olten, 1962), 127–128.

15. Helmut Schmidt in Schmidt et al., *Kindheit und Jugend unter Hitler,* 2nd ed. (Berlin, 1992), 203.

16. Winfried Speitkamp, *Jugend in der Neuzeit: Deutschland vom 16. bis zum 20. Jahrhundert* (Göttingen, 1998), 229.

17. *Das junge Volk* (Aug. 6, 1933): 2; ibid. (Sept. 15, 1933): 2.

18. Report, [July 1934], IfZ, MA-1190/1, FN 1505861-64.

19. Hans-Christian Brandenburg, *Die Geschichte der HJ: Wege und Irrwege einer Generation* (Cologne, 1968), 195–196, 202–203; Matthias von Hellfeld, *Bündische Jugend und Hitlerjugend: Zur Geschichte von Anpassung und Widerstand, 1930–1939* (Cologne, 1987), 169–170.

20. Rietzel to Janssen, July 11, 1934, IfZ, MA-1190/1, FN 1505872-73; Brandenburg, 196.

21. *Vorschriftenhandbuch der Hitler-Jugend (VHB.HJ)* (Jan. 1, 1942), 2: 1068–1070, (IfZ, Db/44.01).

22. ADJ, A166/1.

23. Jürgen W. Falter and Michael H. Kater, "Wähler und Mitglieder der NSDAP: Neue Forschungsergebnisse zur Soziographie des Nationalsozialismus, 1925 bis 1933," *Geschichte und Gesellschaft* 19 (1993): 155–177.

24. "Verordnungsblatt der Reichsjugendführung," Dec. 19, 1933, BA, NSD/43/1; Detlev Peukert, "Protest und Widerstand von Jugendlichen im Dritten Reich," in Richard Löwenthal and Patrick von zur Mühlen, eds., *Widerstand und Verweigerung in Deutschland, 1933 bis 1945* (Bonn, 1982), 191.

25. Manfred Priepke, *Die evangelische Jugend im Dritten Reich, 1933–1936* (Hanover, 1960).

26. Report, [July 1934], as cited in n. 18; Speitkamp, 230–231.

27. Heinrich Roth, *Katholische Jugend in der NS-Zeit unter besonderer Berücksichtigung des Katholischen Jungmännerverbandes: Daten und Dokumente* (Düsseldorf, 1959); Lawrence D. Walker, *Hitler Youth and Catholic Youth, 1933–1936: A Study in Totalitarian Conquest* (Washington, D.C., 1970).

28. Weichinger to Bezirksaussenstelle Bad Reichenhall, May 23, 1934, SAM, LRA/30655. See also the material in SAM, NSDAP/361.

29. Peukert, 192–193.

30. Von Schirach, 232; Gerhard Klemer, *Jugendstrafrecht und Hitler-Jugend: Stellung und Aufgaben der Hitler-Jugend in der Jugendstrafrechtspflege,* 2nd ed. (Berlin, 1941), 24–25; Franz Baaden, *Jugendverfassung und Jugenddienstpflicht* (Berlin, 1943), 23, 25, 32–33.

31. See Von Schirach, 190–191.

32. "Gesetz über die Hitlerjugend," in Heinrich Schönfelder, ed., *Deutsche Reichsgesetze: Sammlung des Verfassungs-, Gemein-, Straf- und Verfahrensrechts für den täglichen Gebrauch,* 13th ed. (Munich, 1943), 1a: 1.

33. Ibid., 2.

34. Calculations based on figures in Von Hellfeld and Klönne, 35.

35. Statistics for Vechta, July 28, 1934, NSAO, 134/1157.

36. Peter Pahmeyer and Lutz van Spankeren, *Die Hitlerjugend in Lippe (1933–1939): Totalitäre Erziehung zwischen Anspruch und Wirklichkeit* (Bielefeld, 1998), 124.

37. *Deutschland-Berichte der Sozialdemokratischen Partei Deutschlands (Sopade), 1934–1940* (Salzhausen, 1980), vol. 2 (1935), 698.

38. Pressenotiz, [Oct. 1935], NSAW, 12 A Neu, 13 h/19596.

39. List of pupils in the HJ, [Brunswick . . . Bad Harzburg], Feb. 15, 1936, NSAW, 12 A Neu, 13/19598; HJ statistics for Bavarian elementary and trade schools, [spring 1936], NSAO, 134/1158.

40. Mergenthaler, "Stärke der Hitlerjugend in den Schulen Württembergs am 1. Juni 1938," NSAW, 12 A Neu, 13 h/19596.

41. Michael Wortmann, *Baldur von Schirach: Hitlers Jugendführer* (Cologne, 1982), 145.

42. Böll cited in Marcel Reich-Ranicki, ed., *Meine Schulzeit im Dritten Reich: Erinnerungen deutscher Schriftsteller* (Munich, 1984), 12.

43. Günter De Bruyn, *Zwischenbilanz: Eine Jugend in Berlin* (Frankfurt am Main, 1995), 92; Jörg Schadt, ed., *Verfolgung und Widerstand unter dem Nationalsozialismus in Baden: Die Lageberichte der Gestapo und des Generalstaatsanwalts Karlsruhe, 1933–1940* (Stuttgart, 1976), 58.

44. Weildorf Schuljugendwalterin report, [Fall 1936], SAM, NSDAP/348.

45. Activity report Jörschke, for Saxony, Dec. 1934, HIS, 13/250; Barbara König's testimony in Reich-Ranicki, 128; Alfons Kenkmann, *Wilde Jugend: Lebenswelt grossstädtischer Jugendlicher zwischen Weltwirtschaftskrise, Nationalsozialismus und Währungsreform* (Essen, 1996), 73.

46. Edith Müller, *Ursel und ihre Mädel* (Reutlingen, [1939]), 70–73.

47. Quotation from Baaden, 79. See also *Jugend im nationalsozialistischen Frankfurt: Ausstellungsdokumentation, Zeitzeugenerinnerungen, Publikum* (Frankfurt am Main, 1987), 52, and Kenkmann, 67, 70.

48. Hermann Melcher, *Die Gefolgschaft: Jugendjahre im Dritten Reich in Heidelberg, 1933–1945* (Berg, 1990), 44; Carola Kuhlmann, *Erbkrank oder erziehbar? Jugendhilfe als Vorsorge und Aussonderung in der Fürsorgeerziehung in Westfalen von 1933–1945* (Weinheim, 1989), 101.

49. *Hitler-Jugend, 1933–1943: Die Chronik eines Jahrzehnts* (Berlin, [1943]), 47.

50. Böhmer to police stations et al., Feb. 10, 1940, BA, Schumacher/239.

51. Landrat Landsberg to Regierungspräsident Munich, Nov. 26, 1940; Klein to Landrat Landsberg, Dec. 12, 1940; Fischer to Landrat Landsberg, Apr. 8, 1941, SAM, LRA/45157.

52. Hindelang to Landräte et al., Aug. 13, 1941, BA, Schumacher/239.

53. Leinfelder to Landrat Wertingen, Apr. 29, 1941, BA, NS28/27.

54. "Der Hitler-Jugend-Richter" 4 (June 1941): 7–8; ibid., 5 (Feb. 1942): 9, (BA, R22/1176); *Das Junge Deutschland* (1942): 183.

55. Helgemeir to Landrat Landsberg, May 22, 1942, SAM, LRA/45157 (quote); Hans Scherer, *Ich war Oberschüler und Luftwaffenhelfer, 1927–1948* (Staffelstein, 1996), vol. 2, 62.

56. Himmler, "Erzwingung der Jugenddienstpflicht," Nov. 24, 1942, BA, R22/1176.

57. "Richterbriefe" 14 (Nov. 1, 1943), (BA, R22/1177); Stumpf to Löfflath, Nov. 8, 1944, BA, NS28/25.

58. See Kreisleitung Darmstadt memo, Feb. 17, 1944, HHSAW, 483/5538, and the evidence for 1942–1944 in BA, NS28/25.

59. For HJ and leadership claim, see Gerhart Wehner, "Die rechtliche Stellung der Hitler-Jugend," Ph.D. dissertation, Dresden, 1939, 55.

60. Maili Hochhuth, *Schulzeit auf dem Lande, 1933–1945: Gespräche und Untersuchungen über die Jahre 1933–1945 in Wattenbach* (Kassel, 1985), 162.

61. Albrecht Möller, *Wir werden das Volk: Wesen und Forderung der Hitlerjugend* (Breslau, 1935), 76; Schirach's speech of September 14, 1942, partially printed in Wortmann, 211–213.

62. Schaar to HJ-Führer Nordmark, May 12, 1944; Peters to Gauhaus Kiel, July 12, 1944, BA, R22/1190.

63. Max von der Grün, *Howl like the Wolves: Growing up in Nazi Germany* (New York, 1980), 219–220; Wapnewski's testimony in Reich-Ranicki, 98–101.

64. *Jugend . . . Frankfurt,* 262.

65. Inge Stolten, *Das alltägliche Exil: Leben zwischen Hakenkreuz und Währungsreform* (Berlin, 1982), 30–31.

66. Rauhut's testimony in Alison Owings, *Frauen: German Women Recall the Third Reich* (New Brunswick, N.J., 1993), 344–345; Rosemarie Heise, "Aufbruch in die Illusion? Eine Jugend in der SBZ/DDR," in Franz-Werner Kersting, ed., *Jugend vor einer Welt in Trümmern: Erfahrungen und Verhältnisse der Jugend zwischen Hitler- und Nachkriegsdeutschland* (Weinheim, 1998), 193.

67. Fest's testimony in Reich-Ranicki, 188–191.

68. Von Schirach on May 23, 1946, in Nuremberg (*Der Prozess,* 419); Artur Axmann, *"Das kann doch nicht das Ende sein": Hitlers letzter Reichsjugendführer erinnert sich,* 2nd ed. (Koblenz, 1995), 230; Hubert Meyer, *Kriegsgeschichte der 12. Panzerdivision "Hitlerjugend"* (Osnabrück, 1982), vol. 1, 17.

69. Hans Volz, *Daten der Geschichte der NSDAP,* 9th ed. (Berlin, 1939), 66; Blomberg quoted in doc. 39 (Apr. 16, 1935), in Karl Heinz Jahnke and Michael Buddrus, eds., *Deutsche Jugend, 1933–1945: Eine Dokumentation* (Hamburg, 1989), 92.

70. *Volksaufklärung und Schule* (no. 29, 1936) (quote), facs. in Von Hellfeld and Klönne, 129; Wortmann, 158.

71. Hein Stünke, "Die Hitlerjugend," in Rudolf Benze and Gustav Gräfer, eds., *Erziehungsmächte und Erziehungshoheit im Grossdeutschen Reich als gestaltende Kräfte im Leben des Deutschen* (Leipzig, 1940), 88–89; Linstow draft, July 8, 1943, BA, Schumacher/239.

72. Hermann Graml, "Integation und Entfremdung: Inanspruchnahme durch Staatsjugend und Dienstpflicht," in Ute Benz and Wolfgang Benz, eds.,

Sozialisation und Traumatisierung: Kinder in der Zeit des Nationalsozialismus (Frankfurt am Main, 1992), 73.

73. Martin Cranz, *Ich, ein Deutscher* (Dülmen, 1987), 63–66; Willy Schumann, *Being Present: Growing up in Hitler's Germany* (Kent, Ohio, 1991), 35–36, 45; Jürgen Peiffer, *Vergangenheit, gebrochener Spiegel: Erinnerungen* (Tübingen, 2000), 47.

74. Camp agendas printed in *HJ erlebt Deutschland: Die Grossfahrten der sächsischen Hitlerjugend* (Leipzig, n.d.), 64; Elke Nyssen, *Schule im Nationalsozialismus* (Heidelberg, 1979), 51; Karl-Heinz Huber, *Jugend unterm Hakenkreuz* (Berlin, 1982), 107–110.

75. Günter Kaufmann, "Die deutsche Jugend im Zeltlager," *Das Junge Deutschland* (1937), 360–365; *Pimpf im Dienst: Ein Handbuch für das Deutsche Jungvolk in der HJ* (Potsdam, 1938), 175–179, 194–197, 204–223.

76. *HJ erlebt Deutschland,* 24, 59; Gottfried Neesse, *Reichsjugendführung* (Berlin, n.d.), 35–39.

77. *Hitler-Jugend . . . Chronik,* 51; Friedrich Grupe, *Jahrgang 1916: Die Fahne war mehr als der Tod* (Munich, 1989), 309–313.

78. Adolf Hitler, *Mein Kampf,* 26th ed. (Munich, 1933), 453–455.

79. Kurt Abels, *Ein Held war ich nicht: Als Kind und Jugendlicher in Hitlers Krieg* (Cologne, 1998), 13; Hans Heinz Pollack, *Verschleppt und verschollen: Geschichte einer Deportation aus Ostpreussen* (Frankfurt am Main, 1990), 30.

80. Möller, 92.

81. Neesse, 28–30; *Hitlerjugend und NS-Reichsbund für Leibesübungen: Richtlinien für die Zusammenarbeit* (n.p., 1940), 37–38; *Hitler-Jugend . . . Chronik,* 20–21, 24.

82. Roman Schnabl, *Das Hitler-Jugend-Schibuch: Grundschule und Leistungssport* (Munich, 1943); Günter Kaufmann, *Das kommende Deutschland: Die Erziehung der Jugend im Reich Adolf Hitlers,* 3rd ed. (Berlin, 1943), 328–329.

83. Dieter Galinski et al., *Nazis und Nachbarn: Schüler erforschen den Alltag im Nationalsozialismus* (Reinbek, 1982), 62, 80–81; Christoph Schubert-Weller, *Hitler-Jugend: Vom "Jungsturm Adolf Hitler" zur Staatsjugend des Dritten Reiches* (Weinheim, 1993), 163–164.

84. Lenz quoted in Reich-Ranicki, 165.

85. Ralf Roland Ringler, *Illusion einer Jugend: Lieder, Fahnen und das bittere Ende: Hitlerjugend in Österreich: Ein Erlebnisbericht* (St. Pölten, 1977), 78 (first quote); Bertram Otto, *"Wussten wir auch nicht, wohin es geht . . .": Erinnerungen, 1927–1947* (Munich, 2000), 77 (second quote).

86. Cranz, 67; Guido Knopp, *Hitlers Kinder,* 2nd ed. (Munich, 2000), 28; Walter Kempowski, *Tadellöser und Wolff: Ein bürgerlicher Roman,* 2nd ed. (Munich, 1975), 406–415; Henry Metelmann, *A Hitler Youth: Growing up in Germany in the 1930s* (London, 1997), 129.

87. *Pimpf im Dienst,* 234–242; *HJ im Dienst: Ausbildungsvorschrift für die Ertüchtigung der deutschen Jugend,* 6th ed. (Berlin, 1940), 200–231; Galinski et al., 67.

88. Bernhard Haupert and Franz Josef Schäfer, *Jugend zwischen Kreuz und Hakenkreuz: Biographische Rekonstruktion als Alltagsgeschichte des Faschismus* (Frankfurt am Main, 1991), 153; Edgar Gielsdorf, *Vom Christkind eine Landsknechtstrommel* (Cologne, 1994), 102.

89. Kaufmann, *Deutschland,* 329; Brandenburg, 230; Huber, 231–233; Boberach, 104.

90. Amtsgericht München, judgment against Rudolf Stimmel, May 16, 1941, ARL, Lü 6.1.2 (München).

91. Alfons Heck, *A Child of Hitler: Germany in the Days when God Wore a Swastika* (Frederick, Colo., 1985), 57; Gabriele Rosenthal, ed., *Die Hitlerjugend-Generation: Biographische Thematisierung als Vergangenheitsbewältigung* (Essen, 1986), 289; Fred Borth, *Nicht zu jung zum Sterben: Die "Hitler-Jugend" im Kampf um Wien, 1945* (Vienna, 1988), 37–38; Schumann, 86–87. On German youth and flying, see Peter Fritzsche, *A Nation of Fliers: German Aviation and the Popular Imagination* (Cambridge, Mass., 1992), esp. 120–124.

92. NSKK-Korpsführer to Reichsjugendführung, Jan. 5, 1940, BA, Schumacher/239; Huber, 167; Haupert and Schäfer, 152; Pahmeyer and Van Spankeren, 194–199.

93. Alfons Heck, *The Burden of Hitler's Legacy* (Frederick, Colo., 1988), 80; Pahmeyer and Van Spankeren, 200.

94. Gielsdorf, 105; Axmann, 329.

95. Peiffer, 64.

96. *Hitler-Jugend . . . Chronik,* 25; Otto Zander, ed., *Weimar: Bekenntnis und Tat: Kulturpolitisches Arbeitslager der Reichsjugendführung, 1938* (Berlin, 1938), 74.

97. Horst Rumpf in Wolfgang Klafki, ed., *Verführung, Distanzierung, Ernüchterung: Kindheit und Jugend im Nationalsozialismus* (Weinheim, 1988), 231; Cranz, 61.

98. Stünke, 86; *Hitler-Jugend . . . Chronik,* 38–39; Zander, 65–67; Michael H. Kater, *The Twisted Muse: Musicians and Their Music in the Third Reich* (New York, 1997), 135–150; Kater, *Composers of the Nazi Era: Eight Portraits* (New York, 2000), 120–121.

99. Wolfgang Klafki in Klafki, 155.

100. Erwin Schwarz-Reiflingen, ed., *HJ Singt: Die schönsten Lieder der Hitler-Jugend: Landsknechts-, Soldaten-, Reiter- und Wanderlieder mit den vollständigen Texten für Klavier in leichter Spielbarkeit* (Mainz, [1933]), 5. See also Cranz, 62; Eva Sternheim-Peters, *Die Zeit der grossen Täuschungen: Eine Jugend im Nationalsozialismus* (Bielefeld, 1992), 38. An excellent analysis of the uses of music in the Hitler Youth toward ideological ends can be found in Baird, 155–171.

101. Cranz, 64.

102. *Das Junge Deutschland* (1939): 137; Gustav Gräfer, "Die Deutsche Schule," in Benze and Gräfer, 55.

103. Stünke, 91.

104. Neesse, 41–42; "Landdienst der Hitler-Jugend," [1942], BA, Schumacher/239; Edith Niehuis, *Das Landjahr: Eine Jugenderziehungseinrichtung in der Zeit des Nationalsozialismus* (Nörten-Hardenberg, 1984).

105. *Hitler-Jugend . . . Chronik*, 22; Erich Blohm, *Hitler-Jugend: Soziale Tatgemeinschaft*, 2nd ed. (Vlotho, 1979), 226–231; Michael H. Kater, "Die Artamanen—Völkische Jugend in der Weimarer Republik," *Historische Zeitschrift* 213 (1971): 577–638.

106. Axmann, 261–265.

107. *Hitler-Jugend . . . Chronik*, 49–50, 59–60.

108. Kaufmann, *Deutschland*, 202.

109. Tritschler report, Oct. 5, 1943, SAG, SF6827, GA/110; Axmann, 324–325.

110. Cranz, 33–36.

111. Example from Katowice (Kattowitz, Silesia) in Jurgen Herbst, *Requiem for a German Past: A Boyhood among the Nazis* (Madison, 1999), 101–102, 107–109.

112. "Die Hitler-Jugend im Kriege," [1944], HIS, 19/358; Heinz Höhne, *Der Orden unter dem Totenkopf: Die Geschichte der SS* (Gütersloh, 1967), 270–273.

113. *Hitler-Jugend . . . Chronik*, 42–43; Horst Rumpf in Klafki, 246–248; Blohm, 302; Axmann, 256–257.

114. Axmann, 257, 330–331.

115. Otto, 128 (quote); Grupe, 304–305; Axmann, 328.

116. Testimony in Johannes Steinhoff et al., eds., *Voices from the Third Reich: An Oral History* (New York, 1994), 212 (quote); *Jungen im Einsatz 1944: Kriegsjahrbuch der Hitler-Jugend* (Munich, n.d.), 22–24; Axmann, 344–346.

117. Hitler, 452.

118. Speech of December 2, 1938, partially printed in Jahnke and Buddrus, 155.

119. Baldur von Schirach, *Die Hitler-Jugend: Idee und Gestalt* (Leipzig, 1934), 165; Hans-Helmut Dietze, *Die Rechtsgestalt der Hitler-Jugend: Eine verfassungsrechtliche Studie* (Berlin, 1939), 221; Pahmeyer and Van Spankeren, 99–100.

120. Neesse, 19–20.

121. Dietze, 218–219; *Das Junge Deutschland* (1937): 47 (quote).

122. Wilhelm Möller-Crivitz, "Das Elternhaus (Vorschulzeit)," in Benze and Gräfer, 34.

123. Act 10, "Der Spitzel," in Bertolt Brecht, *Furcht und Elend des III. Reiches: 24 Szenen* (New York, 1945), 61–70.

124. Heck, *Burden,* 83. See also Pahmeyer and Van Spankeren, 98.

125. Galinski et al., 102; *Jugend . . . Frankfurt,* 133.

126. Robert Gellately, *Backing Hitler: Consent and Coercion in Nazi Germany* (Oxford, 2002), 198.

127. Case of Manfred Sommer in Rosenthal, 234; Gielsdorf, 50.

128. Hüttig memo, June 1, 1934, HIS, 13/248.

129. Gielsdorf, 58; case of Manfred Sommer in Rosenthal, 233; Speitkamp, 212, 225.

130. Melita Maschmann, *Fazit: Keine Rechtfertigung,* 5th ed. (Stuttgart, 1964), 35.

131. Peiffer, 44.

132. *Deutschland-Berichte,* vol. 3 (1936), 174.

133. Speitkamp, 240.

134. Wortmann, 127–130.

135. Von Schirach, *Revolution der Erziehung: Reden aus den Jahren des Aufbaus,* 2nd ed. (Munich, 1939), 110–111 (quote, 111).

136. Alfred Andersch, *Der Vater eines Mörders: Erzählung* (Zurich, 1980). A description of Studienrat Gebhard Himmler from an earlier time is in George W. F. Hallgarten, *Als die Schatten fielen: Erinnerungen vom Jahrhundertbeginn zur Jahrtausendwende* (Frankfurt am Main, 1969), 34–36.

137. Hans-Günter Zmarzlik, *Wieviel Zukunft hat unsere Vergangenheit? Aufsätze und Überlegungen eines Historikers vom Jahrgang 1922* (Munich, 1970), 20–22; De Bruyn, 104–105; Abels, 15; Peiffer, 45–46.

138. Huber, 83; Hans R. Queiser, *"Du gehörst dem Führer!" Vom Hitlerjungen zum Kriegsberichter: Ein autobiographischer Bericht* (Cologne, 1993), 66–67.

139. Entry for March 22, 1933, in Victor Klemperer, *Tagebücher 1933–34,* ed. Walter Nowojski (Berlin, 1999), 14; Ralf Giordano in Geert Platner

et al., eds., *Schule im Dritten Reich—Erziehung zum Tod? Eine Dokumentation*, 2nd ed. (Munich, 1984), 73; Hans Scheuerl in Klafki, 68–69; Wolfgang Klafki in Klafki, 149–150.

140. De Bruyn, 106–107 (quote, 106).

141. Heinrich Böll, *Was soll aus dem Jungen bloss werden? Oder: Irgendwas mit Büchern*, ed. J. H. Reid (Manchester, 1991), 56.

142. Von der Grün, 180–181. See Stefan Zweig, *Decisive Moments in History: Twelve Miniatures* (Riverside, Calif., 1999 [German publ., 1927]).

143. De Bruyn, 106; Hans Scheuerl in Klafki, 67; Hochhuth, 93, 100; Speitkamp, 243.

144. See the text of this chapter at nn. 281f.

145. Otto, 88; Queiser, 69; Ulrich Popplow, "Schulalltag im Dritten Reich: Fallstudie über ein Göttinger Gymnasium," *Aus Politik und Zeitgeschichte: Beilage zur Wochenzeitung Das Parlament*, B18, 80 (1980): 35.

146. Popplow, 35; Harald Buss in Platner et al., 93; Benjamin Ortmeyer, *Schulzeit unterm Hitlerbild: Analysen, Berichte, Dokumente* (Frankfurt am Main, 1996), 63; Peiffer, 45.

147. Albert Böhme and Werner Piutti, eds., *Schulkind im Dritten Reich: Eine Handreichung für Eltern und Erzieher* (Wuppertal-Barmen, [1936]), 41–42; Dietze, 222; A. Kluger, ed., *Die Deutsche Volksschule im Grossdeutschen Reich: Handbuch der Gesetze, Verordnungen und Richtlinien für Erziehung und Unterricht in Volksschulen nebst den einschlägigen Bestimmungen über Hitler-Jugend und Nationalpolitische Erziehungsanstalten* (Breslau, 1940), 387–388.

148. Manfred Rommel in Platner, 62; Schumann, 62; Otto, 88.

149. Maschmann, 31; Huber speech, [early 1939], SAL, PL 512/II, N, 98, 2; Gräfer, 57, 60; Wortmann, 169–173.

150. Nygaard to Kohlmeyer, March 7, 1940, SAH, Jugendbehörde I, 343e; Reichsjugendführung, "Cliquen- und Bandenbildung unter Jugendlichen," Sept. 1942, BA, R22/1177.

151. Möller-Crivitz, 29, 32.

152. Martin Greiffenhagen, *Jahrgang 1928: Aus einem unruhigen Leben* (Munich, 1988), 39; Von der Grün, 247; Karl-Heinz Janssen in Hermann Glaser and Axel Silenius, eds., *Jugend im Dritten Reich* (Frankfurt am Main, 1975), 93; Schumann, 77; Friedrich Juchter, *Formeln, Fahnen, Flakgeschütze: Eine deutsche Jugend zwischen Schule und Kriegsdienst (1934–1947)*, 2nd ed. (Oldenburg, 1999), 108–109.

153. "Aufgaben und Leistungen des NS.-Lehrerbundes im Kriege," [1941/42], HIS, 12/243; Schumann, 73, 115; De Bruyn, 102–103; Harald

Scholtz, *Erziehung und Unterricht unterm Hakenkreuz* (Göttingen, 1985), 105.

154. Grevemühl to Bade, Sept. 18, 1942, NSAW, 12 A Neu, 13 h/19597.

155. De Bruyn, 103.

156. Bormann circular, Sept. 27, 1940, printed in Gerhard Dabel, *KLV: Die erweiterte Kinder-Land-Verschickung: KLV-Lager, 1940–1945* (Freiburg, 1981), 7; "Disziplinarbestimmungen für die Lager der Erweiterten Kinderlandverschickung," in "Der Hitler–Jugend–Richter," no. 5 (Feb. 1942), (BA, R22/1176); Baaden, 120, 123–124; Kaufmann, *Deutschland,* 358.

157. See Gerhard Kock, *"Der Führer sorgt für unsere Kinder . . .": Die Kinderlandverschickung im Zweiten Weltkrieg* (Paderborn, 1997), 178–188; Juchter, 54, 114.

158. Claus Larass, *Der Zug der Kinder: KLV—Die Evakuierung 5 Millionen deutscher Kinder im 2. Weltkrieg* (Munich, 1983), 9, 15; Axmann, 348.

159. Alfred Ehrentreich, *Pädagogische Odyssee: Im Wandel der Erziehungsformen* (Weinheim, 1967), 219; Jost Hermand, *Als Pimpf in Polen: Erweiterte Kinderlandverschickung, 1940–1945* (Frankfurt am Main, 1993), 39; Kock, 192; Ilse Koehn, *Mischling zweiten Grades: Kindheit in der Nazi-Zeit* (Reinbek, 1980), 145.

160. Ehrentreich, 213; Koehn, 51–52; De Bruyn, 109; Knopp, 245.

161. Juchter, 81.

162. Ehrentreich, 211, 237; Koehn, 99–101.

163. Scholtz, *Erziehung,* 104.

164. Koehn, 120–121; Larass, 27, 73–74.

165. De Bruyn, 109; Ehrentreich, 207, 214; Knopp, 245.

166. Koehn, 56, 91–97; Ehrentreich, 208, 237; Juchter, 80, 84, 119; Sigrid Bremer, *Muckefuck und Kameradschaft: Mädchenzeit im Dritten Reich: Von der Kinderlandverschickung 1940 bis zum Studium 1946* (Frankfurt am Main, 1988), 15–17.

167. Kock, 205; Larass, 58–59, 74; De Bruyn, 113; Koehn, 54–55, 91, 116–118.

168. De Bruyn, 111; Ehrentreich, 216; Hermand, 72–73.

169. Dahrendorf quoted in Larass, 166.

170. De Bruyn, 112; Hermand, 73–74.

171. Larass, 63.

172. Hermand, 85; Koehn, 57–60, 99–100.

173. Ehrentreich, 207–208, 210, 216–217; Larass, 211, 223; Koehn, 54, 61, 145; De Bruyn, 112–113.

174. "Die Adolf-Hitler-Schulen," [1944], HIS, 19/358; Wortmann, 146–147; Knopp, 168–170.

175. Gaupersonalamtsleiter to Gauleiter et al., Feb. 20, 1937, BA, Schumacher/270I; "Auslese für den Besuch der Adolf-Hitler-Schule Jahrgang 1940," Gaupersonalamt, BA, Schmacher/372; Durchführungsbestimmungen Härtel, Oct. 2, 1944, SAM, NSDAP/31; Gräfer, 72.

176. Albert Speer, *Erinnerungen,* 8th ed. (Frankfurt am Main, 1970), 137.

177. Dietrich Orlow, "Die Adolf-Hitler-Schulen," *Vierteljahrshefte für Zeitgeschichte* 13 (1965): 278; Scholtz, *NS–Ausleseschulen,* 251–253.

178. Scholtz, *NS–Ausleseschulen,* 175, 210; Blohm, 134.

179. Kaufmann, *Deutschland,* 165; Rolf Eilers, *Die nationalsozialistische Schulpolitik: Eine Studie zur Funktion der Erziehung im totalitären Staat* (Cologne, 1963), 47.

180. Grundmann quoted in Knopp, 196.

181. Baldur von Schirach, *Revolution,* 112.

182. Testimony of Peter E. in Kurt Hass, ed., *Jugend unterm Schicksal: Lebensberichte junger Deutscher, 1946–1949* (Hamburg, 1950), 50, Speitkamp, 247–248.

183. Orlow, 276.

184. Ibid., 280 (quote); Knopp, 176, 190, 192.

185. Kaufmann, *Deutschland,* 170; Knopp, 207, 210–211.

186. Grundmann quoted in Knopp, 176.

187. Hitler quoted for January 1, 1942, in Henry Picker, ed., *Hitlers Tischgespräche im Führerhauptquartier, 1941–42* (Bonn, 1951), 200.

188. Blohm, 133–134; Orlow, 274.

189. David Schoenbaum, *Hitler's Social Revolution: Class and Status in Nazi Germany, 1933–1939* (Garden City, 1967), 268; Orlow, 277; Scholtz, *NS–Ausleseschulen,* 133, 245.

190. Jennes circular, March 24, 1939, BA, NS22/2023; Schoenbaum, 269–271; Dietrich Orlow, *The History of the Nazi Party, 1933–1945* (Pittsburgh, 1973), 188–190.

191. Reinhard Bollmus, "Zum Projekt einer nationalsozialistischen Alternativ-Universität: Alfred Rosenbergs 'Hohe Schule,'" in Manfred Heinemann, ed., *Erziehung und Schulung im Dritten Reich* (Stuttgart, 1980), vol. 2, 125–152.

192. *Verfügungen/Anordnungen Bekanntgaben,* ed. Partei-Kanzlei (Munich, n.d.), 6: 41–43; Schoenbaum, 265–267; Scholtz, *NS–Ausleseschulen,* 299–324; Knopp, 174, 203.

193. Gräfer, 70–71.

194. Christian Schneider et al., *Das Erbe der NAPOLA: Versuch einer Generationengeschichte des Nationalsozialismus* (Hamburg, 1996), 42, 45.

195. Schoenbaum, 268; Scholtz, *NS–Ausleseschulen,* 80, 110, 132–133; Schneider et al., 109.

196. Schneider et al., 55–62 (quote, 57); 161–163; Winfried Maass, *Die Fünfzigjährigen: Portrait einer verratenen Generation* (Hamburg, 1980), 33–37; Knopp, 180–181, 186, 188–189, 194, 208.

197. Eilers, 44; Schneider et al., 54.

198. Heinz W. Kämmer, *Von arm bis braun: Eine Kindheit in der Mitte Deutschlands von den "goldenen" 20ern in die "braunen" 30er* (Essen, 1996), 119.

199. Hitler quoted in Von Schirach, *Ich glaubte,* 180.

200. Hackländer to Oldigs, Wolfsee, Nov. 8, 1933, BA, NS22/342; Veiner to Kommandant, July 15, 1934, BAF, R W6/V67/1; situation report for Lower Franconia, Sept. 7, 1934, GStAM, RE/450; situation report for Wilhelmshaven, May 1938, NSAO, 320/2,2; Martin Broszat et al., eds., *Bayern in der NS-Zeit: Soziale Lage und politisches Verhalten der Bevölkerung im Spiegel vertraulicher Berichte* (Munich, 1977), 83; Von der Grün, 161.

201. Reichsjugendführung circular, June 16, 1934, HIS, 19/360.

202. Jahnke and Buddrus, 88; *Deutschland-Berichte,* vol. 3 (1936), 227.

203. Von Flotow file (1938–39), ARL, Lü 6.1.7 (Jugendgericht Berlin).

204. Situation report for Süd-Hannover-Braunschweig, May 1933, NHSA, Hann. 310I, B13; "Reichs-Jugend-Pressedienst," June 1, 1934, HIS, 19/355; Rabenhofer file (June 1934), SAM, NSDAP/117; Blomquist to Klagges, May 8, 1939, NSAW, 12 A Neu, 13h/16198; *Deutschland-Berichte,* vol. 2 (1935), 969; Broszat et al., 524; Robert Thévoz et al., eds., *Pommern 1934/35 im Spiegel von Gestapo-Lageberichten und Sachakten* (Cologne, 1974), 59.

205. Gendarmerieposten Windischgarsten to Landrat, Sept. 23, 1940, OLA, Pol. Akten/15; Munich Oberlandesgerichtspräsident report, Apr. 30, 1942, BA, R22/1176a; Popp to Weber, Nov. 9, 1942, SAM, LRA/45157; NSDAP "Befehlsblatt," Nov. 1943, BA, NS28/41; Grolmann to Amt für Volkswohlfahrt, Dec. 28, 1943, SAMs, Polit. Polizei, 3. Reich/408.

206. Abelein to Kreisleitung, Jan. 12, 1943, SAL, PL 512/II, 98, 5.

207. Landgericht Berlin, case against Wichmann (1943–44), ARL, Lü 6.1.8 (Jugendgericht Berlin); Kreisamtsleiter Minden to Amt für Volkswohl-

fahrt, Dec. 27, 1943, SAMs, Polit. Polizei, 3. Reich/408; Hermann Stresau, *Von Jahr zu Jahr* (Berlin, 1948), 344.

208. Von Schirach in *Das Junge Deutschland* (1937), 45 (quote); Neesse, 204.

209. Wortmann, 152.

210. Klein, "Jugendführung und politische Leitung," Dec. 15, 1938, SAM, NSDAP/532; Speitkamp, 222.

211. Arno Klönne, "Widersprüche der HJ-Sozialisation," in Ulrich Herrmann, ed., *"Die Formung des Volksgenossen": Der "Erziehungsstaat" des Dritten Reiches* (Weinheim, 1985), 207–208.

212. Activity report Klein, March–Oct. 1933, GStAM, RE/450.

213. Von Schirach, *Revolution,* 19–20; Jahnke and Buddrus, 107–108; Huber, 120.

214. Gabriele Kinz, *Der Bund Deutscher Mädel: Ein Beitrag über die ausserschulische Mädchenerziehung im Nationalsozialismus,* 2nd ed. (Frankfurt am Main, 1991), 33.

215. Von Schirach, *Revolution,* 19–20.

216. Minutes, Jugendrechtsausschuss meeting, Berlin, Dec. 10/11, 1937, BA, R22/1180.

217. Riegraf to Spiess, Feb. 8, 1938, SAL, PL 509/1/3.

218. Entry for March 19, 1943, in Dieter Borkowski, *Wer weiss, ob wir uns wiedersehen: Erinnerungen an eine Berliner Jugend* (Frankfurt am Main, 1980), 28–29.

219. Ringler, 116.

220. Jürgen Schultz, *Die Akademie für Jugendführung der Hitlerjugend in Braunschweig* (Brunswick, 1978), 43; Von Schirach (Dec. 1936) in *Das Junge Deutschland* (1937), 44; Von Schirach, *Revolution,* 11; Dietze, 217.

221. Schultz, *Akademie,* 164, 206; Jahnke and Buddrus, 137–138; Stünke, 84.

222. Scholtz, *Erziehung,* 97.

223. Axmann, 229 (quote); Gielsdorf, 128.

224. Ringler, 79–80.

225. Gielsdorf, 128–131.

226. Ibid., 121.

227. Activity report Klein, March–Oct. 1933, GStAM, RE/450; activity report for Süd-Hannover-Braunschweig, Oct. 1933, NSHA, Hann. 310I, B 13; Galinski et al., 55.

228. Zinsmeier to Bannführer, Apr. 6, 1937, BA, NS28/25; Broszat et al., 93; Von Hellfeld and Klönne, 130.

229. Von Schirach, *Revolution,* 57.

230. Kinz, 63–64; Mahlmann report, Nov. 11, 1940, NSAW, 12 A Neu, 13 h/19596.

231. Voss application, May 19, 1941, NSAW, 12 A Neu, 13h/16123; Silvester Lechner, ed., *Die "Hitlerjugend" am Beispiel der Region Ulm/Neu-Ulm: Ein Aspekt im Umfeld der "Weissen Rose," 1942/43* (Ulm, 1993), 68; Munich Oberlandesgerichtspräsident report, Apr. 30, 1942, BA, R22/1176a.

232. Leiter Wohlfahrtspflege to Hauptamt für Volkswohlfahrt, SAMs, Polit. Polizei, 3. Reich/408; Gielsdorf, 120, 130; Heck, *Child*, 161.

233. Helmut Heiber, ed., *Reichsführer! . . . Briefe an und von Himmler* (Stuttgart, 1968), 270–271.

234. Osterfeld activity report, March 14, 1935, HIS, 13/251; Sieverts, "Jugendgefährdung im Kriege," Oct. 20, 1942, BA, NL/289; K-Führer to Schwarz, June 16, 1944, BA, NS28/25.

235. Galinski et al., 56; political situation report for Party chapter Rothenburg, Feb. 1939, BA, Schumacher/372; Haug to Bannführer, Oct. 9, 1940, BA, NS28/25.

236. Bormann ordinance, March 12, 1940, BA, NS22/856; Pfundtner to Oberste Reichsbehörden et al., Nov. 30, 1942, BA, R18/2958; Kreisleiter Gross-Frankfurt circular, Feb. 2, 1943, HHSAW, 483/5541; Mauer/ Schenke memo, Oct. 5, 1943, BA, Schumacher/368; Walkenhorst memo, Feb. 24, 1945, BA, Schumacher/239; Broszat et al., 588.

237. Entry for Sept. 27, 1934, in Klemperer, *Tagebücher 1933–1934,* 146.

238. Köhler to Ley, Feb. 9, 1937, BA, NS22/739; Oberlandesgerichtspräsident Danzig, situation report, Apr. 10, 1943, BA, R22/1176a.

239. Riegraf to Spiess, Nov. 21, 1938, SAL, PL 509/1/3.

240. Ringler, 80 (quote); Queiser, 63; Koehn, 44–45.

241. Axmann, 370–371; Maschmann, 150–151.

242. Ringler, 123, 134–135 (quote).

243. Ley/Von Schirach agreement, June 1, 1934, BA, NS22/342; *Bremer Nachrichten,* March 3, 1934.

244. Jahnke and Buddrus, 104–105; "Arbeitsanweisung Nr. 13/1938," BA, NS22/2022; Hess ordinance draft, Sept. 9, 1940; Hess to Ley, Sept. 29, 1940, BA, NS22/856.

245. Entry for Aug. 23, 1941, in *TGII,* vol. 1, 299.

246. Entry for Dec. 17, 1941, in *TGII,* vol. 2, 525.

247. Entry for May 5, 1942, in Picker, 238. See also entry for June 23, 1942, in *TGII,* vol. 4, 583; Heiber, 142–143.

248. Bormann to Sauckel, May 27, 1943, BA, Schumacher/378. See also Hitler ordinance A 26/43, April 7, 1943, BA, Schumacher/239.

249. Orlow, *History*, 342; Mauer/Schenke memo, Oct. 5, 1943, BA, Schumacher/368.

250. Maschmann, 153.

251. Ian Kershaw, *The "Hitler Myth": Image and Reality in the Third Reich* (Oxford, 1987).

252. Lauterbacher "Eilbefehl," June 27, 1934, HIS, 18/339; Höhne, 53, 90–124.

253. Lauterbacher memo, Dec. 8, 1934, BA, NSD43/1.

254. Jahnke and Buddrus, 116; *Berliner Zeitung*, May 23, 1936.

255. Jahnke and Buddrus, 124–125, 144–146. See text at n. 120 in Chapter 4.

256. Himmler/Von Schirach memo, Dec. 17, 1938, BA, Schumacher/239; Schindlmayr to Landrat Grafenau, Nov. 30, 1939, BA, Schumacher/239.

257. Jahnke and Buddrus, 327.

258. Files in SAND, unsign. Best., EAP 221-b-20/9; anon. testimony [Feb. 1939] in Huber, 212–213 (quote); *Aschaffenburger Zeitung*, Aug. 16, 1939.

259. See Wolfgang Neuber in Hans Wienicke, ed., *"Schon damals fingen viele an zu schweigen . . .": Quellensammlung zur Geschichte Charlottenburgs von 1933–1945* (Berlin–Charlottenburg, 1986), 158; Queiser, 63, 79.

260. Von Schirach on May 24, 1946, in Nuremberg (*Der Prozess*, 566); Schirach, *Ich glaubte*, 244, 246, 285; Axmann, 220; Herbert Reinecker, *Ein Zeitbericht unter Zuhilfenahme des eigenen Lebenslaufs* (Erlangen, 1990), 98. Critically, see Gisela Miller-Kipp, ed., *"Auch Du gehörst dem Führer": Die Geschichte des Bundes Deutscher Mädel (BDM) in Quellen und Dokumenten* (Weinheim, 2001), 245.

261. Lore Walb, *Ich, die Alte—ich, die Junge: Konfrontation mit meinen Tagebüchern, 1933–1945,* 2nd ed. (Berlin, 1997), 120.

262. Jahnke and Buddrus, 148–151. For HJ action in Vienna, see George E. Berkley, *Vienna and Its Jews: The Tragedy of Success, 1880s–1980s* (Cambridge, Mass., 1988), 311.

263. Albert Bastian in Steinhoff et al., 14–15; Klaus Tischler in Rosenthal, 264; Horst Fuchs Richardson, ed., *Sieg Heil! War Letters of Tank Gunner Karl Fuchs, 1937–1941* (Hamden, Conn., 1987), 36–37.

264. Reinhold Kerstan, *Blood and Honor* (Elgin, Ill., 1980), 34–36; Erhard Eppler, *Als Wahrheit verordnet wurde: Briefe an meine Enkelin,* 3rd. ed. (Frankfurt am Main, 1995), 93–94.

265. Dietrich Strothmann in Glaser and Silenius, 46; Helge Pross, *Memoiren eines Inländers, 1923–1993* (Munich, 1993), 68–70; Peiffer, 73.

266. Rosenthal, 263; Wolfgang Klafki in Klafki, 163; Eppler, 75.

267. Melcher, 199.

268. Neesse, 31; Huber, 91, 108; Schumann, 24, 26, 29.

269. Entry for Feb. 9, 1943, in Borkowski, 21.

270. Funk cited in Jahnke and Buddrus, 141.

271. Otto, 77; entry for May 31, 1943, in Borkowski, 42–43.

272. Wolfgang Hempel, "'Ein kleiner Nazi bis zum letzten Tag': Meine frühe Jugend in der Nazizeit und das Kriegsende," in Kersting, 265.

273. See Stefan Zweig, *Die Welt von Gestern: Erinnerungen eines Europäers* (Berlin, 1965), 367; Berkley, 259–260.

274. Ian Kershaw, *Hitler, 1936–1945: Nemesis* (New York, 2000), 351; Gerhard Botz, *Wohnungspolitik und Judendeportation in Wien, 1938 bis 1945: Zur Funktion des Antisemitismus als Ersatz nationalsozialistischer Sozialpolitik* (Vienna, 1975).

275. Cranz, 105–108.

276. Entries for Aug. 21, 1942, in Klemperer, *Tagebuch 1942*, 217, Feb. 14, 1943, *Tagebuch 1943*, 32, and Oct. 16, 1944, *Tagebuch 1944*, 141.

277. Entry for May 17, 1943, in Borkowski, 40–41; entry for June 23, 1943, in Klemperer, *Tagebuch 1943*, 100; Cranz, 87; Queiser, 79.

278. Kerstan, 32–36; Albert Bastian in Steinhoff et al., 15.

279. Scherer, vol. 1, 51; Karl-Heinz Janssen in Glaser and Silenius, 92; Gielsdorf, 49.

280. Example quoted in Huber, 87. See also Möller, 104–105.

281. Peter Gay, *My German Question: Growing up in Nazi Berlin* (New Haven, 1998), 64 (quote); Gay in *Der Spiegel* (July 21, 2003): 161.

282. Kerstan, 32.

283. Klaus E. quoted in Lothar Steinbach, *Ein Volk, ein Reich, ein Glaube? Ehemalige Nationalsozialisten und Zeitzeugen berichten über ihr Leben im Dritten Reich* (Berlin, 1983), 125.

284. Thea Mandowsky quoted in Platner, 157.

285. Peiffer, 81; Michael Wieck, *Zeugnis vom Untergang Königsbergs: Ein "Geltungsjude" berichtet* (Heidelberg, 1990), 120; Herz quoted in Steinhoff et al., 48.

286. Entry for May 14, 1943, in Borkowski, 40.

287. See Heinz Knobloch, *Eine Berliner Kindheit: Zwischen Olympia und Luftschutzkeller* (Berlin, 1999), 53–54.

288. See the fictionalized chapter, "Adolf Hitler, a Boy, Quick, Tough and

Tenacious," in Hermine Morgenroth and Maria Schmidt, *Kinder, was wisst ihr vom Führer?* (Leipzig, 1933), 25–29; Peiffer, 46; Schumann, 24; Juchter, 93–94; Huber, 110.

289. Janssen in Glaser and Silenius, 88; Klaus E. in Steinbach, 123; Ferdinand B. in *Jugend . . . Frankfurt*, 263; Wolfgang Klafki in Klafki, 152.

290. Klaus Tischler in Rosenthal, 261; Knopp, 29.

291. *Der Kongress zu Nürnberg vom 5. bis 10. September 1934: Offizieller Bericht über den Verlauf des Reichsparteitages mit sämtlichen Reden* (Munich, 1934), 165–167.

292. Otto, 80.

293. Von Schirach's dedication for Horst Kerutt, ed., *Adolf-Hitler-Marsch der deutschen Jugend* (Munich, 1939), n.p.

3. German Girls for Matrimony and Motherhood

1. Raymond Phillips, ed., *Trial of Josef Kramer and Forty-four Others (The Belsen Trial)* (London, 1949), 247–261 (first quote, 260; third quote, 256), 531, 601, 615–616, 641, 644, 711–712, 747; Gisella Perl, *I was a Doctor in Auschwitz* (New York, 1979), 61–65 (second quote, 61); Daniel Patrick Brown, *The Beautiful Beast: The Life and Crimes of SS-Aufseherin Irma Grese* (Venture, Calif., 1996), (fourth quote, 85); Giles Playfair and Derrick Sington, *The Offenders: Society and the Atrocious Crime* (London, 1957), 154–185; Martina Ehlert, "Umerziehung zur Demokratie: Der erste Bergen-Belsen-Prozess in Zeitungsberichten," in Claus Füllberg-Stolberg et al., eds., *Frauen in Konzentrationslagern: Bergen-Belsen, Ravensbrück* (Bremen, 1994), 256–257; Wieslar Kielar, *Anus Mundi: Fünf Jahre Auschwitz* (Frankfurt am Main, 1984), 298–299; Olga Lengyel, *Five Chimneys: The Story of Auschwitz* (Chicago, 1947), 147–150, 186–189.

2. The most vocal exponent of this view has been Claudia Koonz. See her *Mothers in the Fatherland: Women, the Family, and Nazi Politics* (New York, 1987).

3. The victim status has been most aptly portrayed in Gisela Bock's study of females as the most prominent targets of forced sterilizations perpetrated upon them by males: *Zwangssterilisation im Nationalsozialismus: Studien zur Rassenpolitik und Frauenpolitik* (Opladen, 1986). See also Bock, "Die Frauen und der Nationalsozialismus: Bemerkungen zu einem Buch von Claudia Koonz," *Geschichte und Gesellschaft* 15 (1989): 563–579; Atina Grossmann, "Feminist Debates about Women and National Socialism,"

Gender and History 3 (1991): 350–358; Adelheid von Saldern, "Victims or Perpetrators? Controversies about the Role of Women in the Nazi State," in David F. Crew, ed., *Nazism and German Society, 1933–1945* (London, 1994), 141–165.

4. That was NSDAP-Amtsleiter Erich Hilgenfeldt. On the larger issue, see Michael H. Kater, "Frauen in der NS-Bewegung," *Vierteljahrshefte für Zeitgeschichte* 31 (1983): 218–224.

5. Ute Frevert, *Women in German History: From Bourgeois Emancipation to Sexual Liberation* (New York, 1989), 202–203.

6. Personal communication by Annemarie Gensichen to the author, Marbella, June 2, 1993. She herself fit just such a model.

7. See the work of Ute Frevert, Jill Stephenson, and Adelheid von Saldern.

8. For the latter, see Frevert, 171–172, 179–180, 198–199, 208–209; Robert Gellately, *Backing Hitler: Consent and Coercion in Nazi Germany* (Oxford, 2002), 10.

9. Adolf Hitler, *Mein Kampf,* 26th ed. (Munich, 1933), 74, 455 (quote).

10. Schemm as quoted in Bernd Lembeck, *Hans Schemm: Ein Leben für Deutschland* (Munich, 1936), 35.

11. Guida Diehl, *Die Deutsche Frau und der Nationalsozialismus* (Eisenach, 1933), 11, 43, 70, 80; "Nationalsozialistische Frauenschaft," in Paul Meier-Benneckenstein, ed., *Das Dritte Reich im Aufbau: Übersichten und Leistungsberichte* (Berlin, 1939), vol. 2, 361; Michael H. Kater, *The Nazi Party: A Social Profile of Members and Leaders, 1919–1945* (Cambridge, Mass., 1983), 151.

12. Hermann Okrass, *Das Ende einer Parole: "Hamburg bleibt rot,"* 2nd ed. (Hamburg, 1935), 243; Jill Stephenson, *Women in Nazi Germany* (Harlow, 2001), 83–84.

13. Hess speech, 1938 Reich Party rally, SAG, SF 6815, GA/6.

14. Nuremberg-Fürth police report, March 3, 1925, SAN, Rep. 503/99.

15. Report [Aug. 1927] quoted in Ernst Deuerlein, ed., *Der Aufstieg der NSDAP in Augenzeugenberichten* (Munich, 1974), 279.

16. Heinrich Hoffmann, *Hitler Was My Friend* (London, 1955), 142; Ernst Hanfstaengl, *Unheard Witness* (Philadelphia, 1957), 36.

17. NSF-Gauabteilungsleiterin Sachsen to NSDAP-Reichsschulungsamt, June 1, 1935, HIS, 13/254.

18. Joachim C. Fest, *Hitler: Eine Biographie,* 3rd ed. (Frankfurt am Main, 1973), 288; Hitler to Frau Vorsitzende, Nov. 15, 1924, HIS, 13/256 (quote).

19. Albert Speer, *Erinnerungen,* 8th ed. (Frankfurt am Main, 1970), 59.

20. "Nationalsozialistische Frauenschaft," 363; NS-Frauengruppe Leipzig to Doktor, Feb. 1927; Goebbels to NS-Frauengruppe, Feb. 16, 1927, HIS, 13/256 (quote).

21. Jay W. Baird, *To Die for Germany: Heroes in the Nazi Pantheon* (Bloomington, 1990), 73–107.

22. Strasser, "Die Organisation der nationalsozialistischen Frauen in der NS-Frauenschaft," Nov. 1, 1931, BA, Schumacher/230; Rees-Fawerdes to Party archive, Oct. 22, 1936, HIS, 13/254; Friedrich Alfred Beck, *Kampf und Sieg: Geschichte der Nationalsozialistischen Deutschen Arbeiterpartei im Gau Westfalen-Süd von den Anfängen bis zur Machtübernahme* (Dortmund, 1938), 327, 371, 517.

23. Munich police memo, Jan. 27, 1931, BHSAM, Sonderabgabe I/1545; circular no. 3, Oct. 7, 1931, BA, Schumacher/230.

24. "Die Frauenarbeit in der Göttinger Ortsgruppe der NSDAP, 1922–35," HIS, 13/254.

25. Baden police report, Jan. 1, 1928, SAF, 317/1257d; Stein to Gau Brandenburg, Oct. 13, 1932, BA, NS22/1046; Heidrich, "Richtlinien für die Organisation und Arbeit der Frauengruppen," May 1, 1930, SAG, SF6818, GA/31.

26. Diehl, 100–101.

27. Hans-Christian Brandenburg, *Die Geschichte der HJ: Wege und Irrwege einer Generation* (Cologne, 1968), 51; Gisela Miller-Kipp, *"Auch Du gehörst dem Führer": Die Geschichte des Bundes Deutscher Mädel (BDM) in Quellen und Dokumenten* (Weinheim, 2001), 17; Lotte Becker, "Der Bund Deutscher Mädel," in Rudolf Benze and Gustav Gräfer, eds., *Erziehungsmächte und Erziehungshoheit im Grossdeutschen Reich als gestaltende Kräfte im Leben des Deutschen* (Leipzig, 1940), 94 (quote).

28. Okrass, 243; Miller-Kipp, 18, 26; Koonz, 129; Schirach to [Strasser], Nov. 11, 1932, BA, Schumacher/230.

29. Hoffmann, *Hitler,* 142; Hartmann Lauterbacher, *Erlebt und mitgestaltet: Kronzeuge einer Epoche, 1923–1945: Zu neuen Ufern nach Kriegsende* (Preussisch Oldendorf, 1984), 124; Miller-Kipp, 293.

30. Becker, 95 (quote); Artur Axmann, *"Das kann doch nicht das Ende sein": Hitlers letzter Reichsjugendführer erinnert sich,* 2nd ed. (Koblenz, 1995), 81; Dagmar Reese, *Straff, aber nicht stramm—herb, aber nicht derb: Zur Vergesellschaftung von Mädchen durch den Bund Deutscher Mädel im soziokulturellen Vergleich zweier Milieus* (Weinheim, 1989), 40.

31. Personal file, Jutta Rüdiger, BAB; Axmann, 249.

32. Husfeld as quoted in Axmann, 249.

33. See Geoffrey Cocks, *Psychotherapy in the Third Reich: The Göring Institute,* 2nd ed. (New Brunswick, N.J., 1997) and, for the HJ, Ludwig Hemm, *Die unteren Führer in der HJ: Versuch ihrer psychologischen Typengliederung* (Leipzig, 1940).

34. Jutta Rüdiger, "Der Bund Deutscher Mädel in der Hitler-Jugend," in Meier-Benneckenstein, 402; Matthias von Hellfeld and Arno Klönne, *Die betrogene Generation: Jugend in Deutschland unter dem Faschismus* (Cologne, 1985), 35; Gabriele Kinz, *Der Bund Deutscher Mädel: Ein Beitrag über die ausserschulische Mädchenerziehung im Nationalsozialismus,* 2nd ed. (Frankfurt am Main, 1991), 25; Reese, 37.

35. Becker, 109–110; Rüdiger, 398, 412; Waltraut Rath in Wolfgang Klafki, ed., *Verführung, Distanzierung, Ernüchterung: Kindheit und Jugend im Nationalsozialismus: Autobiographisches aus erziehungswissenschaftlicher Sicht* (Weinheim, 1988), 194.

36. Gisela Miller-Kipp, "Der Bund Deutscher Mädel in der Hitler-Jugend: Erziehung zwischen Ideologie und Herrschaftsprozess," *Pädagogische Rundschau* (1982): 88.

37. Lydia Schürer-Stolle, "Jungmädel im BDM," in Hilde Munske, ed., *Mädel im Dritten Reich* (Berlin, [1936]), 46; Karin K. in Kurt Hass, ed., *Jugend unterm Schicksal: Lebensberichte junger Deutscher, 1946–1949* (Hamburg, 1950), 35; Mathilde Mundt, Ellen Frey, and Anna Fest in Alison Owings, *Frauen: German Women Recall the Third Reich* (New Brunswick, N.J., 1993), 88, 174, 314; Elfriede Schuster in Gabriele Rosenthal, ed., *Die Hitlerjugend-Generation: Biographische Thematisierung als Vergangenheitsbewältigung* (Essen, 1986), 163; Eva Sternheim-Peters, *Die Zeit der grossen Täuschungen: Eine Jugend im Nationalsozialismus* (Bielefeld, 1992), 182.

38. Baldur von Schirach, *Revolution der Erziehung: Reden aus den Jahren des Aufbaus,* 2nd ed. (Munich, 1939), 47 (quote); Doris K. in Lothar Steinbach, *Ein Volk, ein Reich, ein Glaube? Ehemalige Nationalsozialisten und Zeitzeugen berichten über ihr Leben im Dritten Reich* (Berlin, 1983), 86.

39. Waltraut Rath in Klafki, 190; Doris K. in Steinbach, 88; Maili Hochhuth, *Schulzeit auf dem Lande, 1933–1945: Gespräche und Untersuchungen über die Jahre 1933–1945 in Wattenbach* (Kassel, 1985), 154; Peter Pahmeyer and Lutz van Spankeren, *Die Hitlerjugend in Lippe (1933–1939): Totalitäre Erziehung zwischen Anspruch und Wirklichkeit* (Bielefeld, 1998), 195, n. 170; Miller-Kipp, *Auch,* 101.

40. Ilse McKee, *Tomorrow the World* (London, 1960), 8 (quote); Silvester Lechner, *Das KZ Oberer Kuhberg und die NS-Zeit in der Region Ulm/Neu-Ulm* (Stuttgart, 1988), 83–87; *HJ erlebt Deutschland: Die Grossfahrten der sächs-*

ischen Hitlerjugend (Leipzig, n.d.), 41–41; Sternheim-Peters, 183, 197; Reese, 135–136; Miller-Kipp, *Auch,* 129–130.

41. Kinz, 215–228.
42. Elisabeth K. and Karin K. in Hass, 103, 126; Reese, 135; Anna Fest in Owings, 314; Eva Amann in Lechner, 111. See the analysis in Rosenthal, 59.
43. Hochhuth, 203; Sternheim-Peters, 178; Reese, 206; Ursula Krezschmar in Owings, 186.
44. Quoted in Reese, 205. See also Roswitha Koslowski in Lutz Niethammer, "Privat-Wirtschaft: Erinnerungsfragmente einer anderen Umerziehung," in Niethammer, ed., *"Hinterher merkt man, dass es richtig war, dass es schiefgegangen ist": Nachkriegserfahrungen im Ruhrgebiet* (Berlin, 1983), 30.
45. Marie Mulde in Rosenthal, 128.
46. Sternheim-Peters, 173.
47. Becker, 104, 112; *Hitler-Jugend, 1933–1945: Die Chronik eines Jahrzehnts* (Berlin, [1943]), 24; Rosenthal, 130.
48. Elfriede Zill, "Die körperliche Schulung im BDM.," in Munske, 24–28; *HJ erlebt Deutschland,* 42–43; Trude Bürkner, *Der Bund Deutscher Mädel in der Hitler-Jugend* (Berlin, 1937), 13–14; Axmann, 175–176.
49. Guido Knopp, *Hitlers Kinder,* 2nd ed. (Munich, 2000), 104.
50. Leni Riefenstahl, *Olympia* (1938); Cooper C. Graham, *Leni Riefenstahl and Olympia* (Metuchen, N.J., 1986).
51. Schirach quoted in Michael Wortmann, *Baldur von Schirach: Hitlers Jugendführer* (Cologne, 1982), 162.
52. Maria Kramarz, *Dies Mädel ist Hanne—später bist Du es* (Berlin-Lichterfelde, 1937), 113; Helmut Stellrecht, *Neue Erziehung* (Berlin, 1942), 160; Sternheim-Peters, 270.
53. Sternheim-Peters, 195; Robert Proctor, *The Nazi War on Cancer* (Princeton, 1999), 218–219.
54. *Mädel im Dienst: Ein Handbuch* (Potsdam, 1934), 78; Edelgard Seidel, entry for March 8, 1944, in Heinrich Breloer, ed., *Mein Tagebuch: Geschichten vom Überleben, 1939–1947* (Cologne, 1984), 218; Reese, 62; Sternheim-Peters, 194.
55. Entry for Aug. 27, 1944, in Ingrid Hammer and Susanne zur Nieden, eds., *Sehr selten habe ich geweint: Briefe und Tagebücher aus dem Zweiten Weltkrieg von Menschen aus Berlin* (Zurich, 1992), 298–299; Sternheim-Peters, 196.
56. Hitler quoted in Stephenson, 141. See also Hitler quoted for May 1936 in Reese, 43.

57. Ulla Kuhlo, "Gesundheitsdienst im Bund deutscher Mädel," *Die Ärztin* 17 (1941): 193–200.

58. Bürkner, 21; Sternheim-Peters, 70.

59. Becker, 115; Bürkner, 16; Kinz, 202; Anne Niessen, *"Die Lieder waren die eigentlichen Verführer!": Mädchen und Musik im Nationalsozialismus* (Mainz, 1999).

60. *Mädel im Dienst,* 97, 183–184, 192, 194, 215 (quote). See also Kinz, 213.

61. Kinz, 267; Frevert, 232–233. Michael Burleigh persuasively exposes Mother's Day as the manipulative Nazi instrument it was: see *The Third Reich: A New History* (New York, 2001), 230.

62. Albrecht Möller, *Wir werden das Volk: Wesen und Forderung der Hitlerjugend* (Breslau, 1935), 120; Reinhold Sautter, *Hitlerjugend: Das Erlebnis einer grossen Kameradschaft* (Munich, 1942), 191; Rosenthal, 61.

63. Frevert, 217–218.

64. Günter Kaufmann, *Das kommende Deutschland: Die Erziehung der Jugend im Reich Adolf Hitlers,* 3rd ed. (Berlin, 1943), 290–292; Axmann, 319; testimony in Erich Blohm, *Hitler-Jugend: Soziale Tatgemeinschaft,* 2nd ed. (Vlotho, 1979), 242; *Jugend im nationalsozialistischen Frankfurt: Ausstellungsdokumentation, Zeitzeugenerinnerungen, Publikum* (Frankfurt am Main, 1987), 118.

65. *Das Junge Deutschland* (1937): 560–562; Bürkner, 19; Rüdiger, 401; Hochhuth, 219–220, 224–225, 228, 232–234. On the issue of proper Nazi "female" occupations, see Jill Stephenson, *Women in Nazi Society* (London, 1975).

66. Miller-Kipp, *Auch,* 175–179.

67. Ibid., 180.

68. Stephenson, *Women in Nazi Germany,* 65–66, 81.

69. Bürkner, 18; Rüdiger, 400; Kaufmann, 288; Miller-Kipp, *Auch,* 168–173.

70. Margarete Hannsmann, *Der helle Tag bricht an: Ein Kind wird Nazi* (Munich, 1984), 157–164; Erika S., entry for Apr. 2, 1943, in Breloer, 157; *Jugend . . . Frankfurt,* 273.

71. For the pre-1939 origins, see Stephan Bajohr, "Weiblicher Arbeitsdienst im 'Dritten Reich': Konflikt zwischen Ideologie und Ökonomie," *Vierteljahrshefte für Zeitgeschichte* 28 (1980): 331–350.

72. Frieda Sopp, *Der Arbeitsdienst der deutschen Mädchen* (Berlin, n.d.); Franz W. Seidler, *Frauen zu den Waffen? Marketenderinnen—Helferinnen—Soldatinnen* (Bonn, 1978) 39; Stephenson, *Women in Nazi Germany,* 89; Manfred Seifert, *Kulturarbeit im Reichsarbeitsdienst: Theorie und Praxis nationalsozialistischer Kulturpflege im Kontext historisch-politischer, organisatorischer und ideologischer Einflüsse* (Münster, 1996), 98.

73. Regina Maria Shelton, *To Lose a War: Memoirs of a German Girl* (Carbondale, Ill., 1982), 52–54; *Frauen im Wehrdienst: Erinnerungen von Ingeborg Hecht, Ruth Henry, Christa Meves* (Freiburg, 1989), 10–20; Ingeborg P. in Hass, 79.

74. See the text of Chapter 5 at nn. 116f.

75. Seidler, 47–50, 64; Gerda Szepansky, ed., *"Blitzmädel," "Heldenmutter," "Kriegerwitwe": Frauenleben im Zweiten Weltkrieg* (Frankfurt am Main, 1986), 93–98; Sigrid Bremer, *Muckefuck und Kameradschaft: Mädchenzeit im Dritten Reich: Von der Kinderlandverschickung 1940 bis zum Studium 1946* (Frankfurt am Main, 1988), 78–79; Ursula von Gersdorff, *Frauen im Kriegsdienst, 1914–1945* (Stuttgart, 1969), 68, 339–340.

76. See the text of Chapter 5 at nn. 276f.

77. Gersdorff, 400, 439–440; Maruta Schmidt and Gabi Dietz, eds., *Frauen unterm Hakenkreuz* (Berlin, 1983), 46.

78. Martin Broszat et al., eds., *Bayern in der NS-Zeit: Soziale Lage und politisches Verhalten der Bevölkerung im Spiegel vertraulicher Berichte* (Munich, 1977), 614; Gersdorff, 68; Szepansky, 95; Seifert, 100.

79. Seifert, 102.

80. Burleigh, 446–450; Martin Broszat, *Nationalsozialistische Polenpolitik, 1939–1945* (Stuttgart, 1961); Robert L. Koehl, *RKFDV: German Resettlement and Population Policy, 1939–1945: A History of the Reich Commission for the Strengthening of Germandom* (Cambridge, Mass., 1957); Gellately, 153–154; Knopp, 247.

81. *Hitler-Jugend . . . Chronik,* 49–50, 57–58; Axmann, 325; Kinz, 82; Knopp, 247; Melita Maschmann, *Fazit: Kein Rechtfertigungsversuch,* 5th ed. (Stuttgart, 1964), 121–123.

82. Maschmann, 121; Renate Finckh, *Mit uns zieht die neue Zeit* (Baden-Baden, 1979), 145.

83. Fridel Pauls, "Einsatz in den neuen Ostgebieten," [Aug. 1943], SAG, SF6827, GA/110.

84. Ibid. (quotes); Finkh, 146.

85. Maschmann, 78.

86. Erna Stahl, *Jugend im Schatten von gestern: Aufsätze Jugendlicher zur Zeit* (Hamburg, 1948), 53–57.

87. Fridel Pauls, "Einsatz in den neuen Ostgebieten," [Aug. 1943], SAG, SF6827, GA/110; Finkh, 145.

88. Finkh, 144. Similarly, see Margarethe Eichberger, *Endlich ehrlich erinnern: Jugend unter Hitler, Kriegs- und Nachkriegszeit* (Frankfurt am Main, 1997), 73–74.

89. Finkh, 145.

90. Ibid., 147–148.

91. Stahl, 55–57.

92. Cited in Martin Klaus, *Mädchen im 3. Reich: Der Bund Deutscher Mädel* (Cologne, 1998), 37–38.

93. See Karl-Heinz Huber, *Jugend unterm Hakenkreuz* (Berlin, 1982), 305.

94. On the boys, see Chapters 2 and 5.

95. "Kriegseinsätze der Hitler-Jugend: Gesamteinsatz der Mädel im 1. Kriegsjahr," [1940], HIS, 19/358; "Aufstellung . . . Gau Mecklenburg," [1943], BA, NS26/150.

96. Hildegard Morgenthal, *"Rotkopf, die Ecke brennt, Feuerwehr kommt angerennt": Leben in der NS-Zeit und zwei Leben danach* (Frankfurt am Main, 2000), 17; Sautter, 199; "Mädelerziehung im Kriege," [1944], HIS, 19/358.

97. Sautter, 307, 312; illustration no. 47 in Huber; "Kriegseinsätze der Hitler-Jugend: Gesamteinsatz der Mädel im 1. Kriegsjahr," [1940], HIS, 19/358.

98. "Kriegseinsätze der Hitler-Jugend: Gesamteinsatz der Mädel im 1. Kriegsjahr," [1940], HIS, 19/358; Kauffmann, 315; "Bannbefehl HJ," HJ-Bann Lech (478), [Fall 1942], BA, NS28/27; Kinz, 243–245.

99. "Kriegseinsätze der Hitler-Jugend: Gesamteinsatz der Mädel im 1. Kriegsjahr," [1940], HIS, 19/358; *Hitler-Jugend . . . Chronik*, 43–44.

100. Kreisleitung Darmstadt memo, Feb. 17, 1944, HHSAW, 483/5538.

101. Blohm, 313–314.

102. Ilse Koehn, *Mischling zweiten Grades: Kindheit in der NS-Zeit* (Reinbek, 1980), 106.

103. Venter, report on journey to Angermünde and Prenzlau, Dec. 29, 1943, HIS, 13/260.

104. "Kriegseinsätze der Hitler-Jugend: Gesamteinsatz der Mädel im 1. Kriegsjahr," [1940], HIS, 19/358.

105. Karl Heinz Jahnke, *Hitlers letztes Aufgebot: Deutsche Jugend im sechsten Kriegsjahr, 1944/45* (Essen, 1993), 146–147.

106. Shelton, 36; Schmidt and Dietz, 41.

107. Marie Mulde in Rosenthal, 135; Martin Cranz, *Ich, ein Deutscher* (Dülmen, 1987), 203–204; Friedrich Grupe, *Jahrgang 1916: Die Fahne war mehr als der Tod* (Munich, 1989), 301–302; Bremer, 29.

108. Shelton, 35.

109. Eisenecker quoted in Knopp, 144.

110. Inge Stolten, *Das alltägliche Exil: Leben zwischen Hakenkreuz und Währungsreform* (Berlin, 1982), 88 (quote); Szepansky, 97; Frevert, 249–250; Stephenson, *Women in Nazi Germany*, 112–113; Knopp, 142.

111. *Hitler-Jugend . . . Chronik,* 38.

112. Speer, 73–74; Leni Riefenstahl, *The Sieve of Time: The Memoirs of Leni Riefenstahl* (London, 1992), 131–306; Anna Maria Sigmund, *Die Frauen der Nazis,* 12th ed. (Munich, 2003), 145–171.

113. Her successor was Annemarie Kaspar who got married in 1943, at which time the organization came under Rüdiger directly (Reese, 27–28).

114. See the photograph in Knopp, 111.

115. Sternheim-Peters, 216.

116. Gustav Memminger, ed., *Die Jugend des Führers Adolf Hitler: Bildbuch über die grossdeutsche Jugend* (Leipzig, 1942), 72–73; Axmann, 250; Kinz, 232; Miller-Kipp, *Auch,* 300.

117. Kinz, 229–231; Blohm, 273.

118. Quoted in Miller-Kipp, *Auch,* 78.

119. Becker, 108 (first two quotes); *Hitler-Jugend . . . Chronik,* 38 (third quote).

120. Erna Benze, "Nationalsozialistische Frauenschaft und das Deutsche Frauenwerk," in Benze and Gräfer, 301; Doris K. in Steinbach, 78; *Jugend . . . Frankfurt,* 110.

121. Felix Kersten, *Totenkopf und Treue: Heinrich Himmler ohne Uniform* (Hamburg, n.d.), 92–104.

122. Maschmann, 151–152.

123. Georg Lilienthal, *Der "Lebensborn e.V.": Ein Instrument national-sozialistischer Rassenpolitik* (Stuttgart, 1985); Dorothee Schmitz-Köster, *"Deutsche Mutter, bist Du bereit . . .": Alltag im Lebensborn* (Berlin, 1997), esp. 10–15; Stephenson, *Women in Nazi Germany,* 39, 150–151. Perhaps not surprisingly, the old myth of the Lebensborn as a stud farm still haunts even the most up-to-date literature. See Miller-Kipp, *Auch,* 194. For an earlier sensationalist version see Louis Hagen, *Follow My Leader* (London, 1951), 263–265.

124. See Himmler's remarks regarding "questions about illegitimate mother-hood," June 15, 1937, BA, R18/5518; Sybille Hübner-Funk, *Loyalität und Verblendung: Hitlers Garanten der Zukunft als Träger der zweiten deutschen Demokratie* (Potsdam, 1998), 259–260; Carola Kuhlmann, *Erbkrank oder erziehbar? Jugendhilfe als Vorsorge und Aussonderung in der Fürsorgeerziehung in Westfalen von 1933–1945* (Weinheim, 1989), 197; Brandt to Frank, Dec. 12, 1944, in Helmut Heiber, ed., *Reichsführer! . . .: Briefe an und von Himmler* (Stuttgart, 1968), 297 (also 196, 198, 219–220), and the case of Sigmund Rascher in Michael H. Kater, *Das "Ahnenerbe" der SS: Ein Beitrag zur Kulturpolitik des Dritten Reiches,* 3rd ed. (Munich, 2001), 239–245.

125. J. Mayerhofer, "Liebe und Ehe," *SS-Leitheft* 9, no. 8 (Aug. 1943): 17.

126. Himmler to all SS and Police, Apr. 6, 1942, BA, R43II/512.

127. Kersten, 92–104 (quotes, 93, 94).

128. "Das BDM-Werk 'Glaube und Schönheit,'" May 1938, in Miller-Kipp, *Auch*, 79.

129. Kater, *Das "Ahnenerbe" der SS;* Sautter, 222.

130. Sautter, 223.

131. Kersten, 156–171 (quote, 157).

132. See Hugh R. Trevor-Roper, ed., *The Bormann Letters* (London, 1954); Anna Maria Sigmund, *Die Frauen der Nazis II* (Munich, 2002), 7–60.

133. Heinz Höhne, *Der Orden unter dem Totenkopf: Die Geschichte der SS* (Gütersloh, 1967), 388.

134. Kersten, 223–236; Stephenson, *Women in Nazi Society*, 69–70; Stephenson, *Women in Nazi Germany*, 43.

135. Reich Ministry of Justice, "Der Frauenüberschuss nach dem Kriege," [1944], BA, R22/4003.

136. Sautter, 223; Rüdiger, 407.

137. Sautter, 197; Edith Müller, *Ursel und ihre Mädel* (Reutlingen, [1939]), 54; *Mädel im Dienst*, 243–246; Miller-Kipp, *Auch*, 130.

138. *Mädel im Dienst*, 241 (quote); Maschmann, 41.

139. *Mädel im Dienst*, 198.

140. Quoted in Knopp, 117.

141. Quoted in Finkh, 168.

142. Bürkner, 24; Hannsmann, 75.

143. *Mädel im Dienst*, 249.

144. Becker, 105–106; Finckh, 120.

145. *Mädel im Dienst*, 198–199, 246–248 (quotes, 246, 248).

146. Entry for Feb. 5, 1940, by Charlotte L. in Breloer, 414.

147. Sternheim-Peters, 144.

148. Bürkner, 15; Becker, 103; Miller-Kipp, *Auch*, 258–259.

149. "Das Raubtier," *Der Stürmer* 13 (1935), reproduced in Walter Wuttke-Groneberg, ed., *Medizin im Nationalsozialismus: Ein Arbeitsbuch* (Tübingen, 1980), 353. On the effect of *Stürmer*, see also Sternheim-Peters, 146.

150. Marie Mulde quoted in Rosenthal, 132.

151. See Knopp, 108.

152. *Mädel im Dienst*, 255.

153. Hannsmann, 164.

154. Friedrichs speech, March 23, 1944, BA, Schumacher/368.

155. *Mädel im Dienst,* 253.

156. *Wir Mädel singen: Liederbuch des Bundes Deutscher Mädel* (Wolfenbüttel, 1938), 172–175; today's recollection of Christa Thorau in Hans Wienicke, ed., *"Schon damals fingen viele an zu schweigen . . .": Quellensammlung zur Geschichte Charlottenburgs von 1933–1945* (Berlin-Charlottenburg, 1986), 157.

157. Möller, quotes on 118 and 119.

158. Ibid., 116–119 (quotes, 118); Rüdiger, 396; Bürkner, 22.

159. Stephenson, *Women in Nazi Germany,* 19.

160. Ibid.

161. "Der Führer spricht zu den deutschen Frauen," in *Der Kongress zu Nürnberg vom 5. bis 10. September 1934: Offizieller Bericht über den Verlauf des Reichsparteitages mit sämtlichen Reden* (Munich, 1934), 168–173 (quote, 169).

162. Rosenthal, 62; Charlotte L. in Breloer, 415.

163. Axmann, 229; Reese, 34; Stephenson, *Women in Nazi Germany,* 74; Miller-Kipp, "Bund," 90; Jürgen Schultz, *Die Akademie für Jugendführung der Hitlerjugend in Braunschweig* (Brunswick, 1978), 171–174.

164. Alfons Heck, *A Child of Hitler: Germany in the Days when God wore a Swastika* (Frederick, Colo., 1985), 131.

165. See the examples in Rosenthal, 112–113; Koehn, 107; Knopp, 106.

166. Sternheim-Peters, (quote, 174), 180; Müller, 50; *Mädel im Dienst,* 219–220; Rosenthal, 60.

167. Quoted in Knopp, 122–123. Also see Doris K. in Steinbach, 96.

168. Stephenson, *Women in Nazi Germany,* 55, 65; Michael H. Kater, *Doctors Under Hitler* (Chapel Hill, N.C., 1989), 87–110.

169. Sternheim-Peters, 215; Reese, 41; Rosenthal, 111.

170. Edith Niehuis, *Das Landjahr: Eine Jugenderziehungseinrichtung in der Zeit des Nationalsozialismus* (Nörten-Hardenberg, 1984), 67.

171. Maschmann, 160.

172. Jürgen Falter, *Hitlers Wähler* (Munich, 1991), 143–144; Ian Kershaw, *Hitler, 1889–1936: Hubris* (New York, 1999); Kershaw, *Hitler, 1936–1945: Nemesis* (New York, 2000).

173. See Gisela Otmar in Rosenthal, 107; Gertraude Wortmann in Knopp, 101.

174. *Mädel im Dienst,* 187, 220 (first quote); *Wir Mädel singen,* 31 (second quote).

175. Liselotte G. in Hammer and Zur Nieden, 278; Sternheim-Peters, 186.

176. Lore Walb, *Ich, die Alte—ich, die Junge: Konfrontation mit meinen Tagebüchern, 1933–1945,* 2nd ed. (Berlin, 1997), 35–36.

177. Doris K. in Steinbach, 85–86.

178. Helga Giessel in Winfried Maass, *Die Fünfzigjährigen: Portrait einer verratenen Generation* (Hamburg, 1980), 59.

179. See *Deutschland-Berichte der Sozialdemokratischen Partei Deutschlands (Sopade),* vol. 3 (1936), 1317–18; partial report of Oberlandesgerichtspräsident Munich, Apr. 30, 1942, BA, R22/1176a. Schirach's quote is from his book *Die Hitler-Jugend: Idee und Gestalt* (Leipzig, 1934), 62.

180. On the freedom, see the remarks of former Hitler Youth Hermann Graml, "Integration und Entfremdung: Inanspruchnahme durch Staatsjugend und Dienstpflicht," in Ute Benz and Wolfgang Benz, eds., *Sozialisation und Traumatisierung: Kinder in der Zeit des Nationalsozialismus* (Frankfurt am Main, 1992), 78–79.

181. Ian Buruma and Avishai Margalit, "Occidentalism," *New York Review of Books* (Jan. 17, 2002): 7.

182. Frevert, 64, 134, 186; Elizabeth Heineman, "Sexuality and Nazism: The Doubly Unspeakable?", *Journal of the History of Sexuality* 11 (2002): 30–31. Note the moralizing in Peter Paul Pauquet, *Gespräche mit der Jugend einer zerschlagenen Nation* (Nuremberg, 1947), 114–115.

183. Brauer to Parteigenossin, March 16, 1934, BA, NS22/342.

184. *Deutschland-Berichte,* vol. 2 (1935), 694–696 (quote, 695).

185. Ibid., vol. 3 (1936), 359; Huber, 185.

186. Miller-Kipp, "Bund," 100 (n. 57).

187. Kinz, 42.

188. Von Saldern, 144.

189. Entry for Dec. 13, 1943, in Heinz Boberach, ed., *Meldungen aus dem Reich: Die geheimen Lageberichte des Sicherheitsdienstes der SS, 1938–1945* (Herrsching, 1984), vol. 15, 6145–6147; entry for Jan. 24, 1944, ibid., vol. 16, 6279; monthly report of Regierungspräsident Regensburg, June 11, 1943, BA, Schumacher/483; Ulrich Herbert, *Hitler's Foreign Workers: Enforced Foreign Labor in Germany under the Third Reich* (Cambridge, 1997), 64–66, 70–77, 96–100, 109, 125–127, 133, 269; Michael Burleigh and Wolfgang Wippermann, *The Racial State: Germany, 1933–1945* (Cambridge, 1991), 264–266.

190. Erhard Eppler, *Als Wahrheit verordnet wurde: Briefe an meine Enkelin,* 3rd ed. (Frankfurt am Main, 1995), 84–85; Lechner, 85.

191. Stephenson, *Women in Nazi Germany,* 29, 171–172.

192. Gellately, 157–158.
193. Huber, 268.
194. Entry for Jan. 22, 1942, in Boberach, vol. 9, 3202.
195. Amtsgericht München, judgment against Moser and Nusskern, Sept. 2, 1942, ARL, Lü 6.1.5 (München).
196. Amtsgericht München, judgment against Krammer, Jan. 26, 1943, ARL, Lü 6.1.5 (München).
197. Friedrichs speech, March 23, 1944, BA, Schumacher/368.
198. Amtsgericht München, judgment against Kreitmeier, May 18, 1943, ARL, Lü 6.1.5 (München); entry for June 6, 1943, in Boberach, vol. 14, 5341 (quote).
199. Testimonies of Dieter Wellershoff and Martin Gregor-Dellin in Marcel Reich-Ranicki, ed., *Meine Schulzeit im Dritten Reich: Erinnerungen deutscher Schriftsteller* (Munich, 1984), 146–147, 179. This is corroborated from a girl's point of view in Sternheim-Peters, 356.
200. W. Knopp, "Kriminalität und Gefährdung der Jugend: Lagebericht bis zum Stande vom 1. Januar 1941," BA, NSD43/96 (p. 165); youth court to Reich justice minister, Apr. 5, 1944, BA, R22/1165.
201. Walb, 151.
202. Entry for Nov. 3, 1939, in Boberach, vol. 2, 416; monthly report of SRD Augsburg, Nov. 1, 1940, SAND, unsign. Bestand, EAP 221-b-20/9; W. Knopp, "Kriminalität und Gefährdung der Jugend" (pp. 164–166); excerpt, report of attorney-general Celle, Apr. 4, 1942, BA, R22/1176a; youth court to Reich justice minister, Apr. 5, 1944, BA, R22/1165.
203. Entry for Nov. 3, 1939, in Boberach, vol. 2, 416 (quote); Ungereiter to Reich interior minister, July 26, 1944, BA, R22/3364.
204. Munding to Scheffelt, Feb. 23, 1941, in Friedrich Munding, *Dass ich nur noch selten schreibe: Briefe aus Berlin, 1940–1943*, ed. Werner Trapp (Berlin, 1985), 18; Howard K. Smith, *Feind schreibt mit: Ein amerikanischer Korrespondent erlebt Nazi-Deutschland* (Frankfurt am Main, 1986), 131. See also entry for March 18, 1943, in Ursula von Kardorff, *Berliner Aufzeichnungen: Aus den Jahren 1942 bis 1945*, 3rd ed. (Munich, 1962), 35.
205. Quoted in Huber, 265.
206. Monthly report, Regierungspräsident Regensburg, March 10, 1943, BA, Schumacher/483; Heck, 133–134.
207. Hoffmeister to Reich justice minister, June 30, 1942; situation report of attorney-general Frankfurt, Jan. 28, 1943; excerpt, situation report Oberlandesgerichtspräsident Nuremberg, March 31, 1943, BA, R22/

1176a; Edelgard Seidel, entry for Nov. 27, 1944, in Breloer, 225; entry for Apr. 13, 1944, in Boberach, vol. 16, 6484; Klaus Tischler's testimony in Rosenthal, 266–267; Helmut Altner, *Totentanz Berlin: Tagebuchblätter eines Achtzehnjährigen* (Offenbach, 1947), 32; Walter Kempowski, *Tadellöser and Wolff: Ein bürgerlicher Roman*, 2nd ed. (Munich, 1975), 456.

208. Winfried Süss, *Der "Volkskörper" im Krieg: Gesundheitspolitik, Gesundheitsverhältnisse und Krankenmord im nationalsozialistischen Deutschland, 1939–1945* (Munich, 2003), 396–397.

209. Nazi Party proceedings against Balnus, Oct. 10, 1942, personal file Balnus, BAB; Edelgard Seidel, entry for Sept. 23, 1944, in Breloer, 223–224; Finckh, 146–147.

4. Dissidents and Rebels

1. Hans Rothfels, *The German Opposition to Hitler: An Appraisal* (Hinsdale, Ill., 1948), 12. On Weimar, see Rothfels, "Deutschlands Krise," in Alfred Bozi and Alfred Niemann, eds., *Die Einheit der Nationalen Politik* (Stuttgart, 1925), 1–15; Rothfels, "Wolfgang Kapp," *Deutsches biographisches Jahrbuch* 4 (1922): 132–143. On Rothfels's (eastern-expansionist) politics and historiography, personal biography, and the resistance book, see, preeminently, Ingo Haar, *Historiker im Nationalsozialismus: Deutsche Geschichtswissenschaft und der "Volkstumskampf" im Osten* (Göttingen, 2000), 86–90; Hans Mommsen, "Geschichtsschreibung und Humanität—Zum Gedenken an Hans Rothfels," in Wolfgang Benz and Hermann Graml, eds., *Aspekte deutscher Aussenpolitik im 20. Jahrhundert: Aufsätze Hans Rothfels zum Gedächtnis* (Stuttgart, 1976), 9–27; Hans-Ulrich Wehler, "Historiography in Germany Today," in Jürgen Habermas, ed., *Observations on "The Spiritual Situation of the Age": Contemporary German Perspectives* (Cambridge, Mass., 1984), 229 (quote). On Rothfels as a Jew, see the seminal article by Peter Loewenberg, "Antisemitismus und jüdischer Selbsthass: Eine sich wechselseitig verstärkende sozialpsychologische Doppelbeziehung," *Geschichte und Gesellschaft* 5 (1979): 455–475. Wehler's plight in 1943–44 is documented in *Der Spiegel* (Jan. 6, 2003): 51. In contrast to Rothfels, compare the almost contemporaneous, more inclusive approach to anti-Nazi resistance by Annedore Leber, ed., *Das Gewissen steht auf: 64 Lebensbilder aus dem deutschen Widerstand, 1933–1945* (Berlin, 1954), esp. 22–24.

2. Robert Gellately, *The Gestapo and German Society: Enforcing Racial Policy, 1933–1945* (Oxford, 1991).

3. George (Jürgen) Wittenstein, "The White Rose: Memories and Reflections," paper presented at the International Conference entitled "CONFRONT! Resistance in Nazi Germany," Boston College, Apr. 17, 2002 (APA).

4. Rohlfing memo, June 7, 1935, SAB, 4,65-II, E, 3, a/13.

5. Andreas von Hellfeld, *Bündische Jugend und Hitlerjugend: Zur Geschichte von Anpassung und Widerstand, 1930–1939* (Cologne, 1987), 121–126.

6. Kurt Schilde, *Jugendorganisationen und Jugendopposition in Berlin-Kreuzberg, 1933–45: Eine Dokumentation* (Berlin, 1983), 92–97; Karl Heinz Jahnke and Michael Buddrus, eds., *Deutsche Jugend, 1933–1945: Eine Dokumentation* (Hamburg, 1989), 239–243.

7. Beck to Landräte et al., May 24, 1939, SAM, LRA/47093.

8. Fritz Molden, *Fepolinski und Waschlapski auf dem berstenden Stern: Bericht einer unruhigen Jugend* (Vienna, 1976), 151–152, 158–159.

9. Von Hellfeld, 140–141.

10. Otto B. Roegele, *Gestapo gegen Schüler: Die Gruppe "Christopher" in Bruchsal* (Constance, 1994), 35–51, 85–101.

11. Karl Heinz Jahnke, *Jugend im Widerstand, 1933–1945*, 2nd ed. (Frankfurt am Main, 1985), 127–132.

12. "Politischer Lagebericht," Ortsgruppe Rothenburg, Feb. 1939, BA, Schumacher/372.

13. "SRD-Monatsbericht Oktober," Nov. 4, 1940, SAND, unsign. Best., EAP 221-b-20/9.

14. Jahnke and Buddrus, 284–285.

15. Von Hellfeld, 162–165.

16. Volksgerichtshof Berlin, judgment against Landgraf et al., Sept. 23, 1942, ARL, Parteikanzlei/Mikrofiches (quotes); Landgraf, "Jugend im Kampf für Freiheit und Vaterland," Vienna, n.d., DAOW, 2542.

17. Christine E. King, *The Nazi State and the New Religions: Five Case Studies in Non-Conformity* (New York, 1982), 63–87.

18. Detlev Peukert, "Protest und Widerstand von Jugendlichen im Dritten Reich," in Richard Löwenthal and Patrick von zur Mühlen, eds., *Widerstand und Verweigerung in Deutschland, 1933 bis 1945* (Bonn, 1982), 194 (quote); Ursula Prückner and Axel Waldhier, "Verweigerung—Opposition—Widerstand: Einblicke in das Leben dreier Nicht-Faschisten," in Brigitte Abramowski et al., *"Ohne uns hätten sie das gar nicht machen können": Nazi-Zeit und Nachkrieg in Altona und Ottensen* (Hamburg, 1985), 51; Blair R. Holmes and Alan F. Keele, eds., *When Truth Was Treason: German Youth against Hitler: The Story of the Helmuth Hübener Group* (Urbana, Ill., 1995).

19. Guido Knopp, *Hitlers Kinder,* 2nd ed. (Munich, 2000), 202.
20. Michael Burleigh, *The Third Reich: A New History* (New York, 2001), 411.
21. Wolf Jobst Siedler in Johannes Steinhoff et al., eds., *Voices from the Third Reich: An Oral History* (New York, 1994), 358 (quotes); Gunter Fahle, *Verweigern—Weglaufen—Zersetzen: Deutsche Militärjustiz und ungehorsame Soldaten, 1939–1945: Das Beispiel Ems-Jade* (Bremen, 1990), 170–176; Hans-Dietrich Nicolaisen, *Die Flakhelfer: Luftwaffenhelfer und Marinehelfer im Zweiten Weltkrieg* (Berlin, 1981), 155–156.
22. Eva Amann's testimony is in Silvester Lechner, *Das KZ Oberer Kuhberg und die NS-Zeit in der Region Ulm/Neu-Ulm* (Stuttgart, 1988), 110–111.
23. Otl Aicher, *Innenseiten des Kriegs* (Frankfurt am Main, 1985), 57, 60, 130.
24. Hartnagel to Sophie Scholl, Sept. 14, 1942, quoted in *Spiegel Online,* Jan. 31, 2003.
25. Christian Petry, *Studenten aufs Schafott: Die Weisse Rose und ihr Scheitern* (Munich, 1968), 28; Scholl quoted on p. 30.
26. Personal communication by George Wittenstein to the author, Santa Barbara, May 4, 2003 (quote); Detlef Bald, *Die "Weisse Rose": Von der Front in den Widerstand* (Berlin, 2003), 130.
27. Aicher, 83. On Inge: personal communication by George Wittenstein to the author, Santa Barbara, May 4, 2003.
28. See the text of Chapter 2 at n. 19.
29. Petry, 25–28 (quotes, 27); Lechner, 97–100; Inge Scholl, *Die Weisse Rose* (Frankfurt am Main, 1965), 18–21, 26–30. Scholl's book has become a virtual bible on the White Rose, in several commercially successful editions, heightening the cachet of the Scholl siblings in the conspiracy immeasurably. But since the author was never personally involved in it, the book's information, as George Wittenstein rightly points out, is only second-hand and, as I have been able to ascertain, frequently skewed or incorrect. Obviously, for self-serving reasons, Inge Scholl placed herself at a point in the movement where she had never been, and gave herself an aura of authority that she had never possessed. It is significant that in the latest book on the White Rose, by Detlef Bald, she is not mentioned at all. See Wittenstein, "The White Rose," as in n. 3.
30. Wittenstein, "The White Rose," as in n. 3.
31. Petry, 21–25 (quote, 24); Gerhard Paul, *Ungehorsame Soldaten: Dissens, Verweigerung und Widerstand deutscher Soldaten (1939–1945)* (St. Ingbert, 1994), 96–97.
32. Wittenstein, "The White Rose," as in n. 3.
33. Petry, 19–21.

34. Heinz A. Brenner, *Dagegen: Bericht über den Widerstand von Schülern des Humanistischen Gymnasiums Ulm/Donau gegen die deutsche national-sozialistische Diktatur* (Leutkirch, [1992]), 22–25, 37; Lechner, 98; Scholl, 33–38, 71–72; Petry, 50–51.

35. Lechner, 101; Scholl, 58.

36. Wittenstein, "The White Rose," as in n. 3 (quotes); Petry, 65–73.

37. Petry, 36–42 (quote, 41).

38. "Denkschrift zur Neugründung und Angliederung der deutschen Schule für Volksmusik und Tanz am Trapp'schen Konservatorium der Musik" [1935], StAM, Kulturamt/480.

39. Kurt Huber, "Der Aufbau deutscher Volksliedforschung und Volksliedpflege," *Deutsche Musikkultur* 1 (1936): 66, 68–69.

40. Petry, 42–47; Maria Bruckbauer, *". . . und sei es gegen eine Welt von Feinden!": Kurt Hubers Volksliedsammlung und -pflege in Bayern* (Munich, 1991), 13–15, 99–204.

    Huber's friend, the Munich composer Carl Orff, claimed in 1945–46 that he, too, had been mentoring, had even co-founded, the White Rose in partnership with Huber. He told this to the U.S. authorities in an effort to get easy denazification clearance, since he knew he was guilty of collaboration with the Nazi regime, although he himself had never been a Nazi. Although his scam worked at the time, it has recently been exposed through research. See Clara Huber to the author, Munich, Sept. 30, 1993; Gertrud Orff to the author, Munich, Nov. 12, 1993; George Wittenstein to the author, Santa Barbara, Oct. 21, 1997, APA; Michael H. Kater, *Composers of the Nazi Era: Eight Portraits* (New York, 2000), 111–143; Kater, "In Answer to Hans Jörg Jans," *Musical Quarterly* 84 (2000): 711–712; Richard Taruskin, "Orff's Musical and Moral Failings," *New York Times,* May 6, 2001.

41. Wittenstein, "The White Rose," as in n. 3.

42. Bald, 18–21, 145; Petry, 92–100 (quote, 99).

43. Petry, 100–106 (quotes, 102); Wittenstein, "The White Rose," as in n. 3.

44. Scheibe to anon., [March 1943], SAM, NSDAP/11.

45. Wittenstein, "The White Rose," as in n. 3.

46. Petry, 107–111; Bald, 154–155.

47. Wittenstein, "The White Rose," as in n. 3.

48. Petry, 175–183, 195–211.

49. Scholl, 112, 114.

50. Facs. of leaflets I–VI in Lechner, 7–17.

51. Ian Kershaw, *Hitler, 1880–1936: Hubris* (New York, 1999); Kershaw, *Hitler, 1936–45: Nemesis* (New York, 2000), esp. 751f.

52. Albrecht Riethmüller, "Wunschbild: Beethoven als Chauvinist," *Archiv für Musikwissenschaft* 58 (2001): 91–109; Michael H. Kater, "Introduction," in Kater and Albrecht Riethmüller, eds., *Music and Nazism: Art under Tyranny, 1933–1945* (Laaber, 2003), 1–2.

53. See Günter De Bruyn, *Zwischenbilanz: Eine Jugend in Berlin* (Frankfurt am Main, 1995), 107; Jahnke and Buddrus, 334.

54. Aicher, 10, 14, 28, 36, 81.

55. Ibid., 61, 80, 82; Scholl.

56. Aicher, 88, 154; Lechner, 104.

57. Lechner, 108, 115.

58. Petry, 138–145; Jahnke, 180–186; Inge Stolten, *Das alltägliche Exil: Leben zwischen Hakenkreuz und Währungsreform* (Berlin, 1982), 64, 69.

59. Paul, 97, 99.

60. Wittenstein, "The White Rose," as in n. 3; Ruth Andreas-Friedrich, *Der Schattenmann: Tagebuchaufzeichnungen, 1938–1945* (Berlin, 1947), 110–116.

61. "Anhang: Einzelbeispiele für die Cliquen- und Bandenbildung neuerer Zeit," Sept. 1942; Reichsjugendführung, "Entwurf: Bekämpfung jugendlicher Cliquen," May 11, 1943; Reichsführer-SS, "Betrifft: Bekämpfung jugendlicher Cliquen," Oct. 1943, BA, R22/1177. See Matthias von Hellfeld and Arno Klönne, *Die betrogene Generation: Jugend in Deutschland unter dem Faschismus* (Cologne, 1985), 268–269; Alfons Kenkmann, *Wilde Jugend: Lebenswelt grossstädtischer Jugendlicher zwischen Weltwirtschaftskrise, Nationalsozialismus und Währungsreform* (Essen, 1996), 342; Winfried Speitkamp, *Jugend in der Neuzeit: Deutschland vom 16. bis zum 20. Jahrhundert* (Göttingen, 1998), 234–237.

62. Jandl in Marcel Reich-Ranicki, ed., *Meine Schulzeit im Dritten Reich: Erinnerungen deutscher Schriftsteller* (Munich, 1984), 120–121.

63. Amtsgericht München, judgment against Hüttner et al., March 7, 1941; minutes of youth courts at Amtsgericht München, March 14, 1941, ARL, Lü 6.1.2. and 6.1.3. (München).

64. Heinz Boberach, ed., *Meldungen aus dem Reich: Die geheimen Lageberichte des Sicherheitsdienstes der SS, 1938–1945* (Herrsching, 1984), vol. 3, 477; "Bericht zur innenpolitischen Lage," Nov. 22, 1939, BA, R58/145.

65. "Anhang: Einzelbeispiele . . .," Sept. 1942 (as in n. 61); Sieverts, "Jugendgefährdung im Kriege," Oct. 20, 1942, BA, NL/289; Studt to Schulverwaltung Hamburg, Dec. 5, 1941 and Jan. 1, 1942, SAH, Oberschulbehörde VI, 2 F VIII a 2/3/1.

66. "Die Jugendkriminalität in Hamburg seit Beginn des Krieges," [May 1943], BA, NL/289.

67. Gernet to Präsident Hanseatisches Oberlandesgericht, Feb. 2, 1945, SAH, 213-1, OLG Hamburg.

68. Eschenbacher to K-Gebietsführer et al., Oct. 18, 1942, SAM, OLG München/278; Kümmerlein, "Auszug," Feb. 1, 1943; "Tagesmeldung des GenStA in Stettin," Feb. 18, 1943, BA, R22/1177.

69. Venter report, Dec. 29, 1943, HIS, 13/260; "Jugendliche Cliquen und Banden," enclosed with Reich justice minister to Oberlandesgerichtspräsidenten, June 10, 1944, BA, R22/1177.

70. Stedtnitz report, Nov. 30, 1944, in Karl Heinz Jahnke, *Hitlers letztes Aufgebot: Deutsche Jugend im sechsten Kriegsjahr, 1944/45* (Essen, 1993), 104–105.

71. See Detlev Peukert, "Edelweisspiraten, Meuten, Swing: Jugendsubkulturen im Dritten Reich," in Ulrich Herrmann, ed., *"Die Formung des Volksgenossen": Der "Erziehungsstaat" des Dritten Reiches* (Weinheim, 1985), 223.

72. Von Hellfeld and Klönne, 86–89; "Anhang: Einzelbeispiele . . .," Sept. 1942 (as in n. 61) (quote); minutes of judgment against Pflocksch et al., June 15, 1942, BA, R22/1177.

73. "Anhang: Einzelbeispiele . . .," Sept. 1942 (as in n. 61).

74. Detlev Peukert and Michael Winter, "'Edelweisspiraten' in Duisburg: Eine Fallstudie zum subkulturellen Verhalten von Arbeiterjugendlichen unter dem Nationalsozialismus," *Duisburger Forschungen* 31 (1982): 259–260; Kenkmann, 161–163, 182.

75. Peukert and Winter, 268.

76. Edgar Gielsdorf, *Vom Christkind eine Landsknechtstrommel* (Cologne, 1994), 125–127.

77. Jahnke, *Jugend,* 169–170; Ulrich Herbert, *Hitler's Foreign Workers: Enforced Foreign Labor in Germany under the Third Reich* (Cambridge, 1997), 366–367.

78. "Anhang: Einzelbeispiele . . .," Sept. 1942 (as in n. 61); Albath, "Wilde Jugendgruppen—Edelweisspiraten," [spring 1943]; Pastor to Amtsgerichtspräsident, Nov. 7, 1943, BA, R22/1177.

79. SS-Reichssicherheitshauptamt memo, March 15, 1943, BA, R22/1177.

80. Albath, "Wilde Jugendgruppen—Edelweisspiraten," [spring 1943], BA, R22/1177; Kenkmann, 256–257; Peukert and Winter, 264.

81. Peukert and Winter, 260.

82. Gieseking, minutes of interrogation, Nov. 1, 1943, SAMs, Polit. Polizei, 3. Reich/408; Pastor to Amtsgerichtspräsident, Nov. 7, 1943, BA, R22/1177; *Jugend im nationalsozialistischen Frankfurt: Ausstellungsdokumentation, Zeitzeugenerinnerungen, Publikum* (Frankfurt am Main, 1987), 179–180;

　　　　　　　　Notes to Pages 140–145

Jurgen Herbst, *Requiem for a German Past: A Boyhood among the Nazis* (Madison, 1999), 175.

83. Kenkmann, 298.

84. "Anhang: Einzelbeispiele . . .," Sept. 1942 (as in n. 61).

85. "Auszug aus einem Lagebericht des GenStA. in Braunschweig v. 26.5.1943," BA, R22/1176a; Anderegg to Schlüter, Apr. 27, 1944, BA, R36/2021; Herbert Koleczek interview, Rüdesheim, June 25, 1988; Kenkmann, 297–298. On Frankfurt's youthful jazz and swing scene, which, in contrast to Hamburg's, was predominantly lower-middle-class, see Wassermann to Reich justice minister, June 3, 1943, BA, R22/3364; Cornelia Rühlig and Jürgen Steen, eds., *Walter: *1926, +1945 an der Ostfront: Leben und Lebensbedingungen eines Frankfurter Jungen im III. Reich* (Frankfurt am Main, 1983), 116–118, 121, 123; *Jugend . . . Frankfurt,* 157–160, 181–186, 297, 300–304; Michael H. Kater, *Different Drummers: Jazz in the Culture of Nazi Germany* (New York, 1992), 148–151, 196–198. For Berlin, see Heinrich Kupffer, *Swingtime: Chronik einer Jugend in Deutschland, 1937–1951* (Berlin, 1987), 44–46, 49, 54–57.

86. "Bericht über eine Veranstaltung am 2.3.40 im Curio-Haus," SAH, Jugendbehörde I, 343 e.

87. "Anhang: Einzelbeispiele . . .," Sept. 1942 (as in n. 61).

88. Ibid.

89. Ibid.

90. Entry for Aug. 21, 1941, *TGII* 1: 284.

91. Interrogation protocol of A.v.d.E., Oct. 16, 1941, SAH, Oberschulbehörde VI, 2 F VIII a 2/40/1; Grell to Amtsgericht Hamburg, July 16, 1942, SAH, Amtsgericht Hamburg, Abtlg. Vormundschaftswesen, 115 XI, R 1886, 1653/Rönn; Kruse memo, [1942], BA, NL/289; Hannelore Evers-Frauboes and Robert Vogel (quote) recorded interviews, Hamburg, June 18 and 21, 1988; Hans-Joachim Scheel recorded interview, Toronto, March 29, 1988.

92. Pereira report, Febr. 28, 1941, BA, NL/289; interrogation protocol of Helga Rönn, Sept. 10, 1941, SAH, Amtsgericht Hamburg, Abtlg. Vormundschaftswesen, 115 XI, R 1886, 1653/Rönn; Hans Engel recorded interview, Mamaroneck, N.Y., March 5, 1988; Evers-Frauboes and Vogel recorded interviews.

93. Interrogation protocol of Helga Rönn, Sept. 9, 1941, SAH, Amtsgericht Hamburg, Abtlg. Vormundschaftswesen, 115 XI, R 1886, 1653/Rönn; Vogel recorded interview. See Gerd Albrecht, *Nationalsozialistische Filmpolitik: Eine soziologische Untersuchung über die Spielfilme des Dritten Reichs* (Stuttgart, 1969), 109, 383, 434, 547.

94. Engel recorded interview.
95. Evers-Frauboes recorded interview.
96. Karsten Witte, "Gehemmte Schaulust: Momente des deutschen Revue-films," in Helga Belach, ed., *Wir tanzen um die Welt: Deutsche Revuefilme, 1933–1945* (Munich, 1979), 24.
97. *Skizzen* (June/July 1938): 20; German Brunswick record catalogs for March and Apr. 1936, and Apr. 1938, APA.
98. Entry for Feb. 10, 1942, *TGII* 3: 282.
99. Günter Lust in Bernd Polster, ed., *"Swing Heil": Jazz im Nationalsozialis-mus* (Berlin, 1989), 166; Werner Burkhardt, "Musik der Stunde Null (II)," *Zeitmagazin* (Nov. 18, 1983): 42.
100. Interrogation protocol of Heinrich Fey, Oct. 13, 1941; of A.v.d.E., Oct. 16, 1941; of H.P., Oct. 18, 1941, SAH, Oberschulbehörde VI, 2 F VIII a 2/40/1; Uhlenhorst Oberschule für Jungen memo, Dec. 16, 1941, SAH, Oberschulbehörde VI, 2 F VIII a 2/3/1; Kruse memo, [n.d.], BA, NL/289; Scheel, Vogel, Evers-Frauboes, and Engel (quote) recorded interviews.
101. Crepon report, Nov. 10, 1941, SAH, Oberschulbehörde VI, 2 F VIII a 2/3/1; Kruse memo, [1942], BA, NL/289; interrogation protocol of Heinrich Fey, Oct. 13, 1941; of A.v.d.E., Oct. 16, 1941; of O.S., Oct. 18, 1941; of W.D., Oct. 18, 1941; of W.R., Oct. 21, 1941, SAH, Oberschul-behörde VI, 2 F VIII a 2/40/1; Engel, Vogel, and Evers-Frauboes recorded interviews; Hans-Joachim Scheel to the author, Toronto, Apr. 7, 1988, APA (quote).
102. Gestapo Hamburg to Gemeindeverwaltung Hamburg, Nov. 13, 1940, SAH, Oberschulbehörde VI, 2 F VIII a 2/3/1; Wege memo, Sept. 10, 1941, SAH, Amtsgericht Hamburg, Abtlg. Vormundschaftswesen, 115 XI, R 1886, 1653/Rönn; interrogation protocol of A.v.d.E., Oct. 16, 1941, SAH, Oberschulbehörde VI, 2 F VIII a 2/40/1; Engel and Vogel recorded interviews.
103. Gestapo Hamburg to Gemeindeverwaltung Hamburg, Nov. 13, 1940, SAH, Oberschulbehörde VI, 2 F VIII a 2/3/1; interrogation protocol of A.v.d.E., Oct. 16, 1941, SAH, Oberschulbehörde VI, 2 F VIII a 2/40/1; interrogation protocols of Helga Rönn, Sept. 9, 10, and 11, 1941, SAH, Amtsgericht Hamburg, Abtlg. Vormundschaftswesen, 115 XI, R 1886, 1653 Rönn; Prinzhorn memo, Dec. 12, 1942, SAH, Oberschulbehörde VI, 2 F VIII a 2/40/1.
104. Inga Madlung-Shelton recorded interview, London, May 9, 1988 (quote); Grell to Amtsgericht Hamburg, July 16, 1942, SAH, Amts-gericht Hamburg, Abtlg. Vormundschaftswesen, 115 XI, R 1886, 1653/Rönn.

105. Interrogation protocol of W.D., Oct. 18, 1941, SAH, Oberschulbehörde VI, 2 F VIII a 2/40/1; Pereira report, Feb. 28, 1941, BA, NL/289; Madlung-Shelton recorded interview; Andreas Panagopoulos recorded interview, Hamburg, June 16, 1988; Harry Stephens (Demitrius Georgiadis), *Swing Threatens Third Reich* (Nicosia, 1988); photograph in Kater, *Drummers,* 97, also 109.

106. Scheel recorded interview.

107. *Das Junge Deutschland* (1937): 441–443; *Deutsches Ärzteblatt* 66 (1936): 541.

108. See Gellately.

109. "Die Entwicklung der Kriminalität, namentlich der Jugendkriminalität während des Krieges," [1942]; Bormann, "Bekanntgabe 204/44 g.," Aug. 29, 1944, BA, R22/1165.

110. See *Das Junge Deutschland* (1937): 443–444; "Die Entwicklung der Kriminalität, namentlich der Jugendkriminalität während des Krieges," [1942], BA, R22/1165; "Die Struktur der Jugendkriminalität im ersten und zweiten Weltkrieg," 1943, BA, R22/1159. See also the text of Chapter 3 at n. 182.

111. "Die Entwicklung der Kriminalität im Deutschen Reich vom Kriegsbeginn bis Mitte 1943," BA, R22/1159.

112. Kenkmann, 151; Von Hellfeld and Klönne, 296.

113. Kenkmann, 151.

114. Hanns Anderlahn, "Führung—Erziehung—Strafe," *Das Junge Deutschland* (1937): 54.

115. HJ-Gebiet Hamburg memo, March 12, 1940, SAH, Jugendbehörde I, 343 c.

116. Stark memo, Feb. 2, 1944 (quote); see also Ofterdinger to Schrewe, Jan. 14, 1944, SAH, Oberschulbehörde VI, 2 F VIII a 2/40/1.

117. Amtsgericht Abteilung 28 (Jugendgericht) to Reich justice minister, Apr. 5, 1944, BA, R22/1165.

118. Oberstudiendirektor to Hitler-Jugend Gebiet Hamburg 26, Nov. 27, 1940, SAH, Oberschulbehörde VI, 2 F VIII a 2/3/1.

119. Kenkmann, 130–131, 211.

120. Gerhard Rempel, *Hitler's Children: The Hitler Youth and the SS* (Chapel Hill, N.C., 1989), 52.

121. Ibid., 52–55; "Vorläufige Dienstvorschrift für den HJ-Streifendienst," May 15, 1936, HIS, 13/338.

122. Jahnke and Buddrus, 311–312.

123. Reithmayr report, HJ-Bann Allgäu, Oct. 1–31, 1940, SAND, unsign. Best., EAP, 221-b-20/9.

124. Kechele report, Augsburg Stadt, Oct. [1941], and similar such reports, SAND, unsign. Best., EAP 221-b-20/6; Kenkmann, 169.
125. Von Hellfeld, 191; Rempel, 97.
126. For a principal admission of powerlessness vis-à-vis those institutions, see Reichsjugendführung, "Cliquen- und Bandenbildung unter Jugendlichen," Sept. 1942, BA, R22/1177.
127. Anon. to Mulzer, June 15, 1940, SAH, Sozialbehörde I, VT 38.10; Carola Kuhlmann, *Erbkrank oder erziehbar? Jugendhilfe als Vorsorge und Aussonderung in der Fürsorgeerziehung in Westfalen von 1933–1945* (Weinheim, 1989), 200.
128. Reichsjugendführung, "Entwurf: Bekämpfung jugendlicher Cliquen," May 11, 1943; Jugendführer to Führer der Gebiete und Banne, Dec. 10, 1944, BA, R22/1177; Landgerichtspräsident, "Betrifft: Zusammenarbeit in der Jugendrechtspflege," March 9, 1944, ARL, Lü 4.6.1.1 (OLG Oldenburg); Lothar Gruchmann, "Jugendopposition und Justiz im Dritten Reich: Die Probleme bei der Verfolgung der 'Leipziger Meuten' durch die Gerichte," in Wolfgang Benz, ed., *Miscellanea: Festschrift für Helmut Krausnick zum 75. Geburtstag* (Stuttgart, 1980), 122.
129. Axmann to Himmler, Jan. 8, 1942, BA, NS 19/neu 219.
130. Artur Axmann, *"Das kann doch nicht das Ende sein": Hitlers letzter Reichsjugendführer erinnert sich,* 2nd ed. (Koblenz, 1995), 380.
131. Richard F. Wetzell, *Inventing the Criminal: A History of German Criminology, 1880–1945* (Chapel Hill, N.C., 2000), esp. 235.
132. Kershaw, *Nemesis,* 511, 689; Richard J. Evans, *Rituals of Retribution: Capital Punishment in Germany, 1600–1987* (Oxford, 1996), 632, 639–640, 686–720; Dietrich Güstrow, *Tödlicher Alltag: Strafverteidiger im Dritten Reich* (Berlin, 1981).
133. Werner Johe, *Die gleichgeschaltete Justiz: Organisation des Rechtswesens und Politisierung der Rechtsprechung 1933–1945, dargestellt am Beispiel des Oberlandesgerichtsbezirks Hamburg* (Frankfurt am Main, 1967); Walter Wagner, *Der Volksgerichtshof im nationalsozialistischen Staat* (Stuttgart, 1974); Robert Gellately, *Backing Hitler: Consent and Coercion in Nazi Germany* (Oxford, 2002), 47–48.
134. Albrecht Wagner, *Die Umgestaltung der Gerichtsverfassung und des Verfahrens- und Richterrechts im nationalsozialistischen Staat* (Stuttgart, 1968); Robert Wistrich, *Who's Who in Nazi Germany* (New York, 1982), 115–117, 315–316; Gellately, *Hitler,* 79.
135. Albrecht Wagner, 348–359; Hans Frank, *Im Angesicht des Galgens: Deutung Hitlers und seiner Zeit auf Grund eigener Erlebnisse und Erkenntnisse* (Munich-Gräfelfing, 1953); Gellately, *Hitler,* 119.

136. Wetzell, 121.
137. Kuhlmann, 201.
138. Oberkommando der Wehrmacht to Reich justice minister, Aug. 3, 1942, BA, R22/1177; Bormann to Reich justice minister, Oct. 26, 1942, BA, R22/1179.
139. Daniel Horn, "Coercion and Compulsion in the Hitler Youth, 1933–1945," *Historian* 41 (1979): 653–654; "In einer Jugendarrest-Anstalt: Die Tendenzen in der Strafrechtspflege für Minderjährige," *Das Reich,* July 13, 1941 (quote).
140. Hische, "Entwicklung der Jugendkriminalität und Neuordnung der Jugendkriminalstatistik," Nov. 1943, BA, R22/1165.
141. Reich justice minister to Oberlandesgerichtspräsidenten et al., Sept. [?], 1942; and to Himmler, Sept. 25, 1942, BA, R22/5018.
142. Amtsgericht München, judgment against Steigenberger et al., March 27, 1941; Neck to Oberstaatsanwalt München, March 31, 1942, ARL, Lü 6.1.5 (München); minutes of youth courts at Amtsgericht München, March 14, 1941, ARL, Lü 6.1.3 (München).
143. Reichsjugendführung, "Cliquen- und Bandenbildung unter Jugendlichen," Sept. 1942, BA, R22/1177; Reich justice minister to Oberlandesgerichtspräsidenten et al., Sept. [?] 1942, BA, R22/5018; Peukert and Winter, 259 (quote).
144. Thierack memo, Oct. 26, 1944, enclosed with Jugendführer to Führer der Gebiete und Banne, Dec. 10, 1944, BA, R22/1177; Arno Klönne, *Jugend im Dritten Reich: Die Hitler-Jugend und ihre Gegner: Dokumente und Analysen* (Düsseldorf, 1982), 253–254; Kenkmann, 202; Jahnke and Buddrus, 239–243; Von Hellfeld, 126, 133, 171.
145. Kenkmann, 130–132, 203; Von Hellfeld, 130–132; Peukert and Winter, 253, 255.
146. Reichsjugendführung, "Cliquen- und Bandenbildung unter Jugendlichen," Sept. 1942, BA, R22/1177.
147. See the reservations expressed in "Vermerk über eine Besprechung am 16. August 1939 über die Behandlung der sogenannten Meuten in Leipzig," BA, R22/25.
148. Minutes of judgment against Hess et al., Oct. 28, 1938, IfZ, Fa 117/6.
149. Minutes of judgment against Pfloksch et al., June 15, 1942, BA, R22/1177; Jahnke and Buddrus, 428–430; Gruchmann, 103–130.
150. Volksgerichtshof Berlin, judgment against Landgraf et al., Sept. 23, 1942, ARL, Parteikanzlei/Mikrofiches; Von Hellfeld and Klönne, 283–285; Jahnke, *Jugend,* 129–131; Prückner and Waldhier, 51.

151. See Gruchmann, 105, 123.

152. Paul Werner, "Die Einweisung in die polizeilichen Jugendschutzlager," *Deutsches Jugendrecht* 4 (1943): 96.

153. Wetzell, 235.

154. See Patrick Wagner, "Das Gesetz über die Behandlung Gemeinschafts-fremder: Die Kriminalpolizei und die 'Vernichtung des Verbrechertums,'" in Wolfgang Ayass et al., *Feinderklärung und Prävention: Kriminalbiologie, Zigeunerforschung und Asozialenpolitik* (Berlin, 1988), 77.

155. Rietzsch quoted in minutes of "Arbeitsgemeinschaft für Jugendstrafrecht in München am 21. u. 23.11.40," BA, R22/1180; Patrick Wagner, 83–84.

156. Bormann to Lammers, Aug. 30, 1941, BA, R43II/520c.

157. "Verordnung über die Vereinfachung und Vereinheitlichung der Jugend-strafvollstreckung vom 6.11.1943 (Reichsjugendgerichtsgesetz)," *Reichs-gesetzblatt I* (1943): 646; Thierack memo, Oct. 26, 1944 (as in n. 144).

158. Entry for Feb. 2, 1940, in *TGI* 4: 30 (quote); Jörg Wolff, *Jugendliche vor Gericht im Dritten Reich: Nationalsozialistische Jugendstrafrechtspolitik und Justizalltag* (Munich, 1992), 114–115.

159. Nebe/Schefe, "Die Handhabung der Pol. VO.," [March 1940], BA, R22/1176a; "Schutz der Jugend," *Mitteilungsblatt des Reichskriminal-polizeiamts* 3 (Apr. 1940): 239–250, (BA, R22/1175); Kriminalrätin Dr. Isa Koch, "Die Durchführung der Polizeiordnung zum Schutze der Jugend," *Die Ärztin* 17 (1941): 65–66.

160. Kater, *Drummers,* 157–158.

161. Ibid., 151; Rühlig and Steen, 122.

162. Kruse memo, [1942], BA, NL/289.

163. Von Hellfeld, 129.

164. Molden, 175–177.

165. Himmler to Axmann, Jan. 26, 1942, and to Heydrich, Jan. 26, 1942, BA, NS19/neu 219 (quote).

166. See Kater, *Drummers,* 111–211.

167. Madlung-Shelton recorded interview; Ursula Nielsen and Herbert Rönn recorded interview, Hamburg, June 20, 1988.

168. Albath, "Wilde Jugendgruppen—Edelweisspiraten," [spring 1943], BA, R22/1177.

169. Von Hellfeld and Klönne, 272.

170. Werner, "Schnellbrief," June 26, 1940, BA, R22/1189; Heinrich Muth, "Das 'Jugendschutzlager' Moringen," *Dachauer Hefte* 5 (Nov. 1989): 251. See also Gellately, *Hitler,* 46.

171. Joachim S. Hohmann, *Robert Ritter und die Erben der Kriminalbiologie:*

"Zigeunerforschung" im Nationalsozialismus und in Westdeutschland im Zeichen des Rassismus (Frankfurt am Main, 1991), 133–135 (quote, 135).

172. Ibid., 135–136; Robert Ritter, *Ein Menschenschlag: Erbärztliche und erbgeschichtliche Untersuchungen über die—durch 10 Geschlechterfolgen erforschten—Nachkommen von "Vagabunden, Jaunern und Räubern"* (Leipzig, 1937).

173. Hohmann, 136–140; Guenter Lewy, *The Nazi Persecution of the Gypsies* (New York, 2000).

174. Robert N. Proctor, *Racial Hygiene: Medicine Under the Nazis* (Cambridge, Mass., 1988); Michael H. Kater, *Doctors Under Hitler* (Chapel Hill, N.C., 1989).

175. Ferdinand von Neureiter, *Kriminalbiologie* (Berlin, 1940), esp. 5, 16 (quotes); Hohmann, 136–137.

176. Heinrich Wilhelm Kranz, *"Die Gemeinschaftsunfähigen" (Ein Beitrag zur wissenschaftlichen und praktischen Lösung des sog. "Asozialenproblems")* (Giessen, [1939]); Robert Ritter, "Erbärztliche Verbrechensverhütung," *Deutsche Medizinische Wochenschrift* (May 22, 1942): 536–539; Kater, *Doctors,* 115–119; Hohmann, 135; Wolff, 183.

177. Friedrich Schaffstein, *Die Erneuerung des Jugendstrafrechts* (Berlin, [1936]), 10.

178. Werner, 95.

179. On the latter concept, see Michael H. Kater, "Aufnordnung und Ausmerze: 'Volksgesundheit' im Nationalsozialismus: Ein biopolitisches Konzept und seine Anwendung," *Frankfurter Rundschau,* July 24, 2001.

180. Paul Werner, "Die Polizei in ihrem Kampf gegen die Gefährdung der Jugend," *Das Junge Deutschland* (1941): 243–244. See Wolfgang Ayass, ed., *"Gemeinschaftsfremde": Quellen zur Verfolgung von "Asozialen," 1933–1945* (Koblenz, 1998), xix.

181. Hohmann, 146–148. See Robert Ritter, "Primitivität und Kriminalität," *Monatsschrift für Kriminalbiologie und Strafrechtsreform* 31 (1940): 197–210.

182. Werner, "Einweisung," 97–106; Werner to Kümmerlein, Sept. 6, 1944, BA, R22/1191 (quote).

183. "Dienstliche Anordnung," Moringen, Apr. 16, 1941 (second quote); Wolter-Pecksen to Direktor Landeswerkhaus, Aug. 7, 1942 (first quote), facs. in Martin Guse et al., "Das Jugendschutzlager Moringen—Ein Jugendkonzentrationslager," in Hans-Uwe Otto and Heinz Sühnker, eds., *Soziale Arbeit und Faschismus: Volkspflege und Pädagogik im Nationalsozialismus* (Bielefeld, 1986), 333, 339; Kümmerlein/Eichler travel re-

port, [Apr. 1942], BA, R22/1176; Schmidhäuser to Reichler, July 31, 1943, BA, R22/1306; Patrick Wagner, *Volksgemeinschaft ohne Verbrecher: Konzeptionen und Praxis der Kriminalpolizei in der Zeit der Weimarer Republik und des Nationalsozialismus* (Hamburg, 1996), 376; Hannah Vogt et al., *KZ Moringen—Männerlager, Frauenlager, Jugendschutzlager— Eine Dokumentation* (Göttingen, n.d.), 55.

184. Michael Hepp, "Vorhof zur Hölle: Mädchen im 'Jugendschutzlager' Uckermark," in Angelika Ebbinghaus, ed., *Opfer und Täterinnen: Frauen-biographien des Nationalsozialismus* (Nördlingen, 1987), 202–214 (quote, 211).

185. Patrick Wagner, *Volksgemeinschaft*, 377.

186. Werner, "Einweisung," 99–101; Maike Merten and Katja Limbächer, "Geschichte des Jugendschutzlagers Uckermark," in Katja Limbächer et al., eds., *Das Mädchenkonzentrationslager Uckermark* (Münster, 2000), 16–43.

187. Kümmerlein/Eichler travel report, [Apr. 1942], BA, R22/1176 (quote); Heermann to Oberlandesgerichtspräsident Hamm, July 31, 1944, BA, R22/1191; Paul Werner, "Die polizeilichen Jugendschutzlager," *Deutsche Jugendhilfe* 35 (1944): 101–105; Patrick Wagner, *Volksgemeinschaft*, 378–379.

188. Hepp, 200–201; Erwin Rehn, "Gedächtnisbericht über das Sonderlager (Jugendschutzlager) Moringen und über das Aussenlager Volpriehausen," *Mitteilungen der Dokumentationsstelle zur NS-Sozialpolitik* 1/9–10 (Nov./ Dec. 1985): 94.

189. Ursula Nielsen Rönn and Herbert Rönn recorded interview.

5. Hitler's Youth at War

1. BAB, SS personal file Herbert Taege. First two quotes, SS-Oberschar-führer Kramer, "Beurteilungsnotiz," Dec. 1, 1943; last quote, SS-Haupt-sturmführer, "Beurteilung," June 16, 1944.

2. Herbert Taege, *Über die Zeiten fort: Das Gesicht einer Jugend im Aufgang und Untergang: Wertung—Deutung—Erscheinung* (Lindhorst, 1978).

3. *Spiegel Online*, Oct. 7, 2002; *www.koninklijkhuis.nl/prinsclaus*.

4. See Omer Bartov, *Hitler's Army: Soldiers, Nazis, and War in the Third Reich* (New York, 1991), esp. 104–105, 108–109, 158–161. On the notorious model of Daniel Jonah Goldhagen, salacious generalizations about *all* German civilians as Nazi racists and *all* German soldiers as

master-race killers have been the subject of less than reliable scholarship. See Clarence Lusane, *Hitler's Black Victims: The Historical Experiences of Afro-Germans, European Blacks, Africans, and African-Americans in the Nazi Era* (New York, 2002), 153; and the egregious Fred Kautz, *Gold-Hagen und die "Hürnen Sewfriedte": Die Holocaust-Forschung im Sperrfeuer der Flakhelfer* (Berlin, 1998).

5. See Detlef Bald et al., *Mythos Wehrmacht: Nachkriegsdebatten und Traditionspflege* (Berlin, 2001), and the convincing testimonies in Michael Burleigh, *The Third Reich: A New History* (New York, 2001), 437, 493, 521, 623.

6. *Der Spiegel* (June 2, 2003): 42–46.

7. On December 30, 1944; quoted in Hermann Langer, "Das 'Gesicht der Schule'—Schüleraufsätze, 1939–1944," in Karl Heinz Jahnke et al., *Deutsche Jugend im Zweiten Weltkrieg* (Rostock, 1991), 77.

8. See the sensible remarks on this by Hans Mommsen, "Kriegserfahrungen," in Ulrich Borsdorf and Mathilde Jamin, eds., *Über Leben im Krieg: Kriegserfahrungen in einer Industrieregion, 1939–1945* (Reinbek, 1983), 8–13.

9. Ursula Baumann, *Vom Recht auf den eigenen Tod: Die Geschichte des Suizids vom 19. bis zum 20. Jahrhundert* (Weimar, 2001), 362.

10. Arne W. G. Zoepf, *Wehrmacht zwischen Tradition und Ideologie: Der NS-Führungsoffizier im Zweiten Weltkrieg* (Frankfurt am Main, 1988).

11. Wladyslaw Szpilman, *The Pianist: The Extraordinary Story of One Man's Survival in Warsaw, 1939–45* (Toronto, 2000), 177–181. See also Hosenfeld's diary, Jan. 18, 1942–Aug. 11, 1944, ibid., 193–208; Michael Beckerman, "The 'Pianist' DVD and the Case of the Missing Nocturne," *New York Times* (June 8, 2003).

12. A condemnable example of this can be found in Andreas Hillgruber, *Zweierlei Untergang: Die Zerschlagung des Deutschen Reiches und das Ende des europäischen Judentums* (Berlin, 1986); see esp. 16, 66–67. The early West German political background to this approach is mentioned in Robert G. Moeller, "War Stories: The Search for a Usable Past in the Federal Republic of Germany," *American Historical Review* 101 (1996): 1018–1019. For Moeller's concise analysis of Hillgruber, see p. 1042. See also Elizabeth Heineman, "The Hour of the Woman: Memories of Germany's 'Crisis Years' and West German National Identity," *American Historical Review* 101 (1996): 372, n. 40.

13. In his new novel *Im Krebsgang: Eine Novelle* (Göttingen, 2002). Grass quoted in *Der Spiegel* (Aug. 25, 2003): 143. On Grass's unsettled boyhood, see Hans Peter Brode, *Günter Grass* (Munich, 1979), 10–14; see also Patrick O'Neill, *Günter Grass Revisited* (New York, 1999), 1–13.

14. John M. Coetzee, "Victims," *New York Review of Books* (June 12, 2003): 24. See also Alan Riding, "Still Intrigued by History's Shadow: Günter Grass Worries About the Effects of War, Then as Now," *New York Times* (Apr. 8, 2003).

15. John Updike, "Suppressed Atrocities," *New Yorker* (Apr. 21/28, 2003): 186.

16. Ingrid Hammer and Susanne zur Nieden, eds., *Sehr selten habe ich geweint: Briefe und Tagebücher aus dem Zweiten Weltkrieg von Menschen in Berlin* (Zurich, 1992), 28–29; Joachim Dollwet, "Menschen im Krieg, Bejahung— und Widerstand? Eindrücke und Auszüge aus der Sammlung von Feldpost- briefen im Landeshauptarchiv Koblenz," *Jahrbuch für Westdeutsche Landes- geschichte* 13 (1987): 309; Walter Manoschek, ed., *"Es gibt nur eines für das Judentum: Vernichtung": Das Judenbild in deutschen Soldatenbriefen, 1939–1944* (Hamburg, 1995), 10; Volker Ullrich, "'Wir haben nichts gewusst'—Ein deutsches Trauma," *1999. Zeitschrift für Sozialgeschichte des 20. und 21. Jahrhunderts*, no. 4 (Oct. 1991): 35.

17. Kreutzer to Melcher, Nov. 24, 1939, in Hermann Melcher, *Die Gefolg- schaft: Jugendjahre im Dritten Reich in Heidelberg, 1933–1945* (Berg, 1990), 45–46.

18. See HJ leader Oskar Riegraf's letters to his wife Lotte from the Danish front, May 1940, SAL, PL 509/1/8; Siegbert Stehmann, *Die Bitternis ver- schweigen wir: Feldpostbriefe, 1940–1945,* ed. Gerhard Sprenger (Hanover, 1992), 30.

19. Quote from Helmut N.'s letter of June 12, 1940, in Marlies Tremper, ed., *Briefe des Soldaten Helmut N., 1939–1945* (Berlin, 1988), 63.

20. Fuchs to Mädi, Sept. 1, 1940, in Horst Fuchs Richardson, ed., *Sieg Heil! War Letters of Tank Gunner Karl Fuchs, 1937–1941* (Hamden, Conn., 1987), 77. See also ibid., 68–69, 72–73; Tremper, 61–62, 67; Herbert Johannes Veigel, *Christbäume: Briefe aus dem Krieg* (Berlin, 1991), 34.

21. Quote from Hans Olte in Poland, Apr. 3, 1941, in Klaus Latzel, *Deutsche Soldaten—nationalsozialistischer Krieg? Kriegserlebnis—Kriegserfahrung, 1939–1945* (Paderborn, 1998), 46.

22. FPN 39690 to family, Nov. 17, 1940, in Manoschek, 18. See also ibid., 16–17, 19; Ullrich, 20.

23. See Wolfgang De Bruyn's undated letter (summer 1941) in Günter De Bruyn, *Zwischenbilanz: Eine Jugend in Berlin* (Frankfurt am Main, 1995), 126. Wehrmacht figure according to Bartov, 36.

24. Hellmut to parents, June 22, 1941, in Hammer and Zur Nieden, 126; also Latzel, 89.

25. Veigel, 53, 89; Jürgen Brautmeier, "'Frontbewährung' in Stalingrad:

Feldpostbriefe des Gefreiten Hans Happe aus Delbrück/Westfalen," *Geschichte im Westen* 8 (1993): 170; Omer Bartov, *The Eastern Front, 1941–45: German Troops and the Barbarisation of Warfare* (New York, 1986), 23–24.

26. Hitler quoted in Jay W. Baird, *The Mythical World of Nazi War Propaganda, 1939–1945* (Minneapolis, 1974), 177.

27. Bartov, *Front,* 83–87; Bartov, *Army,* 83; Lothar Gruchmann, *Der Zweite Weltkrieg: Kriegführung und Politik* (Munich, 1967), 127.

28. Anon. letter, June 26, 1941, in Dollwet, 298 (first two quotes); Korri to Darling, Aug. 3, 1941, in Fuchs Richardson, 122 (last quote). The recurring cattle image is also found in Ortwin Buchbender and Reinhold Sterz, eds., *Das andere Gesicht des Krieges: Deutsche Feldpostbriefe, 1939–1945* (Munich, 1982), 85.

29. Udo von Alvensleben, *Lauter Abschiede: Tagebuch vom Kriege,* ed. Harald von Koenigswald (Frankfurt am Main, 1971), 201.

30. Christian Streit, *Keine Kameraden: Die Wehrmacht und die sowjetischen Kriegsgefangenen, 1941–1945* (Stuttgart, 1978); Gerhard L. Weinberg, *A World at Arms: A Global History of World War II* (Cambridge, 1994), 300; Bartov, *Front,* 107–119; Bartov, *Army,* 88–89.

31. Bartov, *Army,* 83.

32. Hans-Ulrich Greffrath in Johannes Steinhoff et al., eds., *Voices from the Third Reich: An Oral History* (New York, 1994), 277 (quote); Brautmeier, 172.

33. Franzl to parents, July 6, 1941, in Manoschek, 33 (quote); Veigel, 60; Hammer and Zur Nieden, 127.

34. Gruchmann, 131; Weinberg, 300; Bartov, *Army,* 84–87.

35. Bartov, *Front,* 99, 119–126; Bartov, *Army,* 65; Iring Fetscher, *Neugier und Furcht: Versuch, mein Leben zu verstehen* (Hamburg, 1995), 92; Ullrich, 21–22, 24; Ernst Klee et al., eds., *"The Good Old Days": The Holocaust as Seen by Its Perpetrators and Bystanders* (New York, 1991), 107–135. On the soldiers' hatred of Jews on the Russian campaign trail, see Ullrich, 23, 36; Manoschek, 32, 40, 62; Dollwet, 299.

36. Veigel, 53; Hammer and Zur Nieden, 127; Latzel, 55.

37. Latzel, 70; Tremper, 133–134.

38. Guido Knopp, *Hitlers Kinder,* 2nd ed. (Munich, 2000), 285.

39. Hans-Joachim Schröder, "'Man kam sich da vor wie ein Stück Dreck': Schikane in der Militärausbildung des Dritten Reichs," in Wolfram Wette, ed., *Der Krieg des kleinen Mannes: Eine Militärgeschichte von unten,* 2nd ed. (Munich, 1995), 189–194.

40. Jürgen Peiffer, *Vergangenheit, gebrochener Spiegel: Erinnerungen* (Tübingen, 2000), 91.

41. Ralf Roland Ringler, *Illusion einer Jugend: Lieder, Fahnen und das bittere Ende: Hitlerjugend in Österreich: Ein Erlebnisbericht* (St. Pölten, 1977), 98.

42. Melcher, 112–113. Similarly, see Leopold A. in Stefanie Reichelt, *"Für mich ist der Krieg aus!": Deserteure und Kriegsdienstverweigerer des Zweiten Weltkrieges in München* (Munich, 1995), 187.

43. Hans Graf von Lehndorff, *Die Briefe des Peter Pfaff, 1943–1944,* 3rd ed. (Munich, 1988), 95; Kurt Abels, *Ein Held war ich nicht: Als Kind und Jugendlicher in Hitlers Krieg* (Cologne, 1998), 117–118.

44. Willy Schumann, *Being Present: Growing Up in Hitler's Germany* (Kent, Ohio, 1991), 142–153.

45. Bartov, *Army,* 14–15.

46. Weinberg, 270–309 (quote, 298); Gruchmann, 128–132.

47. Stehmann to wife, July 23, 1941, in Stehmann, 116. See also Bartov, *Front,* 21–22.

48. Veigel, 96; Wolfgang Wiesen, ed., *Es grüsst Euch alle, Bertold: Von Koblenz nach Stalingrad: Die Feldpostbriefe des Pioniers Bertold Paulus aus Kastel* (Nonnweiler-Otzenhausen, 1991), 63–64; Bartov, *Front,* 24–25.

49. Von Alvensleben, 217; Veigel, 97, 109; Karl Heinz Jahnke, *Hitlers letztes Aufgebot: Deutsche Jugend im sechsten Kriegsjahr, 1944/45* (Essen, 1993), 155; Bartov, *Front,* 22.

50. Nielsen to family, May 28, 1940, in Walter Bähr and Hans Bähr, eds., *Kriegsbriefe gefallener Studenten, 1939–1945* (Tübingen, 1952), 27.

51. Ibid., 300–301; Bartov, *Front,* 26–27.

52. Friedrich Grupe, *Jahrgang 1916: Die Fahne war mehr als der Tod* (Munich, 1989), 161.

53. Kurt Meyer-Grell quoted in Steinhoff et al., 139.

54. Greffrath quoted ibid., 278.

55. Günter Kaufmann, *Das kommende Deutschland: Die Erziehung der Jugend im Reich Adolf Hitlers,* 3rd ed. (Berlin, 1943), 317.

56. Peter Pechel quoted in Steinhoff et al., 133. See also Hammer and Zur Nieden, 23; Buchbender and Sterz, 54; Peiffer, 94.

57. Horst Lange, *Tagebücher aus dem Zweiten Weltkrieg,* ed. Hans Dieter Schäfer (Mainz, 1979), 87. See also Veigel, 159; Von Alvensleben, 254.

58. Hans Joachim Schröder, *Die gestohlenen Jahre: Erzählgeschichten und Geschichtserzählung im Interview: Der Zweite Weltkrieg aus der Sicht ehemaliger Mannschaftssoldaten* (Tübingen, 1992), 678.

59. Bernhard Haupert and Franz Josef Schäfer, *Jugend zwischen Kreuz und*

Hakenkreuz: Biographische Rekonstruktion als Alltagsgeschichte des Faschismus (Frankfurt am Main, 1991), 220. See the text of this chapter at n. 211.

60. Hermann to Rosl, Feb. 28, 1942, in Anatoly Golovchansky et al., *"Ich will raus aus diesem Wahnsinn": Deutsche Briefe von der Ostfront, 1941–1945: Aus sowjetischen Archiven* (Wuppertal, 1991), 67–68. See also ibid., 180; Bähr and Bähr, 301; Bartov, *Front,* 90–91.

61. Hess to Herta, July 22, 1943, in Latzel, 337.

62. Fetscher, 184.

63. Melcher, 168. See also Bartov, *Army,* 25.

64. Bähr and Bähr, 66; Weinberg, 264, 273, 279, 284; Alan Clark, *Barbarossa: The Russian-German Conflict, 1941–45* (New York, 1965), 167.

65. Von Alvensleben, 254.

66. Fetscher, 129; Henry Metelmann, *A Hitler Youth: Growing up in Germany in the 1930s* (London, 1997), 234–235; Veigel, 200; Claus B. Schröder, *Wolfgang Borchert: Biografie* (Hamburg, 1985), 175–176. For official Wehrmacht condemnation of such liaisons, see Bartov, *Front,* 126–129.

67. Burleigh, 530–531; Andreas Hillgruber, "Einführung," in Hillgruber, ed., *Von El Alamein bis Stalingrad: Aus dem Kriegstagebuch des Oberkommandos der Wehrmacht* (Munich, 1964), 7–13; Weinberg, 408–410; Ian Kershaw, *Hitler, 1936–1945: Nemesis* (New York, 2000), 530.

68. William L. Langer, ed., *An Encyclopedia of World History* (Boston, 1968), 1143; *Spiegel Online* (Jan. 29, 2003); *Der Spiegel* (Dec. 16, 2002): 68; Gruchmann, 187–194; Weinberg, 410–417, 420–425 (first quote, 422); entry for Sept. 19, 1942, in Thomas Mann, *Tagebücher, 1940–43,* ed. Peter de Mendelssohn (Frankfurt am Main, 1982), 475 (second quote).

69. The national cover-up is expertly dealt with in Baird, 175–190.

70. Kershaw, 547.

71. Brautmeier, 186; Wiesen, 112. See also Walter Görlitz, ed., *Paulus und Stalingrad: Lebensweg des Generalfeldmarschalls Friedrich Paulus* (Frankfurt am Main, 1964), 255–258.

72. Brautmeier, 175, 178–179, 184, 186; Wiesen, 108–109, 113; Golovchansky, 234–235.

73. Rüdiger Overmans, "Das andere Gesicht des Krieges: Leben und Sterben der 6. Armee," in Jürgen Förster, ed., *Stalingrad: Ereignis—Wirkung—Symbol,* 2nd ed. (Munich, 1993), 420–424, 427; Brautmeier, 175, 179, 185; Wiesen, 108–109, 112–113; Diether Cartellieri, *Die deutschen Kriegsgefangenen in der Sowjetunion: Die Lagergesellschaft: Eine Untersuchung der zwischenmenschlichen Beziehungen in den Kriegsgefangenenlagern* (Munich, 1967), 12–13; *Der Spiegel* (Dec. 16, 2002): 66.

74. Overmans, 422, 426; Brautmeier, 175, 179; Cartellieri, 12–13.

75. Quoted in Overmans, 426. See also ibid., 427–428; Wiesen, 108; Cartellieri, 12; *Der Spiegel* (Dec. 16, 2002): 51.

76. On this phenomenon see Ian Kershaw, *The "Hitler Myth": Image and Reality in the Third Reich* (Oxford, 1987).

77. Joseph Goebbels, "Was ist ein Opfer?", Dec. 28, 1941, in Goebbels, *Das eherne Herz: Reden und Aufsätze aus den Jahren 1941/42,* ed. M. A. Schirmeister (Munich, 1943), 150.

78. Peiffer, 92, 94; Hammer and Zur Nieden, 227–228.

79. Erhard Eppler, *Als Wahrheit verordnet wurde: Briefe an meine Enkelin,* 3rd ed. (Frankfurt am Main, 1995), 153–154.

80. Bähr and Bähr, 67; Von Alvensleben, 203; Melcher, 243–244.

81. See Emmrich's memoirs under the pen name Peter Bamm, *Die unsichtbare Flagge: Ein Bericht,* 8th ed. (Munich, 1957), 199–200; also, from the ideologically opposite point of view, Joseph Goebbels, *Der steile Aufstieg: Reden und Aufsätze aus den Jahren 1942/43,* ed. M. A. Schirmeister (Munich, 1943), 27–28.

82. Steinhoff et al., 133; Buchbender and Sterz, 92; Melcher, 255.

83. Entry for March 23, 1944, in Heinz Boberach, ed., *Meldungen aus dem Reich: Die geheimen Lageberichte des Sicherheitsdienstes der SS, 1938–1945* (Herrsching, 1984), vol. 16, 6439–6445 (quote, 6443). See also Kurt Hass, ed., *Jugend unterm Schicksal: Lebensberichte junger Deutscher, 1946–1949* (Hamburg, 1950), 33–35.

84. *TGII,* vol. 12, 224; *TGII,* vol. 13, 518; Fetscher, 188; Helmut Altner, *Totentanz Berlin: Tagebuchblätter eines Achzehnjährigen* (Offenbach, 1947), 194–195, 204–205; Fred Borth, *Nicht zu jung zum Sterben: Die "Hitler-Jugend" im Kampf um Wien 1945* (Vienna, 1988), 150–152.

85. Ringler, 112.

86. J. S. quoted in Buchbender and Sterz, 40–41.

87. Hammer and Zur Nieden, 230, 243, 250–251; Hartmut von Hentig, *Aufgeräumte Erfahrung: Texte zur eigenen Person* (Munich, 1983), 34; Bähr and Bähr, 134–135. On the Wehrmacht's looting, burning, and destruction, see Bartov, *Front,* 129–136.

88. Entry for Sept. 4, 1941, in Lange, 26 (quote); Ringler, 97.

89. Veigel, 107.

90. Von Hentig, 40. See also Theo Baumeister in Gudrun Norbisrath, ed., *Gestohlene Jugend: Der Zweite Weltkrieg in Erinnerungen* (Essen, 2000), 38–39.

91. Hammer and Zur Nieden, 138; Bertram Otto, *"Wussten wir auch nicht, wohin es geht . . .": Erinnerungen, 1927–1947* (Munich, 2000), 208; Max

von der Grün, *Howl like the Wolves: Growing up in Nazi Germany* (New York, 1980), 253–254; Jahnke et al., *Jugend,* 187–188.

92. Otto, 198–199; De Bruyn, 227.

93. P. G. quoted in Buchbender and Sterz, 123.

94. Baumann, 358.

95. See excerpt from "Militärstrafgesetzbuch," Oct. 10, 1940, in Reichelt, 28; ibid., 29; Bartov, *Army,* 97–100.

96. Reichelt, 29; Norbert Haase, *Deutsche Deserteure* (Berlin, 1987), 23.

97. Reichelt, 27, 106; Jahnke, *Aufgebot,* 73.

98. Gerhard Paul, *Ungehorsame Soldaten: Dissens, Verweigerung und Widerstand deutscher Soldaten (1939–1945)* (St. Ingbert, 1994), 52; Haase, 41. An example of the latter case is in Steinhoff et al., 109.

99. Horst Krüger, *Das zerbrochene Haus: Eine Jugend in Deutschland,* 2nd ed. (Munich, 1967), 206–213.

100. Heinz A. Brenner, *Dagegen: Bericht über den Widerstand von Schülern des Humanistischen Gymnasiums Ulm/Donau gegen die deutsche nationalsozialistische Diktatur* (Leutkirch, [1992]), 39–41. A similar case is related in Reichelt, 190–191.

101. Dieter Knippschild, "'Für mich ist der Krieg aus': Deserteure in der Deutschen Wehrmacht," in Norbert Haase and Gerhard Paul, eds., *Die anderen Soldaten: Wehrkraftzersetzung, Gehorsamsverweigerung und Fahnenflucht im Zweiten Weltkrieg* (Frankfurt am Main, 1995), 133. See also Paul, 64.

102. Hermine Wüllner, ed., *". . . kann nur der Tod die gerechte Sühne sein": Todesurteile deutscher Wehrmachtsgerichte: Eine Dokumentation* (Baden-Baden, 1997), 40–43.

103. Haase, 52 (quote). See also Krüger, 199–201; Bähr and Bähr, 238–241.

104. See Altner, 20–21.

105. Knippschild, 137. See also Elisabeth Abendroth, ed., *Deserteure im Zweiten Weltkrieg: Vaterlandsverräter oder Widerständler* (Oberursel, 1989), 30–31.

106. Ingrid van Bergen, "Mit 13 begegnete ich zum erstenmal dem Tod," *Bild am Sonntag,* Aug. 14, 1977. See also Altner, 86–87; Erhard Lucas-Busemann, *So fielen Königsberg und Breslau: Nachdenken über eine Katastrophe ein halbes Jahrhundert danach* (Berlin, 1994), 59; Doris K. in Lothar Steinbach, *Ein Volk, ein Reich, ein Glaube? Ehemalige Nationalsozialisten und Zeitzeugen berichten über ihr Leben im Dritten Reich* (Berlin, 1983), 104.

107. "Verordnung über das Sonderstrafrecht im Kriege und bei besonderem

Einsatz (Kriegssonderstrafrechtsverordnung)," Aug. 17, 1938, *Reichsgesetzblatt I* (Aug. 26, 1939): 1455.

108. Michael H. Kater, *Doctors Under Hitler* (Chapel Hill, N.C., 1989), 51, 83.

109. Paul, 91.

110. Reichelt, 29.

111. Jahnke, *Aufgebot,* 73.

112. Overmans, 421, 424.

113. Reichelt, 64–65.

114. Ibid., 62–63.

115. Schröder, *Borchert,* 56, 145, 158–164, 185, 232–322; Peter Rühmkorf, *Wolfgang Borchert in Selbstzeugnissen und Bilddokumenten* (Reinbek, 1966).

116. On the Third Reich's gubernatorial structure, see Peter Hüttenberger, "Nationalsozialistische Polykratie," *Geschichte und Gesellschaft* 2 (1976): 417–442; Reinhard Bollmus, *Das Amt Rosenberg und seine Gegner: Studien zum Machtkampf im nationalsozialistischen Herrschaftssystem* (Stuttgart, 1970); Hans Mommsen, "Hitlers Stellung im nationalsozialistischen Herrschaftssystem," in Gerhard Hirschfeld and Lothar Kettenacker, eds., *Der "Führerstaat": Mythos und Realität: Studien zur Struktur und Politik des Dritten Reiches* (Stuttgart, 1981), 43–72.

117. See the text of Chapter 3 at n. 74.

118. Wolfgang Benz, "Vom Freiwilligen Arbeitsdienst zur Arbeitsdienstpflicht," *Vierteljahrshefte für Zeitgeschichte* 16 (1968): 317–346; Michael H. Kater, *Studentenschaft und Rechtsradikalismus in Deutschland, 1918–1933: Eine sozialgeschichtliche Studie zur Bildungskrise in der Weimarer Republik* (Hamburg, 1975), 115, 167–172; Konstantin Hierl, "Die Leistung des Freiwilligen Arbeitsdienstes (Kongressrede)," in *Der Kongress zu Nürnberg vom 5. bis 10. September 1934: Offizieller Bericht über den Verlauf des Reichsparteitages mit sämtlichen Reden* (Munich, 1934), 180–186; Manfred Seifert, *Kulturarbeit im Reichsarbeitsdienst: Theorie und Praxis nationalsozialistischer Kulturpflege im Kontext historisch-politischer, organisatorischer und ideologischer Einflüsse* (Münster, 1996), 27–89; Kurt Stamm, ed., *Der Reichsarbeitsdienst: Reichsarbeitsdienstgesetz mit ergänzenden Bestimmungen und Erläuterungen,* 3rd ed. (Berlin, 1940), 287; Schumann, 136.

119. Stamm, 1.

120. Hermann Kretzschmann, "Der Reichsarbeitsdienst der männlichen Jugend," in Rudolf Benze and Gustav Gräfer, eds., *Erziehungsmächte und Erziehungshoheit im Grossdeutschen Reich als gestaltende Kräfte im Leben*

des Deutschen (Leipzig, 1940), 124; Ringler, 94; Martin Cranz, *Ich, ein Deutscher* (Dülmen, 1987), 176–177; Eppler, 128; Schumann, 139.

121. Hellmut Petersen, *Die Erziehung der deutschen Jungmannschaft im Reichsarbeitsdienst* (Berlin, 1938), 11, 102.

122. The functionality of the spade cult is justified in Petersen, 70–72.

123. Ibid., 80–91; [Martin] Eisenbeck, ed., *Mit Spaten und Waffe in Feindesland: Reichsarbeitsdienst und seine Bautruppen im Feldzug in Polen 1939* (Leipzig, 1939); Grupe, 67–69; De Bruyn, 178–179; Cranz, 176–177, 181, 186; Eppler, 126–138; Schumann, 136–139. On the ineffectiveness of RAD, see Seifert, 100.

124. Artur Axmann, *"Das kann doch nicht das Ende sein": Hitlers letzter Reichsjugendführer erinnert sich,* 2nd ed. (Koblenz, 1995), 282–288. See also Karl Heinz Jahnke and Michael Buddrus, eds., *Deutsche Jugend, 1933–1945: Eine Dokumentation* (Hamburg, 1989), 328–329, 333–334.

125. *Hitler-Jugend, 1933–1943: Die Chronik eines Jahrzehnts* (Berlin, [1943]), 60; Axmann, 283; Jahnke and Buddrus, 365–366; Christoph Schubert-Weller, *Hitlerjugend: Vom "Jungsturm Adolf Hitler" zur Staatsjugend des Dritten Reiches* (Weinheim, 1993), 202–203; Robert Wistrich, *Who's Who in Nazi Germany* (New York, 1982), 7.

126. Axmann, 285; Reich education minister to Unterrichtsverwaltungen et al., Dec. 20, 1944; Brunswick minister of finance to state bureaucracy, Feb. 13, 1945, NSAW, 12 A, Neu, 13h/19597.

127. *Hitler-Jugend . . . Chronik,* 60; Jahnke and Buddrus, 354; Hans Holzträger, *Die Wehrertüchtigungslager der Hitler-Jugend, 1942–1945: Ein Dokumentarbericht* (Ippesheim, 1991), 17–21.

128. Gerhard Rempel, *Hitler's Children: The Hitler Youth and the SS* (Chapel Hill, N.C., 1989), 186.

129. As Gauleiter, Schirach had proceeded to rule Vienna as a personal fiefdom and, with his particular interest in an autonomous cultural policy, was, next to Hitler, raising the ire of Goebbels. See Oliver Rathkolb, *Führertreu und gottbegnadet: Künstlereliten im Dritten Reich* (Vienna, 1991).

130. Dieter Wellershoff in Marcel Reich-Ranicki, ed., *Meine Schulzeit im Dritten Reich: Erinnerungen deutscher Schriftsteller* (Munich, 1984), 149; Axmann, 284, 286–287; Siegfried Lenz, *Beziehungen: Ansichten und Bekenntnisse zur Literatur* (Hamburg, 1970), 24; Knopp, 25–56.

131. *Der Spiegel* (Jan. 6, 2003): 45; Michael H. Kater, *Different Drummers: Jazz in the Culture of Nazi Germany* (New York, 1992), 112.

132. Burleigh, 744.

133. Weinberg, 418–419; Heinz Bude, *Deutsche Karrieren: Lebenskonstruktio-nen sozialer Aufsteiger aus der Flakhelfer-Generation* (Frankfurt am Main, 1987), 23; Ludwig Schätz, *Schüler-Soldaten: Die Geschichte der Luft-waffenhelfer im Zweiten Weltkrieg* (Frankfurt am Main, 1972), 22; Ludger Tewes, *Jugend im Krieg: Von Luftwaffenhelfern und Soldaten, 1939–1945* (Essen, 1989), 40.

134. *Der Spiegel* (Jan. 6, 2003): 45.

135. Tewes, 38–39, 42; Rolf Schörken, "'Schülersoldaten'—Prägung einer Generation," in Rolf-Dieter Müller and Hans-Erich Volkmann, eds., *Die Wehrmacht: Mythos und Realität* (Munich, 1999), 457; Hans Josef Horchem, *Kinder im Krieg: Kindheit und Jugend im Dritten Reich* (Hamburg, 2000), 142.

136. Jahnke and Buddruss, 359–361; Horchem, 142; Hans-Dietrich Nico-laisen, *Die Flakhelfer: Luftwaffenhelfer und Marinehelfer im Zweiten Welt-krieg* (Berlin, 1981), 11; Schörken, 456; Jahnke, *Aufgebot,* 137. On indus-trial apprentices, see Schätz, 73; Axmann, 332, 349–350; Jahnke, *Aufgebot,* 63; Schörken, 459.

137. Friedhelm Golücke, *Schweinfurt und der strategische Luftkrieg 1943: Der Angriff der US Air Force vom 14. Oktober 1943 gegen die Schweinfurter Kugellagerindustrie* (Paderborn, 1980), esp. 55–57; Thomas Childers, *Wings of Morning: The Story of the Last American Bomber Shot Down over Germany in World War II* (Reading, Mass., 1995); Georg W. Feuchter, *Der Luftkrieg,* 3rd ed. (Frankfurt am Main, 1964), 174–267.

138. Friedrich Juchter, *Formeln, Fahnen, Flakgeschütze: Eine deutsche Jugend zwischen Schule und Kriegsdienst (1934–1947),* 2nd ed. (Oldenburg, 1999), 154; Schörken, 458.

139. Weinberg, 567–568.

140. Tewes, 40, 63; Schumann, 121; Ernst A. Itschert et al., *"Feuer frei—Kinder!": Eine missbrauchte Generation—Flakhelfer im Einsatz* (Saar-brücken, 1984), 34, 37; Juchter, 164, 166.

141. There are not even approximate estimates for dead or wounded. See Tewes, 43.

142. Schätz, 39; Schörken, 460.

143. Mantz quoted in *Der Spiegel* (Jan. 27, 2003): 63.

144. Schätz, 39; Schörken, 460; Peter Boenisch cited in Knopp, 280.

145. Itschert et al., 42.

146. Horchem, 167.

147. Tewes, 43.

148. Cranz, 165.

149. Nicolaisen, 20. See also ibid., 53.
150. Itschert et. al., 45–46, 186; Nicolaisen, 22–23; Abels, 61–62.
151. Itschert et al., 155.
152. Tewes, 127; Nicolaisen, 39.
153. Nicolaisen, 94; Knopp, 281.
154. Schörken, 458.
155. Itschert et al., 123; Cranz, 149.
156. Itschert et al., 49, 85–86; Martin Greiffenhagen, *Jahrgang 1928: Aus einem unruhigen Leben* (Munich, 1988), 49; Wolfgang Klafki in Klafki, *Verführung, Distanzierung, Ernüchterung: Kindheit und Jugend im Nationalsozialismus: Autobiographisches aus erziehungswissenschaftlicher Sicht* (Weinheim, 1988), 141, 161. See the text of Chapter 4 at n. 111.
157. Nicolaisen, 215–216; Itschert et al., 87; Cornelia Rühlig and Jürgen Steen, eds., *Walter: *1926, +1945 an der Ostfront: Leben und Lebensbedingungen eines Frankfurter Jungen im III. Reich* (Frankfurt am Main, 1983), 126; Greiffenhagen, 51.
158. Schörken, 466; Tewes, 137; Schumann, 123; De Bruyn, 142.
159. Schumann, 122 (quote). This complaint is echoed in Horchem, 190; Cranz, 150; Eppler, 121; and Abels, 80. For drill details see Itschert et al., 35–36, 123; Juchter, 166; Gunter Otto in Klafki, 127.
160. Eppler, 120–121; Itschert et al., 33–34; Knopp, 279–280.
161. Eppler, 121.
162. Rommel quoted in Schörken, 462. See also Juchter, 164; Horchem, 168; Abels, 80; Itschert et al., 40.
163. Willy Jung, "Junge Luftwaffenhelfer," *Das Reich,* Feb. 21, 1943 (quote); *Das Junge Deutschland* (1943): 87; Nicolaisen, 168.
164. Nicolaisen, 11.
165. Schätz, 57.
166. Rolf Schörken, *Luftwaffenhelfer und Drittes Reich: Die Entstehung eines politischen Bewusstseins,* 2nd ed. (Stuttgart, 1985), 118; Schörken, "Schülersoldaten," 466; Abels, 80; Greiffenhagen, 51; Itschert et al., 48–49, 86.
167. "Reichsbefehl 32/44 K," Sept. 21, 1944, in Nicolaisen, 164–167.
168. Schätz, 56.
169. Wolfgang Klafki in Klafki, 141; Gunter Otto ibid., 126; De Bruyn, 141; Cranz, 173; Schätz, 56; Heinz Boberach, *Jugend unter Hitler* (Düsseldorf, 1982), 127.
170. Eppler, 124; Itschert et al., 35, 126; De Bruyn, 144; Cranz, 156–157; Tewes, 46.
171. "Luftwaffenhelferzeugnis," July 13, 1944, in Hans Scherer, *Ich war Oberschüler und Luftwaffenhelfer, 1927–1948,* vol. 2 (Staffelstein, 1996),

21; Schörken, "Schülersoldaten," 457; Wolfgang Klafki in Klafki, 141; Itschert et al., 133; De Bruyn, 141.

172. Schörken, "Schülersoldaten," 457.

173. Ibid.; Itschert et al., 133.

174. On this concern and the regime's attempt to alleviate it, see entry for July 22, 1943, in Boberach, *Meldungen,* vol. 14, 5521; General Zenetti, "An die Eltern der Luftwaffenhelfer (HJ)," Apr. 11, 1944, in Itschert et al., n.p.; Tewes, 42; Juchter, 156.

175. Wolfgang Klafki in Klafki, 140–141; Tewes, 44; Itschert et al., 37; Schumann, 127; Greiffenhagen, 48.

176. Itschert et al., 36–37; Greiffenhagen, 48.

177. Juchter, 215; Tewes, 86; Greiffenhagen, 52; De Bruyn, 150–151. On the Russian *Hiwis,* see Bartov, *Front,* 138–139.

178. Wolfgang Klafki in Klafki, 161; Schörken, "Schülersoldaten," 465, 467.

179. For an example, see Hildegard Knef, *The Gift Horse: Report on a Life* (London, 1971), 43.

180. Kater, *Drummers,* 195; Hans-Martin Stimpel in Klafki, 116; De Bruyn, 174; Itschert et al., 43; Tewes, 337; Schörken, "Luftwaffenhelfer," 227; Cranz, 156–157, 173.

181. Heinz Höhne, *Der Orden unter dem Totenkopf: Die Geschichte der SS* (Gütersloh, 1967), 414–421.

182. Ibid., 413–414; Bernd Wegner, *Hitlers Politische Soldaten: Die Waffen-SS, 1933–1945: Studien zu Leitbild, Struktur und Funktion einer national-sozialistischen Elite* (Paderborn, 1982), 217–242; Toni Sch. in *Jugend im nationalsozialistischen Frankfurt: Ausstellungsdokumentation, Zeitzeugenerinnerungen, Publikum* (Frankfurt am Main, 1987), 324–325; Eva Sternheim-Peters, *Die Zeit der grossen Täuschungen: Eine Jugend im Nationalsozialismus* (Bielefeld, 1992), 331; Rempel, esp. 206, 214.

183. See the text of Chapter 2 at n. 255; the text of Chapter 4 at n. 120.

184. George H. Stein, *The Waffen-SS: Hitler's Elite Guard at War, 1939–1945* (Ithaca, N.Y., 1966), 34–35.

185. Franz-Werner Kersting, *Militär und Jugend im NS-Staat: Rüstungs- und Schulpolitik der Wehrmacht* (Wiesbaden, 1989), 92–98, 412–421.

186. Matthias von Hellfeld and Arno Klönne, *Die betrogene Generation: Jugend in Deutschland unter dem Faschismus* (Cologne, 1985), 257, 259–262; Jahnke and Buddrus, 316.

187. Theo Loch in Steinhoff et al., 493; Maili Hochhuth, *Schulzeit auf dem Lande, 1933–1945: Gespräche und Untersuchungen über die Jahre 1933–1945* (Kassel, 1985), 216; Jahnke and Buddrus, 307; Sternheim-Peters, 330.

188. Fetscher, 46; Franz Schönhuber, *Ich war dabei,* 3rd ed. (Munich, 1981), 59–61; Wolfgang Klafki in Klafki, 165; Knopp, 322–323; Eppler, 118; Peter Petersen in Steinhoff et al., 9; Jörg Andrees in Winfried Maass, *Die Fünfzigjährigen: Portrait eine verratenen Generation* (Hamburg, 1980), 38–39; Rempel, 215.

189. Höhne, 428.

190. See Juchter, 264–265.

191. Toni Sch. in *Jugend . . . Frankfurt,* 324; Eppler, 114 (quote).

192. Excerpt report of Navy command, June 17, 1941, in Jahnke and Buddrus, 338 (first quote); Bingger to Ohneberg, Apr. 30, 1942, BA, NS28/25 (second quote).

193. On the former, see Gahrmann to Kaltenbrunner, [summer/fall 1942], BA, Schumacher/474.

194. Höhne, 436–437; Stein, 170–171. Later among ethnic Germans anywhere beyond the Reich's borders. See South Tyrolian Paul Tasser's testimony in Steinhoff et al., 108–109.

195. Eppler, 114–115. See also Alfons Heck, *A Child of Hitler: Germany in the Days when God Wore a Swastika* (Frederick, Colo., 1985), 42.

196. Wolfgang Klafki in Klafki, 165–166; Hans-Martin Stimpel ibid., 117; De Bruyn, 142; Schörken, *Luftwaffenhelfer,* 148–149; Schörken, "Schülersoldaten," 470; entry for March 18–22, 1945, in Nicolaisen, 212; Greiffenhagen, 52.

197. Jüttner to Himmler, Nov. 12, 1942, BA, Schumacher/474; entry for Aug. 1, 1943, in Klaus Granzow, *Tagebuch eines Hitlerjungen, 1943–1945* (Bremen, 1965), 32; Holzträger, 31; Knopp, 285; Rempel, 188–191. On the peremptory skull examination, see Melcher, 228.

198. Stein, 204–205.

199. Martin Broszat et al., eds., *Bayern in der NS-Zeit: Soziale Lage und politisches Verhalten der Bevölkerung im Spiegel vertraulicher Berichte* (Munich, 1977), 165–166; Cranz, 190–191; Knopp, 286.

200. Himmler to Bormann, May 14, 1943, in Jahnke and Buddrus, 368–369.

201. Schlünder to Stinglwagner, Jan. 22, 1944; Brandl to HJ-Banne et al., Feb. 9, 1944; Miller to Führer and K-Führer, Jan. 5, 1945; Flade to Höhere SS- und Polizeiführer, Feb. 11, 1945, BA, Schumacher/239; Broszat et al., 683; Jahnke and Buddrus, 362; Knopp, 286; Rempel, 213.

202. Monthly report of Regierungspäsident Regensburg, Feb. 10, 1944, BA, Schumacher/483 (quote); Axmann to Stinglwagner, Apr. 14, 1944, BA, Schumacher/239; Broszat et al., 179.

203. Hubert Meyer, *Kriegsgeschichte der 12. SS-Panzerdivision "Hitlerjugend"* (Osnabrück, 1982), vol. 1, 24.

204. Ibid., 18.
205. Ibid., 11–16; Himmler in Jahnke and Buddrus, 363–364; Stein, 207–208.
206. Axmann, 337.
207. Schlünder to Stinglwagner, Jan. 22, 1944; Brandl to HJ-Banne et al., Feb. 9, 1944, BA, Schumacher/239.
208. Stein, 206; Meyer, 18–44.
209. Stein, 219; Schubert-Weller, 211; Meyer, 17.
210. Klaus E. in Steinbach, 144.
211. Jahnke, *Aufgebot,* 58.
212. Knopp, 292.
213. Jahnke and Buddrus, 386–387; Axmann, 341–342; Chester Wilmot, *The Struggle for Europe* (London, 1952), 296–297, 413–414; Jack L. Granatstein, *The Generals: The Canadian Army's Senior Commanders in the Second World War* (Toronto, 1993), 169.
214. Höhne, 435; Stein, 277–278. SS-General Kurt Meyer's sentence was later commuted, and he was released in September 1954.
215. Axmann, 337–339.
216. Gruchmann, 292–294; Stein, 225–226, 229.
217. Weinberg, 780–781; Golücke, 393–394; James Dugan and Carroll Stewart, *Ploesti: The Great Ground-Air Battle of 1 August 1943* (London, 1963), esp. 262–277.
218. Weinberg, 810–815; Gruchmann, 422–425.
219. Gruchmann, 432, 434; Weinberg, 817.
220. Weinberg, 799, 822; Gruchmann, 434. Gruchmann and Weinberg differ on the exact date when Vienna was taken.
221. There were over 200,000 of those, mostly Reich Germans. See Gruchmann, 413–414, 417, 419, 448 (second quote); Günter Böddeker, *Die Flüchtlinge: Die Vertreibung der Deutschen im Osten* (Munich, 1981), 197–210; Claus Larass, *Der Zug der Kinder: KLV—Die Evakuierung 5 Millionen deutscher Kinder im 2. Weltkrieg* (Munich, 1983), 245–246; Margarete Schell, *Ein Tagebuch aus Prag, 1945–46* (Bonn, 1957), 9–33; Kershaw, *Hitler,* 764 (first quote); *Der Spiegel* (Jan. 6, 2003): 41, 48.
222. Weinberg, 816–817, 822–825; Gruchmann, 415, 430–431, 441.
223. Albert Speer, *Erinnerungen,* 8th ed. (Berlin, 1970), 274–336; Richard J. Overy, *War and Economy in the Third Reich* (Oxford, 1994), 362–375.
224. Gruchmann, 412.
225. Ibid.; Willy A. Boelcke, ed., *Wollt Ihr den totalen Krieg? Die geheimen Goebbels-Konferenzen, 1939–1943* (Munich, 1969), 24 (quote).
226. Gruchmann, 412.

227. Ibid., 412–413.
228. Jahnke, *Aufgebot,* 89, 96, 106; Hans Wienicke, ed., *"Schon damals fingen viele an zu schweigen . . .": Quellensammlung zur Geschichte Charlottenburgs von 1933–1945* (Berlin-Charlottenburg, 1986), 208–209.
229. Weinberg, 786.
230. See the example of HJ-Volkssturm in Vienna, Jan. 1945, in Ringler, 141; also Holzträger, 98.
231. Jahnke, *Aufgebot,* 123, 135–136, 142–143.
232. Ibid., 151.
233. Entry for March 11, 1945, in *TGII,* vol. 15, 473.
234. Jahnke and Buddrus, 406–408.
235. Ringler, 149.
236. See Von Hellfeld and Klönne, 244–245; Holzträger, 95; Veigel, 281.
237. Entry for Sept. 30, 1944, in *TGII,* vol. 13, 584.
238. Arno Rose, *Werwolf, 1944–1945: Eine Dokumentation* (Stuttgart, 1980), 116; Holzträger, 98–102.
239. Christian Scharnefksy, *Die Gruppe Neupert: Vier Gräber auf dem Einbecker Friedhof* (Oldenburg, 1995), 45–47 (quote, 47).
240. Joe Volmar, *I Learned to fly for Hitler* (Dundee, Mich., 1999), 181–185 (quote, 185). See also Von Lehndorff, 43–44.
241. Otto Lasch, *So fiel Königsberg* (Stuttgart, 1976), 121–122; Silke Spieler, *Vertreibung und Vertreibungsverbrechen, 1945–1948: Bericht des Bundesarchivs vom 28. Mai 1974: Archivalien und ausgewählte Erlebnisberichte* (Bonn, 1989), 166, 212; Jahnke and Buddrus, 404; Lucas-Busemann, 54.
242. Lasch, 125–126.
243. For the Hitler Youths' last stand in and around Vienna, see Ringler, esp. 142–144, 194–205; Borth, esp. 13, 51, 67, 98–99, 106, 133–134, 142, 166–169, 208–209, 277.
244. Rolf Noll in Maass, 18–21; Rose, 114–115; Nicolaisen, 180–181.
245. Hans Holzträger, *Kampfeinsatz der Hitler-Jugend im Chaos der letzten Kriegsmonate* (Dinklage, 1995), 40.
246. Knopp, 324–326; Lucas-Busemann, 68; Nicolaisen, 80–81; Boberach, *Jugend,* 136.
247. Hermann Melcher, *Die Gezeichneten: Das Erleben eines 16jährigen Kriegsfreiwilligen der Waffen-SS beim Endkampf um Prag und in sowjetischer Kriegsgefangenschaft, 1945–1950* (Leoni, 1985), 13 (quote); Böddeker, 206–207.
248. The original report from *Niederdeutscher Beobachter,* March 20, 1945, is reprinted in Jahnke, *Aufgebot,* 155–157.
249. Holzträger, *Kampfeinsatz,* 41.

250. Traudl Junge, *Bis zur letzten Stunde: Hitlers Sekretärin erzählt ihr Leben* (Munich, 2003), 189.

251. Altner, 160–161, 169; Jahnke, *Aufgebot,* 168–169; Rose, 115; Lothar Loewe in Steinhoff et al., 469–471; Melita Maschmann, *Fazit: Kein Rechtfertigungsversuch,* 5th ed. (Stuttgart, 1964), 159.

252. Maschmann, 159; Kurt Schilde, "Artur Axmann auf der Spur: Aktivitäten des letzten Reichsjugendführers nach 1945," in Jahnke et al., *Jugend,* 102–103.

253. Knopp, 222; Altner, 123–124; Axmann, 423.

254. Axmann, 417–442; Holzträger, *Kampfeinsatz,* 54–70; Knopp, 358–359.

255. Axmann, 449–467; Schilde, 100.

256. Charles Whiting, *Hitler's Werewolves: The Story of the Nazi Resistance Movement, 1944–1945* (New York, 1972).

257. Rose, 116.

258. Borth, 102–103.

259. Ibid., 251–252.

260. Cited in Knopp, 299.

261. Boberach, *Jugend,* 138–140. See also Klaus Messmer in Steinhoff et al., 492–493, and Perry Biddiscombe, *Werwolf! The History of the National Socialist Guerilla Movement, 1944–1946* (Toronto, 1998), 59–86. Several of Biddiscombe's assertions regarding HJ Werewolves appear dubious because his documentation is either incomplete or not compelling.

262. Rose, 13–21.

263. Borth, 215–224.

264. Dieter Meichsner, *Versucht's noch mal mit uns* (Hamburg, 1948), 9–112. See also General Vassily Tschuikov's account in Peter Gosztony, ed., *Der Kampf um Berlin 1945 in Augenzeugenberichten* (Düsseldorf, 1970), 251–252.

265. Knopp, 223.

266. De Bruyn, 302–303.

267. *Partei-Statistik* (Munich, [1935]), 10; Ute Frevert, *Women in German History: From Bourgeois Emancipation to Sexual Liberation* (Oxford, 1989), 258; Wolfgang Benz, "Einleitung," in Benz and Angelika Schardt, eds., *Kriegsgefangenschaft: Berichte über das Leben in Gefangenenlagern der Alliierten* (Munich, 1991), 7; Cartellieri, 12; Stefan Karner, "Deutsche Kriegsgefangene und Internierte in der Sowjetunion, 1941–1956," in Müller and Volkmann, 1012.

268. Moeller, 1011; Dennis L. Bark and David R. Gress, *A History of West Germany* (Oxford, 1989), vol. 1, 358–365.

269. Burleigh, 513; Karner, 1012, 1015, 1020; Cartellieri, 38; Heinz Pust in Benz and Schardt, 31, 33, 35.

270. Karner, 1013, 1016, 1020, 1024; Maass, 23–25, 125–126; Bude, 92, 124, 126; Hans R. Queiser, *"Du gehörst dem Führer!": Vom Hitlerjungen zum Kriegsberichter: Ein autobiographischer Bericht* (Cologne, 1993), 211, 217–218, 231; Melcher, *Gezeichneten*, 92, 124–128, 137, 200, 210–211, 247–249, 407; Cartellieri, 16, 25, 50–52, 352–353; Overmans, 431, 446; Hans Heinz Pollack, *Verschleppt und verschollen: Geschichte einer Deportation aus Ostpreussen* (Frankfurt am Main, 1990), 62–70; Heinz Pust in Benz and Schardt, 22–28; Schönhuber, 172–173; Spieler, 33; Jürgen L. in Hass, 150–151.

271. Helmut Wolff, *Die deutschen Kriegsgefangenen in britischer Hand: Ein Überblick* (Munich, 1974), 39; Kurt Glaser in Benz and Schardt, 146–147, 156, 178–180.

272. Hans Jonitz in Benz and Schardt, 85–88.

273. Ibid., 102–104; Johann Möller in Norbisrath, 22.

274. Martin Koch in Norbisrath, 102–103; Cranz, 255–267; Juchter, 272; Paul Carell and Günter Böddeker, *Die Gefangenen: Leben und Überleben deutscher Soldaten hinter Stacheldraht* (Frankfurt am Main, 1980), 147–159. James Bacque, in *Other Losses: An Investigation into the Mass Deaths of German Prisoners at the Hands of the Americans and French after World War II* (Toronto, 1989), has many of the sites and details of the treatment right, but the overall number of captives and resultant deaths is hugely exaggerated, and he misjudges the Americans' intent of killing as many Germans as possible. For definitive rebuttals of his badly documented views, see Günter Bischof and Stephen E. Ambrose, eds., *Eisenhower and the German POWs: Facts against Falsehood* (Baton Rouge, 1992); Rüdiger Overmans, "'Ein untergeodneter Eintrag im Leidensbuch der jüngeren Geschichte'? Die Rheinwiesenlager 1945," in Hans-Erich Volkmann, ed., *Ende des Dritten Reiches—Ende des Zweiten Weltkriegs: Eine perspektivische Rückschau* (Munich, 1995), 259–291.

275. Dan P. Silverman, *Hitler's Economy: Nazi Work Creation Programs, 1933–1936* (Cambridge, Mass., 1998), 203–207, 217; Dörte Winkler, *Frauenarbeit im "Dritten Reich"* (Hamburg, 1977); Jill Stephenson, *Women in Nazi Society* (London, 1975); Kater, *Doctors*, 89–110.

276. See the examples in Maschmann; Renate Finckh, *Mit uns zieht die neue Zeit* (Baden-Baden, 1979); Margarete Hannsmann, *Der helle Tag bricht an: Ein Kind wird Nazi* (Munich, 1984).

277. This figure according to Franz Seidler, *Frauen zu den Waffen? Marketende-rinnen—Helferinnen—Soldatinnen* (Bonn, 1978), 74. See also ibid., 62–72, 77; Seidler, *Blitzmädchen: Die Geschichte der Helferinnen der deutschen Wehrmacht im Zweiten Weltkrieg* (Koblenz, 1979), 11–16; Ursula von Gersdorff, ed., *Frauen im Kriegsdienst, 1914–1945* (Stuttgart, 1969), 61–71, 460–461, 470–473; Jahnke, *Aufgebot*, 119–120; Von Hellfeld and Klönne, 240–241; Elfriede Schade-Bartkowiak, *Sag mir, wo die Blumen sind . . .: Unter der Schwesternhaube: Kriegserinnerungen einer DRK-Schwester im II. Weltkrieg an der Ostfront* (Hamburg, 1989), 7–149.

278. Von Gersdorff, 374, 442; 470; Axmann, 447.

279. Seidler, *Blitzmädchen*, 15–16; Seidler, *Frauen*, 68; Von Gersdorff, 67, 69, 442; Inge Stolten, *Das alltägliche Exil: Leben zwischen Hakenkreuz und Währungsreform* (Berlin, 1982), 117; Knopp, 143; Jahnke, *Aufgebot*, 154; Heinrich Breloer, ed., *Mein Tagebuch, Geschichten vom Überleben, 1939–1947* (Cologne, 1984), 494–495; Von Lehndorff, 24.

280. Karner, 1014–1015; Seidler, *Blitzmädchen*, 28–29; Larass, 245; Carell and Böddeker, 321–325.

281. Seidler, *Blitzmädchen*, 24; Boberach, *Meldungen*, vol. 16, 6485; Golovchansky, 110; Melcher, *Gefolgschaft*, 220; Pahl in Schröder, *Jahre*, 398.

282. Otto, 228, points directly to this connection.

283. Joachim-Ernst Fromann to Kurt Michaelis, Sept. 28, 1940, quoted in Kater, *Drummers*, 120.

284. For discouragement, see Von Gersdorff, 62; Seidler, *Blitzmädchen*, 18, 24.

285. Golovchansky, 82; Von Alvensleben, 263; Von Lehndorff, 56. In Norway alone, 10,000 children were born to local girls, fathered by Wehrmacht soldiers (*New York Times*, Dec. 18, 2002).

286. See the enthusiastic report by soldier Hans Bergese about willing French girls and even more willing German ones, to his musical mentor Carl Orff, in his letter from France of May 6, 1941, CM; Peter Paul Pauquet, *Gespräche mit der Jugend einer zerschlagenen Nation* (Nuremberg, 1947), 76–77, 115. See also Elizabeth Heineman, "Sexuality and Nazism: The Doubly Unspeakable?", *Journal of the History of Sexuality* 11 (2002): 28.

287. See the text of Chapter 3 at n. 204.

288. On avoidability see Otto, 186–187; Von Gersdorff, 334.

289. Ruth Windisch in Jutta Rüdiger, ed., *Zur Problematik von Soldatinnen: Der Kampfeinsatz von Flakwaffenhelferinnen im Zweiten Weltkrieg—Berichte und Dokumentationen* (Lindhorst, 1987), 94–97.

290. Seidler, *Frauen*, 65–69; Von Gersdorff, 417–418.

291. Von Gersdorff, 70; Jahnke, *Aufgebot,* 153–154; *Frauen im Wehrdienst: Erinnerungen von Ingeborg Hecht, Ruth Henry, Christa Meves* (Freiburg, 1989), 23–38; Windisch in Rüdiger, 95; Seidler, *Frauen,* 86.

292. Statement of Nov. 30, 1944, quoted in Jahnke, *Aufgebot.* See also Von Gersdorff, 411, 417–418; Seidler, *Blitzmädchen,* 14.

293. The transition is described by Erna Tietz in Alison Owings, *Frauen: German Women Recall the Third Reich* (New Brunswick, N.J., 1993), 269.

294. Gerda Szepansky, ed., *"Blitzmädel," "Heldenmutter," "Kriegerwitwe": Frauenleben im Zweiten Weltkrieg* (Frankfurt am Main, 1986), 240; Lore Vogt, "Bericht über den Einsatz als Flakwaffenhelferin," in Rüdiger, 12–73.

295. Erna Tietz in Owings, 270. *Z.b.V.* was one of many standard Wehrmacht designations.

296. Nicolaisen, 158; Tewes, 43.

297. Lisa quoted in Szepansky, 48.

298. Ibid., 241.

299. As reported in Knopp, 144.

300. Ruth Windisch in Rüdiger, 99–101; Erna Tietz in Owings, 272–273; Seidler, *Blitzmädchen,* 16; *Frauen im Wehrdienst,* 39–41.

301. Through rejection of a proposed *Wehrdienstgesetz,* which would have conscripted women for the armed forces on a huge scale. See Seidler, *Frauen,* 69.

302. Quoted ibid., 70.

303. Axmann, 428, 435.

304. Jahnke, *Aufgebot,* 151–152; Holzträger, *Kampfeinsatz,* 57; Birthe Kundrus, "Nur die halbe Geschichte: Frauen im Umfeld der Wehrmacht zwischen 1939 und 1945—Ein Forschungsbericht," in Müller and Volkmann, 721; Knopp, 146.

305. Holzträger, *Kampfeinsatz,* 40, 45, 50.

306. Jahnke and Buddrus, 410; Axmann, 430; Heck, 131.

307. Holzträger, *Kampfeinsatz,* 64–65.

308. Hildegard Morgenthal, *"Rotkopf, die Ecke brennt, Feuerwehr kommt angerennt": Leben in der NS-Zeit und zwei Leben danach* (Frankfurt am Main, 2000), 51–76.

309. Doris Schmid-Gewinner quoted in Knopp, 146.

310. Kershaw, *Nemesis,* 738; Lasch, 121–122.

311. See the brilliantly fictionalized account of this drama by Günter Grass.

312. Lasch, 125.

313. Quotes from Gruchmann, 420.

314. Moeller, 1011.

315. Ingrid van Bergen, "Mit 13 begegnete ich zum erstenmal dem Tod," *Bild am Sonntag,* Aug. 14, 1977.

316. Hannelore Sch. in Hass, 69.

317. Ingeborg P. ibid., 80–81.

318. Atina Grossmann, "Eine Frage des Schweigens? Die Vergewaltigung deutscher Frauen durch Besatzungssoldaten," *Sozialwissenschaftliche Informationen* 24 (1995): 109–119. See also Ingrid Schmidt-Harzbach, "Eine Woche im April: Berlin 1945: Vergewaltigung als Massenschicksal," *Feministische Studien* 2 (1984): 52. One (late) example is Hitler's rhetoric of Apr. 13, 1945, published in Gosztony, 163–164.

319. Schmidt-Harzbach, 59.

320. Jill Stephenson, *Women in Nazi Germany* (Harlow, 2001), 175–176.

321. Schmidt-Harzbach, 59; Frevert, 258; John Willoughby, "The Sexual Behavior of American GIs During the Early Years of the Occupation of Germany," *Journal of Military History* 62 (1998): 155–174; Petra Goedde, *GIs and Germans: Culture, Gender, and Foreign Relations, 1945–1949* (New Haven, Conn., 2003), 58, 65, 84–85.

322. Kershaw, *Nemesis,* 738; Freya Klier, *Verschleppt ans Ende der Welt: Schicksale deutscher Frauen in sowjetischen Arbeitslagern* (Berlin, 1996), 32; Lasch, 121.

323. Lucas-Busemann, 102; Lasch, 74.

324. See Ehrenburg's anti-German article in Gosztony, 59–60; Anatol Goldberg, *Ilya Ehrenburg: Writing, Politics and the Art of Survival* (London, 1984), 207–209; Joshua Rubenstein, *Tangled Loyalties: The Life and Times of Ilya Ehrenburg* (New York, 1996), 190 (quote), 220–221.

325. Ilya Ehrenburg, *The War: 1941–1945* (London, 1964), 162–171; Rubenstein, 222–223; Goldberg, 209; Heinrich Grüber, *Erinnerungen aus sieben Jahrzehnten* (Cologne, 1968), 221–222; Spieler, 222; Klier, 71, 80; Schmidt-Harzbach, 54.

326. See a Soviet Major's rationale cited in Gosztony, 58.

327. Spieler, 146–147; Lasch, 74, 124; Von Lehndorff, 40.

328. Quoted for Feb. 2, 1945, in Gosztony, 64.

329. Quoted in Lasch, 115. Also ibid., 126; Von Lehndorff, 66–85.

330. Entry for Apr. 25, 1945, in Granzow, 175–176. For rural Pomerania, see also Käthe von Normann, *Tagebuch aus Pommern, 1945–1946: Aufzeichnungen* (Munich, 1962), 17, 30–31, 56, 74, 82.

331. Spieler, 221–222.

332. Ibid., 165–168, 208–211; Hammer and Zur Nieden, 312–313, 366–368, 396–399.

333. Johannes Kaps, ed., *Die Tragödie Schlesiens, 1945/46* (Munich, 1962), 117–118.
334. Margret Boveri, *Tage des Überlebens: Berlin 1945* (Munich, 1968), 124.
335. Schmidt-Harzbach, 54.
336. Boveri, 94–95.
337. Schmidt-Harzbach, 53.
338. For one of those exceptions, see Boveri, 103.
339. Generally for these scenarios, see the descriptions ibid., and Gosztony.
340. Gosztony, 281.
341. Marie Mulde in Gabriele Rosenthal, ed., *Die Hitlerjugend-Generation: Biographische Thematisierung als Vergangenheitsbewältigung* (Essen, 1986), 146; Elfriede Schuster, ibid., 168.
342. Boveri, 109.
343. Ibid., 84. See also Knef, 101–102.
344. Grüber, 221–223.
345. *Der Spiegel* (Dec. 16, 2002): 56–57.
346. Ehrenburg, 164.
347. For Pomerania, for example, see Von Normann, 31; Klier, 72; for Lower Silesia, see Klier, 79.
348. Cf. Spieler, 53; Karner, "Kriegsgefangene," 1014.
349. Spieler, 196–197, 203–204, 208–210; Irene Burchert in Owings, 146; Klier, 46–47, 59, 67, 79–80, 86–87, 89.
350. Klier, 54, 101.
351. Erna B. ibid., 73–74.
352. Irene Burchert in Owings, 148.
353. Klier, 160, 166; Spieler, 211; Irene Burchert in Owings, 147.
354. Irene Burchert in Owings, 149.
355. See ibid., 149–151; Hildegard N. in Klier, 205; Carell and Böddeker, 325–330.

6. The Responsibility of Youth

1. Wolfgang Borchert, *Draussen vor der Tür: Ein Stück, das kein Theater spielen und kein Publikum sehen will,* in Borchert, *Draussen vor der Tür und ausgewählte Erzählungen* (Reinbek, 1968; originally published 1947), 27.
2. See the text of Chapter 5 at n. 115.
3. Peter Rühmkorf, *Wolfgang Borchert in Selbstzeugnissen und Bilddokumenten* (Reinbek, 1961), 169–171.

4. From a wealth of documented examples, see the one in the diary of Erika S., entry for May 8, 1945, in Heinrich Breloer, ed., *Mein Tagebuch: Geschichten vom Überleben, 1939–1947* (Cologne, 1984), 187; and Johann Raymann in Gudrun Norbisrath, ed., *Gestohlene Jugend: Der Zweite Weltkrieg in Erinnerungen* (Essen, 2000), 60.

5. Hilde Thurnwald, *Gegenwartsprobleme Berliner Familien: Eine soziologische Untersuchung an 498 Familien* (Berlin, 1948), 52–53, 66; *Jugend in Westdeutschland* (Munich, n.d.), 11–12; Annette Kuhn, "Die vergessene Frauenarbeit in der deutschen Nachkriegszeit," in Anna-Elisabeth Freier and Annette Kuhn, eds., *"Das Schicksal Deutschlands liegt in der Hand seiner Frauen": Frauen in der deutschen Nachkriegsgeschichte* (Düsseldorf, 1983), 184–185; Axel Schildt, "Von der Not der Jugend zur Teenager-Kultur: Aufwachsen in den 50er Jahren," in Axel Schildt and Arnold Sywottek, eds., *Modernisierung im Wiederaufbau: Die westdeutsche Gesellschaft der 50er Jahre* (Bonn, 1993), 335–336; Friedhelm Boll, *Auf der Suche nach Demokratie: Britische und deutsche Jugendinitiativen in Niedersachsen nach 1945* (Bonn, 1995), 31–43; *Der Spiegel* (Jan. 27, 2003): 63.

6. Clemens Vollnhals, "Einleitung," in Vollnhals, ed., *Entnazifizierung: Politische Säuberung und Rehabilitierung in den vier Besatzungszonen, 1945–1949* (Munich, 1991), 11.

7. See, for example, Gerhard Fauth, ed., *Ruf an die deutsche Jugend: Ein Bericht* (Munich, 1948), 10, 41.

8. Breloer, 234; Ralf Roland Ringler, *Illusion einer Jugend: Lieder, Fahnen und das bittere Ende: Hitlerjugend in Österreich: Ein Erlebnisbericht* (St. Pölten, 1977), 168; Wolfgang Klafki in Klafki, ed., *Verführung, Distanzierung, Ernüchterung: Kindheit und Jugend im Nationalsozialismus: Autobiographisches aus erziehungswissenschaftlicher Sicht* (Weinheim, 1988), 168; Herbert Johannes Veigel, *Christbäume: Briefe aus dem Krieg* (Berlin, 1991), 276–277, 334; Edgar Gielsdorf, *Vom Christkind eine Landsknechtstrommel* (Cologne, 1994), 198–199.

9. Arnold P. in Kurt Hass, ed., *Jugend unterm Schicksal: Lebensberichte junger Deutscher, 1946–1949* (Hamburg, 1950), 22 (first quote); Erna Stahl, ed., *Jugend im Schatten von gestern: Aufsätze Jugendlicher zur Zeit* (Hamburg, 1948), 80 (second quote).

10. Knut Pipping et al., *Gespräche mit der deutschen Jugend: Ein Beitrag zum Autoritätsproblem* (Helsingfors, 1954), 326, 329–330; Manfred Rommel, "Die überflüssige Generation—Übersteigerte Hoffnungen," in Claus Richter, ed., *Die überflüssige Generation: Jugend zwischen Apathie und Aggression* (Königstein, 1979), 88; Günter De Bruyn, *Zwischenbilanz: Eine*

Jugend in Berlin (Frankfurt am Main, 1995), 307; Anna J. Merritt and Richard L. Merritt, eds., *Public Opinion in Occupied Germany: The OMGUS Surveys* (Urbana, Ill., 1970), 209; *Jugend zwischen 15 und 24: Eine Untersuchung zur Situation der deutschen Jugend im Bundesgebiet* (Bielefeld, 1954), 307.

11. Roland Gröschel, "Jugendarbeit und Jugendpolitik in Berlin zwischen Krieg, Frieden und Systemkonkurrenz, 1944–1949/50: Forschungsstand—Forschungslücken—Forschungsfragen," in Ulrich Herrmann, ed., *Jugendpolitik in der Nachkriegszeit: Zeitzeugen—Forschungsberichte—Dokumente* (Weinheim, 1993), 53; F. Roy Willis, *The French in Germany: 1945–1949* (Stanford, 1962), 147–161.

12. Karl Heinz Jahnke and Michael Buddrus, eds., *Deutsche Jugend, 1933–1945: Eine Dokumentation* (Hamburg, 1989), 445–446.

13. Heinz Pust in Wolfgang Benz and Angelika Schardt, eds., *Kriegsgefangenschaft: Berichte über das Leben in Gefangenenlagern der Alliierten* (Munich, 1991), 43; Gröschel, 53; Rüdiger Kriemann, "Zur sozialen und politischen Situation von Jugendlichen in Mecklenburg im Sommer 1945," in Karl Heinz Jahnke et al., *Deutsche Jugend im Zweiten Weltkrieg* (Rostock, 1991), 108. On rape especially of young women by Red Army personnel as a constant problem in Soviet-occupied Germany, 1945–1948, see Norman M. Naimark, *The Russians in Germany: A History of the Soviet Zone of Occupation, 1945–1949* (Cambridge, Mass., 1995), 83–90.

14. Mann's BBC address of Oct. 24, 1942, in Jahnke and Buddrus, 446–447.

15. Helmut Schmidt in Schmidt et al., *Kindheit und Jugend unter Hitler,* 2nd ed. (Berlin, 1992), 234 (quote); Helmut Wolff, *Die deutschen Kriegsgefangenen in britischer Hand: Ein Überblick* (Munich, 1974), 46–47; Rolf Schörken, *Jugend 1945: Politisches Denken und Lebensgeschichte* (Opladen, 1990), 83, 119–123; Jürgen Reulecke, "Geboren um 1920: Die Altersgenossen von Hans Scholl und Willi Graf: Zur Diskussion um die junge Generation nach dem Zweiten Weltkrieg," in Michael Kissener and Bernhard Schäfers, eds., *"Weitertragen": Studien zur "Weissen Rose": Festschrift für Anneliese Knoop-Graf zum 80. Geburtstag* (Constance, 2001), 72–73.

16. Willy Schumann, *Being Present: Growing Up in Hitler's Germany* (Kent, Ohio, 1991), 175 (quote); Hans-Günter Zmarzlik, *Wieviel Zukunft hat unsere Vergangenheit? Aufsätze und Überlegungen eines Historikers vom Jahrgang 1922* (Munich, 1970), 25; Gröschel, 52; Schörken, 149–150.

17. Manfred Strack, "Amerikanische Kulturbeziehungen zu (West-)Deutschland, 1945–1955," *Zeitschrift für Kulturaustausch* 37 (1987): 286; Axel Schildt, *Moderne Zeiten: Freizeit, Massenmedien und "Zeitgeist" in der*

Bundesrepublik der 50er Jahre (Hamburg, 1995), 403; Richard Pells, *Not Like Us: How Europeans Have Loved, Hated, and Transformed American Culture Since World War II* (New York, 1997), 52–57.

18. Kurt Lewin, "The Special Case of Germany," *Public Opinion Quarterly* 7 (1943): 555–566, esp. 555, 560–561, 564.

19. Donald McGranahan and Morris Janowitz, "A Comparison of Social Attitudes among American and German Youth," *Journal of Abnormal and Social Pathology* 41 (1946): 3–14, esp. 3, 5.

20. Henry J. Kellermann, *The Present Status of German Youth*, U.S. Department of State, Publication 2583, European Series 11 (Washington, D.C., 1946), 1, 17.

21. Hermann Jung, *Die deutschen Kriegsgefangenen in amerikanischer Hand* (Munich, 1972), 218–238; Hans Jonitz in Benz and Schardt, 112; Glaser in Benz and Schardt, 202–203, 208–209; Klaus Tischler in Gabriele Rosenthal, ed., *Die Hitlerjugend-Generation: Biographische Thematisierung als Vergangenheitsbewältigung* (Essen, 1986), 273–276; Schörken, 29–30; Martin Cranz, *Ich, Ein Deutscher* (Dülmen, 1987), 264–265.

22. *Life*, Overseas Edition for the Armed Forces (Oct. 15, 1945): 21.

23. Kellermann, 5, 11; Saul K. Padover, *Experiment in Germany: The Story of an American Intelligence Officer* (New York, 1946), 72–77; Kurt Piehl, *Schieber, Tramps, Normalverbraucher: Unterwegs im Nachkriegsdeutschland* (Frankfurt am Main, 1989), 16–17. For an early criticism of the U.S. attitude, see Howard Becker, *Vom Barette schwankt die Feder: Die Geschichte der deutschen Jugendbewegung* (Wiesbaden, 1949), 223–224, 227. On the negative German attitude well into the 1970s, see Alfons Kenkmann, *Wilde Jugend: Lebenswelt grossstädtischer Jugendlicher zwischen Weltwirtschaftskrise, Nationalsozialismus und Währungsreform* (Essen, 1996), 212; Elke Nyssen and Sigrid Metz-Göckel, " 'Ja, die waren ganz einfach tüchtig'—Was Frauen aus der Geschichte lernen können," in Freier and Kuhn, 338. On Schaffstein before and after 1945, see the text of Chapter 4 at n. 177, and Rolf Seeliger, *Braune Universität: Deutsche Hochschullehrer gestern und heute* (Munich, 1965), vol. 2, 60–62. It is indicative of the myopia with which the subject of youth in the Third Reich has been and still is treated that, following Schaffstein's interpretation, one of its early chroniclers, Arno Klönne, had no use for *Edelweisspiraten, Meuten,* and Swings as late as 1993. See his "Zur Rekonstruktion von 'Jugendöffentlichkeit' in Deutschland nach dem Ende des NS-Regimes—Hinweise und Fragen," in Ingo Koch, ed., *Deutsche Jugend zwischen Krieg und Frieden, 1944–1946* (Rostock, 1993), 25–26. Similarly: Although Perry Biddiscombe, on the basis

of solely British and U.S. sources, concedes that the *Edelweiss* label was hijacked after 1945 by HJ veterans bent on neo-Nazi, anti-Allied sabotage, he generally echoes, based on the same limited sources, contemporary Western Allied suspicions against surviving *Edelweiss* groups so as to validate *post hoc* their collective condemnation as mere criminals. See his " 'The Enemy of Our Enemy': A View of the *Edelweiss Piraten* [*sic*] from the British and American Archives," *Journal of Contemporary History* 30 (1995): 37–62.

24. J. G. Siebert, *The Remaking of German Youth* (London, [1945]), 68.
25. Kellermann, 4.
26. Doris K. in Lothar Steinbach, *Ein Volk, ein Reich, ein Glaube? Ehemalige Nationalsozialisten und Zeitzeugen berichten über ihr Leben im Dritten Reich* (Berlin, 1983), 105–106; Friedrich Grupe, *Jahrgang 1916: Die Fahne war mehr als der Tod* (Munich, 1989), 358–359; Rosenthal, 149; Bodo Brücher, "Jugendarbeit im Spannungsfeld zwischen Überlieferung und Besatzungspolitik: Am Beispiel der 'Falken' nach 1945," in Herrmann, 30–31; Karl-Ernst Bungenstab, *Umerziehung zur Demokratie? Re-education-Politik im Bildungswesen der US-Zone, 1945–1949* (Düsseldorf, 1970), 125–127.
27. "Zeittafel," in Vollnhals, 352.
28. Clemens Vollnhals, "Entnazifizierung: Politische Säuberung unter alliierter Herrschaft," in Hans-Erich Volkmann, ed., *Ende des Dritten Reiches— Ende des Zweiten Weltkriegs: Eine perspektivische Rückschau* (Munich, 1995), 382.
29. On the political objectives, see Schildt, *Zeiten,* 401–402; Strack, 288; Petra Goedde, *GIs and Germans: Culture, Gender, and Foreign Relations, 1945–49* (New Haven, Conn., 2003).
30. Anna J. Merritt and Richard L. Merritt, eds., *Public Opinion in Semi-sovereign Germany: The HICOG Surveys, 1949–1955* (Urbana, Ill., 1980), 39–40; Strack, 290, 297–298; Pells, 50.
31. Maria Höhn, *GIs and Fräuleins: The German-American Encounter in 1950s West Germany* (Chapel Hill, N.C., 2002), 61–62.
32. Ralph Willett, *The Americanization of Germany, 1945–1949* (London, 1989), 91–92; R. Stephen Craig, "American Forces Network in the Cold War: Military Broadcasting in Postwar Germany," *Journal of Broadcasting and Electronic Media* 32 (1988): 309–318.
33. See the articles in *Funk Illustrierte,* no. 17 (1949), and Oliver Hassenkamp, *Der Sieg nach dem Krieg: Die gute schlechte Zeit* (Munich, [1983]), 31–32; Wilfried Breyvogel et al., " 'Der Krieg gibt jedem noch ungeahnte Möglichkeiten der Bewährung': Essener Gymnasiasten zwischen 1930 und

1945," in Wilfried Breyvogel and Heinz-Hermann Krüger, eds., *Land der Hoffnung—Land der Krise: Jugendkulturen im Ruhrgebiet, 1900–1987* (Berlin, 1987), 201; Horst H. Lange, *Jazz in Deutschland: Die deutsche Jazz-Chronik, 1900–1960* (Berlin, 1966), 156.

34. Craig, 309.

35. Fritz Eberhard, *Der Rundfunkhörer und sein Programm: Ein Beitrag zur empirischen Sozialforschung* (Berlin, 1962), 157; Willett, 97; Axel Schildt, "Hegemon der häuslichen Freiheit: Rundfunk in den 50er Jahren," in Schildt and Sywottek, 473–474.

36. McGranahan and Janowitz, 9; Heinz Kluth, "Das Verhältnis der arbeitslosen Jugendlichen zum Staat und zur Politik," in *Arbeitslosigkeit und Berufsnot der Jugend* (Cologne, 1952), vol. 2, 191; Breloer, 417; Schörken, 29; Wilhelm Jurzek, "Von der Hitlerjugend zum 'Berliner Gespräch': Meine Erinnerungen als Politologe und Zeitzeuge," in Franz-Werner Kersting, ed., *Jugend vor einer Welt in Trümmern: Erfahrungen und Verhältnisse der Jugend zwischen Hitler- und Nachkriegsdeutschland* (Weinheim, 1998), 160.

37. Rommel as quoted in Winfried Maass, *Die Fünzigjährigen: Porträt einer verratenen Generation* (Hamburg, 1980), 145.

38. Claus Larass, *Der Zug der Kinder: KLV—Die Evakuierung 5 Millionen deutscher Kinder im 2. Weltkrieg* (Munich, 1983), 211; Roswitha Fröhlich, *Ich konnte einfach nichts sagen: Tagebuch einer Kriegsgefangenen* (Reinbek, 1979), 46, 70.

39. Schumann, 173.

40. Kellermann, 15–16; Heinz Westphal, "Junge Menschen 1945—Am Anfang einer neuen Zeit," in Kersting, 287; De Bruyn, 304, 308; Jurzek, 159–160; Cranz, 48.

41. Christian Schneider et al., *Das Erbe der NAPOLA: Versuch einer Generationengeschichte des Nationalsozialismus* (Hamburg, 1996), 140–142.

42. Stephen Spender, *European Witness* (New York, 1946), 32–33.

43. Steven P. Remy, *The Heidelberg Myth: The Nazification and Denazification of a German University* (Cambridge, Mass., 2002), 124, 167; Anson Rabinbach, *In the Shadow of Catastrophe: German Intellectuals between Apocalypse and Enlightenment* (Berkeley, 1997), 133–134.

44. Kellermann, 3, 10.

45. Boll, 199–222.

46. Bungenstab, 154–155.

47. See the text of Chapter 1 at n. 38.

48. Kellermann, 2.

49. McGranahan and Janowitz, 10.
50. *German Youth between Yesterday and Tomorrow: 1 April 1947–30 April 1948* (Berlin, 1948), 1 (quote); Thurnwald, 148, 151.
51. Helmut Schelsky, *Die skeptische Generation: Eine Soziologie der deutschen Jugend* (Düsseldorf, 1963; first printing 1957).
52. Schelsky, esp. 77–82, 109–110, 355 (quote), 356.
53. On Schelsky's Nazi past, see Seeliger, vol. 3, 79–83. On the SS-infiltrated Reichsuniversität Strassburg, see Michael H. Kater, *Das "Ahnenerbe" der SS: Ein Beitrag zur Kulturpolitik des Dritten Reiches,* 3rd ed. (Munich, 2001), 285–286.
54. For a contemporary critique of Schelsky see Boll, esp. 20, 224.
55. Ernst Samhaber, "Die erste Probe," *Die Zeit* (Feb. 21, 1946): 1.
56. Annemarie Krapp, "Was ist Demokratie?", in Fauth, 43–44. See also ibid., 57.
57. Jost Hermand, *Als Pimpf in Polen: Erweiterte Kinderlandverschickung, 1940–1945* (Frankfurt am Main, 1993), 112; Zmarzlik, 26–28; Heinrich Kupffer, *Swingtime: Chronik einer Jugend in Deutschland, 1937–1951* (Berlin, 1987), 98–100.
58. Stahl, 77; Hass, 39; Grupe, 363; De Bruyn, 307. See also Maass, 145; Westphal, 283–284; Heinz Bude, *Deutsche Karrieren: Lebenskonstruktionen sozialer Aufsteiger aus der Flakhelfer-Generation* (Frankfurt am Main, 1987), esp. 45, 53.
59. Hildegard Milberg, "Zwischen gestern und morgen: Hamburgs Jugend nach 1945—Ist das Dritte Reich überwunden?", *Junges Hamburg* 12 (1958): 4.
60. Milberg, 4–5.
61. Schmidt, 189. See also Kluth, 134–136.
62. Merritt and Merritt, *OMGUS Surveys,* 86.
63. Otto Haase, "Die soziale Lage der Jugend," in Adolf Grimme and Otto Haase, *Befreiter Geist: Vorträge der kulturpädagogischen Woche in Hannover vom 25.–27. September 1945* (Hanover, 1946), 31–33; Hartmut von Hentig, *Aufgeräumte Erfahrung: Texte zur eigenen Person* (Munich, 1983), 38; Kluth, 142.
64. Kluth, 133–158. See already Kellermann, 6.
65. *German Youth,* 1, and Table 3. The timing for the reauthorization of political groups varied according to group type and Allied zone. In the British Zone, for instance, a Social Democratic Student club was functioning at Hamburg University as early as 1945 (Schmidt, 236). See also the text above at n. 45. Politically oriented groups were permitted in the U.S. Zone

only in March 1947 (Bungenstab, 128). For a description of the spectrum of new West German youth groups, see *Jugend in Westdeutschland,* 46–53.

66. Theodor Heuss, *Reden an die Jugend,* ed. Hans Bott (Tübingen, 1956), 80.

67. Hitler's political testament of Apr. 29, 1945, as quoted in Percy Ernst Schramm, ed., *Die Niederlage 1945: Aus dem Kriegstagebuch des Oberkommandos der Wehrmacht* (Munich, 1962), 415.

68. Boll, 133; Kurt Schilde, "Artur Axmann auf der Spur: Aktivitäten des letzten Reichsjugendführers nach 1945," in Jahnke et al., 99–105.

69. Jutta Rüdiger in Gisela Miller-Kipp, ed., *"Auch Du gehörst dem Führer": Die Geschichte des Bundes Deutscher Mädel (BDM) in Quellen und Dokumenten* (Weinheim, 2001), 312–313; Rüdiger, *Die Hitler-Jugend und ihr Selbstverständnis im Spiegel ihrer Aufgabengebiete* (Lindhorst, 1983); Rüdiger, *Der Bund Deutscher Mädel: Eine Richtigstellung* (Lindhorst, 1984).

70. Baldur von Schirach, *Ich glaubte an Hitler* (Hamburg, 1967), 312–318; Michael Wortmann, *Baldur von Schirach: Hitlers Jugendführer* (Cologne, 1982), 10–11.

71. Von Schirach on May 24, 1946, cited in *Der Prozess gegen die Hauptkriegsverbrecher vor dem Internationalen Militärgerichtshof Nürnberg, 14. November 1945 – 1. Oktober 1946* (Munich, 1984), vol. 13, 477.

72. Robert Wistrich, *Who's Who in Nazi Germany* (New York, 1982), 273.

73. Borchert, 59.

74. Peter H. Merkl, *The Origins of the West German Republic* (New York, 1963); Elmer Plischke, *Contemporary Government of Germany* (Boston, 1964); Geoffrey K. Roberts, *West German Politics* (London, 1972); Kurt P. Tauber, *Beyond Eagle and Swastika: German Nationalism since 1945,* vol. 1. (Middletown, Conn., 1967).

Acknowledgments

The idea for this book came to me after years of work, earlier in my career, on both German youth and various institutions of the Nazi movement, in particular the Nazi Party. Over several years, research for the book was generously supported by grants from the Social Sciences and Humanities Research Council of Canada, the Alexander von Humboldt-Stiftung (Konrad Adenauer Research Award), a two-year Senior Killam Fellowship of the Canada Council, and York University. Without this financial assistance, the opportunities for gathering basic materials from German, Austrian, and U.S. archives, as well as university release time to write, could never have been provided.

As my plan for the book took shape, I was able to present and discuss it in colloquia arranged by colleagues in North America and Germany. At York University, the Canadian Centre for German and European Studies, where I am based, arranged a meeting with faculty and students through the good offices of its directors, Jeffrey Peck and Mark Webber. At the Historisches Kolleg in Munich, Jürgen Reulecke, Reinhard Spree, Gerhard A. Ritter, Hans Mommsen, and Wolfgang Hardtwig convened colleagues for several hours of presentation and lively discussion. Hans Rudolf Vaget did the same for me at Smith College. Hartmut Lehmann of the Max Planck-Institut für Geschichte in Göttingen discussed with me some of my earlier ideas for this book, as did Jörg Wolff at the Institut für Rechtswissenschaften (Arbeitsgruppe

Jugend und Strafrecht) of the Universität Lüneburg. Before I spoke there, Jörg Wolff had generously made available to me the entire records of his research for his own important work on the regimentation of youth during the Third Reich. I have benefited immensely from the help I received from these colleagues, and I am very grateful to them.

As always, the experienced librarians at York University helped me to obtain less accessible books and sources, some of which dated from the Nazi period and were available only from other Canadian and American libraries, not to mention European ones. Even if sometimes I monopolized the books for longer than I should have, Mary Lehane, Gladys Fung, and Julie Pippo never lost their patience with me. For this they deserve my gratitude.

I would also like to thank Edward Shorter, who hosted me in 1997–1998 as the Jason A. Hannah Visiting Professor of the History of Medicine at the University of Toronto. This position gave me an opportunity to study problems arising from the psychology of adolescence. My insights into the pathologization and criminalization of youth in the Nazi system resulted, not least, from fruitful conversations with Ned, his colleagues at the university, and several visiting scholars.

I owe a special debt to Joyce Seltzer, my editor at Harvard University Press. The combination of intelligence, experience, intuition, and empathy that she brought to her reading of the manuscript was extremely helpful, especially in the final shaping of the book. Errors which remain, however, are entirely my own liability.

Index